D1324148

ACCA

ADVANCED FINANCIAL MANAGEMENT (AFM)

P
R
A
C
T
I
C
E

&

R
E
V
I
S
I
O
N

K
I
T

BPP Learning Media is an **ACCA Approved Content Provider** for the ACCA qualification. This means we work closely with ACCA to ensure our products fully prepare you for your ACCA exams.

In this Practice & Revision Kit which has been reviewed by the **ACCA examining team**, we:

- Discuss the **best strategies** for revising and taking your ACCA exams

- Ensure you are well **prepared** for your exam

- Provide you with **lots of great guidance** on tackling questions

- Provide you with **three** mock exams

- Provide **ACCA exam answers** as well as our own for selected questions

Our **Passcards** also support the Advanced Financial Management syllabus.

FOR EXAMS IN SEPTEMBER 2018, DECEMBER 2018, MARCH 2019 AND JUNE 2019

BPP
LEARNING MEDIA

First edition 2007
Twelfth edition February 2018

ISBN 9781 5097 1671 5
(previous ISBN 9781 5097 0864 2)
e-ISBN 9781 5097 1701 9

Cataloguing-in-Publication Data
A catalogue record for this book
is available from the British Library

Published by

BPP Learning Media Ltd
BPP House, Aldine Place
London W12 8AA

www.bpp.com/learningmedia
Printed and bound by CPI Group (UK) Ltd
Croydon
CR0 4YY

Your learning materials, published by BPP Learning Media Ltd, are printed on paper obtained from traceable, sustainable sources.

The contents of this book are intended as a guide and not professional advice. Although every effort has been made to ensure that the contents of this book are correct at the time of going to press, BPP Learning Media makes no warranty that the information in this book is accurate or complete and accepts no liability for any loss or damage suffered by any person acting or refraining from acting as a result of the material in this book.

We are grateful to the Association of Chartered Certified Accountants for permission to reproduce past examination questions. The suggested solutions in the Practice & Revision Kit have been prepared by BPP Learning Media Ltd, except where otherwise stated.

Contents

	Page
Finding questions	
Question index	iv
Topic index	vii
Helping you with your revision	viii
Revising AFM	
Topics to revise	x
Question practice	x
Passing the AFM exam	xi
Exam formulae	xv
Exam information	xvii
Useful websites	xx
Questions and answers	
Questions	3
Answers	85
Exam practice	
Mock exam 1 (ACCA March/June 2017 Sample questions)	
• Questions	305
• Plan of attack	313
• Answers	314
Mock exam 2 (Specimen exam)	
• Questions	327
• Plan of attack	335
• Answers	336
Mock exam 3 (ACCA September/December 2017 Sample questions)	
• Questions	351
• Plan of attack	359
• Answers	360
Mathematical tables and formulae	375
Review form	

Question index

The headings in this checklist/index indicate the main topics of questions, but questions are expected to cover several different topics.

Questions set under the old syllabus Paper 3.7 – *Strategic Financial Management (SFM)* and Paper 14 – *Financial Strategy (FS)* are included where their style and/or content are similar to the questions that appear in *Advanced Financial Management (AFM)*.

	Marks	Time allocation Mins	Page number Question	Answer
Part A: Role of the senior financial adviser in the multinational organisation				
1 Preparation question: Mezza (6/11, amended)	25	49	3	85
2 Preparation question: Strom (12/12, amended)	25	49	4	87
3 Preparation question: PMU (12/10, amended)	25	49	4	90
4 Preparation question: Kilenc (6/12, amended)	25	49	5	92
5 Chawan (6/15)	25	49	6	95
6 Limni Co (6/13)	25	49	7	98
7 International Enterprises (12/07, amended)	25	49	8	100
8 Anchorage Retail (12/09, amended)	25	49	10	103
9 High K (Sep/Dec 17)	25	49	12	106
10 Lamri (12/10, amended)	25	49	13	109
11 Moonstar (Sep/Dec 15)	25	49	14	112
Part B: Advanced investment appraisal				
12 Preparation question: Cathlynn	15	29	16	114
13 Preparation question: Faoilean (6/14)	25	49	16	115
14 Preparation question: Bournelorth (Mar/Jun 17)	25	49	17	118
15 Fernhurst (Sep/Dec 16)	25	49	18	120
16 Your business (6/09, amended)	25	49	19	123
17 Tisa Co (6/12, amended)	25	49	20	126
18 Arbore (12/12, amended)	25	49	21	128
19 MMC (6/11, amended)	25	49	22	131
20 Marengo (12/10, amended)	25	49	22	133
21 Furlion Co (Mar/Jun 16)	25	49	23	135
22 Airline Business (12/07, amended)	25	49	24	138
23 Fubuki (12/10)	25	49	24	141
24 Coeden (12/12, amended)	25	49	25	144
25 Levante (12/11, amended)	25	49	26	147
26 GNT (2013 pilot paper)	25	49	27	150
27 Riviere (12/14)	25	49	28	153
28 AWP Co	25	49	29	155

BPP
LEARNING MEDIA

	Marks	Time allocation Mins	Page number Question	Page number Answer

Part C: Acquisitions and mergers

	Marks	Time allocation Mins	Question	Answer
29 Preparation question: Saturn Systems (6/08, amended)	25	49	30	158
30 Mercury Training (6/08, amended)	25	49	30	160
31 Chithurst (Sep/Dec 16)	25	49	31	163
32 Kodiak Company (12/09, amended)	25	49	32	166
33 Louieed (Mar/Jun 16)	25	49	33	169
34 Makonis (12/13)	25	49	34	172
35 Vogel (6/14)	25	49	35	174

Part D: Corporate reconstruction and reorganisation

	Marks	Time allocation Mins	Question	Answer
36 AIR	25	49	37	177
37 Doric (2013 pilot paper)	25	49	38	180
38 Flufftort (Sep/Dec 15)	25	49	39	181
39 BBS Stores (6/09, amended)	25	49	41	185
40 Ennea (6/12)	25	49	42	189
41 Nubo (12/13)	25	49	44	192
42 Bento (6/15)	25	49	45	194
43 Staple Group (Mar/June 16)	25	49	46	197

Part E: Treasury and advanced risk management techniques

	Marks	Time allocation Mins	Question	Answer
44 Retilon (FS, 6/00, amended)	25	49	48	200
45 Kenduri Co (6/13)	25	49	49	204
46 Massie (Sep/Dec 15)	25	49	50	207
47 KYT (FS, 6/99, amended)	25	49	51	211
48 Asteroid Systems (6/08, amended)	25	49	52	213
49 Multidrop (6/10, amended)	25	49	52	216
50 Casasophia (6/11, amended)	25	49	53	218
51 Alecto (2013 pilot paper)	25	49	54	221
52 Awan (12/13)	25	49	55	224
53 Phobos (12/08, amended)	25	49	56	226
54 Keshi (12/14)	25	49	57	229
55 Daikon (6/15)	25	49	58	232
56 Sembilan (6/12, amended)	25	49	59	235
57 Pault (Sep/Dec 16)	25	49	60	238

	Marks	Time allocation Mins	Page number Question	Page number Answer
Part F: 50 mark questions				
58 Yilandwe (6/15)	50	98	61	240
59 Avem (12/14)	50	98	63	244
60 Chmura (12/13)	50	98	64	250
61 Mlima (6/13)	50	98	66	255
62 Lignum (12/12, amended)	50	98	68	260
63 Tramont (2013 pilot paper)	50	98	69	264
64 Cigno (Sep/Dec 15)	50	98	71	269
65 Lirio (Mar/Jun 16)	50	98	73	274
66 Morada (Sep/Dec 16)	50	98	75	279
67 Pursuit (6/11, amended)	50	98	77	284
68 Polytot (SFM, 6/04, amended)	50	98	79	290
69 Nente (6/12, amended)	50	98	80	296

Mock exam 1 (ACCA March/June 2017 Sample questions)

Mock exam 2 (Specimen exam)

Mock exam 3 (ACCA September/December 2017 Sample questions)

BPP
LEARNING MEDIA

Topic index

Listed below are the key AFM syllabus topics and the numbers of the questions in this Kit covering those topics. If you need to concentrate your practice and revision on certain topics or if you want to attempt all available questions that refer to a particular subject, you will find this index useful.

Syllabus topic	Question numbers
A1: Role of senior financial advisor	1, 24, 28, 30, ME2 Q1
A2: Financial strategy formulation	1, 2, 4, 5, 6, 8, 9, 11, 30, 35, 58, 59, 63, 66, 69, ME1 Q1, ME3 Q1
A3: Ethical and governance issues	1, 29, 61, 63, 67, ME1 Q1, ME2 Q1
A4: Management of international trade and finance	2, 4, 5, 28, 45, 59, 60, 67
A5: Strategic business and financial planning	3, 9, 14
A6: Dividend policy and transfer pricing	3, 5, 6, 7, 10, 31, 65, 68
B1: Discounted cash flow techniques	15, 17, 18, 27, 28, 59, 62, ME3 Q2
B2: Option pricing theory	12, 13, 16, 19, 20, 21, 60, 62
B3: Impact of financing and APV	22, 23, 25, 26, 28, 41, 54, 56, 61, 63, ME1 Q3, ME2 Q2, ME3 Q1
B4: Valuation and free cash flows	7, 10, 24, 33, 61, 65, ME3 Q2
B5: International investment and financing	58, 60, 62, 68, ME2 Q1
C1: Acquisitions and other growth strategies	3, 29, 33, 35, 58, 64, ME1 Q1, ME2 Q3
C2: Valuation for acquisition and mergers	30, 31, 32, 33, 34, 35, 59, 61, 64, 65, 67, 69, ME2 Q3
C3: Regulatory issues	64, 67, 69
C4: Financing acquisitions and mergers	33, 34, 67
D1: Financial reconstruction	36, 37, 38, 39, 40, 42, 66, ME3 Q1
D2: Business reorganisation	36, 37, 41, 42, 64, 66, ME1 Q1, ME3 Q2
E1: Treasury function	13, 48, 52, 54, ME3 Q2
E2: Foreign exchange hedging	44, 45, 46, 47, 48, 49, 50, 62, 65, 68, ME1 Q2, ME2 Q1
E3: Interest rate hedging	46, 47, 51, 52, 53, 54, 55, 56, 57, ME3 Q2

ME1 is Mock Exam 1, ME2 is Mock Exam 2 and ME3 is Mock Exam 3.

Helping you with your revision

BPP Learning Media – Approved Content Provider

As an ACCA **Approved Content Provider**, BPP Learning Media gives you the **opportunity** to use revision materials reviewed by the ACCA examining team. By incorporating the ACCA examining team's comments and suggestions regarding the depth and breadth of syllabus coverage, the BPP Learning Media Practice & Revision Kit provides excellent, **ACCA-approved** support for your revision.

These materials are reviewed by the ACCA examining team. The objective of the review is to ensure that the material properly covers the syllabus and study guide outcomes, used by the examining team in setting the exams, in the appropriate breadth and depth. The review does not ensure that every eventuality, combination or application of examinable topics is addressed by the ACCA Approved Content. Nor does the review comprise a detailed technical check of the content as the Approved Content Provider has its own quality assurance processes in place in this respect.

Tackling revision and the exam

Using feedback obtained from the ACCA examining team review:

- We look at the dos and don'ts of revising for, and taking, ACCA exams

- We focus on AFM; we discuss revising the syllabus, what to do (and what not to do) in the exam, how to approach different types of question and ways of obtaining easy marks

Selecting questions

We provide signposts to help you plan your revision.

- A full **question index**

- A **topic index** listing all the questions that cover key topics, so that you can locate the questions that provide practice on these topics, and see the different ways in which they might be examined

Making the most of question practice

At BPP Learning Media we realise that you need more than just questions and model answers to get the most from your question practice.

- Our **Top tips** included for certain questions provide essential advice on tackling questions, presenting answers and the key points that answers need to include

- We show you how you can pick up **Easy marks** on some questions, as we know that picking up all readily available marks often can make the difference between passing and failing

- We include **marking guides** to show you what the examining team rewards

- We include **comments from** the **examining team** to show you where students struggled or performed well in the actual exam

- We refer to the **BPP Study Text** for exams in September 2018, December 2018, March 2019 and June 2019 for detailed coverage of the topics covered in questions.

Attempting mock exams

There are three mock exams that provide practice at coping with the pressures of the exam day. We strongly recommend that you attempt them under exam conditions.

Mock exam 2 is the Specimen exam paper. **Mock exam 1** and **Mock exam 3** are compiled from questions selected by the examining team from the March and June 2017 exams and from the September and December 2017 exams respectively. They do not reflect the entire exams but contain questions most appropriate for students to practice.

Revising AFM

Topics to revise

Any part of the syllabus could be tested in the compulsory Section A question, therefore it is essential that you learn the **entire syllabus** to maximise your chances of passing. There are no short cuts – trying to spot topics is dangerous and will significantly reduce the likelihood of success.

As this is an advanced level exam, it **assumes knowledge** of the topics covered in *Financial Management (FM)*, including business valuation techniques, investment appraisal techniques, cost of capital and risk management. You should revise these topics if necessary as they impact on your understanding of the more advanced techniques.

From September 2018 every exam will contain a question which has a clear focus on syllabus Section B (advanced investment appraisal) and on Section E (treasury and advanced risk management) so these syllabus sections are especially important.

It's also useful to keep reading the business pages during your revision period and not just narrowly focus on the syllabus. Remember that the examining team has stressed that this exam is about how organisations respond to real-world issues, so the more you read, the more practical examples you will have of how organisations have tackled real-life situations.

Question practice

You should use the Passcards and any brief notes you have to revise the syllabus, but you mustn't spend all your revision time passively reading. **Question practice is vital**; doing as many questions as you can in full will help develop your ability to analyse scenarios and produce relevant discussion and recommendations.

Make sure you leave enough time in your revision schedule to practise the longer Section A questions. The scenarios and requirements of Section A questions are more complex and will integrate several parts of the syllabus, so practice is essential. Also ensure that you attempt all three mock exams under exam conditions.

Passing the AFM exam

Displaying the right qualities

The examining team will expect you to display the following qualities.

Qualities required	
Fulfilling the higher level question requirements	This means that when you are asked to show higher level skills such as **assessment or evaluation**, you will only score well if you demonstrate them. Merely describing something when you are asked to evaluate it will not earn you the marks you need.
Identifying the most important features of the organisation and its environment	You must use your **technical knowledge and business awareness** to identify the key features of the scenario.
Sorting the information in the scenario	You will get a lot of information, particularly in the Section A scenario, and will be expected to **evaluate how useful** it is and **use it** to support answers such as comparisons and discussions.
Selecting relevant examples	You will gain credit for using **good** examples from the scenario in the question to establish the relevance of the point that you are making.
Arguing well	You may be expected to discuss both sides of a case, or present an argument in favour or against something. You will gain marks for the **quality** and **logical flow of your arguments**.
Making reasonable recommendations	The measures you recommend must be **appropriate** for the organisation; you may need to discuss their strengths and weaknesses, as there may be costs of adopting them. The recommendations should clearly state what has to be done.

Avoiding weaknesses

Our experience of, and examiner feedback from, other higher level exams enables us to predict a number of weaknesses that are likely to occur in many students' answers. You will enhance your chances significantly if you ensure you avoid these mistakes:

- **Failing to provide what the question verbs require** (discussion, evaluation, recommendation) or to write about the topics specified in the question requirements

- **Repeating the same material** in different parts of answers

- **Stating theories and concepts** rather than applying them

- **Quoting chunks of detail** from the question that don't add any value

- **Forcing irrelevancies into answers**, for example irrelevant definitions or theories, or examples that don't relate to the scenario

- **Giving long lists or writing down all that's known** about a broad subject area, and not caring whether it's relevant or not

- **Focusing too narrowly on one area** – for example only covering financial risks when other risks are also important

- **Letting your personal views prevent you from answering the question** – the question may require you to construct an argument with which you personally don't agree

- **Unrealistic or impractical recommendations**

- **Vague recommendations** – instead of just saying improve risk management procedures, you should discuss precisely **how** you would improve them

- **Failing to answer sufficient questions**, or all parts of a question, because of poor time management

Choosing which questions to answer first

We recommend that you spend time at the beginning of your exam carefully reading through all of the questions in the exam, and each of their requirements. Once you feel familiar with your exam we then recommend that you attempt the compulsory Section A question first, ensuring that you spend adequate time reading and planning before you begin to write up your answer.

During the second half of the exam, you can put Section A aside and concentrate on the two Section B questions.

However our recommendations are not inflexible. If you really think the Section A question looks a lot harder than the Section B questions, then do those first, but **DON'T run over time on them**. You must leave yourself at least 1 hour and 38 minutes to tackle the Section A question. When you come back to it, once you have had time to reflect, you should be able to generate more ideas and find the question is not as bad as it looks.

Remember also that small overruns of time during the first half of the exam can add up to leave you very short of time towards the end.

Tackling questions

You'll improve your chances by following a step-by-step approach to Section A scenarios along the following lines.

Step 1 Read the background

Usually the first couple of paragraphs will give some background on the company and what it is aiming to achieve. By reading this carefully you will be better equipped to relate your answers to the company as much as possible.

Step 2 Read the requirements

There is no point reading the detailed information in the question until you know what it is going to be used for. Don't panic if some of the requirements look challenging – identify the elements you are able to do and look for links between requirements, as well as possible indications of the syllabus areas the question is covering.

Step 3 Identify the action verbs

These convey the level of skill you need to exhibit and also the structure your answer should have. A lower level verb such as define will require a more descriptive answer; a higher level verb such as evaluate will require a more applied, critical answer. It should be stressed that **higher level requirements and verbs** are likely to be most significant in this exam.

Action verbs that are likely to be frequently used in this exam are listed below, together with their intellectual levels and guidance on their meaning.

Intellectual level		
1	Identify/describe	State the meaning of
	Calculate	Perform a specific mathematical technique
2	Discuss	Examine in detail by argument
	Analyse	Examine in detail the structure of...
	Evaluate	Use your judgement to assess the value of...
3	Advise	Use judgement to recommend a course of action
	Report	Present/justify valid recommendations
	Estimate	Make an approximate judgement or calculation

BPP
LEARNING MEDIA

Step 4   Check the mark allocation to each part

This shows you the depth anticipated and helps allocate time.

Step 5   Read the question slowly, focusing on the initial requirements

Once you know what you are expected to do in the first requirement, read the question in detail, trying to focus on the information that will be needed for your first task.

Step 6   Read the scenario carefully

Put points under headings related to requirements (eg by noting in the margin to what part of the question the scenario detail relates).

Step 7   Consider the consequences of the points you've identified

You will often have to provide recommendations based on the information you've been given. Be prepared to criticise the code, framework or model that you've been told to use if required. You may have also to bring in wider issues or viewpoints, for example the views of different stakeholders.

Step 8   Write a brief plan

You may be able to do this on the question paper as often there will be at least one blank page in the question booklet. However any plan you make should be reproduced in the answer booklet when writing time begins. Make sure you identify all the requirements of the question in your plan – each requirement may have sub-requirements that must also be addressed. If there are professional marks available, highlight in your plan where these may be gained (such as preparing a report).

Step 9   Write the answer

Make every effort to present your answer clearly. The pilot paper and exams so far indicate that the examining team will be looking for you to make a number of clear points. The best way to demonstrate what you're doing is to put points into separate paragraphs with clear headers.

Discussion questions

Do not be tempted to write all you know about a particular topic in a discussion part of a question. Markers can easily spot when a student is 'waffling' and you will receive little or no credit for this approach. Keep referring back to the question requirement to ensure you are not straying from the point.

To make it easier for the marker to determine the relevance of the points you are making, you could explain what you mean in one sentence and then why this point is relevant in another.

Remember that **depth of discussion** will be important. Always bear in mind how many marks are available for the discussion as this will give you an indication of the depth that is required. Ask yourself the following questions as you are tackling a discussion question:

- **Have I made a point in a coherent sentence?**
- **Have I explained the point** (to answer the 'so what' or 'why' queries)?
- **Have I related the point to the company in the scenario?**

Gaining the easy marks

As AFM is a Strategic Professional exam, four **professional level marks** will be awarded. Some of these should be easy to obtain. The examining team has stated that some marks may be available for presenting your answer in the form of a letter, presentation, memo, report or briefing notes. You may also be able to obtain marks for the style and layout of your answer.

Reports should always have an appropriate title. They should be **formally written**, with an **introductory paragraph** setting out the aims of the report. You should use **short paragraphs** and **appropriate headings**, with a summary of findings as a conclusion. Detailed calculations should be presented as an appendix, and it will often be appropriate to end the report with a recommendation/conclusion.

Memorandums should have the following information at the beginning:

Subject; name of recipient; name of author; date

The language can be **less formal** than a report but the content should still have an introduction and conclusion, and be divided into small paragraphs with appropriate headings.

Exam formulae

Set out below are the **formulae you will be given in the exam**. If you are not sure what the symbols mean, or how the formulae are used, you should refer to the appropriate chapter in this Study Text.

Chapter in Study Text

Modigliani and Miller Proposition 2 (with tax)

$$k_e = k_e^i + (1-T)(k_e^i - k_d)\frac{V_d}{V_e}$$

7a

The capital asset pricing model

$$E(r_i) = R_f + \beta_i(E(r_m) - R_f)$$

2

The asset beta formula

$$\beta_a = \left[\frac{V_e}{(V_e + V_d(1-T))}\beta_e\right] + \left[\frac{V_d(1-T)}{(V_e + V_d(1-T))}\beta_d\right]$$

7a

The growth model

$$P_0 = \frac{D_0(1+g)}{(r_e - g)}$$

7b

Gordon's growth approximation

$$g = br_e$$

7a

The weighted average cost of capital

$$WACC = \left[\frac{V_e}{V_e + V_d}\right]k_e + \left[\frac{V_d}{V_e + V_d}\right]k_d(1-T)$$

7a

The Fisher formula

$$(1 + i) = (1 + r)(1 + h)$$

5

Purchasing power parity and interest rate parity

$$S_1 = S_0 \times \frac{(1+h_c)}{(1+h_b)}$$

8

$$F_0 = S_0 \times \frac{(1+i_c)}{(1+i_b)}$$

8

Modified internal rate of return

$$\text{MIRR} = \left[\frac{PV_R}{PV_I}\right]^{\frac{1}{n}}(1+r_e) - 1 \qquad\qquad 5$$

The Black-Scholes option pricing model

$$c = P_a N(d_1) - P_e N(d_2)e^{-rt} \qquad\qquad 6$$

$$\text{Where} \quad d_1 = \frac{\ln(P_a/P_e) + (r + 0.5s^2)t}{s\sqrt{t}} \qquad\qquad 6$$

$$d_2 = d_1 - s\sqrt{t} \qquad\qquad 6$$

The put call parity relationship

$$p = c - P_a + P_e e^{-rt} \qquad\qquad 6$$

Formulae to learn

These are the main formulae that are not given in the exam formula sheet. Make sure you learn these as you may be required to use them in the exam. They are used throughout the Study Text and this Practice & Revision Kit.

$$\mathbf{Ke} = \frac{D_1}{P_0} + g$$

$$\mathbf{K_d} = \frac{i(1-t)}{P_0}$$

$$\mathbf{K_{pref}} = \frac{\text{Preference dividend}}{\text{Market value}_{(ex\ div)}} = \frac{d}{P_0}$$

Gearing $\qquad = \qquad \dfrac{\text{Book value of debt}}{\text{Book value of equity}}$

Interest cover $\qquad = \qquad \dfrac{\text{Profit from operations}}{\text{Interest}}$

Current ratio $\qquad = \qquad$ Current assets $\quad : \quad$ Current liabilities

Exam information

Format of the exam

Time allowed: 3 hours and 15 minutes and the **pass mark** remains at 50%.

Section A comprises one compulsory question. The total for this section is 50 marks.

Longer questions will cover topics from across the syllabus but will tend to be based on one major area – for example a cross-border merger question (major topic) might bring in ethical issues (smaller topic).

Four professional marks are available. The examining team has emphasised that in order to gain all the marks available, students must write in the specified format (such as a report or memo). Reports must have terms of reference, conclusion, appendices and appropriate headings. Make sure you are familiar with how different types of documents are constructed to improve your chances of gaining maximum professional marks.

Section B is 50 marks in total (25 marks per question). Both questions are compulsory (from September 2018).

From the September 2018 exam, all topics and syllabus sections will be examinable in either Section A or Section B of the exam, but every exam will have questions which have a focus on syllabus Sections B and E. There will no longer be any wholly narrative questions (although some still appear in this Revision Kit as preparation questions).

Examining team's general comments

If you are preparing to sit AFM you should pay particular attention to the following in order to maximise your chances of success.

1   *Know your stuff*

   - Develop a sound knowledge of the entire AFM syllabus. Augment studying the manuals with wider reading of the financial press, finance textbooks, articles in *Student Accountant* and financial journals.

   - You should expect and be prepared for questions from a range of syllabus areas and more than one area may be tested in a single question. Be prepared for questions that require you to consider a number of areas of the syllabus within one question.

2   *Question practice*

   - Work through the past exam questions under exam conditions and to time. Doing past questions will help you build efficiency in answering questions and help you build knowledge of how to make your answer relevant to the scenario in the question.

3   *Address the requirement and scenario*

   - Your answer must relate to the scenario in question. Context is very important for higher-level exams. General answers will gain fewer or even no marks.

   - In your exams, good time management techniques and habits are essential in ensuring success. Make sure that you are able to answer all parts of each question and manage your time effectively so that you make a reasonable attempt at each part of each question. Good time management skills are essential.

   - Often parts of a requirement may ask for more than one aspect. Make sure that you can answer, and do answer, everything each part of each requirement is asking for.

   - Make sure you answer the requirements correctly. For example, if the question asks you to explain, it is not enough just to list. If the question asks you to assess, it is not enough just to explain.

4   *Communicate concisely*

- For the written parts of any question, remember it is generally a mark for each relevant point. Repeating a point does not get you any extra marks and it wastes time. Avoid repetition.

- Don't use incomplete sentences when making a point. Marks are awarded for complete points made in full sentences. However, you can use bullet points and numbered paragraphs, and headings when appropriate, to structure an answer to a question. But points made should be in complete sentences.

5   *Think before you start and manage your time*

- Pay attention to the number of marks available – this provides you with a clear indication of the amount of time you should spend on each question part.

- Use your exam time effectively. The questions may contain a substantial amount of information that you will need to sort out and apply properly and you should plan your answer before beginning to write it.

Marks available in respect of professional skills

The presentation of your answers is critical. It is very important to pay regard to neatness, organisation and structure of your answers. Professional exams are extremely time-pressured but giving your answers a structure will help you organise your thoughts and work more effectively. Make sure that your answers are legible because markers cannot award marks for something that they cannot read.

Analysis of past exams

The table below provides details of when each element of the syllabus has been examined in the ten most recent sittings and the Section (A or B) in which each element was examined (**Note.** Until September 2018 there was a choice of two questions from three in Section B of the exam).

Since September 2016, ACCA have been issuing two exams each year, after the December and June exam sessions. These exams are compiled from questions selected from the two preceding sessions eg in December 2017, the sample questions were compiled from September 2017 and December 2017 exams.

Covered in Text chapter		Sep/ Dec 2017	Mar /Jun 2017	Sep/ Dec 2016	Mar /Jun 2016	Sep /Dec 2015	Jun 2015	Dec 2014	Jun 2014	Dec 2013	Jun 2013
	ROLE OF SENIOR FINANCIAL ADVISER										
1, 2	Role of senior financial adviser/ financial strategy formulation	A		A, B	A		B	B		A	B
3	Ethical/environmental issues				B						A
4a	Trading in a multinational environment				B	B				A	
4b	Planning in a multinational environment										B
	ADVANCED INVESTMENT APPRAISAL										
5	Discounted cash flow techniques	B		B						A	
6	Application of option pricing theory to investment decisions				B			B	B	A	
7a, 7b	Impact of financing, adjusted present values/valuation and free cash flows	A	B	A		B			A, B	B	A
8	International investment/financing		B		A		A				
	ACQUISITIONS AND MERGERS										
9, 11, 12	Strategic/financial/regulatory issues		A		B	A		A	B		B
10	Valuation techniques	B		B	B	A		A	B	B	A, B
	CORPORATE RECONSTRUCTION AND REORGANISATION										
13	Financial reconstruction	A				B	B				A
14	Business reorganisation	B	A		B		B			B	
	TREASURY AND ADVANCED RISK MANAGEMENT TECHNIQUES										
15	Role of the treasury function	B		A				B			
16	Hedging foreign currency risk		B		A	B			A		B
17	Hedging interest rate risk	B		B		B	B	B	A	B	B

IMPORTANT!

The table above gives a broad idea of how frequently major topics in the syllabus are examined. It should not be used to question spot and predict for example that Topic X will not be examined because it came up two sittings ago. The examining team's reports indicate that the examining team is well aware some students try to question spot. The examining team avoid predictable patterns and may, for example, examine the same topic two sittings in a row.

Additional information

The study guide provides more detailed guidance on the syllabus and can be found by visiting the exam resource finder on the ACCA website: www.accaglobal.com/uk/en/student/exam-support-resources.html

Useful websites

The websites below provide additional sources of information of relevance to your studies for AFM.

*   www.accaglobal.com

    ACCA's website. The students' section of the website is invaluable for detailed information about the qualification, past issues of *Student Accountant* (including technical articles) and even interviews with the examining team.

*   www.bpp.com

    Our website provides information about BPP products and services, with a link to ACCA's website.

*   www.reuters.com

    This website provides information about current international business. You can search for information and articles on specific industry groups as well as individual companies.

Questions

ROLE OF THE SENIOR FINANCIAL ADVISER IN THE MULTINATIONAL ORGANISATION

Questions 1 to 11 cover the role and responsibility towards stakeholders, the subject of Part A of the BPP Study Text for AFM.

1 Preparation question: Mezza (6/11, amended)   49 mins

[Note that from September 2018 questions that are wholly narrative will not be set]

Mezza Co is a large food manufacturing and wholesale company. It imports fruit and vegetables from countries in South America, Africa and Asia, and packages them in steel cans and plastic tubs and as frozen foods, for sale to supermarkets around Europe. Its suppliers range from individual farmers to government-run co-operatives, and farms run by its own subsidiary companies. In the past, Mezza Co has been very successful in its activities, and has an excellent corporate image with its customers, suppliers and employees. Indeed Mezza Co prides itself on how it has supported local farming communities around the world and has consistently highlighted these activities in its annual reports.

However, in spite of buoyant stock markets over the last couple of years, Mezza Co's share price has remained static. Previously announcements to the stock market about growth potential led to an increase in the share price. It is thought that the current state is because there is little scope for future growth in its products. As a result the company's directors are considering diversifying into new areas. One possibility is to commercialise a product developed by a recently acquired subsidiary company. The subsidiary company is engaged in researching solutions to carbon emissions and global warming, and has developed a high carbon absorbing variety of plant that can be grown in warm, shallow sea water. The plant would then be harvested into carbon-neutral bio-fuel. This fuel, if widely used, is expected to lower carbon production levels.

Currently there is a lot of interest among the world's governments in finding solutions to climate change. Mezza Co's directors feel that this venture could enhance its reputation and result in a rise in its share price. They believe that the company's expertise would be ideally suited to commercialising the product. On a personal level, they feel that the venture's success would enhance their generous remuneration package which includes share options. It is hoped that the resulting increase in the share price would enable the options to be exercised in the future.

Mezza Co has identified the coast of Maienar, a small country in Asia, as an ideal location, as it has a large area of warm, shallow waters. Mezza Co has been operating in Maienar for many years and as a result, has a well-developed infrastructure to enable it to plant, monitor and harvest the crop, although a new facility would be needed to process the crop after harvesting. The new plant would employ local people. Mezza Co's directors have strong ties with senior government officials in Maienar and the country's politicians are keen to develop new industries, especially ones with a long-term future.

The area identified by Mezza Co is a rich fishing ground for local fishermen, who have been fishing there for many generations. However, the fishermen are poor and have little political influence. The general perception is that the fishermen contribute little to Maienar's economic development. The coastal area, although naturally beautiful, has not been well developed for tourism. It is thought that the high carbon absorbing plant, if grown on a commercial scale, may have a negative impact on fish stocks and other wildlife in the area. The resulting decline in fish stocks may make it impossible for the fishermen to continue with their traditional way of life.

Required

(a)   Discuss the key issues that the directors of Mezza Co should consider when making the decision about whether or not to commercialise the new product, and suggest how these issues may be mitigated or resolved.   **(17 marks)**

(b)   Advise the board on what Mezza Co's integrated report should disclose about the impact of undertaking the project on Mezza Co's capitals.   **(8 marks)**

(Total = 25 marks)

2 Preparation question: Strom (12/12, amended)   49 mins

[Note that from September 2018 questions that are wholly narrative will not be set]

Strom Co is a clothing retailer, with stores selling mid-price clothes and clothing accessories throughout Europe. It sells its own-brand items, which are produced by small manufacturers located in Africa, who work solely for Strom Co. The recent European sovereign debt crisis has affected a number of countries in the European Union (EU). Consequently, Strom Co has found trading conditions to be extremely difficult, putting pressure on profits and sales revenue.

The sovereign debt crisis in Europe resulted in countries finding it increasingly difficult and expensive to issue government bonds to raise funds. Two main reasons have been put forward to explain why the crisis took place: firstly, a number of countries continued to borrow excessive funds, because their expenditure exceeded taxation revenues; and secondly, a number of countries allocated significant sums of money to support their banks following the 'credit crunch' and the banking crisis.

In order to prevent countries defaulting on their debt obligations and being downgraded, the countries in the EU and the International Monetary Fund (IMF) established a fund to provide financial support to member states threatened by the risk of default, credit downgrades and excessive borrowing yields. Strict economic conditions known as austerity measures were imposed on these countries in exchange for receiving financial support.

The austerity measures have affected Strom Co negatively, and the years 20X1 and 20X2 have been particularly bad, with sales revenue declining by 15% and profits by 25% in 20X1, and remaining at 20X1 levels in 20X2. On investigation, Strom Co noted that clothing retailers selling clothes at low prices and at high prices were not affected as badly as Strom Co or other mid-price retailers. Indeed, the retailers selling low-priced clothes had increased their profits, and retailers selling luxury, expensive clothes had maintained their profits over the last two to three years.

In order to improve profitability, Strom Co's board of directors expects to cut costs where possible. A significant fixed cost relates to quality control, which includes monitoring the working conditions of employees of Strom Co's clothing manufacturers, as part of its ethical commitment.

Required

(a)   Explain the role and aims of the IMF and discuss possible reasons why the austerity measures imposed on EU countries might have affected Strom Co negatively.   **(10 marks)**

(b)   Suggest, giving reasons, why the austerity measures might not have affected clothing retailers at the high and low price range, as much as the mid-price range retailers like Strom Co.   **(4 marks)**

(c)   Discuss the risks to Strom Co of reducing the costs relating to quality control and how the detrimental impact of such reductions in costs could be decreased.   **(6 marks)**

(d)   Discuss the competitive advantages that a global multinational clothing retailer would have over a clothing retailer based in one Eurozone country.   **(5 marks)**

(Total = 25 marks)

3 Preparation question: PMU (12/10, amended)   49 mins

[Note that from September 2018 questions that are wholly narrative will not be set]

Prospice Mentis University (PMU) is a prestigious private institution and a member of the Holly League, which is made up of universities based in Rosinante and renowned worldwide as being of the highest quality. Universities in Rosinante have benefited particularly from students coming from Kantaka, and PMU has been no exception. However, PMU has recognised that Kantaka has a large population of able students who cannot afford to study overseas. Therefore it wants to investigate how it can offer some of its most popular degree programmes in Kantaka, where students will be able to study at a significantly lower cost. It is considering whether to enter into a joint venture with a local institution or to independently set up its own university site in Kantaka.

Offering courses overseas would be a first from a Holly League institution and indeed from any academic institution based in Rosinante. However, there have been less renowned academic institutions from other countries which have formed joint ventures with small private institutions in Kantaka to deliver degree programmes. These have been of low quality and are not held in high regard by the population or the Government of Kantaka.

In Kantaka, government-run universities and a handful of large private academic institutions, none of which have entered into joint ventures, are held in high regard. However, the demand for places in these institutions far outstrips the supply of places and many students are forced to go to the smaller private institutions or to study overseas if they can afford it.

After an initial investigation the following points have come to light:

1   The Kantaka Government is keen to attract foreign direct investment (FDI) and offer tax concessions to businesses which bring investment funds into the country and enhance the local business environment. However, at present the Kantaka Government places restrictions on the profits that can be remitted to foreign companies which set up subsidiaries in the country. There are no restrictions on profits remitted to a foreign company that has established a joint venture with a local company. It is also likely that PMU would need to borrow a substantial amount of money if it were to set up independently. The investment funds required would be considerably smaller if it went into a joint venture.

2   Given the past experiences of poor quality education offered by joint ventures between small local private institutions and overseas institutions, the Kantaka Government has been reluctant to approve degrees from such institutions. The Government has also not allowed graduates from these institutions to work in national or local government, or in nationalised organisations.

3   Over the past two years the Kantaka currency has depreciated against other currencies, but economic commentators believe that this may not continue for much longer.

4   A large proportion of PMU's academic success is due to innovative teaching and learning methods, and high quality research. The teaching and learning methods used in Kantaka's educational institutions are very different. Apart from the larger private and government-run universities, little academic research is undertaken elsewhere in Kantaka's education sector.

Required

(a)   Discuss the benefits and disadvantages of PMU entering into a joint venture instead of setting up independently in Kantaka. As part of your discussion, consider how the disadvantages can be mitigated and the additional information PMU needs in order to make its decision.   **(20 marks)**

(b)   Assuming that there are limits on funds that can be repatriated from Kantaka, briefly discuss the steps PMU could take to get around this, if it set up a subsidiary in Kantaka.   **(5 marks)**

(Total = 25 marks)

4 Preparation question: Kilenc (6/12, amended)   49 mins

[Note that from September 2018 questions that are wholly narrative will not be set]

Kilenc Co, a large listed company based in the UK, produces pharmaceutical products which are exported around the world. It is reviewing a proposal to set up a subsidiary company to manufacture a range of body and facial creams in Lanosia. These products will be sold to local retailers and to retailers in nearby countries.

Lanosia has a small but growing manufacturing industry in pharmaceutical products, although it remains largely reliant on imports. The Lanosian Government has been keen to promote the pharmaceutical manufacturing industry through purchasing local pharmaceutical products, providing government grants and reducing the industry's corporate tax rate. It also imposes large duties on imported pharmaceutical products which compete with the ones produced locally.

Although politically stable, the recent worldwide financial crisis has had a significant negative impact on Lanosia. The country's national debt has grown substantially following a bailout of its banks and it has had to introduce economic measures which are hampering the country's ability to recover from a deep recession. Growth in real wages has been negative over the past three years, the economy has shrunk in the past year and inflation has remained higher than normal during this time.

On the other hand, corporate investment in capital assets, research and development, and education and training has grown recently and interest rates remain low. This has led some economists to suggest that the economy should start to recover soon. Employment levels remain high in spite of low nominal wage growth.

Lanosian corporate governance regulations stipulate that at least 40% of equity share capital must be held by the local population. In addition, at least 50% of members on the board of directors, including the Chairman, must be from Lanosia. Kilenc Co wants to finance the subsidiary company using a mixture of debt and equity. It wants to raise additional equity and debt finance in Lanosia in order to minimise exchange rate exposure. The small size of the subsidiary will have minimal impact on Kilenc Co's capital structure. Kilenc Co intends to raise the 40% equity through an initial public offering (IPO) in Lanosia and provide the remaining 60% of the equity funds from its own cash funds.

Required

(a) Discuss the key risks and issues that Kilenc Co should consider when setting up a subsidiary company in Lanosia, and suggest how these may be mitigated. **(15 marks)**

(b) The directors of Kilenc Co have learnt that a sizeable number of equity trades in Lanosia are conducted using dark pool trading systems.

Required

Explain what dark pool trading systems are and how Kilenc Co's proposed IPO may be affected by these.
(5 marks)

(c) Lanosia has a reputation as a country with significant levels of money laundering.

Required

Explain the steps that Kilenc Co should take to prevent the company being used by money launderers.
(5 marks)

(Total = 25 marks)

5 Chawan (6/15)   49 mins

The treasury department of Chawan Co, a listed company, aims to maintain a portfolio of around $360 million consisting of equity shares, corporate bonds and government bonds, which it can turn into cash quickly for investment projects. Chawan Co is considering disposing of 27 million shares, valued at $2.15 each, which it has invested in Oden Co. The head of Chawan Co's treasury department is of the opinion that, should the decision be made to dispose of its equity stake in Oden Co, this should be sold through a dark pool network and not sold on the stock exchange where Oden Co's shares are listed. In the last few weeks, there have also been rumours that Oden Co may become subject to a takeover bid.

Oden Co operates in the travel and leisure (T&L) sector, and the poor weather conditions in recent years, coupled with a continuing recession, have meant that the T&L sector is underperforming. Over the past three years, sales revenue fell by an average of 8% per year in the T&L sector. However, there are signs that the economy is starting to recover, but this is by no means certain.

Given below are extracts from the recent financial statements and other financial information for Oden Co and the T&L sector.

ODEN CO
YEAR ENDING 31 MAY

	20X3	20X4	20X5
	$m	$m	$m
Total non-current assets	972	990	980
Total current assets	128	142	126
Total assets	1,100	1,132	1,106
Equity			
Ordinary shares ($0.50)	300	300	300
Reserves	305	329	311
Total equity	605	629	611

	20X3	20X4	20X5
	$m	$m	$m
Non-current liabilities			
Bank loans	115	118	100
Bonds	250	250	260
Total non-current liabilities	365	368	360
Current liabilities			
Trade and other payables	42	45	37
Bank overdraft	88	90	98
Total current liabilities	130	135	135
Total equity and liabilities	1,100	1,132	1,106

ODEN CO
YEAR ENDING 31 MAY

	20X3	20X4	20X5
	$m	$m	$m
Sales revenue	1,342	1,335	1,185
Operating profit	218	203	123
Finance costs	(23)	(27)	(35)
Profit before tax	195	176	88
Taxation	(35)	(32)	(16)
Profit for the year	160	144	72

OTHER FINANCIAL INFORMATION (BASED ON ANNUAL FIGURES TILL 31 MAY OF EACH YEAR)

	20X2	20X3	20X4	20X5
Oden Co average share price ($)	2.10	2.50	2.40	2.20
Oden Co dividend per share ($)	0.15	0.18	0.20	0.15
T&L sector average share price ($)	3.80	4.40	4.30	4.82
T&L sector average earnings per share ($)	0.32	0.36	0.33	0.35
T&L sector average dividend per share ($)	0.25	0.29	0.29	0.31
Oden Co's equity beta	1.5	1.5	1.6	2.0
T&L sector average equity beta	1.5	1.4	1.5	1.6

The risk-free rate and the market return have remained fairly constant over the last 10 years at 4% and 10% respectively.

Required

(a) Explain what a dark pool network is and why Chawan Co may want to dispose of its equity stake in Oden Co through one, instead of through the stock exchange where Oden Co's shares are listed. **(5 marks)**

(b) Discuss whether or not Chawan Co should dispose of its equity stake in Oden Co. Provide relevant calculations to support the discussion.

Note. Up to 10 marks are available for the calculations. **(20 marks)**

(Total = 25 marks)

6 Limni Co (6/13)   49 mins

Limni Co is a large company manufacturing hand-held electronic devices such as mobile phones and tablet computers. The company has been growing rapidly over the last few years, but it also has high research and development expenditure. It is involved in a number of projects worldwide, developing new and innovative products and systems in a rapidly changing industry. Due to the nature of the industry, this significant growth in earnings has never been stable, but has depended largely on the success of the new innovations and competitor actions. However, in the last two years it seems that the rapid period of growth is slowing, with fewer products coming to market compared to previous years.

Limni Co has never paid dividends and has financed projects through internally generated funds and with occasional rights issues of new share capital. It currently has insignificant levels of debt. The retained cash reserves have recently grown because of a drop in the level of investment in new projects.

The company has an active treasury division which invests spare funds in traded equities, bonds and other financial instruments; and releases the funds when required for new projects. The division also manages cash flow risk using money and derivative markets. The treasury division is currently considering investing in three companies with the following profit after tax (PAT) and dividend history:

	Company Theta		Company Omega		Company Kappa	
Year	PAT	Dividends	PAT	Dividends	PAT	Dividends
	$'000	$'000	$'000	$'000	$'000	$'000
20X7	57,100	22,840	93,300	60,560	162,400	44,100
20X6	54,400	21,760	90,600	57,680	141,500	34,200
20X5	52,800	21,120	88,000	54,840	108,900	26,300
20X4	48,200	19,280	85,400	52,230	105,700	20,250
20X3	45,500	18,200	82,900	49,740	78,300	15,700

All three companies' share capital has remained largely unchanged since 20X3.

Recently, Limni Co's board of directors (BoD) came under pressure from the company's larger shareholders to start returning some of the funds, currently retained by the company, back to the shareholders. The BoD thinks that the shareholders have a strong case to ask for repayments. However, it is unsure whether to pay a special, one-off large dividend from its dividend capacity and retained funds, followed by small annual dividend payments, or to undertake a periodic share buyback scheme over the next few years.

Limni Co is due to prepare its statement of profit or loss shortly and estimates that the annual sales revenue will be $600 million, on which its profit before tax is expected to be 23% of sales revenue. It charges depreciation of 25% on a straight-line basis on its non-current assets of $220 million. It estimates that $67 million investment in current and non-current assets was spent during the year. It is due to receive $15 million in dividends from its subsidiary companies, on which annual tax of 20% on average has been paid. Limni Co itself pays annual tax at 26%, and the tax authorities where Limni Co is based charge tax on dividend remittances made by overseas subsidiary companies, but give full credit on tax already paid on those remittances. In order to fund the new policy of returning funds to shareholders, Limni Co's BoD wants to increase the current estimated dividend capacity by 10%, by asking the overseas subsidiary companies for higher repatriations.

Required

(a) Discuss Limni Co's current dividend, financing and risk management policies, and suggest how the decision to return retained funds back to the shareholders will affect these policies. **(8 marks)**

(b) Evaluate the dividend policies of each of the three companies that Limni Co is considering investing in, and discuss which company Limni Co might select. **(8 marks)**

(c) Calculate, and briefly comment on, how much the dividends from overseas companies need to increase by, to increase Limni Co's dividend capacity by 10%. **(6 marks)**

(d) Discuss the benefits to Limni Co's shareholders of receiving repayments through a share buyback scheme as opposed to the dividend scheme described above. **(3 marks)**

(Total = 25 marks)

7 International Enterprises (12/07, amended)   49 mins

You are the chief financial officer of International Enterprises, a listed multinational company with interests in Europe and the Far East. You are concerned about certain aspects of the company's financial management. The company has enjoyed a high rate of growth over the last three years as a result of a single product's development. This product has had a big impact in the fast moving mobile communications industry. However, the company does not have any new products in development and is relying on expanding its market share and developing upgraded versions of the current product.

As part of your preparation for the board meeting to discuss the 20X7 draft accounts, you have prepared a projected statement of profit or loss and statement of financial position for the year ending 31 December 20X8. These projections are based upon a number of agreed assumptions taken from the company's strategic plan. As part of the agenda, the board will also consider its dividend target for the forthcoming year.

INTERNATIONAL ENTERPRISES
STATEMENT OF PROFIT OR LOSS FOR THE YEAR

ENDED 31 DECEMBER	20X8 (projected) $m	20X7 (draft) $m	20X6 (actual) $m
Revenue	288.1	261.9	220.0
Cost of sales	143.2	132.6	104.0
Gross profit	144.9	129.3	116.0
Less other operating costs	36.1	27.0	24.0
Operating profit	108.8	102.3	92.0
Finance costs	1.8	2.3	2.3
Profit before tax	107.0	100.0	89.7
Income tax expense (at 30%)	32.1	30.0	26.9
Profit for the period	74.9	70.0	62.8

STATEMENT OF FINANCIAL POSITION AS AT

31 DECEMBER	20X8 (projected) $m	20X7 (draft) $m	20X6 (actual) $m
Non-current assets (see Note)			
Buildings, plant and machinery	168.0	116.0	96.0
Current assets			
Inventories	3.2	3.7	2.3
Receivables	25.6	29.1	19.6
Cash	151.8	155.8	121.7
Total current assets	180.6	188.6	143.6
Total assets	348.6	304.6	239.6
Equity and liabilities			
Paid up share capital			
Ordinary shares (25c)	25.0	25.0	20.0
Other reserves	12.0	12.0	10.0
Retained earnings	216.9	170.0	120.0
Less dividends payable	0.0	−28.0	−20.0
	216.9	142.0	100.0
Total equity	253.9	179.0	130.0
Current liabilities			
Trade payables	8.8	7.7	6.4
Tax payable	28.5	25.6	23.3
Interest	1.8	2.3	2.3
Dividends payable	0.0	28.0	20.0
Total current liabilities	39.1	63.6	52.0
Non-current liabilities			
Loans	35.0	45.0	45.0
Provisions (deferred tax)	20.6	17.0	12.6
Total non-current liabilities	55.6	62.0	57.6
Total liabilities	94.7	125.6	109.6
Total equity and liabilities	348.6	304.6	239.6

Note.	20X8 $m	20X7 $m	20X6 $m
Non-current assets	280.0	200.0	160.0
Less accumulated depreciation	112.0	84.0	64.0
Net book value of non-current assets	168.0	116.0	96.0

Required

(a) Prepare a cash flow forecast for the year ended 31 December 20X8. **Note.** The format does not need to comply with accounting standards. **(6 marks)**

(b) Estimate the company's maximum dividend capacity after the target level of capital reinvestment is undertaken (making any working capital adjustments you deem necessary) and discuss whether International Enterprises' dividend policy is sustainable and whether dividends should be paid at the maximum capacity level or not. **(12 marks)**

(c) Review the potential performance of the business in the year ended 31 December 20X8, if the expectations contained within the strategic plan are fulfilled, using any performance measures you think appropriate. **(7 marks)**

(Total = 25 marks)

8 Anchorage Retail (12/09, amended)   49 mins

Anchorage Retail Company is a large high street and online retailer that has lost its position as the premier quality clothes, household goods and food chain in the European market. Five years previously there had been speculation that the company would be a takeover target for any one of a number of private equity firms. However, a newly appointed and flamboyant Chief Executive Officer, John Bear, initiated a major capital reconstruction and a highly aggressive turnaround strategy.

The reaction to that turnaround strategy was an improvement in the company's share price from $3 to $7 per share over the subsequent 3 years. The private equity firms which had been interested in acquiring the company were deterred for two principal reasons. First, John Bear had a reputation for his aggressive style and his history of defending his companies against takeover. Second, the share price of Anchorage had reached a record high.

In recent months a belief in the investment community had become widespread that the revival of the company's performance had more to do with the reorganisation of the firm's capital than the success of John Bear's turnaround strategy. John Bear insisted, however, that the improvements in the reported 'bottom line' reflected a sustainable improvement in the performance of the business. However, the recession in the European retail market following the 'credit crunch' led to a sharp reduction in Anchorage's share price reinforced by concerns in the financial markets that John Bear has become too dominant in the board of the company.

The most recent accounts for Anchorage, in summary form, are as follows:

Anchorage Retail Company

PROFIT/LOSS STATEMENT

	20X9	20X8
	$m	$m
Revenue	9,000	8,500
Cost of sales	5,500	5,250
Gross profit	3,500	3,250
Less other operating costs	2,250	2,220
Operating profit	1,250	1,030
Finance costs	80	110
Profit before tax	1,170	920
Income tax expense (at 30%)	310	270
Profit for the period	860	650

SUMMARY CASH FLOW STATEMENT

	20X9
	$m
Operating cash flow	1,610
Less interest	(110)
Less taxation	(270)
Free cash flow before reinvestment	1,230
Dividend paid	(270)
CAPEX	(740)
Financing	(70)
Net cash flow	150

STATEMENT OF FINANCIAL POSITION

	20X9 $m	20X8 $m
Assets		
Non-current assets	4,980	4,540
Current assets	1,220	850
Total assets	6,200	5,390
Equity and liabilities		
Ordinary share capital (25c)	400	425
Share premium	230	200
Capital redemption reserve	2,300	2,300
Other reserves	(6,540)	(6,500)
Retained earnings	5,990	5,400
Dividends payable	(350)	(270)
Total equity	2,030	1,555
Non-current liabilities	1,900	1,865
Current liabilities	2,270	1,970
Total equity and liabilities	6,200	5,390

The management of Polar Finance, a large private equity investment fund, has begun a review following the sale of a substantial part of its investment portfolio. It is now considering Anchorage as a potential target for acquisition. They have contacted you and asked if you would provide a brief report on the financial performance of Anchorage and give an independent view on a bid the company is considering for the business. The suggested bid would be in the form of a cash offer of $3.20 a share which would represent a 60¢ premium on the current share price. Reviewing the fund's existing business portfolio prior to acquisition you estimate that its asset beta is 0.285. Polar Finance has equity funds under management of $1,125 million and a market based gearing ratio (debt as a proportion of total capital employed) of 0.85. This acquisition would be financed from additional cash resources and by additional borrowing of $2.5 billion. It is expected that Anchorage's proportion of the total post-acquisition cash flows will be 20%. Polar Finance does not pay tax on its income.

During your investigations you discover the following:

1   The equity beta for Anchorage is 0.75. The current risk-free rate is 5%. In order to estimate the rate of return on the market using the dividend growth model you note that the current dividend yield on a broadly based market index is 3.1% and the growth in GDP is 4% nominal. The growth of the firms in the index is fairly represented by growth in GDP.

2   Anchorage has a gearing ratio based upon market capitalisation of 24%. You estimate that its current cost of debt capital is 6.2%. You may assume that Anchorage's cost of finance has been constant over the last 12 months.

You may use year-end statement of financial position values when calculating performance ratios.

Required

(a)   Outline the principal risks that Polar Finance should consider when assessing an acquisition of this size.

(6 marks)

(b)   Summarise the performance of Anchorage in 20X9 compared with 20X8 using ratios you consider appropriate.

(6 marks)

(c)   Estimate the impact of this acquisition upon the required rate of return of equity investors in Polar Finance.

(7 marks)

(d)   Evaluate the argument that this company may have been systematically undervalued by the market and is therefore a suitable target for acquisition.

(6 marks)

(Total = 25 marks)

9 High K

High K Co is one of the three largest supermarket chains in the country of Townia. Its two principal competitors, Dely Co and Leminster Co, are of similar size to High K Co. In common with its competitors (but see below), High K Co operates three main types of store:

- Town centre stores – these sell food and drink and a range of small household items. High K Co's initial growth was based on its town centre stores, but it has been shutting them over the last decade, although the rate of closure has slowed in the last couple of years.

- Convenience stores – these are smaller and sell food and drink and very few other items. Between 20X3 and 20Y3, High K Co greatly expanded the number of convenience stores it operated. Their performance has varied, however, and since 20Y3, High K Co has not opened any new stores and closed a number of the worst-performing stores.

- Out-of-town stores – these sell food and drink and a full range of household items, including large electrical goods and furniture. The number of out-of-town stores which High K Co operated increased significantly until 20Y0, but has only increased slightly since.

The majority of town centre and out-of-town stores premises are owned by High K Co, but 85% of convenience stores premises are currently leased.

High K Co also sells most of its range of products online, either offering customers home delivery or 'click and collect' (where the customer orders the goods online and picks them up from a collection point in one of the stores).

High K Co's year end is 31 December. When its 20Y6 results were published in April 20Y7, High K Co's chief executive emphasised that the group was focusing on:

- Increasing total shareholder return by improvements in operating efficiency and enhancement of responsiveness to customer needs

- Ensuring competitive position by maintaining flexibility to respond to new strategic challenges

- Maintaining financial strength by using diverse sources of funding, including making use in future of revolving credit facilities

Since April 20Y7, Dely Co and Leminster Co have both announced that they will be making significant investments to boost online sales. Dely Co intends to fund its investments by closing all its town centre and convenience stores, although it also intends to open more out-of-town stores in popular locations.

The government of Townia was re-elected in May 20Y7. In the 18 months prior to the election, it eased fiscal policy and consumer spending significantly increased. However, it has tightened fiscal policy since the election to avoid the economy overheating. It has also announced an investigation into whether the country's large retail chains treat their suppliers unfairly.

BPP
LEARNING MEDIA

Extracts from High K Co's 20Y6 financial statements and other information about it are given below:

HIGH K CO
STATEMENT OF PROFIT OR LOSS EXTRACTS
YEAR ENDING 31 DECEMBER (ALL AMOUNTS IN $m)

	20Y4	20Y5	20Y6
Sales revenue	23,508	23,905	24,463
Gross profit	1,018	1,211	1,514
Operating profit	204	407	712
Finance costs	(125)	(115)	(100)
Profit after tax	52	220	468
Dividends	150	170	274

HIGH K CO STATEMENT OF FINANCIAL POSITION EXTRACTS
YEAR ENDING 31 DECEMBER (ALL AMOUNTS IN $m)

	20Y4	20Y5	20Y6
Non-current assets	10,056	9,577	8,869
Cash and cash equivalents	24	709	1,215
Other current assets	497	618	747
Total non-current and current assets	10,577	10,904	10,831
Equity			
Ordinary shares ($1)	800	800	800
Reserves	7,448	7.519	7,627
Total equity	8,248	8,319	8,427
Non-current liabilities	1,706	1,556	1,246
Current liabilities	623	1,029	1,158
Other information			
Market price per share			
(in $, $3.89 at end of 20Y3, $3.17 currently)	3.54	3.34	3.23
Staff working in shops ('000)	78	75	72
Segment information			
Revenue ($m)			
Town centre stores	5,265	5,189	5,192
Convenience stores	3,786	3,792	3,833
Out-of-town stores	10,220	10,340	10,547
Store revenue	19,271	19,321	19,572
Online sales	4,237	4,584	4,891
Number of stores			
Town centre stores	165	157	153
Convenience stores	700	670	640
Out-of-town stores	220	224	227

Required

(a) Evaluate High K Co's financial performance. You should indicate in your discussion areas where further information about High K Co would be helpful. Provide relevant calculations for ratios and trends to support your evaluation.

Note. Up to 10 marks are available for calculations. **(21 marks)**

(b) Discuss how High K Co may seek to finance an investment programme. **(4 marks)**

(Total = 25 marks)

10 Lamri (12/10, amended) 49 mins

Lamri Co (Lamri), a listed company, is expecting sales revenue to grow to $80 million next year, which is an increase of 20% from the current year. The operating profit margin for next year is forecast to be the same as this year at 30% of sales revenue. In addition to these profits, Lamri receives 75% of the after-tax profits from one of its wholly owned foreign subsidiaries, Magnolia Co (Magnolia), as dividends. However, its second wholly owned foreign subsidiary, Strymon Co (Strymon), does not pay dividends.

Lamri is due to pay dividends of $7.5 million shortly and has maintained a steady 8% annual growth rate in dividends over the past few years. The company has grown rapidly in the last few years as a result of investment in key projects and this is likely to continue.

For the coming year it is expected that Lamri will require the following capital investment.

- An investment equivalent to the amount of depreciation to keep its non-current asset base at the present productive capacity. Lamri charges depreciation of 25% on a straight-line basis on its non-current assets of $15 million. This charge has been included when calculating the operating profit amount.

- A 25% investment in additional non-current assets for every $1 increase in sales revenue.

- $4.5 million additional investment in non-current assets for a new project.

Lamri also requires a 15% investment in working capital for every $1 increase in sales revenue.

Strymon produces specialist components solely for Magnolia to assemble into finished goods. Strymon will produce 300,000 specialist components at $12 variable cost per unit and will incur fixed costs of $2.1 million for the coming year. It will then transfer the components to Magnolia at full cost price, where they will be assembled at a cost of $8 per unit and sold for $50 per unit. Magnolia will incur additional fixed costs of $1.5 million in the assembly process.

Tax-Ethic (TE) is a charitable organisation devoted to reducing tax avoidance schemes by companies operating in poor countries around the world. TE has petitioned Lamri's board of directors to reconsider Strymon's policy of transferring goods at full cost. TE suggests that the policy could be changed to cost plus 40% mark-up. If Lamri changes Strymon's policy, it is expected that Strymon would be asked to remit 75% of its after-tax profits as dividends to Lamri.

Other information

1   Lamri's outstanding non-current liabilities of $35 million, on which it pays interest of 8% per year, and its 30 million $1 issued equity capital will not change for the coming year.

2   Lamri's, Magnolia's and Strymon's profits are taxed at 28%, 22% and 42% respectively. A withholding tax of 10% is deducted from any dividends remitted from Strymon.

3   The tax authorities where Lamri is based charge tax on profits made by subsidiary companies but give full credit for tax already paid by overseas subsidiaries.

4   All costs and revenues are in $ equivalent amounts and exchange rate fluctuations can be ignored.

Required

(a)   Calculate Lamri's dividend capacity for the coming year prior to implementing TE's proposal and after implementing the proposal.
                                                                          (14 marks)

(b)   Comment on the impact of implementing TE's proposal and suggest possible actions Lamri may take as a result.
                                                                          (6 marks)

(c)   Outline the mechanisms that the tax authorities could use to prevent transfer price manipulation by Lamri.
                                                                          (5 marks)

                                                                    (Total = 25 marks)

11 Moonstar (Sep/Dec 15)   49 mins

Moonstar Co is a property development company which is planning to undertake a $200 million commercial property development. Moonstar Co has had some difficulties over the last few years, with some developments not generating the expected returns and the company has at times struggled to pay its finance costs. As a result Moonstar Co's credit rating has been lowered, affecting the terms it can obtain for bank finance. Although Moonstar Co is listed on its local stock exchange, 75% of the share capital is held by members of the family who founded the company. The family members who are shareholders do not wish to subscribe for a rights issue and are unwilling to dilute their control over the company by authorising a new issue of equity shares. Moonstar Co's board is therefore considering other methods of financing the development, which the directors believe will generate higher returns than other recent investments, as the country where Moonstar Co is based appears to be emerging from recession.

Securitisation proposals

One of the non-executive directors of Moonstar Co has proposed that it should raise funds by means of a securitisation process, transferring the rights to the rental income from the commercial property development to a special purpose vehicle. Her proposals assume that the leases will generate an income of 11% per annum to Moonstar Co over a 10-year period. She proposes that Moonstar Co should use 90% of the value of the investment for a collateralised loan obligation which should be structured as follows:

- 60% of the collateral value to support a tranche of A-rated floating rate loan notes offering investors LIBOR plus 150 basis points

- 15% of the collateral value to support a tranche of B-rated fixed rate loan notes offering investors 12%

- 15% of the collateral value to support a tranche of C-rated fixed rate loan notes offering investors 13%

- 10% of the collateral value to support a tranche as subordinated certificates, with the return being the excess of receipts over payments from the securitisation process

The non-executive director believes that there will be sufficient demand for all tranches of the loan notes from investors. Investors will expect the income stream from the development to be low risk, as they will expect the property market to improve with the recession coming to an end and enough potential lessees to be attracted by the new development.

The non-executive director predicts that there would be annual costs of $200,000 in administering the loan. She acknowledges that there would be interest rate risks associated with the proposal, and proposes a fixed for variable interest rate swap on the A-rated floating rate notes, exchanging LIBOR for 9.5%.

However, the Finance Director believes that the prediction of the income from the development that the non-executive director has made is over-optimistic. He believes that it is most likely that the total value of the rental income will be 5% lower than the non-executive director has forecast. He believes that there is some risk that the returns could be so low as to jeopardise the income for the C-rated fixed rate loan note holders.

Islamic finance

Moonstar Co's Chief Executive has wondered whether Sukuk finance would be a better way of funding the development than the securitisation.

Moonstar Co's Chairman has pointed out that a major bank in the country where Moonstar Co is located has begun to offer a range of Islamic financial products. The Chairman has suggested that a Mudaraba contract would be the most appropriate method of providing the funds required for the investment.

Required

(a) Calculate the amounts in $ which each of the tranches can expect to receive from the securitisation arrangement proposed by the non-executive director and discuss how the variability in rental income affects the returns from the securitisation. **(11 marks)**

(b) Discuss the benefits and risks for Moonstar Co associated with the securitisation arrangement that the non-executive director has proposed. **(6 marks)**

(c) (i) Discuss the suitability of Sukuk finance to fund the investment, including an assessment of its appeal to potential investors. **(4 marks)**

    (ii) Discuss whether a Mudaraba contract would be an appropriate method of financing the investment and discuss why the bank may have concerns about providing finance by this method. **(4 marks)**

(Total = 25 marks)

ADVANCED INVESTMENT APPRAISAL

Questions 12 to 28 cover advanced investment appraisal, the subject of Part B of the BPP Study Text for AFM.

12 Preparation question: Cathlynn   29 mins

(a) The current share price of Cathlynn plc is £3.50. Using the Black-Scholes model, estimate the value of a European call option on the shares of the company that has an exercise price of £3.30 and 3 months to run before it expires. The risk-free rate of interest is 8% and the variance of the rate of return on the share has been 12%.

Note. The Black-Scholes formula shows call price for a European option P_c where

$P_c = P_s N(d_1) - Xe^{-rT} N(d_2)$

Where N(d) = cumulative distribution function

$$d_1 = \frac{\ln(P_S/X) + rT}{\sigma\sqrt{T}} + 0.5\sigma\sqrt{T}$$

d_2 = $d_1 - \sigma\sqrt{T}$

P_s = share price

e = the exponential constant 2.7183

X = exercise price of option

r = annual (continuously compounded) risk-free rate of return

T = time of expiry of option in years

σ = share price volatility, the standard deviation of the rate of return on shares

$N(d_x)$ = delta, the probability that a deviation of less than d_x will occur in a normal distribution with a mean of zero and a standard deviation of one

ln = natural log

Normal distribution tables are in the appendix to this Kit.   **(10 marks)**

(b) Discuss the main limitations of the Black-Scholes model.   **(5 marks)**

                                                                                (Total = 15 marks)

13 Preparation question: Faoilean (6/14)   49 mins

[Note that from September 2018 questions that are wholly narrative will not be set]

The Chief Executive Officer (CEO) of Faoilean Co has just returned from a discussion at a leading university on the 'application of options to investment decisions and corporate value'. She wants to understand how some of the ideas which were discussed can be applied to decisions made at Faoilean Co. She is still a little unclear about some of the discussion on options and their application, and wants further clarification on the following:

(i) Faoilean Co is involved in the exploration and extraction of oil and gas. Recently there have been indications that there could be significant deposits of oil and gas just off the shores of the Republic of Ireland. The Government of the Republic of Ireland has invited companies to submit bids for the rights to commence the initial exploration of the area to assess the likelihood and amount of oil and gas deposits, with further extraction rights to follow. Faoilean Co is considering putting in a bid for the rights. The speaker leading the discussion suggested that using options as an investment assessment tool would be particularly useful to Faoilean Co in this respect.

(ii) The speaker further suggested that options were useful in determining the value of equity and default risk, and suggested that this was why companies facing severe financial distress could still have a positive equity value.

(iii) Towards the end of the discussion, the speaker suggested that changes in the values of options can be measured in terms of a number of risk factors known as the 'greeks', such as the 'vega'. The CEO is unclear why option values are affected by so many different risk factors.

Required

(a) With regard to (i) above, discuss how Faoilean Co may use the idea of options to help with the investment decision in bidding for the exploration rights, and explain the assumptions made when using the idea of options in making investment decisions. **(11 marks)**

(b) With regard to (ii) above, discuss how options could be useful in determining the value of equity and default risk, and why companies facing severe financial distress still have positive equity values. **(9 marks)**

(c) With regard to (iii) above, explain why changes in option values are determined by numerous different risk factors and what 'vega' determines. **(5 marks)**

(Total = 25 marks)

14 Preparation question: Bournelorth (Mar/Jun 17)   49 mins

[Note that from September 2018 questions that are wholly narrative will not be set]

Bournelorth Co is an IT company which was established by three friends ten years ago. It was listed on a local stock exchange for smaller companies nine months ago.

Bournelorth Co originally provided support to businesses in the financial services sector. It has been able to expand into other sectors over time due to the excellent services it has provided and the high quality staff whom its founders recruited. The founders have been happy with the level of profits which the IT services have generated. Over time they have increasingly left the supervision of the IT services in the hands of experienced managers and focused on developing diagnostic applications (apps). The founders have worked fairly independently of each other on development work. Each has a small team of staff and all three want their teams to work in an informal environment which they believe enhances creativity.

Two apps which Bournelorth Co developed were very successful and generated significant profits. The founders wanted the company to invest much more in developing diagnostic apps. Previously they had preferred to use internal funding, because they were worried that external finance providers would want a lot of information about how Bournelorth Co is performing. However, the amount of finance required meant that funding had to be obtained from external sources and they decided to seek a listing, as two of Bournelorth Co's principal competitors had recently been successfully listed.

25% of Bournelorth Co's equity shares were made available on the stock exchange for external investors, which was the minimum allowed by the rules of the exchange. The founders have continued to own the remaining 75% of Bournelorth Co's equity share capital. Although the listing was fully subscribed, the price which new investors paid was lower than the directors had originally hoped.

The board now consists of the three founders, who are the executive directors, and two independent non-executive directors, who were appointed when the company was listed. The non-executive directors have expressed concerns about the lack of frequency of formal board meetings and the limited time spent by the executive directors overseeing the company's activities, compared with the time they spend leading development work. The non-executive directors would also like Bournelorth Co's external auditors to carry out a thorough review of its risk management and control systems.

The funds obtained from the listing have helped Bournelorth Co expand its development activities. Bournelorth Co's competitors have recently launched some very successful diagnostic apps and its executive directors are now afraid that Bournelorth Co will fall behind its competitors unless there is further investment in development. However, they disagree about how this investment should be funded. One executive director believes that Bournelorth Co should consider selling off its IT support and consultancy services business. The second executive director favours a rights issue and the third executive director would prefer to seek debt finance. At present Bournelorth Co has low gearing and the director who is in favour of debt finance believes that there is too much uncertainty associated with obtaining further equity finance, as investors do not always act rationally.

Required

(a)   Discuss the factors which will determine whether the sources of finance suggested by the executive directors are used to finance further investment in diagnostic applications (apps).   **(8 marks)**

(b)   (i)   Identify the risks associated with investing in the development of apps and describe the controls which Bournelorth Co should have over its investment in development.   **(6 marks)**

        (ii)   Discuss the issues which determine the information Bournelorth Co communicates to external finance providers.   **(3 marks)**

(c)   (i)   Explain the insights which behavioural finance provides about investor behaviour.   **(3 marks)**

        (ii)   Assess how behavioural factors may affect the share price of Bournelorth Co.   **(5 marks)**

(Total = 25 marks)

15 Fernhurst (Sep/Dec 16)   **49 mins**

Fernhurst Co is a manufacturer of mobile communications technology. It is about to launch a new communications device, the Milland, which its directors believe is both more technologically advanced and easier to use than devices currently offered by its rivals.

Investment in the Milland

The Milland will require a major investment in facilities. Fernhurst Co's directors believe that this can take place very quickly and production be started almost immediately.

Fernhurst Co expects to sell 132,500 units of the Milland in its first year. Sales volume is expected to increase by 20% in Year 2 and 30% in Year 3, and then be the same in Year 4 as Year 3, as the product reaches the end of its useful life. The initial selling price in Year 1 is expected to be $100 per unit, before increasing with the rate of inflation annually.

The variable cost of each unit is expected to be $43.68 in Year 1, rising by the rate of inflation in subsequent years annually. Fixed costs are expected to be $900,000 in Year 1, rising by the rate of inflation in subsequent years annually.

The initial investment in non-current assets is expected to be $16,000,000. Fernhurst Co will also need to make an immediate investment of $1,025,000 in working capital. The working capital will be increased annually at the start of each of Years 2 to 4 by the inflation rate and is fully recoverable at the end of the project's life. Fernhurst Co will also incur one-off marketing expenditure of $1,500,000 post-inflation after the launch of the Milland. The marketing expenditure can be assumed to be made at the end of Year 1 and be a tax-allowable expense.

Fernhurst Co pays company tax on profits at an annual rate of 25%. Tax is payable in the year that the tax liability arises. Tax-allowable depreciation is available at 20% on the investment in non-current assets on a reducing balance basis. A balancing adjustment will be available in Year 4. The realisable value of the investment at the end of Year 4 is expected to be zero.

The expected annual rate of inflation in the country in which Fernhurst Co is located is 4% in Year 1 and 5% in Years 2 to 4.

The applicable cost of capital for this investment appraisal is 11%.

Other calculations

Fernhurst Co's finance director has indicated that besides needing a net present value calculation based on this data for the next board meeting, he also needs to know the figure for the project's duration, to indicate to the board how returns from the project will be spread over time.

Failure of launch of the Milland

The finance director would also like some simple analysis based on the possibility that the marketing expenditure is not effective and the launch fails, as he feels that the product's price may be too high. He has suggested that there is a 15% chance that the Milland will have negative net cash flows for Year 1 of $1,000,000 or more. He would like to know by what percentage the selling price could be reduced or increased to result in the investment having a zero net present value, assuming demand remained the same.

Assessment of new products

Fernhurst Co's last board meeting discussed another possible new product, the Racton, and the finance director presented a range of financial data relating to this product, including the results of net present value and payback evaluations. One of the non-executive directors, who is not a qualified accountant, stated that they found it difficult to see the significance of the different items of financial data. Their understanding was that Fernhurst Co merely had to ensure that the investment had a positive net present value and shareholders were bound to be satisfied with it, as it would maximise their wealth in the long term. The Finance Director commented that, in reality, some shareholders looked at the performance of the investments which Fernhurst Co made over the short term, whereas some were more concerned with the longer term. The financial data he presented to board meetings included both short- and long-term measures.

Required

(a) Evaluate the financial acceptability of the investment in the Milland and calculate and comment on the investment's duration. **(15 marks)**

(b) Calculate the percentage change in the selling price required for the investment to have a zero net present value, and discuss the significance of your results. **(5 marks)**

(c) Discuss the non-executive director's understanding of net present value and explain the importance of other measures in providing data about an investment's short- and long-term performance. **(5 marks)**

(Total = 25 marks)

16 Your business (6/09, amended)   49 mins

You have been conducting a detailed review of an investment project proposed by one of the divisions of your business. Your review has two aims: first to correct the proposal for any errors of principle, and second, to recommend a financial measure to replace payback as one of the criteria for acceptability when a project is presented to the company's board of directors for approval. The company's current weighted average cost of capital is 10% per annum.

The initial capital investment is for $150 million followed by $50 million one year later. The post tax cash flows, for this project, in $ million, including the estimated tax benefit from capital allowances for tax purposes, are as follows:

Year	0	1	2	3	4	5	6
Capital investment (plant and machinery):							
First phase	−127.50						
Second phase		−36.88					
Project post-tax cash flow ($ million)			44.00	68.00	60.00	35.00	20.00

Company tax is charged at 30% and is paid/recovered in the year in which the liability is incurred. The company has sufficient profits elsewhere to recover capital allowances on this project, in full, in the year they are incurred. All the capital investment is eligible for a first year allowance for tax purposes of 50% followed by a writing down allowance of 25% per annum on a reducing balance basis.

You notice the following points when conducting your review:

1 An interest charge of 8% per annum on a proposed $50 million loan has been included in the project's post-tax cash flow before tax has been calculated.

2 Depreciation for the use of company shared assets of $4 million per annum has been charged in calculating the project post-tax cash flow.

3 Activity based allocations of company indirect costs of $8 million have been included in the project's post-tax cash flow. However, additional corporate infrastructure costs of $4 million per annum have been ignored which you discover would only be incurred if the project proceeds.

4 It is expected that the capital equipment will be written off and disposed of at the end of Year 6. The proceeds of the sale of the capital equipment are expected to be $7 million which have been included in the forecast of the project's post-tax cash flow. You also notice that an estimate for site clearance of $5 million

has not been included nor any tax saving recognised on the unclaimed writing down allowance on the disposal of the capital equipment.

Required

(a) Prepare a corrected project evaluation using the net present value technique supported by a separate assessment of the sensitivity of the project to a $1 million change in the initial capital expenditure.

(14 marks)

(b) Estimate the discounted payback period and the duration for this project, commenting on the relative advantages and disadvantages of each method.

(5 marks)

(c) Recommend whether this project is acceptable and also which techniques the board should consider when reviewing capital investment projects in future.

(6 marks)

(Total = 25 marks)

17 Tisa Co (6/12, amended)   49 mins

Tisa Co is considering an opportunity to produce an innovative component which, when fitted into motor vehicle engines, will enable them to utilise fuel more efficiently. The component can be manufactured using either process Omega or process Zeta. Although this is an entirely new line of business for Tisa Co, it is of the opinion that developing either process over a period of four years and then selling the production rights at the end of four years to another company may prove lucrative.

The annual after-tax cash flows for each process are as follows:

Process Omega

Year	0	1	2	3	4
After-tax cash flows ($'000)	(3,800)	1,220	1,153	1,386	3,829

Process Zeta

Year	0	1	2	3	4
After-tax cash flows ($'000)	(3,800)	643	546	1,055	5,990

Tisa Co has 10 million 50c shares trading at 180c each. Its loans have a current value of $3.6 million and an average after-tax cost of debt of 4.50%. Tisa Co's capital structure is unlikely to change significantly following the investment in either process.

Elfu Co manufactures electronic parts for cars including the production of a component similar to the one being considered by Tisa Co. Elfu Co's equity beta is 1.40, and it is estimated that the equivalent equity beta for its other activities, excluding the component production, is 1.25. Elfu Co has 400 million 25c shares in issue trading at 120c each. Its debt finance consists of variable rate loans redeemable in seven years. The loans paying interest at base rate plus 120 basis points have a current value of $96 million. It can be assumed that 80% of Elfu Co's debt finance and 75% of Elfu Co's equity finance can be attributed to other activities excluding the component production. Both companies pay annual corporation tax at a rate of 25%. The current base rate is 3.5% and the market risk premium is estimated at 5.8%.

Required

(a) Provide a reasoned estimate of the cost of capital that Tisa Co should use to calculate the net present value of the two processes. Include all relevant calculations.

(8 marks)

(b) Calculate the internal rate of return (IRR) and the modified internal rate of return (MIRR) for Process Omega. Given that the IRR and MIRR of Process Zeta are 26.6% and 23.3% respectively, recommend which process, if any, Tisa Co should proceed with and explain your recommendation.

(8 marks)

(c) Elfu Co has estimated an annual standard deviation of $800,000 on one of its other projects, based on a normal distribution of returns. The average annual return on this project is $2,200,000.

Required

(i) Estimate the project's value at risk (VaR) at a 99% confidence level for 1 year and over the project's life of 5 years. Explain what is meant by the answers obtained. **(4 marks)**

(ii) Apart from the use of VaR, briefly explain methods that Elfu Co can use to deal with risk and uncertainty in investment appraisal and their drawbacks. **(5 marks)**

(Total = 25 marks)

18 Arbore (12/12, amended) 49 mins

Arbore Co is a large listed company with many autonomous departments operating as investment centres. It sets investment limits for each department based on a three-year cycle. Projects selected by departments would have to fall within the investment limits set for each of the three years. All departments would be required to maintain a capital investment monitoring system, and report on their findings annually to Arbore Co's board of directors.

The Durvo department is considering the following five investment projects with three years of initial investment expenditure, followed by several years of positive cash inflows. The department's initial investment expenditure limits are $9,000,000, $6,000,000 and $5,000,000 for years one, two and three respectively. None of the projects can be deferred and all projects can be scaled down but not scaled up.

Investment required at start of year

Project	Year one (Immediately)	Year two	Year three	Project net present value
PDur01	$4,000,000	$1,100,000	$2,400,000	$464,000
PDur02	$800,000	$2,800,000	$3,200,000	$244,000
PDur03	$3,200,000	$3,562,000	$0	$352,000
PDur04	$3,900,000	$0	$200,000	$320,000
PDur05	$2,500,000	$1,200,000	$1,400,000	Not provided

PDur05 project's annual operating cash flows commence at the end of year four and last for a period of 15 years. The project generates annual sales of 300,000 units at a selling price of $14 per unit and incurs total annual relevant costs of $3,230,000. Although the costs and units sold of the project can be predicted with a fair degree of certainty, there is considerable uncertainty about the unit selling price. The department uses a required rate of return of 11% for its projects, and inflation can be ignored.

The Durvo department's Managing Director is of the opinion that all projects which return a positive net present value (NPV) should be accepted and does not understand the reason(s) why Arbore Co imposes capital rationing on its departments. Furthermore, she is not sure why maintaining a capital investment monitoring system would be beneficial to the company.

Required

(a) (i) Calculate the NPV of project PDur05. Calculate and comment on what percentage fall in the selling price would need to occur before the NPV falls to zero. **(6 marks)**

(ii) Explain the strengths and weaknesses of NPV as a basis for making investment decisions in a capital rationing situation. **(5 marks)**

(b) Formulate an appropriate capital rationing model, based on the above investment limits, that maximises the NPV for department Durvo. Finding a solution for the model is not required. **(3 marks)**

(c) Assume the following output is produced when the capital rationing model in part (b) above is solved:

Category 1: Total Final Value
$1,184,409

Category 2: Adjustable Final Values
Project PDur01: 0.958
Project PDur02: 0.407
Project PDur03: 0.732
Project PDur04: 0.000
Project PDur05: 1.000

Category 3:

Constraints Utilised	Slack
Year one: $9,000,000	Year one: $0
Year two: $6,000,000	Year two: $0
Year three: $5,000,000	Year three: $0

Required

Explain the figures produced in each of the three output categories. **(5 marks)**

(d) Provide a brief response to the Managing Director's opinions by:

(i) Explaining why Arbore Co may want to impose capital rationing on its departments **(2 marks)**

(ii) Explaining the features of a capital investment monitoring system and discussing the benefits of maintaining such a system **(4 marks)**

(Total = 25 marks)

19 MMC (6/11, amended)   49 mins

MesmerMagic Co (MMC) is considering whether to undertake the development of a new computer game based on an adventure film due to be released in 22 months. It is expected that the game will be available to buy two months after the film's release, by which time it will be possible to judge the popularity of the film with a high degree of certainty. However, at present, there is considerable uncertainty about whether the film, and therefore the game, is likely to be successful. Although MMC would pay for the exclusive rights to develop and sell the game now, the directors are of the opinion that they should delay the decision to produce and market the game until the film has been released and the game is available for sale.

MMC has forecast the following end of year cash flows for the four-year sales period of the game.

Year	1	2	3	4
Cash flows ($ million)	25	18	10	5

MMC will spend $7 million at the start of each of the next 2 years to develop the game and the gaming platform, and to pay for the exclusive rights to develop and sell the game. Following this, the company will require $35 million for production, distribution and marketing costs at the start of the 4-year sales period of the game.

It can be assumed that all the costs and revenues include inflation. The relevant cost of capital for this project is 11% and the risk-free rate is 3.5%. MMC has estimated the likely volatility of the cash flows at a standard deviation of 30%.

Required

(a) Estimate the financial impact of the directors' decision to delay the production and marketing of the game. The Black-Scholes option pricing model may be used, where appropriate. All relevant calculations should be shown. **(12 marks)**

(b) Briefly discuss the implications of the answer obtained in part (a) above. **(7 marks)**

(c) Discuss how a decrease in the value of each of the determinants of the option price in the Black-Scholes option pricing model for European options is likely to change the price of a call option. **(6 marks)**

(Total = 25 marks)

20 Marengo (12/10, amended)   49 mins

The treasury division of Marengo Co, a large quoted company, holds equity investments in various companies around the world. One of the investments is in Arion Co, in which Marengo holds 200,000 shares, which is around 2% of the total number of Arion Co's shares traded on the stock market. Over the past year, due to the general strength in the equity markets following optimistic predictions of the performance of world economies, Marengo's investments have performed well. However, there is some concern that the share price of Arion Co may fall in the coming two months due to uncertainty in its markets. It is expected that any fall in share prices will be reversed following this period of uncertainty.

The treasury division managers in Marengo, Wenyu, Lola and Sam, have met with the Chief Executive Officer (CEO), Edward, to discuss what to do with the investment in Arion Co and they each made a different suggestion as follows:

1   Wenyu was of the opinion that Marengo's shareholders would benefit most if no action were taken. He argued that the courses of action proposed by Lola and Sam, below, would result in extra costs and possibly increase the risk to Marengo Co.

2   Lola proposed that Arion Co's shares should be sold in order to eliminate the risk of a fall in the share price.

3   Sam suggested that the investment should be hedged using an appropriate derivative product.

4   Edward does not understand why Marengo Co holds equity investments at all. He believes all shares should be sold.

Although no exchange-traded derivative products exist on Arion Co's shares, a bank has offered over-the-counter (OTC) option contracts at an exercise price of 350 cents per share in a contract size of 1,000 shares each, for the appropriate time period. Arion Co's current share price is 340 cents per share, although the volatility of the share prices could be as high as 40%.

It can be assumed that Arion Co will not pay any dividends in the coming few months and that the appropriate inter-bank lending rate will be 4% over that period.

Required

(a)   Estimate the number of OTC put option contracts that Marengo Co will need to hedge against any adverse movement in Arion Co's share price. Provide a brief explanation of your answer.

   Note. You may assume that the delta of a put option is equivalent to N(–d1).   **(7 marks)**

(b)   Discuss possible reasons for the suggestions made by each of the three managers and the CEO. **(18 marks)**

                                                                                                                 (Total = 25 marks)

21 Furlion Co (Mar/Jun 16)   49 mins

Furlion Co manufactures heavy agricultural equipment and machinery which can be used in difficult farming conditions. Furlion Co's Chief Executive has been investigating a significant opportunity in the country of Naswa, where Furlion Co has not previously sold any products. The Government of Naswa has been undertaking a major land reclamation programme and Furlion Co's equipment is particularly suitable for use on the reclaimed land. Because of the costs and other problems involved in transporting its products, Furlion Co's Chief Executive proposes that Furlion Co should establish a plant for manufacturing machinery in Naswa. He knows that the Naswan Government is keen to encourage the development of sustainable businesses within the country.

Initial calculations suggest that the proposed investment in Naswa would have a negative net present value of $1.01 million. However, Furlion Co's Chief Executive believes that there may be opportunities for greater cash flows in future if the Naswan Government expands its land reclamation programme. The Government at present is struggling to fund expansion of the programme out of its own resources and is looking for other funding. If the Naswan government obtains this funding, the Chief Executive has forecast that the increased demand for Furlion Co's products would justify $15 million additional expenditure at the site of the factory in 3 years' time. The expected net present value for this expansion is currently estimated to be $0.

It can be assumed that all costs and revenues include inflation. The relevant cost of capital is 12% and the risk-free rate is 4%. The Chief Executive has estimated the likely volatility of cash flows at a standard deviation of 30%.

One of Furlion Co's non-executive directors has read about possible changes in interest rates and wonders how these might affect the investment appraisal.

Required

(a)   Assess, showing all relevant calculations, whether Furlion Co should proceed with the significant opportunity. Discuss the assumptions made and other factors which will affect the decision of whether to establish a plant in Naswa. The Black-Scholes pricing model may be used, where appropriate.   **(16 marks)**

(b)   Explain what is meant by an option's rho and discuss the impact of changes in interest rates on the appraisal of the investment.   **(5 marks)**

(c)   Discuss the possibility of the Naswan Government obtaining funding for further land reclamation from the World Bank, referring specifically to the International Development Association.   **(4 marks)**

(Total = 25 marks)

22 Airline Business (12/07, amended)   49 mins

Your company, which is in the airline business, is considering raising new capital of $400 million in the bond market for the acquisition of new aircraft. The debt would have a term to maturity of four years. The market capitalisation of the company's equity is $1.2 billion and it has a 25% market gearing ratio (market value of debt to total market value of the company). This new issue would be ranked for payment, in the event of default, equally with the company's other long-term debt and the latest credit risk assessment places the company at AA. Interest would be paid to holders annually. The company's current debt carries an average coupon of 4% and has 3 years to maturity. The company's effective rate of tax is 30%.

The current yield curve suggests that, at 3 years, government treasuries yield 3.5% and at 4 years they yield 5.1%. The current credit risk spread is estimated to be 50 basis points at AA. If the issue proceeds, the company's investment bankers suggest that a 90 basis point spread will need to be offered to guarantee take-up by its institutional clients.

Required

(a)   Advise on the coupon rate that should be applied to the new debt issue to ensure that it is fully subscribed.

(4 marks)

(b)   Estimate the current and revised market valuation of the company's debt and the increase in the company's effective cost of debt capital.   **(8 marks)**

(c)   Discuss the relative advantages and disadvantages of this mode of capital financing in the context of the company's stated financial objectives.   **(8 marks)**

(d)   Briefly consider company-specific factors that will be used in the credit rating assessment to classify the company as AA.   **(5 marks)**

(Total = 25 marks)

23 Fubuki (12/10)   49 mins

Fubuki Co, an unlisted company based in Megaera, has been manufacturing electrical parts used in mobility vehicles for people with disabilities and the elderly for many years. These parts are exported to various manufacturers worldwide but at present there are no local manufacturers of mobility vehicles in Megaera. Retailers in Megaera normally import mobility vehicles and sell them at an average price of $4,000 each. Fubuki Co wants to manufacture mobility vehicles locally and believes that it can sell vehicles of equivalent quality locally at a discount of 37.5% to the current average retail price.

Although this is a completely new venture for Fubuki Co, it will be in addition to the company's core business. Fubuki Co's directors expect to develop the project for a period of 4 years and then sell it for $16 million to a private equity firm. Megaera's Government has been positive about the venture and has offered Fubuki Co a subsidised loan of up to 80% of the investment funds required, at a rate of 200 basis points below Fubuki Co's borrowing rate. Currently Fubuki Co can borrow at 300 basis points above the 5-year government debt yield rate.

A feasibility study commissioned by the directors, at a cost of $250,000, has produced the following information.

1   Initial cost of acquiring suitable premises will be $11 million, and plant and machinery used in the manufacture will cost $3 million. Acquiring the premises and installing the machinery is a quick process and manufacturing can commence almost immediately.

2   It is expected that in the first year 1,300 units will be manufactured and sold. Unit sales will grow by 40% in each of the next 2 years before falling to an annual growth rate of 5% for the final year. After the first year the selling price per unit is expected to increase by 3% per year.

3   In the first year, it is estimated that the total direct material, labour and variable overhead costs will be $1,200 per unit produced. After the first year, the direct costs are expected to increase by an annual inflation rate of 8%.

4   Annual fixed overhead costs would be $2.5 million of which 60% are centrally allocated overheads. The fixed overhead costs will increase by 5% per year after the first year.

5   Fubuki Co will need to make working capital available of 15% of the anticipated sales revenue for the year, at the beginning of each year. The working capital is expected to be released at the end of the fourth year when the project is sold.

Fubuki Co's tax rate is 25% per year on taxable profits. Tax is payable in the same year as when the profits are earned. Tax-allowable depreciation is available on the plant and machinery on a straight-line basis. It is anticipated that the value attributable to the plant and machinery after 4 years is $400,000 of the price at which the project is sold. No tax-allowable depreciation is available on the premises.

Fubuki Co uses 8% as its discount rate for new projects but feels that this rate may not be appropriate for this new type of investment. It intends to raise the full amount of funds through debt finance and take advantage of the Government's offer of a subsidised loan. Issue costs are 4% of the gross finance required. It can be assumed that the debt capacity available to the company is equivalent to the actual amount of debt finance raised for the project.

Although no other companies produce mobility vehicles in Megaera, Haizum Co, a listed company, produces electrical-powered vehicles using similar technology to that required for the mobility vehicles. Haizum Co's cost of equity is estimated to be 14% and it pays tax at 28%. Haizum Co has 15 million shares in issue trading at $2.53 each and $40 million bonds trading at $94.88 per $100. The 5-year government debt yield is currently estimated at 4.5% and the market risk premium at 4%.

Required

(a)   Evaluate, on financial grounds, whether Fubuki Co should proceed with the project.   **(17 marks)**

(b)   Discuss the appropriateness of the evaluation method used and explain any assumptions made in part (a) above.   **(8 marks)**

(Total = 25 marks)

24 Coeden (12/12, amended)   49 mins

Coeden Co is a listed company operating in the hospitality and leisure industry. Coeden Co's board of directors met recently to discuss a new strategy for the business. The proposal put forward was to sell all the hotel properties that Coeden Co owns and rent them back on a long-term rental agreement. Coeden Co would then focus solely on the provision of hotel services at these properties under its popular brand name. The proposal stated that the funds raised from the sale of the hotel properties would be used to pay off 70% of the outstanding non-current liabilities and the remaining funds would be retained for future investments.

The board of directors is of the opinion that reducing the level of debt in Coeden Co will reduce the company's risk and therefore its cost of capital. If the proposal is undertaken and Coeden Co focuses exclusively on the provision of hotel services, it can be assumed that the current market value of equity will remain unchanged after implementing the proposal.

Coeden Co financial information

EXTRACT FROM THE MOST RECENT STATEMENT OF FINANCIAL POSITION

	$'000
Non-current assets (revalued recently)	42,560
Current assets	26,840
Total assets	69,400
Share capital (25c per share par value)	3,250
Reserves	21,780
Non-current liabilities (5.2% redeemable bonds)	42,000
Current liabilities	2,370
Total capital and liabilities	69,400

Coeden Co's latest free cash flow to equity of $2,600,000 was estimated after taking into account taxation, interest and reinvestment in assets to continue with the current level of business. It can be assumed that the annual reinvestment in assets required to continue with the current level of business is equivalent to the annual amount of depreciation. Over the past few years, Coeden Co has consistently used 40% of its free cash flow to equity on new investments while distributing the remaining 60%. The market value of equity calculated on the basis of the free cash flow to equity model provides a reasonable estimate of the current market value of Coeden Co.

The bonds are redeemable at par in three years and pay the coupon on an annual basis. Although the bonds are not traded, it is estimated that Coeden Co's current debt credit rating is BBB but would improve to A+ if the non-current liabilities are reduced by 70%.

Other information

Coeden Co's current equity beta is 1.1 and it can be assumed that debt beta is 0. The risk-free rate is estimated to be 4% and the market risk premium is estimated to be 6%.

There is no beta available for companies offering just hotel services, since most companies own their own buildings. The average asset beta for property companies has been estimated at 0.4. It has been estimated that the hotel services business accounts for approximately 60% of the current value of Coeden Co and the property company business accounts for the remaining 40%.

Coeden Co's corporation tax rate is 20%. The three-year borrowing credit spread on A+ rated bonds is 60 basis points and 90 basis points on BBB rated bonds, over the risk-free rate of interest.

Required

(a) Calculate, and comment on, Coeden Co's cost of equity and weighted average cost of capital before and after implementing the proposal. Briefly explain any assumptions made. **(20 marks)**

(b) Discuss the validity of the assumption that the market value of equity will remain unchanged after the implementation of the proposal. **(5 marks)**

(Total = 25 marks)

25 Levante (12/11, amended) 49 mins

Levante Co is a large unlisted company which has identified a new project for which it will need to increase its long-term borrowings from $250 million to $400 million. This amount will cover a significant proportion of the total cost of the project and the rest of the funds will come from cash held by the company.

The current $250 million unsubordinated borrowing is in the form of a 4% bond which is trading at $98.71 per $100 and is due to be redeemed at par in 3 years. The issued bond has a credit rating of AA. The new borrowing will also be raised in the form of a traded bond with a par value of $100 per unit. It is anticipated that the new project will generate sufficient cash flows to be able to redeem the new bond at $100 par value per unit in 5 years. It can be assumed that coupons on both bonds are paid annually.

Both bonds would be ranked equally for payment in the event of default and the directors expect that, as a result of the new issue, the credit rating for both bonds will fall to A. The directors are considering the following two alternative options when issuing the new bond:

1   Issue the new bond at a fixed coupon of 5% but at a premium or discount, whichever is appropriate to ensure full take-up of the bond; or

2   Issue the new bond at a coupon rate where the issue price of the new bond will be $100 per unit and equal to its par value.

The following extracts are provided on the current government bond yield curve and yield spreads for the sector in which Levante Co operates:

Current government bond yield curve

Years	1	2	3	4	5
	3.2%	3.7%	4.2%	4.8%	5.0%

Yield spreads (in basis points)

Bond rating	1 year	2 years	3 years	4 years	5 years
AAA	5	9	14	19	25
AA	16	22	30	40	47
A	65	76	87	100	112
BBB	102	121	142	167	193

Required

(a) Calculate the expected percentage fall in the market value of the existing bond if Levante Co's bond credit rating falls from AA to A. **(3 marks)**

(b) Advise the directors on the financial implications of choosing each of the two options when issuing the new bond. Support the advice with appropriate calculations. **(8 marks)**

(c) Among the criteria used by credit agencies for establishing a company's credit rating are the following: industry risk, earnings protection, financial flexibility and evaluation of the company's management.

Briefly explain each criterion and suggest factors that could be used to assess it. **(8 marks)**

(d) The following information is available for the expected situation after the proposed bond issue.

Total assets = $1,050m

Monthly net income = $25m

Annual profit before interest and tax = $450m

Standard deviation of earnings = 8%

Assume the new bond is issued with a 5% coupon.

Use the Kaplan-Urwitz model for unquoted companies to predict whether the credit rating will be AAA, AA or A. **(6 marks)**

Note. The model is $Y = 4.41 + 0.0014F + 6.4 \pi - 2.56S - 2.72L + 0.006C - 0.53 \sigma$

Where

F = total assets (in millions)

π = net income/total assets

S = debt status (subordinated = 1, otherwise 0)

L = gearing (long-term debt/total assets)

C = interest cover

σ = standard deviation of earnings

AAA ratings are given for scores over 6.76, AA ratings are given for scores over 5.19 but less than 6.76, A for scores over 3.28.

(Total = 25 marks)

26 GNT (2013 pilot paper)   49 mins

GNT Co is considering an investment in one of two corporate bonds. Both bonds have a par value of $1,000 and pay coupon interest on an annual basis. The market price of the first bond is $1,079.68. Its coupon rate is 6% and it is due to be redeemed at par in 5 years. The second bond is about to be issued with a coupon rate of 4% and will also be redeemable at par in 5 years. Both bonds are expected to have the same gross redemption yields (yields to maturity). The yield to maturity of a company's bond is determined by its credit rating.

GNT Co considers duration of the bond to be a key factor when making decisions on which bond to invest.

Required

(a)   Estimate the Macaulay duration of the two bonds GNT Co is considering for investment.   **(9 marks)**

(b)   Discuss how useful duration is as a measure of the sensitivity of a bond price to changes in interest rates.
(8 marks)

(c)   Among the criteria used by credit agencies for establishing a company's credit rating are the following: industry risk, earnings protection, financial flexibility and evaluation of the company's management.

Briefly explain each criterion and suggest factors that could be used to assess it.   **(8 marks)**

(Total = 25 marks)

27 Riviere (12/14)   49 mins

Riviere Co is a small company based in the European Union (EU). It produces high quality frozen food which it exports to a small number of supermarket chains located within the EU as well. The EU is a free trade area for trade between its member countries.

Riviere Co finds it difficult to obtain bank finance and relies on a long-term strategy of using internally generated funds for new investment projects. This constraint means that it cannot accept every profitable project and often has to choose between them.

Riviere Co is currently considering investment in one of two mutually exclusive food production projects: Privi and Drugi. Privi will produce and sell a new range of frozen desserts exclusively within the EU. Drugi will produce and sell a new range of frozen desserts and savoury foods to supermarket chains based in countries outside the EU. Each project will last for five years and the following financial information refers to both projects.

PROJECT DRUGI ANNUAL AFTER-TAX CASH FLOWS EXPECTED AT THE END OF EACH YEAR

Year	Current	1	2	3	4	5
Cash flows (€'000)	(11,840)	1,230	1,680	4,350	10,240	2,200

	Privi	*Drugi*
Net present value	€2,054,000	€2,293,000
Internal rate of return	17.6%	Not provided
Modified internal rate of return	13.4%	Not provided
Value at risk (over the project's life)		
95% confidence level	€1,103,500	Not provided
90% confidence level	€860,000	Not provided

Both projects' net present value has been calculated based on Riviere Co's nominal cost of capital of 10%. It can be assumed that both projects' cash flow returns are normally distributed and the annual standard deviation of project Drugi's present value of after-tax cash flows is estimated to be €400,000. It can also be assumed that all sales are made in € (Euro) and therefore the company is not exposed to any foreign exchange exposure.

Notwithstanding how profitable project Drugi may appear to be, Riviere Co's board of directors is concerned about the possible legal risks if it invests in the project because they have never dealt with companies outside the EU before.

Required

(a)   Discuss the aims of a free trade area, such as the EU, and the possible benefits to Riviere Co of operating within the EU.
(5 marks)

(b)   Calculate the figures which have not been provided for project Drugi and recommend which project should be accepted. Provide a justification for the recommendation and explain what the value at risk measures.
(13 marks)

(c)   Discuss the possible legal risks of investing in project Drugi which Riviere Co may be concerned about and how these may be mitigated.
(7 marks)

(Total = 25 marks)

28 AWP Co

AWP Co is a multinational listed company which has a credit rating of AA from major credit rating agencies. AWP Co currently has a financial gearing level measured by debt divided by debt plus equity (Debt/(Debt + Equity)) of 8%. The average gearing ratio for AWP Co's industry is 35%. The Chief Executive understands Modigliani and Miller's theory and wants AWP Co to issue more debt as he believes this will increase the value of AWP Co. The Chief Executive has also been quoted as saying 'I don't understand why the industry average gearing ratio is only 35%. Surely companies should be issuing as much debt as possible, as a 100% geared company would have a much greater value.'

In response to the Chief Executive's wishes, AWP Co will issue bonds of $200 million. There are two different bonds that it is currently considering.

Option 1

A 4-year bond with an annual coupon rate of 5%. The bonds will be redeemable at par.

Option 2

A 3-year bond with an annual coupon rate of 4%, redeemable at a premium of 5% to nominal value.

The current annual spot yield curve for government bonds is as follows:

One-year   3.3%
Two-year   3.8%
Three-year 4.5%
Four-year   5.3%

The following table of spreads (in basis points) is given for the retail sector.

Rating	1 year	2 year	3 year	4 year
AAA	12	23	36	50
AA	27	40	51	60
A	43	55	67	80

Required

(a) (i)   Calculate the theoretical issue prices and the duration of the two bonds.   **(12 marks)**

     (ii) Analyse the results obtained in part (a)(i).   **(4 marks)**

(b) Evaluate the comments made by the Chief Executive, making reference to other theories of capital structure.
                                                                                               (9 marks)

                                                                                      (Total = 25 marks)

ACQUISITIONS AND MERGERS

Questions 29 to 35 cover acquisitions and mergers, the subject of Part C of the BPP Study Text for AFM.

29 Preparation question: Saturn Systems (6/08, amended)

49 mins

[Note that from September 2018 questions that are wholly narrative will not be set]

Mr Moon is the Chief Executive Officer of Saturn Systems, a very large listed company in the telecommunications business. The company is in a very strong financial position, having developed rapidly in recent years through a strategy based upon growth by acquisition. Currently, earnings and earnings growth are at all-time highs, although the company's cash reserves are at a low level following a number of strategic investments in the last financial year. The previous evening Mr Moon gave a speech at a business dinner and during questions made some remarks that Pluto Ltd was an attractive company with 'great assets' and that he would be a 'fool' if he did not consider the possibility 'like everyone else' of acquiring the company. Pluto is a long established supplier to Saturn Systems and if acquired would add substantially to the market capitalisation of the business.

Mr Moon's comments were widely reported in the following morning's financial newspapers and, by 10am, the share price of Pluto had risen 15% in out-of-hours and early trading. The first that you, Saturn's chief financial officer, heard about the issue was when you received an urgent call from Mr Moon's office. You have just completed a background investigation of Pluto, along with three other potential targets instigated at Saturn's last board meeting in May. Following that investigation, you have now commenced a review of the steps required to raise the necessary debt finance for a bid and the procedure you would need to follow in setting up a due diligence investigation of each company.

On arriving at Mr Moon's office you are surprised to see the Chairman of the board in attendance. Mr Moon has just put down the telephone and is clearly very agitated. They tell you about the remarks made by Mr Moon the previous evening and that the call just taken was from the Office of the Regulator for Public Companies. The regulator had wanted to know if a bid was to be made and what announcement the company intended to make. They had been very neutral in their response pending your advice but had promised to get back to the regulator within the hour. They knew that if they were forced to admit that a bid was imminent and then withdrew that they would not be able to bid again for another six months. Looking at you they ask as one: 'what do we do now?' After a short discussion you returned to your office and began to draft a memorandum with a recommendation about how to proceed.

Required

(a) Discuss the advantages and disadvantages of growth by acquisition as compared with growth by internal (or organic) investment. **(5 marks)**

(b) Assess the regulatory, financial and ethical issues in this case. **(15 marks)**

(c) Propose a course of action that the company should now pursue, including a draft of any announcement that should be made, given that the board of Saturn Systems wishes to hold open the option of making a bid in the near future. **(5 marks)**

(Total = 25 marks)

30 Mercury Training (6/08, amended)

49 mins

Mercury Training was established in 20W9 and since that time it has developed rapidly. The directors are considering either a flotation or an outright sale of the company.

The company provides training for companies in the computer and telecommunications sectors. It offers a variety of courses ranging from short intensive courses in office software to high level risk management courses using advanced modelling techniques. Mercury employs a number of in-house experts who provide technical materials and other support for the teams that service individual client requirements. In recent years, Mercury has diversified into the financial services sector and now also provides computer simulation systems to companies for valuing acquisitions. This business now accounts for one-third of the company's total revenue.

Mercury currently has 10 million, 50c shares in issue. Jupiter is one of the few competitors in Mercury's line of business. However, Jupiter is only involved in the training business. Jupiter is listed on a small company investment market and has an estimated beta of 1.5. Jupiter has 50 million shares in issue with a market price of 580c. The average beta for the financial services sector is 0.9. Average market gearing (debt to total market value) in the financial services sector is estimated at 25%.

Other summary statistics for both companies for the year ended 31 December 20X7 are as follows:

	Mercury	Jupiter
Net assets at book value ($ million)	65	45
Earnings per share (c)	100	50
Dividend per share (c)	25	25
Gearing (debt to total market value)	30%	12%
Five-year historic earnings growth (annual)	12%	8%

Analysts forecast revenue growth in the training side of Mercury's business to be 6% per annum, but the financial services sector is expected to grow at just 4%.

Background information:

The equity risk premium is 3.5% and the rate of return on short-dated government stock is 4.5%.
Both companies can raise debt at 2.5% above the risk-free rate.
Tax on corporate profits is 40%.

Required

(a) Estimate the cost of equity capital and the weighted average cost of capital for Mercury Training. **(8 marks)**

(b) Advise the owners of Mercury Training on a range of likely issue prices for the company. **(10 marks)**

(c) Discuss the advantages and disadvantages, to the directors of Mercury Training, of a public listing versus private equity finance as a means of disposing of their interest in the company. **(7 marks)**

(Total = 25 marks)

31 Chithurst (Sep/Dec 16)   49 mins

Chithurst Co gained a stock exchange listing five years ago. At the time of the listing, members of the family who founded the company owned 75% of the shares, but now they only hold just over 50%. The number of shares in issue has remained unchanged since Chithurst Co was listed. Chithurst Co's directors have continued the policy of paying a constant dividend per share each year which the company had before it was listed. However, investors who are not family members have become increasingly critical of this policy, saying that there is no clear rationale for it. They would prefer to see steady dividend growth, reflecting the increase in profitability of Chithurst Co since its listing.

The Finance Director of Chithurst Co has provided its board with details of Chithurst Co's dividends and investment expenditure, compared with two other similar-sized companies in the same sector, Eartham Co and Iping Co. Each company has a 31 December year end.

	Chithurst Co			Eartham Co			Iping Co		
	Profit for year after interest and tax	Dividend paid	New investment expenditure	Profit for year after interest and tax	Dividend paid	New investment expenditure	Profit for year after interest and tax	Dividend paid	New investment expenditure
	$m	$m	$m	$m	$m	$m	$m	$m	$m
20X2	77	33	18	95	38	30	75	35	37
20X3	80	33	29	(10)	15	15	88	17	64
20X4	94	33	23	110	44	42	118	39	75
20X5	97	33	21	120	48	29	132	42	84

Other financial information relating to the three companies is as follows:

	Chithurst Co	Eartham Co	Iping Co
Cost of equity	11%	14%	12%
Market capitalisation $m	608	1,042	1,164
Increase in share price in last 12 months	1%	5%	10%

Chithurst Co's Finance Director has estimated the costs of equity for all three companies.

None of the three companies has taken out significant new debt finance since 20X1.

Required

(a) Discuss the benefits and drawbacks of the dividend policies which the three companies appear to have adopted. Provide relevant calculations to support your discussion.

Note. Up to 5 marks are available for the calculations. **(15 marks)**

(b) Discuss how the market capitalisation of the three companies compares with your valuations calculated using the dividend valuation model. Use the data provided to calculate valuations based on growth rates for the most recent year and for the last three years.

Note. Up to 5 marks are available for the calculations. **(10 marks)**

(Total = 25 marks)

32 Kodiak Company (12/09, amended) 49 mins

Kodiak Company is a small software design business established four years ago. The company is owned by three directors who have relied upon external accounting services in the past. The company has grown quickly and the directors have appointed you as a financial consultant to advise on the value of the business under their ownership.

The directors have limited liability and the bank loan is secured against the general assets of the business. The directors have no outstanding guarantees on the company's debt.

The company's latest statement of profit or loss and the extracted balances from the latest statement of financial position are as follows:

PROFIT/LOSS	$'000	FINANCIAL POSITION	$'000
Revenue	5,000	Opening non-current assets	1,200
Cost of sales	3,000	Additions	66
Gross profit	2,000	Non-current assets (gross)	1,266
Other operating costs	1,877	Accumulated depreciation	367
Operating profit	123	Net book value	899
Interest on loan	74	Net current assets	270
Profit before tax	49	Loan	(990)
Income tax expense	15	Net assets employed	179
Profit for the period	34		

During the current year:

1 Depreciation is charged at 10% per annum on the year-end non-current asset balance before accumulated depreciation, and is included in other operating costs in the statement of profit or loss.

2 The investment in net working capital is expected to increase in line with the growth in gross profit.

3   Other operating costs consisted of:

	$'000
Variable component at 15% of sales	750
Fixed costs	1,000
Depreciation on non-current assets	127

4   Revenue and variable costs are projected to grow at 9% per annum and fixed costs are projected to grow at 6% per annum.

5   The company pays interest on its outstanding loan of 7.5% per annum and incurs tax on its profits at 30%, payable in the following year. The company does not pay dividends.

6   The net current assets reported in the statement of financial position contain $50,000 of cash.

One of your first tasks is to prepare for the directors a forward cash flow projection for three years and to value the firm on the basis of its expected free cash flow to equity. In discussion with them you note the following:

- The company will not dispose of any of its non-current assets but will increase its investment in new non-current assets by 20% per annum. The company's depreciation policy matches the currently available tax write-off for capital allowances. This straight-line write-off policy is not likely to change.

- The directors will not take a dividend for the next three years but will then review the position taking into account the company's sustainable cash flow at that time.

- The level of the loan will be maintained at $990,000 and, on the basis of the forward yield curve, interest rates are not expected to change.

- The directors have set a target rate of return on their equity of 10% per annum which they believe fairly represents the opportunity cost of their invested funds.

Required

(a)   Prepare a three-year cash flow forecast for the business on the basis described above, highlighting the free cash flow to equity in each year.   **(12 marks)**

(b)   Estimate the value of the business based upon the expected free cash flow to equity and a terminal value based upon a sustainable growth rate of 3% per annum thereafter.   **(6 marks)**

(c)   Advise the directors on the assumptions and the uncertainties within your valuation.   **(7 marks)**

(Total = 25 marks)

33 Louieed (Mar/Jun 16)   49 mins

Louieed Co, a listed company, is a major supplier of educational material, selling its products in many countries. It supplies schools and colleges and also produces learning material for business and professional exams. Louieed Co has exclusive contracts to produce material for some examining bodies. Louieed Co has a well-defined management structure with formal processes for making major decisions.

Although Louieed Co produces online learning material, most of its profits are still derived from sales of traditional textbooks. Louieed Co's growth in profits over the last few years has been slow and its directors are currently reviewing its long-term strategy. One area in which they feel that Louieed Co must become much more involved is the production of online testing materials for exams and to validate course and textbook learning.

Bid for Tidded Co

Louieed Co has recently made a bid for Tidded Co, a smaller listed company. Tidded Co also supplies a range of educational material, but has been one of the leaders in the development of online testing and has shown strong profit growth over recent years. All of Tidded Co's initial five founders remain on its board and still hold 45% of its issued share capital between them. From the start, Tidded Co's directors have been used to making quick decisions in their areas of responsibility. Although listing has imposed some formalities, Tidded Co has remained focused on acting quickly to gain competitive advantage, with the five founders continuing to give strong leadership.

Louieed Co's initial bid of five shares in Louieed Co for three shares in Tidded Co was rejected by Tidded Co's board. There has been further discussion between the two boards since the initial offer was rejected and Louieed Co's board is now considering a proposal to offer Tidded Co's shareholders two shares in Louieed Co for one share in Tidded Co or a cash alternative of $22.75 per Tidded Co share. It is expected that Tidded Co's shareholders will choose one of the following options:

1 To accept the 2 shares for 1 share offer for all the Tidded Co shares;

2 To accept the cash offer for all the Tidded Co shares; or

3 60% of the shareholders will take up the 2 shares for 1 share offer and the remaining 40% will take the cash offer.

In the case of the third option being accepted, it is thought that 3 of the company's founders, holding 20% of the share capital in total, will take the cash offer and not join the combined company. The remaining two founders will probably continue to be involved in the business and be members of the combined company's board.

Louieed Co's Finance Director has estimated that the merger will produce annual post-tax synergies of $20 million. He expects Louieed Co's current price/earnings (P/E) ratio to remain unchanged after the acquisition.

Extracts from the two companies' most recent accounts are shown below:

	Louieed	Tidded
	$m	$m
Profit before finance cost and tax	446	182
Finance costs	(74)	(24)
Profit before tax	372	158
Tax	(76)	(30)
Profit after tax	296	128
Issued $1 nominal shares	340 million	90 million
P/E ratios, based on most recent accounts	14	15.9
Long-term liabilities (market value) ($m)	540	193
Cash and cash equivalents ($m)	220	64

The tax rate applicable to both companies is 20%.

Assume that Louieed Co can obtain further debt funding at a pre-tax cost of 7.5% and that the return on cash surpluses is 5% pre-tax.

Assume also that any debt funding needed to complete the acquisition will be reduced instantly by the balances of cash and cash equivalents held by Louieed Co and Tidded Co.

Required

(a) Discuss the advantages and disadvantages of the acquisition of Tidded Co from the viewpoint of Louieed Co.

(6 marks)

(b) Calculate the P/E ratios of Tidded Co implied by the terms of Louieed Co's initial and proposed offers, for all three of the above options.

(5 marks)

(c) Calculate, and comment on, the funding required for the acquisition of Tidded Co and the impact on Louieed Co's earnings per share and gearing, for each of the three options given above.

Note. Up to 10 marks are available for the calculations.

(14 marks)

(Total = 25 marks)

34 Makonis (12/13)

49 mins

Makonis Co, a listed company producing motor cars, wants to acquire Nuvola Co, an engineering company involved in producing innovative devices for cars. Makonis Co is keen to incorporate some of Nuvola Co's innovative devices into its cars and thereby boost sales revenue.

The following financial information is provided for the two companies:

	Makonis Co	Nuvola Co
Current share price	$5.80	$2.40
Number of issued shares	210 million	200 million
Equity beta	1.2	1.2
Asset beta	0.9	1.2

It is thought that combining the two companies will result in several benefits. Free cash flows to firm of the combined company will be $216 million in current value terms, but these will increase by an annual growth rate of 5% for the next 4 years, before reverting to an annual growth rate of 2.25% in perpetuity. In addition to this, combining the companies will result in cash synergy benefits of $20 million per year, for the next 4 years. These synergy benefits are not subject to any inflationary increase and no synergy benefits will occur after the fourth year. The debt to equity ratio of the combined company will be 40:60 in market value terms and it is expected that the combined company's cost of debt will be 4.55%.

The corporation tax rate is 20%, the current risk-free rate of return is 2% and the market risk premium is 7%. It can be assumed that the combined company's asset beta is the weighted average of Makonis Co's and Nuvola Co's asset betas, weighted by their current market values.

Makonis Co has offered to acquire Nuvola Co through a mixed offer of one of its shares for two Nuvola Co shares plus a cash payment, such that a 30% premium is paid for the acquisition. Nuvola Co's equity holders feel that a 50% premium would be more acceptable. Makonis Co has sufficient cash reserves if the premium is 30%, but not if it is 50%.

Required

(a) Estimate the additional equity value created by combining Nuvola Co and Makonis Co, based on the free cash flows to firm method. Comment on the results obtained and briefly discuss the assumptions made.

(13 marks)

(b) Estimate the impact on Makonis Co's equity holders if the premium paid is increased to 50% from 30%.

(5 marks)

(c) Estimate the additional funds required if a premium of 50% is paid instead of 30% and discuss how this premium could be financed.

(7 marks)

(Total = 25 marks)

35 Vogel (6/14)

49 mins

Vogel Co, a listed engineering company, manufactures large-scale plant and machinery for industrial companies. Until ten years ago, Vogel Co pursued a strategy of organic growth. Since then, it has followed an aggressive policy of acquiring smaller engineering companies, which it feels have developed new technologies and methods, which could be used in its manufacturing processes. However, it is estimated that only between 30% and 40% of the acquisitions made in the last 10 years have successfully increased the company's shareholder value.

Vogel Co is currently considering acquiring Tori Co, an unlisted company, which has three departments. Department A manufactures machinery for industrial companies, Department B produces electrical goods for the retail market, and the smaller Department C operates in the construction industry. Upon acquisition, Department A will become part of Vogel Co, as it contains the new technologies which Vogel Co is seeking, but Departments B and C will be unbundled, with the assets attached to Department C sold and Department B being spun off into a new company called Ndege Co.

Given below are extracts of financial information for the two companies for the year ended 30 April 2014.

	Vogel Co	Tori Co
	$m	$m
Sales revenue	790.2	124.6
Profit before depreciation, interest and tax (PBDIT)	244.4	37.4
Interest	13.8	4.3
Depreciation	72.4	10.1
Pre-tax profit	158.2	23.0

	Vogel Co $m	Tori Co $m
Non-current assets	723.9	98.2
Current assets	142.6	46.5
7% unsecured bond	–	40.0
Other non-current and current liabilities	212.4	20.2
Share capital (50c/share)	190.0	20.0
Reserves	464.1	64.5

Share of current and non-current assets and profit of Tori Co's three departments:

	Department A	Department B	Department C
Share of current and non-current assets	40%	40%	20%
Share of PBDIT and pre-tax profit	50%	40%	10%

Other information

1   It is estimated that for Department C, the realisable value of its non-current assets is 100% of their book value, but its current assets' realisable value is only 90% of their book value. The costs related to closing Department C are estimated to be $3 million.

2   The funds raised from the disposal of Department C will be used to pay off Tori Co's other non-current and current liabilities.

3   The 7% unsecured bond will be taken over by Ndege Co. It can be assumed that the current market value of the bond is equal to its book value.

4   At present, around 10% of Department B's PBDIT come from sales made to Department C.

5   Ndege Co's cost of capital is estimated to be 10%. It is estimated that in the first year of operation Ndege Co's free cash flows to firm will grow by 20%, and then by 5.2% annually thereafter.

6   The tax rate applicable to all the companies is 20%, and Ndege Co can claim 10% tax-allowable depreciation on its non-current assets. It can be assumed that the amount of tax-allowable depreciation is the same as the investment needed to maintain Ndege Co's operations.

7   Vogel Co's current share price is $3 per share and it is estimated that Tori Co's price/earnings (P/E) ratio is 25% higher than Vogel Co's P/E ratio. After the acquisition, when Department A becomes part of Vogel Co, it is estimated that Vogel Co's P/E ratio will increase by 15%.

8   It is estimated that the combined company's annual after-tax earnings will increase by $7 million due to the synergy benefits resulting from combining Vogel Co and Department A.

Required

(a)   Discuss the possible reasons why Vogel Co may have switched its strategy of organic growth to one of growing by acquiring companies.   **(4 marks)**

(b)   Discuss the possible actions Vogel Co could take to reduce the risk that the acquisition of Tori Co fails to increase shareholder value.   **(7 marks)**

(c)   Estimate, showing all relevant calculations, the maximum premium Vogel Co could pay to acquire Tori Co, explaining the approach taken and any assumptions made.   **(14 marks)**

(Total = 25 marks)

CORPORATE RECONSTRUCTION AND REORGANISATION

Questions 36 to 43 cover corporate reconstruction and reorganisation, the subject of Part D of the BPP Study Text for AFM.

36 AIR   49 mins

The directors of ER have decided to concentrate the company's activities on three core areas, bus services, road freight and taxis. As a result the company has offered for sale a regional airport that it owns. The airport handles a mixture of short-haul scheduled services, holiday charter flights and air freight, but does not have a runway long enough for long-haul international operations.

The existing managers of the airport, along with some employees, are attempting to purchase the airport through a leveraged management buyout, and would form a new unquoted company, AIR. The total value of the airport (free of any debt) has been independently assessed at $35 million.

The managers and employees can raise a maximum of $4 million towards this cost. This would be invested in new ordinary shares issued at the par value of 50c per share. ER, as a condition of the sale, proposes to subscribe to an initial 20% equity holding in the company, and would repay all debt of the airport prior to the sale.

EPP Bank is prepared to offer a floating rate loan of $20 million to the management team, at an initial interest rate of LIBOR plus 3%. LIBOR is currently at 10%. This loan would be for a period of seven years, repayable upon maturity, and would be secured against the airport's land and buildings. A condition of the loan is that gearing, measured by the book value of total loans to equity, is no more than 100% at the end of 4 years. If this condition is not met the bank has the right to call in its loan at one month's notice. AIR would be able to purchase a 4-year interest rate cap at 15% for its loan from EPP Bank for an upfront premium of $800,000.

A venture capital company, AV, is willing to provide up to $15 million in the form of unsecured mezzanine debt with attached warrants. This loan would be for a 5-year period, with principal repayable in equal annual instalments, and have a fixed interest rate of 18% per year.

The warrants would allow AV to purchase 10 AIR shares at a price of 100 cents each for every $100 of initial debt provided, at any time after 2 years from the date the loan is agreed. The warrants would expire after five years.

Most recent statement of profit or loss for the airport

	$'000
Landing fees	14,000
Other revenues	8,600
	22,600
Labour	5,200
Consumables	3,800
Central overhead payable to ER	4,000
Other expenses	3,500
Interest paid	2,500
	19,000
Taxable profit	3,600
Taxation (33%)	1,188
Retained earnings	2,412

ER has offered to continue to provide central accounting, personnel and marketing services to AIR for a fee of $3 million per year, with the first fee payable in year one. All revenues and cost (excluding interest) are expected to increase by approximately 5% per year.

Required

Prepare a report for the managers of the proposed new company AIR which:

(a)   Analyses the advantages and disadvantages for the management buyout of the proposed financing mix

(9 marks)

(b)   Evaluates whether or not EPP Bank's gearing restriction in four years' time is likely to be a problem

(10 marks)

All relevant calculations must be shown. State clearly any assumptions that you make.

(c)   As a possible alternative to obtaining finance from AV, assume that a venture capital company that you are employed by has been approached by the management buyout (MBO) team for a $10 million loan. Discuss what information, other than that provided above, would be required from the MBO team in order to decide whether or not to agree to the loan.

(6 marks)

(Total = 25 marks)

37 Doric (2013 pilot paper)   49 mins

Doric Co has two manufacturing divisions: parts and fridges. Although the parts division is profitable, the fridges division is not, and as a result its share price has declined to 50c per share from a high of $2.83 per share around 3 years ago. Assume it is now 1 January 20X3.

The board of directors is considering two proposals:

(i)   To cease trading and close down the company entirely.

(ii)   To close the fridge division and continue the parts division through a leveraged management buyout. The new company will continue with manufacturing parts only, but will make an additional investment of $50 million in order to grow the parts division after-tax cash flows by 3.5% in perpetuity. The proceeds from the sale of the fridges division will be used to pay the outstanding liabilities. The finance raised from the management buyout will pay for any remaining liabilities, the funds required for the additional investment, and to purchase the current equity shares at a premium of 20%.The fridges division is twice the size of the parts division in terms of its assets attributable to it.

Extracts from the most recent financial statements:

FINANCIAL POSITION AS AT 31 DECEMBER 20X2	$m
Assets	
Non-current assets	110
Current assets	220
Share capital ($0.40 per share par value)	40
Reserves	10
Liabilities (Non-current and current)	280

STATEMENT OF PROFIT OR LOSS FOR THE YEAR ENDED 31 DECEMBER 20X2

		$m
Sales revenue: Parts division		170
Fridge division		340
Costs prior to depreciation, interest payments and tax:	Parts division	(120)
	Fridge division	(370)
Depreciation, tax and interest		(34)
Loss		(14)

If the entire company's assets are sold, the estimated realisable values of assets are as follows:

	$m
Non-current assets	100
Current assets	110

The following additional information has been provided:

Redundancy and other costs will be approximately $54 million if the whole company is closed, and pro rata for individual divisions that are closed. These costs have priority for payment before any other liabilities in case of closure. The taxation effects relating to this may be ignored.

Corporation tax on profits is 20% and it can be assumed that tax is payable in the year incurred. Annual depreciation on non-current assets is 10% and this is the amount of investment needed to maintain the current level of activity. The new company's cost of capital is expected to be 11%.

Required

(a)   Briefly discuss the possible benefits of Doric Co's parts division being divested through a management buyout.   **(4 marks)**

(b)   Provide an estimate of the return the liability holders and the shareholders would receive in the event that Doric Co is closed and all its assets sold.   **(3 marks)**

(c)   Estimate the amount of additional finance needed and the value of the new company, if only the assets of the fridges division are sold and the parts division is divested through a management buyout. Briefly discuss whether or not the management buyout would be beneficial.   **(10 marks)**

(d)   Doric Co's directors are of the opinion that they could receive a better price if the fridges division is sold as a going concern instead of its assets sold separately. They have been told that they need to consider two aspects when selling a company or part of a company: (i) seeking potential buyers and negotiating the sale price; and (ii) due diligence.

Discuss the issues that should be taken into consideration with each aspect.   **(8 marks)**

(Total = 25 marks)

38 Flufftort (Sep/Dec 15)   **49 mins**

Five years ago the Patel family invested in a new business, Flufftort Co, which manufactures furniture. Some family members became directors of Flufftort Co, others have not been actively involved in management. A venture capital firm, Gupte VC, also made a 20% investment in Flufftort Co. A representative of Gupte VC was appointed to Flufftort Co's board. Flufftort Co also took out a long-term 8.5% bank loan.

Sales have generally been disappointing. As a result, members of the Patel family have been reluctant to invest further in Flufftort Co. Over the last year Gupte VC has taken a tougher attitude towards Flufftort Co. Gupte VC pressurised Flufftort Co to pay a dividend of $2 million for the year ended 30 June 20X5. Gupte VC has also said that if Flufftort Co's financial results do not improve, Gupte VC may exercise its right to compel Flufftort Co to buy back its shares at par on 30 June 20X6.

However, Flufftort Co's most recent product, the Easicushion chair, has been a much bigger success than expected. In order to produce enough Easicushion chairs to affect its results substantially, Flufftort Co will need to make significant expenditure on manufacturing facilities and additional working capital.

EXTRACTS FROM STATEMENT OF PROFIT OR LOSS FOR YEAR ENDED 30 JUNE 20X5 AND FORECAST STATEMENT OF PROFIT OR LOSS FOR YEAR ENDED 30 JUNE 20X6

	20X5	20X6 forecast
	$m	$m
Operating profit	8.0	6.0
Finance cost	(3.0)	(3.0)
Profit before tax	5.0	3.0
Tax on profits (20%)	(1.0)	(0.6)
Profit for the period	4.0	2.4
Dividends	(2.0)	–
Retained earnings	2.0	2.4

Note. The forecast statement of profit or loss for the year ended 30 June 20X6 is not affected by the proposed investment. This can be assumed only to affect results after 30 June 20X6. The figure shown for retained earnings in the 20X6 forecast can be assumed to be the net increase in cash for the year ended 30 June 20X6.

SUMMARISED STATEMENT OF FINANCIAL POSITION AS AT 30 JUNE 20X5

	$m
Assets	
Non-current assets	69.0
Current assets excluding cash	18.0
Cash	7.6
Total assets	94.6
Equity and liabilities	
Share capital ($1 shares)	50.0
Retained earnings	2.6
Total equity	52.6
Long-term liabilities	
8.5% bank loan	30.0
9% loan note	5.0
Total long-term liabilities	35.0
Current liabilities	7.0
Total liabilities	42.0
Total equity and liabilities	94.6

Notes

1   55% of shares are owned by the members of the Patel family who are directors, 25% by other members of the Patel family and 20% by Gupte VC.

2   The bank loan is secured on the non-current assets of Flufftort and is due for repayment on 31 December 20X9. The loan is subject to a covenant that the ratio of equity to non-current liabilities should be greater than 1.3 on a book value basis. Flufftort has also been granted an overdraft facility of up to $5 million by its bank.

3   The loan note is held by Rajiv Patel, a member of the Patel family who is not a director. The loan note is unsecured, is subordinated to the bank loan and has no fixed date for repayment.

4   If no finance is available for investment in manufacturing facilities, non-current assets, current assets excluding cash, the bank loan, loan note and current liabilities can be assumed to be the same at 30 June 20X6 as at 30 June 20X5.

However, the Chief Executive and Finance Director of Flufftort Co intend to propose that the company should be refinanced to fund the expanded production of the Easicushion chair. They have not yet consulted anyone else about their proposals.

Details of the proposed refinancing are as follows:

1   The members of the Patel family who are directors would subscribe to an additional 15 million $1 shares at par.

2   Gupte VC would subscribe to an additional 20 million $1 shares at par.

3   The 8.5% bank loan would be renegotiated with the bank and the borrowing increased to $65 million, to be repaid on 30 June 20Y2. The expected finance cost of the loan would be 10% per annum.

4   Rajiv Patel's loan note would be replaced by 5 million $1 shares.

5   The refinancing would mean non-current assets would increase to $125 million, current assets other than cash would increase to $42 million and current liabilities would increase to $12 million.

6   Operating profits would be expected to increase to $20 million in the first full year after the facilities are constructed (year ended 30 June 20X7) and $25 million in the second year (year ended 30 June 20X8). No dividends would be paid for these two years, as cash surpluses would be used for further investment as required. Tax on company profits can be assumed to remain at 20%.

Required

(a) (i) Prepare a projected statement of financial position as at 30 June 20X6, on the assumption that Gupte VC exercises its rights and Gupte VC's shares are repurchased and cancelled by Flufftort Co.

(4 marks)

(ii) Prepare a projected statement of financial position as at 30 June 20X6 on the assumption that the proposed refinancing and investment take place.

(4 marks)

(iii) Prepare projected statements of profit or loss for the years ended 30 June 20X7 and 30 June 20X8 on the basis that the profit forecasts are correct.

(4 marks)

(b) Evaluate whether the suggested refinancing scheme is likely to be agreed by all finance providers. State clearly any assumptions which you make.

(13 marks)

(Total = 25 marks)

39 BBS Stores (6/09, amended)   49 mins

BBS Stores, a publicly quoted limited company, is considering unbundling a section of its property portfolio. The company believes that it should use the proceeds to reduce the company's medium-term borrowing and to reinvest the balance in the business (Option 1). However, the company's investors have argued strongly that a sale and rental scheme would release substantial cash to investors (Option 2). You are a financial consultant and have been given the task of assessing the likely impact of these alternative proposals on the company's financial performance, cost of capital and market value.

Attached is the summarised BBS Stores' statement of financial position. The company owns all its stores.

	As at year end 20X8 $m	As at year end 20X7 $m
Assets		
Non-current assets		
Intangible assets	190	190
Property, plant and equipment	4,050	3,600
Other assets	500	530
	4,740	4,290
Current assets	840	1,160
Total assets	5,580	5,450
Equity		
Called-up share capital – equity	425	420
Retained earnings	1,535	980
Total equity	1,960	1,400
Liabilities		
Current liabilities	1,600	2,020
Non-current liabilities		
Medium-term loan notes	1,130	1,130
Other non-financial liabilities	890	900
Total liabilities	3,620	4,050
Total liabilities and equity	5,580	5,450

The company's profitability has improved significantly in recent years and earnings for 20X8 were $670 million (20X7: $540 million).

The company's property, plant and equipment within non-current assets for 20X8 are as follows:

	Land and buildings $m	Fixtures, fittings and equipment $m	Assets under construction $m	Total $m
Year end 20X8				
At revaluation	2,297	4,038	165	6,500
Accumulated depreciation		(2,450)		(2,450)
Net book value	2,297	1,588	165	4,050

The property portfolio was revalued at the year end 20X8. The assets under construction are valued at a market value of $165 million and relate to new building. In recent years commercial property values have risen in real terms by 4% per annum. Current inflation is 2.5% per annum. Property rentals currently earn an 8% return.

The proposal is that 50% of the property portfolio (land and buildings) and 50% of the assets under construction would be sold to a newly established property holding company called RPH that would issue bonds backed by the assured rental income stream from BBS Stores. BBS Stores would not hold any equity interest in the newly formed company nor would they take any part in its management.

BBS Stores is currently financed by equity in the form of 25c fully paid ordinary shares with a current market value of 400c per share. The capital debt for the company consists of medium-term loan notes of which $360 million are repayable at the end of 2 years and $770 million are repayable at the end of 6 years. Both issues of medium-term notes carry a floating rate of LIBOR plus 70 basis points. The interest liability on the 6-year notes has been swapped at a fixed rate of 5.5% in exchange for LIBOR which is also currently 5.5%. The reduction in the firm's gearing implied by Option 1 would improve the firm's credit rating and reduce its current credit spread by 30 basis points. The change in gearing resulting from the second option is not expected to have any impact upon the firm's credit rating. There has been no alteration in the rating of the company since the earliest debt was issued.

The BBS Stores equity beta is currently 1.824. A representative portfolio of commercial property companies has an equity beta of 1.25 and an average market gearing (adjusted for tax) of 50%. The risk-free rate of return is 5% and the equity risk premium is 3%. Using CAPM the current cost of equity is 10.47%. The current WACC is 9.55%. The company's current accounting rate of return on new investment is 13% before tax. You may assume that debt betas are zero throughout. The effective rate of company tax is 35%.

Required

On the assumption that the property unbundling proceeds, prepare a report for consideration by senior management which should include the following:

(a)   A comparative statement showing the impact upon the statement of financial position and on the earnings per share on the assumption that the cash proceeds of the property sale are used:

    (i)   To repay the debt, repayable in two years, in full and for reinvestment in non-current assets

    (ii)   To repay the debt, repayable in two years, in full and to finance a share repurchase at the current share price with the balance of the proceeds   **(13 marks)**

(b)   An estimate of the weighted average cost of capital for the remaining business under both options on the assumption that the share price remains unchanged   **(8 marks)**

(c)   An evaluation of the potential impact of each alternative on the market value of the firm (you are not required to calculate a revised market value for the firm)   **(4 marks)**

(Total = 25 marks)

40 Ennea (6/12)   49 mins

Three proposals were put forward for further consideration after a meeting of the executive directors of Ennea Co to discuss the future investment and financing strategy of the business. Ennea Co is a listed company operating in the haulage and shipping industry.

Proposal 1

To increase the company's level of debt by borrow⟨...⟩ ⟨...⟩ to buy back share capital.

Proposal 2

To increase the company's level of deb⟨...⟩ additional non-current assets in the⟨...⟩

Proposal 3

To sell excess non-curre⟨...⟩ more services to the sh⟨...⟩ non-current assets. All the ⟨...⟩ company's debt.

Ennea Co financial information

EXTRACTS FROM THE FORECAST FINAN⟨...⟩

	$m
Non-current assets	282
Current assets	66
Total assets	348
Equity and liabilities	
Share capital (40c per share)	48
Retained earnings	123
Total equity	171
Non-current liabilities	140
Current liabilities	37
Total liabilities	177
Total liabilities and equity	348

Ennea Co's forecast after-tax profit for the coming year is expected to be $26 million and its current share price is $3.20 per share. The non-current liabilities consist solely of a 6% medium-term loan redeemable within 7 years. The terms of the loan contract stipulate that an increase in borrowing will result in an increase in the coupon payable of 25 basis points on the total amount borrowed, while a reduction in borrowing will lower the coupon payable by 15 basis points on the total amount borrowed.

Ennea Co's effective tax rate is 20%. The company's estimated after-tax rate of return on investment is expected to be 15% on any new investment. It is expected that any reduction in investment would suffer the same rate of return.

Required

(a) Estimate and discuss the impact of each of the three proposals on the forecast statement of financial position, the earnings and earnings per share, and gearing of Ennea Co. **(20 marks)**

(b) An alternative suggestion to Proposal 3 was made where the non-current assets could be leased to other companies instead of being sold. The lease receipts would then be converted into an asset through securitisation. The proceeds from the sale of the securitised lease receipts asset would be used to reduce the outstanding loan borrowings.

Required

Explain what the securitisation process would involve and what would be the key barriers to Ennea Co undertaking the process. **(5 marks)**

(Total = 25 marks)

41 Nubo (12/13)   49 mins

Nubo Co has divisions operating in two diverse sectors: production of aircraft parts and supermarkets. Whereas the aircraft parts production division has been growing rapidly, the supermarkets division's growth has been slower. The company is considering selling the supermarkets division and focusing solely on the aircraft parts production division.

Extracts from Nubo Co's most recent financial statements are as follows:

Year ended 30 November	20X3
	$m
Profit after tax	166
Non-current assets	550
Current assets	122
Non-current liabilities	387
Current liabilities	95

About 70% of Nubo Co's non-current assets and current assets are attributable to the supermarkets division and the remainder to the aircraft parts production division. Each of the two divisions generates roughly half of the total profit after tax. The market value of the two divisions is thought to be equivalent to the price/earnings (P/E) ratios of the two divisions' industries. The supermarket industry's P/E ratio is 7 and the aircraft parts production industry's P/E ratio is 12.

Nubo Co can either sell the supermarkets division as a going concern or sell the assets of the supermarkets division separately. If the assets are sold separately, Nubo Co believes that it can sell the non-current assets for 115% of the book value and the current assets for 80% of the book value. The funds raised from the sale of the supermarkets division will be used to pay for all the company's current and non-current liabilities.

Following the sale of the supermarkets division and paying off the liabilities, Nubo Co will raise additional finance for new projects in the form of debt. It will be able to borrow up to a maximum of 100% of the total asset value of the new downsized company.

One of the new projects which Nubo Co is considering is a joint venture with Pilvi Co to produce an innovative type of machinery which will be used in the production of light aircraft and private jets. Both companies will provide the expertise and funding required for the project equally. Representatives from both companies will make up the senior management team and decisions will be made jointly. Legal contracts will be drawn up once profit-sharing and other areas have been discussed by the companies and agreed on.

Pilvi Co has approached Ulap Bank for the finance it requires for the venture, based on Islamic finance principles. Ulap Bank has agreed to consider the request from Pilvi Co but, because the financing requirement will be for a long period of time and because of uncertainties surrounding the project, Ulap Bank wants to provide the finance based on the principles of a Musharaka contract, with Ulap Bank requiring representation on the venture's senior management team. Normally Ulap Bank provides funds based on the principles of a Mudaraba contract, which the bank provides for short-term, low-risk projects, where the responsibility for running a project rests solely with the borrower.

Required

(a)   Advise Nubo Co whether it should sell the supermarkets division as a going concern or sell the assets separately and estimate the additional cash and debt funds which could be available to the new, downsized company. Show all relevant calculations.   **(7 marks)**

(b)   An alternative to selling the supermarkets division would be to demerge both the divisions. In this case, all of Nubo Co's liabilities would be taken over by the demerged supermarkets division. Also, either of the demerged companies can borrow up to 100% of their respective total asset values.

Required

Discuss whether a demerger of the supermarkets division may be more appropriate than a sale.   **(6 marks)**

(c)   Discuss why Ulap Bank may want to consider providing the finance based on a Musharaka contract instead of a Mudaraba contract, and the key concerns Nubo Co may have from the arrangement between Pilvi Co and Ulap Bank.   **(12 marks)**

(Total = 25 marks)

42 Bento (6/15)

In order to raise funds for future projects, the management of Bento Co, a large manufacturing company, is considering disposing of one of its subsidiary companies, Okazu Co, which is involved in manufacturing rubber tubing. It is considering undertaking the disposal through a management buyout (MBO) or a management buy-in (MBI). Bento Co wants $60 million from the sale of Okazu Co.

Given below are extracts from the most recent financial statements for Okazu Co:

YEAR ENDING 30 APRIL

	20X5
	$'000
Total non-current assets	40,800
Total current assets	12,300
Total assets	53,100
Equity	24,600
Non-current liabilities	16,600
Current liabilities	
Trade and other payables	7,900
Bank overdraft	4,000
Total current liabilities	11,900
Total equity and liabilities	53,100

YEAR ENDING 30 APRIL

	20X5
	$'000
Sales revenue	54,900
Operating profit	12,200
Finance costs	1,600
Profit before tax	10,600
Taxation	2,120
Profit for the year	8,480

Notes relating to the financial statements above:

1   Current assets, non-current assets and the trade and other payables will be transferred to the new company when Okazu Co is sold. The bank overdraft will be repaid by Bento Co prior to the sale of Okazu Co.

2   With the exception of the bank overdraft, Bento Co has provided all the financing to Okazu Co. No liabilities, except the trade and other payables specified above, will be transferred to the new company when Okazu Co is sold.

3   It is estimated that the market value of the non-current assets is 30% higher than the book value and the market value of the current assets is equivalent to the book value.

4   The group finance costs and taxation are allocated by Bento Co to all its subsidiaries in pre-agreed proportions.

Okazu Co's senior management team has approached Dofu Co, a venture capital company, about the proposed MBO. Dofu Co has agreed to provide leveraged finance for a 50% equity stake in the new company on the following basis:

• $30 million loan in the form of an 8% bond on which interest is payable annually, based on the loan amount outstanding at the start of each year. The bond will be repaid on the basis of fixed equal annual payments (constituting of interest and principal) over the next four years.

• $20 million loan in the form of a 6% convertible bond on which interest is payable annually. Conversion may be undertaken on the basis of 50 equity shares for every $100 from the beginning of Year 5 onwards.

•   5,000,000 $1 equity shares for $5,000,000.

Okazu Co's senior management will contribute $5,000,000 for 5,000,000 $1 equity shares and own the remaining 50% of the equity stake.

As a condition for providing the finance, Dofu Co will impose a restrictive covenant that the new company's gearing ratio will be no higher than 75% at the end of its first year of operations, and then fall to no higher than 60%, 50% and 40% at the end of Year 2 to Year 4 respectively. The gearing ratio is determined by the book value of debt divided by the combined book values of debt and equity.

After the MBO, it is expected that earnings before interest and tax will increase by 11% per year and annual dividends of 25% on the available earnings will be paid for the next 4 years. It is expected that the annual growth rate of dividends will reduce by 60% from Year 5 onwards following the MBO. The new company will pay tax at a rate of 20% per year. The new company's cost of equity has been estimated at 12%.

Required

(a) Distinguish between an MBO and an MBI. Discuss the relative benefits and drawbacks to Okazu Co if it is disposed through an MBO instead of an MBI. **(5 marks)**

(b) Estimate, showing all relevant calculations, whether the restrictive covenant imposed by Dofu Co is likely to be met. **(12 marks)**

(c) Discuss, with supporting calculations, whether or not an MBO would be beneficial for Dofu Co and Okazu Co's senior management team. **(8 marks)**

(Total = 25 marks)

43 Staple Group (Mar/Jun 16) 49 mins

Staple Group is one of Barland's biggest media groups. It consists of four divisions, organised as follows:

- **Staple National** – the national newspaper, the *Daily Staple*. This division's revenues and operating profits have decreased for the last two years.

- **Staple Local** – a portfolio of 18 local and regional newspapers. This division's operating profits have fallen for the last five years and operating profits and cash flows are forecast to be negative in the next financial year. Other newspaper groups with local titles have also reported significant falls in profitability recently.

- **Staple View** – a package of digital channels showing sporting events and programmes for a family audience. Staple Group's board has been pleased with this division's recent performance, but it believes that the division will only be able to sustain a growth rate of 4% in operating profits and cash flows unless it can buy the rights to show more major sporting events. Over the last year, Staple View's biggest competitor in this sector has acquired two smaller digital broadcasters.

- **Staple Investor** – established from a business which was acquired three years ago, this division offers services for investors including research, publications, training events and conferences. The division gained a number of new clients over the last year and has thus shown good growth in revenues and operating profits.

Some of Staple Group's institutional investors have expressed concern about the fall in profitability of the two newspaper divisions.

The following summarised data relates to the group's last accounting year. The percentage changes in pre-tax profits and revenues are changes in the most recent figures compared with the previous year.

	Total	National	Division Local	View	Investor
Revenues ($m)	1,371.7	602.4	151.7	496.5	121.1
Increase/(decrease) in revenues (%)		(5.1)	(14.7)	8.2	16.5
Pre-tax profits ($m)	177.3	75.6	4.5	73.3	23.9
Increase/(decrease) in pre-tax profits (%)		(4.1)	(12.6)	7.4	19.1
Post-tax cash flows ($m)	120.2	50.7	0.3	53.5	15.7
Share of group net assets ($m)	635.8	267.0	66.6	251.2	51.0
Share of group long-term liabilities ($m)	230.9	104.4	23.1	93.4	10.0

Staple Group's board regards the *Daily Staple* as a central element of the group's future. The directors are currently considering a number of investment plans, including the development of digital platforms for the *Daily Staple*. The Finance Director has costed the investment programme at $150 million. The board would prefer to fund the investment programme by disposing of parts or all of one of the other divisions. The following information is available to help assess the value of each division:

1   One of Staple Group's competitors, Postway Co, has contacted Staple Group's directors asking if they would be interested in selling 15 of the local and regional newspapers for $60 million. Staple Group's Finance Director believes this offer is low and wishes to use the net assets valuation method to evaluate a minimum price for the Staple Local division.

2   Staple Group's Finance Director believes that a valuation using free cash flows would provide a fair estimate of the value of the Staple View division. Over the last year, investment in additional non-current assets for the Staple View division has been $12.5 million and the incremental working capital investment has been $6.2 million. These investment levels will have to increase at 4% annually in order to support the expected sustainable increases in operating profit and cash flow.

3   Staple Group's Finance Director believes that the valuation of the Staple Investor division needs to reflect the potential it derives from the expertise and experience of its staff. The Finance Director has calculated a value of $118.5 million for this division, based on the earnings made last year but also allowing for the additional earnings which he believes that the expert staff in the division will be able to generate in future years.

Assume a risk-adjusted, all-equity financed, cost of capital of 12% and a tax rate of 30%. Goodwill should be ignored in any calculations.

Staple Group's finance and human resources directors are looking at the staffing of the two newspaper divisions. The Finance Director proposes dismissing most staff who have worked for the group for less than two years, two years' employment being when staff would be entitled to enhanced statutory employment protection. The Finance Director also proposes a redundancy programme for longer-serving staff, selecting for redundancy employees who have complained particularly strongly about recent changes in working conditions. There is a commitment in Staple Group's annual report to treat employees fairly, communicate with them regularly and enhance employees' performance by structured development.

Required

(a)   Evaluate the options for disposing of parts of Staple Group, using the financial information to assess possible disposal prices. The evaluation should include a discussion of the benefits and drawbacks to Staple Group from disposing of parts of Staple Group.   **(19 marks)**

(b)   Discuss the significance of the Finance Director's proposals for reduction in staff costs for Staple Group's relationships with its shareholders and employees and discuss the ethical implications of the proposals.
(6 marks)

(Total = 25 marks)

TREASURY AND ADVANCED RISK MANAGEMENT TECHNIQUES

Questions 44 to 57 cover treasury and advanced risk management techniques, the subject of Part E of the BPP Study Text for AFM.

44 Retilon (FS, 6/00, amended) 49 mins

Retilon plc is a medium-sized UK company that trades with companies in several European countries. Trade deals over the next three months are shown below. Assume that it is now 20 April.

	Two months' time		Three months' time	
	Receipts	Payments	Receipts	Payments
France	–	€393,265	€491,011	€60,505
Germany	–	–	€890,217	€1,997,651
Denmark	–	–	Kr 8.6m	–

Foreign exchange rates

	Dkroner/£	Euro €/£
Spot	10.68–10.71	1.439–1.465
Two months forward	10.74–10.77	1.433–1.459
Three months forward	10.78–10.83	1.431–1.456

Annual interest rates (valid for 2 months or 3 months)

	Borrowing %	Investing %
UK	7.50	5.50
France	5.75	3.50
Germany	5.75	3.50
Denmark	8.00	6.00

Futures market rates

Three-month euro contracts (125,000 euro contract size)

Contracts are for buying or selling euros. Futures prices are in £ per euro.

June	0.6964
September	0.6983
December	0.7013

Required

(a) (i) Using the forward market, money market and currency futures market as appropriate, devise a foreign exchange hedging strategy that is expected to maximise the cash flows of Retilon plc at the end of the three-month period.

Transactions costs and margin requirements may be ignored for this part of the question. Basis risk may be assumed to be zero at the time the contracts are closed out. Futures contracts may be assumed to mature at the month end. **(15 marks)**

(ii) Successive daily prices on the futures market for a June contract which you have sold are:

Selling price	0.6916
Day 1	0.6930
Day 2	0.6944
Day 3	0.6940

Initial margins are £1,000 per contract. Variation margin is 100% of the initial margin.

Spot exchange rates may be assumed not to change significantly during these three days.

For each of the three days, show the effect on your cash flow of the price changes of the contract.

(4 marks)

(b)   Discuss the advantages and disadvantages of forward contracts and currency futures for hedging against foreign exchange risk. **(6 marks)**

(Total = 25 marks)

45 Kenduri (6/13)   49 mins

Kenduri Co is a large multinational company based in the UK with a number of subsidiary companies around the world. Currently, foreign exchange exposure as a result of transactions between Kenduri Co and its subsidiary companies is managed by each company individually. Kenduri Co is considering whether or not to manage the foreign exchange exposure using multilateral netting from the UK, with the sterling pound (£) as the base currency. If multilateral netting is undertaken, spot mid-rates would be used.

The following cash flows are due in three months between Kenduri Co and three of its subsidiary companies. The subsidiary companies are Lakama Co, based in the US (currency US$), Jaia Co, based in Canada (currency CAD), and Gochiso Co, based in Japan (currency JPY).

Owed by	Owed to	Amount
Kenduri Co	Lakama Co	US$4.5 million
Kenduri Co	Jaia Co	CAD 1.1 million
Gochiso Co	Jaia Co	CAD 3.2 million
Gochiso Co	Lakama Co	US$1.4 million
Jaia Co	Lakama Co	US$1.5 million
Jaia Co	Kenduri Co	CAD 3.4 million
Lakama Co	Gochiso Co	JPY 320 million
Lakama Co	Kenduri Co	US$2.1 million

Exchange rates available to Kenduri Co

	US$/£1	CAD/£1	JPY/£1
Spot	1.5938–1.5962	1.5690–1.5710	131.91–133.59
3-month forward	1.5996–1.6037	1.5652–1.5678	129.15–131.05

Currency options available to Kenduri Co
Contract size £62,500, Exercise price quotation: US$/£1, Premium: cents per £1

	Call options		Put options	
	3-month expiry	6-month expiry	3-month expiry	6-month expiry
Exercise price				
1.60	1.55	2.25	2.08	2.23
1.62	0.98	1.58	3.42	3.73

It can be assumed that option contracts expire at the end of the relevant month.

Annual interest rates available to Kenduri Co and subsidiaries

	Borrowing rate	Investing rate
UK	4.0%	2.8%
US	4.8%	3.1%
Canada	3.4%	2.1%
Japan	2.2%	0.5%

Required

(a)   Advise Kenduri Co on, and recommend, an appropriate hedging strategy for the US$ cash flows it is due to receive or pay in three months, from Lakama Co. Show all relevant calculations to support the advice given.
(12 marks)

(b)   Calculate, using a tabular format (transactions matrix), the impact of undertaking multilateral netting by Kenduri Co and its three subsidiary companies for the cash flows due in three months. Briefly discuss why some governments allow companies to undertake multilateral netting, while others do not.   **(10 marks)**

(c) When examining different currency options and their risk factors, it was noticed that a long call option had a high gamma value. Explain the possible characteristics of a long call option with a high gamma value.

(3 marks)

(Total = 25 marks)

46 Massie (Sep/Dec 15)   49 mins

The Armstrong Group is a multinational group of companies. Today is 1 September. The treasury manager at Massie Co, one of Armstrong Group's subsidiaries based in Europe, has just received notification from the group's head office that it intends to introduce a system of netting to settle balances owed within the group every six months. Previously inter-group indebtedness was settled between the two companies concerned.

The predicted balances owing to, and owed by, the group companies at the end of February are as follows:

Owed by	Owed to	Local currency Million (m)
Armstrong (US)	Horan (South Africa)	US$12.17
Horan (South Africa)	Massie (Europe)	SA R42.65
Giffen (Denmark)	Armstrong (US)	D Kr21.29
Massie (Europe)	Armstrong (US)	US$19.78
Armstrong (US)	Massie (Europe)	€1.57
Horan (South Africa)	Giffen (Denmark)	D Kr16.35
Giffen (Denmark)	Massie (Europe)	€1.55

The predicted exchange rates, used in the calculations of the balances to be settled, are as follows:

	D Kr	US$	SA R	€
1 D Kr =	1.0000	0.1823	1.9554	0.1341
1 US$ =	5.4855	1.0000	10.7296	0.7358
1 SA R =	0.5114	0.0932	1.0000	0.0686
1 € =	7.4571	1.3591	14.5773	1.0000

Settlement will be made in dollars, the currency of Armstrong Group, the parent company. Settlement will be made in the order that the company owing the largest net amount in dollars will first settle with the company owed the smallest net amount in dollars.

Note. D Kr is Danish Krone, SA R is South African Rand, US$ is United States dollar and € is euro.

Required

(a) (i)   Calculate the inter-group transfers which are forecast to occur for the next period.   **(8 marks)**
     (ii) Discuss the problems which may arise with the new arrangement.   **(3 marks)**

The most significant transaction which Massie Co is due to undertake with a company outside the Armstrong Group in the next six months is that it is due to receive €25 million from Bardsley Co on 30 November. Massie Co's treasury manager intends to invest this money for the six months until 31 May, when it will be used to fund some major capital expenditure. However, the treasury manager is concerned about changes in interest rates. Predictions in the media range from a 0.5% rise in interest rates to a 0.5% fall.

Because of the uncertainty, the treasury manager has decided to protect Massie Co by using derivatives. The treasury manager wishes to take advantage of favourable interest rate movements. Therefore she is considering options on interest rate futures or interest rate collars as possible methods of hedging, but not interest rate futures. Massie Co can invest at LIBOR minus 40 basis points and LIBOR is currently 3.6%.

The treasury manager has obtained the following information on euro futures and options. She is ignoring margin requirements.

Three-month euro futures, €1,000,000 contract, tick size 0.01% and tick value €25.

September	95.94
December	95.76
March	95.44

Options on 3-month euro futures, €1,000,000 contract, tick size 0.01% and tick value €25. Option premiums are in annual %.

	Calls		Strike		Puts	
September	December	March		September	December	March
0.113	0.182	0.245	96.50	0.002	0.123	0.198
0.017	0.032	0.141	97.00	0.139	0.347	0.481

It can be assumed that settlement for the contracts is at the end of the month. It can also be assumed that basis diminishes to zero at contract maturity at a constant rate and that time intervals can be counted in months.

Required

(b)   Based on the choice of options on futures or collars which Massie Co is considering and assuming the company does not face any basis risk, recommend a hedging strategy for the €25 million receipt. Support your recommendations with appropriate comments and relevant calculations.   **(14 marks)**

(Total = 25 marks)

47 KYT (FS, 6/99, amended)   49 mins

KYT Inc is a company located in the US that has a contract to purchase goods from Japan in two months' time on 1 September. The payment is to be made in yen and will total 140 million yen.

The Managing Director of KYT Inc wishes to protect the contract against adverse movements in foreign exchange rates and is considering the use of currency futures. The following data are available.

Spot foreign exchange rate

$1 = 128.15 yen

Yen currency futures contracts on Singapore Monetary Exchange

Contract size 12,500,000 yen, contract prices are US$ per yen.

Contract prices:

September   0.007985
December   0.008250

Assume that futures contracts mature at the end of the month.

Required

(a)   (i)   Illustrate how KYT might hedge its foreign exchange risk using currency futures.   **(3 marks)**

(ii)   Explain the meaning of basis risk and show what basis risk is involved in the proposed hedge.

(4 marks)

(iii)   Assuming the spot exchange rate is 120 yen/$ on 1 September and that basis risk decreases steadily in a linear manner, calculate what the result of the hedge is expected to be. Briefly discuss why this result might not occur. Margin requirements and taxation may be ignored.   **(5 marks)**

(b)   In addition, KYT is concerned about its exposure to variable interest rate borrowing. Discuss the relevant considerations when deciding between futures and options to hedge a company's interest rate risk.

(5 marks)

(c)   The KYT business plan for the next five years shows a significant increase in business with Japan. The general manager tells you that the operations director is presenting the business case for setting up a wholly owned subsidiary in Japan. To that end, he has asked you to prepare a paper, to be presented at the board meeting, explaining the foreign exchange exposure risks which would result from such an investment.

In particular, he tells you he would like to explain transaction and translation exposure as he has heard that translation exposure risk is only a book entry and not a 'real cost' and so can be ignored.   **(8 marks)**

(Total = 25 marks)

48 Asteroid Systems (6/08, amended)

49 mins

Asteroid Systems is a German-based company with a subsidiary in Switzerland. The company's treasury manager expects the Swiss business will remit the equivalent of €1.5 million in 2 months. Her expectations of the future remittance are based upon the current SFr/Euro forward rate.

The current spot and forward rates for Swiss francs against the euro are extracted from the *Financial Times* and are shown in the table below.

	Closing mid-point	Change on day	Bid/offer spread	Days mid High	Low	One month Rate	Annual %	Three month Rate	Annual %
Switzerland (SFr/€)	1.6242	0.0107	239–244	1.6261	1.6147	1.6223	1.4	1.6176	1.6

In the euro money market the company can make fixed interest deposits at LIBOR and can borrow at LIBOR plus 20 basis points for terms of greater than one month but up to six months. The company can borrow at fixed rates in the Swiss money market. LIBOR rates, as quoted in the *Financial Times*, are as follows.

	EUR	CHF
Spot	3.56688	2.06000
1 week	3.57300	2.06000
2 week	3.58438	2.07000
1 month	3.60900	2.08000
2 month	3.72538	2.17000
3 month	3.78238	2.20000

The company's treasury manager is keen to eliminate transaction risk. However, because of the margin requirements and their impact upon the firm's cash flow, she would prefer not to use exchange-traded derivatives. Swiss franc borrowing or lending rates would need to be negotiated with the bank.

The CEO of Asteroid Systems has heard that a local competitor has made substantial gains from using its treasury department to speculate on foreign exchange markets and is interested in adding speculation to the role of the treasury department.

Required

(a) Estimate the lowest acceptable Swiss borrowing or lending rate for a money market hedge maturing in two months. **(10 marks)**

(b) Discuss the relative advantages and disadvantages of the use of a money market hedge compared with using exchange-traded derivatives for hedging a foreign exchange exposure. **(6 marks)**

(c) Discuss the extent to which currency hedging can reduce a firm's cost of capital. **(4 marks)**

(d) Discuss the points to consider when deciding whether the treasury department of Asteroid Systems should operate as a profit centre or a cost centre. **(5 marks)**

(Total = 25 marks)

49 Multidrop (6/10, amended)

49 mins

You are the financial manager of Multidrop (Group), a European-based company which has subsidiary businesses in North America, Europe and Singapore. It also has foreign currency balances outstanding with two non-group companies in the UK and Malaysia. Last year the transaction costs of ad-hoc settlements both within the group and with non-group companies were significant and this year you have reached agreement with the non-group companies to enter into a netting agreement to clear indebtedness with the minimum of currency flows. It has been agreed that Multidrop (Europe) will be the principal in the netting arrangement and that all settlements will be made in euros at the prevailing spot rate.

The summarised list of year-end indebtedness is as follows:

Owed by:	Owed to:	
Multidrop (Europe)	Multidrop (US)	US$6.4 million
Multidrop (Singapore)	Multidrop (Europe)	S$16 million
Alposong (Malaysia)	Multidrop (US)	US$5.4 million
Multidrop (US)	Multidrop (Europe)	€8.2 million
Multidrop (Singapore)	Multidrop (US)	US$5.0 million
Multidrop (Singapore)	Alposong (Malaysia)	Rm25 million
Alposong (Malaysia)	NewRing (UK)	£2.2 million
NewRing (UK)	Multidrop (Singapore)	S$4.0 million
Multidrop (Europe)	Alposong (Malaysia)	Rm8.3 million

Currency cross rates (mid-market) are as follows:

Currency		UK £	US$	Euro	S$	Rm
1 UK £	=	1.0000	1.4601	1.0653	2.1956	5.3128
1 US$	=	0.6849	1.0000	0.7296	1.5088	3.6435
1 Euro	=	0.9387	1.3706	1.0000	2.0649	4.9901
1 S$	=	0.4555	0.6628	0.4843	1.0000	2.4150
1 Rm	=	0.1882	0.2745	0.2004	0.4141	1.0000

You may assume settlement will be at the mid-market rates quoted.

Required

(a) Calculate the inter-group and inter-company currency transfers that will be required for settlement by Multidrop (Europe).   (12 marks)

(b) Discuss the advantages and disadvantages of netting arrangements with both group and non-group companies.   **(9 marks)**

(c) Discuss whether Multidrop (Europe) should adopt a policy of invoicing overseas customers in its home currency (euro).   **(4 marks)**

(Total = 25 marks)

50 Casasophia (6/11, amended)   49 mins

Casasophia Co, based in a European country that uses the euro (€), constructs and maintains advanced energy efficient commercial properties around the world. It has just completed a major project in the US and is due to receive the final payment of US$20 million in 4 months.

Casasophia Co is planning to commence a major construction and maintenance project in Mazabia, a small African country, in six months' time. This government-owned project is expected to last for three years during which time Casasophia Co will complete the construction of state of the art energy efficient properties and provide training to a local Mazabian company in maintaining the properties. The carbon-neutral status of the building project has attracted some grant funding from the European Union and these funds will be provided to the Mazabian Government in Mazabian Shillings (MShs).

Casasophia Co intends to finance the project using the US$20 million it is due to receive and borrow the rest through a € loan. It is intended that the US$ receipts will be converted into € and invested in short-dated treasury bills until they are required. These funds plus the loan will be converted into MShs on the date required, at the spot rate at that time.

Mazabia's Government requires Casasophia Co to deposit the MShs2.64 billion it needs for the project, with Mazabia's central bank, at the commencement of the project. In return, Casasophia Co will receive a fixed sum of MShs1.5 billion after tax, at the end of each year for a period of 3 years. Neither of these amounts is subject to inflationary increases. The relevant risk-adjusted discount rate for the project is assumed to be 12%.

Financial information

Exchange rates available to Casasophia

	Per €1	Per €1
Spot	US$1.3585–US$1.3618	MShs116–MShs128
4-month forward	US$1.3588–US$1.3623	Not available

Currency futures (Contract size €125,000, Quotation: US$ per €1)

2-month expiry	1.3633
5-month expiry	1.3698

Currency options (Contract size €125,000, Exercise price quotation: US$ per €1, cents per euro)

	Calls		Puts	
Exercise price	2-month expiry	5-month expiry	2-month expiry	5-month expiry
1.36	2.35	2.80	2.47	2.98
1.38	1.88	2.23	4.23	4.64

Casasophia Co local government base rate	2.20%
Mazabia government base rate	10.80%
Yield on short-dated euro treasury bills	1.80%
(assume 360-day year)	

Mazabia's current annual inflation rate is 9.7% and is expected to remain at this level for the next 6 months. However, after that, there is considerable uncertainty about the future and the annual level of inflation could be anywhere between 5% and 15% for the next few years. The country where Casasophia Co is based is expected to have a stable level of inflation at 1.2% per year for the foreseeable future. A local bank in Mazabia has offered Casasophia Co the opportunity to swap the annual income of MShs1.5 billion receivable in each of the next 3 years for euros, at the estimated annual MShs/€ forward rates based on the current government base rates.

Required

(a) Advise Casasophia Co on, and recommend, an appropriate hedging strategy for the US$ income it is due to receive in four months. Include all relevant calculations.

(15 marks)

(b) Given that Casasophia Co agrees to the local bank's offer of the swap, calculate the net present value of the project, in six months' time, in €. Discuss whether the swap would be beneficial to Casasophia Co.

(10 marks)

(Total = 25 marks)

51 Alecto (2013 pilot paper)

49 mins

Alecto Co, a large listed company based in Europe, is expecting to borrow €22,000,000 in 4 months' time on 1 May 20X2. It expects to make a full repayment of the borrowed amount nine months from now. Currently there is some uncertainty in the markets, with higher than normal rates of inflation, but an expectation that the inflation level may soon come down. This has led some economists to predict a rise in interest rates and others suggesting an unchanged outlook or maybe even a small fall in interest rates over the next six months.

Although Alecto Co is of the opinion that it is equally likely that interest rates could increase or fall by 0.5% in 4 months, it wishes to protect itself from interest rate fluctuations by using derivatives. The company can borrow at LIBOR plus 80 basis points and LIBOR is currently 3.3%. The company is considering using interest rate futures, options on interest rate futures or interest rate collars as possible hedging choices.

The following information and quotes from an appropriate exchange are provided on euro futures and options. Margin requirements may be ignored.

Three-month euro futures, €1,000,000 contract, tick size 0.01% and tick value €25.

March	96.27
June	96.16
September	95.90

Options on three-month euro futures, €1,000,000 contract, tick size 0.01% and tick value €25. Option premiums are in annual %.

Calls				Puts		
March	June	September	Strike	March	June	September
0.279	0.391	0.446	96.00	0.006	0.163	0.276
0.012	0.090	0.263	96.50	0.196	0.581	0.754

It can be assumed that settlement for both the futures and options contracts is at the end of the month. It can also be assumed that basis diminishes to zero at contract maturity at a constant rate and that time intervals can be counted in months.

Required

(a) Briefly discuss the main advantage and disadvantage of hedging interest rate risk using an interest rate collar instead of options. **(4 marks)**

(b) Based on the three hedging choices Alecto Co is considering and assuming that the company does not face any basis risk, recommend a hedging strategy for the €22,000,000 loan. Support your recommendation with appropriate comments and relevant calculations in €. **(17 marks)**

(c) Explain what is meant by basis risk and how it would affect the recommendation made in part (b) above.

(4 marks)

(Total = 25 marks)

52 Awan (12/13)   49 mins

Awan Co is expecting to receive $48,000,000 on 1 February 2014, which will be invested until it is required for a large project on 1 June 2014. Due to uncertainty in the markets, the company is of the opinion that it is likely that interest rates will fluctuate significantly over the coming months, although it is difficult to predict whether they will increase or decrease.

Awan Co's treasury team want to hedge the company against adverse movements in interest rates using one of the following derivative products:

Forward rate agreements (FRAs);
Interest rate futures; or
Options on interest rate futures.

Awan Co can invest funds at the relevant inter-bank rate less 20 basis points. The current inter-bank rate is 4.09%. However, Awan Co is of the opinion that interest rates could increase or decrease by as much as 0.9% over the coming months.

The following information and quotes are provided from an appropriate exchange on $ futures and options. Margin requirements can be ignored.

Three-month $ futures, $2,000,000 contract size

Prices are quoted in basis points at 100 – annual % yield

December 2013:   94.80
March 2014:   94.76
June 2014:   94.69

Options on three-month $ futures, $2,000,000 contract size, option premiums are in annual %

Calls				Puts		
December	March	June	Strike	December	March	June
0.342	0.432	0.523	94.50	0.090	0.119	0.271
0.097	0.121	0.289	95.00	0.312	0.417	0.520

Voblaka Bank has offered the following FRA rates to Awan Co:

1–7:	4.37%
3–4:	4.78%
3–7:	4.82%
4–7:	4.87%

It can be assumed that settlement for the futures and options contracts is at the end of the month and that basis diminishes to zero at contract maturity at a constant rate, based on monthly time intervals. Assume that it is 1 November 2013 now and that there is no basis risk.

Required

(a) Based on the three hedging choices Awan Co is considering, recommend a hedging strategy for the $48,000,000 investment, if interest rates increase or decrease by 0.9%. Support your answer with appropriate calculations and discussion. **(19 marks)**

(b) A member of Awan Co's treasury team has suggested that if option contracts are purchased to hedge against the interest rate movements, then the number of contracts purchased should be determined by a hedge ratio based on the delta value of the option.

Required

Discuss how the delta value of an option could be used in determining the number of contracts purchased. **(6 marks)**

(Total = 25 marks)

53 Phobos (12/08, amended)   49 mins

Following a collapse in credit confidence in the banking sector globally, there have been high levels of volatility in the financial markets around the world. Phobos Co is a UK listed company and has a borrowing requirement of £30 million arising in 2 months' time on 1 March and expects to be able to make repayment of the full amount 6 months from now. The governor of the central bank has suggested that interest rates are now at their peak and could fall over the next quarter. However, the Chairman of the Federal Reserve in the US has suggested that monetary conditions may need to be tightened, which could lead to interest rate rises throughout the major economies. In your judgement there is now an equal likelihood that rates will rise or fall by as much as 100 basis points depending upon economic conditions over the next quarter.

LIBOR is currently 6.00% and Phobos can borrow at a fixed rate of LIBOR plus 50 basis points on the short-term money market but the company treasurer would like to keep the maximum borrowing rate at or below 6.6%.

Short-term sterling index futures have a contract size of £500,000 and a tick size of £12.50. The open and settlement prices of three-month futures contracts are shown below (settlement at the end of the month):

	Open	Settlement
March	93.800	93.880
June	93.870	93.940
September	93.890	93.970

You may assume that basis diminishes to zero at contract maturity at a constant rate over time and that time intervals can be counted in months.

Options on short sterling futures have a contract size of £500,000 and the premiums (shown as an annual percentage) available against a range of exercise prices are as follows:

	Calls			Puts		
Exercise	March	June	September	March	June	September
93750	0.155	0.260	0.320	0.045	0.070	0.100
94000	0.038	0.110	0.175	0.168	0.170	0.205
94250	0.010	0.040	0.080	0.300	0.350	0.360

(a)   Estimate the effective interest rate cost if the anticipated interest rate exposure is hedged:

     (i)   Using the sterling interest rate futures

     (ii)   Using the options on short sterling futures   **(14 marks)**

(b)   Outline the benefits and dangers to Phobos of using derivative agreements in the management of interest rate risk.   **(6 marks)**

(c)   In addition, Phobos has long-term variable rate borrowing, which is due for repayment in six years. Phobos previously did not consider the risk great enough to hedge the interest rate risk but, with an expectation that interest rates will rise, they are now considering a swap arrangement.

The finance director's assistant has suggested that the company should investigate the use of alternatives to a swap, such as forward rate agreements or interest rate options. The finance director has stated that there is very little point in such an investigation because the alternatives to swaps tend to be designed to deal with short-term interest rate movements and so they would offer very little protection against the movements that could occur over the next six years. The finance director does not believe that there is any point in purchasing a sequence of short-term instruments over the next six years.

Required

Evaluate the finance director's statement that there is no point in purchasing a sequence of short-term instruments to lower exposure to interest rate risks over the remaining six years of the loan.   **(5 marks)**

                                                (Total = 25 marks)

54 Keshi (12/14)   **49 mins**

Keshi Co is a large multinational company with a number of international subsidiary companies. A centralised treasury department manages Keshi Co and its subsidiaries' borrowing requirements, cash surplus investment and financial risk management. Financial risk is normally managed using conventional derivative products such as forwards, futures, options and swaps.

Assume it is 1 December 20X4 today and Keshi Co is expecting to borrow $18,000,000 on 1 February 20X5 for a period of 7 months. It can either borrow the funds at a variable rate of LIBOR plus 40 basis points or a fixed rate of 5.5%. LIBOR is currently 3.8% but Keshi Co feels that this could increase or decrease by 0.5% over the coming months due to increasing uncertainty in the markets.

The treasury department is considering whether or not to hedge the $18,000,000, using either exchange-traded March options or over-the-counter swaps offered by Rozu Bank.

The following information and quotes for $ March options are provided from an appropriate exchange. The options are based on 3-month $ futures and $1,000,000 contract size and option premiums are in annual %.

March calls	Strike price	March puts
0.882	95.50	0.662
0.648	96.00	0.902

Option prices are quoted in basis points at 100 minus the annual percentage yield and settlement of the options contracts is at the end of March 20X5. The current basis on the March futures price is 44 points and it is expected to be 33 points on 1 January 20X5, 22 points on 1 February 20X5 and 11 points on 1 March 20X5.

Rozu Bank has offered Keshi Co a swap on a counterparty variable rate of LIBOR plus 30 basis points or a fixed rate of 4.6%, where Keshi Co receives 70% of any benefits accruing from undertaking the swap, prior to any bank charges. Rozu Bank will charge Keshi Co 10 basis points for the swap.

Keshi Co's Chief Executive Officer believes that a centralised treasury department is necessary in order to increase shareholder value, but Keshi Co's new Chief Financial Officer (CFO) thinks that having decentralised treasury departments operating across the subsidiary companies could be more beneficial. The CFO thinks that this is particularly relevant to the situation which Suisen Co, a company owned by Keshi Co, is facing.

Suisen Co operates in a country where most companies conduct business activities based on Islamic finance principles. It produces confectionery products including chocolates. It wants to use Salam contracts instead of commodity futures contracts to hedge its exposure to price fluctuations of cocoa. Salam contracts involve a commodity which is sold based on currently agreed prices, quantity and quality. Full payment is received by the seller immediately, for an agreed delivery to be made in the future.

Required

(a)   Based on the two hedging choices Keshi Co is considering, recommend a hedging strategy for the $18,000,000 borrowing. Support your answer with appropriate calculations and discussion.   **(15 marks)**

(b)   Discuss how a centralised treasury department may increase value for Keshi Co and the possible reasons for decentralising the treasury department.   **(6 marks)**

(c)   Discuss the key differences between a Salam contract, under Islamic finance principles, and futures contracts.   **(4 marks)**

(Total = 25 marks)

55 Daikon (6/15)   **49 mins**

For a number of years Daikon Co has been using forward rate agreements to manage its exposure to interest rate fluctuations. Recently its Chief Executive Officer (CEO) attended a talk on using exchange-traded derivative products to manage risks. She wants to find out by how much the extra cost of the borrowing detailed below can be reduced, when using interest rate futures, options on interest rate futures, and a collar on the options, to manage the interest rate risk. She asks that detailed calculations for each of the three derivative products be provided and a reasoned recommendation be made.

Daikon Co is expecting to borrow $34,000,000 in 5 months' time. It expects to make a full repayment of the borrowed amount in 11 months' time. Assume it is 1 June 20X5 today. Daikon Co can borrow funds at LIBOR plus 70 basis points. LIBOR is currently 3.6%, but Daikon Co expects that interest rates may increase by as much as 80 basis points in 5 months' time.

The following information and quotes from an appropriate exchange are provided on LIBOR-based $ futures and options.

Three-month $ December futures are currently quoted at 95.84. The contract size is $1,000,000, the tick size is 0.01% and the tick value is $25.

Options on 3-month $ futures, $1,000,000 contract, tick size 0.01% and tick value $25. Option premiums are in annual %.

December calls	Strike price	December puts
0.541	95.50	0.304
0.223	96.00	0.508

Initial assumptions

It can be assumed that settlement for both the futures and options contracts is at the end of the month; that basis diminishes to zero at a constant rate until the contract matures and time intervals can be counted in months; that margin requirements may be ignored; and that if the options are in-the-money, they will be exercised at the end of the hedge instead of being sold.

Further issues

In the talk, the CEO was informed of the following issues:

(i)   Futures contracts will be marked to market daily. The CEO wondered what the impact of this would be if 50 futures contracts were bought at 95.84 on 1 June and 30 futures contracts were sold at 95.61 on 3 June, based on the $ December futures contract given above. The closing settlement prices are given below for four days:

Date	Settlement price
1 June	95.84
2 June	95.76
3 June	95.66
4 June	95.74

(ii) Daikon Co will need to deposit funds into a margin account with a broker for each contract they have opened, and this margin will need to be adjusted when the contracts are marked to market daily.

(iii) It is unlikely that option contracts will be exercised at the end of the hedge period unless they have reached expiry. Instead, they are more likely to be sold and the positions closed.

Required

(a) Based on the three hedging choices available to Daikon Co and the initial assumptions given above, draft a response to the Chief Executive Officer's (CEO's) request made in the first paragraph of the question.

(15 marks)

(b) Discuss the impact on Daikon Co of each of the three further issues given above. As part of the discussion, include the calculations of the daily impact of the mark to market closing prices on the transactions specified by the CEO.

(10 marks)

(Total = 25 marks)

56 Sembilan (6/12, amended)   49 mins

Sembilan Co, a listed company, recently issued debt finance to acquire assets in order to increase its activity levels. This debt finance is in the form of a floating rate bond, with a face value of $320 million, redeemable in 4 years. The bond interest, payable annually, is based on the spot yield curve plus 60 basis points. The next annual payment is due at the end of year one.

Sembilan Co is concerned that the expected rise in interest rates over the coming few years would make it increasingly difficult to pay the interest due. It is therefore proposing to either swap the floating rate interest payment to a fixed rate payment, or to raise new equity capital and use that to pay off the floating rate bond. The new equity capital would either be issued as rights to the existing shareholders or as shares to new shareholders.

Ratus Bank has offered Sembilan Co an interest rate swap, whereby Sembilan Co would pay Ratus Bank interest based on an equivalent fixed annual rate of 3.76¼% in exchange for receiving a variable amount based on the current yield curve rate. Payments and receipts will be made at the end of each year, for the next four years. Ratus Bank will charge an annual fee of 20 basis points if the swap is agreed and will also guarantee the swap. The current annual spot yield curve rates are as follows:

Year	1	2	3	4
Rate	2.5%	3.1%	3.5%	3.8%

The current annual forward rates for years two, three and four are as follows:

Year	2	3	4
Rate	3.7%	4.3%	4.7%

Required

(a) Based on the above information, calculate the amounts Sembilan Co expects to pay or receive every year on the swap (excluding the fee of 20 basis points). Explain why the fixed annual rate of interest of 3.76¼% is less than the 4-year yield curve rate of 3.8%.

(6 marks)

(b) (i) Demonstrate that Sembilan Co's interest payment liability does not change, after it has undertaken the swap, whether the interest rates increase or decrease.

(5 marks)

(ii) Discuss the advantages and disadvantages of the swap for Sembilan Co.

(5 marks)

(c) Discuss the factors that Sembilan Co should consider when deciding whether it should raise equity capital to pay off the floating rate debt.

(9 marks)

(Total = 25 marks)

57 Pault (Sep/Dec 16)   49 mins

Pault Co is currently undertaking a major programme of product development. Pault Co has made a significant investment in plant and machinery for this programme. Over the next couple of years, Pault Co has also budgeted for significant development and launch costs for a number of new products, although its Finance Director believes there is some uncertainty with these budgeted figures, as they will depend upon competitor activity amongst other matters.

Pault Co issued floating rate loan notes, with a face value of $400 million, to fund the investment in plant and machinery. The loan notes are redeemable in ten years' time. The interest on the loan notes is payable annually and is based on the spot yield curve, plus 50 basis points.

Pault Co's Finance Director has recently completed a review of the company's overall financing strategy. His review has highlighted expectations that interest rates will increase over the next few years, although the predictions of financial experts in the media differ significantly.

The Finance Director is concerned about the exposure Pault Co has to increases in interest rates through the loan notes. He has therefore discussed with Millbridge Bank the possibility of taking out a four-year interest rate swap. The proposed terms are that Pault Co would pay Millbridge Bank interest based on an equivalent fixed annual rate of 4.847%. In return, Pault Co would receive from Millbridge Bank a variable amount based on the forward rates calculated from the annual spot yield curve rate at the time of payment minus 20 basis points. Payments and receipts would be made annually, with the first one in a year's time. Millbridge Bank would charge an annual fee of 25 basis points if Pault Co enters the swap.

The current annual spot yield curve rates are as follows:

Year	1	2	3	4
Rate	3.70%	4.25%	4.70%	5.10%

A number of concerns were raised at the recent board meeting when the swap arrangement was discussed.

- Pault Co's chairman wondered what the value of the swap arrangement to Pault Co was, and whether the value would change over time.

- One of Pault Co's non-executive directors objected to the arrangement, saying that in his opinion the interest rate which Pault Co would pay and the bank charges were too high. Pault Co ought to stick with its floating rate commitment. Investors would be critical if, at the end of four years, Pault Co had paid higher costs under the swap than it would have done had it left the loan unhedged.

Required

(a) (i)   Using the current annual spot yield curve rates as the basis for estimating forward rates, calculate the amounts Pault Co expects to pay or receive each year under the swap (excluding the fee of 25 basis points).   **(6 marks)**

     (ii) Calculate Pault Co's interest payment liability for Year 1 if the yield curve rate is 4.5% or 2.9%, and comment on your results.   **(6 marks)**

(b) Advise the chairman on the current value of the swap to Pault Co and the factors which would change the value of the swap.   **(4 marks)**

(c) Discuss the disadvantages and advantages to Pault Co of not undertaking a swap and being liable to pay interest at floating rates.   **(9 marks)**

(Total = 25 marks)

50 MARK QUESTIONS

Questions 58 to 69 are a bank of mixed 50 mark questions which cover a range of syllabus areas.

58 Yilandwe (6/15)

98 mins

Yilandwe, whose currency is the Yilandwe Rand (YR), has faced extremely difficult economic challenges in the past 25 years because of some questionable economic policies and political decisions made by its previous governments. Although Yilandwe's population is generally poor, its people are nevertheless well educated and ambitious. Just over three years ago, a new government took office and since then it has imposed a number of strict monetary and fiscal controls, including an annual corporation tax rate of 40%, in an attempt to bring Yilandwe out of its difficulties. As a result, the annual rate of inflation has fallen rapidly from a high of 65% to its current level of 33%. These strict monetary and fiscal controls have made Yilandwe's Government popular in the larger cities and towns, but less popular in the rural areas which seem to have suffered disproportionately from the strict monetary and fiscal controls.

It is expected that Yilandwe's annual inflation rate will continue to fall in the coming few years as follows:

Year	Inflation rate
1	22.0%
2	14.7%
3 onwards	9.8%

Yilandwe's Government has decided to continue the progress made so far, by encouraging foreign direct investment into the country. Recently, government representatives held trade shows internationally and offered businesses a number of concessions, including:

1   Zero corporation tax payable in the first two years of operation; and

2   An opportunity to carry forward tax losses and write them off against future profits made after the first two years.

The government representatives also promised international companies investing in Yilandwe prime locations in towns and cities with good transport links.

Imoni Co

Imoni Co, a large listed company based in the US with the US dollar ($) as its currency, manufactures high tech diagnostic components for machinery, which it exports worldwide. After attending one of the trade shows, Imoni Co is considering setting up an assembly plant in Yilandwe where parts would be sent and assembled into a specific type of component, which is currently being assembled in the US. Once assembled, the component will be exported directly to companies based in the European Union (EU). These exports will be invoiced in euro (€).

Assembly plant in Yilandwe: financial and other data projections

It is initially assumed that the project will last for four years. The four-year project will require investments of YR21,000 million for land and buildings, YR18,000 million for machinery and YR9,600 million for working capital to be made immediately. The working capital will need to be increased annually at the start of each of the next three years by Yilandwe's inflation rate and it is assumed that this will be released at the end of the project's life.

It can be assumed that the assembly plant can be built very quickly and production started almost immediately. This is because the basic facilities and infrastructure are already in place as the plant will be built on the premises and grounds of a school. The school is ideally located, near the main highway and railway lines. As a result, the school will close and the children currently studying there will be relocated to other schools in the city. The government has kindly agreed to provide free buses to take the children to these schools for a period of six months to give parents time to arrange appropriate transport in the future for their children.

The current selling price of each component is €700 and this price is likely to increase by the average EU rate of inflation from Year 1 onwards.

The number of components expected to be sold every year are as follows:

Year	1	2	3	4
Sales component units ('000)	150	480	730	360

The parts needed to assemble into the components in Yilandwe will be sent from the US by Imoni Co at a cost of $200 per component unit, from which Imoni Co would currently earn a pre-tax contribution of $40 for each component unit. However, Imoni Co feels that it can negotiate with Yilandwe's Government and increase the transfer price to $280 per component unit. The variable costs related to assembling the components in Yilandwe are currently YR15,960 per component unit. The current annual fixed costs of the assembly plant are YR4,600 million. All these costs, wherever incurred, are expected to increase by that country's annual inflation every year from Year 1 onwards.

Imoni Co pays corporation tax on profits at an annual rate of 20% in the US. The tax in both the US and Yilandwe is payable in the year that the tax liability arises. A bilateral tax treaty exists between Yilandwe and the US. Tax-allowable depreciation is available at 25% per year on the machinery on a straight-line basis.

Imoni Co will expect annual royalties from the assembly plant to be made every year. The normal annual royalty fee is currently $20 million, but Imoni Co feels that it can negotiate this with Yilandwe's Government and increase the royalty fee by 80%. Once agreed, this fee will not be subject to any inflationary increase in the project's four-year period.

If Imoni Co does decide to invest in an assembly plant in Yilandwe, its exports from the US to the EU will fall and it will incur redundancy costs. As a result, Imoni Co's after-tax cash flows will reduce by the following amounts:

Year	1	2	3	4
Redundancy and lost contribution	20,000	55,697	57,368	59,089

Imoni Co normally uses its cost of capital of 9% to assess new projects. However, the Finance Director suggests that Imoni Co should use a project-specific discount rate of 12% instead.

Other financial information

Current spot rates

Euro per dollar	€0.714/$1
YR per euro	YR142/€1
YR per dollar	YR101.4/$1

Forecast future rates based on expected inflation rate differentials

Year	1	2	3	4
YR/$1	120.1	133.7	142.5	151.9

Year	1	2	3	4
YR/€1	165.0	180.2	190.2	200.8

Expected inflation rates

EU expected inflation rate: Next two years	5%
EU expected inflation rate: Year 3 onwards	4%
US expected inflation rate: Year 1 onwards	3%

Required

(a) Discuss the possible benefits and drawbacks to Imoni Co of setting up its own assembly plant in Yilandwe, compared to licensing a company based in Yilandwe to undertake the assembly on its behalf. **(5 marks)**

(b) Prepare a report which:

    (i) Evaluates the financial acceptability of the investment in the assembly plant in Yilandwe **(21 marks)**

    (ii) Discusses the assumptions made in producing the estimates, and the other risks and issues which Imoni Co should consider before making the final decision **(17 marks)**

    (iii) Provides a reasoned recommendation on whether or not Imoni Co should invest in the assembly plant in Yilandwe **(3 marks)**

    Professional marks will be awarded in part (b) for the format, structure and presentation of the report.

(4 marks)

(Total = 50 marks)

59 Avem (12/14)

Nahara Co and Fugae Co

Nahara Co is a private holding company owned by the Government of a wealthy oil-rich country to invest its sovereign funds. Nahara Co has followed a strategy of risk diversification for a number of years by acquiring companies from around the world in many different sectors.

One of Nahara Co's acquisition strategies is to identify and purchase undervalued companies in the airline industry in Europe. A recent acquisition was Fugae Co, a company based in a country which is part of the European Union (EU). Fugae Co repairs and maintains aircraft engines.

A few weeks ago, Nahara Co stated its intention to pursue the acquisition of an airline company based in the same country as Fugae Co. The EU, concerned about this, asked Nahara Co to sell Fugae Co before pursuing any further acquisitions in the airline industry.

Avem Co's acquisition interest in Fugae Co

Avem Co, a UK-based company specialising in producing and servicing business jets, has approached Nahara Co with a proposal to acquire Fugae Co for $1,200 million. Nahara Co expects to receive a premium of at least 30% on the estimated equity value of Fugae Co, if it is sold.

Given below are extracts from the most recent statements of financial position of both Avem Co and Fugae Co.

	Avem Co	Fugae Co
	$m	$m
Share capital (50c/share)	800	100
Reserves	3,550	160
Non-current liabilities	2,200	380
Current liabilities	130	30
Total capital and liabilities	6,680	670

Each Avem Co share is currently trading at $7.50, which is a multiple of 7.2 of its free cash flow to equity. Avem Co expects that the total free cash flows to equity of the combined company will increase by $40 million due to synergy benefits. After adding the synergy benefits of $40 million, Avem Co then expects the multiple of the total free cash flow of the combined company to increase to 7.5.

Fugae Co's free cash flow to equity is currently estimated at $76.5 million and it is expected to generate a return on equity of 11%. Over the past few years, Fugae Co has returned 77.3% of its annual free cash flow to equity back to Nahara Co, while retaining the balance for new investments.

Fugae Co's non-current liabilities consist entirely of $100 nominal value bonds which are redeemable in 4 years at the nominal value, on which the company pays a coupon of 5.4%. The debt is rated at B+ and the credit spread on B+ rated debt is 80 basis points above the risk-free rate of return.

Proposed luxury transport investment project by Fugae Co

In recent years, the country in which Fugae Co is based has been expanding its tourism industry and hopes that this industry will grow significantly in the near future. At present tourists normally travel using public transport and taxis, but there is a growing market for luxury travel. If the tourist industry does expand, then the demand for luxury travel is expected to grow rapidly. Fugae Co is considering entering this market through a four-year project. The project will cease after four years because of increasing competition.

The initial cost of the project is expected to be $42,000,000 and it is expected to generate the following after-tax cash flows over its 4-year life:

Year	1	2	3	4
Cash flows ($'000)	3,277.6	16,134.3	36,504.7	35,683.6

The above figures are based on the tourism industry expanding as expected. However, it is estimated that there is a 25% probability that the tourism industry will not grow as expected in the first year. If this happens, then the present value of the project's cash flows will be 50% of the original estimates over its 4-year life.

It is also estimated that if the tourism industry grows as expected in the first year, there is still a 20% probability that the expected growth will slow down in the second and subsequent years, and the present value of the project's cash flows would then be 40% of the original estimates in each of these years.

Lumi Co, a leisure travel company, has offered $50 million to buy the project from Fugae Co at the start of the second year. Fugae Co is considering whether having this choice would add to the value of the project.

If Fugae Co is bought by Avem Co after the project has begun, it is thought that the project will not result in any additional synergy benefits and will not generate any additional value for the combined company, above any value the project has already generated for Fugae Co.

Although there is no beta for companies offering luxury forms of travel in the tourist industry, Reka Co, a listed company, offers passenger transportation services on coaches, trains and luxury vehicles. About 15% of its business is in the luxury transport market and Reka Co's equity beta is 1.6. It is estimated that the asset beta of the non-luxury transport industry is 0.80. Reka Co's shares are currently trading at $4.50 per share and its debt is currently trading at $105 per $100. It has 80 million shares in issue and the book value of its debt is $340 million. The debt beta is estimated to be zero.

General information

The corporation tax rate applicable to all companies is 20%. The risk-free rate is estimated to be 4% and the market risk premium is estimated to be 6%.

Required

(a) Discuss whether or not Nahara Co's acquisition strategies, of pursuing risk diversification and of purchasing undervalued companies, can be valid. **(7 marks)**

(b) Discuss why the European Union (EU) may be concerned about Nahara Co's stated intention and how selling Fugae Co could reduce this concern. **(4 marks)**

(c) Prepare a report for the board of directors of Avem Co, which:

   (i)   Estimates the additional value created for Avem Co, if it acquires Fugae Co without considering the luxury transport project; **(10 marks)**

   (ii) Estimates the additional value of the luxury transport project to Fugae Co, both with and without the offer from Lumi Co; and **(18 marks)**

   (iii) Evaluates the benefit attributable to Avem Co and Fugae Co from combining the two companies with and without the project, and concludes whether or not the acquisition is beneficial. The evaluation should include any assumptions made. **(7 marks)**

   Professional marks will be awarded in part (c) for the format, structure and presentation of the report.

   (4 marks)

   (Total = 50 marks)

60 Chmura (12/13) 98 mins

Since becoming independent just over 20 years ago, the country of Mehgam has adopted protectionist measures which have made it difficult for multinational companies to trade there. However, recently, after discussions with the World Trade Organization (WTO), it seems likely that Mehgam will reduce its protectionist measures significantly.

Encouraged by these discussions, Chmura Co, a company producing packaged foods, is considering a project to set up a manufacturing base in Mehgam to sell its goods there and in other regional countries nearby. An initial investigation costing $500,000 established that Mehgam had appropriate manufacturing facilities, adequate transport links and a reasonably skilled but cheap workforce. The investigation concluded that, if the protectionist measures were reduced, then the demand potential for Chmura Co's products looked promising. It is also felt that an early entry into Mehgam would give Chmura Co an advantage over its competitors for a period of five years, after which the current project will cease, due to the development of new advanced manufacturing processes.

Mehgam's currency, the Peso (MP), is currently trading at MP72 per $1. Setting up the manufacturing base in Mehgam will require an initial investment of MP2,500 million immediately, to cover the cost of land and buildings (MP1,250 million) and machinery (MP1,250 million). Tax-allowable depreciation is available on the machinery at an annual rate of 10% on cost on a straight-line basis. A balancing adjustment will be required at the end of year five, when it is expected that the machinery will be sold for MP500 million (after inflation). The market value of the land

and buildings in 5 years' time is estimated to be 80% of the current value. These amounts are inclusive of any tax impact.

Chmura Co will require MP200 million for working capital immediately. It is not expected that any further injections of working capital will be required for the five years. When the project ceases at the end of the fifth year, the working capital will be released back to Chmura Co.

Production of the packaged foods will take place in batches of product mixes. These batches will then be sold to supermarket chains, wholesalers and distributors in Mehgam and its neighbouring countries, which will repackage them to their individual requirements. All sales will be in MP. The estimated average number of batches produced and sold each year is given below:

Year	1	2	3	4	5
Batches produced and sold	10,000	15,000	30,000	26,000	15,000

The current selling price for each batch is estimated to be MP115,200. The costs related to producing and selling each batch are currently estimated to be MP46,500. In addition to these costs, a number of products will need a special packaging material which Chmura Co will send to Mehgam. Currently the cost of the special packaging material is $200 per batch. Training and development costs, related to the production of the batches, are estimated to be 80% of the production and selling costs (excluding the cost of the special packaging) in the first year, before falling to 20% of these costs (excluding the cost of the special packaging) in the second year, and then nil for the remaining years. It is expected that the costs relating to the production and sale of each batch will increase annually by 10% but the selling price and the special packaging costs will only increase by 5% every year.

The current annual corporation tax rate in Mehgam is 25% and Chmura Co pays annual corporation tax at a rate of 20% in the country where it is based. Both countries' taxes are payable in the year that the tax liability arises. A bi-lateral tax treaty exists between the two countries which permits offset of overseas tax against any tax liabilities Chmura Co incurs on overseas earnings.

The risk-adjusted cost of capital applicable to the project on $-based cash flows is 12%, which is considerably higher than the return on short-dated $ treasury bills of 4%. The current rate of inflation in Mehgam is 8%, and in the country where Chmura Co is based it is 2%. It can be assumed that these inflation rates will not change for the foreseeable future. All net cash flows from the project will be remitted back to Chmura Co at the end of each year.

Chmura Co's Finance Director is of the opinion that there are many uncertainties surrounding the project and has assessed that the cash flows can vary by a standard deviation of as much as 35% because of these uncertainties.

Recently Bulud Co offered Chmura Co the option to sell the entire project to Bulud Co for $28 million at the start of year three. Chmura Co will make the decision of whether or not to sell the project at the end of year two.

Required

(a) Discuss the role of the World Trade Organization (WTO) and the possible benefits and drawbacks to Mehgam of reducing protectionist measures. **(9 marks)**

(b) Prepare an evaluative report for the board of directors of Chmura Co which addresses the following parts and recommends an appropriate course of action:

    (i) An estimate of the value of the project before considering Bulud Co's offer. Show all relevant calculations. **(14 marks)**

    (ii) An estimate of the value of the project taking into account Bulud Co's offer. Show all relevant calculations. **(9 marks)**

    (iii) A discussion of the assumptions made in parts (i) and (ii) above and the additional business risks which Chmura Co should consider before it makes the final decision whether or not to undertake the project. **(14 marks)**

Professional marks will be awarded in part (b) for the format, structure and presentation of the report.

(4 marks)

(Total = 50 marks)

61 Mlima (6/13)

98 mins

Mlima Co is a private company involved in aluminium mining. About eight years ago, the company was bought out by its management and employees through a leveraged buyout (LBO). Due to high metal prices worldwide, the company has been growing successfully since the LBO. However, because the company has significant debt borrowings with strict restrictive covenants and high interest levels, it has had to reject a number of profitable projects. The company has currently two bonds in issue, as follows:

- A 16% secured bond with a nominal value of $80 million, which is redeemable at par in 5 years. An early redemption option is available on this bond, giving Mlima Co the option to redeem the bond at par immediately if it wants to.

- A 13% unsecured bond with a nominal value of $40 million, which is redeemable at par in 10 years.

Mlima Co's board of directors (BoD) has been exploring the idea of redeeming both bonds to provide it with more flexibility when making future investment decisions. To do so, the BoD has decided to consider a public listing of the company on a major stock exchange. It is intended that a total of 100 million shares will be issued in the newly listed company. From the total shares, 20% will be sold to the public, 10% will be offered to the holders of the unsecured bond in exchange for redeeming the bond through an equity-for-debt swap, and the remaining 70% of the equity will remain in the hands of the current owners. The secured bond would be paid out of the funds raised from the listing.

The details of the possible listing and the distribution of equity were published in national newspapers recently. As a result, potential investors suggested that, due to the small proportion of shares offered to the public and for other reasons, the shares should be offered at a substantial discount of as much as 20% below the expected share price on the day of the listing.

Mlima Co, financial information

It is expected that after the listing, deployment of new strategies and greater financial flexibility will boost Mlima Co's future sales revenue and, for the next 4 years, the annual growth rate will be 120% of the previous 2 years' average growth rate. After the 4 years, the annual growth rate of the free cash flows to the company will be 3.5%, for the foreseeable future. Operating profit margins are expected to be maintained in the future. Although it can be assumed that the current tax-allowable depreciation is equivalent to the amount of investment needed to maintain the current level of operations, the company will require an additional investment in assets of 30c per $1 increase in sales revenue for the next four years.

EXTRACTS FROM MLIMA CO'S PAST THREE YEARS' STATEMENT OF PROFIT OR LOSS

Year ended	31 May 20X3	31 May 20X2	31 May 20X1
	$m	$m	$m
Sales revenue	389.1	366.3	344.7
Operating profit	58.4	54.9	51.7
Net interest costs	17.5	17.7	18.0
Profit before tax	40.9	37.2	33.7
Taxation	10.2	9.3	8.4
Profit after tax	30.7	27.9	25.3

Once listed, Mlima Co will be able to borrow future debt at an interest rate of 7%, which is only 3% higher than the risk-free rate of return. It has no plans to raise any new debt after listing, but any future debt will carry considerably fewer restrictive covenants. However, these plans do not take into consideration the Bahari project (see below).

Bahari project

Bahari is a small country with agriculture as its main economic activity. A recent geological survey concluded that there may be a rich deposit of copper available to be mined in the north-east of the country. This area is currently occupied by subsistence farmers, who would have to be relocated to other parts of the country. When the results of the survey were announced, some farmers protested that the proposed new farmland they would be moved to was less fertile and that their communities were being broken up. However, the protesters were intimidated and violently put down by the Government, and the state-controlled media stopped reporting about them. Soon afterwards, their protests were ignored and forgotten.

In a meeting between the Bahari Government and Mlima Co's BoD, the Bahari Government offered Mlima Co exclusive rights to mine the copper. It is expected that there are enough deposits to last at least 15 years. Initial estimates suggest that the project will generate free cash flows of $4 million in the first year, rising by 100% per year in each of the next 2 years, and then by 15% in each of the 2 years after that. The free cash flows are then expected to stabilise at the Year 5 level for the remaining 10 years.

The cost of the project, payable at the start, is expected to be $150 million, comprising machinery, working capital and the mining rights fee payable to the Bahari Government. None of these costs is expected to be recoverable at the end of the project's 15-year life.

The Bahari Government has offered Mlima Co a subsidised loan over 15 years for the full $150 million at an interest rate of 3% instead of Mlima Co's normal borrowing rate of 7%. The interest payable is allowable for taxation purposes. It can be assumed that Mlima Co's business risk is not expected to change as a result of undertaking the Bahari project.

At the conclusion of the meeting between the Bahari Government and Mlima Co's BoD, the president of Bahari commented that working together would be like old times when he and Mlima Co's Chief Executive Officer (CEO) used to run a business together.

Other information

Mlima Co's closest competitor is Ziwa Co, a listed company which mines metals worldwide. Mlima Co's directors are of the opinion that after listing Mlima Co's cost of capital should be based on Ziwa Co's ungeared cost of equity. Ziwa Co's cost of capital is estimated at 9.4%, its geared cost of equity is estimated at 16.83% and its pre-tax cost of debt is estimated at 4.76%. These costs are based on a capital structure comprising of 200 million shares, trading at $7 each, and $1,700 million 5% irredeemable bonds, trading at $105 per $100. Both Ziwa Co and Mlima Co pay tax at an annual rate of 25% on their taxable profits.

It can be assumed that all cash flows will be in $ instead of the Bahari currency and therefore Mlima Co does not have to take account of any foreign exchange exposure from this venture.

Required

(a) Prepare a report for the BoD of Mlima Co that:

   (i) Explains why Mlima Co's directors are of the opinion that Mlima Co's cost of capital should be based on Ziwa Co's ungeared cost of equity and, showing relevant calculations, estimate an appropriate cost of capital for Mlima Co. **(7 marks)**

   (ii) Estimates Mlima Co's value without undertaking the Bahari project and then with the Bahari project. The valuations should use the free cash flow methodology and the cost of capital calculated in part (i). Include relevant calculations. **(14 marks)**

   (iii) Advises the BoD whether or not the unsecured bond holders are likely to accept the equity-for-debt swap offer. Include relevant calculations. **(5 marks)**

   (iv) Advises the BoD on the listing and the possible share price range, if a total of 100 million shares are issued. The advice should also include:

      (1) A discussion of the assumptions made in estimating the share price range

      (2) In addition to the reasons mentioned in the scenario above, a brief explanation of other possible reasons for changing its status from a private company to a listed one

      (3) An assessment of the possible reasons for issuing the share price at a discount for the initial listing **(12 marks)**

   Professional marks will be awarded in part (a) for the format, structure and presentation of the report.
   (4 marks)

(b) Discuss the possible impact on, and response of, Mlima Co to the following ethical issues, with respect to the Bahari project:

   (i) The relocation of the farmers
   (ii) The relationship between the Bahari president and Mlima Co's CEO

   Note. The total marks will be split equally between each part. **(8 marks)**

   (Total = 50 marks)

62 Lignum (12/12, amended)

98 mins

Lignum Co, a large listed company, manufactures agricultural machines and equipment for different markets around the world. Although its main manufacturing base is in France and it uses the euro (€) as its base currency, it also has a few subsidiary companies around the world. Lignum Co's treasury division is considering how to approach the following three cases of foreign exchange exposure that it faces.

Case One

Lignum Co regularly trades with companies based in Zuhait, a small country in South America whose currency is the Zupesos (ZP). It recently sold machinery for ZP140 million, which it is about to deliver to a company based there. It is expecting full payment for the machinery in four months. Although there are no exchange-traded derivative products available for the ZP, Medes Bank has offered Lignum Co a choice of two over-the-counter derivative products.

The first derivative product is an over-the-counter forward rate determined on the basis of the Zuhait base rate of 8.5% plus 25 basis points and the French base rate of 2.2% less 30 basis points.

Alternatively, with the second derivative product Lignum Co can purchase either euro call or put options from Medes Bank at an exercise price equivalent to the current spot exchange rate of ZP142 per €1. The option premiums offered are: ZP7 per €1 for the call option or ZP5 per €1 for the put option.

The premium cost is payable in full at the commencement of the option contract. Lignum Co can borrow money at the base rate plus 150 basis points and invest money at the base rate minus 100 basis points in France.

Case Two

Namel Co is Lignum Co's subsidiary company based in Maram, a small country in Asia, whose currency is the Maram Ringit (MR). The current pegged exchange rate between the Maram Ringit and the euro is MR35 per €1. Due to economic difficulties in Maram over the last couple of years, it is very likely that the Maram Ringit will devalue by 20% imminently. Namel Co is concerned about the impact of the devaluation on its statement of financial position.

Given below is an extract from the current statement of financial position of Namel Co.

	MR'000
Non-current assets	179,574
Current assets	146,622
Total assets	326,196
Share capital and reserves	102,788
Non-current liabilities	132,237
Current liabilities	91,171
Total capital and liabilities	326,196

The current assets consist of inventories, receivables and cash. Receivables account for 40% of the current assets. All the receivables relate to sales made to Lignum Co in euro. About 70% of the current liabilities consist of payables relating to raw material inventory purchased from Lignum Co and payable in euro. 80% of the non-current liabilities consist of a euro loan and the balance are borrowings sourced from financial institutions in Maram.

Case Three

Lignum Co manufactures a range of farming vehicles in France which it sells within the European Union to countries which use the euro. Over the previous few years, it has found that its sales revenue from these products has been declining and the Sales Director is of the opinion that this is entirely due to the strength of the euro. Lignum Co's biggest competitor in these products is based in the US and US$ rate has changed from almost parity with the euro 3 years ago to the current value of US$1.47 for €1. The agreed opinion is that the US$ will probably continue to depreciate against the euro, but possibly at a slower rate, for the foreseeable future.

New machinery

Lignum Co has recently successfully tested a revolutionary new agricultural machine. It is now considering whether to undertake the necessary development work in order to make it a viable commercial product. It believes the development phase will take 3 years costing €2.5 million p.a. (including inflation) following which the machinery will have a market life of 12 years.

Demand is estimated to be 60 units p.a. Production requires the use of a special steel alloy whose prices are quite volatile but would be €800,000 at today's prices and Lignum Co intends to sell at a 12.5% premium. Steel alloy prices are expected to rise at 4% p.a. with a standard deviation of 22%.

Lignum Co would need to take on a new production facility for this engine at the end of the 3-year development phase that will cost €31.4 million. Its cost of capital is 12% and risk-free rate is 5.5%.

Given the volatility involved, Lignum Co is contemplating building a Monte Carlo simulation model to help evaluate this project.

Required

(a)   Prepare a report for Lignum Co's treasury division that:

   (i)   Briefly explains the type of currency exposure Lignum Co faces for each of the above cases.

(3 marks)

   (ii)   Recommends which of the two derivative products Lignum Co should use to manage its exposure in case one and advises on alternative hedging strategies that could be used. Show all relevant calculations. **(9 marks)**

   (iii)   Computes the gain or loss on Namel Co's statement of financial position, due to the devaluation of the Maram Ringit in case two, and discusses whether and how this exposure should be managed.

(8 marks)

   (iv)   Discusses how the exposure in case three can be managed. **(3 marks)**

Professional marks will be awarded for the structure and presentation of the report. **(4 marks)**

(b)   (i)   Using the Black-Scholes model for valuing real options, estimate the current value of the option to produce the new machinery and determine whether the company should proceed, assuming both production revenues and costs arise at the year end. **(12 marks)**

   (ii)   Discuss whether it is appropriate for Lignum Co to use Monte Carlo simulation in the evaluation of this opportunity. **(6 marks)**

(c)   Explain the five input factors that are included in the Black-Scholes model for option valuation.   **(5 marks)**

(Total = 50 marks)

63 Tramont (2013 pilot paper)   98 mins

Tramont Co is a listed company based in the US and manufactures electronic devices. One of its devices, the X-IT, is produced exclusively for the US market. Tramont Co is considering ceasing the production of the X-IT gradually over a period of four years because it needs the manufacturing facilities used to make the X-IT for other products.

The Government of Gamala, a country based in South-East Asia, is keen to develop its manufacturing industry and has offered Tramont Co first rights to produce the X-IT in Gamala and sell it to the US market for a period of four years. At the end of the four-year period, the full production rights will be sold to a government-backed company for Gamalan Rupiahs (GR) 450 million after tax (this amount is not subject to inflationary increases). Tramont Co has to decide whether to continue production of the X-IT in the US for the next four years or to move the production to Gamala immediately.

Currently each X-IT unit sold makes a unit contribution of $20. This unit contribution is not expected to be subject to any inflationary increase in the next four years. Next year's production and sales estimated at 40,000 units will fall by 20% each year for the following 3 years. It is anticipated that after four years the production of the X-IT will stop. It is expected that the financial impact of the gradual closure over the four years will be cost neutral (the revenue from sale of assets will equal the closure costs). If production is stopped immediately, the excess assets would be sold for $2.3 million and the costs of closure, including redundancy costs of excess labour, would be $1.7 million.

The following information relates to the production of the X-IT moving to Gamala. The Gamalan project will require an initial investment of GR 230 million, to pay for the cost of land and buildings (GR 150 million) and machinery (GR 80 million). The cost of machinery is tax allowable and will be depreciated on a straight-line basis over the next four years, at the end of which it will have a negligible value.

Tramont Co will also need GR 40 million for working capital immediately. It is expected that the working capital requirement will increase in line with the annual inflation rate in Gamala. When the project is sold, the working capital will not form part of the sale price and will be released back to Tramont Co.

Production and sales of the device are expected to be 12,000 units in the first year, rising to 22,000 units, 47,000 units and 60,000 units in the next 3 years respectively.

The following revenues and costs apply to the first year of operation:

- Each unit will be sold for $70.

- The variable cost per unit comprising of locally sourced materials and labour will be GR 1,350.

- In addition to the variable cost above, each unit will require a component bought from Tramont Co for $7, on which Tramont Co makes $4 contribution per unit.

- Total fixed costs for the first year will be GR 30 million.

The costs are expected to increase by their countries' respective rates of inflation, but the selling price will remain fixed at $70 per unit for the 4-year period.

The annual corporation tax rate in Gamala is 20% and Tramont Co currently pays corporation tax at a rate of 30% per year. Both countries' corporation taxes are payable in the year that the tax liability arises. A bi-lateral tax treaty exists between the US and Gamala, which permits offset of overseas tax against any US tax liability on overseas earnings. The US and Gamalan tax authorities allow losses to be carried forward and written off against future profits for taxation purposes.

Tramont Co has decided to finance the project by borrowing the funds required in Gamala. The commercial borrowing rate is 13% but the Gamalan Government has offered Tramont Co a 6% subsidised loan for the entire amount of the initial funds required. The Gamalan Government has agreed that it will not ask for the loan to be repaid as long as Tramont Co fulfils its contract to undertake the project for the four years. Tramont Co can borrow dollar funds at an interest rate of 5%.

Tramont Co's financing consists of 25 million shares currently trading at $2.40 each and $40 million 7% bonds trading at $1,428 per $1,000. Tramont Co's quoted beta is 1.17. The current risk-free rate of return is estimated at 3% and the market risk premium is 6%. Due to the nature of the project, it is estimated that the beta applicable to the project if it is all-equity financed will be 0.4 more than the current all-equity financed beta of Tramont Co. If the Gamalan project is undertaken, the cost of capital applicable to the cash flows in the US is expected to be 7%.

The spot exchange rate between the dollar and the GR is GR 55 per $1. The annual inflation rates are currently 3% in the US and 9% in Gamala. It can be assumed that these inflation rates will not change for the foreseeable future. All net cash flows arising from the project will be remitted back to Tramont Co at the end of each year.

There are two main political parties in Gamala: the Gamala Liberal (GL) Party and the Gamala Republican (GR) Party. Gamala is currently governed by the GL Party but general elections are due to be held soon. If the GR Party wins the election, it promises to increase taxes of international companies operating in Gamala and review any commercial benefits given to these businesses by the previous government.

Required

(a)   Prepare a report for the board of directors (BoD) of Tramont Co that:

(i)   Evaluates whether or not Tramont Co should undertake the project to produce the X-IT in Gamala and cease its production in the US immediately. In the evaluation, include all relevant calculations in the form of a financial assessment and explain any assumptions made.

It is suggested that the financial assessment should be based on present value of the operating cash flows from the Gamalan project, discounted by an appropriate all-equity rate, and adjusted by the present value of all other relevant cash flows.   **(27 marks)**

(ii) Discusses the potential change in government and other business factors that Tramont Co should consider before making a final decision. **(8 marks)**

Professional marks will be awarded in part (a) for the format, structure and presentation of the answer.

(4 marks)

(b) Although not mandatory for external reporting purposes, one of the members of the BoD suggested that adopting a triple bottom line approach when monitoring the X-IT investment after its implementation would provide a better assessment of how successful it has been.

Discuss how adopting aspects of triple bottom line reporting may provide a better assessment of the success of X-IT. **(6 marks)**

(c) Another member of the BoD felt that, despite Tramont Co having a wide range of shareholders holding well-diversified portfolios of investments, moving the production of the X-IT to Gamala would result in further risk diversification benefits.

Discuss whether moving the production of the X-IT to Gamala may result in further risk diversification for the shareholders already holding well-diversified portfolios. **(5 marks)**

(Total = 50 marks)

64 Cigno (Sep/Dec 15)   98 mins

Cigno Co is a large pharmaceutical company, involved in the research and development (R&D) of medicines and other healthcare products. Over the past few years, Cigno Co has been finding it increasingly difficult to develop new medical products. In response to this, it has followed a strategy of acquiring smaller pharmaceutical companies which already have successful products in the market and/or have products in development which look very promising for the future. It has mainly done this without having to resort to major cost cutting and has therefore avoided large-scale redundancies. This has meant that not only has Cigno Co performed reasonably well in the stock market, but it has also maintained a high level of corporate reputation.

Anatra Co is involved in two business areas: the first area involves the R&D of medical products, and the second area involves the manufacture of medical and dental equipment. Until recently, Anatra Co's financial performance was falling, but about three years ago a new Chief Executive Officer (CEO) was appointed and she started to turn the company around. Recently, the company has developed and marketed a range of new medical products, and is in the process of developing a range of cancer-fighting medicines. This has resulted in a good performance in the stock market, but many analysts believe that its shares are still trading below their true value. Anatra Co's CEO is of the opinion that the turnaround in the company's fortunes makes it particularly vulnerable to a takeover threat, and she is thinking of defence strategies that the company could undertake to prevent such a threat. In particular, she was thinking of disposing of some of the company's assets and focusing on its core business.

Cigno Co is of the opinion that Anatra Co is being held back from achieving its true potential by its equipment manufacturing business and that by separating the two business areas, corporate value can be increased. As a result, it is considering the possibility of acquiring Anatra Co, unbundling the manufacturing business, and then absorbing Anatra Co's R&D of medical products business. Cigno Co estimates that it would need to pay a premium of 35% to Anatra Co's shareholders to buy the company.

Financial information: Anatra Co

Given below are extracts from Anatra Co's latest statement of profit or loss and statement of financial position for the year ended 30 November 20X5.

	20X5
	$m
Sales revenue	21,400
Profit before interest and tax (PBIT)	3,210
Interest	720
Pre-tax profit	2,490

	20X5
	$m
Non-current liabilities	9,000
Share capital (50c/share)	3,500
Reserves	4,520

Anatra Co's share of revenue and profits between the two business areas are as follows:

	Medical products R&D	Equipment manufacturing
Share of revenue and profit	70%	30%

Post-acquisition benefits from acquiring Anatra Co

Cigno Co estimates that following the acquisition and unbundling of the manufacturing business, Anatra Co's future sales revenue and profitability of the medical R&D business will be boosted. The annual sales growth rate is expected to be 5% and the profit margin before interest and tax is expected to be 17.25% of sales revenue, for the next 4 years. It can be assumed that the current tax-allowable depreciation will remain equivalent to the amount of investment needed to maintain the current level of operations, but that the company will require an additional investment in assets of 40c for every $1 increase in sales revenue.

After the 4 years, the annual growth rate of the company's free cash flows is expected to be 3% for the foreseeable future.

Anatra Co's unbundled equipment manufacturing business is expected to be divested through a sell-off, although other options such as a management buy-in were also considered. The value of the sell-off will be based on the medical and dental equipment manufacturing industry. Cigno Co has estimated that Anatra Co's manufacturing business should be valued at a factor of 1.2 times higher than the industry's average price/earnings ratio. Currently the industry's average earnings per share is 30c and the average share price is $2.40.

Possible additional post-acquisition benefits

Cigno Co estimates that it could achieve further cash flow benefits following the acquisition of Anatra Co, if it undertakes a limited business reorganisation. There is some duplication of the R&D work conducted by Cigno Co and Anatra Co, and the costs related to this duplication could be saved if Cigno Co closes some of its own operations. However, it would mean that many redundancies would have to be made, including employees who have worked in Cigno Co for many years. Anatra Co's employees are considered to be better qualified and more able in these areas of duplication, and would therefore not be made redundant.

Cigno Co could also move its headquarters to the country where Anatra Co is based and thereby potentially save a significant amount of tax, other than corporation tax. However, this would mean a loss of revenue for the Government where Cigno Co is based.

The company is concerned about how the Government and the people of the country where it is based might react to these issues. It has had a long and beneficial relationship with the country and its people.

Cigno Co has estimated that it would save $1,600 million after-tax free cash flows to the firm at the end of the first year as a result of these post-acquisition benefits. These cash flows would increase by 4% every year for the next 3 years.

Estimating the combined company's weighted average cost of capital

Cigno Co is of the opinion that as a result of acquiring Anatra Co, the cost of capital will be based on the equity beta and the cost of debt of the combined company. The asset beta of the combined company is the individual companies' asset betas weighted in proportion of the individual companies' market value of equity. Cigno Co has a market debt to equity ratio of 40:60 and an equity beta of 1.10.

It can be assumed that the proportion of market value of debt to market value of equity will be maintained after the two companies combine.

Currently, Cigno Co's total firm value (market values of debt and equity combined) is $60,000 million and Anatra Co's asset beta is 0.68.

Additional information

- The estimate of the risk-free rate of return is 4.3% and of the market risk premium is 7%.

- The corporation tax rate applicable to all companies is 22%.

- Anatra Co's current share price is $3 per share, and it can be assumed that the book value and the market value of its debt are equivalent.

- The pre-tax cost of debt of the combined company is expected to be 6.0%.

Important note

Cigno Co's board of directors (BoD) does not require any discussion or computations of currency movements or exposure in this report. All calculations are to be presented in $ million. Currency movements and their management will be considered in a separate report. The BoD also does not expect any discussion or computations relating to the financing of acquisition in this report, other than the information provided above on the estimation of the cost of capital.

Required

(a) Distinguish between a divestment through a sell-off and a management buy-in as forms of unbundling.

(4 marks)

(b) Prepare a report for the BoD of Cigno Co which:

(i) Estimates the value attributable to Cigno Co's shareholders from the acquisition of Anatra Co before taking into account the cash benefits of potential tax savings and redundancies, and then after taking these into account

(18 marks)

(ii) Assesses the value created from (b)(i) above, including a discussion of the estimations made and methods used

(8 marks)

(iii) Advises the BoD on the key factors it should consider in relation to the redundancies and potential tax savings

(4 marks)

Professional marks will be awarded in part (b) for the format, structure and presentation of the report.

(4 marks)

(c) Discuss whether the defence strategy suggested by Anatra Co's CEO of disposing assets is feasible.

(6 marks)

(d) Takeover regulation, where Anatra Co is based, offers the following conditions aimed at protecting shareholders: the mandatory-bid condition through sell-out rights, the principle of equal treatment, and squeeze-out rights.

Required

Explain the main purpose of each of the three conditions.

(6 marks)

(Total = 50 marks)

65 Lirio (Mar/Jun 16)

98 mins

Lirio Co is an engineering company which is involved in projects around the world. It has been growing steadily for several years and has maintained a stable dividend growth policy for a number of years now. The board of directors (BoD) is considering bidding for a large project which requires a substantial investment of $40 million. It can be assumed that the date today is 1 March 20X6.

The BoD is proposing that Lirio Co should not raise the finance for the project through additional debt or equity. Instead, it proposes that the required finance is obtained from a combination of funds received from the sale of its equity investment in a European company and from cash flows generated from its normal business activity in the coming two years. As a result, Lirio Co's current capital structure of 80 million $1 equity shares and $70 million 5% bonds is not expected to change in the foreseeable future.

The BoD has asked the company's treasury department to prepare a discussion paper on the implications of this proposal. The following information on Lirio Co has been provided to assist in the preparation of the discussion paper.

Expected income and cash flow commitments prior to undertaking the large project for the year to the end of February 20X7

Lirio Co's sales revenue is forecast to grow by 8% next year from its current level of $300 million, and the operating profit margin on this is expected to be 15%. It is expected that Lirio Co will have the following capital investment requirements for the coming year, before the impact of the large project is considered:

1   A $0.10 investment in working capital for every $1 increase in sales revenue;

2   An investment equivalent to the amount of depreciation to keep its non-current asset base at the present productive capacity. The current depreciation charge already included in the operating profit margin is 25% of the non-current assets of $50 million;

3   A $0.20 investment in additional non-current assets for every $1 increase in sales revenue; and

4    $8 million additional investment in other small projects.

In addition to the above sales revenue and profits, Lirio Co has one overseas subsidiary – Pontac Co, from which it receives dividends of 80% on profits. Pontac Co produces a specialist tool which it sells locally for $60 each. It is expected that it will produce and sell 400,000 units of this specialist tool next year. Each tool will incur variable costs of $36 per unit and total annual fixed costs of $4 million to produce and sell.

Lirio Co pays corporation tax at 25% and Pontac Co pays corporation tax at 20%. In addition to this, a withholding tax of 8% is deducted from any dividends remitted from Pontac Co. A bi-lateral tax treaty exists between the countries where Lirio Co is based and where Pontac Co is based. Therefore corporation tax is payable on profits made by subsidiary companies, but full credit is given for corporation tax already paid.

It can be assumed that receipts from Pontac Co are in $ equivalent amounts and exchange rate fluctuations on these can be ignored.

Sale of equity investment in the European country

It is expected that Lirio Co will receive euro (€) 20 million in 3 months' time from the sale of its investment. The € has continued to remain weak, while the $ has continued to remain strong through 20X5 and the start of 20X6. The financial press has also reported that there may be a permanent shift in the €/$ exchange rate, with firms facing economic exposure. Lirio Co has decided to hedge the € receipt using one of currency forward contracts, currency futures contracts or currency options contracts.

The following exchange contracts and rates are available to Lirio Co.

	Per €1
Spot rates	$1.1585–$1.1618
Three-month forward rates	$1.1559–$1.1601

Currency futures (contract size $125,000, quotation: € per $1)

| March futures | €0.8638 |
| June futures | €0.8656 |

Currency options (contract size $125,000, exercise price quotation € per $1, premium € per $1)

	Calls		Puts	
Exercise price	March	June	March	June
0.8600	0.0255	0.0290	0.0267	0.0319

It can be assumed that futures and options contracts expire at the end of their respective months.

Dividend history, expected dividends and cost of capital, Lirio Co

Year to end of February	20X3	20X4	20X5	20X6
Number of $1 equity shares in issue ('000)	60,000	60,000	80,000	80,000
Total dividends paid ($'000)	12,832	13,602	19,224	20,377

It is expected that dividends will grow at the historic rate, if the large project is not undertaken.

Expected dividends and dividend growth rates if the large project is undertaken:

Year to end of February 20X7	Remaining cash flows after the investment in the $40 million project will be paid as dividends.
Year to end of February 20X8	The dividends paid will be the same amount as the previous year.
Year to end of February 20X9	Dividends paid will be $0.31 per share.
In future years from February 20X9	Dividends will grow at an annual rate of 7%.

Lirio Co's cost of equity capital is estimated to be 12%.

Required

(a)   With reference to purchasing power parity, explain how exchange rate fluctuations may lead to economic exposure.   **(6 marks)**

(b)   Prepare a discussion paper, including all relevant calculations, for the BoD of Lirio Co which:

   (i)   Estimates Lirio Co's dividend capacity as at 28 February 20X7, prior to investing in the large project
                                                                                                                           (9 marks)

   (ii)   Advises Lirio Co on, and recommends, an appropriate hedging strategy for the euro (€) receipt it is due to receive in three months' time from the sale of the equity investment   **(14 marks)**

   (iii)   Using the information on dividends provided in the question, and from (b)(i) and (b)(ii) above, assesses whether or not the project would add value to Lirio Co   **(8 marks)**

   (iv)   Discusses the issues of proposed methods of financing the project which need to be considered further   **(9 marks)**

   Professional marks will be awarded in part (b) for the format, structure and presentation of the discussion paper.   **(4 marks)**

                                                                                                                     (Total = 50 marks)

66 Morada (Sep/Dec 16)   98 mins

Morada Co is involved in offering bespoke travel services and maintenance services. In addition to owning a few hotels, it has built strong relationships with companies in the hospitality industry all over the world. It has a good reputation of offering unique, high quality holiday packages at reasonable costs for its clients. The strong relationships have also enabled it to offer repair and maintenance services to a number of hotel chains and cruise ship companies.

Following a long discussion at a meeting of the board of directors (BoD) about the future strategic direction which Morada Co should follow, three directors continued to discuss one particular issue over dinner. In the meeting, the BoD had expressed concern that Morada Co was exposed to excessive risk and therefore its cost of capital was too high. The BoD feared that several good projects had been rejected over the previous two years, because they did not meet Morada Co's high cost of capital threshold. Each director put forward a proposal, which they then discussed in turn. At the conclusion of the dinner, the directors decided to ask for a written report on the proposals put forward by the first director and the second director, before taking all three proposals to the BoD for further discussion.

First director's proposal

The first director is of the opinion that Morada Co should reduce its debt in order to mitigate its risk and therefore reduce its cost of capital. He proposes that the company should sell its repair and maintenance services business unit and focus just on offering bespoke travel services and hotel accommodation. In the sale, the book value of non-current assets will reduce by 30% and the book value of current liabilities will reduce by 10%. It is thought that the non-current assets can be sold for an after-tax profit of 15%.

The first director suggests that the funds arising from the sale of the repair and maintenance services business unit and cash resources should be used to pay off 80% of the long-term debt. It is estimated that as a result of this, Morada Co's credit rating will improve from Baa2 to A2.

Second director's proposal

The second director is of the opinion that risk diversification is the best way to reduce Morada Co's risk and therefore reduce its cost of capital. He proposes that the company raise additional funds using debt finance and then create a new strategic business unit. This business unit will focus on construction of new commercial properties.

The second director suggests that $70 million should be borrowed and used to invest in purchasing non-current assets for the construction business unit. The new debt will be issued in the form of 4-year redeemable bonds paying an annual coupon of 6.2%. It is estimated that if this amount of debt is raised, then Morada Co's credit rating will worsen to Ca3 from Baa2. Current liabilities are estimated to increase to $28 million.

Third director's proposal

The third director is of the opinion that Morada Co does not need to undertake the proposals suggested by the first director and the second director just to reduce the company's risk profile. She feels that the above proposals require a fundamental change in corporate strategy and should be considered in terms of more than just tools to manage risk. Instead, she proposes that a risk management system should be set up to appraise Morada Co's current risk profile, considering each type of business risk and financial risk within the company, and taking appropriate action to manage the risk where it is deemed necessary.

MORADA CO EXTRACTS FROM THE FORECAST FINANCIAL POSITION FOR THE COMING YEAR

	$'000
Non-current assets	280,000
Current assets	8,000
Total assets	328,000

Equity and liabilities	
Share capital (40c/share)	50,000
Retained earnings	137,000
Total equity	187,000

Non-current liabilities (6.2% redeemable bonds)	120,000
Current liabilities	21,000
Total liabilities	141,000
Total liabilities and equity capital	328,000

Other financial information

Morada Co's forecast after-tax earnings for the coming year are expected to be $28 million. It is estimated that the company will make a 9% return after tax on any new investment in non-current assets, and will suffer a 9% decrease in after-tax earnings on any reduction in investment in non-current assets.

Morada Co's current share price is $2.88 per share. According to the company's finance division, it is very difficult to predict how the share price will react to either the proposal made by the first director or the proposal made by the second director. Therefore it has been assumed that the share price will not change following either proposal.

The finance division has further assumed that the proportion of the book value of non-current assets invested in each business unit gives a fair representation of the size of each business unit within Morada Co.

Morada Co's equity beta is estimated at 1.2, while the asset beta of the repairs and maintenance services business unit is estimated to be 0.65. The relevant equity beta for the new, larger company including the construction unit relevant to the second director's proposals has been estimated as 1.21.

The bonds are redeemable in four years' time at face value. For the purposes of estimating the cost of capital, it can be assumed that debt beta is zero. However, the 4-year credit spread over the risk-free rate of return is 60 basis points for A2 rated bonds, 90 basis points for Baa2 rated bonds and 240 basis points for Ca3 rated bonds.

A tax rate of 20% is applicable to all companies. The current risk-free rate of return is estimated to be 3.8% and the market risk premium is estimated to be 7%.

Required

(a) Explain how business risk and financial risk are related; and how risk mitigation and risk diversification can form part of a company's risk management strategy. **(6 marks)**

(b) Prepare a report for the board of directors of Morada Co which:

   (i) Estimates Morada Co's cost of equity and cost of capital, based on market value of equity and debt, before any changes and then after implementing the proposals put forward by the first and by the second directors; **(17 marks)**

   (ii) Estimates the impact of the first and second directors' proposals on Morada Co's forecast after-tax earnings and forecast financial position for the coming year; and **(7 marks)**

   (iii) Discusses the impact on Morada Co of the changes proposed by the first and second directors and recommends whether or not either proposal should be accepted. The discussion should include an explanation of any assumptions made in the estimates in (b)(i) and (b)(ii) above. **(9 marks)**

   Professional marks will be awarded in part (b) for the format, structure and presentation of the report. **(4 marks)**

(c) Discuss the possible reasons for the third director's proposal that a risk management system should consider each risk, before taking appropriate action. **(7 marks)**

(Total = 50 marks)

67 Pursuit (6/11, amended)   98 mins

Pursuit Co, a listed company which manufactures electronic components, is interested in acquiring Fodder Co, an unlisted company involved in the development of sophisticated but high risk electronic products. The owners of Fodder Co are a consortium of private equity investors who have been looking for a suitable buyer for their company for some time. Pursuit Co estimates that a payment of the equity value plus a 25% premium would be sufficient to secure the purchase of Fodder Co. Pursuit Co would also pay off any outstanding debt that Fodder Co owed. Pursuit Co wishes to acquire Fodder Co using a combination of debt finance and its cash reserves of $20 million, such that the capital structure of the combined company remains at Pursuit Co's current capital structure level.

Information on Pursuit Co and Fodder Co

Pursuit Co

Pursuit Co has a market debt to equity ratio of 50:50 and an equity beta of 1.18. Currently Pursuit Co has a total firm value (market value of debt and equity combined) of $140 million. Pursuit Co makes sales in US, Europe and Asia and has obtained some of its debt funding from international markets.

FODDER CO, EXTRACTS FROM THE STATEMENT OF PROFIT OR LOSS

Year ended	31 May 20X1 $'000	31 May 20X0 $'000	31 May 20W9 $'000	31 May 20W8 $'000
Sales revenue	16,146	15,229	14,491	13,559
Operating profit (after operating costs and tax-allowable depreciation)	5,169	5,074	4,243	4,530
Net interest costs	489	473	462	458
Profit before tax	4,680	4,601	3,781	4,072
Taxation (28%)	1,310	1,288	1,059	1,140
After-tax profit	3,370	3,313	2,722	2,932
Dividends	123	115	108	101
Retained earnings	3,247	3,198	2,614	2,831

Fodder Co has a market debt to equity ratio of 10:90 and an estimated equity beta of 1.53. It can be assumed that its tax-allowable depreciation is equivalent to the amount of investment needed to maintain current operational levels. However, Fodder Co will require an additional investment in assets of 22c per $1 increase in sales revenue, for the next 4 years. It is anticipated that Fodder Co will pay interest at 9% on its future borrowings.

For the next four years, Fodder Co's sales revenue will grow at the same average rate as the previous years. After the forecasted four-year period, the growth rate of its free cash flows will be half the initial forecast sales revenue growth rate for the foreseeable future.

Information about the combined company

Following the acquisition, it is expected that the combined company's sales revenue will be $51,952,000 in the first year, and its profit margin on sales will be 30% for the foreseeable future. After the first year the growth rate in sales revenue will be 5.8% per year for the following 3 years. Following the acquisition, it is expected that the combined company will pay annual interest at 6.4% on future borrowings.

The combined company will require additional investment in assets of $513,000 in the first year and then 18c per $1 increase in sales revenue for the next 3 years. It is anticipated that after the forecasted four-year period, its free cash flow growth rate will be half the sales revenue growth rate.

It can be assumed that the asset beta of the combined company is the weighted average of the individual companies' asset betas, weighted in proportion of the individual companies' market value.

Other information

The current annual government base rate is 4.5% and the market risk premium is estimated at 6% per year. The relevant annual tax rate applicable to all the companies is 28%.

SGF Co's interest in Pursuit Co

There have been rumours of a potential bid by SGF Co to acquire Pursuit Co. Some financial press reports have suggested that this is because Pursuit Co's share price has fallen recently. SGF Co is in a similar line of business as Pursuit Co and, until a couple of years ago, SGF Co was the smaller company. However, a successful performance has resulted in its share price rising, and SGF Co is now the larger company.

The rumours of SGF Co's interest have raised doubts about Pursuit Co's ability to acquire Fodder Co. Although SGF Co has made no formal bid yet, Pursuit Co's board is keen to reduce the possibility of such a bid. The Chief Financial Officer has suggested that the most effective way to reduce the possibility of a takeover would be to distribute the $20 million in its cash reserves to its shareholders in the form of a special dividend. Fodder Co would then be purchased using debt finance. He conceded that this would increase Pursuit Co's gearing level but suggested it may increase the company's share price and make Pursuit Co less appealing to SGF Co.

Required

(a) Prepare a report to the board of directors of Pursuit Co that:

 (i) Evaluates whether the acquisition of Fodder Co would be beneficial to Pursuit Co and its shareholders. The free cash flow to firm method should be used to estimate the values of Fodder Co and the combined company assuming that the combined company's capital structure stays the same as that of Pursuit Co's current capital structure. Include all relevant calculations. **(16 marks)**

 (ii) Discusses the limitations of the estimated valuations in part (i) above. **(4 marks)**

 (iii) Estimates the amount of debt finance needed, in addition to the cash reserves, to acquire Fodder Co and concludes whether Pursuit Co's current capital structure can be maintained. **(3 marks)**

 (iv) Explains the implications of a change in the capital structure of the combined company to the valuation method used in part (i) and how the issue can be resolved. **(4 marks)**

 (v) Assesses whether the Chief Financial Officer's recommendation would provide a suitable defence against a bid from SGF Co and would be a viable option for Pursuit Co. **(5 marks)**

 Professional marks will be awarded in this question for the format, structure and presentation of the report. **(4 marks)**

(b) Assess how the global debt crisis may affect Pursuit Co. **(8 marks)**

(c) The Chief Executive Officer has heard that many companies in the industry use environmental reporting. Discuss what this would involve for Pursuit Co and the advantages and disadvantages to Pursuit Co of adding environmental reporting to its annual report. **(6 marks)**

(Total = 50 marks)

68 Polytot (SFM, 6/04, amended)   98 mins

Assume that it is now 1 July. Polytot plc, a UK-based multinational company, has received an export order valued at 675 million pesos from a company in Grobbia, a country that has recently been accepted into the World Trade Organization, but which does not yet have a freely convertible currency.

The Grobbian company only has access to sufficient US$ to pay for 60% of the goods, at the official US$ exchange rate. The balance would be payable in the local currency, the Grobbian peso, for which there is no official foreign exchange market. Polytot is due to receive payment in four months' time and has been informed that an unofficial market in Grobbian pesos exists in which the peso can be converted into pounds. The exchange rate in this market is 15% worse for Polytot than the 'official' rate of exchange between the peso and the pound.

Exchange rates

	$/£
Spot	1.5475–1.5510
3 months forward	1.5362–1.5398
1 year forward	1.5140–1.5178

	Grobbian peso/£
Official spot rate	156.30

	Grobbian peso/$
Official spot rate	98.20

Philadelphia SE £/$ options £31,250 (cents per pound)

	Calls			Puts		
	Sept	Dec	March	Sept	Dec	March
1.5250	2.95	3.35	3.65	2.00	3.25	4.35
1.5500	1.80	2.25	2.65	3.30	4.60	5.75
1.5750	0.90	1.40	1.80	4.90	6.25	7.35
1.6000	0.25	0.75	1.10	6.75	8.05	9.15

£/$ currency futures (CME, £62,500)

September	1.5350
December	1.5275

Assume that options and futures contracts mature at the relevant month end.

Required

Produce a report which:

(a)   Discusses the alternative forms of currency hedge that are available to Polytot plc and calculate the expected revenues, in £ sterling, from the sale to the company in Grobbia as a result of each of these hedges. Provide a reasoned recommendation as to which hedge should be selected.   **(19 marks)**

Professional marks for format, structure and presentation of report   **(4 marks)**

(b)   The Grobbian company is willing to undertake a countertrade deal whereby 40% of the cost of the goods is paid for by an exchange of 3 million kilos of Grobbian strawberries. A major UK supermarket chain has indicated that it would be willing to pay between 50 and 60 pence per kilo for the strawberries.

Discuss the issues that Polytot should consider before deciding whether or not to agree to the countertrade.   **(6 marks)**

(c)   The Grobbian company has asked for advice in using the Euromarkets to raise international finance.

Required

Provide a briefing memo for the company discussing the advantages of the Euromarkets, and any potential problems for the Grobbian company in using them.   **(7 marks)**

(d)   Polytot also has subsidiaries in three countries – Umgaba, Mazila and Bettuna.

1   The subsidiary in Umgaba manufactures specialist components, which may then be assembled and sold in either Mazila or Bettuna.

2   Production and sales volume may each be assumed to be 400,000 units per year no matter where the assembly and sales take place.

3   Manufacturing costs in Umgaba are $16 per unit and fixed costs (for the normal range of production) $1.8 million.

4   Assembly costs in Mazila are $9 per unit and in Bettuna $7.50 per unit. Fixed costs are $700,000 and $900,000 respectively.

5   The unit sales price in Mazila is $40 and in Bettuna $37.

6   Corporate taxes on profits are at the rate of 40% in Umgaba, 25% in Mazila, 32% in Bettuna and 30% in the UK. No tax credits are available in these three countries for any losses made. Full credit is given by the UK tax authorities for tax paid overseas.

7   Tax-allowable import duties of 10% are payable on all goods imported into Mazila.

8   A withholding tax of 15% is deducted from all dividends remitted from Umgaba.

9   Polytot expects about 60% of profits from each subsidiary to be remitted direct to the UK each year.

10   Cost and price data in all countries is shown in US dollars.

Required

Evaluate and explain:

(i)   If the transfer price from Umgaba should be based upon fixed cost plus variable cost, or fixed cost plus variable cost plus a mark-up of 30%

(ii)   Whether assembly should take place in Mazila or Bettuna   **(10 marks)**

(e)   Comment upon the likely attitude of the governments of each of the four countries towards the transfer price and assembly location selected in (d)(i) and (d)(ii) above.   **(4 marks)**

(Total = 50 marks)

69 Nente (6/12, amended)   98 mins

Nente Co, an unlisted company, designs and develops tools and parts for specialist machinery. The company was formed 4 years ago by 3 friends, who own 20% of the equity capital in total, and a consortium of 5 business angel organisations, which own the remaining 80%, in roughly equal proportions. Nente Co also has a large amount of debt finance in the form of variable rate loans. Initially the amount of annual interest payable on these loans was low and allowed Nente Co to invest internally generated funds to expand its business. Recently, though, due to a rapid increase in interest rates, there has been limited scope for future expansion and no new product development.

The board of directors, consisting of the three friends and a representative from each business angel organisation, met recently to discuss how to secure the company's future prospects. Two proposals were put forward, as follows:

Proposal 1

To accept a takeover offer from Mije Co, a listed company, which develops and manufactures specialist machinery tools and parts. The takeover offer is for $2.95 cash per share or a share-for-share exchange where two Mije Co shares would be offered for three Nente Co shares. Mije Co would need to get the final approval from its shareholders if either offer is accepted.

Proposal 2

To pursue an opportunity to develop a small prototype product that just breaks even financially, but gives the company exclusive rights to produce a follow-on product within two years.

The meeting concluded without agreement on which proposal to pursue.

After the meeting, Mije Co was consulted about the exclusive rights. Mije Co's directors indicated that they had not considered the rights in their computations and were willing to continue with the takeover offer on the same terms without them.

Currently, Mije Co has 10 million shares in issue and these are trading for $4.80 each. Mije Co's price/earnings (P/E) ratio is 15. It has sufficient cash to pay for Nente Co's equity and a substantial proportion of its debt, and believes that this will enable Nente Co to operate on a P/E level of 15 as well. In addition to this, Mije Co believes that it can find cost-based synergies of $150,000 after tax per year for the foreseeable future. Mije Co's current profit after tax is $3,200,000.

The following financial information relates to Nente Co and to the development of the new product.

Nente Co financial information

EXTRACT FROM THE MOST RECENT STATEMENT OF PROFIT OR LOSS

	$'000
Sales revenue	8,780
Profit before interest and tax	1,230
Interest	(455)
Tax	(155)
Profit after tax	620
Dividends	Nil

EXTRACT FROM THE MOST RECENT STATEMENT OF FINANCIAL POSITION

	$'000
Net non-current assets	10,060
Current assets	690
Total assets	10,750
Share capital (40c per share par value)	960
Reserves	1,400
Non-current liabilities: Variable rate loans	6,500
Current liabilities	1,890
Total liabilities and capital	10,750

In arriving at the profit after tax amount, Nente Co deducted tax-allowable depreciation and other non-cash expenses totalling $1,206,000. It requires an annual cash investment of $1,010,000 in non-current assets and working capital to continue its operations.

Nente Co's profits before interest and tax in its first year of operation were $970,000 and have been growing steadily in each of the following three years, to their current level. Nente Co's cash flows grew at the same rate as well, but it is likely that this growth rate will reduce to 25% of the original rate for the foreseeable future.

Nente Co currently pays interest of 7% per year on its loans, which is 380 basis points over the government base rate, and corporation tax of 20% on profits after interest. It is estimated that an overall cost of capital of 11% is reasonable compensation for the risk undertaken on an investment of this nature.

New product development (Proposal 2)

Developing the new follow-on product will require an investment of $2,500,000 initially. The total expected cash flows and present values of the product over its 5-year life, with a volatility of 42% standard deviation, are as follows:

Year(s)	Now	1	2	3 to 7 (total)
Cash flows ($'000)	–	–	(2,500)	3,950
Present values ($'000)	–	–	(2,029)	2,434

Required

(a)   Prepare a report for the board of directors of Nente Co that:

(i)   Estimates the current value of a Nente Co share, using the free cash flow to firm methodology

(7 marks)

(ii)   Estimates the percentage gain in value to a Nente Co share and a Mije Co share under each payment offer **(8 marks)**

(iii)   Estimates the percentage gain in the value of the follow-on product to a Nente Co share, based on its cash flows and on the assumption that the production can be delayed following acquisition of the exclusive rights of production.   **(8 marks)**

(iv)   Discusses the likely reaction of Nente Co and Mije Co shareholders to the takeover offer, including the assumptions made in the estimates above and how the follow-on product's value can be utilised by Nente Co.   **(8 marks)**

Professional marks will be awarded for the presentation, structure and clarity of the answer.   **(4 marks)**

(b)   Evaluate the current performance of Nente Co and comment on what this will mean for the proposed takeover bid.   **(8 marks)**

(c)   Since the approach to Nente Co, Mije Co has itself been the subject of a takeover bid from Tianhe Co, a listed company which specialises in supplying machinery to the manufacturing sector and has a market capitalisation of $245 million.

Required

Evaluate the general post-bid defences and comment on their suitability for Mije Co to try to prevent the takeover from Tianhe Co.   **(7 marks)**

(Total = 50 marks)

BPP
LEARNING MEDIA

Answers

1 Preparation question: Mezza

Marking scheme

		Marks	
(a)	Overarching corporate aim	1–2	
	Discussion of the project adding value and issues relating to return and risk	3–4	
	Possible suggestions for mitigating the negative issues to above discussion	3–4	
	Discussion of the ethical and environmental issues	3–4	
	Possible suggestions for mitigating the ethical and environmental issues	3–4	
	Other relevant key issues and suggestions for mitigation	2–3	
			Max 17
(b)	1–2 marks per capital discussed		Max 8
			25

(a) **Overarching corporate aim**

The main aim of the directors is to maximise shareholder value and any decisions should be taken with this objective in mind. However, the company has other stakeholders and directors should be sensitive to potential negative implications from implementing the project.

Key issue (1) – will the project add value?

The first issue to consider is whether the project will add value to the company.

Positive factors

At first glance it would appear that the project would be adding value, as it is meeting an identifiable market need (tackling climate change). There are likely to be positive effects on the company's reputation and ultimately its share price as Mezza Co is demonstrating a desire and ability to tackle climate change. If Mezza Co champions the work being done by its subsidiary, there are likely to be future opportunities for the subsidiary to work on similar projects.

Other factors to consider

Before progressing with the project, further investigation into its likely value is required. Whilst there is no doubt that such a project should be well received, there are risks that must be considered, not just from the project itself but also from the behaviour of the directors. Share options form part of the directors' remuneration package and they may be tempted to take greater risks as a result, in order to try to boost the share price. This may be against the wishes of shareholders and other stakeholders who may have a more risk-averse attitude.

The project appears to use new technology and ideas which, by their very nature, will be risky. There will therefore be uncertainty surrounding the income stream from the project – the extent of the risk should be assessed prior to progressing with the project. Are the current revenue and cost estimates realistic? What is the likelihood of competitors entering the market and the potential effects on revenue and market share? A full investigation, using such means as sensitivity analysis and duration, is required to answer such questions.

When assessing the extent of the value added by the project, it is important that risk is factored into the process. By doing so, directors will be in a better position (if necessary) to show stakeholders that they are not taking unacceptable risks in proceeding with the project. Other factors that must be investigated include the length of time it will take to get the product to market, any additional infrastructure required and potential expertise needed.

Key issue (2) – plant location

Positive factors

Mezza Co has identified an 'ideal' location for the plant, namely Maienar in Asia. This is due to Mezza already having a significant presence in Maienar and thus a well-developed infrastructure exists. There are also strong ties with senior government officials in this country and the Government is keen to develop new industries. All of these factors are very positive for the potential development of the project. The ties to senior government officials are likely to be particularly useful when trying to deal with legal and administrative issues, thus reducing the time between development and production actually starting.

Other factors to consider

Despite the positive factors mentioned above, there are ethical and environmental issues to consider prior to making a final decision regarding plant location. The likely effect on the fishermen's livelihood could produce adverse publicity, as could potential damaging effects on the environment and wildlife. Environmental impact tends to generate considerable debate and Mezza will want to avoid any negative effects on its reputation (particularly as the project is supposed to be 'environmentally friendly').

The fact that Mezza has close ties with senior political figures and the Government in general may create negative feeling if it is felt that Mezza could influence the Government into making decisions that are not in the best interests of the locality and the country as a whole. This is a relationship that will have to be managed very carefully.

Risk mitigation

Given that Mezza has an excellent corporate image, it is unlikely that it will want to ignore the plight of the fishermen. It could try to work with the fishermen and involve them in the process, pointing out the benefits of the project to the environment as a whole (without ignoring the effects on their livelihood). It could offer the fishermen priority on new jobs that are created and emphasise the additional wealth that the project is likely to create.

Mezza could also consider alternative locations for the plant, although this is likely to be expensive, given the need for certain infrastructure already present in Maienar. Alternatively the company could try to find an alternative process for growing and harvesting the plant that would not have adverse effects on wildlife and fish stocks. Again, this is an expensive option and any such costs would have to be set against expected revenues to determine value added.

As mentioned above, Mezza will have to manage its relationship with Maienar's Government very carefully as it does not want to appear to be influencing government decisions. Mezza needs to make it very clear that it is following proper legal and administrative procedures – and is working with the Government to protect and improve the country, rather than exploit it for its own gains.

Conclusion

It is important that Mezza considers all of the likely benefits and costs related to the project, not just to itself but also to the country and its inhabitants. While gaining prompt approval from the Government will allow the project to proceed and become profitable more quickly, it is important that Mezza focuses on the effects of the project and alternative ways to proceed, in order to avoid an overall negative impact on its reputation.

(b)   **Integrated reporting**

Integrated reporting looks at the ability of an organisation to create value and considers important relationships, both internally and externally. It involves considering the impact of the proposed project and six capitals as follows.

Financial

The integrated report should explain how commercialising the product should generate revenues over time, be an important element in diversification and make a significant contribution to the growth of Mezza. The report should also disclose the financial strategy implications if additional funding was required and what finance cost commitments Mezza will assume.

Manufactured

The report would identify the new facility as an important addition to Mezza's productive capacity. It would also show how the infrastructure that Mezza already has in Maienar will be used to assist in growing and processing the new plant.

Intellectual

The report should show how Mezza intends to protect the plant and hence its future income by some sort of protection, such as the patent. It should also highlight how development of the plant fulfils the aims of the subsidiary, to develop products that have beneficial impacts on other capitals.

Human

Mezza should show how the employment opportunities provided by the new facility link to how Mezza has been using local labour in Maienar. It should highlight the ways in which the new facility allows local labour to develop their skills. However, the report also needs to show whether Mezza is doing anything to help the fishermen deal with their loss of livelihood, since the adverse impact on the fishermen would appear to go against Mezza's strategy of supporting local farming communities.

Social and relationship

The development of the plant and the new facility should be reported in the context of Mezza's strategy of being a good corporate citizen in Maienar. It should explain how the new plant will assist economic development there and in turn how this will enhance the value derived to Mezza from operating in that country.

Natural

The report needs to set the adverse impact on the area and the fishing stock in the context of the longer-term environmental benefits that development of the plant brings. It also needs to show the commitments that Mezza is making to mitigate environmental damage.

2 Preparation question: Strom

Text references. This area is covered in Chapter 4a.

Top tips. In part (a) you need to assume that the marks are evenly split between the two parts of the requirement when writing your answer.

For part (b) ensure that you address each issue separately rather than giving one overall answer.

In part (d) make sure your answers are not generic advantages of multinationals as many of these relate to producers rather than retailers.

Easy marks. In part (c) there are some fairly easy marks available for discussion of obvious risks from reducing the spend on quality control. Remember to tailor your answer to be relevant for Strom Co.

			Marks
(a)	Explanation of the role and aims of the IMF	5–6	
	Reasons for austerity measures affecting Strom Co negatively	4–5	
			Max 10
(b)	Suggestion(s) for not affecting low-price retailers	2	
	Suggestion(s) for not affecting high-price retailers	2	
			4
(c)	Discussion of the risks	3–4	
	Reduction of the detrimental impact	2–3	
			Max 6
(d)	One mark per valid point		Max 5
			25

(a) The role of the IMF is to oversee the global financial system, in particular to stabilise exchange rates, helping countries to achieve a **balance of payments** and influencing economic policies to help in the **development of countries**. The IMF can provide financial support to member countries in the form of a loan which is typically repayable in three to five years. The funds for the loan are raised through the deposits of member countries. The pre-conditions that the IMF places on its loans to debtor countries vary according to the individual situation of each country, but the general position is as follows.

(i) The IMF wants countries which borrow from the IMF to get into a position to start **repaying the loans fairly quickly**. To do this, the countries must take effective action to improve their balance of payments position.

(ii) To make this improvement, the IMF generally believes that a country should take action to **reduce the demand for goods and services** in the economy (eg by increasing taxes and cutting government spending). This will reduce imports and help to put a brake on any price rises. The country's industries should then also be able to divert more resources into export markets and hence exports should improve in the longer term.

(iii) With 'deflationary' measures along these lines, standards of living will fall (at least in the short term) and unemployment may rise. The IMF regards these short-term hardships to be necessary if a country is to succeed in sorting out its balance of payments and international debt problems.

The IMF has been criticised for the conditions imposed on countries, including specific criticism for the suggestion that its policies cause austerity measures which impact more on those with **lower or mid-range incomes**. This in turn hinders long-term growth and development.

Strom Co trades across Europe, where economic activity has been **severely affected in recent years** due to the banking crisis and then due to austerity measures applied by many European governments. For retailers there are two problems posed by this. Firstly, with limited growth and higher taxes, individuals will have **less disposable income**. Secondly, increased unemployment will also limit disposable income. These two problems mean customers may reduce their expenditure on clothing in order to meet other needs.

Companies may need to increase their marketing spend and possibly offer greater discounts or other incentives in order to **remain competitive** or maintain market share. These increased costs will **reduce profit margins**. It can be seen that profit margins have reduced for Strom Co from 20X1 levels. This may be caused by increased spend on marketing or by a failure to reduce the cost base proportionally, but further analysis would be required to determine the cause.

It appears that Strom Co is trying to reduce its costs to address the issue of **declining profitability**. In circumstances where sales revenues are declining and they cannot be stabilised or improved, cost structures may need to be changed in order for Strom Co to make **reasonable profits**.

(b)   Low-price clothing retailers may benefit at the expense of mid-price retailers due to a **switch** from mid-price clothes to low-price clothes by consumers. The austerity measures may result in people having less money to spend or being less willing to spend due to future uncertainty. As stated above it is thought that austerity measures affect the mid-income and low-income earners more negatively. Together with the above this may change their buying preferences to low-priced clothes. This would be the case especially where **brand loyalty is limited** and the low-price clothes are perceived as either similar quality or better **value for money**.

With high-priced clothes, there may be **greater brand loyalty**, meaning customers are less likely to switch to mid-priced clothing. Customers who purchase high-priced clothing may prefer to make **savings elsewhere** to switching to cheaper clothing. Many people who purchase high-priced clothing may be high-income earners who are relatively less affected by austerity measures as argued above.

(c)   The most obvious risk arising from reducing the allocation of resources to quality control is that quality control inspections will be reduced. This **increases the risk of defective goods** being sold. There is a chance that the cost of processing returned goods could outweigh the savings in quality control. A reduction in the monitoring of working conditions of employees may allow **questionable employment practices** to emerge, which could compromise Strom Co's ethical standards.

A further significant risk is the impact on the reputation of Strom Co and its products. Lower quality and defective clothes could cause serious **damage to the reputation** of Strom Co and result in reduced future sales revenue. This damage to reputation would be very **difficult to reverse**. A fall in ethical standards could also badly damage reputation. Customers may switch their custom to alternative suppliers, investors may sell their shares and the public may organise campaigns against Strom Co. Such reputation damage will be **long term** and maybe even permanent.

Strom Co may be able to make savings in quality control without causing the adverse effects discussed above. Savings could be made by reviewing the processes and eliminating any **unnecessary or duplicated procedures**. It should also evaluate whether alternative processes, which are less resource intensive, can be used that will not compromise quality control or the monitoring of working conditions. This review should be performed by experts. **All critical processes must be retained**, regardless of the level of resources required. The risk of the review containing errors should be evaluated and discussed by senior management to ensure that Strom Co is comfortable with the likely risk level.

(d)   A global multinational retailer has the advantage of a presence in different countries which are **not all experiencing the same economic conditions**. For example, a mid-price clothing retailer may still have strong sales in a country which has not been as strongly affected by the sovereign debt crisis as the Eurozone.

Managerial expertise may be fostered in the environment of the larger multinational enterprise, and can be developed from previous knowledge of foreign markets.

Economies of scale can be gained in marketing, finance, research and development, transport and purchasing by virtue of firms being large and having increased bargaining power.

Multinationals enjoy considerable cost advantages in relation to finance. They have the advantage of access to the **full range of financial instruments** such as eurocurrency and eurobonds, which reduces their borrowing costs.

Multinationals' financial strength is also achieved through their ability to **reduce risk by diversifying their operations** and their sources of borrowing.

3 Preparation question: PMU

Text references. Joint ventures are covered in Chapter 4b.

Top tips. The question is asking for benefits and disadvantages of entering into a joint venture rather than setting up independently. It is not asking you to discuss whether or not PMU should move into this market (Kantaka). If you enter into such discussions you will gain no credit.

Make sure your answer is balanced. You are given no indication in the question about the number of marks available for each element of the requirement – it is up to you to address the issues that arise in the scenario. Don't just provide a list of benefits and disadvantages – at this level you are expected to expand each issue and provide potential ways in which disadvantages can be dealt with.

Don't forget to suggest additional information that is required before a final decision can be made.

Easy marks. Even without detailed knowledge of joint ventures, the scenario is sufficiently detailed for you to pick out a number of points that will earn marks.

Examining team's comments. This question was well answered with many candidates gaining a high proportion of the marks for their answers. Answers that gained fewer marks did not give many points or lacked adequate discussion because they were in note form.

Marking scheme

		Marks
(a)	Benefits of joint venture (1 to 2 marks per well-explained point)	4–6
	Disadvantages of joint venture, including ways of mitigating disadvantages (2–3 marks per well-explained point)	10–12
	Additional information (1 mark per point)	3–5
		Max 20
(b)	One point per method explained	Max 5
		25

(a) **Benefits and disadvantages of PMU entering into a joint venture**

Benefits of joint venture

A joint venture with a local partner would give PMU relatively **low cost access** to an overseas market. The Kantaka Government is offering tax concessions to companies bringing FDI into the country and PMU would benefit further by having to borrow less money if it entered into a joint venture.

Given that PMU has no experience of overseas investment and doing business in foreign countries, having a joint venture partner would be beneficial. Such a partner could assist with such issues as **marketing, cultural and language issues and dealing with government restrictions and bureaucracy**.

A joint venture partner could also give easier access to **capital markets** which would reduce any **foreign currency risk** for PMU. If its investment is funded in Rosinante currency but fee income is in Kantaka currency, this will result in long-term foreign currency risk exposure. We have been told that the Kantaka currency has been depreciating against other currencies over the past two years. If this continues the fee income will be worth less when converted into Rosinante currency and could lead to a shortfall in funds available to cover the cost of the investment borrowings.

A joint venture would give PMU the chance to share costs with the local partner. Academic institutions already exist in Kantaka which would eliminate the need to source new premises and a whole new team to run the degree programmes.

Disadvantages of joint venture

The most significant problem with entering into a joint venture for PMU is the potential effects on **reputation**. PMU is a member of the prestigious Holly League and is world-renowned as being of the highest quality. The Kantaka Government has a history of being reluctant to approve degrees from overseas institutions that enter into joint ventures with local partners and those who do graduate with such degrees have been unable to seek employment in national or local government or nationalised organisations. In addition, degree programmes emerging from joint ventures are not held in high regard by Kantaka's population.

With this in mind, PMU could suffer from **negative publicity** if it chooses a poor academic institution with which to have a joint venture. It will have to carry out significant research into potential partners before making a decision. The academic institution chosen should ideally have a high reputation for quality teaching and qualifications to protect PMU's own reputation. It may also be worthwhile for PMU to meet with the Kantaka Government to try to obtain a commitment from the Government to back its degree programmes. All such efforts take time but it is important to do sufficient groundwork before making such a major commitment. PMU should also determine whether the Government will recognise its degrees if it sets up on its own rather than entering into a joint venture.

PMU should also be mindful of the potential impact on the **quality** of its degree programmes. We are told that the teaching and learning methods used in Kantaka's educational institutions are very different to the innovative methods used by PMU (which are instrumental in its academic success). In addition, students will have certain very **high expectations** of the quality of infrastructure, such as IT facilities, halls of residence and lecture halls. Any joint venture partner should be able to adapt to match such expectations. Existing staff will require **sufficient training** to ensure that teaching quality is not compromised. As far as possible, Kantaka students should have the same overall experience that PMU's home-based students in Rosinante enjoy. This may require a higher proportion of Rosinante staff being brought in initially until local staff acquire the necessary skills.

Cultural differences present major challenges to businesses setting up overseas. Steps should be taken to minimise such differences between local staff and expats from Rosinante. We have been told about the differences in teaching and learning methods – there are also differences in **attitudes** towards research, a major activity in Holly League universities. PMU will have to put strategies in place to deal with these and other cultural differences and ensure the availability of programmes to help expat staff settle into a new country. At all costs, a 'them and us' culture should be avoided as this will create resentment and alienation of local staff. One idea might be to encourage **staff exchange programmes** to expose both sets of staff to each other's cultures.

Joint ventures can restrict **managerial freedom of actions** as opinions of both sets of managers may differ. It is important that PMU listens to the opinions of the joint venture partner regardless of how different these may be to the underlying principles of its own managers. Clear guidelines should be developed regarding the aims and objectives of the joint venture and both sets of managers should be involved in the decision-making process.

It is important that PMU considers **government restrictions** on such factors as visas for key staff from Rosinante, proportion of total staff that has to be made up of local employees and repatriation of funds from Kantaka to Rosinante. A meeting with government officials is essential to clarify such issues.

Legal issues must be addressed properly and with due care and attention. Terms and conditions of the joint venture, roles and responsibilities of both parties, profit sharing percentages and ownership percentages must all be discussed by legal representatives of both sides of the contract.

Other information required

- Will tax concessions be lost if PMU decides to 'go it alone' rather than enter into a joint venture? If so the impact on funding required will have to be determined.

- What government restrictions might be imposed on repatriation of funds and visas for key staff?

- Outcome of discussions with the Kantaka Government regarding whether it will recognise PMU degrees and thus allow graduates to gain employment in government and nationalised industries.

- Outcome of research into the availability of potential joint venture partners that will fulfil students' expectations regarding infrastructure, facilities and teaching methods.

- What is the likelihood of PMU's degrees being recognised by Kantaka's own people?

- Will PMU be able to raise funds locally to finance the venture, thus reducing exposure to foreign currency risk?

- Will local staff be willing to undergo training in PMU's teaching and learning methods and to what extent is this likely to breed resentment?

- Will PMU be able to source experts in Kantaka to help set up the venture if it decides to 'go it alone'?

(b)   There are a number of ways PMU could deal with the issue of blocked funds:

(i)   PMU could sell goods or services to the subsidiary and obtain payment. This could be for course materials or teaching staff supplied. The amount of this payment would depend on the volume of sales and also on the transfer price for the sales.

(ii)   PMU could charge a royalty on the courses that the subsidiary runs. The size of the royalty could be adjusted to suit the wishes of PMU's management.

(iii)   PMU could make a loan to a subsidiary at a high interest rate, which would improve PMU's company's profits at the expense of the subsidiary's profits.

(iv)   Management charges may be levied by PMU for costs incurred in the management of international operations.

(v)   The subsidiary could make a loan, equal to the required dividend remittance to PMU.

4 Preparation question: Kilenc

Text references. International investment is covered in Chapter 8 and the global debt crisis is covered in Chapter 4a. Money laundering is also covered in Chapter 4a.

Top tips. Ensure that your answer to part (a) relates to the scenario rather than just a generic list of factors to consider for an overseas investment. Ensure that you comment on the economic situation as this is relevant to the decision.

For part (c) note that the actions to prevent money laundering should not change because Lanosia has a poor reputation. The steps should be in place anyway.

Easy marks. Part (b) offers easy marks if you are familiar with dark pool trading systems.

Examining team's comments. Part (a) of the question which asked candidates to discuss the key risks and issues of setting up an international subsidiary was done well and many responses gained high marks for this part. However, responses got relatively fewer marks for the mitigation of the risks and issues. Nevertheless, generally high marks were achieved in part (a).

On the other hand, few responses were able to provide adequate responses to part (b).

Marking scheme

			Marks
(a)	Discussion of key risks or issues (2–3 marks for each)	8–10	
	Suggestions for management or control of the risk or issue (1–2 marks each)	6–8	
			Max 15
(b)	Explanation of dark pool trading systems	2–3	
	Consequences and how these would affect Kilenc Co	2–3	
			Max 5
(c)	One mark per relevant discussion point		Max 5
			25

(a)   There are several risks and issues that Kilenc Co will need to consider in order to make a decision whether to set up a subsidiary company in Lanosia or not. It will then need to evaluate if these risks and issues can be mitigated or controlled.

Risks and issues

If the subsidiary is set up there is likely to be an impact on Kilenc Co's **current exports to Lanosia** and also to other countries in the same region. Assuming there are existing exports to the region, and that setting up the subsidiary will reduce these exports, there could be adverse effects on the employees and facilities currently supplying these exports. If there are to be redundancies this may damage Kilenc Co's reputation. In addition, Kilenc Co needs to consider how the subsidiary would be perceived and whether the **locally produced products will be seen as the same quality** as the imported ones.

Lanosia is currently in **recession** and this may have a **negative impact on the demand** for the products. The costs of setting up a subsidiary will need to be less than the expected benefits from additional sales and cost reductions. The expected benefits may be less than forecast, especially if the recession continues. On the other hand, there may be additional opportunities from having a subsidiary once recovery from the recession has begun.

The Lanosian Government offers support to pharmaceutical companies and Kilenc Co may find it is subject to restrictions if it is felt that the subsidiary is affecting local companies. For example it may impose repatriation restrictions or increase taxes that the subsidiary has to pay. Alternatively given the fact that 40% of the shares will be locally owned and 50% of the board will also be from Lanosia may mean that the **subsidiary is viewed as a local company** and the government support will also be available to the subsidiary.

Kilenc Co wants to raise debt finance in Lanosia. It needs to consider whether this finance will actually be available. Following the bailout of the banks there may be a shortage of funds for borrowing. Also the high inflation rate may mean that there will be pressure to raise interest rates which may in turn raise borrowing costs.

The Lanosian IPO is likely to result in a **number of minority shareholders**, which combined with the composition of the board may create agency issues for the subsidiary. For example, the board of the subsidiary may make decisions that are in local interests rather than those of the parent company. Alternatively the local board and shareholders may feel that they are dictated to by the parent company and that local interests are not considered at all.

Cultural issues also need to be considered, which include issues arising from dealing with people of a different nationality and also issues of culture within the organisation. A good understanding of cultural issues is important, as is the need to get the **right balance between autonomy and control** by the parent company.

Other risks including foreign exchange exposure, health and safety compliance and physical risks all need to be considered and assessed. There are numerous legal requirements from health and safety legislation which must be understood and complied with. The risk of damage from events such as fire, floods or other natural disasters should also be considered.

Mitigation of risks and issues

The financial costs and benefits need to be fully analysed to establish the viability of the subsidiary. This should include techniques such as **sensitivity analysis** to assess the impact of changes in variables. Any real options should also be analysed to include the value of any follow-on projects in the appraisal.

A marketing campaign could be conducted to ensure that customers' perceptions of the locally produced products are the same as the existing products. Using the **same packaging as the existing products** can help with this. Communication, both external and internal, can be used to minimise any damage to reputation arising from the move to Lanosia. If possible, employees should be redeployed within the organisation to reduce any redundancies.

The Lanosian Government should be negotiated with and communicated with regularly during the setting up of the subsidiary. This should help to **maximise any government support** and/or minimise any restrictions. This may continue after the establishment of the subsidiary to reduce the chance of new regulations or legislation which could adversely affect the subsidiary.

An economic analysis of the likely interest and inflation rates should be conducted. Kilenc Co may want to use fixed rate debt for its financing or use interest rate swaps to effectively fix their interest charge. The costs of such an activity also need to be considered.

The corporate governance structure needs to be negotiated and agreed on in order to get the right balance between autonomy and central control. All major parties should be included in the negotiations and the structure should be clearly communicated.

Cultural differences should be considered from the initial setting up of the subsidiary. Staff handbooks and training sessions can be used to communicate the culture of the organisation to employees.

Foreign exchange exposure can be mitigated through hedging. Health and safety and physical loss risk can be mitigated through a combination of hedging and legal advice.

(b)   Dark pools are **off-exchange facilities** that allow trading of large blocks of shares. They allow brokers and fund managers to place and match large orders **anonymously** to avoid influencing the share price. The transactions are only made public after the trades have been completed. Traders placing large orders on the transparent exchanges risk signalling that they are large buyers or sellers. Such signals could cause the markets to move against them and put the order at risk.

The main argument supporting the use of dark pools is that they **prevent artificial price volatility** that volume sales could cause on an exchange and so the market maintains its efficiency. The counter argument to this is that the regulated exchanges do not know about the transactions taking place until the trades have been completed. As a result, the prices at which these trades are executed remain unknown until after the event. Such a lack of information on significant trades makes **the regulated exchanges less efficient**. Dark pools also take trade away from the regulated exchanges, resulting in reduced transparency as fewer trades are publicly exposed. Such a practice could reduce liquidity in the regulated exchanges and hinder efficient price-setting.

Dark pools are unlikely to impact on the subsidiary company of Kilenc Co because the share price of the subsidiary would be based on the parent company which would not be affected by the Lanosia stock market. The **efficiency of the Lanosian stock market will be important, though**.

(c)   It will be important for Kilenc Co to apply strict customer due diligence in all of its operations in Lanosia and also in the UK.

Applying this should mean the following steps are taken:

When establishing a **business relationship** it is likely that this will be an ongoing relationship. Therefore it is important to establish identity and credibility at the start. Kilenc Co will have to obtain information such as the source and origin of funds that its customer will be using, copies of recent and current financial statements and details of the customer's business.

Customer due diligence should also be carried out if there is a need to carry out an 'occasional transaction' worth 15,000 euros or more – that is, transactions that are not carried out within an ongoing business relationship. Kilenc Co should also look out for 'linked' transactions which are individual transactions of 15,000 euros or more that have been broken down into smaller, separate transactions to avoid due diligence checks.

If there are any **doubts** about identification information that has been obtained previously, then additional checks should be performed.

When the **customer's circumstances change** – for example, a change in the ownership of the customer's business or a significant change in the type of business activity of the customer, then new checks should be performed.

Ongoing monitoring of the business

It is important that Kilenc Co has an effective system of internal controls to protect the business from being used for money laundering. Staff should be suitably trained in the implementation of these internal controls and be alert to any potential issues. A specific member of staff should be nominated as the person to whom any suspicious activities should be reported.

Full documentation of anti-money laundering policies and procedures should be kept and updated as appropriate. Staff should be kept fully informed of any changes.

Maintaining full and up to date records

Kilenc Co is required to keep full and up to date records for financial reporting and auditing purposes, but these can also be used to demonstrate compliance with money laundering regulations. Such records will include receipts, invoices and customer correspondence. European money laundering regulations require that such information be kept for each customer for five years, beginning on either the date a transaction is completed or the date a business relationship ends.

5 Chawan

Text references. Chapter 2.

Top tips. This question required analysis of a company's past performance to help to decide whether or not to dispose of shares in the company. This is a tricky question to interpret; if rushed it can easily be misinterpreted as a valuations question (this was a common error in the exam). Once you have interpreted what is required this question is fairly straightforward in terms of the technical skills required.

Examining team's comments. Good answers for this part, which provided calculations in a tabular format and then discussed the results in a holistic manner, gained the majority of the marks. However, many responses tended to be unstructured, with few calculations to back up what was being said. Some responses also tended to be largely descriptive and piecemeal, where a ratio or trend was calculated and commented on, but the larger picture and discussion were missed. A surprising number of responses made errors in calculating the ratios and/or only gave ratios for one or two years. At this level, such an approach will not gain many marks. It is also difficult to discuss the key findings in any meaningful manner without examining a trend, but this cannot be done from examining one or two years' data.

Marking scheme

			Marks
(a)	Explanation of a dark pool network	3–4	
	Explanation of why Chawan Co may want to use one	1–2	
			Max 5
(b)	Profitability ratios	1–2	
	Investor ratios	3–4	
	Other ratios	1–2	
	Trends and other calculations	3–4	
			Max 10
	Note. Maximum 7 marks if only ratio calculations provided		
	Discussion of company performance over time	2–3	
	Discussion of company performance against competitors	2–3	
	Discussion of actual returns against expected returns	1–2	
	Discussion of need to maintain portfolio and alternative investments	1–2	
	Discussion of future trends and expectations	1–2	
	Discussion of takeover rumour and action as a result	1–2	
	Other relevant discussion/commentary	1–2	
			Max 10
			25

(a) A dark pool network allows shares to be traded anonymously, away from public scrutiny. No information on the trade order is revealed prior to it taking place. The price and size of the order are only revealed once the trade has taken place. Two main reasons are given for dark pool networks: first they prevent the risk of other traders moving the share price up or down; and second they often result in reduced costs because trades normally take place at the mid-price between the bid and offer; and because broker-dealers try to use their own private pools, thereby saving exchange fees.

Chawan Co's holding in Oden Co is 27 million shares out of a total of 600 million shares, or 4.5%. If Chawan Co sold such a large holding all at once, the price of Oden Co shares may fall temporarily and significantly, and Chawan Co may not receive the value based on the current price. By utilising a dark pool network, Chawan Co may be able to keep the price of the share largely intact, and possibly save transaction costs.

Although the criticism against dark pool systems is that they prevent market efficiency by not revealing bid-offer prices before the trade, proponents argue that in fact market efficiency is maintained because a large sale of shares will not move the price down artificially and temporarily.

(b)   **Ratio calculations**

Focus on investor and profitability ratios

Oden Co	20X2	20X3	20X4	20X5
Operating profit/sales revenue		16.2%	15.2%	10.4%
Operating profit/capital employed		22.5%	20.4%	12.7%
Earnings per share		$0.27	$0.24	$0.12
Price to earnings ratio		9.3	10.0	18.3
Gearing ratio (debt/(debt + equity))		37.6%	36.9%	37.1%
Interest cover (operating profit/finance costs)		9.5	7.5	3.5
Dividend yield	7.1%	7.2%	8.3%	6.8%
Travel and leisure (T&L) sector				
Price to earnings ratio	11.9	12.2	13.0	13.8
Dividend yield	6.6%	6.6%	6.7%	6.4%

Other calculations

Oden Co sales revenue annual growth rate average between 20X3 and 20X5 =

$$\left(\frac{1,185}{1,342}\right)^{1/2} - 1 = -6.0\%$$

Between 20X4 and 20X5 = (1,185 – 1,335)/1,335 = –11.2%.

Oden Co average financing cost

20X3: 23/(365 + 88) = 5.1%
20X4: 27/(368 + 90) = 5.9%
20X5: 35/(360 + 98) = 7.6%

Share price changes	20X2–20X3	20X3–20X4	20X4–20X5
Oden Co	19.0%	–4.0%	–8.3%
T&L sector	15.8%	–2.3%	12.1%

Oden Co

Return to shareholders (RTS)	20X3	20X4	20X5
Dividend yield	7.2%	8.3%	6.8%
Share price gain	19.0%	–4.0%	–8.3%
Total	26.2%	4.3%	–1.5%

Average: 9.7%

Required return (based on capital asset pricing model (CAPM))	13.0%	13.6%	16.0%

Average: 14.2%

T&L sector (RTS)	20X3	20X4	20X5
Dividend yield	6.6%	6.7%	6.4%
Share price gain	15.8%	–2.3%	12.1%
Total shareholder return	22.4%	4.4%	18.5%

Average: 15.1%

Required return (based on CAPM)	12.4%	13.0%	13.6%

Average: 13.0%

> **Tutorial note.** Dividend yield, when calculated as part of total shareholder return, is normally calculated as current dividend ÷ **closing** share price of the **previous** year. This is not the case in the calculations shown here because the closing share price is not given (the share price given is the average share price for the year) but a calculation based on the previous year share price would be acceptable in the exam.

Discussion

The following discussion compares the performance of Oden Co over time to the T&L sector and against expectations, in terms of it being a sound investment. It also considers the wider aspects which Chawan Co should take account of and the further information which the company should consider before coming to a final decision.

In terms of Oden Co's performance between 20X3 and 20X5, it is clear from the calculations above that the company is experiencing considerable financial difficulties. Profit margins have fallen and so has the earnings per share (EPS). While the amount of gearing appears fairly stable, the interest cover has deteriorated. The reason for this is that borrowing costs have increased from an average of 5.1% to an average of 7.6% over the 3 years. The share price has decreased over the three years as well and in the last year so has the dividend yield. This would indicate that the company is unable to maintain adequate returns for its investors (please also see below).

Although Oden Co has tried to maintain a dividend yield which is higher than the sector average, its price/earnings (P/E) ratio has been lower than the sector average between 20X3 and 20X4. It does increase significantly in 20X5, but this is because of the large fall in the EPS, rather than an increase in the share price. This could be an indication that there is less confidence in the future prospects of Oden Co, compared to the rest of the T&L sector. This is further corroborated by the higher dividend yield which may indicate that the company has fewer value-creating projects planned in the future. Finally, whereas the T&L sector's average share price seems to have recovered strongly in 20X5, following a small fall in 20X4, Oden Co's share price has not followed suit and the decline has gathered pace in 20X5. It would seem that Oden Co is a poor performer within its sector.

This view is further strengthened by comparing the actual returns to the required returns based on the capital asset pricing model (CAPM). Both the company and the T&L sector produced returns exceeding the required return in 20X3 and Oden Co experienced a similar decline to the sector in 20X4. However, in 20X5, the T&L sector appears to have recovered but Oden Co's performance has worsened. This has resulted in Oden Co's actual average returns being significantly below the required returns between 20X2 and 20X5.

Taking the above into account, the initial recommendation is for Chawan Co to dispose of its investment in Oden Co. However, there are three important caveats which should be considered before the final decision is made.

The first caveat is that Chawan Co should look at the balance of its portfolio of investments. A sale of $58 million worth of equity shares within a portfolio total of $360 million may cause the portfolio to become unbalanced and for unsystematic risk to be introduced into the portfolio. Presumably, the purpose of maintaining a balanced portfolio is to virtually eliminate unsystematic risk by ensuring that it is well diversified. Chawan Co may want to reinvest the proceeds from the sale of Oden Co (if it decides to proceed with the disposal) in other equity shares within the same sector to ensure that the portfolio remains balanced and diversified.

The second caveat is that Chawan Co may want to look into the rumours of a takeover bid of Oden Co and assess how realistic it is that this will happen. If there is a realistic chance that such a bid may happen soon, Chawan Co may want to hold onto its investment in Oden Co for the present time. This is because takeover bids are made at a premium and the return to Chawan Co may increase if Oden Co is sold during the takeover.

The third caveat is that Chawan Co may want to consider Oden Co's future prospects. The calculations above are based on past performance between 20X2 and 20X5 and indicate an increasingly poor performance. However, the economy is beginning to recover, albeit slowly and erratically. Chawan Co may want to consider how well placed Oden Co is to take advantage of the improving conditions compared to other companies in the same industrial sector.

If Chawan Co decides that none of the caveats materially affect Oden Co's poor performance and position, then it should dispose of its investment in Oden Co.

6 Limni Co

Marking scheme

			Marks
(a)	Evaluation of dividend policy	1–2	
	Evaluation of financing policy	3–4	
	Evaluation of risk management policy	1–2	
	Effect of dividends and share buybacks on the policies	2–3	
			Max 8
(b)	2 marks per evaluation of each of the three companies	6	
	Discussion of which company to invest in	2	
			8
(c)	Calculation of initial dividend capacity	3	
	Calculation of new repatriation amount	2	
	Comment	1–2	
			Max 6
(d)	1 mark per relevant point		Max 3
			25

(a) **Dividend policy**

Many high-growth companies, such as Limni Co, retain cash instead of paying dividends and use the cash to help fund the growth. Many such companies declare an intention not to pay dividends and as such the shareholders expect their wealth to increase through **capital gains** rather than dividend payments.

Financing

Capital structure theory suggests that to take advantage of the tax shield on interest payments, companies should have a capital structure which is a mixture of debt and equity. **Pecking order theory** suggests that companies typically use internally generated funds before seeking to raise external funds (initially debt, then equity). The two main factors in deterring companies from seeking external finance are **favouring one investor group at the expense of another** and the agency effect of providing additional information to the market.

Limni Co is following the pecking order theory to the extent that it is using internally generated funds first. However, it is then deviating from pecking order theory in looking to raise equity finance rather than debt even though it currently has insignificant levels of debt and is therefore not making full use of the tax shield. This may be explained by the fact that Limni Co operates in a **high-risk**, **rapidly changing industry**, where business risk is high. It may not want to take on **high levels of financial risk** by using significant levels of debt finance. Other issues such as potentially restrictive debt covenant may also be a factor in the financing decision.

Risk management

Managing the volatility of cash flows enables a company to plan its investment strategy more accurately. Limni Co needs to ensure that it will have **sufficient internally generated cash available when it is needed** for planned investments. More importantly, since Limni Co faces high levels of business risk, as discussed above, the company should look to manage the risks that are beyond the individual control of the company's managers.

Effect on policies by returning funds to shareholders

Returning funds to shareholders will affect each of these policies. The shareholder clientele could change, which may lead to share price fluctuations. However, since the change is being requested by shareholders, there is a good chance that this may not happen. The financing policy is likely to change since there will be less internally generated funds available, so Limni Co may consider taking on additional debt finance and therefore will have to look at the balance of business and financial risk. This could in turn change the risk management policy as interest rate risk will also have to be managed as well.

(b) **Theta**

Company Theta has a **fixed dividend payout ratio of 40%.** As a result the increase in dividends in recent years depends on the increase in profit after tax in these years rather than increasing at a steady rate, which is often preferred by shareholders. If profit after tax was to fall, Theta may reduce its dividend, which could send the wrong signals to shareholders and cause significant fluctuations in the share price. To avoid this, Theta may keep a stable dividend in years of reduced profits.

Omega

Company Omega has a policy of **increasing dividends at approximately 5% per year**, but earnings are only increasing at a rate of approximately 3% per year. This means the **dividend payout ratio is increasing**; it was 60% in 20X3 and is 65% in 20X7. Although this cannot continue in the long term, it suggests that there are less investment opportunities currently and Omega is reducing its retention ratio. This investment would be attractive to an investor looking for a high level of dividend income.

Kappa

Company Kappa has increased its payout ratio from 20% in 20X3 to 27% in 20X7. This is a fairly low payout ratio, but it is growing. **Earnings are growing rapidly** overall, but not at a constant annual rate (35% growth in 20X4, but only 3% in 20X5). Overall dividend growth is at a rate of 29% per year, and the annual dividend growth rate has been fairly constant. This policy seems consistent with a **growing company**, which is now **starting to pay more significant dividends** and return more funds to shareholders. This investment would be attractive to investors seeking a lower level of dividend income and higher levels of capital growth.

Due to uncertainty about whether Theta could decrease its future dividend payments, Limni Co is likely to prefer to invest in either Omega or Kappa. The choice between these two depends on whether Limni Co would **prefer higher dividends or higher capital growth**. Issues such as taxation position or length of time that the funds would be invested for may influence this choice too.

(c) **Current dividend capacity**

		$'000
Profit before tax	(23% × $600m)	138,000
Tax	(26% × $138m)	(35,880)
Profit after tax		102,120
Add back depreciation	(25% × 220m)	55,000
Less investment in assets		(67,000)
Overseas remittances		15,000
Additional tax	(6% × 15m)	(900)
Dividend capacity		104,220

Increase in dividend capacity = 104.22m × 0.1 = $10.422m

Gross up to allow for extra 6% tax = $10.422m/0.94 = $11,087,234

Percentage increase in remittances needed = (11,087,234/15,000,000) × 100% = 73.9%

Dividend repatriations would need to increase by approximately $11.1 million or 73.9% in order to increase dividend capacity by 10%. Limni Co needs to consider both whether this is **possible** for the subsidiaries and the **motivational and operational impact** of doing so on the subsidiaries.

(d) The main benefit of a share buyback scheme to a shareholder is that they can choose whether or not to sell their shares back to the company. This means they **can control the amount of cash they receive and in turn manage their own tax liability**. With dividend payments, especially with large special dividends, there may be a large tax liability as a result. Further benefits include the fact that, as share capital is reduced, the **earnings per share figure is likely to increase and share price may increase** too. Additionally share buybacks are often viewed positively by the markets and share price may increase.

7 International Enterprises

Text references. Dividend capacity is covered in Chapter 2.

Top tips. Being faced with the preparation of a cash flow statement in part (a) might throw you slightly but bear in mind that it doesn't have to be in a form that complies with accounting standards. You should be familiar with cash flow statements from earlier studies and this one is not so bad. Remember that the figures for interest, taxation and dividends in the cash flow statement will be the accrued figures at the end of the previous year and also the treatment of changes in working capital components.

The calculation of the maximum dividend capacity in part (b) is complicated by the requirement to adjust working capital. As cost of sales is not fully funded, resources will have to be drawn from working capital to cover the shortfall. Ensure your discussion in part (b) is related to the scenario and not just a generic list of points.

Part (c) looks daunting but make sure you follow the instructions to provide key summary information and then use this to create an analysis that goes beyond stating simply that a ratio has increased or decreased. Ensure your points are supported from the scenario and by the calculations that are needed to support the performance judgement.

Easy marks. The preparation of the cash flow statement in part (a) is straightforward, as is the calculation of free cash flow before reinvestment in part (b).

Examining team's comments. Many candidates appreciated that this was a firm with substantial cash reserves, a low level of gearing and a relatively weak profit performance. The technical skills required by this question were largely drawn from earlier levels of study, reflecting the broad levels of competency required of the financial manager.

All but a small proportion of candidates knew how to extract a cash flow forecast but a substantial number made incorrect adjustments leading to cash changes which bore no resemblance to the movement in the statement of financial position. Most candidates understood the concept of free cash flow to equity, although only a small minority were able to make reasonable adjustments for net reinvestment.

		Marks	
(a)	Operating cash flow	3	
	Other items	3	
			Max 6
(b)	Calculation of free cash flow before reinvestment	1	
	Reinvestment deduction	2	
	Working capital adjustment	2	
	Summary of dividend capacity	1	
	Discussion – 1 mark per relevant point	6	
			Max 12
(c)	Calculations	3	
	Analysis	4	
			Max 7
			25

(a) CASH FLOW STATEMENT FOR THE YEAR ENDED 31 DECEMBER 20X8

	$m
Operating profit	108.8
Add depreciation ($112.0 – 84.0m)	28.0
	136.8
Changes in working capital:	
Increase in trade payables	1.1
Reduction in inventories	0.5
Reduction in trade receivables	3.5
Operating cash flow	141.9
Less interest (20X7 figure paid in 20X8)	(2.3)
Less taxation (20X7 figure paid in 20X8)	(25.6)
Free cash flow before reinvestment	114.0
Less capital expenditure	(80.0)
Less dividends (20X7 figure paid in 20X8)	(28.0)
Less financing (repayment of loan)	(10.0)
Net change in cash	(4.0)

(b) **Dividend capacity**

International Enterprises' dividend capacity is determined by its free cash flow to equity holders after net reinvestment (where reinvestment is the level of investment required to maintain the required operating capacity of the business).

In this case, **free cash flow before reinvestment** is $114 million. **Capital expenditure** is $80 million; **repayment of loan** is $10 million. This would give a **maximum dividend capacity** of $24 million.

However, what about the **working capital requirement**?

International Enterprises appears to be funding working capital by reducing its inventories and the time it takes to receive money from its customers whilst at the same time increasing the time it takes to pay its suppliers. Total change in working capital is $5.1 million ($1.1 + 0.5 + 3.5 – see cash flow statement in (a) above). This should be taken out-of-the-money available to pay dividends.

Dividend capacity is now reduced to $24 million – 5.1 million = $18.9 million.

International Enterprises' **actual dividend** is $28 million, which suggests that the company has over-distributed funds. The shortfall would need to be taken from its cash reserves. Clearly this is not a sustainable dividend policy in the long run.

There appears to be limited opportunity for International Enterprises to achieve further growth through introducing new products. Therefore, unless steps can be taken to increase free cash flow in the next few years then dividends will need to be reduced so that they are paid out of earnings.

International Enterprises appears to have a large cash balance which may not be required and therefore could be paid out to shareholders in the form of dividends. This would be better if it was done as a special dividend so as not to give shareholders **unrealistic expectations** about future dividend levels. However, if this cash balance is earmarked for future investment that can be used to increase shareholder wealth, then it should be used for this purpose and not distributed to shareholders.

In theory, the entire free cash flow to equity can be paid as dividends as this is the amount that is available for this purpose. In practice however only a portion of this figure will be given to the shareholders as dividends, as the management team tends to prefer a smooth dividend pattern.

(c)   Review of potential performance for year ended 31 December 20X8

$$ROCE = \frac{\text{Profit before interest and tax}}{\text{Capital employed}}$$

ROCE (20X6) $= 92/(130 + 45) = 52.6\%$

ROCE (20X7) $= \dfrac{102.3}{(179 + 45)} = 45.7\%$

ROCE (20X8) $= \dfrac{108.8}{(253.9 + 35)} = 37.7\%$

Operating margin = PBIT/sales
Operating margin (20X6) = 92.0/220.0 = 41.8%
Operating margin (20X7) = 102.3/261.9 = 39.1%
Operating margin (20X8) = 108.8/288.1 = 37.8%

Asset turnover = Sales/capital employed

Asset turnover (20X6) = 220/(130 + 45) = 1.26
Asset turnover (20X7) = 261.9/(179 + 45) = 1.17
Asset turnover (20X8) = 288.1/(253.9 + 35) = 1.00

Looking to 20X8 there are some positive signs. Sales (+10%) and net profits (+7%) are continuing to rise. Our financial risk is also projected to fall, as can be seen by the reduction in our loan capital in 20X8. ROCE remains at a high level.

However, the growth rate in sales and profits has fallen compared to 20X7 (sales growth in 20X7 was 19%, profit growth was 11%). ROCE has also fallen to approximately 70% of its 20X6 level. This is due to a fall in operating margins and a slowdown in asset turnover. The slowdown in asset turnover in 20X8 is partly due to a major investment of $80 million in capital expenditure.

The share price could fall as a result of these estimates, as the market is likely to view them as an indication of declining performance. Revenue has not increased in line with the increase in capital base – management should be investigating why this has occurred. Operating margins are projected to decline from 39.1% to 37.7%. This suggests that stricter operating cost control measures are needed.

Use of capital

The main issue appears to be the relative lack of revenue and value generation by the capital employed. This is a particular concern given the reliance on a single product which has generated most of the growth in recent years, and appears to be in a degree of decline.

There appears to be a large amount of cash being generated, the effective use of which will have to be reviewed, whether it is reinvested in new capital projects, used for paying off loan capital or perhaps for acquiring competitors with new products in the pipeline. If none of these are undertaken then the cash should be returned to the shareholders.

8 Anchorage Retail

Marking scheme

			Marks
(a)	Identification of principal risks (2 each) Disclosure/valuation/regulation/other		
			Max 6
(b)	Calculations	3	
	Commentary	3	
			Max 6
(c)	Ungearing betas	2	
	Combined beta	2	
	Estimation of impact on equity rate of return	3	
			Max 7
(d)	Undervaluation and the implication of inefficiency	2	
	Behavioural factors	2	
	Review of current price attractiveness of the acquisition	2	
			Max 6
			25

(a) **Principal general risks associated with a large acquisition**

Regulatory risk

This is a large acquisition and may therefore be subject to scrutiny from the Government or other regulatory agencies if there is a threat to public interest. However, Polar Finance is not in the retail trade therefore is unlikely to attract attention from agencies regulating competition or restrictions to it. One potential issue is the lack of accountability of private equity funds and the background to Anchorage may result in scrutiny from regulatory authorities.

Disclosure risk

An acquisition of this size must be supported by reliable information that reflects the potential earning power and financial business of the company. It is essential to ensure that all supporting information, such as the financial statements, have not been manipulated to give a more favourable picture. The statement of profit or loss must be supported by the relevant cash flow for example and all other supporting documents should be subject to scrutiny to verify their authenticity.

Valuation risk

This size of acquisition may change the risk of Polar Finance due to changes in exposure to financial risk or market risk. As a result, investors' or potential investors' perceived risk of Polar Finance may also be altered. Such changes to risk mean that the post-acquisition value of Polar Finance is unlikely to be a simple sum of its pre-acquisition value and the value of Anchorage.

(b)   **Performance of Anchorage in 20X8 and 20X9**

(i)   **Return on capital employed (ROCE)**

ROCE is a measure of the return that is being earned on total capital employed. Any reduction in the ratio indicates that funds are being used less efficiently than in previous years. There are numerous ways in which ROCE can be calculated but the following formula has been used for the purpose of this report:

$$ROCE = \frac{PBIT}{Capital\ employed}$$

Where capital employed = total equity + non-current liabilities

	20X9	20X8
	$m	$m
PBIT (operating profit)	1,250	1,030
Capital employed		
Total equity	2,030	1,555
Non-current liabilities	1,900	1,865
Capital employed	3,930	3,420
ROCE	31.8%	30.1%

ROCE has improved slightly, indicating that capital is being used more efficiently than in 20X8.

A major driver of this is an increase in operating margin from 12.1% (1,030/8,500) to 13.9% (1,250/9,000).

(ii)   **Return on equity**

This ratio measures the return on equity funds only – that is, the funds provided by the shareholders – and is calculated by dividing total equity funds by profit after interest and tax.

	20X9	20X8
	$m	$m
Profit after interest and tax	860	650
Total equity funds	2,030	1,555
Return on equity	42.4%	41.8%

Similar to ROCE, return on equity has shown a slight improvement in 20X9. The improvement is not as high as with ROCE because the 20X9 equity figure has risen quite strongly (by $475 million). This is because the company is reinvesting most ($475m/$860m = 55%) of its profits after tax.

Based on the ratios analysed Anchorage appears to be providing a good return to its investors. Sales and profits are rising, and its financial gearing is falling and it is cash generating. Without any industry yardsticks to compare against, it is not possible to give a definite conclusion about Anchorage's performance over this time period, but such strong ratios give little indication of any reason for the concerns over Anchorage's performance; this is surprising if a recession is having an impact on the retail sector.

(c)   **Impact of acquisition on the required rate of return of equity investors in Polar Finance**

One of the differences between Anchorage and Polar Finance is the fact that Polar Finance does not pay tax on its income. This means that there is no benefit to be gained from the tax shield on debt. In order to calculate the asset beta of Polar Finance we would use the following formula:

$$\beta_a = \beta_e \times \frac{V_e}{V_e + V_d}$$

The asset beta of Polar Finance is given as 0.285.

However, as Anchorage gains benefit from the tax shield on debt, its asset beta should be calculated using the following formula:

$$\beta_a = \beta_e \times \frac{V_e}{V_e + V_d(1-T)}$$

$\beta_a = 0.75 \times [0.76/(0.76 + 0.24 \times 0.7)] = 0.614$

Anchorage's proportion of post-acquisition cash flows is expected to be 20%, meaning that Polar Finance will have 80%. The **combined asset beta** post-acquisition is therefore estimated as:

$(0.8 \times 0.285) + (0.2 \times 0.614) = 0.351$

Before we can determine the required return from investors in the combined company and compare it with that of investors in Polar Finance only, we need to calculate the **equity betas** of Polar Finance and the combined entity.

Polar Finance's debt is given as 85% of the total company, meaning that equity of $1,125 million makes up 15%. Debt can be calculated as:

($1,125 million/0.15) $\times$ 0.85 = $6,375 million

Post-acquisition level of debt = $6,375 million (Polar) + $2,500 million (additional borrowing)

= $8,875 million

Equity beta post-acquisition can be calculated using the following formula:

$$\beta_e = \beta_a \left(\frac{V_e + V_d(1-T)}{V_e} \right)$$

There is no benefit from the tax shield therefore $(1 - T)$ can be ignored.

$\beta_e = 0.351 \times [(1,125 + 8,875)/1,125] = 3.12$

Equity beta of Polar Finance is:

$\beta_e = 0.285 \times [(1,125 + 6,375)/1,125] = 1.9$

The capital asset pricing model (CAPM) can now be used to calculate the required return on equity pre- and post-acquisition.

Pre-acquisition

$r_e = R_f + \beta_i(E(r_m) - R_f)$

$r_e = 5\% + 1.9 \times 2.224\%$ (calculated in Appendix 1)

$r_e = 9.23\%$

Post-acquisition

$r_e = 5\% + 3.12 \times 2.224\%$

$r_e = 11.94\%$

As a result of the acquisition, shareholders in Polar will require an increase in return of 2.71%.

(d)   **Evaluation of argument that Anchorage may have been undervalued by the market**

The argument that the market may have undervalued Anchorage suggests **market inefficiency**. The **efficient market hypothesis** (EMH) suggests that this argument is unlikely. Further support for the EMH is given by the number of investors that operate in the market for a business such as Anchorage – it is unlikely that this number of investors would misprice the company. Although there is evidence of investors being deterred by Anchorage's reputation in the past, which may affect current investors' rational expectations about the company, the effect of such expectations is likely to be diversified away during the pricing process.

However, share prices may be affected by a number of behavioural factors. For example, **availability bias** can occur when people will often focus more on information that is **prominent (available)**. In this case the share price of Anchorage may be depressed because of **recent** rumours or press articles about the success of Anchorage's strategy.

The current share price of Anchorage is $2.60. With 1,600 million shares in issue, this represents a market capitalisation of $4,160 million. Return on equity is 6.668% (see Working 1). If dividend payments were capitalised at this return on equity, this would suggest a market capitalisation of $4,049 million. The market appears to expect very little growth in Anchorage in the future, perhaps partly due to its reputation. As a result, a bid price of $3.20 should be attractive to Anchorage's shareholders.

Working 1: Anchorage – estimation of cost of equity

Calculate the cost of equity

(i)   Calculate expected market return using dividend growth model:

$$P_0 = \frac{D_0(1+g)}{(r_e - g)}$$

Rearranging the formula to express in terms of r_e:

$$r_e = \frac{D_0(1+g)}{P_0} + g$$

$$r_e = \frac{0.031(1+0.04)}{1} + 0.04$$

$$r_e = 7.224\%$$

This result suggests that the market will have an expected return of 7.224%. The risk-free rate is given as 5% therefore the market risk premium is 2.224%.

(ii)   Use the CAPM to calculate return on equity:

$$r_e = R_f + \beta_i(E(r_m) - R_f)$$
$$r_e = 5\% + (0.75 \times 2.224\%)$$
$$r_e = 6.668\%$$

9 High K

Text references. Analysis of financial strategy is covered in Chapter 2 of the Study Text.

Easy Marks. The ratio analysis required here should have been a source of easy marks.

Examining team's comments. The performance of candidates who attempted this question was good. Sometimes candidates merely stated that a ratio/trend was increasing or decreasing, without attempting to address why this may be happening.

Marking scheme

			Marks
(a)	**Ratios**		
	Profitability	1–2	
	Liquidity	1	
	Solvency	1–2	
	Investor	3–4	
	Other ratios and trends	2–3	
			Max 10
	Discussion		
	Profitability	2–3	
	Liquidity	1–2	
	Gearing	1–2	

Investor	2–3
Stores and online sales	3–4
Conclusion	1–2
	Max 11

(b) 1 mark per relevant point   Max 4

25

(a) **Profitability**

Revenues from the different types of store and online sales have all increased this year, despite a drop in store numbers. The increase in revenue this year may be largely due, however, to the government-induced pre-election boom in consumer expenditure, which appears unlikely to be sustained. Because the split of profits is not given, it is impossible to tell what has been the biggest contributor to increased profit. Profit as well as revenue details for different types of store would be helpful, also profit details for major product lines.

Improvements in return on capital employed derive from increases in profit margins and asset turnover.

The improvements in gross margins may be due to increased pressure being put on suppliers, in which case they may not be sustainable because of government pressure. The increased sales per store employee figures certainly reflects a fall in staff numbers, improving operating profit, although it could also be due to staff being better utilised or increased sales of higher value items in larger stores. If staff numbers continue to be cut, however, this could result in poorer service to customers, leading ultimately to decreased sales, so again it is questionable how much further High K Co can go.

The asset turnover shows an improvement which partly reflects the increase in sales. There have been only limited movements in the portfolio of the larger stores last year. The fall in non-current assets suggests an older, more depreciated, asset base. If there is no significant investment, this will mean a continued fall in capital employed and improved asset turnover. However, in order to maintain their appeal to customers, older stores will need to be refurbished and there is no information about refurbishment plans. Information about recent impairments in asset values would also be helpful, as these may indicate future trading problems and issues with realising values of assets sold.

Liquidity

The current ratio has improved, although the higher cash balances have been partly reflected by higher current liabilities. The increase in current liabilities may be due to a deliberate policy of taking more credit from suppliers, which the government may take measures to prevent. Being forced to pay suppliers sooner will reduce cash available for short-term opportunities.

Gearing

The gearing level in 20Y6 is below the 20Y4 level, but it would have fallen further had a fall in debt not been partly matched by a fall in High K Co's share price. It seems surprising that High K Co's debt levels fell during 20Y6 at a time of lower interest rates. Possibly lenders were (rightly) sceptical about whether the cut in central bank lending rate would be sustained and limited their fixed rate lending. Interest cover improved in 20Y6 and will improve further if High K Co makes use of revolving credit facilities. However, when High K Co's loans come up for renewal, terms available may not be as favourable as those High K Co has currently.

Investors

The increase in after-tax profits in 20Y5 and 20Y6 has not been matched by an increase in share price, which has continued to fall. The price/earnings ratio has been falling from an admittedly artificially high level, and the current level seems low despite earnings and dividends being higher. The stock market does not appear convinced by High K Co's current strategy. Return to shareholders in 20Y6 has continued to rise, but this has been caused by a significant % increase in dividend and hence increase in dividend yield. The continued fall in share price after the year end suggests that investors are sceptical about whether this increase can be maintained.

Revenue analysis

Town centre stores

High K Co has continued to close town centre stores, but closures have slowed recently and revenue increased in 20Y6. This suggests High K Co may have selected wisely in choosing which stores to keep open, although Dely Co believes there is no future for this type of store. Arguably though, town centre stores appeal to some customers who cannot easily get to out-of-town stores. Town centre stores may also be convenient collection points for customers using online click and collect facilities.

Convenience stores

High K Co has invested heavily in these since 20X3. The figures in 20Y4 suggest it may have over-extended itself or possibly suffered from competitive pressures and saturation of the market. The 20Y6 results show an improvement despite closures of what may have been the worst-performing stores. The figures suggest Dely Co's decision to close its convenience stores may be premature, possibly offering High K Co the opportunity to take over some of its outlets. Maintaining its convenience store presence would also seem to be in line with High K Co's commitment to be responsive to customer needs. Profitability figures would be particularly helpful here, to assess the impact of rental commitments under leases.

Out-of-town stores

Although the revenue per store for out-of-town stores has shown limited improvement in 20Y6, this is less than might have been expected. The recent consumer boom would have been expected to benefit the out-of-town stores particularly, because expenditure on the larger items which they sell is more likely to be discretionary expenditure by consumers which will vary with the business cycle. Where Dely Co sites its new out-of-town stores will also be a major issue for High K Co, as it may find some of its best-performing stores face more competition. High K Co again may need to consider significant refurbishment expenditure to improve the look of these stores and customer experience in them.

Online sales

Online sales have shown steady growth over the last few years, but it is difficult to say how impressive High K Co's performance is. Comparisons with competitors would be particularly important here, looking at how results have changed over the years compared with the level of investment made. It is also impossible to tell from the figures how much increases in online sales have been at the expense of store sales.

Conclusion

If High K Co's share price is to improve, investors need it to make some sort of definite decision about strategy the way its competitors have since its last year end. What the chief executive has been saying about flexibility and keeping a varied portfolio has not convinced investors. If High K Co is to maintain its competitive position, it may well have no choice but to make a significant further investment in online operations. Possibly as well it could review where its competitor is closing convenience stores, as it may be able to open, with limited investment, new stores in locations with potential.

However, it also must decide what to do about the large out-of-town stores, as their performance is already stagnating and they are about to face enhanced competition. High K Co will also need to determine its dividend policy, with maybe a level of dividend which is considered the minimum acceptable to shareholders allowed for in planning cash outflows.

Appendix

	20Y4	20Y5	20Y6
Profitability			
Gross profit %	4.33	5.07	6.19
Operating profit %	0.87	1.70	2.91
Asset turnover (sales revenue/(total assets − current liabilities))	2.36	2.42	2.53
Return on capital employed % (operating profit % × asset turnover)	2.05	4.11	7.36
Liquidity			
Current ratio	0.84	1.29	1.69
Solvency			
Gearing (non-current liabilities/non-current liabilities + share capital)			
(Market values of share capital) %	37.6	36.8	32.5
Interest cover	1.63	3.54	7.12
Investors			

	20Y4	*20Y5*	*20Y6*
Dividend cover	0.35	1.29	1.71
Price/earnings ratio	54.46	12.15	5.52
Return to shareholders			
Dividend yield %	5.30	6.36	10.60
Share price gain/(loss) %	(9.00)	(5.65)	(3.29)
Total	(3.70)	0.71	7.31
Revenue/store ($m)			
Town centre	31.91	33.05	33.93
Convenience	5.41	5.66	5.99
Out-of-town	46.45	46.16	46.46
Store revenue per store staff member ($'000)	247	258	272

(**Note.** Credit will be given for alternative relevant calculations and discussion. Candidates are not expected to complete all of the calculations or evaluation above to obtain the available marks.)

(b) High K Co has not raised any equity finance over the last five years. Its falling share price means that a new share issue may not be successful. It may not only need debt finance to be renewed, but additional funding to be obtained.

High K Co intends to make more use of revolving credit facilities, which it need not draw on fully, rather than loans, which will mean that its finance costs are lower than on ordinary debt. However, these facilities are likely to be at floating rates, so if the government increases the central bank rate significantly, they could come at significant cost if High K Co decides to utilise them fully.

Finance costs on new debt, whatever form it takes, may therefore be significant and lower interest cover. High K Co may have to investigate selling some of the stores it owns either outright or on a sale or leaseback basis.

10 Lamri

Text references. Dividend capacity is covered in Chapter 2.

Top tips. The bulk of the marks relate to calculations in this question therefore it is important to show all your workings. However, there is a lot to do for 14 marks so try to identify shortcuts where you can – for example, the cash from domestic activities both prior to and subsequent to the implementation of the proposal is the same so there is no need to calculate this twice.

Don't be afraid to state what you might think is the obvious. There are marks available for identifying the irrelevance of adjusting for depreciation so make sure you mention your reasons for not including this calculation.

In part (b) it is important to recognise that the implementation of the proposal would result in a shortfall in dividend capacity (don't forget to uplift existing dividend by 8%). By recognising this issue, you can then make suggestions as to how the problem can be overcome.

Easy marks. There are several easy marks to be gained in part (a) – for example, calculating operating profit, interest and tax. Part (c) is a straightforward discussion of mechanisms to prevent transfer price manipulation.

Examining team's comments. This question required a logical and systematic approach as a lot was being asked (particularly in part (a)). Good attempts at part (a) achieved high marks but sometimes the answers were not appropriately structured which resulted in mixed-up answers. Few appropriate answers were received for part (b) and mostly reflected the disorganised approach to part (a).

		Marks
(a)	Calculation of operating profit, interest and domestic tax	3	
	Calculation of investments in working capital and non-current assets (including correct treatment of depreciation)	3	
	Calculation of dividend remittance before new policy implementation	2	
	Calculation of additional tax payable on Magnolia profits before new policy implementation	1	
	Calculation of dividend remittance after new policy implementation	3	
	Calculation of additional tax payable on Magnolia profits after new policy implementation	1	
	Dividend capacity	1	
			14
(b)	Concluding comments and explanation of reason	2	
	Possible actions (1 mark per suggestion)	4	
			6
(c)	1 mark per valid point		5
			25

(a) **Dividend capacity**

Prior to implementing TE's proposal

	$m
Operating profit (30% of $80m)	24.00
Less interest (8% of $35m)	(2.80)
Profit before tax	21.20
Less tax (28%)	(5.94)
Profit after tax	15.26
Less investment in working capital [15% of (20/120 × $80m)]	(2.00)
Less investment in non-current assets [25% of (20/120 × $80m)]	(3.33)
Less investment in new project	(4.50)
Cash flow from domestic activities	5.43
Overseas subsidiaries dividend remittances (W1)	3.16
Less tax paid on Magnolia's profits [(28 – 22)% of $5.40m]	(0.32)
Dividend capacity	8.27

> **Tutorial note.** There is no need to add back depreciation to obtain cash flow as the investment that amounts to the total depreciation charged will cancel out this calculation. The effect is therefore neutral.

After implementing TE's proposal

	$m
Cash flows from domestic activities (see above)	5.43
Overseas subsidiaries dividend remittances (W2)	2.71
Additional tax on Magnolia's profits (6% of $3.12m)	(0.19)
Dividend capacity	7.95

Workings

1   *Overseas subsidiaries dividend remittances prior to TE's proposal*

	Magnolia	Strymon
	$m	$m
Sales revenue	15.00	5.70
Less variable costs	(2.40)	(3.60)
Less transferred costs	(5.70)	Nil
Less fixed costs	(1.50)	(2.10)
Operating profit	5.40	Nil
Less tax	(1.19)	Nil
Profit after tax	4.21	Nil
Remitted to Lamri	(3.16)	Nil
Retained in company	1.05	Nil

2   *Overseas subsidiaries dividend remittances after implementing TE's proposal*

	Magnolia	Strymon
	$m	$m
Sales revenue	15.00	7.98
Less variable costs	(2.40)	(3.60)
Less transferred costs	(7.98)	Nil
Less fixed costs	(1.50)	(2.10)
Operating profit	3.12	2.28
Less tax	(0.69)	(0.96)
Profit after tax	2.43	1.32
Remitted to Lamri	(1.82)	(0.89)
Withholding tax		(0.1)
Retained in company	0.61	0.33

(b)   **Comments on impact of TE's proposal**

If the proposal is implemented, Lamri's dividend capacity will fall from $8.27m to $7.95m. Whilst the dividend capacity prior to implementation of the proposal exceeds the dividend to be paid ($7.5m × 1.08 = $8.1m), the proposal would lead to a shortfall in dividend capacity. The shortfall arises due to the high tax rate paid on Strymon's profits that Lamri cannot obtain credit for. Not only does Lamri lose the withholding tax on the remittances (10%), it is also paying an additional 14% in corporation tax (42 – 28).

There are several ways in which the problem of this relatively small shortfall could be overcome. Lamri might consider reducing the growth rate of its dividends to a level that would be covered by the dividend capacity of $7.95m. However, this might send adverse signals to the market given that a steady 8% growth has been maintained over the last few years.

Another alternative would be to borrow the shortfall. This may not be a popular option if Lamri wishes to avoid increasing its borrowings, particularly to fund dividend payments. Given that it would have to borrow to fund current shortfalls, there is a possibility that this problem would continue in the future, leading to even greater borrowings or the potential of having to reduce dividend growth.

Lamri might wish to consider postponing the project to a later date but the potential impact on company business would have to be evaluated. We are told in the scenario that a number of projects are in the pipeline for the future. Therefore postponing a current investment may not be feasible without impacting on future investments.

The final possibility would be to ask for a higher remittance from Strymon or Magnolia. The main problem with this would be the potential negative impact on morale of the subsidiaries' managers if they are required to pay over greater proportions of their profits (which may affect any profit-related benefits they may have).

(c)   Transfer price manipulation is said to occur where Lamri uses transfer prices to avoid payment of taxes and tariffs, or other controls that the Government of the host country has put in place.

The most common solution that tax authorities have adopted to reduce the probability of transfer price manipulation is to develop particular transfer pricing regulations as part of the corporate income tax code. These regulations are generally based on the concept of the arm's length standard, which states that all intra-firm activities of Lamri should be priced as if they took place between unrelated parties acting at arm's length in a competitive market.

The arm's length standard is defined as the prices which would have been agreed upon between unrelated parties engaged in the same or similar transactions under the same or similar conditions in the open market. In the absence of the existence of data to allow a reasonable estimate of the arm's length standard then the alternative methods used to establish the arm's length transfer price include:

(i) **Comparable uncontrolled price**
This method looks for a comparable product to the transaction in question being traded by Lamri in a comparable transaction with an unrelated party or the same or similar product being traded between two unrelated parties.

(ii) **Resale price method**
This method focuses on one side of the transaction, either the manufacturer or distributor, to estimate the transfer price using a functional approach.

(iii) **Cost plus method**
This method starts with the costs of production, measured using recognised accounting principles and then adds an appropriate mark-up over costs. The appropriate mark-up is estimated from those earned by similar manufacturers.

(iv) **Profit split method**
This method allocates the profit earned on a transaction between related parties.

11 Moonstar

Text references. Securitisation is covered in Chapter 4a, Islamic finance in Chapter 7a, and interest rate swaps in Chapter 17.

Top tips. It is important to review the articles on the ACCA website in the lead up to the exam; these often signal that a topic is likely to be tested. An article on securitisation appeared on the ACCA website shortly before this exam sitting.

Easy marks. There are a few easy marks to be picked up in part (c) but only if you have a good working knowledge of this area.

Marking scheme

				Marks
(a)		Calculation of receivable	1	
		Loan note amounts attributable to the A, B and C tranches	1	
		Impact of swap	2	
		Calculation of interest payable on interest for tranches A-, B- and C-rated tranches	3	
		Estimation of return to subordinated certificates	1	
		Comments and calculation relating to sensitivity	3	
				11
(b)		Benefits of securitisation	3–4	
		Risks associated with securitisation	2–3	
				Max 6
(c)	(i)	Explanation/discussion of suitability of Sukuk finance	2–3	
		Discussion of investors' views	1–2	
				Max 4

(ii)	Explanation/discussion of suitability of Mudaraba contract	2–3	
	Discussion of bank's views	1–2	
		Max	4
			25

(a) An annual cash flow account compares the estimated cash flows receivable from the property against the liabilities within the securitisation process. The swap introduces leverage into the arrangement.

Cash flow receivable	$m	Cash flow payable	$m
$200 million × 11%	22.00	A-rated loan notes	
Less service charge	(0.20)	Pay $108 million (W1) × 11% (W2)	11.88
		B-rated loan notes	
		Pay $27 million (W1) × 12%	3.24
		C-rated loan notes	
		Pay $27 million (W1) × 13%	3.51
	21.80		18.63
		Balance to the subordinated certificates	3.17

Workings

1   *Loan notes* $m

    A $200m × 0.9 × 0.6   108

    B $200m × 0.9 × 0.15   27

    C $200m × 0.9 × 0.15   27

2   *Swap*

Pay fixed rate under swap	9.5%
Pay floating rate	LIBOR + 1.5%
Receive floating rate under swap	(LIBOR)
Net payment	11%

The holders of the certificates are expected to receive $3.17 million on $18 million, giving them a return of 17.6%. If the cash flows are 5% lower than the non-executive director has predicted, annual revenue received will fall to $20.90 million, reducing the balance available for the subordinated certificates to $2.07 million, giving a return of 11.5% on the subordinated certificates, which is below the returns offered on the B- and C-rated loan notes. The point at which the holders of the certificates will receive nothing and below which the holders of the C-rated loan notes will not receive their full income will be an annual income of $18.83 million (a return of 9.4%), which is 14.4% less than the income that the non-executive director has forecast.

(b) **Benefits**

The finance costs of the securitisation may be lower than the finance costs of ordinary loan capital. The cash flows from the commercial property development may be regarded as lower risk than Moonstar Co's other revenue streams. This will impact upon the rates that Moonstar Co is able to offer borrowers.

The securitisation matches the assets of the future cash flows to the liabilities to loan note holders. The non-executive director is assuming a steady stream of lease income over the next ten years, with the development probably being close to being fully occupied over that period.

The securitisation means that Moonstar Co is no longer concerned with the risk that the level of earnings from the properties will be insufficient to pay the finance costs. Risks have effectively been transferred to the loan note holders.

Risks

Not all of the tranches may appeal to investors. The risk-return relationship on the subordinated certificates does not look very appealing, with the return quite likely to be below what is received on the C-rated loan notes. Even the C-rated loan note holders may question the relationship between the risk and return if there is continued uncertainty in the property sector.

If Moonstar Co seeks funding from other sources for other developments, transferring out a lower risk income stream means that the residual risks associated with the rest of Moonstar Co's portfolio will be higher. This may affect the availability and terms of other borrowing.

It appears that the size of the securitisation should be large enough for the costs to be bearable. However, Moonstar Co may face unforeseen costs, possibly unexpected management or legal expenses.

(c)   (i)   Sukuk finance could be appropriate for the securitisation of the leasing portfolio. An asset-backed Sukuk would be the same kind of arrangement as the securitisation, where assets are transferred to a special purpose vehicle and the returns and repayments are directly financed by the income from the assets. The Sukuk holders would bear the risks and returns of the relationship.

The other type of Sukuk would be more like a sale and leaseback of the development. Here the Sukuk holders would be guaranteed a rental, so it would seem less appropriate for Moonstar Co if there is significant uncertainty about the returns from the development.

The main issue with the asset-backed Sukuk finance is whether it would be as appealing as certainly the A-tranche of the securitisation arrangement which the non-executive director has proposed. The safer income that the securitisation offers A-tranche investors may be more appealing to investors than a marginally better return from the Sukuk. There will also be costs involved in establishing and gaining approval for the Sukuk, although these costs may be less than for the securitisation arrangement described above.

(ii)   A Mudaraba contract would involve the bank providing capital for Moonstar Co to invest in the development. Moonstar Co would manage the investment which the capital funded. Profits from the investment would be shared with the bank, but losses would be solely borne by the bank. A Mudaraba contract is essentially an equity partnership, so Moonstar Co might not face the threat to its credit rating which it would if it obtained ordinary loan finance for the development. A Mudaraba contract would also represent a diversification of sources of finance. It would not require the commitment to pay interest that loan finance would involve.

Moonstar Co would maintain control over the running of the project. A Mudaraba contract would offer a method of obtaining equity funding without the dilution of control which an issue of shares to external shareholders would bring. This is likely to make it appealing to Moonstar Co's directors, given their desire to maintain a dominant influence over the business.

The bank would be concerned about the uncertainties regarding the rental income from the development. Although the lack of involvement by the bank might appeal to Moonstar Co's directors, the bank might not find it so attractive. The bank might be concerned about information asymmetry – that Moonstar Co's management might be reluctant to supply the bank with the information it needs to judge how well its investment is performing.

12 Preparation question: Cathlynn

Text references. Chapter 6.

Top tips. If you can work your way through the formula and are able to use the normal distribution table, this question is actually not that bad. In (i), we need the standard deviation, σ, so therefore we need to take the square root of the variance which we are given in the question. We have used interpolation to find the values in (ii).

(a)   (i)   Find (d_1) and (d_2).

Note. Standard deviation = square root of the variance so $s = \sqrt{0.12} = 0.346$

$$d_1 = \frac{\ln(P_a/P_e) + (r + 0.5s^2)t}{s\sqrt{t}}$$

$$d_1 = \frac{\ln(3.5/3.3) + (0.08 + 0.5 \times 0.346^2)0.25}{0.346\sqrt{0.25}}$$

$$d_1 = \frac{0.059 + (0.14)0.25}{0.173}$$

$$d_1 = \frac{0.094}{0.173} = 0.54$$

$$d_2 = d_1 - s\sqrt{T}$$

$$d_2 = 0.54 - (\sqrt{0.12}\sqrt{0.25})$$

$$= 0.54 - 0.17 = 0.37$$

(ii)   Find N (d_1) and N (d_2) using normal distribution tables.

N (0.54)   = 0.5 + 0.2054 = 0.7054
N (0.37)   = 0.5 + 0.1443 = 0.6443

(iii)   Using the Black-Scholes formula:

$$C_0 = (3.50 \times 0.7054) - ((3.30e^{-0.08 \times 0.25}) \times 0.6443)$$
$$= 2.47 - 2.08 = 0.39$$

(b)   The main limitations of the Black-Scholes model are:

(i)   The model is **only designed** for the valuation of **European call options**.

(ii)   The basic model is based on the assumption that **shares pay no dividends**.

(iii)   The model assumes that there will be **no transaction costs**.

(iv)   The model assumes knowledge of the **risk-free rate of interest,** and also assumes the risk-free rate will be constant throughout the option's life.

(v)   Likewise the model also assumes accurate knowledge of the **standard deviation of returns**, which is also assumed to be constant throughout the option's life.

13 Preparation question: Faoilean

Text references. The Black-Scholes model and its use in the valuation of real options are covered in Chapter 6.

Top tips. Note that in part (a) you need to do more than state the types of real option – you need to **apply** each type to the scenario to spell out how they can help with the investment decision.

Easy marks. If you can identify general limitations of the Black-Scholes option pricing (BSOP) model in part (a) and the general factors that cause option values to change you can score up to seven marks.

Examining team's comments. From the answers it was evident that this question was selected by candidates either because the candidates knew the topic area well and were able to gain good marks, or because they felt that by writing a lot on the area, they would be able to gain sufficient marks to achieve a pass. Unfortunately marks were only awarded for answers which were relevant and where the answer was directed to the question asked in each part.

Part (a) – on the whole, this part was not answered very well. Whereas in past examinations candidates were asked, and could do, numerical calculations of real options, candidates this time around found discussing the concept of real options and its application particularly difficult.

Part (b) – it seems that candidates' knowledge of this area was very poor.

Part (c) – most answers listed the greeks but few explained why option values were determined by the greeks. The part on what vega determines was addressed better, but again this was in a minority of answers and not the majority.

			Marks
(a)	Discussion of the idea of using options in making the project investment decision	7–8	
	Explanation of the assumptions	3–4	
			Max 11
(b)	Discussion of using options to value equity	4–5	
	Discussion of using options to assess default risk	2–3	
	Discussion of financial distress and time value of an option	2–3	
			Max 9
(c)	Explanation of why option values are determined by different risk factors	2–3	
	Explanation of what determines 'vega'	2–3	
			Max 5
			25

(a)   Conventional investment appraisal techniques such as net present value analysis often do not capture the full strategic benefits of a project in terms of either features of a project that allow risk to be managed or features that allow further follow-on gains to be made.

For example a situation may exist where a project is easy to abandon, or uses assets that are easy to switch to another use if the project fails. This **abandonment/redeployment option** adds value to a project because it limits the project's downside risk.

With this project Faoilean Co could negotiate a get-out clause which gives it the right to **sell the project back** to the Government at a later date at a pre-agreed price. Alternatively, it could build facilities in such a way that it can **redeploy** them to other activities, or scale the production up or down more easily and at less cost. These options give the company the opportunity to step out of a project at a future date, if uncertainties today become negative outcomes in the future.

Another type of real option is the **option to delay**. A project can be structured to allow a company to react to improved information about the prospects of the project eg by staggering the capital expenditure over a period of time instead of investing in one block at the start of the project.

In the situation which Faoilean Co is considering, the initial **exploration rights** may give it the **option to delay** the decision of whether to undertake the **extraction** of oil and gas to a later date. In that time, using previous knowledge and experience, it can estimate the quantity of oil and gas which is present more accurately. It can also use its knowledge to assess the variability of the likely quantity. Faoilean Co may be able to negotiate a longer timescale with the Government of Ireland for undertaking the initial exploration, before it needs to make a final decision on whether and how much to extract.

Finally, some projects may create an **option to expand into other areas** using the benefit of the experience gained during the project. For example, Faoilean Co can explore whether or not applying for the rights to undertake this exploration project could give it priority in terms of future projects, perhaps due to the new knowledge or technologies it builds during the current project. These opportunities would allow it to gain competitive advantage over rivals which, in turn, could provide it with greater opportunities in the future, but which are uncertain at present.

Faoilean Co can use the Black-Scholes option valuation formulae to assess the value of any real options associated with the project. This value can be added to the conventional net present value computation to give a more accurate assessment of the project's value.

The option price formula used with investment decisions is based on the BSOP model. The BSOP model makes a number of assumptions as follows:

(i)   The option is assumed to be exercised at a specific point in time (ie a European option); this may not be true in reality eg an option to redeploy may be exercised at any time.

(ii)   The BSOP model uses the risk-free rate of interest. It is assumed that this is known and remains constant, which may not be the case where the time it takes for the option to expire is long;

(iii)   The most significant drawback of the BSOP model is the **estimation of the standard deviation** of the price of the asset. The BSOP model assumes that volatility can be assessed and stays constant throughout the life of the project; again with long-term projects these assumptions may not be valid.

(iv)   The BSOP model assumes that the underlying asset can be traded freely. This is probably not accurate where the underlying asset is an investment project.

These assumptions mean that the value based around the BSOP model is indicative and not definitive.

(**Note**. Credit will be given for alternative relevant comments.)

(b)   The value of a firm can be thought of in these terms:

(i)   If the firm fails to generate enough value to repay its loans, then its value = 0; shareholders have the **option** to let the company die at this point.

(ii)   However, if the firm does generate enough value then the extra value belongs to the shareholders and in this case shareholders can pay off the debt (this is the **exercise price**) and continue in their **ownership** of the company.

Therefore, the BSOP model can be applied because shareholders have a **call option** on the business. The protection of limited liability creates the same effect as a call option because there is an upside if the firm is successful, but shareholders lose nothing other than their initial investment if it fails. So the value of a company can be calculated as the amount that you would pay as a **premium for this call option**.

If, at expiry of the debt, the value of the company is greater than the face value of debt, then the option is in-the-money, otherwise if the value of the firm is less than the face value of debt, then the option is out-of-the-money and equity is worthless.

Prior to expiry of the debt, the call option (value to holders of equity) will also have a time value attached to it.

The BSOP model can be used to assess the value of the option to the equity holders, the value of equity, which can consist of both time value and intrinsic value if the option is in-the-money, or just time value if the option is out-of-money.

Within the BSOP model, N(d1), the delta value, shows how the value of equity changes when the value of the company's assets changes. N(d2) depicts the probability that the call option will be in-the-money (ie have intrinsic value for the equity holders).

Debt can be regarded as the debt holders writing a put option on the company's assets, where the premium is the receipt of interest when it falls due and the capital redemption. If N(d2) depicts the probability that the call option is in-the-money, then 1 − N(d2) depicts the probability of default.

Therefore the BSOP model and options are useful in determining the value of equity and default risk.

Option pricing can be used to explain why companies facing severe financial distress can still have positive equity values. A company facing severe financial distress would presumably be one where the equity holders' call option is well out-of-money and therefore has no intrinsic value. However, as long as the debt on the option is not at expiry, then that call option will still have a time value attached to it. Therefore, the positive equity value reflects the time value of the option, even where the option is out-of-money, and this will diminish as the debt comes closer to expiry. The time value indicates that even though the option is currently out-of-money, there is a possibility that due to the volatility of asset values, by the time the debt reaches maturity, the company will no longer face financial distress and will be able to meet its debt obligations.

(**Note**. Credit will be given for alternative relevant comments.)

(c)   According to the BSOP model, the value of an option is dependent on five variables: the value of the underlying asset, the exercise price, the risk-free rate of interest, the implied volatility of the underlying asset, and the time to expiry of the option. These five variables are input into the BSOP formula, in order to compute the value of a call or a put option. The different risk factors determine the impact on the option value of the changes in the five variables, and collectively these are known as the 'Greeks'.

In the case of a call option the option will be more valuable if:

- The exercise price is lower; or

- The value of the underlying asset, the risk-free rate of interest, the volatility, or the time period is higher.

The 'vega' determines the sensitivity of an option's value to a change in the implied volatility of the underlying asset. Implied volatility is what the market is implying the volatility of the underlying asset will be in the future. The value of an option will rise as volatility increases because it will increase the potential extent to which an option may be in-the-money which will benefit the option holder – but if an option is out-of-the-money it will simply not be exercised and therefore if the extent to which an option is out-of-the-specifmoney rises then it has no impact on the option holder. Therefore as the 'vega' increases, so will the value of the option.

(**Note.** Credit will be given for alternative relevant comments.)

14 Preparation question: Bournelorth

			Marks
(a)	Shareholder wealth maximisation and need for further investment	1–2	
	Sell-off of IT services business	1–2	
	Rights issue	2–3	
	Debt finance	2–3	
		Max	8
(b)	(i) Risks associated with investment in development	up to 4	
	Controls over development	up to 4	
		Max	6
	(ii) 1 mark per point		3
(c)	(i) Explanation that behavioural finance departs from rational decision-making		3
	(ii) Impacts of behavioural factors on share price – Up to 2 marks per well-explained point	Max	5
			25

(a)   According to traditional finance theory, Bournelorth Co's directors will wish to strive for long-term shareholder wealth maximisation. The directors may not have been fully committed to long-term wealth maximisation, as they seemed to have focused on the development aspects which interested them most and left the original business mostly to others. However, now they are likely to come under pressure from the new external shareholders to maximise shareholder wealth and pay an acceptable level of dividend. To achieve this, it seems that Bournelorth Co will have to commit further large sums to investment in development of diagnostic applications (apps) in order to keep up with competitors.

Selling off the IT services business

At present the IT services business seems to be a reliable generator of significant profits. Selling it off would very likely produce a significant cash boost now, when needed. However, it would remove the safety net of reasonably certain income and mean that Bournelorth Co followed a much riskier business model. The IT services business also offers a possible gateway to reach customers who may be interested in the apps which Bournelorth Co develops.

Rights issue

If the executive directors wish to maintain their current percentage holdings, they would have to subscribe to 75% of the shares issued under the rights issue. Even though the shares would be issued at a discount, the directors might well not have the personal wealth available to subscribe fully. Previously they had to seek a listing to obtain enough funds for expansion, even though they were reluctant to bring in external investors, and this suggests their personal financial resources are limited.

However, the directors may need to take up the rights issue in order to ensure its success. If they do not, it may send out a message to external investors that the directors are unwilling to make a further commitment themselves because of the risks involved. There are also other factors which indicate that the rights issue may not be successful. The directors did not achieve the initial market price which they originally hoped for when Bournelorth Co was listed and shareholders may question the need for a rights issue soon after listing.

If the executive directors do not take up all of their rights, and the rights issue is still successful, this may have consequencesfor the operation of the business. The external shareholders would own a greater percentage of Bournelorth Co's equity share capital and may be in a position to reinforce the wishes of non-executive directors for improved governance and control systems and change of behaviour by the executive directors. Possibly they may also demand additional executive and non-executive directors, which would change the balance of power on the board.

The level of dividend demanded by shareholders may be less predictable than the interest on debt. One of the directors is also concerned whether the stock market is efficient or whether the share price may be subject to behavioural factors (discussed in (c) below).

Debt finance

Debt providers will demand Bournelorth Co commits to paying interest and ultimately repaying debt. This may worry the directors because of the significant uncertainties surrounding returns from new apps. Significant debt may have restrictive covenants built in, particularly if Bournelorth Co cannot provide much security. The directors may be faced with restrictions on dividends, for example, which may upset external shareholders.

Uncertainties surrounding funding may also influence directors' decisions. Loan finance may be difficult to obtain, but the amount and repayments would be fixed and could be budgeted, whereas the success of a rights issue is uncertain.

(b)   (i)   The main risks connected with development work are that time and resources are wasted on projects which do not generate sales or are not in line with corporate strategy. Directors may choose apps which interest them rather than apps which are best for the business. There is also the risk that projects do not deliver benefits, take too long or are too costly. Bournelorth Co's directors' heavy involvement in development activities may have made it easier to monitor them. However, the dangers with this are that the directors focus too much on their own individual projects, do not consider their projects objectively and do not step back to consider the overall picture.

The board must decide on a clear strategy for investment in development and needs to approve major initiatives before they are undertaken. There must be proper planning and budgeting of all initiatives and a structured approach to development. The board must regularly review projects, comparing planned and actual expenditure and resource usage. The board must be prepared to halt projects which are unlikely to deliver benefits. One director should be given responsibility for monitoring overall development activity without being directly involved in any of the work. Post-completion reviews should be carried out when development projects have been completed.

(ii)   Communication with shareholders and other important stakeholders, such as potential customers, may be problematic. Bournelorth Co faces the general corporate governance requirement of transparency and has to comply with the specific disclosure requirements of its local stock market.

However, governance best practice also acknowledges that companies need to be allowed to preserve commercial confidentiality if appropriate, and clearly it will be relevant for Bournelorth Co.

However, the less that it discloses, the less information finance providers will have on which to base their decisions.

Another issue with disclosure is that product failures may be more visible now that Bournelorth Co has obtained a listing and may have to include a business review in its accounts.

(c)   (i)   Sewell defines behavioural finance as the influence of psychology on the behaviour of financial practitioners and the subsequent effect on markets. Behavioural finance suggests that individual decision-making is complex and will deviate from rational decision-making. Under rational decision-making, individual preferences will be clear and remain stable. Individuals will make choices with the aim of maximising utility, and adopt a rational approach for assessing outcomes.

Under behavioural finance, individuals may be more optimistic or conservative than appears to be warranted by rational analysis. They will try to simplify complex decisions and may make different decisions based on the same facts at different times.

(ii)   Bournelorth Co's share price may be significantly influenced by the impact of behavioural factors, as it is a newly listed company operating in a sector where returns have traditionally been variable and unpredictable. The impact of behavioural factors may be complex, and they may exert both upward and downward pressures on Bournelorth Co's share price. Investors may, for example, compensate for not knowing much about Bournelorth Co by anchoring, which means using information which is irrelevant, but which they do have, to judge investment in Bournelorth Co.

The possibility of very high returns may add to the appeal of Bournelorth Co's shares. Some investors may want the opportunity of obtaining high returns even if it is not very likely that they will. The IT sector has also been subject to herd behaviour, notably in the dotcom boom. The herd effect is when a large number of investors have taken the same decision, for example to invest in a particular sector, and this influences others to conform and take the same decision.

However, even if Bournelorth Co produces high returns for some time, the fact that it is in a volatile sector may lead to investors selling shares before it appears to be warranted on the evidence, on the grounds that by the laws of chance Bournelorth Co will make a loss eventually (known as the gambler's fallacy).

Under behavioural finance, the possible volatility of Bournelorth Co's results may lead to downward pressure on its share price for various reasons. First some investors have regret aversion, a general bias against making a loss anyway. This, it is claimed, means that the level of returns on equity is rather higher than the returns on debt than is warranted by a rational view of the risk of equity.

Similarly under prospect theory, investors are more likely to choose a net outcome which consists entirely of small gains, rather than an identical net outcome which consists of a combination of larger gains and some losses. At present also, Bournelorth Co does not have much of a history of results for the market to analyse. Even when it has been listed for some time, however, another aspect of behavioural finance is investors placing excessive weight on the most recent results.

If the market reacts very well or badly to news about Bournelorth Co, the large rise or fall in the share price which resultsmay also not be sustainable, but may revert back over time.

15 Fernhurst

Text references. Investment appraisal methods are covered in Chapter 5.

Top tips. In part (a) time management will be important, there are a lot of calculations to do (tax, inflation, working capital, duration) and it will be important to move on if a particular calculation is proving to be time consuming.

Easy marks. Parts (b) and (c) are opportunities to score strongly. Part (b) asked for a calculation (and discussion) of the sensitivity of the project to a reduction in the selling price. Good exam technique could have been employed here to deal with the only area of complexity (the 15% chance of negative cash flows in Year 1) as a brief discussion point in your answer. Part (c) required a discussion of the meaning and significance of NPV and whether short-term measures were also important. This allowed candidates to identify the important of risk and uncertainty in investment appraisal.

		Marks
(a)	Sales revenue	2
	Variable costs	2
	Fixed costs	1
	Tax-allowable depreciation	2
	Tax payable	1
	Working capital	2
	NPV of project	1
	Comment on NPV	1
	Duration calculation	2
	Comment on duration	1
		15
(b)	Reduction in selling price	3
	Discussion	2–3
	Max	5
(c)	Significance of net present value	1–2
	Shareholders' attitude to the longer and shorter term	2–3
	Time frame measures	1–2
	Max	5
		25

(a)

	0	1	2	3	4
	$'000	$'000	$'000	$'000	$'000
Sales revenue (W1)		13,250	16,695	22,789	23,928
Variable costs (W2)		(5,788)	(7,292)	(9,954)	(10,452)
Contribution		7,462	9,403	12,835	13,476
Marketing expenditure		(1,500)			
Fixed costs		(900)	(945)	(992)	(1,042)
Tax-allowable depreciation (W3)		(3,200)	(2,560)	(2,048)	(8,192)
Taxable profits/(losses)		1,862	5,898	9,795	4,242
Taxation (25%)		(466)	(1,475)	(2,449)	(1,061)
Add back tax-allowable depreciation		3,200	2,560	2,048	8,192
Cash flows after tax		4,596	6,983	9,394	11,373
Initial investment	(16,000)				
Working capital	(1,025)	(41)	(53)	(56)	1,175
Cash flows	(17,025)	4,555	6,930	9,338	12,548
Discount factor	1.000	0.901	0.812	0.731	0.659
Present values	(17,025)	4,104	5,627	6,826	8,269
Net present value	7,801				

The net present value (NPV) is positive, which indicates the project should be undertaken.

Workings

1   *Sales revenue*

Year		$'000
1	132,500 × 100	13,250
2	132,500 × 100 × 1.05 × 1.2	16,695
3	132,500 × 100 × 1.05² × 1.2 × 1.3	22,789
4	132,500 × 100 × 1.05³ × 1.2 × 1.3	23,928

2   *Variable costs*

Year		$m
1	132,500 × 43.68	5,788
2	132,500 × 43.68 × 1.05 × 1.2	7,292
3	132,500 × 43.68 × 1.05² × 1.2 × 1.3	9,954
4	132,500 × 43.68 × 1.05³ × 1.2 × 1.3	10,452

3   *Tax-allowable depreciation*

Year		$'000
		16,000
1	Tax-allowable depreciation	(3,200)
		12,800
2	Tax-allowable depreciation	(2,560)
		10,240
3	Tax-allowable depreciation	(2,048)
		8,192
4	Balancing allowance	(8,192)
		0

Duration

Year	1	2	3	4
Present value (PV) $'000	4,104	5,627	6,826	8,269
Percentage of total PV	16.5%	22.7%	27.5%	33.3%

Duration = (1 × 0.165) + (2 × 0.227) + (3 × 0.275) + (4 × 0.333) = 2.78 years

The result indicates that it will take approximately 2.78 years to recover half the PV of the project. Duration considers the time value of money and all of the cash flows of a project.

(b)   **Reduction in selling price**

Discounted revenue cash flows = (13,250 × 0.75 × 0.901) + (16,695 × 0.75 × 0.812) + (22,789 × 0.75 × 0.731) + (23,928 × 0.75 × 0.659) = $43,441,000

Reduction in selling price = 7,801/43,441 = 18.0%

Fernhurst Co would appear to have some scope to reduce the price in order to guarantee the success of the product launch. It would be useful to know whether the Finance Director's views on the success of the product would change if the product was launched at a lower price. There may be scope to launch at a price which is more than 18.0% lower than the planned launch price, and increase the sales price subsequently by more than the rate of inflation if the launch is a success.

If the directors are unwilling to reduce the price, then their decision will depend on whether they are willing to consider other ways of mitigating a failed launch or take a chance that the product will make a loss and be abandoned. They will take into account both the probability (15%) of the loss and the magnitude (at least $1,000,000 but possibly higher).

Presumably the Finance Director's assessment of the probability of a loss is based more on doubts about the demand level rather than the level of costs, as costs should be controllable. Possibly Fernhurst Co's directors may consider a smaller-scale launch to test the market, but then Fernhurst Co would still be left with expensive facilities if the product were abandoned. The decision may therefore depend on what alternative uses could be made of the new facilities.

(c)   The non-executive director has highlighted the importance of long-term maximisation of shareholders' wealth. The NPV is the most important indicator of whether an investment is likely to do that. However, the assessment of investments using NPV has to be modified if the company is undertaking a number of different investments and capital is rationed. It is not necessarily the case that the investments with the highest NPV will be chosen, as account has to be taken of the amount of capital invested as well.

However, investors are not necessarily concerned solely with the long term. They are also concerned about short-term indicators, such as the annual dividend which the company can sustain. They may be concerned if the company's investment portfolio is weighted towards projects which will produce good long-term returns, but limited returns in the near future.

Risk will also influence shareholders' views. They may prefer investments where a higher proportion of returns are made in the shorter term, if they feel that longer-term returns are much more uncertain. The NPV calculation itself discounts longer-term cash flows more than shorter-term cash flows.

The payback method shows how long an investment will take to generate enough returns to pay back its investment. It favours investments which pay back quickly, although it fails to take into account longer-term cash flows after the payback period. Duration is a better measure of the distribution of cash flows, although it may be less easy for shareholders to understand.

16 Your business

Text references. NPV, sensitivity analysis and duration are covered in Chapter 5. Discounted payback is assumed knowledge from FM.

Top tips. When making the adjustments to cash flows in part (a), make sure these are made net of tax as you are given the post-tax cash flows. There is only one mark available for discussion in part (b) so don't write too much. Discounted payback should be familiar to you from previous studies. Part (c) requires two types of recommendation – on the project and on the techniques used – so this gives you a useful structure for your answer.

Easy marks. A lot of this question covers techniques that were previously covered in FM. You should be able to pick up a number of relatively easy marks in all parts of the question.

Marking scheme

			Marks
(a)	Add back net interest	1	
	Add back depreciation	1	
	Add back indirect cost charge	1	
	Deduct infrastructure costs	1	
	Estimation of site clearance	1	
	Calculation of tax on unrecovered capital allowances	3	
	Deduct site clearance and reinstatement	1	
	Calculation of NPV	1	
	Sensitivity to change in CAPEX	4	
			14
(b)	Calculation of discounted payback	2	
	Calculation of duration	2	
	Comparative assessment of the techniques	1	
			5

(c)   Review of techniques and recommendation   2
       Definition and interpretation of duration measure   2
       Review of sensitivity and its deficiencies   2

                                                                               6
                                                                              25

(a)   The first thing to do in this question is to determine how to correct the errors of principle.

       (i)   Interest should not be included as this is already accounted for in the discount rate. The annual
              interest charge of $4 million (less tax of 30%) should be added back to the cash flow in each year.

       (ii)   Depreciation is **not** a cash flow and should be ignored in NPV calculations. The annual charge of
              $4 million (less tax at 30%) should be added back to the cash flow in each year.

       (iii) Indirect allocated costs are not relevant. These should be added back to the annual cash flows (net of
              tax). Corporate infrastructure costs are relevant to the project and should have been included. These
              costs should be deducted from annual cash flow figures (net of tax), as should the estimates for site
              clearance.

       (iv)   Capital allowances in Year 6 should be accounted for.

Corrected project evaluation

Year	0	1	2	3	4	5	6
	$m	$m	$m	$m	$m	$m	$m
Project post-tax cash flow	(127.50)	(36.88)	44.00	68.00	60.00	35.00	20.00
Add net interest			2.80	2.80	2.80	2.80	2.80
Add depreciation net of tax			2.80	2.80	2.80	2.80	2.80
Add indirect costs			5.60	5.60	5.60	5.60	5.60
Add capital allowances (W1)							3.68
Less site clearance costs							(3.50)
Less infrastructure costs			(2.80)	(2.80)	(2.80)	(2.80)	(2.80)
Revised cash flows	(127.50)	(36.88)	52.40	76.40	68.40	43.40	28.58
Discount factor 10%	1.000	0.909	0.826	0.751	0.683	0.621	0.564
DCF	(127.50)	(33.52)	43.28	57.38	46.71	26.95	16.12

NPV = $29.42m

Working: Calculation of unclaimed capital allowances

	$m	Tax benefit at 30% $m
Year 0: Capital investment	150.00	
First year allowance (50%)	(75.00)	
Tax written down value	75.00	
Year 1: New investment	50.00	
First year allowance on new investment	(25.00)	
WDA on Year 0 investment (25%)	(18.75)	
Tax written down value	81.25	
Year 2: WDA	(20.31)	
Tax written down value	60.94	
Year 3: WDA	(15.24)	
Tax written down value	45.70	
Year 4: WDA	(11.43)	
Tax written down value	34.27	

	$m	Tax benefit at 30% $m
Year 5: WDA	(8.57)	
Tax written down value	25.70	
Year 6: WDA	6.43	
Tax written down value	19.27	
Proceeds from sale	7.00	
Balancing allowance	12.27	3.68

Sensitivity analysis of project to a $1m increase in initial capital expenditure

Extra capital expenditure will affect not only the cash outflow of the project but also the capital allowances.

Year	0	1	2	3	4	5	6
	$m	$m	$m	$m	$m	$m	$m
Purchase cost/Tax WDV	(1.0)	0.5	0.37	0.28	0.21	0.16	0.12
FYA (50%)	(0.5)						
WDA (25%)	—	(0.13)	(0.09)	(0.07)	(0.05)	(0.04)	(0.03)
Balance	0.5	0.37	0.28	0.21	0.16	0.12	0.09
Impact on cap ex	(1.0)						
Tax saved on capital allowances	0.15	0.039	0.027	0.021	0.015	0.012	0.009
Unrecovered allowance at Year 6							0.027
Impact on cash flow	(0.85)	0.039	0.027	0.021	0.015	0.012	0.036
DCF at 10%	(0.85)	0.0355	0.0223	0.0158	0.0102	0.0075	0.0203

Net impact on NPV = $(0.738)m

This means that every additional $1m spent on capital equipment will only cost the project $0.738m due to tax savings resulting from capital allowances.

(b) Discounted payback and duration

Discounted payback is used to determine how long it will take the project to repay its original investment. As the name suggests this method uses discounted cash flows in the calculations.

Year	0	1	2	3	4	5	6
	$m	$m	$m	$m	$m	$m	$m
Discounted cash flow	(127.50)	(33.52)	43.28	57.38	46.71	26.95	16.12
Cumulative DCF	(127.50)	(161.02)	(117.74)	(60.36)	(13.65)	13.30	29.42

The discounted payback period is approximately 4.5 years.

Project duration is the average time it takes the project to deliver its value. It is calculated by weighting each year of the project by the percentage of the present value recovered in that year.

Year	0	1	2	3	4	5	6
	$m	$m	$m	$m	$m	$m	$m
Discounted cash flow			43.28	57.38	46.71	26.95	16.12
PV of return phase	190.44						
Proportion of PV			0.2273	0.3013	0.2453	0.1415	0.0846
Weighted years			0.4546	0.9039	0.9812	0.7075	0.5076

Duration = sum of weighted years = 3.55 years

Discounted payback overcomes one of the problems of the ordinary payback technique – that is, it uses discounted cash flows rather than ignoring the time value of money. However, the problem with payback (discounted or not) is that it **ignores** cash flows that occur beyond the payback period. Thus projects that have very high initial cash flows but few (if any) in later years may be favoured over those projects that might add greater value to the firm but over a longer period.

The advantage of **duration** is that it considers the cash flows over the **entire life** of the project. It measures how long it will be before the project recovers the bulk of its present value. However, it can be more **difficult to understand** the concept behind duration and for this reason it may not be widely used.

(c)   **Recommendation on capital investment project**

The current project under review has an NPV of **$29.42m** which means that the value of the business will be increased by this amount if the project is undertaken. It has also been found that for every additional $1m spent on capital equipment for this project, the project's NPV will be reduced by $0.738m (due to tax savings made on the capital allowances available on capital expenditure). However, given the size of the NPV it is expected that any variations in capital expenditure should not significantly affect the value added to the firm.

By using **discounted payback**, it has been found that the project will wholly recover its investment within 4.5 years. As the majority of the cash flows occur in the earlier years of the project's life, there is an average recovery of total present value of 3.55 years.

On the basis of the above analysis, it is recommended that the board **approves** this project for commencement.

Investment appraisal techniques

Payback is a technique that has been employed in the appraisal of this project. However, although the discounted version of payback reflects the cost of finance in the results, there is still the problem that it ignores any cash flows that occur after the payback period has been reached. This may result in vital information being missed, such as very few or no cash flows beyond the payback point. **Duration** removes this problem as it focuses on all cash flows of the project, regardless of when they occur. It is a measure of the average time taken for a project to deliver its value. It is a superior technique to payback and its implementation should be considered for future investment appraisal exercises.

Whilst sensitivity analysis is highly useful, there is the problem of **high degrees of correlation** between variables. There is a risk that concentrating too much on one variable will be at the expense of other variables whose movements may be more critical to the project's profitability. The use of **simulation** would help to alleviate this problem. This technique generates thousands of values for the variables of interest and uses those variables to derive the NPV for each possible simulated outcome. The priority of each individual variable in the determination of the overall NPV can then be established.

It is therefore recommended that simulation is incorporated into the investment appraisal in future.

17 Tisa Co

Text references. Investment appraisal is covered in Chapter 5.

Top tips. For part (a) you need to calculate the weighted average cost of capital (WACC). This can be done by estimating the project's asset beta, then using Tisa Co's capital structure to estimate the equity beta, then calculate the WACC.

Part (c)(i) requires an understanding of how to calculate VaR, but you could still get marks from the explanations of what the figures mean even if you have not calculated them correctly.

For part (b) do not neglect the requirement to explain the recommendation you have made.

Easy marks. Part (c)(ii) offers some straightforward discussion marks, some of which will be brought forward knowledge from FM.

Examining team's comments. In part (a) most candidates made a reasonably good attempt at determining the cost of capital, although few candidates were able to calculate the asset beta of other activities and therefore the component asset beta. A small number of candidates used an average of equity and debt weightings and, where this was done correctly, appropriate credit was given. Many responses did not give reasons for the approach taken and thereby did not achieve some relatively easy marks.

Few responses calculated the annual and five-year VaR figures in part (c), and very few provided explanations of the values obtained.

				Marks
(a)		Reasoning behind cost of capital calculation	2	
		Calculation of component asset beta	3	
		Calculation of component equity beta, and Ke and WACC	3	
				8
(b)		Calculation of IRR for Process Omega	3	
		Calculation of MIRR for Process Omega	1	
		Resolution and advice	4	
				8
(c)	(i)	Annual and five-year VaR	2	
		Explanation	2	
				4
	(ii)	1 mark per relevant discussion point	Max 5	
				25

(a) Use the information for Elfu Co to estimate the component project's asset beta. Then use Tisa Co's capital structure to estimate the project's equity beta and WACC. It is assumed that the beta of debt is zero.

Elfu Co MV_e = $1.20 × 400m shares = $480m

Elfu Co MV_d = $96m

Elfu Co portfolio asset beta = $1.40 × $480m/($480m + $96m × (1 − 0.25))$ = 1.217

Elfu Co asset beta of other activities = $1.25 × $360m/($360m + $76.8m × (1 − 0.25))$ = 1.078

1.217 = component asset beta × 0.25 + 1.078 × 0.75

Component asset beta = $(1.217 − (1.078 × 0.75))/0.25$ = 1.634

Component equity beta based on Tisa Co capital structure

$1.634 × [($18m + $3.6m × 0.75)/$18m]$ = 1.879

Using CAPM

$K_e = 3.5\% + 1.879 × 5.8\%$ = 14.40%

$WACC = (14.40\% × $18m + 4.5\% × $3.6m)/($18m + $3.6m)$ = 12.75%, say 13%.

(b) **Process Omega**

Year	Cash flow $'000	Discount factor 13%	PV $'000	Discount factor 20%	PV $'000
0	(3,800)	1.000	(3,800)	1.000	(3,800)
1	1,220	0.885	1,080	0.833	1,016
2	1,153	0.783	903	0.694	800
3	1,386	0.693	960	0.578	801
4	3,829	0.613	2,347	0.482	1,846
			1,490		663

IRR is approximately $13\% + (1,490/(1,490 − 663)) × (20\% − 13\%)$ = 25.6%

Tutorial note. You are unlikely to have used these exact discount rates, in which case you may reach a different conclusion to the one below. As long as your conclusion is based on your calculations you will gain credit, whichever discount rates have been used.

MIRR

$$\text{MIRR} = \left[\frac{PVr}{PVi} \right]^{1/n} \times \left(1 + r_e\right) - 1$$

PVi = PV of investment phase = 3,800

PVr = PV of return phase = 3,800 + NPV of 1,490 = 5,290

$$\text{MIRR} = \left[\frac{5,290}{3,800} \right]^{1/4} \times \left(1 + 0.13\right) - 1 = 0.227 \text{ or } \underline{\textbf{22.7\%}}$$

IRR assumes that positive cash flows are **reinvested and earn a return at the same rate as the project's IRR**. The MIRR assumes that positive cash flows are reinvested at the cost of capital. The assumption is more **reasonable** and the result produced is consistent with the net present value. Process Zeta should be adopted as a result, although the difference between the two projects is not significant.

(c) (i) A 99% confidence level requires the VaR to be within 2.33 standard deviations from the mean, based on a single tail measure.

Annual VaR = 2.33 × $800,000 = $1,864,000

Five-year VaR = $1,864,000 × $5^{0.5}$ = $4,168,031

This means that Elfu Co can be 99% confident that the cash flows will not fall by more than $1,864,000 in any one year or $4,168,031 in total over the 5-year period. This means that it can be 99% sure that the returns will be at least ($2,200,000 – $1,864,000) = $336,000 each year. The company can also be 99% sure that the total 5-year returns will be at least ($11,000,000 – $4,168,031) = $6,831,969. There is only a 1% chance that the returns will be less than $336,000 each year or $6,831,969 in total.

(ii) Risk is most commonly dealt with by using **expected value** analysis, which involves assigning probabilities to all possible outcomes. The major drawback is that the assignment of probabilities is highly subjective. This method is also not suitable for a one-off project, as it may give an expected value that is not possible. It also does not indicate the maximum loss or the probability of making a loss, factors which will impact managers' decision making when they consider project risks.

Uncertainty can be dealt with using a variety of methods. One of these is **sensitivity analysis**. This involves altering the variables in the investment appraisal and seeing how this affects the outcome. The main drawbacks are that variables are looked at in isolation, but in reality they may be **interdependent** and that it does not assess the likelihood of the changes in the variables occurring.

Payback and **discounted payback** can be used to determine how long it will take to recover the initial cost of the investment. The major drawback is that any cash flows after payback has occurred are ignored.

18 Arbore

Text references. Chapter 5 covers net present value and capital rationing.

Top tips. In part (a)(i) ensure you tackle both parts of the requirement. For part (ii) it is important to consider the factors which are different in a capital rationing scenario.

For part (d) ensure that you take the mark allocation for each sub-part into account when determining the length of your answer.

Easy marks. If you have studied multi-period capital rationing, full marks should be obtained on parts (b) and (c).

				Marks
(a)	(i)	Calculation of project PDur05 net present value	2	
		Calculation of percentage fall of selling price	3	
		Comment	1	
				6
	(ii)	1 mark per relevant point		Max 5
(b)		Formulation of objective function	1	
		Formulation of constraints	2	
				3
(c)		Category 1	1	
		Category 2	2	
		Category 3	2	
				5
(d)	(i)	Explanation		2
	(ii)	Explanation of the features of a CIMS	1–2	
		Benefits of maintaining a CIMS (1 mark per benefit)	2–3	
				Max 4
				25

(a)   (i)   **PDur05 NPV**

Annual sales revenue = $14 × 300,000 = $4.2m

Annual costs = $3.23m

Annual cash flows = $0.97m

This cash flow will be a 15-year annuity, starting from Year 4.

NPV   = (2.5m) + (1.2m × 0.901) + (1.4m × 0.812) + (0.97m × 7.191 × 0.731)
        = (2.5m) + (1.081m) + (1.137m) + 5.099m
        = $0.381m

Sensitivity

To get an NPV of zero, the total present value (PV) of the project's annual cash flows needs to equal the sum of the PV of the investment amounts.
2.5m + 1.081m + 1.137m = $4.718m

This would mean annual cash flows would need to fall to:
4.718m/(7.191 × 0.731) = $0.897m
Sales revenue would need to fall to:
0.897m + 3.23m = $4.127m
Sales price would need to fall to:
4.127m/300,000 = $13.76
or a percentage decrease of:
(14 − 13.76)/14 × 100 = 1.7%

Conclusion

The NPV of the project is very sensitive to changes in the selling price of the product. Just a small decrease in the selling price could make the NPV zero or negative, meaning the project would not be worthwhile.

(ii) The **NPV method** gives an absolute figure which shows the increase in shareholders' funds as a result of the investment in a particular project. If capital is unlimited then this is the measure that should determine the projects to be invested in. If capital is limited then it is also necessary to consider the amount of limited capital required by the project.

Capital rationing decisions are often **more complicated** than identifying the ranking by NPV. Some of the complications of capital rationing problems are as follows:

(1) If capital is restricted in one period then it is highly likely to also be restricted in the next and **subsequent periods** as well. A multi-period model will therefore be required.

(2) Projects are unlikely to possess the same characteristics. For example, some projects may contain real options with follow-on opportunities. Other projects may have greater **strategic significance**, which outweigh other financial considerations.

(3) Some projects may be **'one-off' opportunities** which can only be undertaken in a particular period. Other projects may be able to be delayed and then commence in the following period.

(b) A multi-period capital rationing model would use linear programming as follows:

Let: X1 = investment in project PDur01; X2 = investment in project PDur02; X3 = investment in project PDur03; X4 = investment in project PDur04; and X5 = investment in project PDur05

Then the objective is to maximise:

464X1 + 244X2 + 352X3 + 320X4 + 383X5

Given the following constraints:

Constraint Year 1: 4,000X1 + 800X2 + 3,200X3 + 3,900X4 + 2,500X5 ≤ 9,000

Constraint Year 2: 1,100X1 + 2,800X2 + 3,562X3 + 0X4 + 1,200X5 ≤ 6,000

Constraint Year 3: 2,400X1 + 3,200X2 + 0X3 + 200X4 + 1,400X5 ≤ 5,000

And where X1, X2, X3, X4, X5 ≥ 0

(c) **Category 1**

This figure is the maximum NPV that can be earned with the given constraints on capital expenditure. This is why this figure is less than the total NPV of all five of the projects.

Category 2

These are the proportions of each project that should be undertaken to achieve the maximum NPV given in category 1. In this situation all of PDur05, 95.8% of PDur01, 73.2% of PDur03 and 40.7% of PDur02 should be undertaken. There should be no investment at all in project PDur04.

Category 3

These figures show the use of the constraints in each period and also any slack or investment funds unused in each period. As can be seen here, the constraints are fully utilised and there is no slack in any of the periods.

(d) (i) Generally speaking, a project with a positive NPV should be undertaken by a company and it **increases shareholder wealth** by generating returns in excess of the required rate. In this case, Arbore Co appears to be imposing **internal limits** on the amount of capital available for investment for each department. This may be due to budgetary limits on the amount the company wants to borrow. This is known as **soft capital rationing**.

(ii) A capital investment monitoring system (CIMS) is used to monitor the ongoing progress of a capital investment project once the decision to proceed has been taken. The CIMS will set a plan of how the project is to proceed and also a budget for the project. It will set project milestones and when they need to be achieved by. It will also consider the potential **external and internal risks** to the project. Contingency plans will be drawn up to deal with these identified risks if it is considered necessary. The CIMS will then ensure that the project progresses in line with the plan and the budget.

The benefits of a CIMS to Arbore include the fact that it attempts to ensure that the project **meets its budgeted revenue and expenditure**. It also helps to ensure that the project is completed on time and that the identified risk factors are still valid. Part of the role of the CIMS will be to identify a **critical path** of linked activities which will be vital to delivering the project on time. The participating departments should also take a **proactive** approach towards managing the risks of the project and may be able to reduce costs as a result. In addition, CIMS could be used as a means of communication between the project managers and the monitoring team.

19 MMC

Marking scheme

		Marks	
(a)	Value of project without considering option to delay decision and conclusion	2	
	Current price variable (P_a) for Black-Scholes formula	1	
	Additional cost (P_e) for Black-Scholes formula	1	
	Other variables for Black-Scholes formula	1	
	Calculation of $N(d_1)$	3	
	Calculation of $N(d_2)$	1	
	Value of option to delay decision	1	
	Revised value of project and conclusion	2	
		12	
(b)	1 to 2 marks per well-explained point		Max 7
(c)	1 to 2 marks per well-explained point		Max 6
			25

(a) **Financial impact of option to delay**

First of all we calculate the present value (PV) of the project without the option to delay.

Year	0	1	2	3	4	5	6
	$m	$m	$m	$m	$m	$m	$m
Cash flows	(7.0)	(7.0)	(35.0)	25.0	18.0	10.0	5.0
Discount factor (11%)	1.000	0.901	0.812	0.731	0.659	0.593	0.535
DCF	(7.0)	(6.31)	(28.42)	18.28	11.86	5.93	2.68

NPV = $(2.98)m

Without the option to delay the project would be rejected.

Option to delay – use the Black-Scholes model to value this option

$$c = P_a N(d_1) - P_e N(d_2)e^{-rt}$$

Where $d_1 = \dfrac{\ln\left(P_a / P_e\right) + (r + 0.5s^2)t}{s\sqrt{t}}$

$d_2 = d_1 - s\sqrt{t}$

P_a = current value of the project (that is the PV of its cash inflows)
= $18.28m + $11.86m + $5.93m + $2.68m
= $38.75m

P_e = 'exercise price' of the project (that is, the cost of production etc that can be delayed)
= $35m

t = exercise date (that is, when the exercise price is paid) = 2 years

r = risk-free rate = 3.5%

s = standard deviation = 0.3

d_1 = [ln(38.75/35) + (0.035 + 0.5 × 0.3²) × 2]/[0.3 × $\sqrt{2}$] = 0.62

d_2 = 0.62 – (0.3 × $\sqrt{2}$) = 0.20

Using the normal distribution tables:

$N(d_1)$ = 0.5 + 0.2324 = 0.7324

$N(d_2)$ = 0.5 + 0.0793 = 0.5793

Value of option to delay = (38.75 × 0.7324) – (35 × 0.5793 × $e^{(-0.035 \times 2)}$) = $9.127m

Total value of project = $9.127m – $2.98m = $6.147m

The project would therefore be accepted with the option to delay included.

(b) **Implications of the results**

The option to delay the project gives management time to consider and monitor the potential investment before committing to its execution. This extra time will allow management to assess the popularity of similar launches and also to monitor competition. The success of the film will be heavily reliant on the marketing campaign launched by the film's promoters prior to its release – management will be able to monitor the extent of this campaign before committing to an expensive (and potentially unsuccessful) project.

However, the calculations of the value of the option to delay are subject to several limiting assumptions, primarily the volatility of the cash flows. The value of the option to delay ($9.127m) is not an exact figure but rather an **indication** of how much management would value the opportunity to delay. The result shows that management should not dismiss the project immediately, despite the current negative NPV.

There may be other options embedded within the project. The technology used to develop the game may be used for other projects in the future (option to **redeploy**). Alternatively the project could lead to follow-on projects if the film is successful enough to generate sequels.

(c) The value of the option depends on the following variables.

(i) **The price of the security**

A decrease in the price of the security will mean that a call option becomes **less valuable**. Exercising the option will mean purchasing a security that has a lower value.

(ii) **The exercise price of the option**

A decrease in the exercise price will mean that a call option becomes **more valuable**; the profit that can be made from exercising the option will have increased.

(iii) **Risk-free rate of return**

A decrease in the risk-free rate will mean that a call option becomes **less valuable**. The purchase of an option rather than the underlying security will mean that the option holder has spare cash available which can be invested at the risk-free rate of return. A decrease in that rate will mean that it becomes less worthwhile to have spare cash available, and hence to have an option rather than having to buy the underlying security.

(iv) **Time to expiry of the option**

A decrease in the time of expiry will mean that a call option becomes **less valuable**, as the time premium element of the option price has been decreased.

(v) **Volatility of the security price**

A decrease in volatility will mean that a call option becomes **less valuable**. A decrease in volatility will decrease the chance that the security price will be above the exercise price when the option expires.

20 Marengo

Text references. Option pricing is covered in Chapter 6.

Top tips. There are several ways in which part (b) can be approached and the examining team stated that he would award marks for alternative relevant approaches. What is important is that you assess the advantages and disadvantages of each suggestion to provide a balanced discussion.

Easy marks. Part (a) offers some easy marks for calculating the delta of options and the number of options required.

Examining team's comments. Part (a) was either done well with candidates calculating the delta and then applying it correctly, or done poorly where candidates went on to calculate the value of a call and put option (which were not required). Very few candidates explained the numerical answer. Candidates need to be aware that some question parts may have more than a single requirement and all the requirements need to be addressed correctly in order to achieve full marks. Some reasonable points were made in part (b) but in many cases these lacked depth or substance.

Marking scheme

		Marks
(a)	Identifying the need to calculate $N(d_1)$ for hedge ratio	2
	Calculation of d_1	2
	Calculation of $N(-d_1)$	2
	Calculation of number of put options required	1
		7

(b)   Discussing the theoretical argument for not hedging   3–4
       Discussing the limitations/risks/costs of selling the shares   3–4
       Discussing the risks/costs of using OTC options to hedge   2–3
       Discussing whether to hold shares at all   2–3
       Discussing the potential benefits of hedging and application to scenario   2–3
       Relevant concluding remarks   1–2

                                                                                   Max 18
                                                                                        25

(a)   The number of put options to be purchased depends on the hedge ratio, which in turn is determined by the option's delta. We can estimate delta using $N(-d_1)$.

$$d_1 = \frac{\ln\left(P_a / P_e\right) + (r + 0.5s^2)t}{s\sqrt{t}}$$

$d_1 = [\ln(340/350) + (0.04 + 0.5 \times 0.4^2) \times 2/12]/(0.4 \times \sqrt{(2/12)})$

$d_1 = (-0.0290 + 0.02)/0.163$

$d_1 = -0.06$

$-d1 = 0.06$

$N(-d1) = 0.5 + 0.0239 = 0.5239$

Number of put options needed = 200,000 shares/(0.5239 × 1,000 shares) = 382 contracts

(b)   **Possible reasons for the suggestions made by each of the three managers**

       (i)   *No hedging at all*

              This argument is based on the theory that corporate risk should not be hedged. This theory states that, where a company holds a well-diversified portfolio and securities are priced correctly, unsystematic risk will be at least reduced to a minimal level or eliminated completely. There is, therefore, no apparent gain to shareholders of any further hedging or management of corporate risk (that is, unsystematic risk cannot be reduced further). Should hedging take place in a perfect market it is likely that shareholders will actually lose out, as the benefits derived from hedging will be outweighed by the costs of doing so.

              In an imperfect market, however, shareholders are more likely to benefit from hedging. By reducing the volatility of the firm's earnings, cash flows are likely to increase, which will increase shareholders' wealth. Such a situation is likely to arise:

              (1)   If stable earnings increase the certainty of being able to pay for future investments which would encourage a more stable investment policy

              (2)   If tax rates are increasing

              (3)   If a high volatility of earnings could lead to financial distress for the company

              None of the above reasons for hedging appears to exist for Marengo Co and the case for hedging seems to be weak. Marengo is a large company with numerous investments, therefore it is unlikely that reducing the volatility of one such investment will have a significant effect on its cash flows.

       (ii)   *Sell Arion Co's shares in order to eliminate risk of a fall in share price*

              This is based on the assumption that Marengo will be protected from a fall in Arion's share price if it gets rid of the shares in Arion. However, there are a few issues with this proposal.

              It is assumed that Marengo holds shares in Arion as an investment and generates a return greater than the risk-free rate. If Marengo sells these shares, an alternative investment offering similar returns should have to be found for the surplus funds, to prevent a reduction in Marengo's shareholder value. If such investments are not available, the shares should not be sold.

Another issue is the potential effect on Arion's share price if Marengo does 'dump' a large number of shares on the market. Managers have to ask whether they are likely to be able to sell such a large proportion of Arion's shares, although there is the chance that investors want to take the opportunity of purchasing shares at a lower price now, in the expectation that the price will increase again following the projected period of uncertainty.

(iii)   *Hedge the investment using an appropriate derivative product*

If this proposal was undertaken, Marengo would be required to purchase 382 OTC put options from the bank (see calculations above). This could prove to be expensive, as Marengo will have to pay a premium on each option for the flexibility of having the right, but not the obligation, to exercise the options. Should the option not be exercised, Marengo will have suffered the cost of the premiums for no reason. However, if the options are exercised, Marengo will have protected itself against downside movements in the share price.

Hedging using options involves several risks. Delta is not stable, which means that the number of options that should have been taken out may change (thus Marengo may not be fully protected). Option values also change, the closer they come to the exercise date (measured by theta) and the underlying asset's volatility changes (measured by vega).

Despite the risks associated with derivative products, a stable hedging policy can be used to reduce agency conflicts between shareholders and managers. A single hedging transaction is unlikely to have much impact, but it is important to maintain a consistent approach to hedging against investment risks. This protects not only shareholders' wealth but also managers, who may not be as well diversified as the shareholders.

(iv)   *Do not hold any equity investments at all*

Edward may be correct that Marengo Co should not hold equity investments. This is not a core area of business for Marengo Co and it may be best not to focus on it and therefore sell all the shares. However, it is the job of the treasury department to manage excess funds and liquidity and it may be that the equity holdings deliver a valuable dividend stream which contributes to a healthy cash flow for the business. The treasury department will be able to show if their investment choices outperform the market return.

There is no easy way to justify or discourage hedging. Each case should be examined on its individual merits, but it is important for a company to have a risk management strategy on which such decisions can be based.

21 Furlion Co

Text references. The Black-Scholes model and its use in the valuation of real options are covered in Chapter 6, the World Bank is covered in Chapter 4a and rho is covered in Chapter 17.

Top tips. A number of articles on the Black-Scholes model were published on the ACCA website in the lead up to these exams, so make sure you are checking the ACCA website for recently published articles.

If you have studied – and are comfortable with – the valuation of real options using the Black-Scholes model, part (a) of this question should be relatively straightforward. The main issues you have to deal with are recognising that you are dealing with real options rather than traded options and appreciating that the option to delay is a call option.

Part (a) is a straightforward application of the Black-Scholes model. Make sure you make clear to the marker the value you are attaching to each of the components of the formulae being used. Remember to deal with the discussion areas of the question too – an easy thing to forget in the midst of large calculations!

Part (b), for five marks, required a discussion of the impact of changes in the interest rate on the value of a call option. The impact of changes in any of 'the greeks' is a commonly examined area.

Part (c) should be fairly brief. A couple of points about the role and limitations of the World Bank (and the International Development Association) are all that is needed.

Easy marks. Discussion of the limitations of Black-Scholes and other factors to be taken into account in part (a).

Marks

(a) Current price variable (P_a) in BSOP formula — 1
Other variables in BSOP formula — 1
Calculation of d_1 and d_2 — 3
Determination of $N(d_1)$ and $N(d_2)$ — 2
Value of the option to expand decision — 1
Revised value of projects and comments — Max 3
Assumptions — Max 3
Other factors — Max 3

Max 16

(b) Explanation of rho — 2
Impact of interest rate movements — 3

5

(c) Role of World Bank — 1
Usefulness of World Bank as a source of finance — 1–2
Role of IDA — 1
Usefulness of IDA as a source of finance — 1–2

Max 4

25

(a) **Value of option to expand**

Variables

Volatility = 30%

Current price (value of project including option exercise price) = $15m × 0.712 = $10.68m

Exercise price (capital expenditure) = $15m

Exercise date = 3 years

Risk-free rate = 4%

$d_1 = [\ln(10.68/15) + (0.04 + 0.5 \times 0.3^2) \times 3]/(0.3 \times \sqrt{3}) = -0.1630$

$d_2 = -0.1630 - 0.3 \times \sqrt{3} = -0.6826$

$N(d_1) = 0.5 - 0.0636 = 0.4364$ (using 0.16 for d_1)

$N(d_2) = 0.5 - 0.2517 = 0.2483$ (using 0.68 for d_2)

Value of call option = $P_a \times N(d_1) - P_e \times N(d_2) \times e^{-rt}$

$= (10.68 \times 0.4364) - (15 \times 0.2483 \times e^{-0.04 \times 3})$

$= 4.66 - 3.30$

$= \$1.36m$

Overall value = $1.36m - $1.01m = $0.35m

The investment has a positive net present value, so should be accepted on those grounds. Furlion Co should also consider the value of an abandonment option if results turn out to be worse than expected or a delay option if it wants to see how the reclamation programme is going to continue.

Assumptions made and other factors

Using real options for decision making has limitations. Real options are built around uncertainties surrounding future cash flows, but real option theory is only useful if management can respond effectively to these uncertainties as they evolve. The Black-Scholes model for valuing real options has a number of assumptions which may not be true in practice. It assumes that there is a market for the underlying asset and the volatility of returns on the underlying asset follows a normal distribution. The model also assumes perfect markets, a constant risk-free interest rate and constant volatility.

Furlion Co will also consider expectations about the future of the land reclamation programme. Has the programme been as quick and as effective as the Naswan Government originally expected? Furlion Co will also want to consider how the programme will be affected by the amount of funding the Government obtains and any conditions attached to that funding.

Furlion Co may also wish to consider whether its investment of this type will be looked on favourably by the Naswan Government and whether tax or other concessions will be available. These may come with conditions, given the Government's commitment to a sustainable economy, such as the way production facilities operate or the treatment of employees.

Given that this is a market which may expand in the future, Furlion Co should also consider the reaction of competitors. This may be a market where establishing a significant presence quickly may provide a significant barrier if competitors try to enter the market later.

As the investment is for the manufacture of specialist equipment, it is possible that there is insufficient skilled labour in the local labour pool in Naswa. As well as training local labour, supervision is likely to be required, at least initially, from staff based in other countries. This may involve cultural issues such as different working practices.

(b) The sensitivity of the valuation of options to interest rate changes can be measured by the option's rho. The option's rho is the amount of change in the option's value for a 1% change in the risk-free interest rate. The rho is positive for calls and so will be positive if the risk-free interest rate does increase.

However, interest rates tend to move quite slowly and the interest rate is often not a significant influence on the option's value, particularly for short-term options. However, many real options are longer term and will have higher rhos than short-term options. A change in interest rates will be more significant the longer the time until expiry of an option.

In addition, there are possible indirect economic effects of interest rate changes, such as on the return demanded by finance providers and hence on the cost of capital.

(c) The World Bank provides loans, often direct to governments, on a commercial basis, for capital projects. Loans are generally for a long-term period, which may suit the Naswan Government. However, the terms of the loan may be onerous; not just the finance costs but the other conditions imposed on the scope of the projects.

Given the circumstances of the investment, Naswa may be able to obtain assistance from the International Development Association, which is part of the World Bank. This provides loans on more generous terms to the poorest countries. However, it is designed for countries with very high credit risk which would struggle to obtain funding by other means, and Naswa may not be eligible.

22 Airline Business

Marking scheme

		Marks	
(a)	Advice on the appropriate coupon rate		4
(b)	Estimate of current value of debt	2	
	Estimate of market value of debt following new issue	3	
	Calculation of revised cost of debt capital	3	
			8
(c)	Relative advantages and disadvantages		
	Asset specificity and matching	2	
	Agency effects	2	
	Static trade-off arguments	2	
	Pecking order	2	
			8
(d)	One mark per explained factor		Max 5
			25

(a) The appropriate coupon rate for the new debt issue should be the same as the yield for the four-year debt, which is calculated as follows:

Yield for 4-year debt = risk-free rate + credit spread

= 5.1% + 0.9% (0.9% is the 90 base point spread) = 6%

The investment bankers have suggested that at a spread of 90 base points will guarantee that the offer will be taken up by the institutional investors. If the spread was set too high, the debt would be issued at a premium; if it was too low then it would have to be issued at a discount as there would not be a full take-up.

(b) **Impact of new issue on the company's cost of debt and market valuation**

When new debt is issued this will increase the risk of the company, resulting in a reduction in the company's credit rate and/or an increase in the company's cost of debt.

Current amount of debt in issue

Using the company's current gearing ratio of 25%, we can calculate the current amount of debt in issue:

$$\text{Gearing} = \frac{\text{MV of debt}}{\text{MV of debt} + \text{MV of equity}}$$

$$0.25 = \frac{\text{MV of debt}}{1.2\text{bn} + \text{MV of debt}}$$

0.25 (1.2bn + MV of debt) = MV of debt

0.25 × 1.2bn + 0.25MV of debt = MV of debt

0.3bn = 0.75MV of debt

MV of debt = 0.4bn

Thus the current market value of debt in issue is $0.4bn. This is actually the par value as well, given that the coupon rate of 4% and the market yield (3.5% + 50 basis points) are the same.

Effect of new debt on market value of current debt

As mentioned in part (a) above, the yield on the new debt will be 6% (5.1% + 90 basis points). If we assume that this new debt is issued at par at 6%, the market value of existing debt will be reduced by the reduction in credit rating and the increase in yield to 4.4% (that is, original yield of 4% + [90 – 50] basis points).

$$\text{Effect} = \frac{0.4}{1.044} + \frac{0.4}{1.044^2} + \frac{0.4}{1.044^3} = 110 \text{ basis points reduction}$$

This means that the new market value of current debt will be 98.9% (100 – 1.1%) of the current market value.

New market value = 98.9% of $400 million = $395.6 million

If the new debt of $400 million is – as expected – taken up at the par value then total market value of debt in issue will be:

$395.6 million + 400 million = $795.6 million

Effect of new debt on cost of debt capital

Using the yields calculated above (6% for new debt; 4.4% for existing debt), the revised cost of debt capital can be calculated on a weighted average basis, adjusted for the effect of tax:

$$\text{Cost of debt} = \left[\frac{400\text{m}}{(400\text{m} + 395.6\text{m})} \times 6\% + \frac{395.6\text{m}}{(400\text{m} + 395.6\text{m})} \times 4.4\% \right] \times (1 - 0.30)$$

$$= [3.02\% + 2.19\%] \times 0.7 = 3.64\%$$

Current cost of debt = 4% × (1 – 0.30) = 2.8%

The effect of the new debt issue on cost of debt is to increase it by 84 basis points (3.64% – 2.8%).

What should be borne in mind is that part of this increase will be due to the longer term to maturity (4 years rather than 3 years).

(c) **Advantages and disadvantages of debt as a method of financing**

Relative lower cost of debt compared with equity

One of the advantages of debt is that, due to the tax shield on interest payments, it is a relatively cheaper form of financing than equity (whose dividends are paid out of earnings **after** tax). As such we would expect the higher level of gearing to lead to a fall in the weighted average cost of capital.

Appropriate to the industry and specific assets

The company is in the airline industry where debt tends to be a more appropriate method of finance, given that many of the assets can be sold when they are being replaced. In this case, the company is using debt to acquire new aircraft where a secondhand market does exist.

Signalling and agency effects

Companies tend to prefer debt to equity as a method of financing. This is mainly due to the tax shield offered by interest payments on debt. If the company increases its level of debt financing, the market could interpret this as meaning that management believe the company is undervalued. There is a significant agency effect arising from the legal obligation to make interest payments. Managers are less inclined to divert money towards financing their own incentives and perks if they know they have such legal obligations to meet.

Alteration of capital structure

One of the problems with debt financing is that it could be viewed as increasing the risk of the company to equity holders, given that there is a legal obligation to pay interest before dividends can be paid. As a result, investors may require a higher rate of return before they will be tempted to invest money in the company.

(d) **Management evaluation**

The rating agencies will look at the overall quality of management and succession planning, as well as performance from mergers and acquisitions and financial performance based on financial statements.

Financial gearing

The level of financial gearing will be considered; typically, companies with a low level of gearing will have a higher credit rating.

Position in the airline industry

The relative position of the company within the airline industry in terms of operating efficiency will be taken into account.

Accounting quality

There will be a general consideration of the accounting policies which could be used to manipulate profits (such as goodwill and depreciation) and whether there have been any qualifications to the audit report.

Earnings protection

Existing and projected measures such as return on capital and profit margins will be considered. Sources of future earnings growth will also be taken into account.

Cash flow adequacy

The relationship between cash flow and gearing and the ability to finance the cash needs of the business are important factors to be considered.

Financial flexibility

Financing needs will be evaluated, including alternatives in situations of financial stress. Agencies will also consider banking relationships and any restrictive debt covenants.

23 Fubuki

Marking scheme

		Marks	
(a)	Sales revenue, direct costs and additional fixed costs	4	
	Incremental working capital	1	
	Taxation	2	
	Estimation of k_e (ungeared)	2	
	Net cash flows, present value and base case NPV	2	
	Issue costs	1	
	Calculation of tax shield impact	2	
	Calculation of subsidy impact	1	
	APV and conclusion	2	
			17
(b)	Discussion of using APV	2–3	
	Assumption about Haizum as proxy and MM proposition 2	3–4	
	Other assumptions	2–3	
		Max	8
			25

(a) **Net present value**

	0	1	2	3	4
	$m	$m	$m	$m	$m
Sales (W1)		3.250	4.687	6.757	7.308
Direct costs (W2)		(1.560)	(2.359)	(3.567)	(4.045)
Specific fixed costs (W2)		(1.000)	(1.050)	(1.102)	(1.157)
Taxable cash flows		0.690	1.278	2.088	2.106
Tax (25%)		(0.173)	(0.320)	(0.522)	(0.527)
Capital allowances (W3)		0.163	0.163	0.163	0.163
Capital expenditure	(14.0)				
Sale of project					16.000
Working capital (W4)	(0.488)	(0.215)	(0.311)	(0.082)	1.096
Net cash flows	(14.488)	0.465	0.810	1.647	18.838
Discount factor (W5)	1.000	0.909	0.826	0.751	0.683
DCF	(14.488)	0.423	0.669	1.237	12.866

Base case NPV = $0.707m (positive but marginal)

Workings

1   *Sales*

	1	2	3	4
Sales units	1,300	1,820	2,548	2,675
Selling price (3% increase p.a.)	$2,500	$2,575	$2,652	$2,732
Sales revenue	$3.250m	$4.687m	$6.757m	$7.308m

2   *Costs*

> **Tutorial note.** Remember that only specific fixed costs should be included in the NPV calculation – allocated fixed costs are not relevant.

	1	2	3	4
Sales units	1,300	1,820	2,548	2,675
Direct costs/unit (8% increase p.a.)	$1,200	$1,296	$1,400	$1,512
Total direct costs	$1.560m	$2.359m	$3.567m	$4.045m
Specific fixed costs (5% increase p.a.)	$1m	$1.05m	$1.102m	$1.157m

3   *Capital allowances*

Capital allowances (tax-allowable depreciation) are available on plant and machinery at a rate of 25% (straight-line basis).

Annual capital allowance will be 25% of $3 – 0.4m = $0.65m

Tax benefit = $0.65m × 25% = $0.163m p.a.

> **Tutorial note.** You could also have assumed that capital allowances were $0.75m in the first 3 years and $0.35m in the final year. You would gain full credit for this.

4   *Working capital*

> **Tutorial note.** It is only the **extra** working capital required each year that should be included in the NPV calculation. Don't be tempted to include the full 15% of each year's sales revenue as the annual working capital requirement. You should only include the difference between this year's working capital requirement and that required for next year.

Working capital requirement

	1	2	3	4
Total sales revenue	$3.250m	$4.687m	$6.757m	$7.308m
Total working capital required for the year (15% of sales revenue)	$0.488m	$0.703m	$1.014m	$1.096m
Incremental working capital	$0.488m	$0.215m	$0.311m	$0.082m
Year in which accounted for	0	1	2	3

5 *Discount factor*

We assume that the ungeared cost of equity will be used to discount the project as this represents the business risk associated with this new venture.

$$k_e = k_e^i + (1-T)(k_e^i - k_d)\frac{V_d}{V_e}$$

$V_d = \$40m \times 0.9488 = \$37.952m$ (where 0.9488 represents the fraction of the par value at which the debt is trading)

$V_e = 15m \text{ shares} \times \$2.53 = \$37.95m$

We are not told the ratio of V_d to V_e therefore we will assume that it is 1.

$14 = k_e^i + 0.72 \times (k_e^i - 4.5) \times 1$

$14 = 1.72 k_e^i - 3.24$

$k_e^i = 10.02\%$ (say 10%)

> **Tutorial note.** You could also have estimated the discount rate by calculating the asset beta and then using that to calculate the cost of equity.

Financing side effects

Issue costs (4%) are on the gross (ie total) finance required which is the time 0 project cash flow of $14.488m divided by 96% (1 minus 4% issue costs) = $15.092m.

The subsidy benefit of 2% is available on 80% of the project finance ($14.488m) and needs to be multiplied by 1 minus the tax rate to capture the after tax effect.

	$m
Issue costs (4% × $15.092m)	(0.604)
Tax shield on debt (W6)	0.764
Subsidy benefit ($14.488m × 80% × 0.02 × 75% × 3.588)	0.624
Net benefits of financing side effects	0.784
Add base case NPV	0.707
Adjusted NPV	1.491

When the side effects of financing are taken into consideration the project looks more attractive. The NPV is less marginal and the project is likely to be accepted.

> **Tutorial note.** You might have included the issue costs in the funds borrowed. This would still give you the full credit of marks.

6 *Tax shield*

Fubuki Co can borrow at 300 basis points above the 5-year government debt yield rate of 4.5% – that is, 7.5%.

The Government has offered Fubuki a subsidised loan of up to 80% of the funds required ($14.488m) at a rate of 200 basis points below Fubuki's borrowing rate of 7.5% (that is, 5.5%).

Annual tax relief

	$m
Subsidised loan ($14.488m × 80% × 5.5% × 25%)	0.159
Remainder of loan ($14.488m × 20% × 7.5% × 25%)	0.054
Total	0.213
Discounted at 4.5% debt yield rate for 4 years – annuity factor of	3.588
Present value of tax shield	0.764

> **Tutorial note.** Instead of using 4.5% to discount the tax relief, you could have used 7.5% as this is Fubuki's normal borrowing rate and reflects its normal risk.

(b) **Appropriateness of the evaluation method**

APV can be used when the impact of debt financing is considerable. As can be seen from the calculations above, the side effects of debt financing are significant and are shown separately rather than being integrated into the cost of capital. Base case NPV is marginal but when the financing side effects are taken into consideration the project becomes much more acceptable (NPV is increased by more than 100% even after issue costs have been deducted).

Assumptions

Some of the assumptions made in (a) above are quite general.

(i)   Cash flows occur at the end of the year (unless otherwise specified).
(ii)   The feasibility study is treated as a sunk cost.
(iii) We have assumed that the five-year debt yield is equivalent to the risk-free rate.
(iv)   Annual reinvestment needed on plant and machinery is equal to the tax-allowable depreciation.

However, other assumptions were made that warrant further discussion.

(i)   Initial working capital represents part of the funds borrowed but subsequent increments will be financed by the project itself. The company may not have the necessary funds at the start of the project to finance the working capital. Therefore it is reasonable to include the required amount in the initial borrowings. However, the company should assess whether it is reasonable to expect the project to fund the incremental requirements, as these represent quite large amounts.

(ii)   Haizum Co's ungeared cost of equity is used as it is assumed to represent the business risk attributable to the new venture and is calculated on the assumption that Modigliani and Miller's Proposition 2 holds.

(iii) This assumes that the ungeared cost of equity does not include financial distress costs which may or may not be reasonable. It is difficult to determine an accurate ungeared cost of equity in practice and the figure used is based on a company in a similar, but not identical, line of business to the new venture. However it is likely that such approximations of the cost of capital are acceptable given that the discount rate tends to be the least sensitive factor in investment appraisal.

24 Coeden

> **Text references.** Cost of capital is covered in Chapter 7a.
>
> **Top tips.** In part (a) there are a series of related calculations to get to the answer for the post-implementation weighted average cost of capital (WACC). It may not be immediately obvious how to get to the final answer. If you cannot see how to get to the next stage, state a simplifying assumption and move on.
>
> The pre-implementation WACC is relatively straightforward to calculate and does represent half of the marks for this requirement.
>
> **Easy marks.** The requirement for part (b) gives you a clue that the assumption is highly questionable.

Marks

(a)   *Prior to implementation of the proposal*
    Cost of equity   1
    Cost of debt   1
    Market value of debt   2
    Market value of equity   3
    WACC   1
    After implementing the proposal
    Coeden Co's current asset beta   1
    Asset beta of hotel services business only   2
    Equity beta of hotel services business only   2
    Cost of equity   1
    WACC   1
    Assumptions (1–2 marks per explained assumption)   2–3
    Discussion   2–3
                                                                                       Max 20
(b)   Discussion (1–2 marks per point)   Max   5
                                                                                            25

(a)   **Before implementing proposal**

Cost of equity = 4% + (1.1 × 6%) = 10.6%
Cost of debt = 4% + 0.90 = 4.9%

Market value of debt (MV$_d$)

($5.20 × 1/1.049) + ($5.20 × 1/1.049^2) + ($105.20 × 1/1.049^3) = $100.82
Total value = $42 million × 100.82/100 = $42,344,400

Market value of equity (MV$_e$)

As stated in the question the free cash flow to equity model provides a reasonable estimate of the market value of the company.

Assumption

The growth rate can be estimated using the rb model. It is assumed that the retained free cash flows to equity will be invested to generate a return at least equal to the shareholders' required rate of return.

r = 10.6% and b = 0.4

g = rb = 10.6% × 0.4 = 4.24%

$MV_e = \dfrac{FCF \times g}{k_e - g}$ = 2.6m × 1.0424/(0.106 − 0.0424) = $42,614,000 (rounded)

The proportion of MV$_e$ to MV$_d$ is close to 50:50, which will be used here to simplify the calculations.

WACC = 10.6% × 0.5 + 4.9% × 0.5 × 0.8 = 7.3%

After implementing the proposal

The estimate of the asset beta for Coeden Co is:

β_a = 1.1 × 0.5/(0.5 + 0.5 × 0.8) = 0.61

Asset beta for hotel services

It has been assumed that Coeden Co's asset beta is a weighted average of the average property company beta and the hotel services beta.

Therefore:

$0.61 = \text{(Asset beta (hotel services)} \times 0.6) + (0.4 \times 0.4)$

$0.45 = \text{Asset beta (hotel services)} \times 0.6$

Asset beta (hotel services) = 0.75

Equity beta for Coeden Co, hotel services only

MV_e is unchanged as stated in the question.

$MV_e = \$42,614,000$

$k_d = 4 + 0.6 = 4.6\%$

$MV_d = (\$5.20 \times 1/1.046) + (\$5.20 \times 1/1.046^2) + (\$105.20 \times 1/1.046^3) = \$101.65$

Total value = $12.6 million × 101.65/100 = $12,808,000 (rounded)

Equity beta calculation

$0.75 = \beta_e \times (42,614/(42,614 + 12,808 \times 0.8))$

$0.75 = \beta_e \times 0.806$

$\beta_e = 0.93$

Hotel services cost of equity and WACC

$k_e = 4\% + 0.93 \times 6\% = 9.6\%$

$\text{WACC} = 9.6\% \times (42,614/(42,614 + 12,808)) + 4.6\% \times 0.8 \times (12,808/(42,614 + 12,808)) = 8.2\%$

Comment

	Before proposal	After proposal
Cost of equity	10.6%	9.6%
WACC	7.3%	8.2%

The proposal will increase the asset beta of Coeden Co because the hotel services industry has a **higher business risk** than a business that also owns hotels. However, the equity beta and the cost of equity are both lower because of the **reduction in the level of debt**. This is because the reduction in debt means that the financial risk of Coeden Co is lower. However, the WACC increases because this lower debt level means there is less cheap debt in the financing mix. As a result the board of directors' assertion that the lower level of debt will reduce WACC is incorrect.

(b)   The assumption that the market value of equity will not change is unlikely to hold in reality. The change in the growth rate of free cash flows and sales revenue and the changes in the business and financial risks of the new business are all likely to have an effect.

In estimating the asset beta of Coeden Co for offering hotel services only there has been no consideration of the **change in business risk** as a result of renting rather than owning the hotels. A revised asset beta should be estimated to reflect the change in business risk.

The market value of equity has been used to estimate the post-implementation equity beta and cost of equity of the business. However, the market value of equity is dependent on the cost of equity, which is itself dependent on the equity beta. Therefore both the cost of equity and the market value of equity will **change** as a result of the implementation of this proposal.

25 Levante

Marking scheme

			Marks
(a)	Calculation of company-specific yield curve	1	
	Calculation of bond value based on credit rating of A	1	
	Calculation of percentage fall in the value of the bond	1	
			3
(b)	Calculation of bond value based on 5% coupon	1	
	Calculation of new coupon rate	4	
	Advice on which type of bond to issue	2–3	
			Max 8
(c)	For each of the four criteria:		
	2 marks for explanation and suggestion of factors		8
(d)	Determine components	3	
	Apply formula	2	
	Conclude on rating	1	
			6
			25

(a) Spot yield rates based on A credit rating

Year	
1	3.2% + 0.65% = 3.85%
2	3.7% + 0.76% = 4.46%
3	4.2% + 0.87% = 5.07%
4	4.8% + 1% = 5.8%
5	5.0% + 1.12% = 6.12%

Bond value (A rating) – to be redeemed in 3 years' time

Year
1 $\$4 \times 1.0385^{-1}$ =   3.852
2 $\$4 \times 1.0446^{-2}$ =   3.666
3 $\$104 \times 1.0507^{-3}$ = 89.660

                                                            97.178 per $100

Current price (AA rating) = $98.71 per $100

Fall in price due to drop in rating = (98.71 – 97.178)/98.71 × 100 = 1.55%

(b) **Financial implications of each of the two options**

    (i)   *Value of 5% bond*

        Spot rates applicable to Levante Co are those calculated above:

Year	
1	3.85%
2	4.46%
3	5.07%
4	5.80%
5	6.12%

        Value of 5% fixed coupon bond

Year		
1	5×1.0385^{-1}	4.815
2	5×1.0446^{-2}	4.582
3	5×1.0507^{-3}	4.311
4	5×1.0580^{-4}	3.991
5	105×1.0612^{-5}	78.019
	Total value	95.718

        This means that the bond would have to be issued at a discount if a 5% coupon was offered.

    (ii)   *New coupon rate for bond valued at $100 by the market*

        As a 5% coupon means that the bond would have to be issued at a discount, a higher coupon must be offered. The coupon rate can be calculated by finding the yield to maturity of the 5% bond discounted at the yield curve given above. This will then be the coupon of the new bond to ensure the face value is $100.

$$\$5 \times (1 + YTM)^{-1} + \$5 \times (1 + YTM)^{-2} + \$5 \times (1 + YTM)^{-3} + \$5 \times (1 + YTM)^{-4} + \$105 \times (1 + YTM)^{-5}$$

$$= \$95.718$$

        We solve this equation by trial and error – it doesn't have to work out exactly but we are looking for a coupon rate that will be close to $95.718.

        If we try 6%, we obtain a result of $95.78 which is close enough to the target of $95.718.

        This means that if the coupon payment is $6 per $100 (6%) the market value of the bond will be equal to the face value of $100.

$$\$6 \times 1.06^{-1} + \$6 \times 1.06^{-2} + \$6 \times 1.06^{-3} + \$6 \times 1.06^{-4} + \$106 \times 1.06^{-5} = \$100$$

        Advice to directors

        If a coupon of 5% was chosen then the bond would be issued at a discount of approximately 4.28%. To raise $150 million the company would have to issue ($150 million/95.718) $156,710,337 of bonds in terms of their nominal value. When the bonds come to be redeemed in 5 years' time, Levante will have to pay an additional $6,710,337 to redeem these bonds.

However, a lower coupon rate will mean that interest payments each year will fall. Issuing $150 million at 6% would mean that annual interest payments would be $9 million (6% of $150 million). In comparison, issuing $156,710,337 of bonds at 5% is an annual interest payment of $7,835,517 which lower by $1,164,483.

The choice depends on whether the directors feel that that project's profit will be sufficient to cover the additional redemption charges in five years' time. If they are reasonably confident that profits will be sufficient then they should choose the lower coupon rate bond. If they wish to spread the cost rather than paying it in one lump sum then the higher coupon rate should be chosen.

(c)   **Industry risk**

Industry risk refers to the strength of the industry within the country and how resilient it is to changes in the country's economy. Industry risk could be assessed using such factors as the impact of economic forces on **industry performance**, the **cyclical nature** of the industry (and the extent of the peaks and troughs) and the extent to which **industry demand** is affected by economic forces.

Earnings protection

Earnings protection refers to how well the industry will be able to protect its earnings in the wake of changes in the economy. This could be assessed using such factors as **diversity** of the customer base, sources of **future earnings growth** and **profit margins** and return on capital.

Financial flexibility

Financial flexibility refers to the ease with which companies can raise finance in order to pursue profitable investment opportunities. This could be assessed by **evaluating future financial needs**, the range of **alternative sources of finance** available, the company's **relationship with its bank** and any **debt covenants** that may restrict operations.

Evaluation of the company's management

This refers to how well management is managing the company and planning for its future. This could be assessed by looking at the company's **planning, controls, financing policies and strategies**; merger and acquisition performance and **record of achievement** in financial results; and the **overall quality** of management and succession planning.

(d)   Here:

$F = 1,050$

$\pi = (25 \times 12)/1,050 = 0.286$

$S = 0$

$L = 400/1,050 = 0.381$

Interest $= (250 \times 0.04) + (150 \times 0.05) = 17.5$

$C = 450/17.5 = 25.7$

$\sigma = 0.08$

$Y = 4.41 + (0.0014 \times 1,050) + (6.4 \times 0.286) - 0 - (2.72 \times 0.381) + (0.006 \times 25.7) - (0.53 \times 0.08)$

$Y = 4.41 + 1.47 + 1.830 - 1.036 + 0.154 - 0.042 = 6.79$

The Kaplan-Urwitz model predicts that the credit rating will be AAA.

26 GNT

Marking scheme

		Marks	
(a)	Calculation of the gross redemption yield	2	
	PV of cash flows and the duration of bond 1	3	
	PV of cash flows and the duration of bond 2	4	
			9
(b)	Duration as a single measure of sensitivity of interest rates	3–4	
	Explanation of convexity	2–3	
	Explanation of the change in the shape of the yield curve and other limitations	2–3	
			Max 8
(c)	For each of the criteria – 2 marks for explanation and suggestion of factors		8
			25

(a) To calculate the duration of both bonds, the PV of the cash flows and the selling price of the bonds need to be calculated first. To obtain the PVs of the cash flows they need to be discounted by the gross redemption yield. This requires an IRR style calculation.

The market price of the first bond, which is $1,079.68, can be used to find the gross redemption yield that is common to both bonds.

Period	Cash flow	Amount $	Discount factor 5%	PV	Discount factor 4%	PV
1–4	Interest	60	3.546	212.76	3.630	217.80
5	Interest plus redemption	1,060	0.784	831.04	0.822	871.32
				1,043.80		1,089.12

Gross redemption yield = 4% + [(1,089.12 – 1,079.68)/(1,089.12 – 1,043.80)] = 4.21% say 4.2%

Bond 1

Period	Cash flow	Amount $	Discount factor at 4.2%	PV
1	Interest	60	0.9597	57.58
2	Interest	60	0.9210	55.26
3	Interest	60	0.8839	53.03
4	Interest	60	0.8483	50.89
5	Interest plus redemption	1,060	0.8141	862.95
				1,079.71

Note. This should be the market price; difference is due to rounding.

Period	PV	Duration multiplier	
1	57.58	1	57.58
2	55.26	2	110.52
3	53.03	3	159.09
4	50.89	4	203.56
5	862.95	5	4,314.75
	1,079.71		4,845.50

Duration = 4,845.50/1,079.71 = 4.49 years

Bond 2

Period	Cash flow	Amount $	Discount factor at 4.2%	PV
1	Interest	40	0.9597	38.39
2	Interest	40	0.9210	36.84
3	Interest	40	0.8839	35.36
4	Interest	40	0.8483	33.93
5	Interest plus redemption	1,040	0.8141	846.66
				991.18

This is the market price of Bond 2.

Period	PV	Duration multiplier	
1	38.39	1	38.39
2	36.84	2	73.68
3	35.36	3	106.08
4	33.93	4	135.72
5	846.66	5	4,233.30
	991.18		4,587.17

Duration = 4,587.17/991.18 = 4.63 years

(b) The sensitivity of a particular bond to a change in interest rates will depend on its **redemption date**. Bonds that have a later maturity date are **more price sensitive** to interest rate changes.

Duration measures the average time that a bond takes to 'pay back' its market price. The average time taken to recover the cash flow from an investment is not only affected by the maturity date of the investment but also by the coupon rate (which determines the interest payments). We want to be able to **compare bonds** quickly – this is where duration is useful.

Duration can be used to assess a bond's change in value following an interest rate change by using the following formula:

$$\Delta P = -D/(1 + Y) \times \Delta Y \times P$$

Where:

ΔP = change in bond price   P = current market price of the bond

ΔY = change in yield   Y = gross redemption yield

D = duration

The main limitation of duration is that it **assumes a linear relationship** between interest rates and price. That is, it assumes that for a certain percentage change in interest rates, there will be an equal percentage change in price.

However, as interest rates change the bond price is unlikely to change in a linear fashion. Rather, it will have some kind of convex relationship with interest rates (see below).

Relationship Between Bond Price and Yield

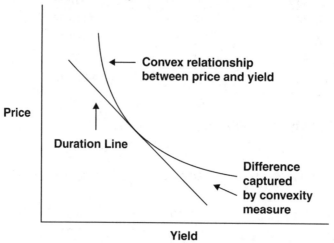

From the diagram above, the more convex the relationship the more inaccurate duration is for measuring interest rate sensitivity. Therefore **duration should be treated with caution** in predictions of interest rate/price relationships, for any interest rate changes that are not small.

Duration can only be applied to measure the **approximate change** in bond price due to changes in interest rates if the interest rate change does not lead to a change in the shape of the yield curve. This is because it is an average measure based on the GRY (yield to maturity).

(c)   **Industry risk**

Industry risk is a measure of the resilience of the company's industry to changes in the wider economy. The following factors could be used to assess this:

- The strength of the industry measured by the impact of economic forces
- Cyclical nature of the industry and the scale of the peaks and troughs
- Demand factors within the industry

Earnings protection

Earnings protection is a measure of how well the company can maintain or protect its current level of earnings in changing circumstances. The following factors could be used to assess this:

- Sources of earnings growth
- Customer base
- Return on capital, pre-tax and net profit margins

Financial flexibility

Financial flexibility is a measure of the ability of the company to raise the finance it needs to pursue its investment goals. The following factors could be used to assess this:

- Relationships with banks
- Any existing debt covenants
- Evaluation of financing needs
- Plans and alternatives under stress

Evaluation of company management

Evaluation of company management is a measure of how well management is managing and planning the future of the company. The following factors could be used to assess this:

- The company's planning, controls, financing policies and strategies
- Overall quality of management and succession
- Merger and acquisition performance
- Record of achievement in financial and non-financial results

27 Riviere

Marking scheme

			Marks
(a)	Discussion of the EU as a free trade area	2–3	
	Discussion of the possible benefits to Riviere Co	2–3	Max 5
(b)	Calculation of IRR	2	
	Calculation of MIRR	2	
	Standard deviation calculations	1	
	Value at risk calculations	2	
	Discussion of merits of NPV and MIRR	2–3	
	Explanation of VaR	2–3	
	Recommendation	1–2	
			Max 13
(c)	Discussion of possible legal risks	3–4	
	Discussion of how to deal with these	3–4	
			Max 7
			25

(a) **A free trade area** like the EU aims to remove barriers to trade and allow **freedom of movement** of production resources such as capital and labour within the EU. The EU also has a **common legal structure** across all member countries and tries to **limit any discriminatory practice** against companies operating in these countries.

The EU also erects **common external trade barriers** to trade against countries which are not member states.

Riviere Co may benefit from operating within the EU in a number of ways.

It may be protected from non-EU competition because companies outside the EU may find it **difficult to enter the EU** markets due to barriers to trade.

A common legal structure should ensure that the standards of food quality and packaging apply equally across all the member countries. This will **reduce compliance costs** for Riviere, which may be an important issue for a small company with limited financial resources.

Having access to capital and labour within the EU may make it easier for the company to set up branches inside the EU, if it wants to. The company may also be able to access any grants which are available to companies based within the EU.

(b) **Project Drugi internal rate of return (IRR)**

Net present value (NPV): €2,293,000 approximately using a cost of capital of 10%

Time	0	1	2	3	4	5
Cash flows (€'000)	(11,840)	1,230	1,680	4,350	10,240	2,200
Try 20%	1.0	0.833	0.694	0.579	0.482	0.402
Present value	(11,840)	1,025	1,166	2,519	4,936	884

NPV = €(1,310,000)

IRR = 10% + 2,293/(2,293 + 1,310) × 10% approximately = **16.4%**

Modified internal rate of return (MIRR)

Total present values (PVs) of inflows from time 1 to 5 at 10% discount rate = outlay + NPV of project = €11,840,000 + €2,293,000 = €14,133,000

MIRR (using formula provided) = $\left[\dfrac{PVr}{PVi}\right]^{1/n} \times \left(1 + r_e\right) - 1$

MIRR = $\left[\dfrac{14,133}{11,840}\right]^{1/5} \times (1 + 0.1) - 1 =$ **14%**

Value at risk (VaR)

A 95% confidence level requires the annual present value VaR to be within approximately 1.645 standard deviations from the mean.

A 90% confidence level requires annual present value VaR to be within approximately 1.282 standard deviations from the mean.

(**Note.** An approximation of standard deviations to two decimal places is acceptable.)

95%, 5-year present value VaR = $400,000 × 1.645 × square root of 5 (since it is a 5-year project) = approx. **€1,471,000**

90%, 5-year present value VaR = $400,000 × 1.28 (approx.) × square root of 5 (since it is a 5-year project) = approx. **€1,145,000**

	Privi	Drugi
NPV (10%)	€2,054,000	€2,293,000
IRR	17.6%	16.4%
MIRR	13.4%	14.0%
VaR (over the project's life)		
95% confidence level	€1,103,500	€1,471,000
90% confidence level	€860,000	€1,145,000

The IRR for project Privi is higher. However, where projects are mutually exclusive, the **IRR can give an incorrect answer**. One reason for this is that the IRR assumes that returns are reinvested at the internal rate of return, whereas NPV and the MIRR assume that they are reinvested at the cost of capital (discount rate) which in this case is 10%. The cost of capital is a more realistic assumption as this is the minimum return required by investors in a company.

The NPV and the MIRR both indicate that project Drugi would create more value for Riviere Co.

Therefore, based purely on cash flows, **project Drugi should be accepted due to the higher NPV and MIRR, as they give the theoretically correct answer of the value created.**

The VaR provides an indication of the potential riskiness of a project. For example, if Riviere Co invests in project Drugi then it can be 95% confident that the PV will not fall by more than €1,471,000 over its life. Hence the project will still produce a positive NPV. However, there is a 5% chance that the loss could be greater than €1,471,000. With project Privi, the potential loss in value is smaller and therefore it is less risky.

When risk is also taken into account, the choice between the projects is not clear cut and depends on Riviere Co's attitude to risk and return. Project Drugi gives the higher potential NPV but is riskier, whereas project Privi is less risky but gives a smaller NPV. This is before taking into account additional uncertainties such as trading in an area in which Riviere Co is not familiar.

It is therefore recommended that Riviere Co should only proceed with project Drugi if it is willing to accept the higher risk and uncertainty.

(c)   There are a number of possible **legal risks** which Riviere Co may face:

(i)   The countries where the product is sold may have **different legal regulations** on food preparation, quality and packaging.

(ii)   The legal regulations may be more lax in countries outside the EU but Riviere Co needs to be aware that **complying only with the minimum standards may impact its image negatively overall**, even if they are acceptable in the countries concerned.

(iii) There may be **trade barriers** eg **import quotas** in the countries concerned which may make it difficult for Riviere Co to compete.

(iv)   The legal system in some countries **may not recognise the trademarks** or production patents which the company holds on its packaging and production processes. This may enable competitors to copy the food and the packaging.

(v)   Different countries may have different regulations regarding **product liability** from poorly prepared and/or stored food which cause harm to consumers.

Possible mitigation strategies:

(i)   Riviere Co needs to undertake sufficient **research** into the countries' **current laws** and regulations to ensure that it complies with the standards required. It may even want to ensure that it exceeds the required standards to ensure that it maintains its reputation.

(ii)   Riviere Co needs to ensure that it also keeps abreast of **potential changes** in the law. It may also want to ensure that it complies with best practice, even if it is not the law yet. Often current best practices become enshrined in future legislation.

(iii) Strict **contracts** need to be set up between Riviere Co and any agents it uses to transport and sell the food. These could be followed up by **regular checks** to ensure that the standards required are maintained.

(**Note.** Credit will be given for alternative, relevant discussion for parts (a) and (c).)

28 AWP

Text references. Duration and theories of capital structure are both covered in Chapter 7a.

Top tips. This question covers some parts of the syllabus that students typically struggle with.

In part (a)(i) you need to calculate the yield to maturity to get the discount rate for the duration calculation. Don't forget to adjust the spot rate with the AA credit spread. Part (a)(ii) requires you to know the general features of duration and to comment on the results you have found.

Easy marks. Part (b) offers some relatively straightforward discussion marks as long as you have covered these topics.

(a)   (i)   **Issue price**

The spot yield curve should be used to calculate a likely issue price. This government bond yield curve needs to be adjusted by the credit spread for an AA rated company.

	1 year	2 year	3 year	4 year
Gov't bond annual spot yield curve	3.30	3.80	4.50	5.30
AA rated spread	0.27	0.40	0.51	0.60
	3.57	4.20	5.01	5.90

Each of the bonds can be separated into separate bonds.

Option 1

	1 year	2 year	3 year	4 year
Bond 1	5			
Bond 2		5		
Bond 3			5	
Bond 4				105

Option 2

	1 year	2 year	3 year
Bond 1	4		
Bond 2		4	
Bond 3			109

The present values of these payments (using the yield curve calculated above) will be the likely issue price.

Option 1

$$\text{Issue price} = (5 \times \frac{1}{1.0357}) + (5 \times \frac{1}{1.0420^2}) + (5 \times \frac{1}{1.0501^3}) + (105 \times \frac{1}{1.0590^4}) = \$97.24$$

Option 2

$$\text{Issue price} = (4 \times \frac{1}{1.0357}) + (4 \times \frac{1}{1.0420^2}) + (109 \times \frac{1}{1.0501^3}) = \$101.68$$

Yield to maturity (YTM)

The YTM for each bond can be calculated as follows:

Option 1

Year	Cash flow	DF 5%	PV	DF 6%	PV
0	(97.24)	1.000	(97.24)	1.000	(97.24)
1–4	5	3.546	17.73	3.465	17.33
4	100	0.823	82.30	0.792	79.20
			2.79		(0.71)

For Option 1 the YTM is $5 + \left[\left(\frac{2.79}{2.79 + 0.71} \right)(6 - 5) \right] = 5.80\%$

Option 2

Year	Cash flow	DF 4%	PV	DF 5%	PV
0	(101.68)	1.000	(101.68)	1.000	(101.68)
1–3	4	2.775	11.10	2.723	10.89
3	105	0.889	93.35	0.864	90.72
			2.77		(0.07)

For Option 2 the YTM is $4 + \left[\left(\frac{2.77}{2.77 + 0.07} \right)(5 - 4) \right] = 4.98\%$

Duration

Option 1

	Year 1	Year 2	Year 3	Year 4	Total
Cash flows	5	5	5	105	
Discount factor (5.80%)	0.945	0.893	0.844	0.798	
Present value	4.725	4.465	4.220	83.790	97.20
% of total present value	0.05	0.05	0.04	0.86	
Year multiplied by % (eg Year 3 value = 3 × 0.04 = 0.12)	0.05	0.10	0.12	3.44	3.71

Duration = 3.71 years

Option 2

	Year 1	Year 2	Year 3	Total
Cash flows	4	4	109	
Discount factor (4.98%)	0.953	0.907	0.864	
Present value	3.812	3.628	94.176	101.616
% of total present value	0.04	0.04	0.92	
Year multiplied by %	0.04	0.08	2.76	2.88

Duration = 2.88 years

(ii) Duration gives each bond an overall risk weighting which allows bonds of different maturities and coupon rates to be directly compared. Duration is a composite measure of risk expressed in terms of years. In general terms longer-dated bonds will have longer durations and lower-coupon bonds will have longer durations. A bond that is redeemed at a premium will also have a longer duration to one redeemed at par or even at a discount.

The first of these general points is shown by the calculations in part (a)(i) where the longer-dated bond has the longer duration. The points about lower coupons and bonds redeemed at a premium is also shown as the duration of Option 2 is only marginally less than the three-year length of the bond. This is because the vast majority of the returns are in the redemption payment received in Year 3.

(b) The Chief Executive understands that the use of debt financing can increase the value of a company due to the tax relief available on the debt. This comes from Modigliani and Miller's theory which assumes that debt is risk free.

However, an increase in debt financing will also result in an **increase in the chance of bankruptcy** because of the increased commitment in interest payments. Failure to meet those interest payments because of inadequate cash on hand will cause the firm some financial distress, and the ultimate form of financial distress is bankruptcy.

As a result of these **increased distress costs** the gearing-adjusted value of the firm should be decreased. The value of the company in this case will be: Value of the ungeared company + (tax rate × interest payments) – present value of the bankruptcy costs.

Starting from the empirical observation that firms in AWP Co's industry **do not have 100% gearing ratios**, it is plausible that a firm's weighted average cost of capital (WACC) will start to increase and its value will start to decrease after a certain value of the gearing ratio, to reflect the increasing costs of gearing.

The conclusion is that a company should gear up to take advantage of any tax benefits available, but only to the extent that the **marginal benefits exceed** the **marginal costs** of **financial distress**. After this point, the market value of the firm will start to fall and its WACC will start to rise. This is known as the **static trade-off theory** of capital structure. In this scenario it may well be that the optimum point is around the average industry gearing ratio.

Agency theory provides a rationale for an optimal structure based on the existence of agency costs associated with the issue of debt and equity. There are agency problems in directors trying to reconcile the interests of debt holders and equity holders as well as potentially trying to reconcile the interests of new and old shareholders following an issue of equity. Agency theory states that the optimal capital structure of the company will be formed at the particular level of debt and equity where the benefits of the debt that can be received by the shareholders equal the costs of debt imposed by the debt holders. It could be argued that, given AWP Co's relatively low level of gearing, it has not reached this optimum point.

Pecking order theory states that the preferred order for sources of finance is initially retained earnings, then debt and lastly equity. It is this order that the Chief Executive appears to want AWP Co to move towards, although in the past it seems likely that equity was preferred to debt.

29 Preparation question: Saturn Systems

Text references. Ethics are covered in Chapter 3. Regulations relating to takeovers are covered in Chapter 11.

Top tips. This is a relatively straightforward question if you can identify the issues involved.

Requirement (b) is divided neatly into three types of issues so deal with each type under a separate heading to make it easy for the marker to identify your points.

The solution given relates to the UK City Code but you can refer to your own country's codes instead and still gain the available marks.

Make sure you relate your answer to the specific scenario and do not just write everything you know about takeover and acquisition regulations.

Easy marks. Part (a) is a fairly straightforward discussion. Also it should have been easy to identify that the financial risk of Saturn could change if more debt was introduced into the capital structure to fund the acquisition of Pluto.

Examining team's comments. Under most jurisdictions, what was said could be taken as notice of intention to bid, whereas the company had neither estimated the value nor undertaken a due diligence study of the potential target.

The many good answers to this question recognised the significance of the CEO's remarks and the weak position of the company in terms of both its state of preparation for an announcement and the regulatory implications of the remarks. A small minority of candidates did not recognise that there was a problem with the CEO's comments and spent considerable space discussing ways in which the bid might be defended.

Overall many candidates performed well on this question, providing well-written and well-argued answers. More attention to the wider implications, and particularly those relating to the ethical issues concerning the transparency and availability of price-sensitive information, would have earned more marks.

Marking scheme

		Marks
(a)	Per explained point	1–2
		Max 5
(b)	Identification of the problems created by Mr Moon's remarks	3
	Significance of the price reaction	3
	The firm's current position and identification of the holding option on the PR	4
	Ethical problems of insider information, fairness to stakeholders, avoidance of dissembling	5
		15
(c)	Issue of immediate press release	2
	Draft of statement reserving the company's position under the six-month rule	3
		5
		25

(a) Advantages of growth by acquisition

Acquiring an **existing company** is a speedier method of entering a new business than setting up a project using internal resources, because an acquired business will already have **customers** and, hopefully, **goodwill**. An acquisition may also effectively **eliminate a competitor** and may **allow higher profitability**. Other advantages may come from the **combination of complementary resources** of the acquiring and acquired companies.

Also, because Pluto is a **major supplier** of Saturn, the acquisition will help to secure Saturn's supply chain and could help reduce costs, which can be important in a competitive industry such as telecommunications. The acquisition could also mean that competitors are forced to seek alternative and perhaps lower quality suppliers.

Problems of growth by acquisition

Frequently, a **significant premium** must be **paid** in order to **encourage existing shareholders** to sell, or to outbid, a rival. This may make it difficult to show a **respectable return** on the cost of the acquisition.

The acquired company may **not produce the exact product or service** that the acquirer needs, or may need **significant investment** before it conforms to quality requirements.

Management problems are also quite common, particularly when the acquiring and acquired companies have different organisational cultures. **Disputes** may cause the loss of key staff members, resulting in reduced quality or even in the establishment of competing businesses.

(b) There are several **regulatory, financial and ethical issues** that must be considered if Saturn Systems wants to make a bid for Pluto Ltd.

Regulatory issues

As a large listed company we have an obligation to ensure that any remarks made in the public domain will not mislead investors. The **City Code** in the UK requires the maintenance of **absolute secrecy** prior to an announcement being made. This requirement falls on the person or persons who hold **confidential information** (particularly information that might affect share price) and every effort should be made to prevent **accidental disclosure** of such information.

The City Code specifically states that a **false market must not be created** in the shares of the 'target' company. The remarks made last night no doubt contributed to the 15% rise in Pluto's share price. In accordance with the City Code, Saturn Systems will be expected to make a **statement of intention** in the light of the effect of the remarks at the dinner.

If it is stated that Saturn Systems are not interested in making a bid, it will not be able to make another bid **for six months**, unless Pluto's board **recommends** a bid that might be made by Saturn Systems. Another way in which this restriction could be waived is if another offer is made by a **third party**.

Financial issues

Saturn Systems are in a strong **financial position** at the moment which may be one of the reasons the market interpreted the remarks as being significant. The 15% increase in Pluto's share price indicates that the market now sees Pluto as being a **target for takeover** and that Saturn may be interested in buying the company.

One problem is that Saturn Systems is only in the early stages of investigating Pluto and has not yet conducted a **due diligence** study. It does not know what the company is worth as a valuation has not yet taken place. As the remarks apparently contributed to a 15% increase in share price, Saturn Systems will now have to pay more for Pluto if it decides to make a bid. This could affect the financial position as it may be unable to raise the extra finance required to cover the additional cost.

As well as the issues above, there is the likelihood of the extra debt affecting the **financial risk profile**. The acquisition of Pluto could also affect the **business risk exposure**. As a result, Saturn Systems cannot value Pluto without revaluing the existing business. If Pluto's value exceeds the increase in Saturn's value if the acquisition took place, it should not proceed with the purchase.

Ethical issues

There is now a dilemma of how to proceed. Saturn Systems has made no secret of the fact that it wants to growth by acquisition rather than organically therefore it would not be ethical to deny any interest in Pluto. It was one of four potential targets discussed at the last board meeting and investigations have been conducted into the company as well as reviewing the steps necessary to raise the finance for acquisition. In order to maintain its commitment to transparency of information, it is recommended that Saturn Systems clarifies its intentions.

(c) **Proposed course of action**

Saturn Systems should release a statement to **clarify the position** regarding Pluto. It should confirm that it is looking into the possibility of an acquisition of Pluto but make it clear that the board has decided not to make a bid at this time. However, it should be made clear that Saturn Systems **reserves the right** to make a bid or take any action that would otherwise be prohibited under the **six-month rule** should Pluto's board agree to an acquisition or if any other company announced its intention to make an offer. This means Saturn Systems still has the chance to complete its investigations and develop a bid proposal before entering into negotiations with Pluto's board.

30 Mercury Training

Text references. Cost of equity and weighted average cost of capital (WACC) are covered in Chapters 2 and 7a. Valuation of shares is covered in Chapter 10. Financing methods are discussed in Chapters 2 and 7a.

Top tips. In part (a), the asset beta of Mercury is calculated using the revenue weightings from Jupiter and the financial services sector. This is quite a tough section for eight marks and it is important to show all your workings to ensure you gain as many marks as possible.

Part (b) requires the use of the dividend valuation model to calculate share price at the higher end of the range of possible prices. There are three possible growth rates that could be used. You should recognise that the historic earnings growth rate actually exceeds the cost of equity capital and therefore cannot be sustained in the long run. As you are calculating the higher end of the range, use the higher of the other two possible growth rates.

Part (c) requires knowledge of the advantages and disadvantages of public listings and private equity finance. Remember to make it relevant to the scenario.

Easy marks. The discussion in part (c) is more straightforward than some of the calculations. However, it can be seen from the examining team's comments below that the easiest way of losing marks is not to read/answer the question set.

Examining team's comments. Candidates were invited to combine market risk measures for the two aspects of Mercury Training. Another company is publicly quoted and has a beta that matches two-thirds of the business of Mercury Training. The remainder of its business has a beta matching that of the financial services sector. Using the portfolio beta concept, a combined beta can be estimated. Given the different levels of gearing involved, candidates faced the common problem of ungearing the risk measures for the proxies to create an asset beta. They must then be combined and geared again to match the business profile of Mercury Training. Tax also complicated matters as this affected both the cost of debt and its weighting in the calculation of the respective asset betas.

A substantial majority of candidates understood what the question required and made a good attempt at answering it. Similarly in part (b) many candidates attempted to calculate a likely issue price but did not 'advise' the owners of Mercury Training on the range that might be negotiable in the event of an issue or sale of the business. The overall lesson for candidates here is to focus carefully on the verbs expressing what is required in each part of the question and to construct their answers in a way that clearly focuses on the requirements of the question.

Common problems or issues in candidates' answers were:

(a)   Ignoring tax in the estimation of asset betas
(b)   Failing to recognise the application of the portfolio beta concept in creating a proxy estimate for the company
(c)   Using long-term growth estimates that were in excess of the equilibrium rate of equity return generated by the capital asset pricing model (CAPM) and therefore unsustainable
(d)   Lack of understanding of the advantages and disadvantages of private equity finance

Marking scheme

		Marks	
(a)	Calculation of tax-adjusted gearing for Jupiter and the FS sector	2	
	Calculation of the proxy asset beta for Mercury and its estimated equity beta	4	
	Estimation of Mercury's equity cost of capital and WACC	2	
			8
(b)	Lowest rate set at liquidated value of the business	2	
	Calculation of reinvestment rate and growth	3	
	Estimation of upper boundary price per share	3	
	Identification of control premium	2	
			10

		Marks
(c)	Advantages and disadvantages of listing (regulatory, takeover, process)	4
	Nature of private equity finance and its advantages and disadvantages	4

$$\text{Max} \quad \underline{7}$$
$$\underline{25}$$

(a) ## Step 1

Ungear beta of Jupiter and financial services sector

$$\beta_a = \beta_g \frac{V_e}{V_e + V_d (1-T)}$$

Jupiter $= 1.5 \times \dfrac{88}{88 + (12 \times 0.6)} = 1.3865$

FS sector $= 0.9 \times \dfrac{75}{75 + (25 \times 0.6)} = 0.75$

Step 2

Calculate average asset beta for Mercury

$\beta_a = (0.67 \times 1.3865) + (0.33 \times 0.75) = 1.175$

Step 3

Regear Mercury's beta

$$\beta_a \qquad = \beta_e \times \frac{V_e}{V_e + V_d(1-T)}$$

$$1.175 \qquad = \beta_e \times \frac{70}{70 + 30(1 - 0.4)}$$

$1.175 \qquad = \beta_e \times 0.795$

$\beta_e \qquad = 1.48$

Step 4

Calculate cost of equity capital and WACC

Using CAPM:

Cost of equity capital $= R_f + \beta_i(E(r_m) - R_f) = 4.5 + 1.48 \times 3.5 = 9.68\%$

$$\textbf{WACC} \qquad = \left[\frac{V_e}{V_e + V_d} \right] k_e + \left[\frac{V_d}{V_e + V_d} \right] k_d (1 - T)$$

$$= (0.7 \times 0.0968) + (0.3 \times [0.045 + 0.025]) \times 0.6$$

$$= 8.04\%$$

Where k_d = risk-free rate (4.5%) + premium on risk-free rate (2.5%)

When to use cost of equity and WACC

Cost of equity is the rate of return required by the company's ordinary shareholders. The return includes **a risk-free rate** (to reflect that investors are rational) and a **risk premium** (to reflect that investors are risk averse). Cost of equity is used to value income streams to the **shareholders** (that is, dividends).

WACC is the average cost of capital of the business and is based on the company's **level of gearing**. WACC is used to value income streams to the **business as a whole** ie free cash flow (for example, it is used as the **discount rate** to appraise potential investments).

(b)   **Range of likely issue prices**

Lower range of issue price will be the net assets at fair value divided by the number of shares

= $65 million/10 million shares

= $6.50 per share

Upper range – use **dividend valuation model**

Three possible earnings rates:

(i)   **Historical earnings growth rate** of 12% is greater than the cost of equity capital, therefore cannot be sustained in the long run

(ii)   The **weighted anticipated growth rate** of the two business sectors in which Mercury operates (0.67 × 6% + 0.33 × 4% = 5.34%)

(iii)   **The rate implied from the firm's reinvestment** (9.68% – see part (a) Step 4 above)

$$g = br_e = \frac{(100-25)}{100} \times 0.0968 = 7.26\%$$

The higher of the two feasible rates – that is, 7.26% – should be used to calculate the higher issue price

$$P_0 = \frac{d_0(1+g)}{(k_e - g)}$$

$$P_0 = \frac{25(1+0.0726)}{(0.0968-0.0726)} = \$11.08 \text{ per share}$$

If the company was floated, the higher price above (which is based on a minority shareholding earning a dividend from the shares) could be achieved. This implies that a portion of the equity and **effective control** is retained. **Private equity investors** are likely to be willing to pay a premium for the benefits of control (**control premium**) – often as much as 30–50% of the share price. In this case negotiations may start at a share price of $16.62 ($11.08 × 1.5).

(c)   To: Directors of Mercury Training
       From: Treasury department
       Subject: Public listing versus private equity finance

As you are currently considering either a flotation or an outright sale of Mercury Training, I would like to outline the relative advantages and disadvantages of a public listing versus private equity finance.

Public listing

This is the traditional method of raising finance by firms which have reached a certain size. Where a public listing is sought, owners will be looking to **release their equity stake** in the firm (either partially or in total). A public listing gives the company access to **a wider pool of finance** and makes it easier to grow by acquisition. As owners, you will be able to release your holding and use the money to fund other projects.

However, public listings lead to the company being subject to **increased scrutiny, accountability and regulation**. There are greater **legal requirements** and the company will also be required to adhere to the **rules of the stock exchange**.

Obtaining a public listing is **expensive** – for example brokerage commission and underwriting fees.

New investors may have **more exacting requirements** and different ideas of how the business should progress. This may put additional strain on the directors responsible for the company's overall strategy.

Private equity

Private equity finance is raised via **venture capital companies** or private equity businesses. There are **fewer regulatory restrictions** attached to private equity finance than there are to public listings. The cost of accessing private equity finance is lower and in certain jurisdictions there are **favourable tax advantages** to private equity investors.

Directors of a company seeking private equity finance must realise however that the financial institution will require an **equity stake** in the company. The directors responsible for the overall company strategy will still be subject to **considerable scrutiny** as the finance providers may want to have a **representative** appointed to the company's board to look after their interests. They may even require the appointment of an **independent director**.

Private equity providers will need to be convinced that the company can **continue its business operations successfully**, otherwise there will be no incentive to invest.

I hope this information is useful but please contact me if you wish to discuss further.

31 Chithurst

Text references. Valuing a firm using the dividend valuation model is covered in Chapter 7a. Dividend policy is covered in Chapters 2 and 4b.

Top tips. In part (a), the key is to spend time analysing the actual policies being followed, not in righting generalised answers on the relevance or irrelevance of dividend poliies in general. A similar question was set in June 2013.

Easy marks. Part (b), should have been easier because of the clear instructions as to the nature of the analysis that was required, however in the exam many students did not read the question properly and did not provide valuations based on 2 growth assumptions as specified by the question.

Marking scheme

			Marks
(a)	Benefits of dividend policy – 1–2 marks for each company	Max	5
	Drawbacks of dividend policy – 2–3 marks for each company	Max	7
	Calculations – Dividend payout ratios – 1 mark per company		3
	Other calculations		2
		Max	15
(b)	Comments on valuation of each company, max 4 marks per company		
	(max 5 marks for valuation calculation(s))	Max	10
			25

(a) **Dividend payout ratio**

	Chithurst Co %	Eartham Co %	Iping Co %
20X2	42.9	40.0	46.7
20X3	41.3	(150.0)	19.3
20X4	35.1	40.0	33.1
20X5	34.0	40.0	31.8

Residual profit (after-tax profit for the year – dividend – new investment)

	Chithurst Co	Eartham Co	Iping Co
	%	%	%
20X2	26	27	3
20X3	18	(40)	7
20X4	38	24	4
20X5	43	43	6

Chithurst Co's policy

Benefits

Chithurst Co's policy provides shareholders with a stable, predictable income each year. As profits have grown consistently, dividend cover has increased, which suggests that, for now, dividend levels are sustainable. These are positive signals to the stock market.

Drawbacks

Chithurst Co's dividend policy is unpopular with some of its shareholders. They have indicated a preference for dividend levels to bear a greater relation to profit levels. Although they are still in a minority and cannot force the directors to pay more dividends, they are now possibly a significant minority. Ultimately, Chithurst Co's share price could fall significantly if enough shareholders sell their shares because they dislike the dividend policy.

The dividend policy may also have been established to meet the financial needs of the shareholders when Chithurst Co was unquoted. However, it is now difficult to see how it fits into Chithurst Co's overall financial strategy. The greater proportion of funds retained does not appear to be linked to the levels of investment Chithurst Co is undertaking. Chithurst Co's shareholders may be concerned that best use is not being made of the funds available. If there are profitable investments which Chithurst Co could be making but is not doing so, then Chithurst Co may find it more difficult in future to sustain the levels of profit growth. Alternatively, if profitable investments do not exist, some shareholders may prefer to have funds returned in the form of a special dividend or share repurchase.

Eartham Co

Benefits

For three out of four years, Eartham Co has been paying out dividends at a stable payout ratio. This may be attractive to some investors, who have expectations that the company's profits will keep increasing in the longer term and wish to share directly in increases in profitability.

The year when Eartham Co's dividend payout ratio differed from the others was 20X3, when Eartham Co made a loss. A dividend of $15m was paid in 20X3, which may be a guaranteed minimum. This limits the downside risk of the dividend payout policy to shareholders, as they know they will receive this minimum amount in such a year.

Drawbacks

Although shareholders are guaranteed a minimum dividend each year, dividends have been variable. Eartham Co's shareholders may prefer dividends to increase at a steady rate which is sustainable over time, even if this rate is lower than the rate of increase in some years under the current policy.

If Eartham Co had another poor year of trading like 20X3, shareholders' expectations that they will be paid a minimum dividend may mean that cash has to be earmarked to pay the minimum dividend, rather than for other, maybe better, uses in the business.

Having a 'normal' dividend policy results in expectations about what the level of dividend will be. Over time Eartham Co's managers may be reluctant to change to a lower payout ratio because they fear that this will give shareholders an adverse signal. Even if its directors maintain a constant ratio normally, shareholders may question whether the proportion of funds being retained is appropriate or whether a higher proportion could be paid out as dividends.

Eartham Co appears to be linking investment and dividend policy by its normal policy of allocating a constant proportion of funds for dividends and therefore a constant proportion of funds to invest. However, the actual level of new investments does not seem to bear much relation to the proportion of funds put aside for investment. When deciding on investments, the directors would also take into account the need to take advantage of opportunities as they arise and the overall amount of surplus funds built up over the years, together with the other sources of external finance available.

Iping Co

Benefits

Iping Co seems to have adopted a residual dividend policy, which links investment and dividend decisions. The strategy appears to be to make investments if they offer sufficient return to increase long-term company value and only pay dividends if there are no more profitable investments. They are assuming that internal funds are cheaper than external funds, or maybe Iping Co cannot raise the funds required from external sources.

The policy is likely to appeal to shareholders who are more concerned with capital growth than short-term income.

Drawbacks

Dividend payments are totally unpredictable, as they depend on the investment choices. Shareholders cannot rely on having any dividend income in a particular year.

Many shareholders may be prepared to sacrifice dividends for a while in order for funds to be available for investment for growth. However, at some point they may consider that Iping Co is well established enough to be able to maintain a consistent dividend policy as well as invest sufficiently for future growth.

(b) **Use of dividend valuation model**

Chithurst Co

Valuation = 33/0.11 = $300m

Chithurst Co's market capitalisation of $608m is considerably in excess of the valuation suggested by the dividend valuation model. This may suggest that investors have some positive expectations about the company and the lower cost of equity compared with the other two companies suggests it is regarded as a more stable investment. Investors could also be valuing the company using earnings growth rather than dividend growth. However, the lower market capitalisation compared with the other two companies and the smaller increase in share price suggest that investors have higher expectations of long-term growth from Eartham Co and Iping Co.

Eartham Co

One-year growth rate = $(48/44) - 1 = 9.1\%$

Valuation using one-year growth rate = $48 (1 + 0.091)/(0.14 - 0.091) = \$1,068.7m$

Three-year growth rate = $\sqrt[3]{(48/38)} - 1 = 8.1\%$

Valuation using three-year growth rate = $48 (1 + 0.081)/(0.14 - 0.081) = \$879m$

Eartham Co's market capitalisation is closer to the valuation suggested by the dividend growth model using the one-year growth rate between 20X4 and 20X5 rather than the three-year growth rate between 20X2 and 20X5. This, together with the recent increase in share price, suggests that Eartham Co's shareholders have an optimistic view of its ability to sustain the profit growth and hence the dividend growth of the last two years, although its higher cost of equity than the other companies suggests that they are more wary about the risks of investing in Eartham Co. It indicates confidence in the directors' strategy, including the investments they have made.

Iping Co

One-year growth rate = $(42/39) - 1 = 7.7\%$

Valuation using one-year growth rate = $42 (1 + 0.077)/(0.12 - 0.077) = \$1,052.0m$

Three-year growth rate = $\sqrt[3]{(42/35)} - 1 = 6.3\%$

Valuation using three-year growth rate = $42 (1 + 0.063)/(0.12 - 0.063) = \$783.3m$

The market capitalisation of Iping Co is higher than is suggested by the dividend valuation model, but the dividend valuation model may not provide a realistic valuation because dividends payable are dependent on investment opportunities.

The larger increase in share price compared with the other two companies suggests that Iping Co's investors expect its investments to produce high long-term returns and hence are presumably satisfied with its dividend policy.

32 Kodiak Company

Text references. Valuing a firm using free cash flow to equity and terminal values is covered in Chapters 5, 7b and 10.

Top tips. In part (a), layout is very important, not just to make things clear for the marker, but also for you to ensure that no figures are missed. There are numerous workings involved in this part of the question therefore you need to be able to keep track of where figures are coming from. Remember that cash flow statements never include depreciation so ensure you account for this when calculating the free cash flow to equity. Make sure you answer the question – you are asked for the free cash flow to equity so you will have to deduct any new investment in non-current assets.

Part (b) is straightforward if you can remember the formula but remember to show your workings. Also write the formula in notation form in your answer to show the marker which formula you are using!

Part (c) is testing your understanding of how estimates can affect the valuation figure. Two of the more important figures are growth rates and required rate of return so make sure you comment on those. There are several other factors you can comment on but remember this part is only worth six marks so don't get carried away!

Easy marks. The calculations in part (a) should be quite straightforward and you should be expecting to gain all, or almost all, of the available marks. As mentioned above, part (b) is also quite straightforward if you remember the formula for calculating terminal value.

Marking scheme

			Marks
(a)	Estimation of depreciation	1	
	Estimation of taxation	1	
	Estimation of changes in working capital	2	
	Projection of statements of profits	4	
	Projection of cash flows	4	
			12
(b)	Calculation/identification of free cash flow	1	
	Calculation of terminal value	2	
	Calculation of present values and business value	3	
			6
(c)	Commentary on required rate of return	2–3	
	Assumptions about the growth rates	2–3	
	Other relevant points	1–2	
			Max 7
			25

(a) Using the information in the question it is clear that in order to produce a projected cash flow statement we must first produce a projected statement of profit or loss for each of the next three years.

PROJECTED STATEMENT OF PROFIT OR LOSS

	Year 1	Year 2	Year 3
	$'000	$'000	$'000
Revenue (9% growth per annum)	5,450	5,941	6,476
Cost of sales (9% growth per annum)	(3,270)	(3,564)	(3,885)
Gross profit	2,180	2,377	2,591
Other operating costs (W1)	(2,013)	(2,160)	(2,318)
Operating profit	167	217	273

PROJECTED CASH FLOW STATEMENT

	Year 1	Year 2	Year 3
	$'000	$'000	$'000
Operating profit	167	217	273
Add depreciation (W2)	135	144	155
Less incremental working capital (W3)	(20)	(22)	(24)
Less interest	(74)	(74)	(74)
Less taxation (W4)	(15)	(28)	(43)
	193	237	287
Less new additions to non-current assets (W2)	(79)	(95)	(114)
Free cash flow to equity	114	142	173

Workings

1 *Operating costs*

	Year 1	Year 2	Year 3
	$'000	$'000	$'000
Variable costs (9% growth per annum)	818	892	972
Fixed costs (6% growth per annum)	1,060	1,124	1,191
Depreciation (10%) (Working 2)	135	144	155
Total operating costs	2,013	2,160	2,318

2 *Depreciation and non-current assets*

	Year 1	Year 2	Year 3
	$'000	$'000	$'000
Non-current assets at start of year	1,266	1,345	1,440
Additions (20% growth)	79	95	114
Non-current assets at end of year	1,345	1,440	1,554
Depreciation (10%)	135	144	155

3 *Working capital*

	Year 1	Year 2	Year 3
	$'000	$'000	$'000
Working capital requirements (9% growth p.a.)	240	262	286
Incremental working capital	(240 – 220) = 20	(262 – 240) = 22	(286 – 262) = 24

Note that the working capital figure excludes cash, therefore the current (Year 0) working capital figure is $270,000 – $50,000 = $220,000.

4   Taxation

	Year 1 $'000	Year 2 $'000	Year 3 $'000
Charged on previous year's profit after interest			
Given in question	15		
Previous year's operating profit (from projected statement of profit or loss)		167	217
Interest		(74)	(74)
Profit before tax		93	143
Tax at 30%		28	43

(b)   **Value of business using free cash flow to equity and terminal value**

	Year 1 $'000	Year 2 $'000	Year 3 $'000
Free cash flow to equity (from (a))	114	142	173
Terminal value (Working)			2,546
Total			2,719
Discount factor (10%)	0.909	0.826	0.751
Present value	104	117	2,042

Value of the business = $2,263,000

Working: Terminal value

$$\text{Terminal value} = \frac{FCF_N(1+g)}{k-g}$$

where g = growth rate
        k = required rate of return

$$\text{Terminal value} = \frac{173(1+0.03)}{0.10-0.03} = \$2,546$$

(c)   **Assumptions and uncertainties within the valuation**

Whilst the valuation of the business is a useful estimate, it should be treated with caution as it is subject to certain assumptions.

Rate of return

The rate of return of 10% is assumed to fairly reflect the required **market rate of return** for a business of this type, which compensates you for the business risk to which you are exposed. Whilst the required return for an investment held in a widely diversified portfolio should only compensate you for **market risk**, if you hold the same investment individually you may expect a higher return due to your increased exposure to risk.

Growth rates

The growth rate applied to terminal value is assumed to be **certain** into the indefinite future. In the case of a three-year projection this is unlikely to be the case, due to unexpected economic conditions and the type of business. In order to reduce the effects of such uncertainties, different growth rates could be applied to the calculations to determine business valuation in a variety of scenarios.

Interest rates and tax rates

Similar to the growth rate, it has been assumed that interest rates and tax rates will remain **unchanged** during the three-year period. If economic conditions suggest that changes may take place revised calculations could reflect different possible rates to update the estimate of business valuation.

Costs, revenues and non-current assets

It has been assumed that the figures used for these factors are certain and that the business is a going concern. It may be worth investigating the **potential variability** of these factors and the range of values that may result for such variability. Changes in estimates will obviously affect operating profit and projected cash flows, which in turn will affect the estimated value of the business.

33 Louieed

Marking scheme

		Marks
(a)	Reasons for acquisition	3
	Reasons against acquisition	3
		6
(b)	Calculations: 1 mark for EPS, 1 mark each for P/E ratio for original offer, and for each of the three options for the proposed offer	5
(c)	Funding of bid: 1 mark for cash option, 1 mark for mixed option	2
	Earnings per share: 1 mark for share-for-share option, 2 marks for cash option, 2 marks for mixed option	5
	Gearing: 1 mark for each option	3
	Comments	4–5
		Max 14
		25

(a)   **Advantages of the acquisition**

Louieed Co and Tidded Co appear to be a good strategic fit for a number of reasons. Louieed Co appears to have limited potential for further growth. Acquiring Tidded Co, a company with better recent growth, should hopefully give Louieed Co the impetus to grow more quickly.

Acquiring a company which has a specialism in the area of online testing will give Louieed Co capabilities quicker than developing this function in-house. If Louieed Co does not move quickly, it risks losing contracts to its competitors.

Acquiring Tidded Co will give Louieed Co access to the abilities of some of the directors who have led Tidded Co to becoming a successful company. They will provide continuity and hopefully will help integrate Tidded Co's operations successfully into Louieed Co. They may be able to lead the upgrading of Tidded Co's existing products or the development of new products which ensures that Louieed Co retains a competitive advantage.

It appears that Tidded Co's directors now want to either realise their investment or be part of a larger company, possibly because it will have more resources to back further product development. If Louieed Co does not pursue this opportunity, one of Louieed Co's competitors may purchase Tidded Co and acquire a competitive advantage itself.

There may also be other synergistic benefits, including savings in staff costs and other savings, when the two companies merge.

Disadvantages of the acquisition

It is not known what the costs of developing in-house capabilities will be. Although the process may be slower, the costs may be less and the process less disruptive to Louieed Co than suddenly adding on Tidded Co's operations.

It is not possible to tell which of Tidded Co's directors are primarily responsible for its success. Loss of the three directors may well represent a significant loss of its capability. This will be enhanced if the three directors join a competitor of Louieed Co or set up in competition themselves.

There is no guarantee that the directors who remain will fit into Louieed Co's culture. They are used to working in a less formal environment and may resent having Louieed Co's way of operating imposed upon them. This could result in departures after the acquisition, jeopardising the value which Tidded Co has brought.

Possibly Tidded Co's leadership in the online testing market may not last. If competitors do introduce major advances, this could mean that Tidded Co's current growth is not sustainable.

(b) **P/E ratio calculations**

Value of Louieed Co's share = $296m × 14/340m = $12.19

Value of Tidded Co share per original bid = $12.19 × (5/3) = $20.32

Tidded Co earnings per share = $128m/90 = $1.42

Tidded Co P/E ratio implied by original bid = $20.32/$1.42 = 14.3

Tidded Co P/E ratio implied by all Tidded Co's shareholders taking up the share offer = $12.19 × 2/$1.42 = 17.2

Tidded Co P/E ratio implied by mixed cash and share offer = ($22.75 × 0.4 + $12.19 × 2 × 0.6)/$1.42 = 16.7

Tidded Co P/E ratio implied by all Tidded Co's shareholders taking up the cash offer = $22.75/$1.42 = 16.0

(c) **Funding of bid**

No extra finance will be required if all Tidded Co's shareholders take up the share offer.

All Tidded Co's shareholders take up cash offer

Cash required = 90m × $22.75 = $2,048m
Extra debt finance required = $2,048m – $220m – $64m = $1,764m

60% share-for-share offer, 40% cash offer
Cash required = 40% × 90m × $22.75 = $819m
Extra debt finance required = $819m – $220m – $64m = $535m

Impact of bid on earnings per share (EPS)

Louieed Co's EPS prior to acquisition = $296m/340 = $0.87

All Tidded Co's shareholders take up share offer
Number of shares after acquisition = 340m + (90m × 2) = 520m
EPS after acquisition = ($296m + $128m + $20m)/520m = $0.85

All Tidded Co's shareholders take up cash offer
Number of shares after acquisition = 340m
EPS after acquisition = ($296m + $128m + $20m – $11.36m – $105.84m)/340m = $0.96

$105.84m is the post-tax finance cost on the additional loan finding required of $1,764m. Therefore $1,764m × 7.5% × 80% = $105.84m.

$11.36m is the post-tax opportunity cost of lost interest on the cash and cash equivalents surpluses of the two companies of $220m + $64m = $284m. Therefore $284m × 5% × 80% = $11.36m.

60% share-for-share offer, 40% cash offer
Number of shares after acquisition 340m + (90m × 2 × 0.6) = 448m
EPS after acquisition = ($296m + $128m + $20m – $11.36m – $32.1m)/448m = $0.89

$32.1m is the post-tax finance cost on the additional loan funding required of $535m. Therefore $535m $\times$ 7.5% $\times$ 80% = $32.1m.

Impact of bid on gearing (using market values)

Louieed Co's gearing (debt/(debt + equity)) prior to bid = 540/(540 + (340 $\times$ 12.19)) = 11.5%

All Tidded Co's shareholders take up share offer
Debt/(Debt + equity) after bid = (540 + 193)/(540 + 193 + (520 $\times$ $0.85 $\times$ 14)) = 10.6%

All Tidded Co's shareholders take up cash offer
Debt/(Debt + equity) after anticipated bid = (540 + 193 + 1,764)/(540 + 193 + 1,764 + (340 $\times$ $0.96 $\times$ 14)) = 35.3%

60% share-for-share offer, 40% cash offer
Debt/(Debt + equity) after bid = (540 + 193 + 535)/(540 + 193 + 535 + (448 $\times$ $0.89 $\times$ 14)) = 18.5%

Comments

The calculations suggest that if Tidded Co's shares are acquired on a share-for-share exchange on the terms required by its shareholders, Louieed Co's shareholders will suffer a fall in EPS attributable to them from $0.87 to $0.85. This is because Tidded Co is being bought on a higher P/E ratio than Louieed Co and the synergies arising from the acquisition are insufficient to compensate for this.

Use of loan finance to back a cash offer will attract tax relief on interest. The cost of debt will be lower than the cost of equity.

Issuing extra shares will lead to a dilution of the power of Louieed Co's existing shareholders. If all of Tidded Co's shareholders take up the share-for-share offer, they will hold around one-third of the shares of the combined company (180m/520m) and this may be unacceptable to Louieed Co's shareholders.

The benefits which Tidded Co's shareholders will gain will be fixed if they take up a cash offer and do not acquire shares in the combined company. If there are significant gains after the acquisition, these will mostly accrue to Louieed Co's existing shareholders if a significant proportion of Tidded Co's shareholders have taken a cash offer.

If the forecast for take-up of the offer is correct, even by combining the cash flows of the two companies, the new company will have insufficient funds to be able to pay all the shareholders who are expected to take up the cash offer. Further finance will be required.

The alternative to loan finance is financing the bid by issuing shares. Depending on the method used, this may also result in dilution of existing shareholders' ownership and also there is no guarantee that the issue will be successful.

There is also no guarantee that the forecast of 40% of the shareholders taking up the cash offer is correct. If all five of the major shareholders decide to realise their investment rather than just two, this will increase the cash required by $512 million (25% $\times$ $22.75 $\times$ 90m), for example.

Gearing will increase if loan finance is needed to finance the cash offer. If the mixed share and cash offer is taken up in the proportions stated, the gearing level of the combined company will increase from 11.5% to 18.5%. Current shareholders may not be particularly concerned about this. However, if all or most of the share capital is bought for cash, the gearing level of the combined company will be significantly greater, at a maximum of 35.3%, than Louieed Co's current gearing. This may be unacceptable to current shareholders and could mean an increase in the cost of equity, because of the increased risk, and also possibly an increase in the cost of debt, assuming in any case that debt finance at the maximum level required will be available. To guard against this risk, Louieed Co's board may want to limit the cash offer to a certain percentage of share value.

34 Makonis

Marking scheme

			Marks
(a)	Market values of Makonis Co and Nuvola Co	1	
	Combined company asset beta	1	
	Combined company equity beta	1	
	Combined company: cost of capital	1	
	Combined company value: Years 1 to 4	3	
	Combined company value: Years 5 to perpetuity	1	
	Combined company value: value to equity holders and additional value	2	
	Comment and discussion of assumptions	3–4	
			Max 13
(b)	Impact on Makonis Co's equity holders if the premium paid to Nuvola Co's equity holders is 30%	2	
	Impact on Makonis Co's equity holders if the premium paid to Nuvola Co's equity holders is 50%	2	
	Impact	1	
			5
(c)	Impact on the cash payable under each of 30% and 50% premiums	3	
	Discussion of how Makonis Co would pay the high premium	4–5	
			Max 7
			25

(a) **Combined company, cost of capital**

Asset beta

$(1.2 \times 480 + 0.9 \times 1,218)/(480 + 1,218) = 0.985$

Equity beta

$0.985 \times (60 + 40 \times 0.8)/60 = 1.51$

Cost of equity

$2\% + 1.51 \times 7\% = 12.57\%$

Cost of capital

$12.57\% \times 0.6 + 4.55\% \times 0.8 \times 0.4 = 9.00\%$

Combined company equity value

Year

	1	2	3	4
	$m	$m	$m	$m
Free cash flows before synergy (growing at 5%)	226.80	238.14	250.05	262.55
Synergies	20.00	20.00	20.00	20.00
Free cash flows	246.80	258.14	270.05	282.55
PV of free cash flows at 9%	226.42	217.27	208.53	200.17

(**Note.** The present value (PV) figures are slightly different if discount table factors are used, instead of formulae. Full credit will be given if discount tables are used to calculate PV figures.)

Total PV of cash flows (Years 1 to 4) = $852.39 million

Total PV of cash flows (Years 5 to perpetuity) = $262.55 \times 1.0225/(0.09 - 0.0225) \times (1.09$ to the power of $-4) = \$2,817.51$ million

Total value to firm = $3,669.90 million

Value attributable to equity holders = $3,669.90 million $\times$ 0.6 = $2,201.94 million

Additional value created from the combined company = $2,201.94 million − ($1,218 million + $480 million) = $2,201.94 million − $1,698.00 million = $503.94 million (or 29.7%)

Although the equity beta and therefore the risk of the combined company is more than Makonis Co on its own, probably due to Nuvola Co's higher business risk (reflected by the higher asset beta), overall the benefits from growth in excess of the risk-free rate and additional synergies have led to an increase in the value of the combined company of just under 30% when compared to the individual companies' values.

However, a number of assumptions have been made in obtaining the valuation, for example:

- The assumption of growth of cash flows in perpetuity and whether this is realistic or not

- Whether the calculation of the combined company's asset beta when based on the weighted average of market values is based on good evidence or not

- It has been assumed that the figures such as growth rates, tax rates, free cash flows, risk-free rate of return and risk premium are accurate and do not change in the future

In all these circumstances, it may be appropriate to undertake sensitivity analysis to determine how changes in the variables would impact on the value of the combined company, and whether the large increase in value is justified.

(b)   If 30% premium is paid to Nuvola Co's equity holders, they will receive = 30% $\times$ $480 million = $144 million of the additional value created.

Makonis Co's equity holders will receive about $359.94 million or $1.71 per share of the additional value created, which is 29.5% of the current share price.

If 50% premium is paid to Nuvola Co's equity holders, they will receive = 50% $\times$ $480 million = $240 million of the additional value created.

Makonis Co's equity holders will receive about $263.94 million or $1.26 per share of the additional value created, which is 21.7% of the current share price.

Hence, Makonis Co's equity holders will receive almost 8% less return if a premium of 50% were paid.

(c)   One Makonis Co share for two Nuvola Co shares implies a premium of $0.50 ([$5.80 − $4.80]/2) per Nuvola Co share.

If a 30% premium is offered to Nuvola Co's equity holders, then they will expect $144 million premium or $0.72 per share, and therefore the cash paid will be $0.22 for each Nuvola Co share or $44 million in total.

If a 50% premium is offered to Nuvola Co's equity holders, then they will expect $240 million premium or $1.20 per share, and therefore the cash paid will be $0.70 per Nuvola Co share or $140 million in total.

The amount of cash required will increase substantially, by about $96 million, if Makonis Co agrees to the demands made by Nuvola Co's equity holders and pays the 50% premium. Makonis Co needs to determine how it is going to acquire the additional funds and the implications from this. For example, it could borrow the money required for the additional funds, but taking on more debt may affect the cost of capital and therefore the value of the company. It could raise the funds by issuing more equity shares, but this may not be viewed in a positive light by the current equity holders.

Makonis Co may decide to offer a higher proportion of its shares in the share-for-share exchange instead of paying cash for the additional premium. However, this will affect its equity holders and dilute their equity holding further. Even the current proposal to issue 100 million new shares will mean that Nuvola Co's equity holders will own just under one-third of the combined company and Makonis Co's shareholders would own just over two-thirds of the combined company.

Makonis Co should also consider what Nuvola Co's equity holders would prefer. They may prefer less cash and more equity due to their personal tax circumstances but, in most cases, cash is preferred by the target firm's equity holders.

35 Vogel

Text references. Acquisitions are covered in Chapters 9 and 10.

Top tips. Part (a) of this question is straightforward and this tempted a lot of candidates to choose this question. However, part (a) is only worth four marks. Be careful to read all parts of a question before choosing it; parts (b) and (c) of this question were not easy!

Easy marks. You should be able to pick up some relatively straightforward marks in part (a) by outlining the motives for an acquisition strategy.

Examining team's comments. This was a popular question with the first part of the question answered well by the majority of the candidates, but parts (b) and (c) were answered less well. It seems that many candidates chose this question because they liked the first part of the question, without considering the subsequent parts.

In part (c) there was little coherent presentation and structure to the answer, with many numbers and calculations presented in a haphazard manner. This approach did not gain many marks as it was not clear where the answer was heading and gave little confidence that the candidate knew what they were doing.

Marking scheme

		Marks
(a)	1–2 marks per point	Max 4
(b)	2–3 marks per point	Max 7
(c)	Cash gained from sales of Department C assets	1
	Calculation of free cash flows for Ndege Co	2
	Calculation of present values of Ndege Co cash flows and value	2
	Vogel Co P/E ratios before and after acquisition	2
	Tori Co P/E ratio and value	1
	Value created from combining Department A with Vogel Co	1
	Maximum premium payable	1
	Approach taken	1–2
	Assumptions made	2–3
		Max 14
		25

(a) Vogel Co may have switched from a strategy of organic growth to one of growth by acquisition, if it was of the opinion that such a change would result in increasing the value for the shareholders.

Acquiring a company to gain access to new products, markets, technologies and expertise will almost certainly be quicker and may be less costly than developing these internally. Horizontal acquisitions may help Vogel Co eliminate key competitors and thereby reduce rivalry and possible overcapacity in its industry; they may also have enabled Vogel Co to take advantage of economies of scale and to compete against large rivals. Vertical acquisitions may help Vogel Co to secure the supply chain and maximise returns from its value chain.

Organic growth may take a long time, can be expensive and may result in little competitive advantage being established due to the time taken. Also organic growth, especially into a new area, would need managers to gain knowledge and expertise of an area or function, which they are not currently familiar with. Furthermore, in a saturated market, there may be little opportunity for organic growth.

(**Note.** Credit will be given for alternative relevant comments.)

(b) Vogel Co can take the following actions to reduce the risk that the acquisition of Tori Co fails to increase shareholder value.

Since Vogel Co has a poor track record of adding value from its acquisitions it needs to review recent acquisitions to understand why they have not added value ie it should do a post-audit of these acquisitions.

Vogel Co should also ensure that the valuation is based on reasonable input figures and that proper due diligence of the perceived benefits is undertaken prior to the offer being made. Often it is difficult to get an accurate picture of the target when looking at it from the outside. Vogel Co needs to ensure that it has sufficient data and information to enable a thorough and sufficient analysis to be undertaken.

The sources of synergy need to be properly assessed to ensure that they are achievable and to identify what actions Vogel Co needs to undertake to ensure their achievement. Targets should be set for all areas of synergy and responsibility for achieving these targets should be clearly allocated to members of Vogels' senior management team.

The board of directors of Vogel Co needs to ensure that there are good reasons to undertake the acquisition, and that the acquisition should result in an increase in value for the shareholders. The non-executive directors should play a crucial role in ensuring that acquisitions are made to enhance the value for the shareholders. Procedures need to be established to ensure that the acquisition is not overpaid. Vogel Co should determine the maximum premium it is willing to pay and not go beyond that figure. Research indicates that often too much is paid to acquire a company and the resultant synergy benefits are not sufficient to cover the premium paid. Often this is the result of the management of the acquiring company wanting to complete the deal at any cost, because not completing the deal may be perceived as damaging to both their own, and their company's, reputation. Vogel Co needs to ensure that it has proper procedures in place to integrate the staff and systems of the target company effectively, and also to recognise that such integration takes time. Vogel Co may decide instead to give the target company a large degree of autonomy and thus make integration less necessary; however, this may result in a reduction in synergy benefits.

Vogel Co should also have strategies in place to retain key staff in the companies that it is acquiring – these people need to be identified at an early stage and given assurances over their role and responsibilities post-acquisition. Vogel Co should also be mindful that its own and the acquired company's staff and management need to integrate and ensure a good working relationship between them.

(**Note.** Credit will be given for alternative relevant comments.)

(c) **Approach taken**

The maximum premium payable is equal to the maximum additional benefit created from the acquisition of Tori Co, with no increase in value for the shareholders of Vogel Co. It should be noted that the shareholders of Vogel Co would probably not approve of the acquisition if they do not gain from it, but certainly they would not approve a bid in excess of this.

The additional benefit can be estimated as the sum of the cash gained (or lost) from selling the assets of Department C, spinning off Department B and integrating Department A, less the sum of the values of Vogel Co and Tori Co as separate companies.

Estimation of cash gained from selling the assets of Department C:

Non-current assets = (20% × $98.2m)	= $19.64m
Current assets = (20% × $46.5m × 0.9)	= $8.37m
Liabilities and closure costs = ($20.2 + $3m)	= $23.2m
Total $19.64m + $8.37m − $23.2m	= **$4.81m**

Value created from spinning off Department B into Ndege Co

Free cash flow of Ndege Co	$m
Current share of PBDIT (0.4 × $37.4m)	14.96
Less PBIT attributable to Department C (10% × 14.96)	(1.50)
Less tax-allowable depreciation (0.4 × 98.2 × 0.10)	(3.93)
Profits before tax	9.53
Tax (20%)	(1.91)
Free cash flows	7.62

Value of Ndege Co =
Present value of $7.62m free cash flow growing at 20% in the first year and discounted at 10%:
$7.62m × 1.2 × 0.909 = $8.31m
Add present value of cash flows from Year 2 onwards:
($9.14m × 1.052)/(0.1 − 0.052) × 0.909 = $182.11m
Less bond taken over by Ndege = $40m
Value to shareholders of Ndege Co = 8.31 + 182.11 − 40 = **$150.42m**

Current values

Vogel Co's current value = $3 × 380m = $1,140m
Vogel Co, profit after tax = $158.2m × 0.8 = $126.56m
Vogel Co, P/E ratio before acquisition = $1,140.0m/$126.56m = 9.01 say 9
Vogel Co, P/E ratio after acquisition = 9 × 1.15 = 10.35
Tori Co, P/E ratio before acquisition = 9 × 1.25 = 11.25

Tori Co post-tax profit = $23m × 0.8 = $18.4m
Tori Co's current value = 11.25 × $18.4m = $207.0m

Value created from combined company

Post-acquisition 50% of Tori's earnings will remain after the disposal of Department C and the spin-off of Department B. So earnings will become:

$126.56m + (0.5 × $18.4m) + $7m synergy) = $142.76m

So the combined company should be worth the P/E of 10.35 × $142.76m = $1,477.57m.

Maximum premium =

	$m
Value of combined firm	1,477.57
Value of Ndege	150.42
Value for disposal of C	4.81
Less current value ($1,140m + $207.0m)	1,347
	285.80

Assumptions

Based on the calculations given above, it is estimated that the value created will be $285.80m.

However, Vogel Co needs to assess whether the numbers it has used in the calculations and the assumptions it has made are reasonable. For example, Ndege Co's future cash flows seem to be growing without any additional investment in assets and Vogel Co needs to establish whether or not this is reasonable. It also needs to establish how the increase in its P/E ratio was determined after acquisition.

Perhaps sensitivity analysis would be useful to show the impact on value changes, if these figures are changed. Given its poor record in generating value previously, Vogel Co needs to pay particular attention to these figures.

36 AIR

> **Text references.** Financial reconstruction is covered in Chapter 13 and management buyout issues in Chapter 14.
>
> **Top tips.** Don't fall into the trap of discussing the advantages and disadvantages of buyouts; the question asked for an assessment of the financing mix.
>
> **Easy marks.** It's best to do the calculations first, but don't spend more than around ten minutes on them. That should give you enough to make sufficient reasonable points in the discussion to pass. Part (c) should also provide some easy marks.

(a)   **Financing mix**

If the airport can be purchased for $35 million, **the financing mix** is proposed as:

Equity: 50 cents ordinary shares

	$m
8 million purchased by managers and employees	4
2 million purchased by ER	1
EPP Bank: secured floating rate loan at LIBOR + 3%	20
AV: mezzanine debt with warrants (balancing figure)	10
Total finance	35

Up to $15 million of the mezzanine debt is available, which could be used to replace some of the floating rate loan. However, this possibility has been rejected because its cost is 18% compared with 13% and the warrants, if exercised, could dilute the manager/employee shareholding.

Leveraged buyout

A **leveraged buyout** of the type proposed allows managers and employees to own 80% of the equity while only contributing $4 million out of $35 million capital (11%). However, it is important that the managers and employees agree on the company's strategy at the outset. If the shareholders break into rival factions, **control** over the company might be **difficult to exercise**. It would be useful to know the disposition of shareholdings among managers and employees in more detail.

Gearing

The initial **gearing** of the company will be extremely **high**: the **debt to equity ratio** is 600% ($30 million debt to $5 million equity). Clearly one of the main medium-term goals following a leveraged buyout is to **reduce gearing** as rapidly as possible, sacrificing high dividend payouts in order to repay loans. For this reason EPP Bank, the major creditor, has imposed a covenant that capital gearing (debt/equity) must be reduced to 100% within four years or the loan will be called in.

Repayment of mezzanine finance

The gearing will be reduced substantially by steady repayment of the unsecured mezzanine finance. This carries such a **high interest** rate because it is a very risky investment by the venture capital company AV. A premium of 5% over secured debt is quite normal. The debt must be repaid in 5 equal annual instalments; that is, $2 million each year. If profits dip in any particular year, AIR might experience cash flow problems, necessitating some **debt refinancing**.

Warrants

If the **warrants** attached to the mezzanine debt are exercised, AV will be able to purchase 1 million new shares in AIR for $1 each. This is a cheap price considering that the book value per share at the date of buyout is $3.50 ($35m/10 million shares). The **ownership** by managers and staff will be **diluted** from 80%

to approximately 73%, with ER holding 18% and AV holding 9%. This should not affect management control provided that managers and staff remain as a unified group.

(b)   **Gearing at period end**

Using these assumptions and ignoring the possible issue of new shares when warrants are exercised, the **gearing** at the end of 4 years is predicted to be 132%, which is **significantly above the target** of 100% needed to meet the condition on EPP's loan. If warrants are exercised, $1 million of new share capital will be raised, reducing the Year 4 gearing to 125%, still significantly above the target.

No dividends

A key assumption behind these predictions is that **no dividends are paid** over this period. This may not be acceptable to managers or employees. It is also assumed that cash generated from operations is sufficient to repay $2 million of mezzanine debt each year, which is by no means obvious from the figures provided.

Increase in LIBOR

Results will be worse if **LIBOR rises** above 10% over the period. However, the purchase of the cap will stop interest payments on EPP's loan rising above 15%. Conversely if **LIBOR falls**, the **increase in profit** could be **considerable**, but it is still very unlikely that the loan condition will be met by Year 4.

Problems in meeting loan condition

There will therefore definitely be a problem in meeting EPP Bank's loan conditions. However, if the company is still showing steady growth by Year 4, and there have been no problems in meeting interest payments, EPP Bank will probably **not exercise its right** to recall the loan. If the loan condition is predicted to be a problem, the directors of AIR could consider:

(i)   Aiming for **continuous improvement** in **cost effectiveness**

(ii)   **Renegotiating** the **central services** contract with ER, or providing central services in-house, in order to save costs

(iii) **Renegotiating** the **allowed gearing ratio** to a more realistic figure

(iv)   Going for further expansion after, say, one or two years (eg extension of a runway in order to handle long-haul flights) and financing this expansion with an **issue of equity funds**; however, this may affect control of the company

(v)   Looking **for possible alternative sources** of debt or equity finance if the EPP Bank loan is recalled, including the possibility of flotation on the stock market

Appendix

AIR: FORECAST STATEMENTS OF PROFIT OR LOSS FOR FIRST FOUR YEARS AND COMPUTATION OF DEBT/EQUITY GEARING RATIOS

	Estimates from				
	Year 0	*Year 1*	*Year 2*	*Year 3*	*Year 4*
	$'000	$'000	$'000	$'000	$'000
Landing fees	14,000				
Other revenues	8,600				
	22,600				
Labour	5,200				
Consumables	3,800				
Other expenses	3,500				
	12,500				

	Estimates from				
	Year 0	Year 1	Year 2	Year 3	Year 4
	$'000	$'000	$'000	$'000	$'000
Direct operating profit growing at 5% p.a.	10,100	10,605	11,135	11,692	12,277
Central services from ER		(3,000)	(3,150)	(3,308)	(3,473)
EPP loan interest at 13% on $20m		(2,600)	(2,600)	(2,600)	(2,600)
Mezzanine debt interest at 18%					
on $10m		(1,800)			
on $8m			(1,440)		
on $6m				(1,080)	
on $4m					(720)
Profit before tax		3,205	3,945	4,704	5,484
Tax at 33%		1,058	1,302	1,552	1,810
Profit after tax		2,147	2,643	3,152	3,674
Reserves b/f		0	2,147	4,790	7,942
Reserves c/f		2,147	4,790	7,942	11,616
Share capital + reserves		7,147	9,790	12,942	16,616
Total debt at end of year		28,000	26,000	24,000	22,000
Gearing: debt/equity		392%	266%	185%	132%

If warrants are exercised, $1 million of new share capital is issued, reducing the gearing at Year 4 to 22,000/17,616 = 125%.

Assumptions

(i) The **central services** will be **provided** by ER for the full four-year period.

(ii) **No dividend** will be paid during the first four years.

(iii) **Sufficient cash** will be **generated** to repay $2 million of mezzanine finance each year and to fund increased working capital requirements.

(iv) **LIBOR** is **assumed to remain at 10%**.

(v) Tax is payable one year in arrears.

(c) In order to decide whether the management buyout can be considered for a $10 million loan, the venture capital company would need the following information:

(i) The **purpose** of the buyout.

(ii) Full **details of the management team**, in order to evaluate expertise and experience and to check that there are no 'gaps' in the team.

(iii) The company's **business plan**, based on a realistic set of strategies (apparently most approaches to venture capital companies fail on this criterion).

(iv) **Detailed cash flow forecasts** under different scenarios for economic factors such as growth, and interest rates. Forecasts of profit and statements of financial position.

(v) Details of the **management team's investment** in the buy-out. Venture capital companies like to ensure that the team is prepared to back their idea with their own money.

(vi) Availability of **security** for the loan, including personal guarantees from the management team. Any other **'sweeteners'** that could be offered to the lender, such as warrants.

(vii) The possibility of appointing a representative of the venture capital company as a director of AIR.

37 Doric

Marking scheme

			Marks
(a)	1 mark per benefit discussed		Max 4
(b)	Calculation of funds used to pay proportion of liabilities	2	
	Comment	1	
			3
(c)	Calculation of funds required from MBO	4	
	Calculation of value of the business	4	
	Discussion	2–3	
			Max 10
(d)	Seeking buyers	4–5	
	Due diligence	3–4	
			Max 8
			25

(a)   There are a number of possible benefits from disposing of a division through an MBO. These include: It may be the **fastest way of raising funds** compared to other divestment methods. It is likely that there would be **less resistance from the managers** and employees which would make a smoother process. It may also offer a **better price** to the selling company as the current management has knowledge of the division and is able to make it successful. Costs associated with an MBO may be less than other methods.

(b)   If the company is closed, the net proceeds will be:

	$m
Sale of all assets	210
Less redundancy and other costs	(54)
Net proceeds from sale of all assets	156

Total liabilities are $280m.

Therefore liability holders will receive $0.56 per $1 owing to them ($156m/$280m). Shareholders will not receive anything.

(c)   If the fridges division is sold:

	$m
Sale of fridge division (2/3 × 210)	140
Redundancy and other costs (2/3 × 54)	(36)
Net proceeds from sale of all assets	104
Amount of current and non-current liabilities	280
Amount of MBO funds needed to pay current and non-current liabilities (280 – 104)	176
Amount of MBO funds needed to pay shareholders	60
Investment needed for new venture	50
Total funds required	286

Value of new company following buyout

	$m
Sales revenue	170.0
Costs	(120.0)
Profits before depreciation	50.0
Depreciation (((1/3 × 100m) + 50m) × 10%) *	(8.3)
Profits before tax	41.7
Tax at 20%	(8.3)
Cash flows before interest payments *	33.4

* It has been assumed that depreciation is available on the revalued non-current assets plus the new investment. It is also assumed that no further investment in non-current assets or working capital is needed.

Estimated value based on cash flows in perpetuity = $33.4m × $\dfrac{1.035}{(0.11 - 0.035)}$ = $461m

This is about 61% over and above the funds invested in the new venture and therefore the MBO is likely to be beneficial. However, this assessment is based on estimates. Small changes in variables, particularly the growth rate, will have a large impact on the value. The assumption of growth in perpetuity may not be accurate either. Sensitivity analysis should be performed before a final decision is made.

(d)   The search for a potential buyer will either involve an **open tender** or the use of an **intermediary**. It may be that a single bidder is sought or maybe Doric Co will look to have an auction of the business among interested parties. Potential purchasers may be found amongst industry competitors as well as Doric Co's suppliers and distributors. A good deal of discretion will be needed to protect the value of the business for sale from adverse competitive action. If this did not happen a dominant competitor in the industry could start a price war which would reduce prices and also the value of the division prior to them making a bid.

Once a potential purchaser is found, it will want to conduct its own **due diligence** to ensure that **everything is as expected** / as it has been told. Access should be given to the potential purchaser for this, including up to date accounts and any legal documentation relating to the assets to be transferred. Doric Co should also perform some due diligence, on the ability of the potential purchaser to complete the transaction. It is necessary to establish how it will be able to finance the purchase and the timescale involved in obtaining this finance. Doric Co's lawyers will also need to assess any possible contractual issues relating to the sale, the transfer of employment rights, the transfer of intellectual property and any rights and responsibilities that will remain with Doric Co.

A sale price is likely to be **negotiated** and should be negotiated in a way that will maximise the return to Doric. **Professionals** should be used to conduct the negotiations and they must be fully informed of the situation around the sale, including any conditions and legal requirements. The consideration for the sale, the title deeds of the assets and terms for the transfer of staff and any accrued employment benefits (such as pension rights) will be **subject to agreement**.

38 Flufftort

> **Text references.** Financial reconstruction is covered in Chapter 13.
>
> **Easy marks.** You should be able to pick up some relatively easy marks in part (b). This required an evaluation of the acceptability of the financing scheme to all parties. There were up to two marks per well-explained point. This should have picked up the breach of a loan covenant in part (a)(i) as well as issues relating to control and risk.
>
> **Examining team's comments.** In part (a), it is worth reminding candidates that occasionally, as in this part of the question, there are marks available for relatively straightforward calculations without needing to apply complex techniques.

			Marks
(a)	(i)	**SOFP if shares purchased and cancelled**	
		Cash and other assets	2
		Equity	1
		Liabilities	1
			4
	(ii)	**SOFP if full refinancing takes place**	
		Cash and other assets	2
		Equity	1
		Liabilities	1
			4
	(iii)	20X7 forecast	2
		20X8 forecast	2
			4
(b)		Up to 2 marks for each well-discussed point	Max 13
			25

(a) (i) **Statement of financial position (SOFP) if Gupte VC shares are purchased by Flufftort Co and cancelled**

	$m
Assets	
Non-current assets	69
Current assets excluding cash	18
Cash	–
Total assets	87
Equity and liabilities	
Share capital	40
Retained earnings	5
Total equity	45
Long-term liabilities	
Bank loan	30
Loan note	5
Total long-term liabilities	35
Current liabilities	7
Total liabilities	42
Total equity and liabilities	87

(ii) **SOFP if full refinancing takes place**

	$m
Assets	
Non-current assets	125
Current assets excluding cash	42
Cash (balancing figure)	5
Total assets	172
Equity and liabilities	
Share capital	90
Retained earnings	5

		$m
Total equity		95
Long-term liabilities		
Bank loan		65
Loan note		–
Total long-term liabilities		65
Current liabilities		12
Total liabilities		77
Total equity and liabilities		172

(iii) **Projected SOPL**

	20X7	20X8
	$m	$m
Operating profit	20.0	25.0
Finance cost	(6.5)	(6.5)
Profit before tax	13.5	18.5
Taxation 20%	(2.7)	(3.7)
Profit after tax	10.8	14.8
Dividends	–	–
Retained earnings	10.8	14.8

(b) **Current situation**

Initial product developments have not generated the revenues required to sustain growth. The new Easicushion chair appears to offer Flufftort Co much better prospects of commercial success. At present, however, Flufftort Co does not have the resources to make the investment required.

Purchase of Gupte VC's shares

In the worst case scenario, Gupte VC will demand repayment of its investment in a year's time. The calculations in (a) show the financial position in a year's time, assuming that there is no net investment in non-current assets or working capital, the purchase of shares is financed solely out of cash reserves and the shares are cancelled. Repayment by this method would mean that the limits set out in the covenant would be breached (45/35 = 1.29) and the bank could demand immediate repayment of the loan.

The directors can avoid this by buying some of Gupte VC's shares themselves, but this represents money which is not being put into the business. In addition, the amount of shares which the directors would have to purchase would be greater if results, and therefore reserves, were worse than expected.

Financing the investment

The calculations in (a) show that the cash flows associated with the refinancing would be enough to finance the initial investment. The ratio of equity to non-current liabilities after the refinancing would be 1.46 (95/65), in line with the current limits in the bank's covenant. However, financing for the subsequent investment required would have to come from surplus cash flows.

Shareholdings

The disposition of shareholdings will change as follows:

	Current shareholdings		Shareholdings after refinancing	
	Million	%	Million	%
Directors	27.5	55.0	42.5	47.2
Other family members	12.5	25.0	12.5	13.9
Gupte VC	10.0	20.0	30.0	33.3
Loan note holder	–	–	5.0	5.6
	50.0	100.0	90.0	100.0

Gupte VC's percentage shareholding will rise from 20% to 33.3%, enough possibly to give it extra rights over the company. The directors' percentage shareholding will fall from 55% to 47.2%, which means that collectively they no longer have control of the company. The percentage of shares held by family members who are not directors falls from 25% to around 19.5%, taking into account the conversion of the loan note. This will mean, however, that the directors can still maintain control if they can obtain the support of some of the rest of the family.

Position of finance providers

The refinancing has been agreed by the Chief Executive and Finance Director. At present, it is not clear what the views of the other directors are, or whether the $15 million contributed by directors will be raised from them in proportion to their current shareholdings. Some of the directors may not be able to, or wish to, make a significant additional investment in the company. On the other hand, if they do not, their shareholdings, and perhaps their influence within the company, will diminish. This may be a greater concern than the board collectively losing control over the company, since it may be unlikely that the other shareholders will combine to outvote the board.

The other family shareholders have not been actively involved in Flufftort Co's management out of choice, so a reduction in their percentage shareholdings may not be an issue for them. They may have welcomed the recent dividend payment as generating a return on their investment. However, as they appear to have invested for the longer term, the new investment appears to offer much better prospects in the form of a capital gain on listing or buyout than an uncertain flow of dividends. The new investment appears only to have an upside for them in the sense that they are not being asked to contribute any extra funding towards it.

Rajiv Patel is unlikely to be happy with the proposed scheme. He is exchanging a guaranteed flow of income for an uncertain flow of future dividends sometime after 20X8. On the other hand, his investment may be jeopardised by the realisation of the worst case scenario, since his debt is subordinated to the bank's debt.

The most important issue from Gupte VC's viewpoint is whether the extra investment required is likely to yield a better outcome than return of its initial investment in a year's time. The plan that no dividends would be paid until after 20X8 is a disadvantage. On the other hand, the additional investment seems to offer the only prospect of realising a substantial gain by Flufftort Co being either listed or sold. The arrangement will mean that Gupte VC may be able to exercise greater influence over Flufftort Co, which may provide it with a greater sense of reassurance about how Flufftort Co is being run. The fact that Gupte VC has a director on Flufftort Co's board should also give it a clear idea of how successful the investment is likely to be.

The bank will be concerned about the possibility of Flufftort Co breaching the covenant limits and may be concerned whether Flufftort Co is ultimately able to repay the full amount without jeopardising its existence. The bank will be concerned if Flufftort Co tries to replace loan finance with overdraft finance. The refinancing provides reassurance to the bank about gearing levels and a higher rate of interest. The bank will also be pleased that the level of interest cover under the refinancing is higher and increasing (from 2.0 in 20X6 to 3.1 in 20X7 and 3.8 in 20X8). However, it will be concerned about how Flufftort Co finances the additional investment required if cash flows from the new investment are lower than expected. In those circumstances Flufftort Co may seek to draw on its overdraft facility.

Conclusion

The key players in the refinancing are Gupte VC, the bank and the directors other than the Chief Executive and the Finance Director. If they can be persuaded, then the scheme has a good chance of being successful. However, Rajiv Patel could well raise objections. He may be pacified if he retains the loan note. This would marginally breach the current covenant limit (90/70 = 1.29), although the bank may be willing to overlook the breach as it is forecast to be temporary. Alternatively, the refinancing would mean that Flufftort Co just had enough spare cash initially to redeem the loan note, although it would be more dependent on cash surpluses after the refinancing to fund the additional investment required.

39 BBS Stores

Marking scheme

		Marks	
(a)	Comparative statement of financial position under the two alternatives (2 each)	4	
	Revision of earnings figure for each alternative and calculation of EPS (3 each)	6	
	Discussion of the unbundling impact upon the statements of financial position and earnings	3	
			13
(b)	Ungearing of current beta and estimation of retail beta	2	
	Estimation of the cost of equity under each alternative	4	
	Estimation of the WACC under each alternative	2	
			8
(c)	Note on problems of taking property assets off the statement of financial position	2	
	Difficulty of predicting net impact of unbundling on shareholder value	2	
	Conclusion	2	
		Max	4
			25

(a) The proposal would involve the following:

	$m
Sell 50% of land and buildings	1,148.50
Sell 50% of assets under construction	82.50
	1,231.00

Impact on statement of financial position

Option 1 is the proposal to use the proceeds ($1,231m) to reduce medium-term borrowing and reinvest the balance in the business (non-current assets). The effect would be as follows:

	Borrowings and other financial liabilities $m	Property, plant and equipment $m	Sales proceeds received (used) $m
Balance at end 20X8 (before adjustment)	1,130	4,050	
Sales proceeds		(1,231)	1,231
Repayment of medium-term notes	(360)		(360)
Reinvestment in company		871	(871)
Balance after adjustment	770	3,690	Nil

Option 2 is the sale and rental scheme proposed by the company's investors on the assumption that this scheme would release substantial cash to them. The proposal would involve the repayment of the medium-term notes and the balance ($871m) used to execute a share buyback. This would involve ($871m/$4) **217.75m shares** with a nominal value of **$54.44m**.

	Borrowings and other financial requirements $m	Property, plant and equipment $m	Called-up share capital – equity $m	Retained earnings $m
Balance at end 20X8 (before adjustment)	1,130	4,050	425	1,535
Sales proceeds		(1,231)		
Repayment of medium-term notes	(360)			
Share buyback			(54.44)	(817)
Balance at end 20X8 after adjustment	770	2,819	370.56	718

Comparative statements of financial position

	20X8 (original) $m	Sales proceeds $m	Option 1 $m	Option 1 $m	Option 2 $m	Option 2 $m
Non-current assets						
Intangible	190			190		190
Property etc	4,050	(1,231)	871	3,690	(1,231)	2,819
Other	500			500		500
	4,740			4,380		3,509
Current assets	840	1,231	(1,231)	840		840
Total assets	5,580			5,220		4,349
Equity						
Called-up equity capital	425			425	(54)	371
Retained earnings	1,535			1,535	(817)	718
Total equity	1,960			1,960		1,089
Liabilities						
Current liabilities	1,600			1,600		1,600
Non-current liabilities						
Borrowings etc	1,130		(360)	770	(360)	770
Other	890			890		890
Total liabilities	3,620			3,260		3,260
Total liabilities and equity	5,580			5,220		4,349

Gearing is affected as follows:

	20X8 (Option 1)	20X8 (Option 2)	20X8 (before adjustment)
Long-term debt (borrowings and other financial liabilities)	770	770	1,130
Total capital employed (total assets – current liabilities)	3,620	2,749	3,980
Gearing ratio	21.27%	28.01%	28.39%

Gearing has been reduced substantially with Option 1. Whilst gearing is also reduced slightly under Option 2, it is considerably higher than the gearing ratio that would result from paying off the medium-term notes and reinvesting the balance in the company.

Impact on earnings per share (EPS)

Both options will result in a reduction in interest payable due to paying off the medium-term notes. In addition, credit spread on the 6-year debt would be reduced by 30 basis points with Option 1. The sale of the property would reduce property rent with both options. Under Option 1, the funds reinvested in the company would earn a return of 13%.

The total effect would be as follows:

	Current position $m	Option 1 $m	Option 2 $m
Earnings for 20X8	670.00	670.00	670.00
Add interest saved on medium-term notes (net of tax): $360m × 6.2% × 65% (interest is charged at LIBOR 5.5% + 70 basis points)		14.51	14.51
Add return on reinvested funds ($871m × 13% × 65%)		73.60	
Add reduction in credit spread on 6-year debt (0.3% × $770m × 65%)		1.50	
Less property rent forgone ($1,231m × 8% × 65%)		(64.01)	(64.01)
Adjusted earnings	670.00	695.60	620.50
Number of shares	1,700.00m	1,700.00m	1,482.00m
Adjusted EPS in cents per share	39.41	40.92	41.87

(b)   **Impact of unbundling on the company's WACC**

Our starting point for this part of the report is to estimate the asset beta for the retail part of the business.

Current k_e = 10.47% and the current WACC = 9.55%

There are 1,700m shares ($425/0.25) so V_e = 1,700 × 4 = $6,800m

V_d = $1,130m

We now ungear the current company beta using the formula:

$$\beta_a = \beta_e \times \frac{V_e}{V_e + V_d(1-T)} = 1.824 \times (6,800/(6,800 + 1,130(1 - 0.35)))$$

β_a = 1.646

The retail asset beta is the weighted average of the individual asset betas:

$$\beta_a = \left[\frac{V_R}{V_T} \times \beta_R \right] + \left[\frac{V_P}{V_T} \times \beta_P \right]$$

Where V_R = value of retail section β_R = asset beta of retail section

V_T = total value of business

β_P = asset beta of property section (this is calculated from the equity beta of other portfolio companies 1.25 × market gearing adjusted for tax of 0.5 = 0.625).

V_P = value of property

$$1.646 = \frac{4,338}{6,800} \times \beta_R + \frac{2,462}{6,800} \times 0.625$$

V_T = $4 × no of shares = $4 × (425m ÷ 0.25) = $6,800m

V_P = 2,297 + 165 = $2,462m

V_R = V_T − V_P = 6,800 − 2,462 = $4,338m

Rearranging the equation we find:

β_R = **2.225**

The asset beta of the company will be a combination of the retail beta (2.225) and the property beta (0.625). We can now calculate the cost of equity under each option.

Value of equity	Option 1	Option 2
	$= 425\text{m} \times 4 \times 4$ $= \$6{,}800\text{m}$	$[(425\text{m} \times 4) - 217.75\text{m}] \times 4$ $= \$5{,}929\text{m}$

The value of **property** (half of which is sold) is now $2,462m \times 0.5 = \$1,231$m

The remaining value of the equity (as above) is the value of the retail section (eg for **Option 1** 6,800 – 1,231 = 5,569, and for **Option 2** 5,929 – 1,231 = 4,698).

The average asset beta can now be calculated as a weighted average of the asset betas for property and retail as follows.

Average asset beta	Option 1	Option 2
	$\dfrac{5{,}569}{6{,}800} \times 2.225 + \dfrac{1{,}231}{6{,}800} \times 0.625$ $= 1.935$	$\dfrac{4{,}698}{5{,}929} \times 2.225 + \dfrac{1{,}231}{5{,}929} \times 0.625$ $= 1.893$

Now using $\beta_a = \beta_e \times \dfrac{V_e}{V_e + V_d(1-T)}$ we can find the equity beta for either option.

Equity beta (adjusted for gearing)	Option 1	Option 2
	$\beta_a = \beta_e \times \dfrac{6{,}800}{(6{,}800 + (770 \times 0.65))}$ $1.935 = \beta_e \times 0.931$ $\beta_e = 1.935/0.931 = 2.078$	$\beta_a = \beta_e \times \dfrac{5{,}929}{(5{,}929 + (770 \times 0.65))}$ $1.893 = \beta_e \times 0.922$ $\beta_e = 1.893/0.922 = 2.053$

Now the cost of equity can be calculated, as follows.

Cost of equity	Option 1	Option 2
	$5\% + (2.078 \times 3\%)$ $= 11.23\%$	$5\% + (2.053 \times 3\%)$ $= 11.16\%$

Option (1) WACC

$$= \left[\frac{6{,}800}{(6{,}800 + 770)} \times 11.23\%\right] + \left[\frac{770}{(6{,}800 + 770)} \times 5.9\% \times 0.65\right] = 10.48\%$$

(where 5.9% = LIBOR + 70bp – 30bp)

Option (2) WACC

$$= \left[\frac{5{,}929}{(5{,}929 + 770)} \times 11.16\%\right] + \left[\frac{770}{(5{,}929 + 770)} \times 6.2\% \times 0.65\right] = 10.34\%$$

Note that both options will increase the current WACC of 9.55% by a considerable margin.

(c) **Potential impact of each alternative on the market value of the firm**

It is difficult to assess the impact of unbundling on the value of BBS Stores. Although the equity beta will increase with the removal of part of the existing property portfolio, this will be countered by a reduction in gearing. We have assumed that the balance of $871 million in Option 1 could be reinvested at the current rate of return of 13%. If we fail to do so then shareholders' value will be significantly reduced. To reduce this risk, shareholders appear to favour Option 2 where they are guaranteed a cash return through a share buyback.

Whether the property is owned or leased should have no effect on the company's value if we can assume that the current use of the assets and the resultant value gained remain unchanged. If a separate property company can be set up we may be able to remove ownership from the statement of financial position. However, we must bear in mind that the ease with which this can be done will depend on accounting regulations in the country concerned.

A final observation is the assumption of a constant and known share price (400 cents). Share prices are not constant nor are they certain. In order to assess the potential impact of any movements in this variable, we should set up a simulation model and run the model for various share prices and equity betas.

40 Ennea

Text references. Chapter 1 for the role and responsibilities of management; Chapter 7a for sources of finance; Chapter 4a for securitisation.

Top tips. In part (a) it is important to include the discussion as well as the forecast statements of financial position and ratios. Don't state just what has happened, but also what this means for Ennea Co to get more marks.

Remember to relate the answer in part (b) to the scenario and the relatively small amount of finance makes a securitisation less likely to be appropriate.

Easy marks. There are some easy marks to be gained in part (a) in the forecasts under each of the three different proposals.

Examining team's comments. Part (a) revolved around the impact of changes in financing of a company and how the impact of changing financial structure affected the financial position, earnings per share and the gearing of the company.

The answers to this part tended to be varied. Candidates, who presented the changed financial position and calculated the changes in earnings for each proposal, which were then incorporated into the calculations of EPS and gearing, gained the majority of marks. However, overall this part of the question was not done well.

Many responses tended to discuss or try to explain the changes and therefore gained fewer marks. Many responses did not consider the impact on interest of increased or reduced debt financing, and therefore did not incorporate the impact into the profit after tax and the financial position. In a notable minority of responses, candidates did not calculate the earnings per share (EPS) and gearing correctly. Such responses gained few marks.

Part (b) tested what securitisation was and the key barriers to Ennea Co undertaking the process. This part was done poorly by most candidates. Few responses gave an adequate explanation of the securitisation process, often confusing it with what leasing was and/or assuming securitisation meant providing asset security or collateral for a loan. Very few responses considered the barriers to Ennea Co in any detail.

		Marks
(a)	Financial position calculations: proposal 1	3
	Financial position calculations: proposal 2	2
	Financial position calculations: proposal 3	3
	Adjustments to forecast earnings	
	Interest payable on additional borrowing and higher coupon	2
	Interest saved on lower borrowing and lower coupon	1
	Return on additional investment	1
	Return lost on less investment and profit on sale of non-current assets	1
	Gearing and EPS calculations	2
	Discussion of the results of the proposals	2–3
	Discussion of the implications (eg risk, market reaction)	2–3
		Max 20

(b)   Explanation of the process   2–3

           Key barriers in undertaking the process   2–3

                                                                   Max   5

                                                                                   25

(a)   **Forecast financial position**

	Current $'000	Proposal 1 $'000	Proposal 2 $'000	Proposal 3 $'000
Non-current assets	282,000	282,000	302,000	257,000
Current assets	66,000	64,720	67,720	63,682
Total assets	348,000	346,720	369,720	320,682
Current liabilities	37,000	37,000	37,000	37,000
Non-current liabilities	140,000	160,000	160,000	113,000
Total liabilities	177,000	197,000	197,000	150,000
Share capital (40c per share)	48,000	45,500	48,000	48,000
Retained earnings	123,000	104,220	124,720	122,682
Total equity	171,000	149,720	172,720	170,682
Total equity and capital	348,000	346,720	369,720	320,682

	Current $'000	Proposal 1 $'000	Proposal 2 $'000	Proposal 3 $'000
Initial profit after tax	26,000	26,000	26,000	26,000
Interest payable on additional borrowing ($20m × 6% × (1 – 0.2))		(960)	(960)	
Additional interest payable ($160m × 0.25% × (1 – 0.2))		(320)	(320)	
Interest saved on reduced borrowing ($27m × 6% × (1 – 0.2))				1,296
Interest saved on lower coupon ($113m × 0.15% × (1 – 0.2))				136
Return on additional investment ($20m × 15%)			3,000	
Return lost on reduced investment ($25m × 15%)				(3,750)
Profit on sale of non-current assets				2,000
Total assets	26,000	24,720	27,720	25,682
Gearing (non-current liabilities/non-current liabilities + equity)	45.0%	51.7%	48.1%	39.8%
Number of shares ('000)	120,000 ($48m/$0.4 per share)	113,750 ($20m/$3.2 = 6.25m shares bought back)	120,000	120,000
Adjusted EPS	21.67c	21.73c	23.10c	21.40c

Note. Other calculations of gearing would be acceptable.

> **Tutorial note.** These explanations are not required for the answer, but are presented here to aid understanding.

Explanations of figures above

Proposal 1

Non-current liabilities are increased by $20 million from the additional debt and capital is reduced by the same amount. Given that the share price is $3.20, the $20 million will buy back $20m / $3.20 = 6.25m shares. These shares have a nominal value of 6.25m × $0.4 = $2.5 million. The split between share capital and retained earnings will therefore be $2.5 million to share capital and the balance of $17.5 million to retained earnings (actually to the share premium account, but this is included in retained earnings for simplicity).

The additional interest payable of $1.28 million is taken off retained earnings due to the reduction in profit after tax and also deducted from cash as it is assumed to be paid in cash. It would be acceptable to include as a current liability if it was assumed to be unpaid.

Proposal 2

Non-current liabilities and non-current assets are increased by $20 million from the additional debt and purchase of assets. Additional interest is payable as for Proposal 1 and the new investment will generate an additional return of 15% which is $3 million in income. The net impact is income of $1.72 million, which is added to retained earnings and to current assets as it represents either cash or a receivable.

Proposal 3

Non-current assets are reduced by the net value at disposal ($25 million) and the proceeds of $27 million are used to reduce non-current liabilities. The profit of $2 million is added to retained earnings.

The reduction of investment in non-current assets means there will be a lower return on investment of 15% of the $25 million. However, interest will be saved on the non-current liabilities which will be paid off. The net impact is a loss of $2.318 million which is subtracted from retained earnings and deducted from current assets as a cash expense. Again it would be acceptable to include as a current liability if it was assumed to be unpaid.

Discussion

Proposal 1 would lead to a small increase in EPS, due to the reduction in the number of shares since earnings fall by about 5% because of the higher interest payments from the additional debt. However, gearing significantly increases by approximately 6%.

Under Proposal 3 EPS will fall, although total earnings will be higher than under Proposal 1. Total earnings fall because the interest saved and the profit on disposal are less than the loss of the return on the non-current asset investment. Gearing would also reduce significantly, by 5%.

Proposal 2 significantly increases EPS, which the other proposals do not. This is due to the return on the additional non-current asset investment. However, gearing will also increase by just over 3%, although this is less than under Proposal 1.

Proposal 1 is the least attractive. The choice between Proposals 2 and 3 will depend on whether the board of Ennea Co would prefer a higher EPS figure or a lower level of financial gearing. This may depend on industry averages for both of these figures, how the stock market would react to the proposals and the implications of the proposals on changes to the risk profile of the company and whether this would change the overall cost of capital. It should also be noted that the above forecasts and estimates and actual results may well differ from those stated.

(b) Asset securitisation for Ennea Co would involve converting the future lease income, from the non-current asset leases, into assets and **selling these assets as bonds** now. The future income is then used to pay the coupons on the bonds. In effect Ennea Co forgoes the interest payments on the leases in favour of the bond sale proceeds.

The lease income would be aggregated and pooled and new bonds would be created based on these. The pooled assets are divided into **tranches** and the tranches are **credit rated**. The higher rated tranches would carry less risk and also have a lower return than tranches with a lower rating. If default occurs, the income of the lower tranches gets reduced first and any subsequent default is applied to the lowest tranche with any income left. This process means an asset with a low level of liquidity can be transformed into a security with high liquidity.

There are a number of barriers to undertaking a securitisation process. It is **very expensive** due to management costs, legal fees and ongoing administration and compliance costs. Ennea Co is looking at selling a relatively small amount of non-current assets and therefore the costs would be a significant proportion of the potential income. This high cost means that securitisation is **not feasible for a small asset pool**.

It is usual to not offer the full value of the asset in the form of securities, but to leave say 10% of the asset value as a buffer against default and converting the other 90% into securities. The method of credit enhancement would give the tranches a **higher credit rating** and therefore **improve their marketability**. However, if Ennea Co was to use this method it would not be able to take advantage of the full value of the assets.

41 Nubo

Text references. Demergers are covered in Chapter 14 and Islamic finance is covered in Chapter 7a.

Easy marks. Part (c) offers easy marks if you answer both parts of the question.

Examining team's comments. Part (a) – many candidates made a reasonable attempt at calculating the financial impact of each of the two options but few candidates were then able to calculate the impact on the debt capacity and the additional funds available to the downsized company.

Part (b) – few candidates were able to give responses beyond a general discussion of demergers and many candidates did not relate their answers to the scenario. Very few candidates discussed the impact on the debt capacity for the downsized company if it undertook a demerger instead of a sale as its divestment option.

Part (c) – the discussion between using Musharaka and Mudaraba contracts was generally done well and it was pleasing to see that candidates had paid due attention to this area.

Marking scheme

		Marks
(a)	Sale of supermarkets division's assets	1
	Sale of supermarkets division as going concern	1
	Advice	2
	Extra cash after liabilities are paid	1
	Maximum debt which can be borrowed	1
	Additional funds available to Nubo Co	1
		7
(b)	1–2 marks per relevant point	Max 6
(c)	Discussion of why Ulap Bank might prefer a Musharaka contract	6–7
	Discussion of key concerns over the joint venture relationship	5–6
		Max 12
		25

(a) Current and non-current liabilities = $387m + $95m = $482m

Sale of assets of supermarkets division

Proportion of assets to supermarkets division
Non-current assets = 70% × $550m = $385m; Current assets = 70% × $122m = $85.4m

Sale of assets = $385m × 1.15 + $85.4m × 0.80 = $511.07m

Sale of supermarkets division as a going concern

Profit after tax attributable to the supermarkets division: $166m/2 = $83m

Estimate of value of supermarkets division based on the P/E ratio of supermarket industry: $83 × 7 = $581m

Although both options generate sufficient funds to pay for the liabilities, the sale of the supermarkets division as a going concern would generate higher cash flows and the spare cash of $99m [$581m – $482m] can be used by Nubo Co for future investments. This is based on the assumption that the value based on the industries' P/E ratios is accurate.

Proportion of assets remaining within Nubo Co

30% × ($550m + $122m) = $201.6m

Add extra cash generated from the sale of $99m

Maximum debt capacity = $300.6m

Total additional funds available to Nubo Co for new investments = $300.6m + $99m = $399.6m

(b)   A demerger would involve splitting Nubo Co into two separate companies which would then operate independently of each other. The equity holders in Nubo Co would continue to have an equity stake in both companies.

Normally demergers are undertaken to ensure that each company's equity values are fair. For example, the value of the aircraft parts production division based on the P/E ratio gives a value of $996m (12 × $83m) and the value of the supermarkets division as $581m. If the current company's value is less than the combined values of $1,577m, then a demerger may be beneficial. However, the management and shareholders of the new supermarkets company may not be keen to take over all the debt.

Nubo Co's equity holders may view the demerger more favourably than the sale of the supermarkets division. At present their equity investment is diversified between the aircraft parts production and supermarkets. If the supermarkets division is sold, then the level of their diversification may be affected. With the demerger, since the equity holders will retain an equity stake in both companies, the benefit of diversification is retained.

However, the extra $99m cash generated from the sale will be lost in the case of a demerger. Furthermore, if the new aircraft parts production company can only borrow 100% of its asset value, then its borrowing capacity and additional funds available to it for new investments will be limited to $201.6m instead of $399.6m.

(c)   With a Mudaraba contract, the profits which Pilvi Co makes from the joint venture would be shared according to a pre-agreed arrangement when the contract is constructed between Pilvi Co and Ulap Bank. Losses, however, would be borne solely by Ulap Bank as the provider of the finance, although provisions can be made where losses can be written off against future profits. Ulap Bank would not be involved in the executive decision-making process. In effect, Ulap Bank's role in the relationship would be similar to an equity holder holding a small number of shares in a large organisation.

With a Musharaka contract, the profits which Pilvi Co makes from the joint venture would still be shared according to a pre-agreed arrangement similar to a Mudaraba contract, but losses would also be shared according to the capital or other assets and services contributed by both parties involved in the arrangement. Therefore a value could be put to the contribution-in-kind made by Pilvi Co and any losses would be shared by Ulap Bank and Pilvi Co accordingly. Within a Musharaka contract, Ulap Bank can also take the role of an active partner and participate in the executive decision-making process. In effect, the role adopted by Ulap Bank would be similar to that of a venture capitalist.

With the Mudaraba contract, Pilvi Co would essentially be an agent to Ulap Bank, and many of the agency issues facing corporations would apply to the arrangement, where Pilvi Co can maximise its own benefit at the expense of Ulap Bank. Pilvi Co may also have a propensity to undertake excessive risk because it is essentially holding a long call option with an unlimited upside and a limited downside.

Ulap Bank may prefer the Musharaka contract in this case, because it may be of the opinion that it needs to be involved with the project and monitor performance closely due to the inherent risk and uncertainty of the venture, and also to ensure that the revenues, expenditure and time schedules are maintained within initially agreed parameters. In this way, it may be able to monitor and control agency related issues more effectively and control Pilvi Co's risky actions and decisions. Being closely involved with the venture would change both Pilvi Co's and Ulap Bank's roles and make them more like stakeholders rather than principals and agents, with a more equitable distribution of power between the two parties.

Nubo Co's concerns would mainly revolve around whether it can work with Ulap Bank and the extra time and cost which would need to be incurred before the joint venture can start. If Pilvi Co had not approached Ulap Bank for funding, the relationship between Nubo Co and Pilvi Co would be less complex within the joint venture. Although difficulties may arise about percentage ownership and profit sharing, these may be resolved through negotiation and having tight specific contracts. The day to day running, management and decision-making process could be resolved through negotiation and consensus. Therefore having a third party involved in all aspects of the joint venture complicates matters.

Nubo Co may feel that it was not properly consulted about the arrangements between Pilvi Co and Ulap Bank, and Pilvi Co would need to discuss the involvement of Ulap Bank with Nubo Co and get its agreement prior to formalising any arrangements. This is to ensure a high level of trust continues to exist between the parties, otherwise the venture may fail.

Nubo Co may want clear agreements on ownership and profit-sharing. It would want to ensure that the contract clearly distinguishes it as not being part of the Musharaka arrangement which exists between Pilvi Co and Ulap Bank. Hence negotiation and construction of the contracts may need more time and may become more expensive.

Nubo Co may have felt that it could work with Pilvi Co on a day to day basis and could resolve tough decisions in a reasonable manner. It may not feel the same about Ulap Bank initially. Clear parameters would need to be set up on how executive decision making will be conducted by the three parties. Therefore, the integration process of bringing a third partner into the joint venture needs to be handled with care and may take time and cost more money. The above issues would indicate that the relationship between the three parties is closer to that of stakeholders, with different levels of power and influence, at different times, as opposed to a principal–agent relationship. This would create an environment which would need ongoing negotiation and a need for consensus, which may make the joint venture hard work. Additionally, it would possibly be more difficult and time consuming to accomplish the aims of the joint venture.

(**Note.** Credit will be given for alternative relevant comments and suggestions for parts (b) and (c) of the question.)

42 Bento

Text references. MBOs are covered in Chapter 14.

Easy marks. Part (a) offers easy marks if you address the question accurately.

Examining team's comments. In part (b) few candidates could apply the annuity factor to calculate the annual amount payable. Instead they opted to do it on a straight-line basis but this ignored the time value of money. However, a good number of responses then structured the profit or loss statement appropriately to take account of interest, tax and dividends, to get to the retained earnings figures. Nonetheless, some responses did not do this and therefore kept the book value of equity unchanged, casting doubt about whether or not they understand the relationship between the profit or loss statement and the statement of financial position.

In part (c), candidates were asked to assess whether or not the MBO was beneficial. Although not specified in the requirements, the appropriate way to assess benefit was to compare the value of the investment, the MBO in this case, with the cost of that investment, the price to be paid for the MBO. This part of the question was not done well.

		Marks
(a)	Distinguish between an MBI and an MBO	2
	Discuss the relative benefits and drawbacks	4
		Max 5
(b)	Annual annuity on 8% bond	1
	Split between interest and capital repayment	2
	Operating profit for the first 4 years	1
	Finance costs	2
	Tax and dividend payable for the first 4 years (1 mark each)	2
	Book values of debt and equity in Years 1 to 4	2
	Gearing and concluding comment	2
		Max 12
(c)	Valuation methods (1 for net assets, 3 for dividend valuation)	4
	Discussion (1 to 2 marks per point)	4
		Max 8
		25

(a) An MBO involves the purchase of a business by the management team running that business. Hence, an MBO of Okazu Co would involve the takeover of that company from Bento Co by Okazu Co's current management team. However, an MBI involves purchasing a business by a management team brought in from outside the business.

The benefits of an MBO relative to an MBI to Okazu Co are that the existing management is likely to have detailed knowledge of the business and its operations. Therefore they will not need to learn about the business and its operations in a way which a new external management team may need to. It is also possible that an MBO will cause less disruption and resistance from the employees when compared to an MBI. If Bento Co wants to continue doing business with the new company after it has been disposed of, it may find it easier to work with the management team which it is more familiar with. The internal management team may be more focused and have better knowledge of where costs can be reduced and sales revenue increased, in order to increase the overall value of the company.

The drawbacks of an MBO relative to an MBI to Okazu Co may be that the existing management may lack new ideas to rejuvenate the business. A new management team, through their skills and experience acquired elsewhere, may bring fresh ideas into the business. It may be that the external management team already has the requisite level of finance in place to move quickly and more decisively, whereas the existing management team may not have the financial arrangements in place yet. It is also possible that the management of Bento Co and Okazu Co have had disagreements in the past and the two teams may not be able to work together in the future if they need to. It may be that an MBI is the only way forward for Okazu Co to succeed in the future.

(b) Annuity (8%, 4 years) = 3.312
Annuity payable per year on loan = $30,000,000/3.312 = $9,057,971
Interest payable on convertible loan, per year = $20,000,000 × 6% = $1,200,000

Annual interest on 8% bond

Year end	1	2	3	4
	$'000	$'000	$'000	$'000
Opening loan balance	30,000	23,342	16,151	8,385
Interest at 8%	2,400	1,867	1,292	671
Annuity	(9,058)	(9,058)	(9,058)	(9,058)
Closing loan balance	23,342	16,151	8,385	(2)*

*The loan outstanding in Year 4 should be zero. The small negative figure is due to rounding.

Estimate of profit and retained earnings after MBO

Year end	1	2	3	4
	$'000	$'000	$'000	$'000
Operating profit	13,542	15,032	16,686	18,521
Finance costs	(3,600)	(3,067)	(2,492)	(1,871)
Profit before tax	9,942	11,965	14,194	16,650
Taxation	(1,988)	(2,393)	(2,839)	(3,330)
Profit for the year	7,954	9,572	11,355	13,320
Dividends	(1,989)	(2,393)	(2,839)	(3,330)
Retained earnings	5,965	7,179	8,516	9,990

Estimate of gearing

Year end	1	2	3	4
	$'000	$'000	$'000	$'000
Book value of equity	15,965 *	23,144	31,660	41,650
Book value of debt	43,342	36,151	28,385	20,000
Gearing	73%	61%	47%	32%
Covenant	75%	60%	50%	40%
Covenant breached?	No	Yes	No	No

* The book value of equity consists of the sum of the 5,000,000 equity shares which Dofu Co and Okazu Co's senior management will each invest in the new company (total 10,000,000), issued at their nominal value of $1 each, and the retained earnings from Year 1. In subsequent years the book value of equity is increased by the retained earnings from that year.

The gearing covenant is forecast to be breached in the second year only, and by a marginal amount. It is forecast to be met in all the other years. It is unlikely that Dofu Co will be too concerned about the covenant breach.

(c) **Net asset valuation**

Based on the net asset valuation method, the value of the new company to its investors (debt holders plus equity holders) is approximately:

1.3 × $40,800,000 (market value of non-current assets) + $12,300,000 (current assets) – $7,900,000 approx. (trade and other payables) = $57,440,000.

The new company will have $50m of non-current liabilities so the value to equity investors will be $57,440,000 – $50,000,000 = $7,440,000.

Dividend valuation model

Year	Dividend	DF (12%)	PV
	$'000		$'000
1	1,989	0.893	1,776
2	2,393	0.797	1,907
3	2,839	0.712	2,021
4	3,330	0.636	2,118
Total			7,822

Annual dividend growth rate, Years 1 to 4 = (3,330/1,989)1/3 – 1 = 18.7%
Annual dividend growth rate after Year 4 = 7.5% [40% × 18.7%]
Value of dividends after Year 4 = ($3,330,000 × 1.075)/(0.12 – 0.075) × 0.636 = $50,594,000 approximately

Based on the dividend valuation model, the value of the equity in the new company is approximately: $7,822,000 + $50,594,000 = $58,416,000

The $60m asked for by Bento Co is payable as $50m of debt finance and $10m of equity; $10m is higher than the current value of the new company's net assets ($7.44m) but $10m is considerably lower than the value of the company based on the present value of future dividends based on the dividend valuation model ($58.4m).

It can be argued that the future growth potential of the company is better represented by the dividend valuation model, rather than the current value of the assets, so the price of $60m does not seem excessive.

However, the dividend valuation model can produce a large variation in results if the model's variables are changed by even a small amount. Therefore, the basis for estimating the variables should be examined carefully to judge their reasonableness, and sensitivity analysis applied to the model to demonstrate the impact of the changes in the variables. The value of the future potential of the new company should also be estimated using alternative valuation methods including free cash flows and price/earnings methods.

It is therefore recommended that the MBO should be accepted.

(**Note.** Credit will be given for alternative, relevant discussion for parts (a) and (c).)

43 Staple Group

Text references. Valuations are covered in Chapter 10, and reorganisations in Chapter 14.

Easy marks. Part (b) offers easy marks if you address both parts of the question.

Examining team's comments. A sizeable number of candidates attempted to value the whole of the company instead of parts of the company.

		Marks
(a)	Sale of Staple Local	
	Calculations/comments on figures	2
	Discussion of benefits/drawbacks	3–4
	Sale of Staple View	
	Calculations/comments on figures	3
	Discussion of benefits/drawbacks	3–4
	Sale of Staple Investor	
	Comments on figures	2
	Discussion of benefits/drawbacks	3–4
	Other points/conclusion	2–3
		Max 19
(b)	Discussion of importance of different stakeholders and possible conflicts	3–4
	Discussion of other ethical issues	2–3
		Max 6
		25

(a) **Staple Local**

Net assets valuation = 15/18 × $66.6m = $55.5m.

It is assumed that the titles in this division are equal in size.

The division's pre-tax profits are $4.5m and post-tax cash flows are $0.3m, with losses forecast for the next year. Therefore any valuation based on current or future expected earnings is likely to be lower than the net assets valuation.

Benefits of selling Staple Local

The local newspapers seem to have the poorest prospects of any part of the group. Further investment may not make a big difference, if the market for local newspapers is in long-term decline.

The offer from Postway Co gives Staple Group the chance to gain cash immediately and to dispose of the papers. The alternative of selling the titles off piecemeal is an uncertain strategy, both in terms of the timescale required and the amounts which can be realised for individual titles. It is very likely that the titles with the best prospects would be sold first, leaving Staple Group with a remaining portfolio which is of very little value.

Drawbacks of selling Staple Local

The offer is not much more than a net asset valuation of the titles. The amount of cash from the sale to Postway Co will be insufficient for the level of investment required in the *Daily Staple*.

The digital platforms which will be developed for the *Daily Staple* could also be used to boost the local papers. Staff on the local titles could have an important role to play in providing content for the platforms.

Loss of the local titles may mean loss of economies of size. In particular, printing arrangements may be more economic if both national and local titles are printed at the same locations.

Staple View

Free cash flows to equity = $53.5m – $12.5m – $6.2m = $34.8m

Free cash flow valuation to equity = $34.8m (1.04)/(0.12 – 0.04) = $452.4m

The assumption of constant growth is most important in this valuation. It is possibly fairly conservative but, just as faster growth could be achieved by gaining the rights to broadcast more sporting events, results may be threatened if Staple View loses any of the rights which it currently has.

Benefits of selling Staple View

Present circumstances may be favourable for selling the television channels, given their current profitability. Staple Group may be able to obtain a better offer from a competitor than in the future, given recent acquisition activity in this sector.

Selling Staple View will certainly generate more cash than selling either of the smaller divisions. This will allow investment not only in the *Daily Staple*, but also in the other divisions, and possibly targeted strategic acquisitions.

Drawbacks of selling Staple View

The television channels have become a very important part of Staple Group. Investors may believe that the group should be focusing on further investment in this division rather than investing in the *Daily Staple*, which may be in decline.

Selling the television channels removes an important opportunity for cross-selling. Newspaper coverage can be used to publicise important programmes on the television channels and the television channels can be used for advertising the newspaper.

Staple View is a bigger part of the group than the other two divisions and therefore selling it is likely to mean a bigger reduction in the group's borrowing capacity.

Staple Investor

The valuation made by the Finance Director is questionable as it is based on one year's profits, which may not be sustainable. There is no information about how the additional earnings have been calculated whether the Finance Director has used a widely accepted method of valuation or just a best estimate. If a premium for additional earnings is justified, there is also no information about whether the benefit from staff's expertise and experience is assumed to be perpetual or just to last for a certain number of years.

Benefits of selling Staple Investor

This division appears to have great potential. Staple Group will be able to sell this division from a position of strength, rather than it being seen as a forced sale like selling the Staple Local division might be.

The division is in a specialist sector which is separate from the other areas in which Staple Group operates. It is not an integral part of the group in terms of the directors' current core strategy.

Drawbacks of selling Staple Investor

The division currently has the highest profit margin at 19.7% compared with Staple National (12.5%), Staple Local (3.0%) and Staple View (14.8%). It seems likely to continue to deliver good results over the next few years. Investors may feel that it is the part of the group which offers the safest prospect of satisfactory returns.

Investors may be happy with the structure of the group as it is, as it offers them some diversification. Selling the Staple Investor division and focusing more on the newspaper parts of the group may result in investors seeking diversification by selling some of the shareholding in Staple Group and investing elsewhere.

Although Staple Group's management may believe that the valuation gives a good indication of the division's true value, they may not be able to sell the division for this amount now. If the division remains within the group, they may achieve a higher price in a few years' time. Even if Staple Investor could be sold for the $118.5 million valuation, this is less than the $150 million required for the planned investment.

Conclusion

Selling the Staple View division offers the directors the best chance to obtain the funds they require for their preferred strategy of investment in the *Daily Staple*. However, the directors are not considering the possibility of selling the *Daily Staple*, perhaps in conjunction with selling the local newspapers as well. Although this could be seen as selling off the part of the group which has previously been essential to its success, it would allow Staple Group to raise the funds for further investment in the television channels and the Staple Investor division. It could allow the directors to focus on the parts of the group which have been the most successful recently and offer the best prospects for future success.

(b) **Stakeholder conflicts**

If Staple Group takes a simple view of the role of stakeholders, it will prioritise the interest of shareholders over other stakeholders, particularly employees here, and take whatever actions are required to maximise profitability. However, in Staple Group's position, there may be a complication because of the differing requirements of shareholders. Some may want high short-term profits and dividends, which may imply significant cost cutting in underperforming divisions. Other shareholders may wish to see profits maximised over the long term and may worry that short-term cost cutting may result in a reduction of investment and adversely affect staff performance at an important time.

Transformational change of the newspaper business is likely to require the co-operation of at least some current employees. Inevitably redundancy will create uncertainty and perhaps prompt some staff to leave voluntarily. Staple Group's management may want to identify some key current employees who can lead the change and try to retain them.

Also the policy of making employees who have not been with the group very long redundant is likely to make it difficult to recruit good new employees. The group will probably create new roles as a result of its digital investment, but people may be unwilling to join the group if it has a reputation for bad faith and not fulfilling promises to develop its staff.

Ethical issues

The significance of what the firm's annual report says about its treatment of employees may depend on how specific it is. A promise to treat employees fairly is rather vague and may not carry much weight, although it broadly commits the firm to the ethical principle of objectivity. If, however, the policy makes more specific statements about engaging with employees and goes further in the statement beyond what is required by law, then Staple Group is arguably showing a lack of honesty if it does not fulfil the commitments it has made.

The suggestion that managers should ensure that employees who are perceived to be 'troublemakers' should be the first to be chosen for redundancy is dubious ethically. If managers do this, then they may be breaking the law, and would certainly be acting with a lack of honesty and transparency.

44 Retilon

Marking scheme

			Marks	
(a)	(i)	Calculation of net receipts/payments	1	
		Forward market hedge calculations	2	
		Money market hedge – two-month payment calculation	2	
		Money market hedge – three-month payment calculation	2	
		Money market hedge – three-month receipt calculation	2	
		Type of futures contract	1	
		No of contracts	1	
		Calculation of gain/loss on future	2	
		Net position on futures	2	
				15
	(ii)	Calculation of Day 1	2	
		Calculation of Day 2	1	
		Calculation of Day 3	1	
				4
(b)		Advantages of forward contracts	Max 2	
		Disadvantages of forward contracts	Max 2	
		Advantages of currency futures	Max 2	
		Disadvantages of currency futures	Max 2	
			Max 6	
				25

(a) (i)

	Receipts	Payments
Two months		€393,265
Three months	Kr8.6m	491,011 + 890,217 − 60,505 − 1,997,651 = €676,928

Forward market hedge

Two months

Payment $\dfrac{€393,265}{1.433}$ = £274,435

Three months

Payment $\dfrac{€676,928}{1.431} = £473,045$

Receipt $\dfrac{Kr8,600,000}{10.83} = £794,090$

Money market hedge

(1) **Two months payment**

We need to invest now to match the €393,265 we require.

The interest rates are quoted per year so they need to be adjusted to become 2-month rates – this means multiplying the annual rate of 3.5% by 2/12, which gives 0.5833%.

Amount to be invested = €393,265/(1 + 0.005833)
= €390,984

Converting at spot rate $\dfrac{390,984}{1.439} = £271,705$

To obtain £271,705, we have to borrow for 2 months.

Again, the interest rates are quoted per year so they need to be adjusted to become 2-month rates, so 7.5% × 2/12 = 1.25%.

Amount to be paid to lender = 271,705 × 1.0125
= £275,101

(2) **Three months payment**

Again we need to invest and the interest rates are quoted per year so they need to be adjusted to become 3-month rates, so 3.5% × 3/12 = 0.875%.

Amount to be invested = €676,928/(1 + 0.00875) = €671,056

Converting at spot rate $\dfrac{671,056}{1.439} = £466,335$

Borrowing £466,335 for 3 months

Again, the interest rates are quoted per year so they need to be adjusted to become 3-month rates, so 7.5% × 3/12 = 1.875%.

Amount to be paid to lender = 466,335 × (1 + 0.01875)
= £475,079

(3) **Three months receipt**

The interest rates are for borrowing over 3 months – this means multiplying the annual rate of 8% by 3/12, which gives 2%.

We need to borrow now to match the receipt we shall obtain.

Amount to be borrowed = 8,600,000/1.02
= Kr8,431,373

Converting at spot rate $\dfrac{8,431,373}{10.71} = £787,243$

Investing in the UK for 3 months will be at a rate of 5.5% × 3/12 = 1.375%.

Amount to be received = 787,243 × 1.01375
= £798,068

Futures – 2 months

- Buy June futures as they mature just after the payment date

- Buy euro futures

- Number of contracts = $\dfrac{€393,265}{125,000}$ = 3.146 (say 3 contracts)

- Tick size = 125,000 × 0.0001 = £12.50

Set up today (20 April)

1 Euros of cover needed =   393,265

2 Contract size   125,000
   Number of contracts   3 contracts

3 June future: Buy euros at 0.6964

Outcome (20 June)

4 **Actual transaction at June spot rate**

   Actual cover (393,265)

   Spot rate 1.433   £(274,435)

   Compare to April spot (1.439)

   = £273,291 ∴ bad news in June

5 **Futures – profit or loss**

   April – to buy   0.6964
   June – to sell   0.6978 (1)
                       0.0014 profit (14 ticks)

   Profit per contract = £12.50 × 14 = £175
   Total profit (3 × 175)   = £525

6 **Net position**

   Actual   £(274,435)
   Future   525
                              £(273,910)

(1)

	End of April	*End of June*
June future	0.6964	0.6978
Spot (1/1.433)	0.6978	0.6978
Basis	(0.0014)	NIL
	2 months' timing difference	0 months remaining

Alternative solution

Effective futures rate = opening futures price – closing basis

= 0.6964 – 0 = 0.6964

€393,265 × 0.6964 = (£273,870)

This solution is slightly less accurate (because it ignores the fact that the actual transaction and the amount hedged on the futures markets are in fact based on slightly different amounts) but is acceptable under exam conditions.

For the 3-month payment

- Buy September futures as they mature just after the payment date
- Buy euro futures
- Number of contracts = 676,928 ÷ 125,000 = 5.4 (say 5 contracts)
- Tick size = 125,000 × 0.0001 = £12.50

Set up today (20 April)

1 Euros needed = 676,928

2 Contract size €125,000

Number of contracts = $\dfrac{676,928}{125,000}$

$\approx$ 5 contracts

3 September future: Buy euros at 0.6983

Outcome (20 July)

4 **Actual transaction at July spot rate**

€676,928 @ 1.431 = £(473,045)

Compare to April spot:

€676,928 @ 1.439 =

= £470,416 ∴ bad news in July

5 **Profit or loss**

April – to buy   0.6983

July – to sell   0.7002 (1)

0.0019 profit

Profit per contract = 19 ticks × £12.50

= £237.50

Total profit   = £237.50 × 5

= £1,187.50

6 **Net position**

Actual transaction at
July spot rate   £(473,045)

Future   1,188

£(471,857)

(1)

	End of April		End of July	
September future	0.6983		0.7002	
Spot (1/1.439)	0.6949		0.6988	(1/1.431)
	0.0034	× 2/5 =	0.0014	
	5 months' timing difference		2 months' timing difference	

Alternative solution

Effective futures rate = opening futures price – closing basis

= 0.6983 – 0.0014 = 0.6969

€676,928 × 0.6969 = (£471,751)

This solution is slightly less accurate (because it ignores the fact that the actual transaction and the amount hedged on the futures markets are in fact based on slightly different amounts) but is acceptable under exam conditions.

Conclusion

For the three-month Kr receipt, the money market will maximise cash flow. For the two euro payments, the futures market should maximise cash flow assuming basis risk is negligible. If basis risk does have a significant impact, the forward market may be the best choice.

(ii) **Day 1** movement 0.6930 – 0.6916 = 14 ticks loss. Extra payment of £175 (14 × £12.50) is required. If the extra payment is not made, the contract will be closed out. Therefore:

Day 2 movement 0.6944 – 0.6930 = 14 ticks loss, extra payment of £175.

Day 3 movement 0.6940 – 0.6944 = 4 ticks profit. Profit = 4 × £12.50 = £50; this can be taken in cash.

(b) **Advantages of forward contracts**

(i) The contract can be tailored to the user's **exact requirements** with quantity to be delivered, date and price all flexible.

(ii) The trader will **know in advance** how much money will be received or paid.

(iii) **Payment** is **not required** until the contract is settled.

Disadvantages of forward contracts

(i) The user may not be able to negotiate **good terms**; the price may depend upon the **size** of the **deal** and how the user is rated.

(ii) Users have to **bear** the **spread** of the contract between the buying and selling price.

(iii) Deals can only be **reversed** by going back to the original party and offsetting the original trade.

(iv) The **creditworthiness** of the other party may be a problem.

Advantages of currency futures

(i) There is a **single specified price** determined by the market, and not the negotiating strength of the customer.

(ii) **Transactions costs** are generally **lower** than for forward contracts.

(iii) The exact date of **receipt** or **payment** of the currency does not have to be **known**, because the futures contract does not have to be closed out until the actual cash receipt or payment is made.

(iv) **Reversal** can easily take place in the market.

(v) Because of the process of **marking to market**, there is no default risk.

Disadvantages of currency futures

(i) The **fixing** of **quantity** and **delivery dates** that is necessary for the future to be traded means that the customer's risk may not be fully covered.

(ii) Futures contracts may not be **available** in the **currencies** that the customer requires.

(iii) **Volatile trading conditions** on the futures markets mean that the potential loss can be high.

45 Kenduri

Text references. Hedging foreign currency transactions is covered in Chapter 16. Gamma is covered in Chapter 17.

Top tips. In part (b) make sure you don't confuse payments and receipts in your matrix. Also it was important to read the scenario carefully to see that the spot mid-rate should be used, rather than any other rate.

For part (c) don't waste time if you don't know what a gamma value is.

Easy marks. There are some easy marks to be gained in part (a) for money market hedging and forward market calculations as these should be brought forward knowledge from FM.

Examining team's comments. For part (a), in many cases the advice was limited to a recommendation but without proper justification, and therefore few marks were gained.

Answers to part (c) were poor and few candidates were aware of what gamma is and what a high gamma meant in relation to a long call option. There also appeared to be some confusion about what a long call meant. A long call is buying the right to buy an underlying asset at a predetermined price, whereas a short call is selling the right to buy an underlying asset at a predetermined price (and similarly for put options).

			Marks
(a)	Calculation of net US$ amount	1	
	Calculation of forward market US$ amount	1	
	Calculation of US$ money market amount	2	
	Calculation of one put option amount (1.60 or 1.62)	3	
	Calculation of the second put option amount or if the preferred exercise price is explained	2	
	Advice and recommendation	3–4	
			Max 12
(b)	Construction of the transactions matrix	1	
	Calculation of the £ equivalent amounts of US$, CAD and JPY	4	
	Calculation of the net receipt/payment	2	
	Explanation of government reaction to hedging	3	
			10
(c)	1 mark per valid point	Max	3
			25

(a) Only transactions between Kenduri Co and Lakama Co are relevant, which are:

Payment of $4.5 million
Receipt of $2.1 million
Net payment = $2.4 million

The hedging options are: using the forward market, money market hedging and currency options.

Forward market

As selling £ for $, receive at lower rate.
2,400,000/1.5996 = £1,500,375

Money market hedge

Invest US$ now: 2,400,000/(1 + 0.031/4) = $2,381,543
Converted at spot: 2,381,543/1.5938 = £1,494,255
Borrow in £ now: 1,494,255 × (1 + 0.04/4) = £1,509,198

The forward market is cheaper and therefore is preferred.

Options

Kenduri would buy sterling put options to protect against a depreciating £.

Exercise price $1.60/£1

£ payment = 2,400,000/1.6 = £1,500,000
1,500,000/62,500 = 24 contracts
24 3-month put options purchased
Premium = 24 × 0.0208 × 62,500 = $31,200
Premium in £ = 31,200/1.5938 = £19,576
Total payments = 1,500,000 + 19,576 = £1,519,576

Exercise price $1.62/£1

£ payment = 2,400,000/1.62 = £1,481,481
1,481,481/62,500 = 23.7 contracts
23 3-month put options purchased
£ payment = 23 × 62,500 = £1,437,500
Premium = 23 × 0.0342 × 62,500 = $49,163

Premium in £ = 49,163/1.5938 = £30,846
Unhedged amount = 2,400,000 – (1,437,500 × 1.62) = $71,250
Hedging using forward market = 71,250/1.5996 = £44,542
Total payments = 1,437,500 + 30,846 + 44,542 = £1,512,888

Both options hedges are worse than using the forward or money markets as a result of the premiums payable for the options. However, options have an advantage over forwards and money markets because the prices are not fixed and the buyer can let the option lapse if exchange rates move favourably. Therefore the options have a limited downside, but an unlimited upside. Only with options can Kenduri Co take advantage of the $ weakening against the £.

Conclusion

The forward market is preferred to the money market hedge. The choice between options and forwards will depend on whether management wants to risk the higher cost for the potential upside if exchange rates move in Kenduri Co's favour.

(b)   Spot mid-rates are as follows:

US$1.5950/£1
CAD 1.5700/£1
JPY 132.75/£1

Paying subsidiary

Receiving subsidiary	UK £'000	US £'000	Canada £'000	Japan £'000	Total receipts (add across) £'000	Total payments (add down) £'000	Net receipt / (payment) £'000
UK	–	1,316.6	2,165.6	–	3,482.2	3,521.9	(39.7)
US	2,821.3	–	940.4	877.7	4,639.4	3,727.1	912.3
Canada	700.6	–	–	2,038.2	2,738.8	3,106.0	(367.2)
Japan	–	2,410.5	–	–	2,410.5	2,915.9	(505.4)

Kenduri Co will make a payment of £39,700 to Lakama Co.
Jaia Co will make a payment of £367,200 to Lakama Co.
Gochiso Co will make a payment of £505,400 to Lakama Co.

Multilateral netting will minimise the number of transactions taking place through the banks of each country. This limits the amount paid in fees to these banks. Governments which do not allow multilateral netting are therefore looking to **maximise the transactions and fees** that the local banks will receive. Other countries may choose to allow multilateral netting in the belief that this makes them more attractive to multinational companies and the lost banking fees are **more than compensated for** by the extra business brought to the country.

(c)   Gamma measures the **rate of change of the delta** of an option. Deltas can be near zero for a long call option which is deep out-of-the-money, where the price of the option will be insensitive to changes in the price of the underlying asset. Deltas can also be near 1 for a long call option which is deep in-the-money, where the price of the option and the value of the underlying asset move mostly in line with each other. When a long call option is at-the-money, the delta is 0.5 but also changes rapidly. Therefore, the **highest gamma values are when a call option is at-the-money**. Gamma values are also higher when the option is closer to expiry. In this case, it appears that the option is trading near at-the-money and that it has a relatively short period before expiry.

46 Massie

Marking scheme

				Marks
(a)	(i)	Dollar amounts owed and owing		2
		Totals owed and owing		3
		Net amounts owed		1
		Payments and receipts		2
				8
	(ii)	1–2 marks per problem discussed	Max	3
(b)		Recommendation to purchase calls		1
		Number and month of contracts		1
		Calculation of basis		1
		Options contracts calculations		4
		(only one option contract needs to be used, with a justification for choosing this exercise price, lose 1 mark if no justification)		
		Collars approach and calculations		5
		Comments and conclusion		2–3
			Max	14
				25

(a) (i)

Owed by	Owed to	Local currency (m)	$m
Armstrong (US)	Horan (South Africa)	US$12.17	12.17
Horan (South Africa)	Massie (Europe)	SA R42.65	3.97
Giffen (Denmark)	Armstrong (US)	D Kr21.29	3.88
Massie (Europe)	Armstrong (US)	US$19.78	19.78
Armstrong (US)	Massie (Europe)	€1.57	2.13
Horan (South Africa)	Giffen (Denmark)	D Kr16.35	2.98
Giffen (Denmark)	Massie (Europe)	€1.55	2.11

Owed to			Owed by		
	Giffen (De) $m	Armtg (US) $m	Horan (SA) $m	Massie (Eu) $m	Total $m
Giffen (De)			2.98		2.98
Armtg (US)	3.88			19.78	23.66
Horan (SA)		12.17			12.17
Massie (Eu)	2.11	2.13	3.97		8.21
Owed by	(5.99)	14.30	(6.95)	(19.78)	
Owed to	2.98	23.66	12.17	8.21	
Net	(3.01)	9.36	5.22	(11.57)	

Under the terms of the arrangement, Massie, as the company with the largest debt, will pay Horan $5.22m, as the company with the smallest amount owed. Then Massie will pay Armstrong $6.35m and Giffen will pay Armstrong $3.01m.

(ii) The Armstrong Group may have problems if any of the governments of the countries where the subsidiaries are located object to multilateral netting. However, this may be unlikely here.

The new system may not be popular with the management of the subsidiaries because of the length of time before settlement (up to six months). Not only might this cause cash flow issues for the subsidiaries, but also the length of time may mean that some of the subsidiaries face significant foreign exchange risks. The system may possibly have to allow for immediate settlement in certain circumstances, for example, if transactions are above a certain size or if a subsidiary will have significant cash problems if amounts are not settled immediately.

(b) Need to hedge against a fall in interest rate, therefore buy call options. Require 50 contracts $(25,000,000/1,000,000) \times 6/3$.

As Massie is looking to invest on 30 November, December contracts are needed.

Basis
Futures price – current price (1 September) = basis
$95.76 – (100 – 3.6) = –0.64$
Unexpired basis = $\frac{1}{4} \times 0.64 = –0.16$

Option
Amount received will be $(LIBOR – 0.4\%) \times 25,000,000 \times 6/12$

If interest rates increase by 0.5% to 4.1%
Expected futures price = $(100 – 4.1) – 0.16 = 95.74$

Exercise price	97.00	96.50
Futures price	95.74	95.74
Exercise option?	No	No
Gain in basis points	–	–
	€	€
Interest received $(€25m \times 6/12 \times (4.1 – 0.4)\%)$	462,500	462,500
Gain on options	–	–
Premium		
$(3.2 \times €25 \times 50)$	(4,000)	
$(18.2 \times €25 \times 50)$		(22,750)
Net receipt	458,500	439,750
Effective interest rates	3.67%	3.52%

Alternative solution:

Exercise rate (100 – price)	3%	3.5%
Futures rate (100 – price)	4.26%	4.26%
Exercise option?	No	No
Gain in %	–	–
	%	%
Interest received $(4.1 – 0.4)\%$	3.7	3.70
Gain on options	–	–
Premium		
	(0.032)	(0.182)
Effective interest rates	3.668%	3.518%
Net receipt (€25m × effective interest rate × 6/12)	458,500	439,750

If interest rates fall by 0.5% to 3.1%

Expected futures price = (100 − 3.1) − 0.16 = 96.74

Exercise price	97.00	96.50
Futures price	96.74	96.74
Exercise option?	No	Yes
Gain in basis points	–	24
	€	€
Interest received		
(€25m × 6/12 × (3.1 − 0.4)%)	337,500	337,500
Gain on options		
(0 and 24 × €25 × 50)	–	30,000
Premium		
(3.2 × €25 × 50)	(4,000)	
(18.2 × €25 × 50)		(22,750)
Net receipt	333,500	344,750
Effective interest rates	2.67%	2.76%

Alternative solution:

Exercise rate (100 − price)	3%	3.5%
Futures rate (100 − price)	3.26%	3.26%
Exercise option?	No	Yes
Gain in %	–	0.24%
	%	%
Interest received		
(3.1 − 0.4)%	2.7	2.70
Gain on options	–	0.24
Premium		
	(0.032)	(0.182)
Effective interest rates	2.668%	2.758%
Net receipt (€25m × effective interest rate × 6/12)	333,500	344,750

Using a collar

Buy December call at 97.00 for 0.032 and sell December put at 96.50 for 0.123. Net premium received = 0.091.

If interest rates increase to 4.1%

	Buy call	Sell put
Exercise price	97.00	96.50
Futures price	95.74	95.74
Exercise option?	No	Yes
Gain in basis points	–	
	€	
Interest received	462,500	
Loss on exercise		
(76 × €25 × 50)	(95,000)	
Premium		
(9.1 × €25 × 50)	11,375	
Net receipt	378,875	
Effective interest rates	3.03%	

Alternative solution:

Futures rate	4.26%
Exercise call option at 3%?	No
Exercise put option at 3.5%?	Yes
Loss on option (futures rate 4.26 – 3.5% put rate)	(0.76)%

	%
Interest received (4.1 – 0.4)%	3.7
Loss on options	(0.76)
Premium (cost of call – revenue from put)	0.091
Effective interest rates	3.031%
Net receipt (€25m × effective interest rate × 6/12)	378,875

If interest rates fall to 3.1%

	Buy call	Sell put
Exercise price	97.00	96.50
Futures price	96.74	96.74
Exercise option?	No	No
Gain in basis points	–	

	€
Interest received	337,500
Loss on exercise	–
Premium (9.1 × €25 × 50)	11,375
Net receipt	348,875
Effective interest rates	2.79%

Alternative solution:

Futures price	3.26%
Exercise call option at 3%?	No
Exercise put option at 3.5%?	No

	%
Interest received (3.1 – 0.4)%	2.7
Premium (cost of call – revenue from put)	0.091
Effective interest rates	2.791%
Net receipt (€25m × effective interest rate × 6/12)	348,875

Summary

	97.00	96.50	Collar
Interest rates rise to 4.1%	3.67%	3.52%	3.03%
Interest rates fall to 3.1%	2.67%	2.76%	2.79%

The collar gives a significantly worse result than either of the options if interest rates rise, because Massie cannot take full advantage of the increase. It is marginally the better choice if interest rates fall.

The recommendation would be to choose the option with the 97.00 exercise price, which has a cheaper premium, unless interest rates are virtually certain to fall.

47 KYT

Text references. Foreign exchange hedging is covered in Chapter 16, interest rate hedging is covered in Chapter 17.

Top tips. Part (a) is what can be generally expected from a futures currency hedging calculation question; make sure that you read all of the information and be careful not to make any basic errors with the calculations.

Easy marks. Part (c) is a fairly straightforward discussion requirement that could be attempted without having completed parts (a) or (b) first.

(a) (i) KYT can **hedge using futures** as follows:

- Use September futures, since these expire soon after 1 September, price of 1/0.007985 = 125.23 ¥/$.

- **Buy** futures, since it wishes to acquire yen to pay the supplier, and the futures contracts are in yen.

- Number of contracts 140m/12.5m = 11.2 contracts ~ 11 contracts

- Tick size

  0.000001 × 12.5m = $12.50

(ii) **Basis risk** arises from the fact the price of a futures contract may not move as expected in relation to the value of the instrument being hedged. Basis changes do occur and thus represent potential profits/losses to investors. Typically, this risk is much smaller than the risk of remaining unhedged.

Basis is the **difference between the spot and futures prices**.

Spot price = 1/128.15
            = 0.007803

Basis = futures rate – spot rate = 0.007985 – 0.007803 = 182 ticks with 3 months to expiry

Basis with one month to expiry, assuming uniform reduction = $\frac{1}{3} \times 182$ = 61 ticks

Spot price on 1 September = 1/120 = 0.008333

Therefore predicted futures price = 0.008333 + 0.000061 = 0.008394

(iii) **Outcome**

Futures market

Opening futures price	0.007985
Closing futures price	0.008394
Movement in ticks	409 ticks

Futures market profit 409 × 11 × $12.50 = $56,238

Net outcome

	$
Spot market payment (¥140m/120)	(1,166,667)
Futures market profit	56,238
	(1,110,429)

Hedge efficiency

The spot rate has moved against KYT. At the original spot rate the payment would have been 140m/128.15 = 1,092,470 which means that the spot rate has moved against KYT by $74,197 (ie 1,166,667 – 1,092,470). The efficiency of the hedge is therefore:

$$\frac{56,238}{74,197} = 76\%$$

This hedge is not perfect because there is **not** an **exact match** between the exposure and the number of contracts, and because the **spot price** has moved more than the futures price due to the reduction in basis. The actual outcome is likely to differ since basis risk does not decline uniformly in the real world.

(b)   **Interest rate futures**

Hedging

A future is an agreement on the future price of a variable. Hedging with futures offers protection against **adverse movements in the underlying asset**; if these occur they will more or less be offset by a gain on the futures market. The person hedging may be worried about **basis risk**, the risk that the futures price may move by a different amount from the underlying asset being hedged.

Terms

The **terms, sums involved and periods** are **standardised** and hedge inefficiencies will be caused by either having too many contracts or too few, and having to consider what to do with the unhedged amount.

Deposit

Futures require the payment of a **small deposit**; this transaction cost is likely to be lower than the premium for a tailored forward rate agreement or any type of option.

Timescale

The majority of futures are taken out to **hedge borrowing** or **lending** for short periods.

Interest rate options

Guaranteed amounts

The main advantage of options is that the buyer cannot lose on the interest rate and can take advantage of any favourable rate movements. An interest rate option provides the **right to borrow a specified amount** at a **guaranteed rate of interest**. On the date of expiry of the option the buyer must decide **whether or not to exercise their right to borrow**. They will only exercise the option if actual interest rates have risen above the option rate.

Premium cost

However, a premium must be paid regardless of whether or not the option is exercised, and the **premium cost** can be quite **high**, high enough not to make an option worthwhile if interest rate movements are expected to be marginal.

Types of option

Options can be **negotiated directly** with the bank (over the counter, OTC) or traded in a standardised form on the LIFFE. **OTC options** will be preferable if the buyers require an option **tailored to their needs** in terms of maturity date, contract size, currency or nature of interest. **OTC options** are also generally more appropriate if the buyer requires a **long time** to maturity or a large contract size. **Traded options** will be more appropriate if the buyers are **looking for options** that can be **exercised at any time**, are looking for a **quick, straightforward** deal, or might want to sell the options before the expiry date if they are not required.

(c)   **Foreign exchange exposure risks resulting from overseas subsidiary**

If a wholly owned subsidiary is established overseas then KYT Inc will face exposure to foreign exchange risk. The magnitude of the resulting risk can, if not properly managed, eliminate any financial benefits we would be hoping to achieve by setting up the overseas subsidiary.

The **foreign exchange risks resulting from a wholly owned overseas subsidiary** are as follows:

(i)   **Transaction risk**

This is the risk of adverse exchange rate movements occurring in the course of normal trading transactions. This would typically arise as a result of exchange rate fluctuations between the date when the price is agreed and the date when the cash is paid.

This form of exposure can give rise to real cash flow gains and losses. It would be necessary to set up a treasury management function whose role would be to assess and manage this risk through various hedging techniques.

(ii)   **Translation risk**

This arises from fluctuations in the exchange rate used to convert any foreign denominated assets or liabilities, or foreign denominated income or expenses when reporting back to the head office and thereby impacting on the investment performance.

This type of risk has no direct cash flow implications as it typically arises when the results of the subsidiary denominated in a foreign currency are translated into the home currency for consolidation purposes. Although there is no direct impact on cash flows, it could influence investors' and lenders' attitudes to the financial worth and creditworthiness of the company. Given that translation risk is effectively an accounting measure and not reflected in actual cash flows, normal hedging techniques are not normally relevant. However, given the possible impact the translated results have on the overall group's performance and the possible influence on any potential investment decision-making process it is imperative that such risks are reduced by balancing assets and liabilities as far as possible.

48 Asteroid Systems

Text references. Foreign currency hedging is covered in Chapter 16.

Top tips. At first glance this appears to be a straightforward foreign currency hedging question but there is a twist involved. The money is being remitted to Asteroid Systems rather than the company making a commitment to pay – therefore a reverse money market hedge will be needed.

In part (a) you will have to calculate the two-month rate using an average of the one-month and three-month rates. When using the interest rate parity formula for calculating the acceptable interest rate, remember that you are dealing with a reverse money market hedge – that is, the foreign currency is borrowed in the overseas market, converted at spot rate and then deposited in the domestic market. You are also trying to find the overseas country's interest rate (i_c) rather than the forward rate (f_0). Remember that you are trying to calculate a two-month rate, therefore you will have to adjust the interest rate parity formula accordingly.

Easy marks. The effects of hedging on cost of capital should offer a fairly easy four marks and the discussion on the treasury department operating as a profit or cost centre should be fairly straightforward.

Examining team's comments. This was not a popular question and only a minority of candidates who attempted it were able to identify the money market requirements and the procedure for setting up a hedge of this type. Whilst straightforward, the calculations focused attention on identifying the minimum Swiss borrowing rate that would make the hedge worthwhile.

The discursive parts of the question asked candidates to discuss the relative merits of money market hedging compared with hedging through the use of exchange-traded derivatives. Good answers focused on the range of hedging instruments available and commonly used in this type of business scenario (currency futures and forex options). Part (c) of the question asked candidates to consider whether hedging of this type would impact on the company's cost of capital. Good answers recognised that this depended on the significance of currency risk in the assessment of a firm's exposure to market risk (in the case of equity) and overall risk (in the case of debt). Many candidates ignored this part of the question.

Common errors in this question were:

(a)   Incorrect estimation of the appropriate forward rate

(b)   Being unable to use the money market hedge in a situation where there is a remittance as opposed to a commitment in the foreign currency concerned

(c)   Not recognising the role of the interest rate parity relationship in determining the minimum acceptable rate for borrowing

(d)   Not appreciating the significance of the correlation between the domestic and the counter currency in determining the potential gains from hedging

Marks

(a)	Calculation of forward rates	4
	Calculation of minimum rate at LIBOR + 7 through reverse money market hedge	5
	Conclusion	1
		Max 10
(b)	Advantages and disadvantages of OTC versus ET derivatives	
	Basis risk	2
	Under/over hedging	1
	Counterparty risk	1
	Flexibility	1
	Margin	1
		6
(c)	Impact upon the cost of equity capital	2
	Impact upon cost of debt capital	2
		4
(d)	One mark per well-explained point	Max 5
		25

(a)   **Money market hedge**

Calculate two-month forward rate

Two-month forward rate is the average of one-month and three-month rates

= (1.6223 + 1.6176)/2 = 1.6199 SFr/€

Exposure to transaction risk could be eliminated by entering into a forward contract to purchase Swiss francs at a rate of SFr/€1.6199 – that is, you would purchase SFr1.6199 × 1.5 million = SFr2.4299 million.

Use interest rate parity formula to calculate lowest acceptable Swiss borrowing or lending rate.

Interest rate parity:

$$f_0 = s_0 \frac{(1+i_c)}{(1+i_b)}$$

Where f_0 is the forward rate (calculated above as 1.6199)
$\quad$ s_0 is the spot rate (1.6244)
$\quad$ i_c is the interest rate in the country overseas (in this case, Switzerland)
$\quad$ i_b is the interest rate in the base country (Germany)

As we are looking for a two-month interest rate, we have to multiply i_c by (2/12) in all cases.

$$1.6199 = 1.6244 \times \frac{1+i_c \times 2/12}{(1+0.03725 \times 2/12)}$$

$$(1 + i_c \times 2/12) = \frac{1.6199 \times (1+0.03725 \times 2/12)}{1.6244}$$

$$(1+ i_c \times 2/12) = 1.0034$$

$$(i_c \times 2/12) = 0.0034$$

$$i_c = 0.0204 \text{ or } 2.04\%$$

If Asteroid Systems can borrow at less than 2.04% in the Swiss market, the money market hedge will be preferable to selling Swiss francs in the forward market.

(b)　**Relative advantages and disadvantages of a money market hedge versus exchange-traded derivatives**

Money market hedge

A money market hedge is the **manufacture of a forward rate** using the spot exchange rate and interest rates of the home and overseas countries. It requires **preferential access** to the short-term money markets and can be a **substitute** for forward contracts.

The **main problems** with a money market hedge are that it is **difficult to reverse** and it can be **relatively expensive**. It is not always possible to construct a money market hedge depending on the currencies with which you are dealing, as you may not be able to get access to the short-term money market in the overseas country.

Exchange-traded derivatives

Exchange-traded derivatives such as futures and options can be set up quickly and closed out easily.

Futures, for example, are normally closed out before maturity with the profit/loss being used to offset the gain or loss in the underlying. These derivatives tend to have **relatively low costs** for small deals and they are **marked to market**; they offer relatively low risk. **Options** offer flexibility in that the holder is **not obliged** to exercise the option on maturity if the market position is such that it would be more profitable not to do so.

However, exchange-traded derivatives are only available for **certain currencies** and offer **few maturity dates**. They are also only available in **fixed amounts** which may mean an **inexact hedge**. In the case of futures, there can also be **cash flow problems** as marking-to-market requires any daily shortfalls to be paid immediately. With exchange-traded options, there will be a premium to be paid which could prove to be expensive for the privilege of flexibility.

Conclusion

For **small, infrequent hedges** the forward market may be more suitable for hedging risk. However, you must take the **costs** of setting up loans and deposits into consideration before making a decision.

(c)　**Currency hedging and cost of capital**

Cost of equity

As hedging reduces a firm's exposure to foreign currency risk, there should be a **favourable impact** on the company's **beta value** and hence its cost of equity. The extent of the impact will depend on **the size and importance** of the potential foreign currency exposure and the **correlation of the currency with the market**. If the currency and the company have the same correlations with the market then the removal of currency risk would have **little or no effect** on the company's cost of capital, as the company's exposure to market risk would not change. The reverse would be true for different correlations with the market and the company's cost of equity would be affected by changes in levels of foreign currency risk.

Cost of debt

The reduction in foreign currency risk may have a **favourable impact** on the company's exposure to **default risk**. The risk of defaulting on debt payments is closely related to the volatility of the company's cash flows – the greater the volatility, the greater will be the default risk. Reduction in foreign currency risk will have a **smoothing effect** on the company's cash flows which will therefore **reduce** the risk of defaulting on debt. This should have a downward impact on the cost of debt and hence the overall cost of capital.

(d)　**Competence of staff**

Local managers may not have sufficient expertise in the area of treasury management to carry out speculative treasury operations competently. Mistakes in this specialised field may be costly. This would make a treasury department more likely to operate as a cost centre.

Controls

Adequate controls must be in place to prevent costly errors and overexposure to risks such as foreign exchange risks in a profit centre.

Information

A treasury department which acts as a profit centre would be competing with other traders employed by major financial institutions who may have better knowledge of the market. In order to compete effectively, the team needs to have detailed and up to date market information.

Attitudes to risk

The more aggressive approach to risk taking may be difficult to reconcile with the attitude to risk that the directors have. The recognition of treasury operations as profit making activities may not fit well with the main business operations of the company.

Internal charges

If the department is to be a true profit centre, then market prices should be charged for its services to other departments. It may be difficult to put realistic prices on some services, such as arrangement of finance or general financial advice.

Performance evaluation

Even with a profit centre approach, it may be difficult to measure the success of a treasury team for the reason that successful treasury activities sometimes involve **avoiding** the incurring of costs, for example when a currency devalues.

49 Multidrop

Text references. Netting is covered in Chapter 16.

Top tips. You should convert all amounts to the settlement currency first – it is important to have read the question thoroughly to pick up this point! A tabular approach makes finding the net amounts owing and owed much easier, both for you and for the marker. Don't forget to refer to both group and non-group companies in part (b) when discussing advantages and disadvantages of netting.

Easy marks. Part (c) should be a discussion using brought forward knowledge from FM.

			Marks
(a)	Set principal as European business	1	
	Conversion to euros	3	
	Initial amounts owed and owing	2	
	Totals owed and owing	2	
	Net amounts owed	2	
	Conclusion: Payments and receipts to Multidrop (Europe)	2	
			12
(b)	Minimisation of number of transactions	1–2	
	Minimisation of cost of transacting	1–2	
	Avoidance of exchange controls	1–2	
	Minimisation of hedging costs	1–2	
	Limiting exposure to net	1–2	
	Taxation issues	1–2	
	Acceptance of liability	1–2	
	Re-invoicing and re-contracting	1–2	
		Max	9
(c)	Removal of transaction risk	1–2	
	Customers not willing to bear risk	1–2	
	Loss of gains on foreign exchange	1	
		Max	4
			25

BPP
LEARNING MEDIA

(a) **Netting**

There are several ways in which this question could be approached. We have shown what we believe to be the most straightforward approach – using a **transactions matrix**.

All settlements are to be made in euros – the first step is therefore to convert all amounts owed to euros.

Owed by	Owed to	Local currency	
		m	€m
Multidrop (Europe)	Multidrop (US)	6.4	4.67
Multidrop (Singapore)	Multidrop (Europe)	16.0	7.75
Alposong (Malaysia)	Multidrop (US)	5.4	3.94
Multidrop (US)	Multidrop (Europe)	8.2	8.20
Multidrop (Singapore)	Multidrop (US)	5.0	3.65
Multidrop (Singapore)	Alposong (Malaysia)	25.0	5.01
Alposong (Malaysia)	NewRing (UK)	2.2	2.34
NewRing (UK)	Multidrop (Singapore)	4.0	1.94
Multidrop (Europe)	Alposong (Malaysia)	8.3	1.66

The next step is to determine how much is owed by (and owed to) each company and net the results off.

Owed to	Europe	US	Malaysia	Singapore	UK	Owed by
Owed by	€m	€m	€m	€m	€m	€m
Europe		4.67	1.66			6.33
US	8.20					8.20
Malaysia		3.94			2.34	6.28
Singapore	7.75	3.65	5.01			16.41
UK				1.94		1.94
Owed to	15.95	12.26	6.67	1.94	2.34	
Owed by	6.33	8.20	6.28	16.41	1.94	
Net	9.62	4.06	0.39	(14.47)	0.40	

Net result

The amounts paid by Multidrop (Europe) are as follows:

US	€4.06m
Malaysia	€0.39m
UK	€0.40m
Total	€4.85m

Multidrop (Europe) receives €14.47m from Singapore.

The net result is a gain of €9.62m for Multidrop (Europe).

(b) **Advantages and disadvantages of netting arrangements**

Advantages

Netting reduces **foreign exchange exposure** as balances are offset between countries. This limits the number of foreign currency exchange **transactions** and thus reduces the transaction costs involved.

Transaction risks (and transaction costs) are also reduced as a result of fewer foreign currency exchanges and this will enable the group to focus their hedging activities on a smaller number of transactions. Fewer hedging activities mean **lower hedging costs** (such as arrangement costs and premiums).

If **exchange controls** are in place (that limit cross-border currency flows), netting allows balances to be offset which minimises total exposure and helps to keep such currency flows to a legally acceptable level.

Disadvantages

One of the main issues with netting arrangements is making netting contracts **legally enforceable**. A netting system cannot operate effectively without resolving the legal status of contracts in numerous jurisdictions. As well as cross-border issues, there may be **taxation** problems to resolve before the netting arrangements can be approved.

There is also the issue of **liabilities** being accepted. This is a particular issue when external parties (in this case, Alposong and NewRing) are involved. The success of the netting arrangement depends on **acceptance of liabilities** by all parties, both internal and external to the group.

Costs in establishing the netting system have to be considered and compared with the savings. If there are no net benefits to be gained from the system then it should be abandoned.

Where third parties are involved, the netting arrangement may involve **re-invoicing** for the net amount or, in some cases, a completely **new contract** may be required.

(c)   The main advantage of this policy is that Multidrop (Europe)'s foreign customers would have to translate their own currencies into euro to pay Multidrop (Europe) and so they would have to bear the currency risk. This would mean Multidrop (Europe) **does not face transaction risk**. If there are time delays between the invoice and payment, the exposure could be significant.

The main disadvantage is likely to be loss of customers who are not prepared to bear the currency risk or possibly even the transaction cost of exchanging currency. These transaction costs will make Multidrop (Europe) less competitive than local companies which invoice in the local currency.

The removal of exchange rate risk also removes the chance for Multidrop (Europe) to make **gains on foreign exchange**.

50 Casasophia

Text references. Net present value (NPV) is covered in Chapter 5 and currency hedging in Chapter 16.

Top tips. In part (a) you are looking for the strategy that maximises receipts for the company. If you are faced with a fraction of a contract when dealing with options, round down and hedge the remainder using a forward contract. Note that the futures contracts will be closed out before expiry therefore you will have to estimate the futures rate (either of the two ways given is acceptable).

Be careful in part (b) as the project is due to start in six months' time rather than the more usual one year's time. This means that you will have to calculate forward rates for six months' time and then go up in increments of one year.

Easy marks. This is quite a challenging question but you should be able to pick up some marks in performing the forward contract and futures contract calculations and adding comments.

Examining team's comments. This question was not done well. In part (a) many students presented adequate calculations of the cash flows using different derivative products but failed to advise adequately (for example although options are generally more expensive they do provide more flexibility). In some cases students had difficulty in calculating an estimate for the basis remaining and occasionally students tried to use money market hedges despite the necessary information not being available in the question.

Few attempts were made to calculate future spot rates based on purchasing power parity for part (b) and some answers just discounted the project in the local currency rather than in euro.

		Marks
(a)	Forward contract calculation	1
	Forward contract comment	1
	Futures contracts calculations	3
	Futures contracts comments	2
	Option contracts calculations	4
	Option contracts comments	2–3
	Conclusion	1
		Max 15

		Marks
(b)	Estimates of forward rates	3
	Estimates of present values and net present value in euros	3
	Discussion	4–5
		Max 10
		25

(a) **Hedging strategy**

Forward contract

The company will be receiving US$ therefore we use US$1.3623 as the rate.

Receipt in € = US$20m/1.3623 = €14,681,054

The hedge fixes the rate at €1 = US$1.3623. This rate is legally binding.

Futures contract

A two-month contract is too short for the required hedge period therefore we must use a five-month contract. The contract will be closed out in four months' time.

Number of contracts = €14,624,159/€125,000 = 117 contracts

You can estimate the futures rate using the five-month price, the spot rate and the four-month forward rate:

We could estimate the number of contracts needed as:

$'000		€'000	Contract size	No contracts
20,000	1.3698	14,601	125	117

Outcome

The outcome will depend on the spot and future prices, the futures price can be estimated as follows:

	Now		4 months	
5-month future	1.3698		1.3714	balance
Spot rate	1.3618		1.3698	assumed
Basis	0.0080	× 1/5 =	0.0016	
	5 months		1 month remaining	

Assuming that the spot rate in four months is the same as the futures rate, the outcome will be:

		$'000	€'000
Actual			
		$20,000	
Assumed spot in 4 months			1.3698 (alternative assumptions are possible)
In euros ('000)			€14,601
Future			
Opening	1.3698	to buy	
Closing	1.3714	to sell	
Ticks	(0.0016)		
Profit ('000)		€17	
(117 × 125,000 × 0.0016/spot 1.3698)			
			€14,618
Effective rate	(20,000/14,618)		1.3682

Comments

The futures rate is worse than the forward rate. Futures contracts are marked to market on a daily basis and require margin payments as a result. As with forward contracts, futures contracts fix the rates and are legally binding.

Options

With options the holder has the right but not the obligation to exercise the option (that is, the option will be exercised if it is beneficial to the holder). However, there is a premium to be paid for this flexibility, making options more expensive than futures and forward contracts.

To protect itself against a weakening US$, Casasophia will purchase euro call options.

Exercise price = $1.36

Receipts = $20m/1.36 = €14,705,882

Number of contracts = €14,705,882/€125,000 = 117.6 contracts (117 contracts)

With 117 contracts, receipts = €125,000 × 117 = €14,625,000

Premium payable = $0.0280 × 117 × 125,000 = $409,500 (or $409,500/1.3585 = €301,435)

Amount not hedged = US$20m – (117 × €125,000 × 1.36) = US$110,000

This amount can be hedged using a 4-month forward contract as follows:

US$110,000/1.3623 = €80,746

Total receipts = €14,625,000 – €301,435 + €80,746 = **€14,404,311**

Exercise price = $1.38

Receipts = $20m/1.38 = €14,492,754

Number of contracts = €14,492,754/€125,000 = 115.9 contracts (purchase 115 contracts)

With 115 contracts, receipts = €125,000 × 115 = €14,375,000

Premium payable = $0.0223 × 115 × 125,000 = US$320,563 (or $320,563/1.3585 = €235,968)

Amount not hedged = US$20m – (115 × €125,000 × 1.38) = US$162,500

This amount can be hedged using a 4-month forward contract as follows:

US$162,500/1.3623 = €119,284

Total receipts = €14,375,000 – €235,968 + €119,284 = **€14,258,316**

The receipts from either of the options are considerably lower than those from either the futures contract or the forward contract. This is primarily due to the premiums payable to secure the flexibility that options offer. The US$ would have to move significantly against the € to allow Casasophia to cover the cost of the premiums.

Conclusion

Based on the calculations above, it is recommended that Casasophia uses forward contracts to hedge against the US$ depreciating against the € in order to maximise receipts. The company should be aware that once the contract is agreed, the price is fixed and is legally binding. In addition, there is no formal exchange for forward contracts, thus giving rise to default risk.

(b)   **Project NPV**

Expected forward rates (using interest rate parity)

$$F_0 = S_0 \times \frac{(1+i_c)}{(1+i_b)}$$

Year	Forward rate (€1 = MShs)
Half year	128 × (1.108/1.022) = 138.77
	128 + [(138.77 − 128)/2] = 133.38
1.5 years	133.38 × (1.108/1.022) = 144.60
2.5 years	144.60 × (1.108/1.022) = 156.77
3.5 years	156.77 × (1.108/1.022) = 169.96

NPV calculation (note that Year 1 actually means 1.5 years from now as project starts in 6 months' time)

Year	1	2	3
Income (MShs, million)	1,500	1,500	1,500
Forward rate	144.60	156.77	169.96
Income (€m)	10.37	9.57	8.82
Discount factor (12%)	0.893	0.797	0.712
DCF	9.26	7.63	6.28

Total present value = €23.17m

Expected spot rate (MShs) in 12 months' time (using purchasing power parity):

$$S_1 = S_0 \times \frac{(1+h_c)}{(1+h_b)}$$

$S_1 = 116 \times (1 + 0.097)/(1 + 0.012) = 125.74$

In 6 months' time expected spot rate = 116 + (125.74 − 116)/2 = 120.9

Total investment required in € = MShs2.64 billion/120.9 = €21.84m

NPV = €1.33m

Will the swap be beneficial for Casasophia?

Forward rates based on interest rate parity show that MShs is depreciating against the € as interest rates are much higher in Mazabia (10.8%) than in the European country (2.2%). However, even with a depreciating MShs the project is still worthwhile (positive NPV).

When forward rates are estimated using purchasing power parity, it is assumed that forward rates will change according to differences between the two countries' inflation rates. If Mazabia's inflation rate is greater than the European country's rate, the MShs will depreciate against the €.

We are told that Mazabia's inflation rate could vary between 5% and 15% over the next few years therefore a swap would appear to be advantageous (as it would fix the future exchange rates). Without the swap there will be uncertainty over the NPV of the project.

Default risk should also be taken into consideration and Casasophia may ask the Government of Mazabia to act as a guarantor in order to reduce the risk.

The grant funding will be provided directly to the Mazabian Government in MShs. It may be worthwhile for Casasophia to explore the possibility of receiving the grant directly in € as this would reduce currency exposure.

51 Alecto

Text references. Interest rate hedging is covered in Chapter 17.

Top tips. Remember that interest rate hedging involves finding the best interest rate whilst protecting yourself against interest rate movements. You are told that interest rates can move by 0.5% in either direction, therefore you really have six calculations to do in part (b) – three techniques with two interest rate movements. Use the tabular approach demonstrated in the Study Text as far as possible.

When tackling hedging questions on interest rates establish immediately whether the company is borrowing or lending. This will help when trying to decide whether it should be buying or selling contracts.

Make sure that you set-up the contracts correctly as your marks will be capped to a low level if you get this wrong.

You do not have to tackle the hedging techniques in the order given in the question – just make sure you label your workings to make it clear which technique you are dealing with. Remember that the net cost of a future when the interest rate rises or falls should be the same (subject to rounding).

As the company is borrowing money and is using a collar, it should buy a put (the right to sell a future) and sell a call. The put will be at the higher interest rate (and the lower strike price) and the call will be at the lower interest rate (the higher strike price).

Whilst the calculations in part (b) may seem quite long, remember that you can use a number of the figures you calculated early on in your later calculations (such as expected futures price) – don't rework these calculations as you will just be wasting valuable time.

Easy marks. You should be able to pick up some relatively straightforward marks in part (c) – you should know what basis risk is.

		Marks	
(a)	Discussion of the main advantage	2	
	Discussion of the main disadvantage	2	
			4
(b)	Recommendation to go short if futures are used and purchase puts if options are used	1	
	Calculation of number of contracts and remaining basis	2	
	Futures contracts calculations	4	
	Options contracts calculations	4	
	Collar approach and calculations	4	
	Supporting comments and conclusion	2–3	
			Max 17
(c)	Explanation of basis risk	2–3	
	Effect of basis risk on recommendation made	2–3	
			Max 4
			25

(a) An interest rate collar involves the purchase of a **put option** and the **simultaneous selling of a call option** at different exercise prices. The main advantage is that it is **cheaper** than just purchasing the put option. This is because the premium received from selling the call option reduces the higher premium payable for the put option.

The main disadvantage is that the **benefit** from any upside movement in interest rates is **capped** by the sale of the call option. With just the put option, the full upside benefit would be realised.

(b) **Futures**

As Alecto is looking to protect against a rise in interest rates it needs to sell futures. As the borrowing is required on 1 May, June contracts are needed.

No of contracts needed = €22,000,000/€1,000,000 × 5/3 months = 36.67

Need 37 contracts

Basis
Current price (1 Jan) – futures price = basis
100 – 3.3 – 96.16 = 0.54
Unexpired basis = 2/6 × 0.54 = 0.18

	Interest rates increase to 3.8%		Interest rates decrease to 2.8%	
Cost of borrowing	$(3.8\% + 0.8\%) \times$ 5/12 × €22m	€421,667	$(2.8\% + 0.8\%) \times$ 5/12 × €22m	€330,000
Expected futures price	100 − 3.8 − 0.18	96.02	100 − 2.8 − 0.18	97.02
Gain/loss on futures market	$(9,616 - 9,602) \times$ €25 × 37	(€12,950)	$(9,616 - 9,702) \times$ €25 × 37	€79,550
Net cost		€408,717		€409,550
Effective interest rate	408,717/22m × 12/5	4.46%	409,550/22m × 12/5	4.47%

The difference in interest rates comes from the rounding of the contracts.

Using options on futures

As Alecto is looking to protect against a rise in interest rates it needs to buy June put options. As before 37 contracts are needed.

Interest rates	Increase to 3.8%		Decrease to 2.8%	
Put option exercise price	4%	3.5%	4%	3.5%
June futures price	3.98%	3.98%	2.98%	2.98%
Exercise option?	No	Yes	No	No
Gain	–	0.48%	–	–
	%	%	%	%
Actual interest cost	(4.60)	(4.60)	(3.60)	(3.60)
Value of option gain	–	0.48	–	–
Premium	(0.16)	(0.58)	(0.16)	(0.58)
Net cost of loan	(4.76)	(4.70)	(3.76)	(4.18)

In each case the cost in euros can be calculated as interest rate × 5/12 × size of loan eg 0.0476 × 5/12 × 22m = 436,333 euros.

Using a collar

Buy June put at 96.00 for 0.163 and sell June call at 96.50 for 0.090. Net premium payable = 0.073. As before 37 contracts are required.

If interest rates increase to 3.8%

	Buy put	Sell call
Exercise price	4%	3.5%
June futures price	3.98%	3.98%
Exercise option?	No	No
	%	
Actual interest cost	(4.60)	
Value of option gain	–	
Premium	(0.07)	
Net cost of loan	(4.67)	

If interest rates decrease to 2.8%

	Buy put	Sell call
Exercise price	4%	3.5%
June futures price	2.98%	2.98%
Exercise option?	No	Yes
	%	
Actual interest cost	(3.60)	
Value of option loss	(0.52)	
Premium	(0.07)	
Net cost of loan	(4.19)	

The cost in euros can be calculated as interest rate × 5/12 × size of loan ie 0.0419 × 5/12 × 22m = 384,083 euros.

If the interest rate futures market is used, the interest cost will be fixed at 4.47%, but if options on futures or an interest rate collar is used the cost will change. If interest rates were to fall then the options hedge gives the more favourable rates. However, if interest rates rise, then the futures hedge gives the lowest interest cost and the options hedge has the highest cost. If Alecto wants to fix its interest rate irrespective of the circumstances, then the futures hedge should be selected.

This recommendation does not include margin payments or other transaction costs, which should be considered in full before a final decision is made.

(c)   **Basis risk** arises from the fact the price of a futures contract may not move as expected in relation to the value of the instrument being hedged. Basis changes do occur and thus represent potential profits/losses to investors. Basis risk is the **difference between the spot and futures prices** and so there is no basis risk where a futures contract is held until maturity. In this case, however, the June contracts are closed two months before expiry and there is no guarantee that the price of the futures contract will be the same as the predicted price calculated by basis at that date. It is assumed that the unexpired basis above is 0.18 but it could be either more or less.

This creates a problem in that the futures contract, which in theory gives a fixed interest cost, may vary and therefore the amount of interest is not fixed or predictable. Typically, this risk is much smaller than the risk of **remaining unhedged** and therefore the impact of this risk is smaller and **preferable** to not hedging at all.

52 Awan

Text references. Interest rate hedging is covered in Chapter 17.

Examining team's comments. Part (a) looked at hedging an investment that was going to be made in a few months' time using interest rate FRAs, futures and options. Responses to this part of the question were mixed. Some responses made more fundamental errors like going short in futures, purchasing put options or choosing the incorrect contract month (June instead of March), and therefore limiting the number of marks that were awarded.

Few responses were able to calculate the basis correctly.

A number of responses chose the incorrect FRA rate.

The discussion of the outcomes tended to be general, as opposed to specifically relating to the scenario, and therefore the recommendation tended to be general as well. At this level it is important for candidates to recognise that contextualised discussion and conclusion will result in higher marks.

The presentation quality of the responses tended to be mixed. Some candidates' answers were presented well, while others were presented in a haphazard way without any coherent flow. This made it very difficult for markers to award marks.

Responses to part (b) of the question were generally weak.

Marking scheme

		Marks
(a)	Calculation of impact of FRA for interest rate increase and decrease	4
	Decision to go long on futures	1
	Selection of March futures and options	1
	Unexpired basis calculation	1
	Impact of interest rates increase/decrease with futures	4
	Decision to buy call options	1
	Impact of interest rates increase/decrease with options	5
	Discussion	2–3
		Max __19__
(b)	1–2 marks per well-explained point	Max __6__
		__25__

(a)   **Using FRAs**

FRA rate 4.82% (3–7), since the investment will take place in 3 months' time for a period of 4 months.

If interest rates increase by 0.9% to 4.99%

Investment return = 4.79% × 4/12 × $48,000,000 =	$766,400
Payment to Voblaka Bank = (4.99% − 4.82%) × $48,000,000 × 4/12 =	$(27,200)
Net receipt =	$739,200
Effective annual interest rate = 739,200/48,000,000 × 12/4 =	4.62%

If interest rates decrease by 0.9% to 3.19%

Investment return = 2.99% × 4/12 × $48,000,000 =	$478,400
Receipt from Voblaka Bank = (4.82% − 3.19%) × $48,000,000 × 4/12 =	$260,800
Net receipt =	$739,200
Effective annual interest rate (as above)	4.62%

Using futures

Need to hedge against a fall in interest rates, therefore go long in the futures market. Awan Co needs March contracts as the investment will be made on 1 February.

No. of contracts needed = $48,000,000/$2,000,000 × 4 months/3 months = 32 contracts.

Basis
Current price (on 1/11) − futures price = total basis
(100 − 4.09) − 94.76 = 1.15
Unexpired basis = 2/5 × 1.15 = 0.46

If interest rates increase by 0.9% to 4.99%

Investment return (from above) =	$766,400
Expected futures price = 100 − 4.99 − 0.46 =	94.55
Loss on the futures market = (0.9455 − 0.9476) × $2,000,000 × 3/12 × 32 =	$(33,600)
Net return =	$732,800
Effective annual interest rate = $732,800/$48,000,000 × 12/4 =	4.58%

If interest rates decrease by 0.9% to 3.19%

Investment return (from above) =	$478,400
Expected futures price = 100 − 3.19 − 0.46 = 96.35	
Gain on the futures market = (0.9635 − 0.9476) × $2,000,000 × 3/12 × 32 =	$254,400
Net return =	$732,800
Effective annual interest rate (as above) =	4.58%

Using options on futures

Need to hedge against a fall in interest rates, therefore buy call options. As before, Awan Co needs 32 March call option contracts ($48,000,000/$2,000,000 × 4 months/3 months).

If interest rates increase by 0.9% to 4.99%

Exercise price	94.50	95.00
Futures price	94.55	94.55
Exercise?	Yes	No
Gain in basis points	5	0
Underlying investment return (from above)	$766,400	$766,400
Gain on options (0.0005 × 2,000,000 × 3/12 × 32, 0)	$8,000	$0
Premium		
0.00432 × $2,000,000 × 3/12 × 32	$(69,120)	
0.00121 × $2,000,000 × 3/12 × 32		$(19,360)
Net return	$705,280	$747,040
Effective interest rate	4.41%	4.67%

If interest rates decrease by 0.9% to 3.19%

	94.50	95.00
Exercise price	94.50	95.00
Futures price	96.35	96.35
Exercise?	Yes	Yes
Gain in basis points	185	135
Underlying investment return (from above)	$478,400	$478,400
Gain on options		
(0.0185 × 2,000,000 × 3/12 × 32)	$296,000	
(0.0135 × 2,000,000 × 3/12 × 32)		$216,000
Premium		
As above	$(69,120)	
As above		$(19,360)
Net return	$705,280	$675,040
Effective interest rate	4.41%	4.22%

Discussion

The FRA offer from Voblaka Bank gives a slightly higher return compared to the futures market; however, Awan Co faces a credit risk with over-the-counter products like the FRA, where Voblaka Bank may default on any money owing to Awan Co if interest rates should fall. The March call option at the exercise price of 94.50 seems to fix the rate of return at 4.41%, which is lower than the return on the futures market and should therefore be rejected. The March call option at the exercise price of 95.00 gives a higher return compared to the FRA and the futures if interest rates increase, but does not perform as well if the interest rates fall. If Awan Co takes the view that it is more important to be protected against a likely fall in interest rates, then that option should also be rejected. The choice between the FRA and the futures depends on Awan Co's attitude to risk and return; the FRA gives a small, higher return, but carries a credit risk. If the view is that the credit risk is small and it is unlikely that Voblaka Bank will default on its obligation, then the FRA should be chosen as the hedge instrument.

(b)   The delta value measures the extent to which the value of a derivative instrument, such as an option, changes as the value of its underlying asset changes. For example, a delta of 0.8 would mean that a company would need to purchase 1.25 option contracts (1/0.8) to hedge against a rise in price of an underlying asset of that contract size, known as the hedge ratio. This is because the delta indicates that when the underlying asset increases in value by $1, the value of the equivalent option contract will increase by only $0.80.

The option delta is equal to $N(d_1)$ from the Black-Scholes option pricing formula. This means that the delta is constantly changing when the volatility or time to expiry change. Therefore even when the delta and hedge ratio are used to determine the number of option contracts needed, this number needs to be updated periodically to reflect the new delta.

53 Phobos

Text references. Interest rate risk and hedging are covered in Chapter 17.

Top tips. If you are familiar with interest rate hedging using derivatives, this should be a relatively straightforward question. Use the BPP proforma for setting up futures and options to ensure you do not forget any of the steps. Make sure you answer the question in part (a) – you are asked for the effective interest rates for each type of derivative. For options, the effective rate will be the average of the two annualised rates for each possible interest rate.

In part (b) divide your answer into pros and cons to make it easier for you and the marker to identify key points.

Part (c) requires a good knowledge of the Black-Scholes model formula.

Easy marks. Part (a) allows you to pick up a number of easy marks such as in the calculation of the number of contracts. You can gain easy marks in part (b) if you are familiar with the pros and cons of derivatives for interest rate hedging purposes.

		Marks
(a)	Calculation of current interest rate	1
	Identification of appropriate future and hedge strategy	1
	Calculation of number of contracts	3
(i)	Calculation of basis for interest rate futures	2
	Calculation of gain/loss on alternative close-outs	2
(ii)	Identification of most appropriate option strategy	1
	Calculation of premium payable	1
	Calculation of loan cost under alternative payoffs	2
	Estimation of expected payoff given equal likelihoods	1
		14
(b)	Problems of making efficient match	1
	Hedge efficiency issues	1
	Default and basis risk	1
	Leveraged swaps and FRAs	2
	Dangers of leveraging	1
		6
(c)	One mark per fully explained point	Max 5
		25

(a) **Estimation of effective interest rate cost using different hedging techniques**

(i) **Futures**

Current interest = Length of exposure × amount of exposure × (LIBOR + 50 basis points)

= $4/12$ × £30 million × 6.5%

= **£650,000**

Type of future = **March** future with an open price of 93.800 and a settlement price of 93.880

Number of contracts = $\dfrac{\text{Amount of exposure}}{\text{Contract size}} \times \dfrac{\text{Length of exposure}}{\text{Contract period}}$

= $\dfrac{\text{£30 million}}{\text{£500,000}} \times \dfrac{4 \text{ months}}{3 \text{ months}}$ = **80 contracts**

Basis = Current spot price – settlement price = 94.00 – 93.88 = 12 basis points (ticks)

Between the closure and maturity of the contract (one month), movement will be 4 ticks (12/3).

Close-out price if interest rate (a) increases, or (b) decreases by 100 basis points

Interest rate at close-out	7%	5%
Open price	93.88	93.88
Futures price at close-out	92.96	94.96
Number of ticks	92	(108)
Total value (80 contracts at £12.50 per tick)	92,000	(108,000)
Cost of loan in spot market	750,000	550,000
Less profit/(loss) on futures	92,000	(108,000)
Net cost of loan	658,000	658,000
Annual equivalent	**6.58%**	**6.58%**

(ii)   **Traded options**

Type of option = March put option

Number of contracts = 80 (see above)

Premium = Number of contracts × premium on March put option × tick size
= 80 × 16.8 × £12.50
= £16,800

Basis = 4 ticks (see (a)(i) above)

Outcomes versus expected movements in interest rates

	7%	5%
Interest rate at close-out	7%	5%
Futures price at close-out	92.96	94.96
Exercise price	94.00	94.00
Exercise option?	Yes	No
Option payoff (ticks)	104.00	Nil
80 contracts at £12.50 per tick	104,000	Nil
Cost of loan in spot market	750,000	550,000
Less option payoff	(104,000)	Nil
Less premium	16,800	16,800
Net cost of loan	662,800	566,800
Annual equivalent	6.63%	5.67%
Effective interest rate (average)	**6.15%**	

(b)   **Pros and cons of using derivatives to manage interest rate risk**

Pros

In a climate of volatile interest rates, exposure to potential interest rate risk is more acute. Companies can use various financial derivative instruments to hedge against such risk, including futures, forward rate agreements (FRA), options and swaps.

The most obvious advantage of using derivatives is that the interest rate that will be applied in the future is **fixed** and there are no surprises. This helps with **financial planning** as companies know how much interest they will have to pay and can budget accordingly.

Futures and FRAs allow companies to **perfectly match** their hedged amounts with the amount of exposure as they can be tailored to the particular needs of the company in question. Whilst **traded options** do not offer this facility, they do offer **flexibility**. If the prevailing interest rate at the time at which options should be exercised is better than the 'locked-in' rate, companies can just let the options lapse – that is, options offer companies **the right but not the obligation** to accept the locked-in rate at the date of maturity.

To avoid the expensive premiums that come with the flexibility of options, companies may use **interest rate swaps** – for example, a company may swap a fixed rate stream of interest payments for a variable rate stream. This allows companies to take advantage of **favourable movements** in interest rates.

Cons

Traded options do not allow perfect hedging as they come in standardised amounts. This could lead to a company purchasing more options than required (expensive and unnecessary) or less than required (leading to some of the exposure being unhedged). In order to hedge the outstanding exposure the company may have to purchase **futures or FRAs**.

Options are **expensive** means of hedging as their flexibility comes at a high price. Regardless of whether the option is exercised, the company must pay a **premium** for the right (but not the obligation) to exercise.

Whilst **swaps** allow companies to exchange fixed rate interest payment streams for variable rate streams, it is often **difficult to gauge the extent of the risk exposure** and to ensure that the exposure (and the swaps) are effectively managed by the company. This can lead to companies suffering **losses** that may be on such a scale as to threaten their survival.

(c) **Short-term nature of instruments**

The Finance Director's assertion about the nature of instruments is correct. Most are designed to hedge for interest rate changes over months rather than years. They are a form of **insurance** for the buyer, where the seller assumes the risk in return for a premium. They are not designed to deal with interest rate changes over a long period, where movements are less certain and the **risks to the provider of the option** would be **greater**.

Renewal of instruments

Costs to Phobos will become **less certain** if a succession of short-term instruments are used to hedge the risk. Phobos may find that once the term of the instrument has expired, an instrument offering the same rate is not available or only available at an **increased premium**, because **expectations about rate rises** have **changed**.

Pricing of instruments

The pricing of instruments will take account of **predicted interest rate movements, uncertainties in predictions** and build in a **profit element** as well. Every time Phobos buys a new instrument, it will be paying a premium to the sellers of the instrument that reflects these considerations. The cumulative cost of these premiums over the time period will be greater than the increased interest costs that Phobos will incur if it purchases the fixed interest rate swap.

54 Keshi

Text references. Treasury management is covered in Chapter 15 and interest rate hedging is covered in Chapter 17.

Top tips. Do not be put off this question if you are unsure of part (b) but are comfortable with interest rate hedging questions. Remember to lay out your calculations in an easy to follow way. You can also work in percentage terms, which is easier than working in monetary amounts.

For part (c) don't spend too long on this if you aren't sure what a Salam contract is.

Easy marks. You should be able to pick up some relatively straightforward marks in part (a) for the option calculations. Ensure your recommendation is based on your calculations.

Marking scheme

			Marks
(a)	Buy put options and number of contracts	1	
	Future prices if interest rates rise or fall	1	
	Option contract calculations for any exercise price	3	
	Second set of option calculations if provided	1	
	Swap and resulting advantage	2	
	Swap impact	2	
	Effective borrowing rate	2	
	Discussion and recommendation	3–4	
			Max 15
(b)	Discussion of merits of centralising	3–4	
	Discussion of merits of decentralising	2–3	Max 6
(c)	1–2 marks per well-explained point		Max 4
			25

BPP LEARNING MEDIA

Answers **229**

(a) **Options**

Keshi needs to hedge against a rise in interest rates, therefore it needs to buy **put options**.

Keshi Co needs 42 March put option contracts ($18,000,000/$1,000,000 × 7 months/3 months).

Basis

Current March futures price – spot price = total basis = 44 basis points as at 1 December

Unexpired basis as at 1 February = 22 **or 0.22% (given in the question)**

If 95.50 options (ie 4.5%) are used:

	Rates fall – 0.5%	Rates rise + 0.5%
	%	%
LIBOR rate (currently 3.8%)	3.3	4.3
Borrowing rate for Keshi	3.7	4.7
Closing future LIBOR + basis of 0.22%	3.52	4.52
Exercise option at 4.5%?	No	Yes
Premium	(0.662)	(0.662)
Option gain/(loss)		0.02
Net effective annual interest rate	**4.362%**	**5.342**
	(3.7 + 0.662)	(4.7 + 0.662 – 0.02)

Alternative solution:

Expected futures price on 1 February if interest rates increase by 0.5% =

100 – (3.8 + 0.5) – 0.22 = 95.48

Expected futures price on 1 February if interest rates decrease by 0.5% =

100 – (3.8 – 0.5) – 0.22 = 96.48

If interest rates increase by 0.5% to 4.3%

Exercise price 95.50

Futures price 95.48

Exercise?   Yes

Gain in basis points 2

Underlying cost of borrowing

4.7% × 7/12 × $18,000,000 = $493,500

Gain on options

0.0002 × $1,000,000 × 3/12 × 42 = $2,100

Premium

0.00662 × $1,000,000 × 3/12 × 42 = $69,510

Net cost $560,910

Effective interest rate **5.342%** (560,910 / 18,000,000 × 12/7)

If interest rates decrease by 0.5% to 3.3%

Exercise price 95.50

Futures price 96.48

Exercise?   No

Underlying cost of borrowing

$3.7\% \times 7/12 \times \$18{,}000{,}000 = \$388{,}500$

Premium $69,510

Net cost $458,010

Effective interest rate **4.362%** ($458{,}010 / 18{,}000{,}000 \times 12/7$)

Using swaps

Keshi will want to swap into fixed rate finance in order to hedge the risk of interest rates rising.

With this type of swap the outcome will be as follows:

	Keshi Co
No swap:	(5.5%)
Swap:	
Loan	(LIBOR + 0.4%)
Fixed rate paid	(4.6%)
Floating rate received	LIBOR + 0.3%
Net cost pre-fee	(4.7%)
Total gain (5.5 vs 4.7)	0.8%
Gain to Keshi (70% of 0.8)	0.56%
Outcome pre-fees (5.5 − 0.56)	4.94%
Outcome post-fees (4.94 + 0.1)	**5.04%**

Discussion and recommendation

Under each choice the interest rate cost to Keshi Co will be as follows:

	Doing nothing	95.50 option	Swap
If rates increase by 0.5%	4.7% floating;	5.342%	5.04%
	5.5% fixed		
If rates decrease by 0.5%	3.7% floating;	4.362%	5.04%
	5.5% fixed		

Borrowing at the floating rate and undertaking a **swap** effectively fixes the rate of interest at 5.04% for the loan, which is **significantly lower than the market fixed rate of 5.5%**.

On the other hand, **doing nothing** and borrowing at the floating rate minimises the interest rate at 4.7%, against the next best choice which is the swap at 5.04% if interest rates increase by 0.5%. And, should interest rates decrease by 0.5%, then doing nothing and borrowing at a floating rate of 3.7% minimises cost, compared to the next best choice which is the 95.50 option.

On the face of it, **doing nothing and borrowing at a floating rate seems to be the better choice** if interest rates increase or decrease by a small amount, but if interest rates increase substantially then this choice will no longer result in the lowest cost.

The swap minimises the variability of the borrowing rates, while doing nothing and borrowing at a floating rate maximises the variability. If Keshi Co wants to eliminate the risk of interest rate fluctuations completely, then it should borrow at the floating rate and swap it into a fixed rate.

(b)   A **centralised** treasury department should be able to evaluate the financing requirements of Keshi Co's group as a whole and it may be able to **negotiate better rates when borrowing in bulk**. The department could operate as an internal bank and undertake **matching** of funds. Therefore it could transfer funds from subsidiaries which have spare cash resources to ones which need them, and thus **avoid going into the costly external market to raise funds**.

The department may be able to undertake **multilateral internal netting** and thereby reduce costs related to hedging activity. **Experts** and resources within one location could **reduce duplication costs**.

The concentration of experts and resources within one central department may result in a **more effective decision-making** environment and higher quality risk monitoring and control. Further, having access to the Keshi Co group's entire cash funds may give the company access to larger and more diverse investment markets.

Decentralising Keshi Co's treasury function to its subsidiary companies may be beneficial in several ways. Each subsidiary company may be better placed to take **local regulations and customs** into consideration. An example is the case of Suisen Co's need to use Salam contracts instead of conventional derivative products which the centralised treasury department may use as a matter of course.

Giving subsidiary companies more **autonomy** over how they undertake their own fund management may result in increased **motivation** and effort from the subsidiary's senior management and thereby increase future income. Subsidiary companies which have access to their own funds may be able to respond to opportunities **quicker** and establish competitive advantage more effectively.

(c)   Islamic principles stipulate the need to avoid uncertainty and speculation. In the case of Salam contracts, payment for the commodity is made at the start of the contract. The buyer and seller of the commodity know the price, the quality and the quantity of the commodity and the date of future delivery with certainty. Therefore, **uncertainty and speculation** are avoided.

On the other hand, futures contracts are marked to market daily and this could lead to uncertainty in the amounts received and paid every day. Furthermore, **standardised futures contracts have fixed expiry dates and predetermined contract sizes**.

This may mean that the underlying position is not hedged or covered completely, leading to limited speculative positions even where the futures contracts are used entirely for hedging purposes.

Finally, only a few commodity futures contracts are offered to cover a range of different quality grades for a commodity, and therefore price movement of the futures market may not be completely in line with the price movement in the underlying asset.

(**Note**. Credit will be given for alternative, relevant discussion for parts (b) and (c).)

55 Daikon

Text references. Interest rate hedging is covered in Chapter 17.

Easy marks. You should be able to pick up some relatively straightforward marks in part (a) for the option calculations. Ensure your recommendation is based on your calculations.

Examining team's comments. Part (b) was done unsatisfactorily by most candidates. Very few candidates got the calculations of the marked to market correct. What was required was to identify the change in ticks or basis points and multiply the three numbers together.

Marking scheme

		Marks
(a)	Additional interest cost	1
	Contract types	1
	Number of contracts and remaining basis	2
	Futures calculations	1
	Options calculations	4
	Collar	4
	Comments and conclusion	3
		Max 15

(b) Marked to market calculations   3
Impact of daily marked to market   3
Impact of margin requirements   3
Impact of selling options instead of exercising   3

Max 10

25

(a) Borrowing period is 6 months (11 months – 5 months).

Current borrowing cost = $34,000,000 × 6 months/12 months × 4.3% = $731,000
Borrowing cost if interest rates increase by 80 basis points (0.8%) = $34,000,000 × 6/12 × 5.1% = $867,000
Additional cost = $136,000 [$34,000,000 × 6/12 × 0.8%]

Using futures to hedge

Need to hedge against a rise in interest rates, therefore go short (contracts to sell) in the futures market.

Borrowing period is 6 months
No. of contracts needed = $34,000,000/$1,000,000 × 6 months/3 months = 68 contracts.

Basis

Current price (on 1 June 20X5) – futures price = total basis
(100 – 3.6) – 95.84 = 0.56
Unexpired basis (at beginning of November) = 2/7 × 0.56 = 0.16

Assume that interest rates increase by 0.8% (80 basis points) to 4.4%

Expected futures price = 100 – 4.4 – 0.16 = 95.44 (or 100 – 95.44 = 4.56%)

Gain on the futures market = (95.84 – 95.44) × $25 × 68 = $68,000 (or 4.56% closing future – 4.16% opening future = 0.4%)

Net additional cost = ($136,000 – $68,000) $68,000 (or 0.8% – 0.4% gain on future = 0.4%)

Using options on futures to hedge

Need to hedge against a rise in interest rates, therefore buy put options. As before, 68 put option contracts are needed ($34,000,000/$1,000,000 × 6 months/3 months).

Assume that interest rates increase by 0.8% (80 basis points) to 4.4%

Exercise price	95.50	96.00
Futures price	95.44	95.44
Exercise?	Yes	Yes
Gain in basis points	6	56
Gain on options		
6 × $25 × 68	$10,200	
56 × $25 × 68		$95,200
Premium		
30.4 × $25 × 68	$51,680	
50.8 × $25 × 68		$86,360
Option benefit/(cost)	$(41,480)	$8,840
Net additional cost		
($136,000 + $41,480)	$177,480	
($136,000 – $8,840)		$127,160

Alternative solution (shown in %)

	%	%
Borrow	−5.1	−5.1
Opening	4.5	4.0
Closing	4.56	4.56
	0.06	0.56
Premium	−0.304	−0.508
NET	−5.344	−5.048
Extra vs 4.3%	−1.044	−0.748
	(0.01044 × $34m × 6/12)	(0.00748 × $34m × 6/12)
In $s	**−177,480**	**−127,160**

Using a collar on options to hedge

Buy put options at 95.50 for 0.304 and sell call at 96.00 for 0.223
Net premium payable = 0.081

Assume that interest rates increase by 0.8% (80 basis points) to 4.4%

	Buy put	Sell call
Exercise price	95.50	96.00
Futures price	95.44	95.44
Exercise?*	Yes	No

(*The put option is exercised since, by exercising the option, the option holder has the right to sell the instrument at 95.50 instead of the market price of 95.44 and gain 6 basis points per contract. The call option is not exercised since, by not exercising the option, the option holder can buy the instrument at a lower market price of 95.44 instead of the higher option exercise price of 96.00.)

Gain on options	
6 × $25 × 68	$10,200
Premium payable	
8.1 × $25 × 68	$13,770
Net cost of the collar	$3,570
Net additional cost	
($136,000 + $3,570)	$139,570

Alternative solution for collar (in %)

	%	
Borrow	−5.1	
Put	0.06	gain (as before)
Call not exercised		
Premium	−0.081	(0.304% − 0.223%)
	−5.121	
	−0.821%	extra vs 4.3%

in $s this is a cost of −$139,570
(0.00821 × $34m × 6/12)

Based on the assumption that interest rates increase by 80 basis points in the next 5 months, the futures hedge would lower the additional cost by the greatest amount and is significantly better than either the options hedge or the collar hedge. In addition to this, futures fix the amount which Daikon Co is likely to pay, assuming that there is no basis risk. The benefits accruing from the options are lower, with the 95.50 option and the collar option actually increasing the overall cost. In each case, this is due to the high premium costs. However, if interest rates do not increase and actually reduce, then the options (and to some extent the collar) provide more flexibility because they do not have to be exercised when interest rates move in the company's favour. But the movement will need to be significant before the cost of the premium is covered.

On that basis, on balance, it is recommended that hedging using futures is the best choice as they will probably provide the most benefit to Daikon Co.

However, it is recommended that the points made in part (b) are also considered before a final conclusion is made.

(b)   **Mark to market: Daily settlements**

2 June: 8 basis points (95.76 – 95.84) × $25 × 50 contracts = $10,000 loss

3 June: 10 basis points (95.66 – 95.76) × $25 × 50 contracts + 5 basis points (95.61 – 95.66) × $25 × 30 contracts = $16,250 loss

[Alternatively: 15 basis points (95.61 – 95.76) × $25 × 30 contracts + 10 basis points (95.66 – 95.76) × $25 × 20 contracts = $16,250 loss]

4 June: 8 basis points (95.74 – 95.66) × $25 × 20 contracts = $4,000 profit

Both mark to market and margins are used by markets to reduce (eliminate) the risk of non-payment by purchasers of the derivative products if prices move against them.

Mark to market closes all the open deals at the end of each day at that day's settlement price, and opens them again at the start of the following day. The notional profit or loss on the deals is then calculated and the margin account is adjusted accordingly on a daily basis. The impact on Daikon Co is that if losses are made, then the company may have to deposit extra funds with its broker if the margin account falls below the maintenance margin level. This may affect the company's ability to plan adequately and ensure it has enough funds for other activities. On the other hand, extra cash accruing from the notional profits can be withdrawn from the broker account if needed.

Each time a market-traded derivative product is opened, the purchaser needs to deposit a margin (initial margin) with the broker, which consists of funds to be kept with the broker while the position is open. As stated above, this amount may change daily and would affect Daikon Co's ability to plan for its cash requirements, but also open positions require that funds are tied up to support these positions and cannot be used for other purposes by the company.

The value of an option prior to expiry consists of time value, and may also consist of intrinsic value if the option is in-the-money. If an option is exercised prior to expiry, Daikon Co will only receive the intrinsic value attached to the option but not the time value. If the option is sold instead, whether it is in-the-money or out-of-the-money, Daikon Co will receive a higher value for it due to the time value. Unless options have other features, like dividends, attached to them, which are not reflected in the option value, they would not normally be exercised prior to expiry.

56 Sembilan

Text references. Chapter 17 for interest rate hedging, Chapter 13 for debt-equity swaps.

Top tips. For part (a) you need to use the forward rates rather than the current yield curve rates for Years 2 to 4. Don't forget the second part of the requirement!

For part (b)(ii) it is important to note that the bank has guaranteed the swap.

Part (c) requires you to think about the implications of raising equity to pay off debt, including the willingness of the shareholders to participate.

Easy marks. Part (b)(i) is fairly straightforward, it just requires you to choose a higher and lower rate to use for the illustration.

Examining team's comments. Part (a) required the candidates to calculate the variable amounts received and the fixed amounts paid by Sembilan Co to Ratus Bank based on forward rates. A number of candidates incorrectly included the 60 basis points, which is part of the original loan contract but would not be part of the swap; and some answers used the spot rates instead of the forward rates. It is surprising that the responses contained basic errors when there was a recent article in the *Student Accountant* on how a swap contract can be valued based on forward rates and a fixed rate. Few candidates could explain why the fixed rate was lower than the four-year spot rate.

In part (b) many responses gave explanations, rather than a demonstration, that the payment liability did not change. Many of the explanations lacked adequate detail. The requirement 'Demonstrate' means that the candidates should show, by examples or otherwise, that the payment does not change whether interest rates increase or decrease. Few managed to do this with any clarity.

Marking scheme

				Marks
(a)		Gross amount receivable by Sembilan Co	1	
		Gross amounts payable by Sembilan Co	1	
		Net amounts receivable or payable every year	2	
		Explanation of why fixed rate is less than the four-year yield curve rate	2	
				6
(b)	(i)	Demonstration of impact of interest rate changes	4	
		Explanation and conclusion	1	
				5
	(ii)	1 mark per relevant discussion point	Max	5
(c)		1–2 marks per relevant discussion point	Max	9
				25

(a)   Gross amounts of interest receivable from Ratus Bank based on Year 1 spot rate and Years 2–4 forward rates.

Year 1 = 0.025 × $320m = $8m
Year 2 = 0.037 × $320m = $11.84m
Year 3 = 0.043 × $320m = $13.76m
Year 4 = 0.047 × $320m = $15.04m

Fixed gross amount of interest payable to Ratus Bank in each of the Years 1–4
3.7625% × $320m = $12.04m

Therefore the expected receipts/(payments) are:

Year 1 = $8.00m − $12.04m = ($4.04m)
Year 2 = $11.84m − $12.04m = ($0.20m)
Year 3 = $13.76m − $12.04m = $1.72m
Year 4 = $15.04m − $12.04m = $3.00m

The equivalent fixed rate of 3.7625% is less than the 3.8% 4-year yield curve rate because the 3.8% represents a zero-coupon bond with one payment in the fourth year. The relevant bond here pays coupons at different time periods when the yield curve rates are lower, hence the fixed rate is lower.

(b)   (i)

	% impact	Yield interest 3%	Yield interest 5%
	%	$m	$m
Borrow at yield + 60 basis points	(Yield + 0.6)	(11.52)	(17.92)
Receive yield	Yield	9.60	16.00
Pay fixed	(3.7625)	(12.04)	(12.04)
Fee 20 basis points	(0.2)	(0.64)	(0.64)
	4.5625	(14.60)	(14.60)

The receipt and payment based on the yield curve remove the fluctuating element, leaving the 60 basis points borrowing charge, the 20 basis points fee and the fixed payment rate: 0.6% + 3.7625% + 0.2% = 4.5625%.

(ii) Sembilan Co is using the swap to manage its **interest rate risk** and is protecting against a rise in interest rates. This has been done without changing the initial debt of $320 million, which is already in issue.

The interest rate payments are fixed, which means that it is much easier for Sembilan Co to **forecast its future cash flows** and also helps to budget accurately.

The cost to Sembilan Co is relatively small, especially when compared to **potential losses** if interest rates are to rise. Other derivatives, such as options, are typically more expensive.

The swap will be relatively **straightforward**, with the bank undertaking all the relevant administration and organisation. Other derivatives would be more time consuming to arrange.

The main disadvantage is that Sembilan Co will be unable to take advantage of a **favourable movement** in interest rates.

There is no **counterparty risk** involved as the bank is guaranteeing the swap and will make good any default.

(c) Issuing equity and using the proceeds to reduce the amount of debt will **change the capital structure** of Sembilan Co and there are a number of implications of this which need to be considered.

As the proportion of debt compared to equity increases, **financial distress also increases** and associated costs along with it. Companies with high levels of financial distress may find that suppliers demand more onerous credit terms, and that they may have to give longer credit terms to attract customers and pay higher wages to attract employees. Also providers of equity may **demand a higher level of return** because financial risk has increased. In addition, there may be restrictive covenants that make it more difficult to raise funds (either debt or equity). On the other hand, there will be greater levels of tax relief from the higher interest payments. However, this is only available while the company is making taxable profits or **tax exhaustion** will set in. Sembilan Co is assumed to have judged the relative benefits of high and low levels of financial gearing in making its original decision on debt and equity levels.

The proposed equity issue will change the existing balance and therefore the value of Sembilan Co may not be maximised. However, a **lower debt level** would result in a **higher credit rating** for the company as well as reduce the scale of restrictive covenants. Increasing the level of equity would also increase the debt capacity of the company, which would help to raise finance for future projects more easily. Reduced financial distress may make it easier to deal with stakeholders such as suppliers and customers.

Changing the financial structure of a company can be expensive. There are likely to be costs for the early redemption of debt which can be found in the contractual clauses of the debt to be repaid. **A new issue of equity may also be expensive**, especially if shares are offered to new shareholders as there will be marketing costs and underwriting costs as well. Although a rights issue may be less expensive, the costs may still be significant.

If a rights issue is undertaken, Sembilan Co will need to decide on whether the current shareholders will be able to take up the rights and the level of discount to the current market price that should be offered to ensure a full take-up of rights. The impact of the rights issue on the current price should be considered as well. Studies have shown that **typically markets view rights issues positively** and the share price does not reduce to the theoretical ex-rights price. However, this is because the funds are usually spent on profitable projects and the reaction may not be so positive if the funds are to be used to repay debt.

The move will need to be justified to the market and so Sembilan Co will need to provide information to existing and any new shareholders which shows that one group will not be favoured at the expense of another. Sufficient information is required to **prevent issues with information asymmetry**, but if too much information is produced it may reduce the competitive position of Sembilan Co.

57 Pault

Marking scheme

			Marks
(a)	(i)	Gross amount payable by Pault Co	1
		Calculation of forward rates	3
		Basis point reduction	1
		Net amounts receivable or payable each year	1
			6
	(ii)	Yield interest calculations	5
		Comment on interest payment liability	1
			6
(b)	Up to 2 marks per point		Max 4
(c)	Advantages (up to 2 marks per relevant point)		Max 5
	Disadvantages (up to 2 marks per relevant point)		Max 5
			9
			25

(a) (i) Gross amount of annual interest paid by Pault Co to Millbridge Bank = 4.847% × $400m = $19.39m.

Gross amounts of annual interest receivable by Pault Co from Millbridge Bank, based on Year 1 spot rates and Years 2–4 forward rates:

Year

1    $0.0350 \times \$400m = \$14m$
2    $0.0460 \times \$400m = \$18.4m$
3    $0.0541 \times \$400m = \$21.64m$
4    $0.0611 \times \$400m = \$24.44m$

Workings

Year 2 forward rate: $(1.0425^2/1.037) - 1 = 4.80\%$

Year 3 forward rate: $(1.0470^3/1.0425^2) - 1 = 5.61\%$

Year 4 forward rate: $(1.0510^4/1.0470^3) - 1 = 6.31\%$

Rates are reduced by 20 basis points in calculation.

At the start of the swap, Pault will expect to pay or receive the following net amounts at each of the next four years:

Year

1    $14m – $19.39m = $(5.39m) payment
2    $18.4m – $19.39m = $(0.99m) payment
3    $21.64m – $19.39m = $2.25m receipt
4    $24.44m – $19.39m = $5.05m receipt

(ii)   **Interest payment liability**

	Impact %	Yield interest 2.9% $m	Yield interest 4.5% $m
Borrow at yield interest + 50 bp	(Yield + 0.5)	(13.60)	(20.00)
Receive yield – 20 bp	Yield – 0.2	10.80	17.20
Pay fixed 4.847%	(4.847)	(19.39)	(19.39)
Bank fee – 25 bp	(0.25)	(1.00)	(1.00)
	(5.797)	(23.19)	(23.19)

The interest payment liability will be $23.19m, whatever the yield interest, as the receipt and payment are based on the yield curve net of interest rate fluctuations.

(b)   At the start of the contract, the value of the swap will be zero. The terms offered by Millbridge Bank equate the discounted value of the fixed rate payments by Pault Co with the variable rate payments by Millbridge Bank.

However, the value of the swap will not remain at zero. If interest rates increase more than expected, Pault Co will benefit from having to pay a fixed rate and the value of the swap will increase. The value of the swap will also change as the swap approaches maturity, with fewer receipts and payments left.

(c)   **Disadvantages of swap arrangement**

The swap represents a long-term commitment at a time when interest rates appear uncertain. It may be that interest rate rises are lower than expected. In this case, Pault Co will be committed to a higher interest rate and its finance costs may be higher than if it had not taken out the finance arrangements. Pault Co may not be able to take action to relieve this commitment if it becomes clear that the swap was unnecessary.

On the basis of the expected forward rates, Pault Co will not start benefiting from the swap until Year 3. Particularly during Year 1, the extra commitment to interest payments may be an important burden at a time when Pault Co will have significant development and launch costs.

Pault Co will be liable for an arrangement fee. However, other methods of hedging which could be used will have a cost built into them as well.

Advantages of swap arrangement

The swap means that the annual interest payment liability will be fixed at $23.19m over the next 4 years. This is a certain figure which can be used in budgeting. Having a fixed figure may help planning, particularly as a number of other costs associated with the investment are uncertain.

The directors will be concerned not just about the probability that floating rates will result in a higher commitment than under the swap, but also about how high this commitment could be. The directors may feel that rates may possibly rise to a level which would give Pault Co problems in meeting its commitments and regard that as unacceptable.

Any criticism after the end of the loan period will be based on hindsight. What appeared to be the cheapest choice at that stage may not have been what appeared most likely to be the cheapest choice when the loan was taken out. In addition, criticism of the directors for not choosing the cheapest option fails to consider risk. The cheapest option may be the most risky. The directors may reasonably take the view that the saving in cost is not worth the risks incurred.

The swap is for a shorter period than the loan and thus allows Pault Co to reconsider the position in four years' time. It may choose to take out another swap then on different terms, or let the arrangement lapse and pay floating rate interest on the loan, depending on the expectations at that time of future interest rates.

58 Yilandwe

> **Text references.** Overseas investment appraisal is covered in Chapter 8 of the Study Text.
>
> **Examining team's comments.** Many candidates found the calculations required in this question difficult and appeared to spend a significant amount of time on them. This created pressure on them to complete the rest of the requirements of the question in less time and also the structure of the report was often unsatisfactory. This meant that candidates failed to gain many of the easier marks available for discussing the assumptions and the majority of the professional marks. Many candidates' scripts which had marks of between 40% and 49% could have passed if these marks had been gained.
>
> In part (a), generally this part of the question was done well with many candidates getting between three and five marks out of five. Where marks were lower, the candidates did not compare between the two options but merely talked about the benefits and drawbacks of setting up a plant in another country. Sometimes candidates made too many points on this part and spent too long on it. Good time management within questions, as well as between questions, is essential.
>
> In part (b), unsatisfactory answers tried to convert all cash flows into dollars from the outset, instead of keeping them in Yilandwe currency. This was not a good approach, as it made the subsequent inflationary impact very difficult to calculate and often the answers were incorrect. Therefore, such answers received few marks.
>
> **Easy marks.** There are numerous easy marks to be picked up in part (a) and (b)(ii) of this question.

Marking scheme

				Marks
(a)		Benefits	2–3	
		Drawbacks	2–3	
				Max 5
(b)	(i)	Sales revenue	3	
		Parts costs	3	
		Variable costs	2	
		Fixed costs	1	
		Royalty fee	1	
		Tax payable in Yilandwe	3	
		Working capital	2	
		Remittable cash flows ($)	1	
		Contribution from parts ($)	2	
		Tax on parts' contribution and royalty	1	
		Impact of lost contribution and redundancy	1	
		NPV of project	1	
				21
	(ii)	Up to 2 marks per assumption discussed	Max 9	
		2–3 marks per issue/risk discussed	Max 11	
				Max 17
	(iii)	Reasoned recommendation		3
		Professional marks		
		Report format	1	
		Layout, presentation and structure	3	
				4
				50

(a) Benefits of own investment as opposed to licensing

Imoni Co may be able to benefit from setting up its own plant as opposed to licensing in a number of ways.

First, Yilandwe wants to attract foreign investment and is willing to offer a number of financial concessions to foreign investors which may not be available to local companies.

The company may also be able to control the quality of the components more easily, and offer better and targeted training facilities, if it has direct control of the labour resources.

The company may also be able to maintain the confidentiality of its products, whereas assigning the assembly rights to another company may allow that company to imitate the products more easily.

Investing internationally may provide opportunities for risk diversification, especially if Imoni Co's shareholders are not well diversified internationally themselves.

Finally, direct investment may provide Imoni Co with new opportunities in the future, such as follow-on options.

Drawbacks of own investment as opposed to licensing

Direct investment in a new plant will probably require higher, upfront costs from Imoni Co compared to licensing the assembly rights to a local manufacturer. It may be able to utilise these saved costs on other projects.

Imoni Co will most likely be exposed to higher risks involved with international investment, such as political risks, cultural risks and legal risks. With licensing these risks may be reduced somewhat.

The licensee, because it would be a local company, may understand the operational systems of doing business in Yilandwe better. It will therefore be able to get off the ground quicker. Imoni Co, on the other hand, will need to become familiar with the local systems and culture, which may take time and make it less efficient initially.

Similarly, investing directly in Yilandwe may mean that it costs Imoni Co more to train the staff and possibly require a steeper learning curve from them. However, the scenario does say that the country has a motivated and well-educated labour force and this may mitigate this issue somewhat.

(**Note.** Credit will be given for alternative, relevant suggestions.)

(b) **Report on the proposed assembly plant in Yilandwe**

This report considers whether or not it would be beneficial for Imoni Co to set up a parts assembly plant in Yilandwe. It takes account of the financial projections, presented in detail in Appendices 1 and 2, discusses the assumptions made in arriving at the projections and discusses other non-financial issues which should be considered. The report concludes by giving a reasoned recommendation on the acceptability of the project.

Assumptions made in producing the financial projections

It is assumed that all the estimates such as sales revenue, costs, royalties, initial investment costs, working capital, and costs of capital and inflation figures are accurate. There is considerable uncertainty surrounding the accuracy of these and a small change in them could change the forecasts of the project quite considerably. A number of projections using sensitivity and scenario analysis may aid in the decision-making process.

It is assumed that no additional tax is payable in the US for the profits made during the first two years of the project's life when the company will not pay tax in Yilandwe either. This is especially relevant to Year 2 of the project.

No details are provided on whether or not the project ends after four years. This is an assumption which is made, but the project may last beyond four years and therefore may yield a positive net present value. Additionally, even if the project ceases after four years, no details are given about the sale of the land, buildings and machinery. The residual value of these non-current assets could have a considerable bearing on the outcome of the project. It is assumed that the increase in the transfer price of the parts sent from the US directly increases the contribution which Imoni Co earns from the transfer. This is probably not an unreasonable assumption. However, it is also assumed that the negotiations with Yilandwe's Government will be successful with respect to increasing the transfer price and the royalty fee. Imoni Co needs to assess whether or not this assumption is realistic.

The basis for using a cost of capital of 12% is not clear and an explanation is not provided about whether or not this is an accurate or reasonable figure. The underpinning basis for how it is determined may need further investigation.

Although the scenario states that the project can start almost immediately, in reality this may not be possible and Imoni Co may need to factor in possible delays.

It is assumed that future exchange rates will reflect the differential in inflation rates between the respective countries. However, it is unlikely that the exchange rates will move fully in line with the inflation rate differentials.

Other risks and issues

Investing in Yilandwe may result in significant political risks. The scenario states that the current political party is not very popular in rural areas and that the population remains generally poor. Imoni Co needs to assess how likely it is that the Government may change during the time it is operating in Yilandwe and the impact of the change. For example, a new government may renege on the current government's offers and/or bring in new restrictions. Imoni Co will need to decide what to do if this happens.

Imoni Co needs to assess the likelihood that it will be allowed to increase the transfer price of the parts and the royalty fee. Whilst it may be of the opinion that currently Yilandwe may be open to such suggestions, this may depend on the interest the Government may get from other companies to invest in Yilandwe. It may consider that agreeing to such demands from Imoni Co may make it obligated to other companies as well.

The financial projections are prepared on the basis that positive cash flows from Yilandwe can be remitted back to the US. Imoni Co needs to establish that this is indeed the case and that it is likely to continue in the future.

Imoni Co needs to be careful about its ethical stance and its values, and the impact on its reputation, given that a school is being closed in order to provide it with the production facilities needed. Whilst the Government is funding some of the transport costs for the children, the disruption this will cause to the children and the fact that after six months the transport costs become the parents' responsibility may have a large, negative impact on the company's image and may be contrary to the ethical values which the company holds. The possibility of alternative venues should be explored.

Imoni Co needs to take account of cultural risks associated with setting up a business in Yilandwe. The way of doing business in Yilandwe may be very different and the employees may need substantial training to adapt to Imoni Co's way of doing business. On the other hand, the fact that the population is well educated, motivated and keen may make this process easier to achieve.

Imoni Co also needs to consider fiscal and regulatory risks. The company will need to assess the likelihood of changes in tax rates, laws and regulations, and set up strategies to mitigate eventualities which can be predicted. In addition to these, Imoni Co should consider and mitigate, as far as possible, operational risks such as the quality of the components and maintenance of transport links.

Imoni Co should assess and value alternative real options which it may have. For example, it could consider whether licensing the production of the components to a local company may be more financially viable; it could consider alternative countries to Yilandwe, which may offer more benefits; it could consider whether the project can be abandoned if circumstances change against the company; and entry into Yilandwe may provide Imoni Co with other business opportunities.

Recommendation

The result from the financial projections is that the project should be accepted because it results in a positive net present value. It is recommended that the financial projections should be considered in conjunction with the assumptions, the issues and risks, and the implications of these, before a final decision is made.

There is considerable scope for further investigation and analysis. It is recommended that sensitivity and scenario analysis be undertaken to take into consideration continuing the project beyond four years and so on. The value of any alternative real options should also be considered and incorporated into the decision.

Consideration must also be given to the issues, risks and factors beyond financial considerations, such as the impact on the ethical stance of the company and the impact on its image, if the school affected is closed to accommodate it.

Report compiled by:

Date:

Appendices

Appendix 1

Year	0	1	2	3	4
	YRm	YRm	YRm	YRm	YRm
Sales revenue (W2)		18,191	66,775	111,493	60,360
Parts costs (W2)		(5,188)	(19,060)	(31,832)	(17,225)
Variable costs (W2)		(2,921)	(10,720)	(17,901)	(9,693)
Fixed costs		(5,612)	(6,437)	(7,068)	(7,760)
Royalty fee (W3)		(4,324)	(4,813)	(5,130)	(5,468)
Tax-allowable depreciation		(4,500)	(4,500)	(4,500)	(4,500)
Taxable profits/(loss)		(4,354)	21,245	45,062	15,714
Tax loss carried forward				(4,354)	
				40,708	
Taxation (40%)		0	0	(16,283)	(6,286)
Add back loss carried fwd				4,354	
Add back depreciation		4,500	4,500	4,500	4,500
Cash flows after tax		146	25,745	33,279	13,928
Working capital	(9,600)	(2,112)	(1,722)	(1,316)	14,750
Land, buildings and machinery	(39,000)				
Cash flows (YRm)	(48,600)	(1,966)	24,023	31,963	28,678

Year	0	1	2	3	4
	YRm	YRm	YRm	YRm	YRm
Exchange rate	101.4	120.1	133.7	142.5	151.9
Remittable flows	(479,290)	(16,370)	179,678	224,302	188,795
Contribution (parts sales)					
($120 + inflation per unit, W4)		18,540	61,108	95,723	48,622
Royalty (W3)		36,000	36,000	36,000	36,000
Tax on contribution and royalty					
(20%)		(10,908)	(19,422)	(26,345)	(16,924)
Cash flows	(479,290)	27,262	257,364	329,680	256,493
Discount factors (12%)	1	0.893	0.797	0.712	0.636
Present values	(479,290)	24,345	205,119	234,732	163,130

Net present value of the project before considering the impact of the lost contribution and redundancy is approximately $148.0 million.

Lost contribution and redundancy cost

The lost contribution and redundancy costs are small compared to the net present value and would therefore have a minimal impact of reducing the net present value by $0.1 million approximately.

(**Note**. Full credit will be given if the assumption is made that the amounts are in $'000 instead of $.)

Appendix 2

Workings

1   *Unit prices and costs including inflation*

Year	1	2	3	4
Selling price (€)	735	772	803	835
Parts ($)	288	297	306	315
Variable costs (YR)	19,471	22,333	24,522	26,925

2   *Sales revenue and costs*

Year	1	2	3	4
	YRm	YRm	YRm	YRm
Sales revenue	$150 \times 735 \times 165$ = 18,191	$480 \times 772 \times 180.2$ = 66,775	$730 \times 803 \times 190.2$ = 111,493	$360 \times 835 \times 200.8$ = 60,360
Parts costs	$150 \times 288 \times 120.1$ = 5,188	$480 \times 297 \times 133.7$ = 19,060	$730 \times 306 \times 142.5$ = 31,832	$360 \times 315 \times 151.9$ = 17,225
Variable costs	$150 \times 19,471$ = 2,921	$480 \times 22,333$ = 10,720	$730 \times 24,522$ = 17,901	$360 \times 26,925$ = 9,693

3   *Royalty fee*

$20 million $\times$ 1.8 = $36 million

This is then converted into YR at the YR/$ rate for each year: 120.1, 133.7, 142.5 and 151.9 for Years 1 to 4 respectively.

4   *Contribution from parts*

Year	1	2	3	4
Revenue per unit in $	280×1.03 = $288.4	288.4×1.03 = $297.052	297.052×1.03 = $305.964	305.964×1.03 = $315.143
Parts costs	200 (current price) − 40 (contribution at current price) = $160 So $160 $\times$ 1.03 = $164.8	164.8×1.03 = $169.744	169.744×1.03 = $174.836	174.836×1.03 = $180.081
Contribution per unit	$288.4 - 164.8$ = $123.6	$297.052 - 169.744$ = $127.308	$305.964 - 174.836$ = $131.128	$315.143 - 180.081$ = $135.062
Contribution in $m	$123.6 \times 150m$ (volume) = $18,540m	$127.308 \times 480m$ = $61,108m	$131.128 \times 730m$ = $95,723m	$135.062 \times 360m$ = $48,622m

(**Note.** Credit will be given for alternative, relevant approaches to the calculations, and to the discussion of the assumptions, risks and issues.)

59 Avem

Text references. Acquisition strategies and valuation issues are covered in Chapters 9 and 10 of the Study Text.

Top tips. For part (a) make sure that you answer **both** aspects to the question (risk diversification **and** identifying undervalued companies).

For part (b) you can score some easy marks by referring to general concerns of competition authorities.

To tackle part (c)(i) you need to realise that what is required is an assessment of the value of the combined entity compared to the value of the two companies as independent entities. If you are working on these lines then you are likely to score a pass mark even if your answer is not perfect.

Part (c)(ii) requires an attempt to assess the present value of the project and also whether to accept an offer at the end of Year 1 to abandon the project. There are many possible approaches here, but the ingredients to success are to have a reasonable attempt at a project-specific cost of capital and to use expected values in a sensible way.

Part (c)(iii) should be attempted even if the numerical analysis in (c)(i) and (c)(ii) has not been completed and gives an opportunity to score some easy marks.

Easy marks. There are numerous easy marks to be picked up in part (a), (b) and (c)(iii) of this question.

Marking scheme

				Marks
(a)		Risk diversification	2–3	
		Purchasing undervalued companies	4–5	
				Max 7
(b)		1–2 marks per point	1	Max 4
(c)	(i)	Avem current value	1	
		Avem free cash flow to equity	1	
		Fugae estimated growth rate	2	
		Fugae estimate of current value	2	
		Combined company – value created	2	
		Gain to Nahara	1	
		Gain to Avem	1	
				10
	(ii)	Reka asset beta	2	
		Project asset beta	1	
		Fugae market value of debt	2	
		Project equity beta and cost of equity	2	
		Project risk-adjusted cost of capital	1	
		Annual PVs of project	1	
		PVs of different outcomes	2	
		Expected NPV before Limni offer	3	
		PV of Limni offer	1	
		Expected NPV of project with Limni offer	3	
				18
	(iii)	Benefits with and without the project	2–3	
		Assumptions	3–4	
		Conclusion	1–2	
				Max 7
		Professional marks		
		Report format	1	
		Layout, presentation and structure	3	
				4
				50

(a) Like individuals holding well-diversified portfolios, a company could reduce its exposure to unsystematic risk by creating a number of subsidiaries in **different sectors**.

This may lead to a **reduction in the volatility of cash flows**, which may lead to a better credit rating and a **lower cost of capital**.

The argument against this states that since **individual shareholders can do this themselves both quickly and cheaply**, there is little reason for companies to do this. Indeed, research suggests that markets do not reward this risk diversification because diversified portfolios are **often managed inefficiently** because head office struggles to cope with the different issues facing each subsidiary. As a result decision making may be **ineffective and slow**.

For Nahara Co, undertaking mergers and acquisitions (M&As) may have beneficial outcomes **if the sovereign fund has its entire investment in the holding company and is not well-diversified itself**. In such a situation unsystematic risk reduction can be beneficial. The case study does not state whether or not this is the case and therefore a definitive conclusion cannot be reached.

If Nahara Co is able to identify undervalued companies and after purchasing the company can increase the value for the holding company overall, by increasing the value of the undervalued companies, then such activity would benefit their shareholders. However, for this strategy to work, Nahara Co must:

(i)   Possess a superior capability or knowledge in identifying bargain buys ahead of its competitor companies. To achieve this, it must have access to better information, which it can tap into quicker and/or have superior analytical tools. This implies that the stock market is **less than semi-strong form efficient**; if the stock market is accurately valuing companies using all available public information then share prices are unlikely to be undervalued.

(ii) Ensure that it has quick access to the necessary funds to pursue an undervalued acquisition. Even if Nahara Co possesses superior knowledge, it is unlikely that this will last for a long time before its competitors find out; therefore it needs to have the funds ready, **to move quickly**. Given that it has access to sovereign funds from a wealthy source, access to funds is probably not a problem.

(iii) Ensure it has competences in turning around underperforming companies – this will require a measure of understanding of the sector that the acquired company is operating in. It is likely that Nahara can develop expertise in a wide range of sectors, but not in all sectors. So there will be **limits to the validity of a diversification strategy**.

(b)   In a similar manner to the Competition and Markets Authority in the UK, the EU will assess significant M&A impact in terms of whether they will lead to **a substantial lessening** of competition within a country's market.

It will, for example, use tests such as worldwide revenue and European revenue of the group after the M&A.

It may **block the M&A** if it feels that the M&A will give the company monopolistic powers or enable it to carve out a dominant position in the market so as to negatively affect consumer choice and prices.

Sometimes the EU may ask for the company to **sell some of its assets** to reduce its dominant position rather than not allow an M&A to proceed. It would appear that this may be the case behind the EU's concern and the reason for its suggested action.

(c)   **Report**

To: Board of Directors, Avem Co
From: AN Consultant
Subject: Proposed acquisition of Fugae Co
Date: XX/XX/XX

Introduction

This report considers whether Avem Co should acquire Fugae Co. In order to assess the additional value created from bringing the two companies together the value of the two companies is determined separately and then as a combined entity. The report concludes by considering whether or not the acquisition will be beneficial to Avem Co and to Nahara Co.

(i)   **Additional value created for Avem without considering the luxury transport project**

Appendix 1 shows that the additional value created from combining the two companies is approximately $451.5m. $276.8m of this will go to Nahara Co, which represents a premium of about 30% which is the minimum acceptable to Nahara Co. The balance of the additional value will go to Avem Co which is about $174.7m. This represents an increase in value of 1.46% [$174.7m/$12,000m].

(ii) **Additional value created for Avem including the luxury transport project**

Appendix 2 shows that accepting **the project would increase Fugae Co's value** as the expected net present value is positive.

After taking into account Lumi Co's offer, the expected net present value is higher. Therefore, it would be **beneficial for Fugae Co to take on the project and accept Lumi Co's offer, if the tourism industry does not grow as expected**, as this will increase Fugae Co's value.

(iii) **Assumptions**

It is assumed that all the figures relating to synergy benefits, betas, growth rates, multipliers, risk-adjusted cost of capital and the probabilities are accurate. There is considerable **uncertainty** surrounding the accuracy of these. A **sensitivity analysis** is probably needed to assess the impact of these uncertainties.

It is assumed that the br model provides a reasonably good estimate of the growth rate, and that perpetuity is not an unreasonable assumption when assessing the value of Fugae Co.

It is assumed that the **capital structure would not change substantially when the new project is taken on**. Since the project is significantly smaller than the value of Fugae Co itself, this is not an unreasonable assumption.

There may be more outcomes in practice than the ones given and financial impact of the outcomes may not be known with such certainty. The **Black-Scholes option pricing model** may provide an alternative and more accurate way of assessing the value of the project.

It is assumed that Fugae Co can rely on Lumi Co paying the $50m at the beginning of Year 2 with certainty. Fugae Co may want to assess the reliability of Lumi Co's offer and whether formal contracts should be drawn up between the two companies.

Concluding comments

Although Nahara Co would gain more than Avem Co from the acquisition both in percentage terms and in monetary terms, **both companies benefit from the acquisition**. As long as all the parties are satisfied that the value is reasonable despite the assumptions highlighted above, it would appear that the acquisition should proceed.

Appendices

Appendix 1: Additional value created from combining Avem Co and Fugae Co

Avem Co, current value = $7.5/share × 1,600m shares = $12,000m

To estimate Fugae's current value we need to estimate the growth rate. This is calculated on the basis of the br_e model.

b = 1 − 0.773 = 0.267

r_e = 0.11

Fugae Co, estimate of growth rate = 0.227 × 0.11 = 0.025 = 2.5%

Fugae Co, current value estimate = $76.5m × 1.025/(0.11 − 0.025) = $922.5m

So the value of the two companies before the combination is approximately $12,000m + $922.5m = $12,922.5m.

The **combined company** is expected to have a value that is 7.5 times its free cash flow. Avem Co's free cash flow to equity = $12,000m/7.2 = $1,666.7m

Fugae's free cash flow is $76.5 million and is expected to increase by the expected synergy of $40 million.

So we can estimate the additional value created by the combined company as:

Value as a combined company − value of Avem and Fugae as independent companies

([$1,666.7m + $76.5m + $40m] × 7.5) − ($12,922.5m) = **$451.5m**

Nahara will expect a 30% return so the gain to Nahara for selling Fugae Co, 30% × $922.5m = **$276.8m**

Therefore Avem Co will gain $174.7m of the additional value created, $451.5m – $276.8m = **$174.7m**

Appendix 2: Value of project to Fugae Co

Appendix 2.1 Project cost of capital

Estimate of risk-adjusted cost of capital to be used to discount the project's cash flows

The project value is calculated based on its cash flows which are discounted at the project's risk-adjusted cost of capital, to reflect the business risk of the project.

To determine the beta of the project we first need to calculate Reka Co's asset beta

Reka Co equity value = $4.50 × 80m shares = $360m

Reka Co debt value = 1.05 × $340m = $357m

Asset beta = 1.6 × $360m/($360m + $357m × 0.8) = 0.89

Now we can calculate the project's asset beta

0.89 = project's asset beta × 0.15 + 0.80 × 0.85

Project's asset beta = 1.4

Before we can calculate the cost of equity for this project we will need to adjust it for Fugae Co's debt levels.

Fugae has $380m of debt in terms of its book value. To calculate the market value of this debt we need to take into account the return required by debt holders. This can be estimated as

Cost of debt = Risk-free rate of return plus the credit spread

= 4% + 0.80% = 4.80%

So the current market value of a $100 bond =

$5.4 × 1.048^{-1} + $5.4 × 1.048^{-2} + $5.4 × 1.048^{-3} + $105.4 × 1.048^{-4} =

$102.14 per $100 book value.

So the total market value of debt = 1.0214 × $380m = $388.1m.

The market value of Fugae's equity has been previously estimated as $922.5m.

So now we can take the asset beta of 1.4 and estimate the project's risk-adjusted equity beta using

$$\beta a = \left(\frac{Ve}{(Ve + Vd\,(1-t))} \right) \beta e + \left(\frac{Vd\,(1-t)}{(Ve + Vd\,(1-t))} \right) \beta d$$

so

1.4 = ($922.5m/($922.5m + $388.1m × 0.8) βe

1.4 × ($922.5m + $388.1m × 0.8)/$922.5m = βe = 1.87

So the project's risk-adjusted cost of equity is:

(ri) = R_f + β $(E(R_m - R_f))$

4% + 1.87 × 6% = **15.2%**

And finally the project's risk-adjusted cost of capital

$$WACC = \left(\frac{V_e}{V_e + V_d} \right) K_e + \left(\frac{V_d}{V_e + V_d} \right) K_d\,(1-t)$$

(922.5/(922.5 + 388.1)) 15.2% + (388.1m/(922.5m + 388.1m)) 4.8% × 0.8

= 11.84%, say 12%

Appendix 2.2 Estimate of expected value of the project without the offer from Lumi Co

If the first year is as expected

($'000)

Year	1	2	3	4
Cash flows	3,277.6	16,134.3	36,504.7	35,683.6
Discount factor 12%	0.893	0.797	0.712	0.636
Present values	2,926.9	12,859.0	25,991.3	22,694.8
Probabilities	1.0	0.8	0.8	0.8
Expected value	**2,926.9**	**10,287.8**	**20,793.0**	**18,155.8**
Present values (40% time 2 – 4)		$12,859.0 \times 0.4$ = 5,143.6	$25,991.3 \times 0.4$ = 10,396.5	$22,694.8 \times 0.4$ = 9,077.9
Probabilities		0.2	0.2	0.2
Expected value		**1,029.3**	**2,079.3**	**1,815.6**
Total expected value	**2,926.9**	**11,317.1**	**22,872.3**	**19,971.4**

Total expected value from time 1–4 if the first year is as expected is therefore 2,926.9 + 11,317.1 + 22,872.3 + 19,971.4 = $57,087.7 (000).

There is a 75% chance of this occurrence.

If the first year is NOT as expected

($'000)

Year	1	2	3	4
Present values (50% fall from original projections)	$2,926.9 \times 0.5$ = 1,463.5	$12,859.0 \times 0.5$ = 6,429.5	$25,991.3 \times 0.5$ = 12,995.7	$22,694.8 \times 0.5$ = 11,347.4

Total expected value from time 1–4 if the first year is **not** as expected is therefore 1,463.5 + 6,429.5 + 12,995.7 + 11,347.4 = $32,236.1 (000).

There is a 25% chance of this occurrence.

The **overall present value (PV) of the project inflows** is $(75\% \times 57,087.7) + (25\% \times 32,236.1)$ = $50,874.8 (000).

So the **project net present value (NPV)** is 50,874.8 – 42,000 = **$8,874.8 (000)**.

Estimate of expected value of the project with the offer from Lumi Co

PV of $50m = $50,000,000 \times 0.893 = $44,650,000$

If the tourism industry does not grow as expected in the first year, then it is more beneficial for Fugae Co to exercise the offer made by Lumi Co, given that Lumi Co's offer of $44.65m (PV of $50m) is greater than the PV of the Years 2 to 4 cash flows for that outcome. This figure is then incorporated into the expected NPV calculations.

So, if the first year is **not** as expected the PV of the inflows becomes 1,463.5 + 44,650 = $46,113.5 (000).

There is a 25% chance of this occurrence.

The **overall PV of the project inflows** now becomes $(75\% \times 57,087.7) + (25\% \times 46,113.5)$ = $54,344.2 (000).

So the **project NPV** is 54,344.2 – 42,000 = **$12,344.2 (000)**.

(**Note.** Credit will be given for alternative, relevant approaches to the calculations, comments and suggestions/recommendations.)

60 Chmura

Marking scheme

			Marks
(a)	Role of the World Trade Organization		4–5
	Benefits of reducing protectionist measures		2–3
	Drawbacks of reducing protectionist measures		2–3
		Max	9
(b)	(i)	Future exchange rates predicted on inflation rate differential	1
		Sales revenue	1
		Production and selling costs	1
		Special packaging costs	2
		Training and development costs	1
		Correct treatment of tax and tax-allowable depreciation	2
		Years 1 to 5 cash flows in $ and present values of cash flows	2
		Ignoring initial investigation cost and additional taxation in Chmura Co host country	1
		Correct treatment of land, buildings, machinery and working capital	2
		Net present value of the project	1
			14

	Marks
(ii) Inputting correct values for the variables	2
Calculation of d1 and d2	2
Establishing N(d1) and N(d2)	2
Call value	1
Put value	1
Value of the project	1
	9

	Marks
(iii) Estimated value and initial recommendation	2–3
Up to 2 marks per assumption discussed	5–6
Up to 2 marks per additional business risk discussed	5–6
Overarching recommendation(s)	1–2
Max	14

	Marks
Professional marks	1
Report format	3
Structure and presentation of the report	4
	50

(a) The WTO was set up to continue to implement the General Agreement on Tariffs and Trade (GATT), and its main aims are to reduce the barriers to international trade. It does this by seeking to prevent protectionist measures such as tariffs, quotas and other import restrictions. It also acts as a forum for negotiation and offering settlement processes to resolve disputes between countries.

The WTO encourages free trade by applying the most favoured nation principle between its members, where a reduction in tariffs offered to one country by another should be offered to all members.

Whereas the WTO has had notable success, some protectionist measures between groups of countries are nevertheless allowed and some protectionist measures, especially non tariff based ones, have been harder to identify and control.

Mehgam could benefit from reducing protectionist measures because its actions would make other nations reduce their protectionist measures against it. Normally countries retaliate against each other when they impose protectionist measures. A reduction in these may allow Mehgam to benefit from increased trade and economic growth. Such a policy may also allow Mehgam to specialise and gain competitive advantage in certain products and services, and compete more effectively globally. Its actions may also gain political capital and more influence worldwide.

Possible drawbacks of reducing protectionist policies mainly revolve around the need to protect certain industries. It may be that these industries are developing and in time would be competitive on a global scale. However, inaction to protect them now would damage their development irreparably. Protection could also be given to old, declining industries which, if not protected, would fail too quickly due to international competition, and would create large-scale unemployment making such inaction politically unacceptable. Certain protectionist policies are designed to prevent 'dumping' of goods at a very cheap price, which hurts local producers.

Note. Credit will be given for alternative relevant discussion.

(b) **Report to the BoD, Chmura Co**

This report recommends whether or not Chmura Co should invest in a food packaging project in Mehgam, following Mehgam reducing its protectionist measures. It initially considers the value of the project without taking into account the offer made by Bulud Co to purchase the project after two years. Following this, Bulud Co's offer is considered. The report concludes by recommending a course of action for the BoD to consider further.

Estimated value of the Mehgam project and initial recommendation

The initial net present value of the project is negative at approximately $(451,000) (see Appendix 1). This would suggest that Chmura Co should not undertake the project.

Bulud Co's offer is considered to be a real option for Mehgam Co. Since it is an offer to sell the project as an abandonment option, a put option value is calculated based on the Finance Director's assessment of the standard deviation and using the Black-Scholes option pricing (BSOP) model. The value of the put option is added to the initial net present value of the project without the option, to give the value of the project. Although Chmura Co will not actually obtain any immediate cash flow from Bulud Co's offer, the real option computation indicates that the project is worth pursuing because the volatility may result in increases in future cash flows.

After taking account of Bulud Co's offer and the Finance Director's assessment, the net present value of the project is positive at approximately $2,942,000 (see Appendix 2). This would suggest that Chmura Co should undertake the project.

Assumptions

It is assumed that all the figures relating to variables such as revenues, costs, taxation, initial investments and their recovery, inflation figures and cost of capital are accurate. There is considerable uncertainty surrounding the accuracy of these, and in addition to the assessments of value conducted in Appendices 1 and 2, sensitivity analysis and scenario analysis are probably needed to assess the impact of these uncertainties.

It is assumed that future exchange rates will reflect the differential in inflation rates between the two countries. It is, however, unlikely that exchange rates will move fully in line with the inflation rate differentials.

It is assumed that the value of the land and buildings at the end of the project is a relevant cost, as it is equivalent to an opportunity benefit, even if the land and buildings are retained by Chmura Co.

It is assumed that Chmura Co will be given and will utilise the full benefit of the bi-lateral tax treaty and therefore will not pay any additional tax in the country where it is based.

It is assumed that the short-dated $ treasury bills are equivalent to the risk-free rate of return required for the BSOP model. And it is assumed that the Finance Director's assessment of the 35% standard deviation of cash flows is accurate.

It is assumed that Bulud Co will fulfil its offer to buy the project in two years' time and there is no uncertainty surrounding this. Chmura Co may want to consider making the offer more binding through a legal contract.

The BSOP model makes several assumptions such as perfect markets, constant interest rates and lognormal distribution of asset prices. It also assumes that volatility can be assessed and stays constant throughout the life of the project, and that the underlying asset can be traded. Neither of these assumptions would necessarily apply to real options. Therefore the BoD needs to treat the value obtained as indicative rather than definitive.

Additional business risks

Before taking the final decision on whether or not to proceed with the project, Chmura Co needs to take into consideration additional risks, including business risks, and where possible mitigate these as much as possible. The main business risks are as follows:

Investing in Mehgam may result in political risks. For example, the current Government may be unstable and if there is a change of government, the new Government may impose restrictions, such as limiting the amount of remittances which can be made to the parent company. Chmura Co needs to assess the likelihood of such restrictions being imposed in the future and consider alternative ways of limiting the negative impact of such restrictions.

Chmura Co will want to gain assurance that the countries to which it will sell the packaged food batches remain economically stable and that the physical infrastructure such as railways, roads and shipping channels are maintained in good repair. Chmura Co will want to ensure that it will be able to export the

BPP LEARNING MEDIA

special packaging material into Mehgam. Finally, it will need to assess the likelihood of substantial protectionist measures being lifted and not re-imposed in the future.

As much as possible, Chmura Co will want to ensure that fiscal risks such as imposition of new taxes and limits on expenses allowable for taxation purposes do not change. Currently, the taxes paid in Mehgam are higher than in Chmura Co's host country and, even though the bi-lateral tax treaty exists between the countries, Chmura Co will be keen to ensure that the tax rate does not change disadvantageously.

Chmura Co will also want to protect itself, as much as possible, against adverse changes in regulations. It will want to form the best business structure, such as a subsidiary company, joint venture or branch, to undertake the project. Also, it will want to familiarise itself on regulations such as employee health and safety law, employment law and any legal restrictions around land ownership.

Risks related to the differences in cultures between the host country, Mehgam, and the countries to which the batches will be exported would be a major concern to Chmura Co. For example, the product mix in the batches which are suitable for the home market may not be suitable for Mehgam or where the batches are exported. It may contain foods which would not be saleable in different countries and therefore standard batches may not be acceptable to the customers. Chmura Co will also need to consider the cultural differences and needs of employees and suppliers.

The risk of the loss of reputation through operational errors would need to be assessed and mitigated. For example, in setting up sound internal controls, segregation of duties is necessary. However, personal relationships between employees in Mehgam may mean that what would be acceptable in another country may not be satisfactory in Mehgam. Other areas Chmura Co will need to focus on are the quality control procedures to ensure that the quality of the food batches is similar to the quality in the host country.

Recommendation

With Bulud Co's offer, it is recommended that the BoD proceed with the project, as long as the BoD is satisfied that the offer is reliable, the sensitivity analysis/scenario analysis indicates that any negative impact of uncertainty is acceptable and the business risks have been considered and mitigated as much as possible.

If Bulud Co's offer is not considered, then the project gives a marginal negative net present value, although the results of the sensitivity analysis need to be considered. It is recommended that, if only these results are taken into consideration, the BoD should not proceed with the project. However, this decision is marginal and there may be other valid reasons for progressing with the project such as possibilities of follow-on projects in Mehgam.

Report compiled by:

Date:

Appendices

Appendix 1: Estimated value of the Mehgam project excluding the Bulud Co offer

(Cash flows in MPm)

Year	1	2	3	4	5
Sales revenue (W2)	1,209.6	1,905.1	4,000.8	3,640.7	2,205.4
Production and selling costs (W3)	(511.5)	(844.0)	(1,856.7)	(1,770.1)	(1,123.3)
Special packaging costs (W4)	(160.1)	(267.0)	(593.7)	(572.0)	(366.9)
Training and development costs	(409.2)	(168.8)	0	0	0
Tax-allowable depreciation	(125)	(125)	(125)	(125)	(125)
Balancing allowance					(125)
Taxable profits/(loss)	3.8	500.3	1,425.4	1,173.6	465.2
Taxation (25%)	(1.0)	(125.1)	(356.4)	(293.4)	(116.3)
Add back depreciation	125	125	125	125	250
Cash flows (MPm)	127.8	500.2	1,194.0	1,005.2	598.9

(All amounts in $'000)

Year	1	2	3	4	5
Exchange rate (W1)	76.24	80.72	85.47	90.50	95.82
Cash flows ($'000)	1,676.3	6,196.7	13,969.8	11,107.2	6,250.3
Discount factor for 12%	0.893	0.797	0.712	0.636	0.567
Present values ($'000)	1,496.9	4,938.8	9,946.5	7,064.2	3,543.9

Present value (PV) of cash flows approx. = $26,990,000

PV of value of land, buildings and machinery in Year 5 = (80% × MP1,250m + MP500m)/95.82 × 0.567 approx. = $8,876,000

PV of working capital = MP200m/95.82 × 0.567 approx. = $1,183,000

Cost of initial investment in $ = (MP2,500m + MP200m)/72 = $37,500,000

NPV of project = $26,990,000 + $8,876,000 + $1,183,000 − $37,500,000 = $(451,000)

Workings

1   *Exchange rates*

Year	1	2	3	4	5
MP/$1	72 × 1.08/1.02 = 76.24	76.24 × 1.08/1.02 = 80.72	80.72 × 1.08/1.02 = 85.47	85.47 × 1.08/1.02 = 90.50	90.50 × 1.08/1.02 = 95.82

2   *Sales revenue (MPm)*

Year	1	2	3	4	5
	10,000 × 115,200 × 1.05 = 1,209.6	15,000 × 115,200 × 1.05^2 = 1,905.1	30,000 × 115,200 × 1.05^3 = 4,000.8	26,000 × 115,200 × 1.05^4 = 3,640.7	15,000 × 115,200 × 1.05^5 = 2,205.4

3   *Production and selling (MPm)*

Year	1	2	3	4	5
	10,000 × 46,500 × 1.1 = 511.5	15,000 × 46,500 × 1.1^2 = 844.0	30,000 × 46,500 × 1.1^3 = 1,856.7	26,000 × 46,500 × 1.1^4 = 1,770.1	15,000 × 46,500 × 1.1^5 = 1,123.3

4   *Special packaging (MPm)*

Year	1	2	3	4	5
	10,000 × 200 × 76.24 × 1.05 = 160.1	15,000 × 200 × 80.72 × 1.05^2 = 267.0	30,000 × 200 × 85.47 × 1.05^3 = 593.7	26,000 × 200 × 90.50 × 1.05^4 = 572.0	15,000 × 200 × 95.82 × 1.05^5 = 366.9

Appendix 2: Estimated value of the Mehgam project including the Bulud Co offer

Present value of underlying asset (Pa) = $30,613,600 (approximately)

(This is the sum of the PVs of the cash flows forgone in Years 3, 4 and 5)

Price offered by Bulud Co (Pe) = $28,000,000

Risk-free rate of interest (r) = 4% (assume government treasury bills are a valid approximation of the risk-free rate of return)

Volatility of underlying asset (s) = 35%

Time to expiry of option (t) = 2 years

$d_1 = [\ln(30,613.6/28,000) + (0.04 + 0.5 × 0.35^2) × 2]/[0.35 × 2^{1/2}] = 0.59$

$d_2 = 0.59 − 0.35 × 2^{1/2} = 0.10$

$N(d_1) = 0.5 + 0.2224 = 0.7224$

$N(d_2) = 0.5 + 0.0398 = 0.5398$

Call value = $30,613,600 \times 0.7224 - $28,000,000 \times 0.5398 \times e^{-0.04 \times 2}$ = approx. $8,160,000

Put value = $8,160,000 - $30,613,600 + $28,000,000 \times e^{-0.04 \times 2}$ = approx. $3,393,000

Net present value of the project with put option = $3,393,000 - $451,000 = approx. $2,942,000

(**Note.** Credit will be given for relevant discussion and recommendation.)

61 Mlima

Text references. Cost of capital and adjusted present value (APV) is covered in Chapter 7a and free cash flow valuations in Chapter 7b. Stock exchange listings are covered in Chapter 2 and ethical issues in Chapter 3.

Top tips. For part (a)(i) you have to know which formula to use to calculate the ungeared cost of equity. It is the MM Proposition 2 formula which is given to you in the exam.

For part (a)(ii) you should have picked up from the question information that the Bahari project needs to be valued using the APV method.

To tackle part (a)(iii) you need to work out what the bond holders stand to gain from the swap and compare it to the current value of the bond in order to decide whether or not they are likely to accept it.

For part (b) make sure you only use the information contained in the question. Note that there is nothing saying the relationship between the president of Bahari and the CEO is inappropriate. Also consider what would happen to the farmers if Mlima Co does not take up the mining option. Note that your answer should be split evenly between the two issues.

Easy marks. There are numerous easy marks to be picked up in part (a)(ii) for calculating the values for Mlima. Part (a)(iv) also offers some easy marks for some straightforward observations.

Examining team's comments. Many candidates spent far too long on this question to the detriment of the rest of the exam. Good time management, an ability to work under pressure and making a reasonable attempt at all the requirements of all the questions are the key ingredients for success.

In part (a)(iii) few candidates could calculate the current value of the bonds, most incorrectly discounting by the coupon rate to get back to the $40m. The subsequent advice given was poor, with little insight given as to why might the bond holders accept or not accept the offer, except to say in very general terms that if the equity value was greater than the current bond value they would probably accept the offer. Many answers displayed a lack of sound understanding of the subject.

For part (a)(iv) a sizeable number of candidates ignored or answered this part very superficially and therefore did not gain the majority of the 12 marks.

For part (b) answers tackled the first issue of relocation of farmers better than the second issue of the relationship between the leaders of the country and the company.

Marking scheme

				Marks
(a)	(i)	Explanation of Mlima Co's cost of capital based on Ziwa Co's ungeared cost of equity	3	
		Ziwa Co, cost of ungeared equity	4	
				7
	(ii)	Sales revenue growth rates	1	
		Operating profit rate	1	
		Estimate of free cash flows and PV of free cash flows for Years 1 to 4	4	
		PV of free cash flows after Year 4	2	
		Base case Bahari project value	2	
		Annual tax shield benefit	1	
		Annual subsidy benefits	1	
		PV of tax shield and subsidy benefits	1	
		Value of the Bahari project	1	
				14

				Marks
(iii)	Calculation of unsecured bond value	2		
	Comment	2		
	Limitation	1		
			5	
(iv)	Comments on the range of values	3–4		
	Discussion of assumptions	3–4		
	Explanation for additional reasons for listing	2–3		
	Assessment of reasons for discounted share price	2–3		
	Conclusion	1–2		
			Max 12	

Professional marks

	Report format	1		
	Layout, presentation and structure	3		
			4	
(b)	Discussion of relocation of farmers	4–5		
	Discussion of relationship between Bahari president and Mlima Co CEO	4–5		
			Max	8
				50

(a) **Report**

To: Board of Directors, Mlima Co
From: AN Consultant
Subject: Initial public listing: price range and implications
Date: XX/XX/XX

This report considers a range of values for Mlima Co to consider in preparation for the proposed public listing. These values are based on 100 million shares being issued. The assumptions made in determining these values are discussed and the likelihood of the equity-for-debt swap being successful is also considered. Finally the report will evaluate other reasons for listing and also why the shares should be issued at a discount.

Mlima Co cost of capital

Ziwa Co's ungeared cost of equity represents the return Ziwa Co's shareholders would require if Ziwa Co was financed entirely by equity. This return would compensate the shareholders for the business risk of Ziwa Co's operations.

Since Mlima Co is in the same industry, and therefore faces the **same business risk**, this required rate of return should also compensate Mlima Co's shareholders. This rate would be used as Mlima Co's cost of capital as it is expecting to have no debt and therefore this rate **does not need adjusting for financial risk**. Therefore the cost of equity is also the cost of capital. This cost of capital is calculated in Appendix 1 as 11%.

Mlima Co estimated value

Using the cost of capital of 11%, the value of Mlima Co is calculated as $564.9 million (see Appendix 2 for full calculation), before considering the proposed Bahari project. The value of the Bahari investment, without considering the tax shield and subsidy benefits from the subsidised government loan, does not exceed the initial investment. When the tax and subsidy benefits are considered, the present value of the Bahari project is $21.5 million (see Appendix 3 for full calculation). This gives a total value for Mlima Co of just over $586 million. This gives the **following potential share prices**, based on 100 million shares, including the effect of the suggested 20% share price discount.

Potential share price	Excluding Bahari project	Including Bahari project
Full value	$5.65 per share	$5.86 per share
20% discount	$4.52 per share	$4.69 per share

Equity-for-debt swap

The unsecured bond is currently estimated to be worth $56.8 million (see Appendix 4 for full calculation). It is proposed that the existing bond holders will be offered a 10% stake in Mlima Co post-listing, which means that **only the value at $5.86 per share would leave the bond holders better off**, and therefore would be the only acceptable price. If the lowest price of $4.52 per share is used, then the equity stake would need to be around 12.6% for the bond holders to accept the offer (56.8m/4.52 = 12.566).

The bond value is based on a yield to maturity of 7%, because Mlima Co can borrow at 7%, so this is therefore its current yield. The yield could be **more accurately estimated** if it was based on future risk-free rates and the credit spreads for the company.

Assumptions

The main assumptions are over the **accuracy of the estimates** used in producing the valuation. The value of Mlima Co is based on estimated future growth rates, profit margins, tax rates and capital investment. The future growth rates and margins are based on **past data, which may not be a reliable indicator of future prospects**. The Bahari project includes estimated cash flows for 15 years and the reasonableness of these estimates needs to be considered to see if they are realistic.

The cost of capital used for Mlima Co is based on Ziwa Co's ungeared cost of equity, on the basis that the business risk is the same for both companies as they operate in the same industry. However, it is possible that the **business risks are different**, for example due to geographical locations, and therefore the cost of capital is not appropriate for Mlima Co. Accepting the Bahari project could also affect the business risk of Mlima Co.

The value of the Bahari project is based on the Bahari Government providing the promised subsidised loan. Mlima Co needs to consider whether the full subsidy will definitely be provided for the full 15 years and whether a change of government may change the position. There may also be other **political risks** which need to be assessed fully.

Transaction costs for the listing have been ignored as they are assumed to be insignificant. It should be confirmed that this is the case before making a final decision.

Reasons for a public listing

The main reason behind this public listing is to remove the debt from the company. Other reasons for pursuing a public listing include: a **gain in prestige** for the company by listing on a recognised stock exchange, having **greater access to sources of finance** and being able to raise funds more quickly as a result, providing shareholders with a value for their equity stake and enabling them to **realise their investment** if they wish to do so.

Issuing shares at a discount

Since the public will only be issued 20% of the share capital from the initial listing, they will be **minority shareholders** and have a limited ability to influence the decision making of Mlima Co. Even if they voted as a bloc, they would not be able to overturn the decision on their own. The discounted share price, would therefore compensate the shareholders for the **additional risk** of being minority shareholders. The position of the unsecured bond holders should also be considered. On the assumption that they hold 12.6% of the equity (as discussed earlier) they could form a bloc with the new shareholders of 32.6%, which would be **enough to influence company decisions**. Whether they would form a bloc with new shareholders or are more closely aligned with the interests of the current owners is something that should be looked into.

Shares are often issued at a discount to ensure that they all get sold. This is even more common for a new listing and the price of the shares does usually rise immediately after the listing.

Conclusion

A price range for the listing of between $4.52 and $5.86 per share has been calculated, depending on whether the Bahari project is undertaken and whether the shares are offered at a discount of 20%. It is recommended that Mlima Co consults the underwriters for the share issue, to carry out book-building to assess the price that potential investors are willing to pay.

If 20% of the shares (20 million shares) are sold to the public at $4.52 per share, the listing will raise just over $90 million. $80 million would then be spent redeeming the secured bond, leaving just in excess of $10 million of funds remaining. Mlima Co needs to consider whether these funds will be **sufficient to carry on its operations**. The Bahari investment may result in a change to the desired capital structure of the company, which may also have an impact on the cost of capital.

Becoming a listed company will also result in listing costs and **additional annual costs** to meet compliance and reporting requirements. These factors will need to be balanced against the benefits of listing before making a decision whether or not to proceed.

Appendices

Appendix 1: Mlima cost of capital

Ziwa Co market value of debt = 105/100 × 1,700m = $1,785m
Ziwa Co market value of equity = 200m × $7 = $1,400m
Ziwa Co ungeared cost of equity using $k_{eg} = k_{eu} + (1 - t)(k_{eu} - k_d)$ D/E
16.83% = k_{eu} + 0.75(k_{eu} − 4.76%) × 1,785/1,400
16.83% + 4.55% = 1.9563k_{eu}
k_{eu} = 10.93% (say 11%)

Appendix 2: Value of Mlima Co prior to Bahari project

Past 2 years' sales growth = $\sqrt{\dfrac{389.1}{344.7}} - 1 = 0.0625$ or 6.25%

Expected growth for 4 years = 1.2 × 6.25% = 7.5%

Operating profit margin (historic)

20X3   58.4/389.1 = 0.150
20X2   54.9/366.3 = 0.150
20X1   51.7/344.7 = 0.150

Operating profit margin is expected to be 15%.

Year	1	2	3	4	4+
	$m	$m	$m	$m	$m
Sales revenue (increasing at 7.5%)	418.3	449.7	483.4	519.7	
Operating profit (15%)	62.7	67.5	72.5	78.0	
Tax at 25%	(15.7)	(16.9)	(18.1)	(19.5)	
Additional capital investment (W1)	(8.8)	(9.4)	(10.1)	(10.9)	
Free cash flows	38.2	41.2	44.3	47.6	49.3*
Discount factor (11%)	0.901	0.812	0.731	0.659	8.787**
PV of free cash flows	34.4	33.5	32.4	31.4	433.2

Value of company = $564.9m

* 47.6 × 1.035 = 49.3

** 1/(0.11 − 0.035) × 0.659 = 8.787

Working

Year	1	2	3	4
	$m	$m	$m	$m
Sales revenue	418.3	449.7	483.4	519.7
Increase in revenue	29.2	31.4	33.7	36.3
30% of increase	8.8	9.4	10.1	10.9

Appendix 3: Value of Bahari project

Base case

Year	Free cash flow $m	Discount factor 11%	PV $m
0	(150)	1.000	(150.0)
1	4	0.901	3.6
2	8	0.812	6.5
3	16	0.731	11.7
4	18.4	0.659	12.1
5	21.2	0.593	12.6
6–15	21.2	3.492	74.0
			(29.5)

10-year annuity discounted for 5 years = 5.889 × 0.593

Annual tax shield benefit = 3% × 150m × 25% = $1.1m

Subsidy benefit = 4% × 150m × 0.75 = $4.5m

Total annual benefit = $5.6m

Annuity factor (7%, 15 years) = 9.108

PV of tax shield and subsidy benefit = 5.6m × 9.108 = $51.0m

APV = ($29.5m) + $51.0m = $21.5m

Appendix 4: Value of unsecured bond

Annual interest = 13% × 40m = $5.2m

Assume a yield to maturity of 7%. A 10-year annuity factor at 7% is 7.024

Discount factor for redemption of bond (7%, 10 years) is 0.508

Bond value = 5.2m × 7.024 + 40m × 0.508 = $56.8m

(b) The activities of Mlima Co are likely to be of greater interest and be **scrutinised more closely** once it is listed. The company needs to consider the ethical implications of both situations and whether Mlima Co is complying with its own ethical code (if it has one).

Regarding the relocation of the farmers, Mlima Co needs to judge where its responsibility lies. It may decide that this is a **matter between the farmers and the Government**, and that Mlima Co is not responsible (either directly or indirectly) for the current situation. If Mlima Co does not agree to the offer, it seems likely that the **mining rights would be given to another company** and so the farmers' situation would not improve by Mlima Co walking away from the deal. Mlima may be better off by influencing the Government over this issue by asking it to keep the farmers together and to offer them more fertile land. In addition, Mlima Co could offer jobs and training to any farmers who choose to remain where they are.

In the case of the Bahari president and Mlima Co's CEO, Mlima Co must ensure that any negotiation was transparent and there was **no bribery or other illegal practice involved**. If the company and the Government can show that decisions have been made in the **best interests** of the country and Mlima Co, and no individuals benefited from the decision, then it should not be seen negatively. Indeed, it is good for business to have strong relationships and this can create a **competitive advantage**.

Mlima should consider how it would respond to public scrutiny of these issues, possibly even pre-empting issues by releasing press statements to explain positions.

62 Lignum

(a)

To:	Treasury Division, Lignum Co
From:	Financial Adviser
Date:	December 20X2
Subject:	Foreign exchange exposure management

This report considers three separate situations involving foreign exchange exposure for Lignum Co and makes recommendations to the treasury department on how to manage these situations.

Types of exposure

In case one, there is a foreign currency receipt in four months' time. There is an exposure due to the possibility that the exchange rates may move against Lignum Co between now and the receipt. This is known as **transaction exposure**. In case two, Lignum Co is faced with **translation exposure** where a subsidiary's assets are translated from the home currency into euro. The local currency is likely to devalue by 20% in the very near future. Lastly, in case three, there is **economic exposure** where the present value of future sales of a locally produced and sold good is being reduced due to overseas produced goods being sold at a relatively cheaper price. The case appears to show that because the US$ has depreciated against the euro, goods can be sold at the same dollar price but a lower euro price.

Hedging strategies

Case one

Transaction exposure is short term in nature and can usually be managed by a variety of hedging techniques, including derivative products. Lignum Co has a choice of two derivative products, an over-the-counter (OTC) forward rate and an OTC option. The forward rate gives a **higher return** of €963,988 compared to the option return of €936,715. Detailed calculations can be found in Appendix 1.

However, the forward rate **locks Lignum Co** into a rate of ZP145.23 per €1 irrespective of the actual movement in the exchange rates. With the option, the company has a choice and if exchange rates move in its favour, ie the Zupeso strengthens against the euro, then Lignum Co can let the option lapse. The decision needs to be made whether a **guaranteed higher amount** is preferable to a guaranteed minimum of €936,715 with the possibility of gains if the Zupeso appreciates.

There may be **other alternatives** to derivatives available to Lignum Co. There may be money market hedging and leading and lagging or a Zupeso bank account may be possible. The Zupeso account may allow **natural hedges** with only periodic currency conversions required to minimise transaction costs. Information on the investment rate in Zupesos would be required in order to consider a money market hedge.

Case two

It would not be necessary to hedge translation risk if the stock market on which Lignum Co is listed is efficient. The translation of the subsidiary's assets is **purely an accounting entry** that occurs for consolidation of group accounts. There is **no actual cash flow** in or out of the company. If money was spent on hedging this risk, then the group will lose money overall, meaning there is less cash available for

distribution to shareholders. However, translation losses may not be fully understood by shareholders, who may **view them negatively**, and there may be associated negative impacts on analytical trends or ratios. As a result Lignum Co may choose to hedge the risk.

The most efficient hedge for such a situation would be to **match assets and liabilities**. In this case, Namel Co has greater asset exposure to the MR and as a result, the expected weakening of the currency would make a translation loss of €1,018,000 (see Appendix 2 for full calculations). This translation exposure could be reduced by **matching liabilities** more closely to assets, for example by converting non-current liability loans in euro to loans in MR.

Case three

Economic exposure is **long term in nature** and as a result is harder to manage/hedge. Few derivatives are offered that cover a long period of time, although some swaps are long term. There is a further issue in that if Lignum Co is exposed to this situation for a long period there will be a sustained negative impact to the company cash flows and value. Lignum Co would find it difficult to maintain an advantage against the US competitor. As a result a **long-term strategic view** is required to manage this risk. For example, if a decision was made to locate production in countries with favourable exchange rates and cheap inputs such as raw materials and labour, the risk will be reduced. A further alternative would be to set up a US subsidiary to create a **natural hedge** for the US$ cash flows.

Appendices

Appendix 1: Case one calculations

Forward rate

Forward rate = 142 × (1 + (0.085 + 0.0025) / 3)/(1 + (0.022 − 0.0030)/3) = 145.23

Receipt due = 140,000,000/145.23 = €963,988

Option

Call options should be purchased to cover the currency depreciation.

Income from option = 140,000,000/142 = €985,915

Option cost

€985,915 × ZP7 = ZP6,901,405

Converting to €

ZP6,901,405/142 = €48,601

It is assumed that the funds for this cost need to be borrowed, so this cost is multiplied by the borrowing rate for the total cost.

€48,601 × (1 + 0.037/3) = €49,200

Net income = €985,915 − €49,200 = €936,715

Tutorial note. The investing rate could have been used above instead of the borrowing rate to calculate the opportunity cost of not investing the funds that were used to pay this cost if this is assumed instead.

Appendix 2: Case two calculations

Devalued rate = MR35 × 1.2 = MR42 per €1

	MR'000	Exposure	€'000 at MR35 per €1	€'000 at MR42 per €1
Non-current assets	179,574	100%	5,131	4,276
Current assets	146,622	60%	2,514	2,095
Non-current liabilities	(132,237)	20%	(756)	(630)
Current liabilities	(91,171)	30%	(781)	(651)
	102,788		6,108	5,090

Total translation loss = €6,108,000 − €5,090,000 = €1,018,000

(b) (i) Lignum Co must pay today (development cost) in order to have the opportunity/option to enter into production in three years' time. It will only choose to do this if the production option value exceeds the present value of the development cost.

Development cost

Time	Cash flow	DF	AV
	€m		€m
0	2.5	1	2.50
1	2.5	$\dfrac{1}{1.12^1}$	2.23
2	2.5	$\dfrac{1}{1.12^2}$	1.99
PV of development cost			6.72

Production option

To evaluate this real call option we need to establish:

P_a = PV of all volatile future cash flows if the project is undertaken

P_e = PV **at the option expiry date** of any non-volatile cash flows arising if the project is undertaken.

s = Volatility of the returns from S

r_f = Risk-free rate

T = Time of expiry

Considering the future volatile cash flows, at today's prices the unit production cost will be €0.8m with a selling price at €0.9m (12½% margin) giving a net cash inflow at €0.1m per unit or €6m p.a. (60 units p.a.). These figures are exposed to an average annual inflation at 4% subject to 22% volatility.

With a cost of capital of 12% and inflation at 4% there is a real required return that can be calculated as:

$1.12 = (1 + r) \times 1.04$

$(1 + r) = \dfrac{1.12}{1.04} = 1.07692$

$r = 0.07692$ or 7.692% p.a.

From the date the production commences we can view the return as a 12-year annuity at €6m to be discounted at a rate of 7.692%, ie:

Time	Cash flow	DF	AV
	€m		€m
1–12	6	$\dfrac{1}{0.07692}(1 - \dfrac{1}{1.07692^{12}})$	45.95

PV of volatile production cash flows at time = 3	45.95
Discount factor to bring to time = 0	45.95
	$\dfrac{1}{1.07692^3}$
PV at volatile production cash flows at time = 0 (S)	36.79

So we have

P_a = €36.79m P_e = €31.4m   s = 22% p.a. r_f = 5.5% p.a.

t = 3 years

$d_1 = \dfrac{\ln\left[\dfrac{36.79}{31.4}\right] + (0.055 + 0.5 \times 0.22^2) \times 3}{0.22 \times \sqrt{3}} = 1.039$

$d_2 = d_1 - s\sqrt{t} = 1.039 - 0.22 \times \sqrt{3} = 0.658$

$N(d_1) = N(1.04) = 0.5 + 0.3508 = 0.8508$

$N(d_2) = N(0.66) = 0.5 + 0.2454 = 0.7454$

$C = P_a N(d_1) - P_e e^{-rt} N(d_2)$

$C = 36.79 \times 0.8508 - 31.4 \times 0.7454 \times e^{-0.055 \times 3} = €11.45m$

Conclusion

	€m
Value of developments call option	11.45
PV of development costs	(6.72)
NPV of development opportunity	4.73

Hence Lignum Co should proceed with the development.

(ii) **Monte Carlo simulation**

A great advantage of using Monte Carlo simulation is that a number of simulations can be run in a **short space of time** on a computer.

It is also possible to build a model with lots of variables, such as level of demand and volatility in steel alloy prices and test changes in each of these variables.

The main disadvantage is in constructing a model that accurately reflects the real world. Although certain economic relationships can be predicted, it is unlikely that a detailed sophisticated model could be produced without significant **time and expense**. Even then, this may not accurately model real world conditions.

In addition, a Monte Carlo simulation will not necessarily generate the optimal solution for Lignum Co; rather, it shows the best option after a number of simulations.

As long as the model is not prohibitively expensive, it is recommended that Lignum Co uses Monte Carlo simulation as part of the evaluation of the opportunity, but that other factors are also considered, particularly if there are any **follow-on opportunities** arising from this project.

(c) The **Black-Scholes pricing model** was developed to value traded call options on quoted shares and can be adapted to value any options. The input variables are:

(i) **The market price of the underlying share**

If the **share price rises**, the value of the call option will increase.

(ii) **The exercise price (or strike price)**

A **call option** gives the holder the **right to buy** the share at a fixed price, known as the **exercise price**. The **higher the price of the underlying share** compared with the exercise price (above), the **more valuable** is the **option**.

(iii) **The time to expiry**

The longer an option has to run before it expires, the more chance there is that the **value of the underlying share will increase**. Time to expiry therefore **adds value** to an option.

(iv) **The volatility of the underlying share (standard deviation of share price variations)**

Options provide **unlimited opportunities for gains** but **losses** are **limited to the purchase price**. This asymmetrical probability distribution of gains/losses means that volatility of the underlying share **adds value** to the option.

(v) **The interest rate**

This is the **risk-free rate of interest**, which gives the **time value of money** and is relevant because the option is valued today but is exercisable on a future date.

The difference between (i) and (ii) is known as the '**intrinsic value**' of the option, but it has a minimum value of zero. The combination of (iii), (iv) and (v) gives its '**time value**'. The total value of the option is the sum of intrinsic and time values.

63 Tramont

Marking scheme

		Marks	
(a)(i)	Estimated future rates based on purchasing power parity	1	
	Sales revenue, variable costs, component cost and fixed costs (in GR)	4	
	Taxable profits and taxation	2	
	Investment, terminal value and working capital	2	
	Cash flows in GR	1	
	Cash flows in $	1	
	Discount rate of all-equity financed project	2	
	Base case PVs and NPV	2	
	PVs of additional contribution, additional tax and opportunity cost	4	
	PV of tax shield and subsidy benefits	4	
	Closure costs and benefits	1	
	Initial comments and conclusion	1–2	
	Assumptions and sensitivity analysis	2–3	
			Max 27
(ii)	Implications of change of government	2–3	
	Other business factors (1–2 marks per factor)	5–6	
			Max 8
	Professional marks		
	Report format	1	
	Layout, presentation and structure	3	
			4

BPP
LEARNING MEDIA

		Marks
(b)	1 mark per relevant point	6
(c)	General commentary regarding benefits of risk diversification	2–3
	Relating specifically to Tramont Co and the Gamalan investment	2–3

Max <u>5</u>
<u>50</u>

(a)

To:	The Board of Directors of Tramont Co
From:	Accountant
Date:	XX/X/XX
Subject:	Evaluation of proposal to relocate production of X-IT to Gamala

The report considers the proposal to relocate production of X-IT from the US to Gamala. The report includes an initial evaluation and then considers the key assumptions made in the evaluation, the potential effects of a change in the Government of Gamala following the upcoming elections and also other business factors that should be taken into account before a decision is made.

The initial evaluation is a base case NPV calculation that assesses the impact of production in Gamala. This is then adjusted to show the impact of cash flows in the US, including the impact of ceasing production, the impact of the subsidy and the tax shield benefits arising from the loan.

Based on the calculations, which can be found in the appendix, the move will generate a positive APV of just over $2.3 million. Based on these calculations it is recommended that production of X-IT should move to Gamala.

Assumptions

The **borrowing rate of 5%** has been used to calculate the present value of the tax shield benefits. The risk-free rate of 3% could have been used instead, but it was felt more prudent to use the 5% rate.
An APV calculation would normally use the debt capacity for the tax shield benefit calculation rather than the amount of debt finance used, but as this is not known it has been **assumed that the increase in debt capacity is equal to the debt finance used**.

There are a number of variables included in the calculations. It is assumed that these will change as stated over the four-year period. Exchange rates have been forecast using purchasing power parity, which it is assumed will hold for the four-year period. In reality these variables may not alter as has been assumed and therefore **it is recommended that sensitivity analysis is used** to calculate the effect of changes in these key variables on the overall conclusion.

Government change

A change of government in Gamala may have a significant impact on the project as a result of changes threatened by the opposition party. The **proposed tax increase may be significant** as this would reduce the total tax shield and subsidy benefits as well as creating higher cash outflows in Years 3 and 4 of the project. An even more significant change may arise, however, from the review of 'commercial benefits'. Approximately 45% (1,033/2,317) of the APV comes from the tax shield and subsidy benefits. If these arrangements were to change then Tramont could lose a significant amount of value from the project.

The new Government may also review whether remittances are allowed every year as has been assumed in these calculations. This issue may be fairly minor as the majority of the value comes from the final year of operation anyway.

Other business factors

Tramont needs to also consider whether being based in Gamala will lead to any **follow-on projects**. The real options that are present within any such projects should be factored into the assessment of whether to relocate.

Tramont also needs to ensure that this project **fits within its overall strategy**. Even if the decision to cease production in the US is made there may be other, better alternatives than the Gamalan option. These other options should also be assessed.

Tramont also needs to consider whether its **systems can be adapted to the culture in Gamala**. If Tramont has experience in international ventures then its directors may be surer of this. Tramont will need to develop strategies to combat any cultural differences. There may be further training costs as part of these strategies which have not been factored into this assessment.

Another factor to consider is whether the project can be delayed as this will reduce the opportunity cost of lost contribution, which is greater in Years 1 and 2. Therefore **a delay could increase the overall value** of the project.

There are possible redundancies from the closure of production of X-IT in the US. Since production will probably cease in the US anyway the strategy should be clearly communicated to employees and other stakeholders in order to ensure its reputation is not damaged. As a result it may be even more important to consider alternatives to this plan.

Conclusion

The initial evaluation suggests that moving production of X-IT to Gamala would be beneficial. Before making a final decision, the board should conduct a detailed sensitivity analysis, analysis of the effects of a change in government and the financial effects of the other factors identified above.

Appendix

NPV of Gamalan project

Year	0	1	2	3	4
	GR'000	GR'000	GR'000	GR'000	GR'000
Sales revenue (W2)		48,888	94,849	214,442	289,716
Variable costs – local (W3)		(16,200)	(32,373)	(75,385)	(104,897)
Imported components (W4)		(4,889)	(9,769)	(22,750)	(31,658)
Fixed costs (inflating at 9%)		(30,000)	(32,700)	(35,643)	(38,851)
Profit before tax		(2,201)	20,007	80,664	114,310
Tax (W5)		0	0	(7,694)	(18,862)
Investment	(230,000)				450,000
Working capital	(40,000)	(3,600)	(3,924)	(4,277)	51,801
Total GR cash flows	(270,000)	(5,801)	16,083	68,693	597,249
Exchange rate GR/$ (W1)	55.00	58.20	61.59	65.18	68.98

Year	0	1	2	3	4
	$'000	$'000	$'000	$'000	$'000
Total $ cash flows	(4,909)	(100)	261	1,054	8,658
$ discount factor (W6)	1.000	0.909	0.826	0.751	0.683
Present value	(4,909)	(91)	216	792	5,913

NPV = $1,921,000

APV	$'000
Base case NPV	1,921
Additional US tax, opportunity cost and additional component contribution (W7)	(1,237)
Closure revenues and costs ($2.3m – $1.7m)	600
Tax shield and subsidy benefits (W8)	1,033
APV	2,317

Workings

1   *Exchange rates*

GR/$

Now   55.00
Year 1 $55.00 \times (1.09/1.03) = 58.20$
Year 2 $58.20 \times (1.09/1.03) = 61.59$
Year 3 $61.59 \times (1.09/1.03) = 65.18$
Year 4 $65.18 \times (1.09/1.03) = 68.98$

2   *Sales revenue*

Revenue = price × units × exchange rate

Year	1	2	3	4
	GR'000	GR'000	GR'000	GR'000
Sales revenue	$70 \times 12,000 \times 58.20$ = 48,888	$70 \times 22,000 \times 61.59$ = 94,849	$70 \times 47,000 \times 65.18$ = 214,442	$70 \times 60,000 \times 68.98$ = 289,716

3   *Variable costs – local*

Unit cost × units × inflation after Year 1

Year	1	2	3	4
	GR'000	GR'000	GR'000	GR'000
Cost	$1,350 \times 12,000$ = 16,200	$1,350 \times 22,000 \times 1.09$ = 32,373	$1,350 \times 47,000 \times 1.09^2$ = 75,385	$1,350 \times 60,000 \times 1.09^3$ = 104,897

4   *Imported components*

Price × units × inflation after Year 1 × exchange rate

Year	1	2	3	4
	GR'000	GR'000	GR'000	GR'000
Cost	$7 \times 12,000 \times 58.20$ = 4,889	$7 \times 22,000 \times 1.03 \times 61.59$ = 9,769	$7 \times 47,000 \times 1.03^2 \times 65.18$ = 22,750	$7 \times 60,000 \times 1.03^3 \times 68.98$ = 31,658

5   *Taxation*

Year	1	2	3	4
	GR'000	GR'000	GR'000	GR'000
Profit/(loss) before tax	(2,201)	20,007	80,664	114,310
Tax-allowable depreciation	(20,000)	(20,000)	(20,000)	(20,000)
Revised profit/(loss)	(22,201)	7	60,664	94,310
Offset against previous losses	0	(7)	(22,194)	0
Losses carried forward	(22,201)	(22,194)	0	0
Tax base	0	0	38,470	94,310
Taxation @ 20%	0	0	(7,694)	(18,862)

6   *Discount rate*

Tramont Co equity beta = 1.17

$MV_e = \$2.40 \times 25m$ shares = \$60m
$MV_d = \$40m \times \$1,428/\$1,000 = \$57.12m$

Tramont Co asset beta (assume debt is risk free)

$1.17 \times 60m/(60m + (57.12 \times 0.7)) = 0.70$

Project asset beta = 0.70 + 0.40 = 1.10
Project discount rate if all-equity financed = 3% + (1.1 × 6%) = 9.6% say 10%

7   *Additional tax, additional contribution and opportunity cost ($'000)*

Year	1	2	3	4
Additional tax*	0	0	(59)	(137)
Opportunity cost**	(560)	(448)	(358)	(287)
Additional contribution***	34	63	140	184
Total cash flows	(526)	(385)	(277)	(240)
7% discount factor	0.935	0.873	0.816	0.763
Present value	(492)	(336)	(226)	(183)

Total present value = $(1,237,000)

* Taxable profits/exchange rate × 10%
** Units × contribution × (1 – tax rate)
*** Units × contribution × inflation × (1 – tax rate)

8   *Tax shield and subsidy benefits (GR'000/$'000)*

Year	1	2	3	4
	GR'000	GR'000	GR'000	GR'000
Annual tax shield*	3,240	3,240	3,240	3,240
Annual subsidy benefit**	15,120	15,120	15,120	15,120
Total benefit	18,360	18,360	18,360	18,360
Exchange rate	58.20	61.59	65.18	68.98
	$'000	$'000	$'000	$'000
Cash flow	315	298	282	266
5% discount rate	0.952	0.907	0.864	0.823
PV	300	270	244	219

Total present value = $1,033,000

* Interest × loan × tax rate = 6% × 270m × 20% = 3.24m
** Interest gain × loan × (1 – tax rate) = 7% × 270m × 0.8 = 15.12m

(b)   Triple bottom line (TBL) reporting involves providing a quantitative summary in terms of social, financial and environmental performance.

The **underlying principle** is that in order to evaluate a company's true performance against its objectives, and assess the risk to the investor, the investor must consider all three areas.

Under the TBL approach decision making should ensure that **each perspective is growing** but not at the **expense** of the others. That is, economic performance should not come at the expense of the environment or society. The idea is that an organisation which accommodates all three areas will enhance shareholder value as long as the costs of producing the report are less than the benefits that arise from it.

In the case of Tramont and production of X-IT, reporting on the impact of moving production to Gamala, including the environmental impact, will show Tramont in a good light and improve its reputation. This should in turn make it easier to attract and retain the best employees.

(c)   Portfolio theory states that shareholders who hold a well-diversified portfolio will have diversified away the unsystematic or company-specific risk and will be left with systematic risk. Following this a shareholder cannot reduce risk further by undertaking **additional diversification** in the same system or market. A company may be able to achieve further diversification for its shareholders by investing in a system or market that the individual shareholders do not invest in themselves. Some studies have shown that well-diversified investors **can benefit from risk diversification** when companies invest in **emerging markets**.

In the case of Tramont and X-IT, it is unclear whether there will be any diversification benefits from the Gamalan investment. Any benefits are dependent on the **size of the investment** and the **nature** of the business operations in Gamala. Another issue is whether the investment represents an investment in a different system or market. If the investment is large and the operations are similar to undertaking a Gamalan company then shareholders in Tramont who do not hold similar companies' shares **may gain risk diversification benefits** from the investment.

64 Cigno

Marking scheme

			Marks
(a)		Up to 2 marks for distinguishing the two forms of unbundling	4
(b)	(i)	Appendix 1	
		Anatra Co, manufacturing business, P/E ratio	1
		Estimate of the value created from sell-off	3
		Appendix 2	
		Cigno Co asset beta	1
		Combined company asset beta	1
		Combined company equity beta	1
		Combined company cost of capital	1

Appendix 3

	Marks
Sales revenue, Years 1 to 4	1
Operating profit, Years 1 to 4	1
Taxation, Years 1 to 4	1
Capital investment, Years 1 to 4	1
Value from Years 1 to 4	1
Value from Year 5 onwards	1
Value for Cigno Co shareholders before impact of savings from tax and employee cost reduction	2

Appendix 4

	Marks
Value created from tax and employee cost savings	1
Value for Cigno Co shareholders after impact of savings from tax and employee cost reduction	1
	18

				Marks
(ii)	Discussion of values for the equity holders, additional costs/benefits not given			3–4
	Methods used and assumptions made			4–5
			Max	8
(iii)	Reputation factors			1–2
	Ethical factors			1–2
	Comment on value			1–2
			Max	4

Professional marks for part (b)

	Marks
Report format	1
Structure and presentation of the report	3
	4

			Marks
(c)	1 to 2 marks per point	Max	6
(d)	Up to 2 marks for explaining the purpose of each condition		6
			50

(a)   Both forms of unbundling involve disposing of the non-core parts of the company.

The divestment through a sell-off normally involves selling part of a company as an entity or as separate assets to a third party for an agreed amount of funds or value. This value may comprise of cash and non cash based assets. The company can then utilise the funds gained in alternative, value-enhancing activities.

The MBI is a particular type of sell-off which involves selling a division or part of a company to an external management team, who will take up the running of the new business and have an equity stake in the business. An MBI is normally undertaken when it is thought that the division or part of the company can probably be run better by a different management team compared to the current one.

(b)   **Report to the BoD, Cigno Co**

This report assesses the potential value of acquiring Anatra Co for the equity holders of Cigno Co, both with and without considering the benefits of the reduction in taxation and in employee costs. The possible issues raised by reduction in taxation and in employee costs are discussed in more detail below. The assessment also discusses the estimates made and the methods used.

Assessment of value created

Cigno Co estimates that the premium payable to acquire Anatra Co largely accounts for the benefits created from the acquisition and the divestment, before considering the benefits from the tax and employee costs saving. As a result, before these savings are considered, the estimated benefit to Cigno Co's shareholders of $128 million (see Appendix 3) is marginal. Given that there are numerous estimations made and the methods used make various assumptions, as discussed below, this benefit could be smaller or larger. It would appear that without considering the additional benefits of cost and tax reductions, the acquisition is probably too risky and would probably be of limited value to Cigno Co's shareholders.

If the benefits of the taxation and employee costs saved are taken into account, the value created for the shareholders is $5,609 million (see Appendix 4), and therefore significant. This would make the acquisition much more financially beneficial. It should be noted that no details are provided on the additional pre-acquisition and post-acquisition costs or on any synergy benefits that Cigno Co may derive in addition to the cost savings discussed. These should be determined and incorporated into the calculations.

Basing corporate value on the P/E method for the sell-off, and on the free cash flow valuation method for the absorbed business, is theoretically sound. The P/E method estimates the value of the company based on its earnings and on competitor performance. With the free cash flow method, the cost of capital takes account of the risk the investors want to be compensated for and the non-committed cash flows are the funds which the business can afford to return to the investors, as long as they are estimated accurately.

However, in practice, the input factors used to calculate the organisation's value may not be accurate or it may be difficult to assess their accuracy. For example, for the free cash flow method, it is assumed that the sales growth rate, operating profit margin, the taxation rate and incremental capital investment can be determined accurately and remain constant. It is assumed that the cost of capital will remain unchanged and it is assumed that the asset beta, the cost of equity and cost of debt can be determined accurately. It is also assumed that the length of the period of growth is accurate and that the company operates in perpetuity thereafter. With the P/E model, the basis for using the average competitor figures needs to be assessed; for example, have outliers been ignored; and the basis for the company's higher P/E ratio needs to be justified as well. The uncertainties surrounding these estimates would suggest that the value is indicative, rather than definitive, and it would be more prudent to undertake sensitivity analysis and obtain a range of values.

Key factors to consider in relation to the redundancies and potential tax savings

It is suggested that the BoD should consider the impact of the cost savings from redundancies and from the tax payable in relation to corporate reputation and ethical considerations.

At present, Cigno Co enjoys a good reputation and it is suggested that this may be because it has managed to avoid large-scale redundancies. This reputation may now be under threat and its loss could affect Cigno Co negatively in terms of long-term loss in revenues, profits and value; and it may be difficult to measure the impact of this loss accurately.

Whilst minimising tax may be financially prudent, it may not be considered fair. For example, currently there is ongoing discussion and debate from a number of governments and other interested parties that companies should pay tax in the countries they operate and derive their profits, rather than where they are based. Whilst global political consensus in this area seems some way off, it is likely that the debate in this area will increase in the future. Companies that are seen to be operating unethically with regard to this may damage their reputation and therefore their profits and value.

Nonetheless, given that Cigno Co is likely to derive substantial value from the acquisition, because of these savings, it should not merely disregard the potential savings. Instead it should consider public relations exercises it could undertake to minimise the loss of reputation, and perhaps meet with the Government to discuss ways forward in terms of tax payments.

Conclusion

The potential value gained from acquiring and unbundling Anatra Co can be substantial if the potential cost savings are taken into account. However, given the assumptions that are made in computing the value, it is recommended that sensitivity analysis is undertaken and a range of values obtained. It is also recommended that Cigno Co should undertake public relations exercises to minimise the loss of reputation, but it should probably proceed with the acquisition, and undertake the cost saving exercise because it is likely that this will result in substantial additional value.

Report compiled by:

Date:

Appendix 1: Estimate of value created from the sell-off of the equipment manufacturing business

Average industry P/E ratio = $2.40/$0.30 = 8
Anatra Co's equipment manufacturing business P/E ratio = 8 × 1.2 = 9.6

Value from sell-off of equipment manufacturing business
Share of pre-tax profit = 30% × $2,490m = $747m

After-tax profit = $747m $\times$ (1 – 0.22) = $582.7m
Value from sell-off = $582.7m $\times$ 9.6 = $5,594m (approximately)

Appendix 2: Estimate of the combined company cost of capital

Anatra Co, asset beta = 0.68

Cigno Co, asset beta:
Equity beta = 1.10
Proportion of market value of debt = 40%; Proportion of market value of equity = 60%
Asset beta = 1.10 $\times$ 0.60/(0.60 + 0.40 $\times$ 0.78) = 0.72

Combined company, asset beta
Market value of equity, Anatra Co = $3 $\times$ 7,000m shares = $21,000m
Market value of equity, Cigno Co = 60% $\times$ $60,000m = $36,000m
Asset beta = (0.68 $\times$ 21,000 + 0.72 $\times$ 36,000)/(21,000 + 36,000) = 0.71 (approximately)

Combined company equity beta = 0.71 $\times$ (0.6 + 0.4 $\times$ 0.78)/0.6 = 1.08

Combined company, cost of equity = 4.3% + 1.08 $\times$ 7% = 11.86%
Combined company, cost of capital = 11.86% $\times$ 0.6 + 6.00% $\times$ 0.78 $\times$ 0.4 = 8.99, say 9%

Appendix 3: Estimate of the value created for Cigno Co's equity holders from the acquisition

Anatra Co, medical R&D value estimate:

Sales revenue growth rate = 5%
Operating profit margin = 17.25%
Tax rate = 22%
Additional capital investment = 40% of the change in sales revenue
Cost of capital = 9% (Appendix 2)
Free cash flow growth rate after 4 years = 3%
Current sales revenue = 70% $\times$ $21,400m = $14,980m

Cash flows, Years 1 to 4

Year	1	2	3	4
	$m	$m	$m	$m
Sales revenue	15,729	16,515	17,341	18,208
Profit before interest and tax	2,713	2,849	2,991	3,141
Tax	597	627	658	691
Additional capital investment	300	314	330	347
Free cash flows	1,816	1,908	2,003	2,103
Present value of cash flows (9% discount)	1,666	1,606	1,547	1,490

Value, Years 1 to 4: $6,309m
Value, Year 5 onwards: [$2,103 $\times$ 1.03/(0.09 – 0.03)] $\times$ 1.09^{-4} = $25,575m
Total value of Anatra Co's medical R&D business area = $31,884m

Total value of Anatra Co following unbundling of equipment manufacturing business and absorbing medical R&D business:

$5,594m (Appendix 1) + $31,884m = $37,478m (approximately)

Anatra Co, current market value of equity = $21,000m
Anatra Co, current market value of debt = $9,000m
Premium payable = $21,000m $\times$ 35% = $7,350m

Total value attributable to Anatra Co's investors = $37,350m

Value attributable to Cigno Co's shareholders from the acquisition of Anatra Co before taking into account the cash benefits of potential tax savings and redundancies = Value following unbundling ($37,478m) – Anatra's debt ($9,000m) – price paid for Anatra ($21,000m + $7,350m) = $128m

Appendix 4: Estimate of the value created from savings in tax and employment costs following possible redundancies

Cash flows, Years 1 to 4

Year	1	2	3	4
	$m	$m	$m	$m
Cash flows (4% increase p.a.)	1,600	1,664	1,731	1,800
Present value of cash flows (9%)	1,468	1,401	1,337	1,275

Total value = $5,481m

Value attributable to Cigno Co's shareholders from the acquisition of Anatra Co after taking into account the cash benefits of potential tax savings and redundancies = $5,609m

(c)   The feasibility of disposing of assets as a defence tool against a possible acquisition depends upon the type of assets sold and how the funds generated from the sale are utilised.

If the type of assets are fundamental to the continuing business then this may be viewed as disposing of the corporation's 'crown jewels'. Such action may be construed as being against protecting the rights of shareholders (similar to the conditions discussed in part (d) below). In order for key assets to be disposed of, the takeover regulatory framework may insist on the corporation obtaining permission from the shareholders first before carrying it out.

On the other hand, the assets may be viewed as not being fundamental to the core business and may be disposed of to generate extra funds through a sell-off (see part (a) above). This may make sense if the corporation is undertaking a programme of restructuring and reorganisation.

In addition to this, the company needs to consider what it intends to do with the funds raised from the sale of assets. If the funds are used to grow the core business and therefore enhancing value, then the shareholders would see this positively and the value of the corporation will probably increase. Alternatively, if there are no profitable alternatives, the funds could be returned to the shareholders through special dividends or share buybacks. In these circumstances, disposing of assets may be a feasible defence tactic.

However, if the funds are retained but not put to value-enhancing use or returned to shareholders, then the share price may continue to be depressed. And the corporation may still be an attractive takeover target for corporations which are in need of liquid funds. In these circumstances, disposing of assets would not be a feasible defence tactic.

(d)   Each of the three conditions aims to ensure that shareholders are treated fairly and equitably.

The mandatory-bid condition through sell out rights allows remaining shareholders to exit the company at a fair price once the bidder has accumulated a certain number of shares. The amount of shares accumulated before the rule applies varies between countries. The bidder must offer the shares at the highest share price, as a minimum, which had been paid by the bidder previously. The main purpose for this condition is to ensure that the acquirer does not exploit their position of power at the expense of minority shareholders.

The principle of equal treatment condition stipulates that all shareholder groups must be offered the same terms, and that no shareholder group's terms are more or less favourable than another group's terms. The main purpose of this condition is to ensure that minority shareholders are offered the same level of benefits as the previous shareholders from whom the controlling stake in the target company was obtained.

The squeeze-out rights condition allows the bidder to force minority shareholders to sell their stake, at a fair price, once the bidder has acquired a specific percentage of the target company's equity. The percentage varies between countries but typically ranges between 80% and 95%. The main purpose of this condition is to enable the acquirer to gain a 100% stake of the target company and prevent problems arising from minority shareholders at a later date.

Note. Credit will be given for alternative, relevant approaches to the calculations, comments and suggestions/recommendations.

65 Lirio

Marking scheme

				Marks
(a)		Up to 2 marks per well-explained point	Max	6
(b)	(i)	Appendices 1 and 1.1		
		Operating profit		1
		Interest paid		1
		Tax paid for normal activities		1
		Investment in working capital		1
		Investment in additional non-current assets		1
		Correct treatment of depreciation		1
		Cash flows remitted from Pontac Co		2
		Additional tax payable		1
				9

(ii)   Appendix 2

Amount received based on forward contracts	1
Correctly identifying long contracts and purchasing call options	1
Expected futures price based on linear narrowing of basis	1
Amount received based on futures contracts	1
Recognition of small over-hedge when using futures contracts	1
Option contracts or futures contracts purchased	1
Premium paid in dollars	1
Amount received based on options contracts	2
1–2 marks for each well-discussed point	4
Reasonable recommendation	1
	14

(iii) Appendix 3 and project assessment

Estimate of dividend growth rate (prior to project undertaken)	2
Estimate of corporate value (prior to project undertaken)	1
Annual dividend per share after transfer of funds to project	2
Estimate of value after project is undertaken	2
Concluding comments on project assessment	1
	8

(iv) Discussion of issues

Limitations of method used	1–2
Signalling impact of change in dividend policy	1–2
Clientele impact of change in dividend policy	2–3
Rationale for not considering debt or equity	3–4
Other relevant discussion points	2–3
Max	9

Professional marks for part (b)

Structure and presentation of the discussion paper	3
Clearly highlighting/emphasising areas for further discussion/detailed summary	1
	4
	50

(a)   Purchasing power parity (PPP) predicts that the exchange rates between two currencies depend on the relative differences in the rates of inflation in each country. Therefore, if one country has a higher rate of inflation compared to another, then its currency is expected to depreciate over time. However, according to PPP the 'law of one price' holds because any weakness in one currency will be compensated by the rate of inflation in the currency's country (or group of countries, in the case of the euro).

Economic exposure refers to the degree by which a company's cash flows are affected by fluctuations in exchange rates. It may also affect companies which are not exposed to foreign exchange transactions, due to actions by international competitors.

If PPP holds, then companies may not be affected by exchange rate fluctuations, as lower currency value can be compensated by the ability to raise prices due to higher inflation levels. This depends on markets being efficient.

However, a permanent shift in exchange rates may occur, not because of relative inflation rate differentials, but because a country (or group of countries) lose their competitive positions. In this case the 'law of one price' will not hold, and prices readjust to a new and long-term or even permanent rate. For example, the UK £ to US$ rate declined in the 20th century, as the US grew stronger economically and the UK grew weaker. The rate almost reached parity in 1985 before recovering. Since the financial crisis in 2009, it has fluctuated between roughly $1.5 to £1 and $1.7 to £1.

In such cases, where a company receives substantial amounts of revenue from companies based in countries with relatively weak economies, it may find that it is facing economic exposure and its cash flows decline over a long period of time.

(b)   **Discussion paper to the BoD, Lirio Co**

Discussion paper compiled by:

Date:

Purpose of the discussion paper

The purpose of this discussion paper is:

(i)   To consider the implications of the BoD's proposal to use funds from the sale of its equity investment in the European company and from its cash flows generated from normal business activity over the next two years to finance a large project, instead of raising funds through equity and/or debt

(ii)   To assess whether or not the project adds value for Lirio Co or not

Background information

The funds needed for the project are estimated at $40,000,000 at the start of the project. $23,118,000 of this amount is estimated to be received from the sale of the equity investment (Appendices 2 and 3). This leaves a balance of $16,882,000 (Appendix 3), which will be obtained from the free cash flows to equity (the dividend capacity) of $21,642,000 (Appendix 1) expected to be generated in the first year. However, this would leave only $4,760,000 available for dividend payments in the first year, meaning a cut in expected dividends from $0.27/share to $0.0595/share (Appendix 3). The same level of dividends will be paid in the second year as well.

Project assessment

Based on the dividend valuation model, Lirio Co's market capitalisation, and therefore its value, is expected to increase from approximately $360 million to approximately $403 million, or by just under 12% (Appendix 3). This would suggest that it would be beneficial for the project to be undertaken.

Possible issues

1   The dividend valuation model is based on a number of factors such as: an accurate estimation of the dividend growth rate, a non-changing cost of equity and a predictable future dividend stream growing in perpetuity. In addition to this, it is expected that the sale of the investment will yield €20,000,000 but this amount could increase or reduce in the next 3 months. The dividend valuation model assumes that dividends and their growth rate are the sole drivers of corporate value, which is probably not accurate.

2   Although the dividend irrelevancy theory proposed by Modigliani and Miller suggests that corporate value should not be affected by a corporation's dividend policy, in practice changes in dividends do matter for two main reasons. First, dividends are used as a signalling device to the markets and unexpected changes in dividends paid and/or dividend growth rates are not generally viewed positively by them. Changes in dividends may signal that the company is not doing well and this may affect the share price negatively.

3   Second, corporate dividend policy attracts certain groups of shareholders or clientele. In the main this is due to personal tax reasons. For example, higher rate taxpayers may prefer low dividend payouts and lower rate taxpayers may prefer higher dividend payouts. A change in dividends may result in the clientele changing and this changeover may result in excessive and possibly negative share price volatility.

4   It is not clear why the BoD would rather not raise the required finance through equity and/or debt. The BoD may have considered increasing debt to be risky. However, given that the current level of debt is $70 million compared to an estimated market capitalisation of $360 million (Appendix 3), raising another $40 million through debt finance will probably not result in a significantly higher level of financial risk. The BoD may have been concerned that going into the markets to raise extra finance may result in negative agency type issues, such as having to make proprietary information public, being forced to give extra value to new equity owners, or sending out negative signals to the markets.

Areas for further discussion by the BoD

Each of these issues should be considered and discussed further by the BoD. With reference to point 1, the BoD needs to discuss whether the estimates and the model used are reasonable in estimating corporate value or market capitalisation. With reference to points 2 and 3, the BoD needs to discuss the implications of such a significant change in the dividend policy and how to communicate Lirio Co's intention to the market so that any negative reaction is minimised. With reference to point 4, the BoD should discuss the reasons for any reluctance to raise finance through the markets and whether any negative impact of this is perhaps less than the negative impact of points 2 and 3.

Appendix 1: Expected dividend capacity prior to large project investment

	$'000
Operating profit (15% × (1.08 × $300 million))	48,600
Less interest (5% of $70 million)	(3,500)
Less taxation (25% × ($48.6 million – 3.5 million))	(11,275)
Less investment in working capital ($0.10 × (0.08 × $300 million))	(2,400)
Less investment in additional non-current assets ($0.20 × (0.08 × $300 million))	(4,800)
Less investment in projects	(8,000)
Cash flows from domestic operations	18,625
Cash flows from Pontac Co's dividend remittances (see Appendix 1.1)	3,297
Additional tax payable on Pontac Co's profits (5% × $5.6 million)	(280)
Dividend capacity	21,642

Appendix 1.1: Dividend remittances expected from Pontac Co

	$'000
Total contribution $24 × 400,000 units	9,600
Less fixed costs	(4,000)
Less taxation (20% × $5.6 million)	(1,120)
Profit after tax	4,480
Remitted to Lirio Co (80% × $4.48 million × 92%)	3,297

Appendix 2: Euro (€) investment sale receipt hedge

Lirio Co can use one of forward contracts, futures contracts or option contracts to hedge the € receipt.

Forward contract

Since it is a € receipt, the 1.1559 rate will be used.
€20,000,000 × 1.1559 = $23,118,000

Futures contracts

Go long to protect against a weakening € and use the June contracts to hedge as the receipt is expected at the end of May 20X6 or beginning of June 20X6 (in three months' time).

Opening basis = futures rate – spot rate

Here the June futures rate (per $) is 0.8656 and the March spot rate (per $) = 1 / 1.1585 = 0.8632.

So opening basis is 0.8656 – 0.8632 = 0.0024

There are 4 months to the expiry of the June futures contract so we can assume that when the futures contracts are closed out, one month before expiry, then ¼ of this basis will remain. So closing basis is estimated as 0.0024 × ¼ = 0.0006.

The effective futures rate can be estimated as opening futures rate – closing basis

---
Tutorial note. Other methods are possible.

Here this gives 0.8656 – 0.0006 = 0.8650.

Expected receipt = €20,000,000/0.8650 = $23,121,387

Number of contracts bought = $23,121,387/$125,000 = approximately 185 contracts (resulting in a very small over-hedge and therefore not material)

(Full credit will be given where the calculations are used to show the correction of the over-hedge using forwards.)

Option contracts

Purchase the June call option to protect against a weakening € and because receipt is expected at the end of May 20X6 or beginning of June 20X6.

Exercise price is 0.86, therefore expected receipt is €20,000,000/0.8600 = $23,255,814
Contracts purchased = $23,255,814/$125,000 = 186.05, say 186
Amount hedged = $125,000 × 186 = $23,250,000
Premium payable = 186 × 125,000 × 0.0290 = €674,250
Premium in $ = €674,250 × 1.1618 = $783,344
Amount not hedged = €20,000,000 − (186 × 125,000 × 0.8600) = €5,000
Use forward contracts to hedge €5,000 not hedged. €5,000 × 1.1559 = $5,780

(Full credit will be given if a comment on the under-hedge being immaterial and therefore not hedged is made, instead of calculating the correction of the under-hedge.)

Total receipts = $23,250,000 + $5,780 − $783,344 = $22,472,436

Advice and recommendation

Hedging using options will give the lowest receipt at $22,472,436 from the sale of the investment, while hedging using futures will give the highest receipt at $23,127,387, with the forward contracts giving a receipt of $23,118,000.

The lower receipt from the option contracts is due to the premium payable, which allows the option buyer to let the option lapse should the € strengthen. In this case, the option would be allowed to lapse and Lirio Co would convert the € into $ at the prevailing spot rate in three months' time. However, the € would need to strengthen significantly before the cost of the option is covered. Given market expectation of the weakness in the € continuing, this is not likely to be the case.

Although futures and forward contracts are legally binding and do not have the flexibility of option contracts, they both give higher receipts. Hedging using futures gives the higher receipt, but futures require margin payments to be made upfront and contracts are marked to market daily. In addition to this, the basis may not narrow in a linear fashion and therefore the amount received is not guaranteed. All these factors create uncertainty in terms of the exact amounts of receipts and payments resulting on a daily basis and the final receipt.

On the other hand, when using forward contracts to hedge the receipt exposure, Lirio Co knows the exact amount it will receive. It is therefore recommended that Lirio Co use the forward markets to hedge the expected receipt.

(Note. It could be argued that in spite of the issues when hedging with futures, the higher receipt obtained from using futures markets to hedge means that they should be used. This is acceptable as well.)

Appendix 3: Estimate of Lirio Co's value based on the dividend valuation model

If the large project is not undertaken and dividend growth rate is maintained at the historic level

Dividend history

Year to end of February	20X3	20X4	20X5	20X6
Number of $1 equity shares in issue ('000)	60,000	60,000	80,000	80,000
Total dividends paid ($'000)	12,832	13,602	19,224	20,377
Dividend per share	$0.214	$0.227	$0.240	$0.255

Average dividend growth rate = $(0.255/0.214)^{1/3} - 1 = 1.0602$ (or say 6%)

Expected dividend in February 20X7 = $0.255 × 1.06 = $0.270

Lirio Co, estimate of value if large project is not undertaken =
$0.270/(0.12 – 0.06) = $4.50 per share or $360 million market capitalisation

If the large project is undertaken

Funds required for project	$40,000,000
Funds from sale of investment (Appendix 2)	$23,118,000
Funds required from dividend capacity cash flows	$16,882,000
Dividend capacity funds before transfer to project (Appendix 1)	$21,642,000
Dividend capacity funds left after transfer	$4,760,000
Annual dividend per share after transfer	$0.0595
Annual dividend paid (end of February 20X7 and February 20X8)	$0.0595
Dividend paid (end of February 20X9)	$0.3100
New growth rate	7%

Lirio Co, estimate of value if large project is undertaken =

$0.0595 \times 1.12^{-1} + $0.0595 \times 1.12^{-2} + $0.3100 \times 1.12^{-3} + [$0.3100 \times 1.07/(0.12 – 0.07)] \times 1.12^{-3} = 5.04 per share or $403 million market capitalisation

(**Note.** A discussion paper can take many formats. The answer provides one possible format. Credit will be given for alternative and sensible formats; and for relevant approaches to the calculations and commentary.)

66 Morada

Text references. Risk management is covered in Chapter 2; cost of capital in Chapter 7a.

Top tips. Part (b)(i) 17 marks – this was the hardest part of this question. It was important here to keep your nerve and to score the easier marks; these were available for calculating the current cost of equity and cost of capital (6 marks were available for this).

The key points in calculating the revised cost of capital were:

- Remembering that the market value of debt is needed for a WACC calculation and that this is not the same as the book value of debt. To work out the market value you need to calculate the present value of the future cash flows and discount at the company's pre-tax cost of debt.

- Read the question carefully, this told you to assume that the value of equity is unchanged under any proposal.

- Being aware that the information provided on movements in assets and liabilities was mainly relevant to part (bii).

Easy marks. Parts of this question are extremely challenging but it is important to target the easier areas and not to worry about getting every aspect of the calculations correct (this is unlikely to be achievable under exam conditions).

The discussion parts of this question – parts (a), (b)(iii) and (c) were worth about half of the marks (including the professional marks in part (b) and therefore need (almost) as much effort as the numerical areas.

In part (b)(iii) the easiest marks are for stating your assumptions – this was requested in the question and was worth up to 3 marks. Key assumptions include the assumption that the value of equity is unaffected by each proposal (which seems highly unlikely) and that the weightings used to calculate the asset beta in proposal 2 are accurate, and that any increase in earnings affects retained profits.

		Marks
(a)	Relationship between business and financial risk	3
	Risk mitigation and risk diversification as part of a company's risk management strategy	3
		6

(b) (i) Appendix 1

Prior to implementation of any proposal

Cost of equity	1
Cost of debt	1
Market value of equity	1
Market value of debt	2
Cost of capital	1

After implementing the first director's proposal

Market value of debt	2
Morada Co, asset beta	1
Asset beta of travel services only	1
Equity beta of travel services only	1
Cost of equity	1
Cost of capital	1

After implementing the second director's proposal

Market value of debt	2
Cost of equity	1
Cost of capital	1
	17

(ii) Appendix 2

Adjusted earnings, first director's proposal	2
Financial position, first director's proposal	2
Adjusted earnings, second director's proposal	2
Financial position, second director's proposal	1
	7

(iii)	Discussion		5–6
	Assumptions		2–3
	Reasoned recommendation		1–2
	(**Note.** Maximum 8 marks if no recommendation given)	Max	9

Professional marks for part (b)

Report format	1
Structure and presentation of the report	3
	4

(c)	1 to 2 marks per point	Max	7
			50

(a) The owners or shareholders of a business will accept that it needs to engage in some risky activities in order to generate returns in excess of the risk-free rate of return. A business will be exposed to differing amounts of business and financial risk depending on the decisions it makes. Business risk depends on the decisions a business makes with respect to the services and products it offers and consists of the variability in its profits. For example, it could be related to the demand for its products, the rate of innovation, actions of competitors, etc. Financial risk relates to the volatility of earnings due to the financial structure of the business and could be related to its gearing, the exchange rate risk it is exposed to, its credit risk, its liquidity risk, etc. A business exposed to high levels of business risk may not be able to take excessive financial risk, and vice versa, as the shareholders or owners may not want to bear risk beyond an acceptable level.

Risk management involves the process of risk identification, of assessing and measuring the risk through the process of predicting, analysing and quantifying it, and then making decisions on which risks to assume, which to avoid, which to retain and which to transfer. As stated above, a business will not aim to avoid all risks, as it will want to generate excess returns. Dependent on factors such as controllability, frequency and severity of the risk, it may decide to eliminate or reduce some risks from the business through risk transfer. Risk mitigation is the process of transferring risks out of a business through, for example, hedging or insurance, or avoiding certain risks altogether. Risk diversification is a process of risk reduction through spreading business activity into different products and services, different geographical areas and/or different industries to minimise being excessively exposed by focusing exclusively on one product/service.

(b) **Report to the BoD, Morada Co**

This report provides a discussion on the estimates of the cost of equity and the cost of capital and the impact on the financial position and the earnings after tax, as a result of the proposals put forward by the first director and the second director. The main assumptions made in drawing up the estimates will also be explained. The report concludes by recommending which of the two directors' proposals, if any, should be adopted.

Discussion

The table below shows the revised figures of the cost of equity and the cost of capital (Appendix 1), and the forecast earnings after tax for the coming year (Appendix 2), following each proposal from the first and second directors. For comparison purposes, figures before any changes are given as well.

	Cost of equity Appendix 1	Cost of capital Appendix 1	Earnings after tax Appendix 2
Current position	12.2%	10.0%	$28.0 million
Following first director's proposal	11.6%	11.1%	$37.8 million
Following second director's proposal	12.3%	9.8%	$30.8 million

Under the first director's proposal, although the cost of equity falls due to the lower financial risk in Morada Co because of less debt, the cost of capital actually increases. This is because, even though the cost of debt has decreased, the benefit of the tax shield is reduced significantly due to the lower amount of debt borrowing. Added to this is the higher business risk, reflected by the asset beta, of Morada Co just operating in the travel services sector. This higher business risk and reduced tax shield more than override the lower cost of debt resulting in a higher cost of capital.

Under the second director's proposal, the cost of equity is almost unchanged. There has been a significant increase in the cost of debt from 4.7% to 6.2%. However, the cost of capital has not reduced significantly because the benefit of the tax shield is also almost eroded by the increase in the cost of debt.

If no changes are made, then the forecast earnings after tax as a percentage of non-current assets is 10% ($28m/$280m). Under the first director's proposal, this figure almost doubles to 19.3% ($37.8m/$196m) and, even if the one-off profit from the sale of non-current assets is excluded, this figure is still higher at 12.9% ($25.2m/$196m). Under the second director's proposal, this figure falls to 8.8% ($30.8m/$350m).

Assumptions

1   It is assumed that the asset beta of Morada Co is a weighted average of the asset betas of the travel services and the maintenance services business units, using non-current assets invested in each business unit as a fair representation of the size of each business unit and therefore the proportion of the business risk which that business unit represents within the company.

2   The assumption of the share price not changing after either proposal is not reasonable. It is likely that due to changes in the business and financial risk from implementing either proposal, the risk profile of the company will change. The changes in the risk profile will influence the cost of equity, which in turn will influence the share price.

3   In determining the financial position of Morada Co, it is assumed that the current assets will change due to changes in the profit after tax figure; therefore this is used as the balancing figure for each proposal.

Recommendation

It is recommended that neither the first director's proposal nor the second director's proposal should be adopted. The second director's proposal results in a lower return on investment and a virtually unchanged cost of capital. So there will not be a meaningful benefit for Morada Co. The first director's proposal does increase the return on investment but results in a higher cost of capital. If the reason for adopting either proposal is to reduce risk, then this is not achieved. The main caveat here is that where the assumptions made in the calculations are not reasonable, they will reduce the usefulness of the analysis.

Report compiled by:

Date:

(**Note.** Credit will be given for alternative and relevant points.)

Appendix 1: Estimates of cost of equity and cost of capital

Before either proposal is implemented

Cost of equity (Ke) = 3.8% + 1.2 $\times$ 7% = 12.2%
Cost of debt (Kd) = 3.8% + 0.9% = 4.7%

Market value of equity (MV_e) = $2.88 $\times$ 125m shares = $360m

Market value of debt (MVd)
Per $100 $6.20 $\times$ 1.047^{-1} + $6.20 $\times$ 1.047^{-2} + $6.20 $\times$ 1.047^{-3} + $106.20 $\times$ 1.047^{-4} = $105.36
Total MVd = $105.36/$100 $\times$ $120m = $126.4m

Cost of capital = (12.2% $\times$ $360m + 4.7% $\times$ 0.8 $\times$ $126.4m)/$486.4m = 10.0%

If the first director's proposal is implemented

MV_e = $360m
BV_d = $120m $\times$ 0.2 = $24m
Kd = 4.4%

MV_d per $100 $6.20 $\times$ 1.044^{-1} + $6.20 $\times$ 1.044^{-2} + $6.20 $\times$ 1.044^{-3} + $106.20 $\times$ 1.044^{-4} = $106.47

Total MV_d = 106.47/$100 $\times$ $24 = $25.6m

Morada Co, asset beta

1.2 $\times$ $360m/($360m + $126.4m $\times$ 0.8) = 0.94

To calculate the asset beta of travel services it will be assumed that it represents 70% of the value of the company (the question says that the % of the total book value of non-current assets can be used to represent the total size of each division, and says that 30% of the non-current assets belong to the repairs and maintenance division).

This means that the asset beta of travel $\times$ 0.7 + asset beta of the repairs and maintenance division $\times$ 0.3 = 0.94.

We are told that the asset beta of the repairs and maintenance division is 0.65 so:

Beta of travel $\times$ 0.7 + 0.65 $\times$ 0.3 = 0.94

So beta of travel $\times$ 0.7 = 0.94 − 0.195

So asset beta of travel = 0.745 / 0.7 = 1.06

This is now re-geared to calculate the equity beta of travel services.

Equity beta of travel services = 1.06 × ($360m + $25.6m × 0.8)/$360m = 1.12

Ke = 3.8% + 1.12 × 7% = 11.6%
Cost of capital = (11.6% × $360m + 4.4% × 0.8 × $25.6m)/$385.6 = 11.1%

If the second director's proposal is implemented

MV_e = $360m

The basis points for the Ca3 rated bond is 240 basis points higher than the risk-free rate of interest, giving a cost of debt of 6.2%, therefore:

MV_d = BV_d = $190m

Equity beta of the new, larger company = 1.21

Ke = 3.8% + 1.21 × 7% = 12.3%
Cost of capital = (12.3% × $360m + 6.2% × 0.8 × $190m)/$550m = 9.8%

Appendix 2: Estimates of forecast after-tax earnings and forecast financial position

MORADA CO EXTRACTS FROM THE FORECAST AFTER-TAX EARNINGS FOR THE COMING YEAR

	Current forecast $'000	Forecast: first director proposal $'000	Forecast: second director proposal $'000
Current forecast after-tax earnings	28,000	28,000	28,000
Interest saved due to lower borrowing ($96m × 6.2% × 0.8)		4,762	
Interest payable on additional borrowing ($70m × 6.2% × 0.8)			(3,472)
Reduction in earnings due to lower investment (9% × $84m)		(7,560)	
Additional earnings due to higher investment (9% × $70m)			6,300
Profit on sale of non-current assets (15% × $84m)		12,600	
Revised forecast after-tax earnings	28,000	37,802	30,828
Increase in after-tax earnings		9,802	2,828

MORADA CO EXTRACTS FROM THE FORECAST FINANCIAL POSITION FOR THE COMING YEAR

	Current forecast $'000	Forecast: first director proposal $'000	Forecast: second director proposal $'000
Non-current assets	280,000	196,000	350,000
Current assets (balancing figure)	48,000	43,702	57,828
Total assets	328,000	239,702	407,828
Equity and liabilities			
Share capital (40c/share)	50,000	50,000	50,000
Retained earnings**	137,000	146,802	139,828
Total equity	187,000	196,802	189,828
Non-current liabilities (6.2% redeemable bonds)	120,000	24,000	190,000
Current liabilities	21,000	18,900	28,000
Total liabilities	141,000	42,900	218,000
Total liabilities and capital	328,000	239,702	407,828

** **Note.** With the two directors' proposals, the retained earnings amount is adjusted to reflect the revised forecast after-tax earnings.

(c)   (**Note.** This is an open-ended question and a variety of relevant answers can be given by candidates depending on how the question requirement is interpreted. The following answer is just one possible approach which could be taken. Credit will be given for alternative, but valid, interpretations and answers therein.)

According to the third director, risk management involves more than just risk mitigation or risk diversification as proposed by the first and second directors. The proposals suggested by the first and the second directors are likely to change the makeup of the company, and cause uncertainty amongst the company's owners or clientele. This in turn may cause unnecessary fluctuations in the share price. She suggests that these changes are fundamental and more than just risk management tools.

Instead, it seems that she is suggesting that Morada Co should follow the risk management process suggested in part (a) above, where risks should be identified, assessed and then mitigated according to the company's risk appetite.

The risk management process should be undertaken with a view to increasing shareholder wealth, and therefore the company should consider what drives this value and what are the risks associated with these drivers of value. Morada Co may assess that some of these risks are controllable and some not controllable. It may assess that some are severe and others less so, and it may assess that some are likely to occur more frequently than others.

Morada Co may take the view that the non-controllable, severe and/or frequent risks should be eliminated (or not accepted). On the other hand, where Morada Co is of the opinion that it has a comparative advantage or superior knowledge of risks, and therefore is better able to manage them, it may come to the conclusion that it should accept these. For example, it may take the view that it is able to manage events such as flight delays or hotel standards, but would hedge against currency fluctuations and insure against natural disasters due to their severity or non-controllability.

Theory suggests that undertaking risk management may increase the value of a company if the benefits accruing from the risk management activity are more than the costs involved in managing the risks. For example, smoothing the volatility of profits may make it easier for Morada Co to plan and match long-term funding with future projects or to take advantage of market imperfections by reducing the amount of taxation payable, or it may reduce the costs involved with incidences of financial distress. In each case, though, the benefits accrued should be assessed against the costs involved.

Therefore, a risk management process is more than just mitigating risk through reducing financial risk as the first director is suggesting or risk diversification as the second director is suggesting. Instead it is a process of risk analysis and then about judgement of which risks to hedge or mitigate, and finally, which risk reduction mechanisms to employ, depending on the type of risk, the cost of the risk analysis and mitigation, and the benefits accruing from the mitigation.

67 Pursuit

Text references. Valuation of companies for acquisition purposes is covered in Chapter 10. Financing acquisitions is covered in Chapter 12. Environmental reporting is covered in Chapter 3 and the global debt crisis in Chapter 4a.

Top tips. Your entire answer should be in report format so don't just produce a set of calculations with some explanations – you are expected to produce a professional-looking report with all the necessary details. It is up to you how you structure your report – for example, calculations could be in appendices – but make sure all the required elements are addressed.

There are numerous calculations required in part (a) before you can actually evaluate the benefits of the acquisition. If you are not sure where to start, ask yourself how benefits of acquisitions are calculated (the difference between the synergy benefits and any premiums paid to acquire the target company). You can then work back from there – synergy is the difference between the value of the combined company and the individual values of the separate companies. You are only given the value of Pursuit so you will have to start with trying to determine the value of Fodder.

The examining team's comments noted that many students struggled with finding a suitable discount rate. If you find yourself in this situation, assume a discount rate and carry on with the rest of the question (just state in your answer that you have assumed this rate). The marking scheme shows that there is only one mark available for this calculation – it is better to forgo this mark than the rest of the marks in the question!

Easy marks. There are numerous straightforward calculations in part (a) where you can pick up marks. The implications of a change in capital structure should provide some easy discussion marks in part (iv).

Examining team's comments. Students generally answered part (a)(i) quite well, although common errors included putting interest in the cash flows (it is already built into weighted average cost of capital (WACC)) and making mistakes in determining a suitable discount rate for the combined company using asset betas.

Answers were generally good for part (a)(ii) but students should study the range of factors from the solution as discussion was limited in some cases.

Parts (a)(iii) and (iv) were answered less well, with many students being unable to calculate whether capital structure could be maintained. Answers regarding the implication of the change in capital structure to the valuation method used were poor in most cases.

Part (a)(v) was answered well when students focused on the particular defence tactic. Poor answers included other defence tactics, which was not required by the question.

Marking scheme

			Marks
(a)	(i)	Ignore interest in calculations	1	
		Estimate cost of capital of Fodder Co	1	
		Estimates of growth rates and profit margins for Fodder Co	2	
		Estimate of intrinsic value of Fodder Co	3	
		Equity beta of combined company	3	
		Cost of capital of combined company	1	
		Estimate of value of combined company	3	
		Synergy benefits, value to Pursuit Co shareholders and conclusion	2–3	
				Max 16
	(ii)	1–2 marks per point discussed (credit will be given for alternative, relevant points)		Max 4
	(iii)	Estimate of the increase in debt capacity after acquisition	1	
		Estimate of the funds required to acquire Fodder Co	1	
		Conclusion	1	
				3
	(iv)	Explanation of the problem of the changing capital structure	2	
		Explanation of the resolution of the problem using the iterative process	2	
				4
	(v)	Assessment of suitable defence	2–3	
		Assessment of viability	2–3	
		(Credit will be given for alternative, relevant points)		Max 5
		Professional marks		
		Report format	1	
		Layout, presentation and structure	3	
				4
(b)	Up to 2 marks for each well-explained point			Max 8

	Marks
(c) Environmental policy	2
Contents of environmental report	2
Long-term increase in shareholder value	1
Additional cost	1
	6
	50

(a)

Report to: **Board of directors of Pursuit Co**
From: Strategic Financial Consultant
Date: June 20X1
Re: Potential acquisition of Fodder Co

Introduction

This report focuses on various issues related to the proposed acquisition of Fodder Co. It evaluates whether the acquisition would be beneficial to Pursuit Co's shareholders and estimates how much finance is likely to be needed to fund the acquisition. As the capital structure may change as a result of the finance required, the report highlights the potential implications of such a change and possible ways in which any issues could be resolved.

The Chief Financial Officer has recommended reducing Pursuit Co's cash reserves as a defence against a potential takeover by SGF Co. This report assesses the suitability of such a defence and whether it would be a viable option.

Valuation of Fodder Co

Tutorial note. This forms the answer to part (a). Remember to ignore interest as it is already included in the discount rate.

Year	1	2	3	4
	$'000	$'000	$'000	$'000
Sales revenue (W1) – growth rate 6%	17,115	18,142	19,231	20,385
Operating profit (6% growth rate)	5,479	5,808	6,156	6,525
Tax at 28%	(1,534)	(1,626)	(1,724)	(1,827)
Less additional investment (W2)	(213)	(226)	(240)	(254)
Free cash flow	3,732	3,956	4,192	4,444
Discount factor 13% (W3)	0.885	0.783	0.693	0.613
Discounted cash flow	3,303	3,098	2,905	2,724

	$'000
Total discounted cash flows (Years 1–4)	12,030
Terminal value (W4)	28,059
Total value of Fodder Co	40,089

Workings

1   *Sales revenue growth*

Growth rate = $(16,146/13,559)^{1/3} - 1 = 0.0599$ or 5.99% (say 6%)

Alternatively:

Growth rate (20X8–20X9) = (14,491 – 13,559)/13,559 = 6.87%
Growth rate (20X9–20Y0) = (15,229 – 14,491)/14,491 = 5.09%
Growth rate (20Y0–20Y1) = (16,146 – 15,229)/15,229 = 6.02%

Average growth rate = (6.87 + 5.09 + 6.02)/3 = 5.99% (say 6%)

2   Additional investment

Year	Sales revenue increase ($'000)	22% of increase
1	(17,115 − 16,146) = 969	213
2	(18,142 − 17,115) = 1,027	226
3	(19,231 − 18,142) = 1,089	240
4	(20,385 − 19,231) = 1,154	254

3   Cost of capital – Fodder Co

Using capital asset pricing model

Cost of equity (k_e) = 4.5% + 6 × 1.53 = 13.68%

WACC = (13.68% × 0.9) + [9% × (1 − 0.28) × 0.1] = 12.96% (say 13%)

4   Terminal value

Growth rate is halved to 3% p.a.

Present value (PV) of cash flows in perpetuity = 4,444 × [1.03/(0.13 − 0.03)] = $45,773

Discounted back to Year 0 = $45,773 × 0.613 = $28,059

Value of combined company

Year	1	2	3	4
	$'000	$'000	$'000	$'000
Sales revenue – growth rate 5.8%	51,952	54,965	58,153	61,526
Operating profit (30% of sales)	15,586	16,490	17,446	18,458
Tax at 28%	(4,364)	(4,617)	(4,885)	(5,168)
Less additional investment (W5)	(513)	(542)	(574)	(607)
Free cash flow	10,709	11,331	11,987	12,683
Discount factor 9% (W6)	0.917	0.842	0.772	0.708
Discounted cash flow	9,820	9,541	9,254	8,980

	$'000
Total discounted cash flows (Years 1–4)	37,595
Terminal value (W7)	151,475
Total value of combined company	189,070

Synergy benefits ($'000s) = Total value of combined company − total value of individual companies
= $189,070 − ($140,000 + $40,089)
= $8,981

Premium required to purchase Fodder Co = 25% of equity

Equity = 90% of $40,089 = $36,080

Premium = $9,020 (in 000s).

Net benefits to Pursuit's shareholders = $8,981 − 9,020 = −$39,000 approx

5   Additional investment

Year	Sales revenue increase ($'000)	18% of increase
1	See note below	
2	54,965 − 51,952 = 3,013	542
3	58,153 − 54,965 = 3,188	574
4	61,526 − 58,153 = 3,373	607

Note. The additional investment for Year 1 is given in the question.

6   Combined company cost of capital

Asset beta is calculated using the formula:

$$\beta_a = \left[\frac{V_e}{(V_e + V_d(1-T))} \beta_e \right] + \left[\frac{V_d(1-T)}{(V_e + V_d(1-T))} \beta_d \right]$$

Asset beta (Pursuit) = 1.18 × (0.5/[0.5 + 0.5 × (1 − 0.28)]) = 0.686   (assume debt beta = 0)

Asset beta (Fodder) = 1.53 × (0.9/[0.9 + 0.1 × (1 − 0.28)]) = 1.417   (assume debt beta = 0)

Asset beta (combined company)

= [(0.686 × $140m) + (1.417 × $40.1m)]/(140m + 40.1m) = 0.849

Equity beta (combined company) = 0.849 × [0.5 + (0.5 × 0.72)]/0.5 = 1.46

Cost of equity (k_e) = 4.5% + 1.46 × 6% = 13.26%

WACC = [13.26% × 0.5] + [6.4% × (0.5 × 0.72)] = 8.93% (say 9%)

7   *Terminal value*

Growth rate is halved to 2.9% p.a.

PV of cash flows in perpetuity = 12,683 × [1.029/(0.09 − 0.029)] = $213,948

Discounted back to Year 0 = $213,948 × 0.708 = $151,475

Comments

The extent of the benefits to Pursuit's shareholders depends on the additional synergy from the acquisition of Fodder Co. The calculations above show the synergy to be about $9 million. However, once Fodder's debts have been cleared (as per the acquisition agreement) and equity shareholders paid there is a negative net present value (NPV) of approximately $39,000. It is therefore unlikely that Pursuit's shareholders will see this acquisition as beneficial.

Limitations of the estimated valuations of Fodder and the combined company

Tutorial note. This forms the answer to part (a)(ii) of the question.

Whilst the valuation techniques used above are useful for providing estimates of company value, it is important to treat the results with caution. The valuation techniques use numerous limiting assumptions, such as constant growth rates both in the early years and for the remainder of the project – there is no way of guaranteeing that these growth rates will be sustainable. Other assumptions include those relating to debt beta (assumed to be zero), discount rates, profit margins and fixed tax rates. As the negative NPV from the acquisition is minimal, changes in any of these variables could potentially change the investment decision.

In addition, no information has been given about **post-acquisition integration costs** or pre-acquisition expenses such as legal fees. These should be taken into consideration when trying to determine the net benefits to shareholders as such costs can be quite substantial.

Pursuit's ability to estimate such variables as sales revenue growth, additional investment required and operating profit growth for Fodder may be **limited** due to lack of detailed information. This means that the value of Fodder may be significantly **inaccurate** and thus synergy benefits will be more difficult to predict.

In view of the issues above, it would appear to be **unwise to rely on a single value**. It would be better to have a range of values based on different assumptions and the likelihood of their occurrence.

Amount of debt finance needed and likelihood of maintaining current capital structure

Tutorial note. This forms the answer to part (a)(iii) of the question.

Pursuit is currently valued at $140 million – with a 50/50 split between debt and equity this means $70 million debt and $70 million equity. If this capital structure was to be maintained, the combined company (with an approximate value before payments to Fodder's shareholders of $189 million) would have debt of $94.5 million and equity of the same amount. Debt capacity would thus have to increase by about $24.5 million.

Amount payable for Fodder

	$'000
Debt obligations (10% of $40,089)	4,009
Shareholders ($36,080 × 1.25)	45,100
	49,109

Part of the price for Fodder could be paid using the extra debt capacity of $24.5 million and also the $20 million cash reserves that Pursuit currently has. However, there would still be a shortfall of $4.6 million. It is therefore impossible to maintain the current capital structure if Pursuit only uses cash reserves and debt finance to fund the acquisition.

Implications of changes in capital structure

> **Tutorial note.** This forms the answer to part (a)(iv) of the question.

The use of either of the two proposals for funding the acquisition of Fodder (a combination of debt finance and cash reserves or the Chief Financial Officer's suggestion of debt finance only) will mean a change in capital structure.

Such a fundamental change will have significant implications for the combined company. The cost of capital will have to be recalculated, which will have an effect on the valuation of the combined company. As the valuation of the company changes, so will the market value of debt and market value of equity. This will have a subsequent effect on cost of capital and the cycle will continue.

This is the type of scenario that is consistent with an acquisition where both financial and business risk change.

The issue can be resolved by using an **iterative process** (which may be performed on an Excel spreadsheet). This process involves recalculating beta and cost of capital and then applying these to determine a revised company valuation. The process is then repeated until the assumed capital structure is close to the one that has been recalculated.

Another alternative would be to use **adjusted present value** which first calculates a value assuming an all-equity financial structure and then makes adjustments for the effects of the method of financing used.

Suggested defence against a potential bid by SGF Co

> **Tutorial note.** This forms the answer to part (a)(v) of the question.

The Chief Financial Officer has suggested a distribution of the $20 million cash reserves to shareholders in the form of a special dividend in order to defend against the potential bid by SGF Co. This type of defence is known as the **'crown jewels'** approach, whereby a company dispenses with its most valuable assets (which may have been the main reason for the takeover bid).

Returning the cash to the shareholders may have a positive effect on the currently depressed share price. It may be that the shareholders do not agree with the board's policy to retain large cash reserves and a reduction in these reserves may push up the share price and reduce the likelihood of a takeover bid.

A formal bid has not been made to date and it would be wise for Pursuit's board to determine whether the large cash reserves are the attraction or if SGF has another reason for wishing to acquire Pursuit. In addition, before the cash is returned to the shareholders, it should be determined whether this is actually what the shareholders want. There would be no point returning the money to them if they would prefer it to be reinvested in the company.

If the cash reserves are returned to the shareholders this will have implications for funding the acquisition of Fodder. Even with the $20 million reserves to partially finance the purchase, the capital structure would have to change. If this money was not available then there would be a much more significant change in capital structure as an additional $20 million in debt finance would have to be found (if possible). This will have an effect on cost of capital and also on the value of the combined firm (see discussion above).

It may be the case that the amount of debt required is not feasible due to the considerable increase in gearing it would mean. The board of Pursuit should consider whether the acquisition is worth pursuing due to its minimal benefit to shareholders.

Conclusion

This report has focused on the potential acquisition of Fodder Co and a possible defence against a takeover bid by SGF Co. There are numerous issues that must be resolved prior to making a final decision regarding going ahead with the acquisition, but it is clear that (if the valuations are correct) the capital structure cannot remain unchanged. The implications of this must be considered prior to a final decision being made. The board should also consider whether the acquisition should go ahead at all, given the minimal benefit to shareholders.

Should you require any further information please do not hesitate to contact me.

(b)   The global debt crisis may affect Pursuit Co in a number of ways.

Lack of availability of debt finance for Pursuit Co

The global debt crisis has meant there is a lack of liquidity in the debt finance markets. This means that companies such as Pursuit Co find it more difficult to raise debt finance and as such may not be able to raise the debt finance required for the acquisition of Fodder Co.

Contraction in demand for Pursuit Co's product

The global debt crisis and ensuing lack of confidence in the economic system have meant that many consumers have restricted their spending and this may affect demand for electronic goods, or other products which have Pursuit Co's components in them. This will mean that the manufacturers of the end products reduced their purchases from Pursuit Co, meaning Pursuit Co's revenue will fall.

Supply chain disruption

The events described above to reduce the demand for Pursuit Co could also happen to reduce demand for members of Pursuit Co's supply chain. In the most extreme case members of the supply chain could go out of business, forcing Pursuit Co to seek new suppliers.

Positive aspects

If Pursuit Co is in a relatively strong position in its industry, it may still be able to obtain debt finance and may be able to acquire competitors in various countries that are struggling to achieve the level of financing they require to operate successfully. Alternatively Pursuit Co may be able to attract key personnel from competitors that are struggling as a result of the global financial crisis.

(c)   Many companies believe that development of a green environment policy will mean a **long-term improvement in profitability**. Environmental and social factors are seen to contribute to a sustainable business that will enhance long-term shareholder value by addressing the needs of its stakeholders – employees, customers, suppliers, the community and the environment.

Many companies are now including environmental performance as part of their annual reports. If Pursuit Co does the same, it could include the following items: what the business does and how it impacts on the environment, environmental objectives (eg use of 100% recyclable materials within $\times$ years), Pursuit Co's approach to achieving and monitoring these objectives, and any progress to date. If there are any measures used these should be backed by independent verification where possible.

The main advantage for Pursuit Co is that it can strengthen its corporate image and long-term shareholder wealth by portraying itself as an environmentally friendly company.

The main disadvantage for Pursuit Co is the additional cost of monitoring and reporting performance.

68 Polytot

Text references. Chapter 16 covers hedging techniques, Chapter 8 covers raising capital overseas, Chapter 4a covers international trade and Chapter 4b covers transfer pricing.

Top tips. With the futures and options contracts, calculating the outcome is slightly different from some other questions:

- With futures you are told enough about basis to work out the price in four months' time, and you have to use that in this question to find the number of contracts. Strictly you should also take into account the over-hedge and take the difference to the forward market to make the results strictly comparable with the forward market result; however, you are unlikely to be penalised for not doing so.

- With the options you use the 1.5250 to calculate the number of contracts but again should calculate the over-hedge. Remember the premium is translated at the opening rate. It would also be possible (although it would give you an extra calculation) to calculate the outcome using an option price of $1.55 as it is not that much worse than the forward market, and does mean the company can choose not to exercise the option if necessary.

(a)   **Report**

To: The Board of Directors Polytot plc

From: A Financial Adviser

Subject: Currency hedging for Polytot plc

Date: XX/XX/XXXX

This report considers the alternative forms of currency hedge that are available to Polytot plc and calculates the expected sterling revenue that would be received as a result of the sale of goods to Grobbia. The report also recommends the most appropriate hedging strategy.

Currency hedges available to Polytot

Polytot's receipt will be in four months' time, on 31 October.
60% of the sales price is $675 \times 60\% = 405$m pesos.
Converted to dollars at the spot rate this is worth $405/98.20 = \$4,124,236$

From the information given, the company could try a forward market hedge, a currency futures hedge or a currency options hedge for this receipt of dollars.

The remainder of the sales price will in each case be converted at the unofficial rate of 1.15×156.30 pesos to the £, ie 179.745 peso/£, $\frac{675-405}{179.745}$ giving £1,502,128.

Forward market hedge

On 1 July, Polytot will enter into a contractual obligation to sell $4,124,236 for £ on 31 October at a rate to be agreed on 1 July.

The four-month $/£ forward rate will have to be interpolated between the three-month and the one-year rates.

Interpolating, the rate for 4 months forward $= 1.5398 - ((1.5398 - 1.5178)/9)$
$$= 1.5398 - 0.0024$$
$$= 1.5374$$

$4,124,236/1.5374 = £2,682,604.

Futures hedge

Set up

(i)   December £ futures
(ii)   Buy futures
(iii)   Number of contracts

$$\frac{4,124,236 / 1.5275}{62,500} = 42.98, \text{ say 43 contracts}$$

(iv)   Tick size $0.0001 \times 62,500 = \$6.25$

(v)   The basis now is: 1.5275 future
                                             1.5510 spot
                                             ___(235) ticks

If basis reduces evenly over the six-month life of the contract, in four months' time basis will be $1/3 \times 235$ ticks $= (78)$ ticks.

Closing futures price

As an example, use opening futures rate of 1.5275 as the predicted **spot** rate.

Using basis of 78 ticks as above, closing futures price = 1.5275 − 0.0078 = 1.5197

Hedge outcome

(i) **Outcome in futures market**

Opening futures price	1.5275 buy
Closing futures price	1.5197 sell
Movement in ticks	78 ticks loss

Futures loss 43 × $6.25 × 78 = $20,963

(ii) **Net outcome**

	£
Spot market receipt ($4,126,236/1.5275)	2,701,300
Futures loss, translated at closing rate ($20,963/1.5275)	(13,724)
	2,687,576

Effective rate = $4,126,236/2,687,576 = 1.5353

Alternative calculation of the effective rate (a quick approximate method)

Opening future − closing basis = 1.5275 − (78) = 1.5353

The outcome using this is $4,126,236 / 1.5353 = £2,687,576

Basis risk

The basis calculation is subject to **basis risk**, which means that the basis of 0.78 cents is subject to a margin of error, which may give a better or worse result.

Initial margin

Unlike forward contracts, when Polytot enters into a futures contract, a deposit known as **initial margin** must be paid. Daily gains or losses on the futures market, known as variation margin, are then marked to Polytot's account and, in the case of losses, must be financed.

Impact of uncertainties

The futures market hedge aims to give the same locked-in exchange rate as is obtainable from the forward market, but a few more **uncertainties** are involved. For Polytot the exchange rate obtainable may be better than on the forward market, if it is prepared to accept the risks.

Currency options hedge

Currency options **provide protection against losses** in the event of unfavourable exchange rate movements, but allow the company to take advantage of exchange gains in the event of favourable movements. This is because an option does not have to be exercised unless it is to the investor's advantage.

Set up the hedge

(i) December options

(ii) Call options as we need to buy £

(iii) Strike price 1.5250 as better than the forward rate

(iv) How many contracts

$$\frac{4,124,236 \div 1.525}{31,250} = 87 \text{ contracts}$$

Amount hedged on forward market = (31,250 × 87 × 1.525) − 4,124,236 = $21,858

(v) Premium $= \dfrac{3.35}{100} \times 31{,}250 \times 87$

$= \$91{,}078 \ @ \ 1.5475$

$= £58{,}855$

(vi) Amount to be hedged on forward market

$= (87 \times £31{,}250 \times 1.5250) - \$4{,}124{,}236$

$= \$4{,}146{,}094 - \$4{,}124{,}236 = \$21{,}858$

Outcome

	£
Option market (31,250 × 87)	2,718,750
Over-hedge on forward ($21,858/1.5374)	(14,217)
Premium	(58,855)
	2,645,678

Effect of premium

As with all options, the **minimum guaranteed outcome** will be less than that obtainable on the forward or futures markets because of the cost of the option premium. However, if the dollar strengthens, the option can be allowed to lapse, enabling Polytot to make currency gains that would not be possible if the forward or futures contracts were used.

Recommendations

The hedge taken will depend on Polytot's **overall strategy** and **attitude towards currency gains and losses**.

Not hedging

Given that the forward markets are indicating that the dollar is likely to strengthen, Polytot may **decide not to hedge** at all, which is unwise, as an unexpected decline in the dollar could produce embarrassing losses.

Forward and futures market

The forward and futures markets are effective at **eliminating losses**, which is the prime requirement for a risk-averse policy. Of these two methods, the forward contract has **less risk** and requires **less administration**, though in this case it is predicted to produce slightly worse results.

Option

The option is a **compromise** between these two possible approaches, providing a degree of protection against losses but the opportunity of making a gain if the chance arises.

Conclusion

Assuming the company is reasonably risk averse, the best hedge would probably be the simple, **risk-averse forward contract**.

If you have any questions about this report, please do not hesitate to contact me.

(b) **Sale of strawberries**

Three million kilos of strawberries could be sold at between 50 and 60 pence per kilo, providing receipts of £1.5 to £1.8 million. This is in comparison with the receipt of £1,502,128 if the pesos are exchanged on the unofficial market.

Potential problems

The strawberries therefore can potentially provide a better income. However, there are important questions to be answered before the deal can be accepted.

(i) Does the import of strawberries **contravene food quotas** set under the European common agricultural policy?

(ii) How **reliable is the offer** to provide strawberries? Is it realistically possible to organise the supply? Will they be provided all at once, or in several lots?

(iii) What is the **general quality** of Grobbian strawberries? Are they likely to be rejected by large buyers? How will the quality be determined and inspected? What are the costs of this?

(iv) Strawberries are perishable goods. How will they be **transported** and **insured**? Who will bear the cost of this?

(v) What **other additional costs** might be incurred?

(vi) How will the **receipt and sale** of strawberries be **taxed**?

(c) To: Directors of Polytot plc

From: Financial adviser

Briefing note

Using Euromarkets to raise international finance

Raising finance on Euromarkets has a number of advantages compared with domestic capital markets.

Regulation

Euromarkets are subject to fewer regulatory controls than domestic markets. This results in relatively low issue costs, smaller differentials between lending and borrowing rates and hence cheaper borrowing costs. Interest is usually payable gross of tax, which is attractive to some investors.

Range of products

The Euromarkets provide a flexible range of products, including interest rate swaps and currency swaps, and there is an active secondary market in many of the securities. They are capable of handling very large loan offers within a short lead time, compared with domestic markets that have queuing processes.

Need for high rating

In order to borrow on the Euromarkets the Grobbian company would need to achieve a high rating by an international rating agency or, as an alternative, would need to have any issue of funds guaranteed by the Grobbian Government. Since the loan would be in a hard currency, the market will need to be sure that the company will have access to sufficient hard currency to pay interest and repay the principal.

(d) **Fixed plus variable cost**

	Umbaga $'000	Mazila $'000	Bettuna $'000
Sales	8,200	16,000	14,800
Costs			
Variable costs	6,400	3,600	3,000
Fixed costs	1,800	700	900
Transfer price	–	8,200	8,200
Import duty	–	820	–
	8,200	13,320	12,100
Taxable profit	–	2,680	2,700
Tax	–	670	864
Profit after tax	–	2,010	1,836
Withholding tax	–	–	–
Remittance	–	1,206	1,101.6
UK tax on remittance (W)	–	(134)	–
	–	1,072	1,101.6
Retained (40% after-tax profit)	–	804	734.4
Total profit		1,876	1,836.0

Total profit ($'000)

Umbaga + Mazila 0 + 1,876 = 1,876.0

Umbaga + Bettuna 0 + 1,836 = 1,836.0

Working

UK tax = (2,680,000 × 0.3) − 670,000 = 134,000

Fixed plus variable cost plus 30%

	Umbaga $'000	Mazila $'000	Bettuna $'000
Sales	10,660	16,000	14,800
Costs			
Variable costs	6,400	3,600	3,000
Fixed costs	1,800	700	900
Transfer price	−	10,660	10,660
Import duty	−	1,066	−
	8,200	16,026	14,560
Taxable profit	2,460	(26)	240
Tax	984	−	76.8
Profit/(Loss) after tax	1,476	(26)	163.2
Withholding tax			
(Umbaga 1,476 × 0.6 × 0.15)	132.84	−	−
Remittance			
(Umbaga 1,476 × 0.6 × 0.85)	752.76	−	97.92
UK tax on remittance	−	−	−
	752.76	−	97.92
Retained (40% after-tax profit)	590.4	(26)	65.28
Total profit	1,343.16	(26)	163.2

Total profit ($'000)

Umbaga + Mazila 1,343.16 − 26 = 1,317.16
Umbaga + Bettuna 1,343.16 + 163.2 = 1,506.36

Conclusion

The best plan is to charge sales at fixed plus variable costs, and manufacture in Mazila. This avoids tax in the country of highest tax, Umbaga.

(e) **Likely government attitudes**

Umbaga

The Government may query whether the **transfer price** is at a **commercial rate** and, depending on the tax laws, may be able to impart an artificial profit to the transaction and hence charge tax.

Mazila

The Government's attitude is likely to be **favourable** as manufacturing is taking place in the country, and hence boosting its economy. Although the import duty is lower than under the mark-up scenario, this is more than outweighed by the company tax that the Government will be able to collect.

Bettuna

The Government can take **no action** against the company as the company is not doing anything. It can try to attract the company by offering a subsidy, which would only need to be greater than $40,000 (1,876,000 − 1,836,000) for the decision to be changed.

UK

The UK Government would be happy with this arrangement, since it is the only arrangement of those considered that will mean that the company pays tax.

69 Nente

Marking scheme

		Marks
(a)	Appendix 1	
	Based on PBIT, calculation of the growth rate	2
	Calculation of free cash flows	2
	Calculation of company value, equity value and value of each share	3
		7
	Appendix 2	
	Cash offer	
	Estimate of value of combined company	3
	Value created per share for Nente Co shareholders	1
	Share-for-share offer	
	Expected share price for the combined company	2
	Value created for a Nente Co share	1
	Value created for a Mije Co share	1
		8
	Appendix 3	
	PV of underlying asset	1
	Value of exercise price	1
	$N(d_1)$	2
	$N(d_2)$	2
	Value of call	1
	Value added to Nente Co share	1
		8

		Marks
Discussion		
Nente Co shareholders	2–3	
Mije Co shareholders	1–2	
Assumptions made	2–3	
Use of value of follow-on product	2–3	
		Max 8
Professional marks		
Report format	1	
Layout, presentation and structure	3	
		4

(b)
Profit level discussion	1–2	
Financial gearing	2–3	
Growth rates and dividends	2–3	
Impact of follow-on product	1–2	
		Max 8
(c) 1–2 marks for each defence covered		Max 7
		50

(a) **REPORT**

To: **The Board of Directors of Nente Co**
From: **A N Accountant**
Date: **X/X/XX**
Re: **Impact of the takeover proposal from Mije Co and the follow-on project**

This report considers the value, to both Nente Co and Mije Co shareholders, based on a cash offer and also on a share-for-share offer. It discusses the potential reactions of these groups of shareholders to the alternative offers and how best to make use of the follow-on opportunity. All significant assumptions made in the assessments are also explained.

The appendices to this report show the detailed calculations for estimating an equity value for Nente Co, the value to shareholders of Nente Co and Mije Co of the acquisition under both a cash offer and a share-for-share exchange and the value of the follow-on product rights to Nente Co.

The results of the detailed calculations are shown here.

Estimated current price of a Nente Co share	$2.90 (Appendix 1)	

Estimated increase in share price	Nente Co	Mije Co
	%	%
Cash offer (Appendix 2)	1.7	9.4
Share-for-share offer (Appendix 2)	17.9	6.9

Estimated value per share of the follow-on product   8.7% (Appendix 3)

The cash offer is **unlikely to be accepted** by Nente Co shareholders because the estimated gains are only slightly higher than the current share price, although being unlisted Nente Co shareholders may not be able to realise the current price should they wish to sell. The share-for-share exchange gives a much larger increase of 17.9% and is much more likely to be acceptable to Nente Co shareholders. It is also **higher than the expected return** from the follow-on product and therefore based on the financial data the most attractive option for Nente Co shareholders is the takeover on a share-for-share exchange basis.

Mije Co shareholders are likely to **prefer the cash offer** so that they can maximise their own returns and not dilute their control of the company, but they may accept the share-for-share offer as this still offers an increase in value. Mije Co shareholders would need to consider whether these returns are in excess of any other investment opportunities that are available and whether the acquisition of Nente Co is the **best use of funds**.

There are a number of assumptions present in the calculations. For example, for calculating the current value of a Nente Co share the free cash flow model is used. This assumes that the growth rate and free cash flow exist in **perpetuity** and that the estimated cost of capital is appropriate. The takeover offer analysis is based on the assumption that the proposed synergy savings will be achieved and that the P/E **bootstrapping** approach is valid. For the calculation of the follow-on product value the option variables are estimates and an assumption is made that these will not change in the period before the decision is taken. The calculated value is based on the scenario that the option can only be exercised after two years, but it appears that the option can be exercised at any time within the two-year period.

The follow-on product has been treated separately from the takeover, but Nente Co could ask Mije Co to **take this into account** in its takeover offer. The value of the rights to Nente Co is $609,021 (Appendix 3) and adds around 25c or 8.8% to the value of a Nente Co share. If Mije were to increase its offer by this value, or the rights could be sold prior to the takeover, then the return to a Nente Co shareholder would be 17.9% + 8.8% = 26.7%.

In conclusion, the preferred outcome for Nente Co shareholders would be to accept the share-for-share offer and to convince Mije Co to take the value of the follow-on product into consideration. Nente Co shareholders will need to be assured of the **accuracy of the calculations** provided in the appendices before they accept the offer.

Appendices

Appendix 1

Estimate of current value of Nente Co's equity based on free cash flows

Total value = Free cash flows × (1 + growth rate (g))/(Cost of capital (k) − g)
k = 11%
Past growth rate = (latest profit before interest and tax (PBIT)/Earliest PBIT) $^{1/\text{no of periods of growth}}$ − 1
Past g = $(1,230/970)^{1/3}$ − 1 = 0.0824
Future g = 0.25 × 0.0824 = 0.0206

Free cash flow calculation
Free cash flow (FCF) = PBIT + non-cash flows − cash investment − tax
FCF = 1,230,000 + 1,206,000 − 1,010,000 − (1,230,000 × 20%) = $1,180,000

Total value = $1,180,000 × 1.0206/(0.11 − 0.0206) = $13,471,007
Equity value = $13,471,007 − $6,500,000 = $6,971,007
Number of shares = $960,000/$0.40 = 2.4 million
Equity value per share = $6,971,007/2.4 million shares = $2.90

Appendix 2

Cash offer

Gain in value to a Nente Co shareholder = ($2.95 − $2.90)/$2.90 = 1.7%

Additional earnings post-acquisition = $620,000 + $150,000 = $770,000
Additional earnings per share (EPS) = $770,000/10m = 7.7c per share
Using the P/E ratio to calculate the increase in share price = 15 × 7.7c = $1.16
Additional value created = $1.16 × 10 million = $11.6 million
Less cost of acquisition = ($2.95 × 2.4 million) = $7.08 million
Value added for Mije Co shareholders = 11.6 million − 7.08 million = $4.52 million

Gain in value to a shareholder of Mije = $4.52 million/10 million = 45.2c
45.2c/480c = 9.4%

Share-for-share offer

Earnings of combined company = $770,000 (from above) + $3,200,000 = $3,970,000
Total number of shares in combined number = 10 million + (2.4 million × 2/3) = 11,600,000
EPS of combined company = $3.97 million/11.6 million = 34.2c

Expected share price using P/E ratio = 34.2 × 15 = 513c = $5.13

Gain in value to a shareholder of Mije Co = ($5.13 – $4.80)/$4.80 = 6.9%
Current value of three shares in Nente Co = $2.90 × 3 = $8.70
Gain in value to a shareholder of Nente Co = ((2 × $5.13) – $8.70)/$8.70 = 17.9%

Appendix 3

Value of follow-on product

Present value (PV) of the cash inflows	2,434,000
PV of the option cost	(2,029,000)
Net present value (NPV) of the new product	405,000

Based on NPV, without considering the option to delay, the project would increase the value of Nente Co by $405,000.

Value of the option to delay

Price of asset (PV of future positive cash flows)	$2,434,000
Exercise price (initial cost – not discounted)	$2,500,000
Time to expiry of option	2 years
Risk-free rate (government base rate = 7% – 380 basis points)	3.2%
Volatility	42%

$d_1 = [\ln(2,434/2,500) + (0.032 + 0.5 \times 0.42^2) \times 2]/(0.42 \times 2^{0.5}) = 0.359$
$d_2 = 0.359 – (0.42 \times 2^{0.5}) = –0.235$
$N(0.36) = 0.5 + 0.1406 = 0.6406$
$N(–0.24) = 0.5 – 0.0948 = 0.4052$

Value of option = $2,434,000 \times 0.6406 – 2,500,000 \times 0.4052 \times e^{-(0.032 \times 2)}$
= $1,559,220 – $950,199 = $609,021

This project increases the value of the company by $609,021 or 25.4c per share ($609,021/2.4 million).

In percentage terms this is an increase of about 8.8% (25.4c/290c).

(b)   Nente Co has an **operating profit** margin of 14% (1,230/8,780) but the significant interest payments mean that profit after tax is approximately half of the PBIT figure. This profit after tax figure is less than the required annual investment in non-current assets and working capital.

Nente Co has a high level of **financial gearing**. When measured by book value, the gearing level is 73% (6,500/(2,360 + 6,500)). This high level of debt, coupled with rising interest rates, means that the interest payments are high and **interest coverage** is currently 2.7 times.

Given that future growth levels are only expected to be 2% (from part (a) above) profit after tax is unlikely to **increase significantly** unless interest rates fall dramatically. The low level of profit after tax means that **no dividend** has been paid in the most recent period. The business angels will want to see a **return on their investment**, which is unlikely to be in the form of future dividends given these prospects. Therefore they are likely to be attracted by the prospect of an exit route through a sale of their equity stake.

The **follow-on product** should help to increase Nente Co's growth rate, but with the limited scope for expansion and lack of other product development it would appear that the business angels would need to sell their equity stakes to generate significant returns.

(c)   There are a number of possible post-bid defences available to Mije Co.

Attempting to have the bid referred to the **competition authorities** seems unlikely to be successful, based on the size of Mije Co, and because this is a vertical merger rather than a horizontal one – which means Tianhe Co is unlikely to significantly increase its existing market share.

If it is specifically the Tianhe Co takeover that Mije Co wishes to defend against, then a **white knight** defence could be a successful tactic. This involves finding a friendly company to join in the bidding process and eventually acquire Mije Co. The difficulty will be in finding a willing friendly company.

A **counter-bid** does not seem to be appropriate given the relative market capitalisation of Mije Co compared to Tianhe Co. Tianhe Co has a current market value of $245 million which is over 5 times the current market capitalisation of Mije Co of $48 million.

A **crown jewels** defence would involve selling off Mije Co's most valuable assets to make it less attractive as an acquisition. This may mean that Tianhe Co is uninterested in continuing the takeover bid, but it could compromise Mije Co's current operations and as such the existing shareholders may object to this.

A **poison pill** defence attempts to make a company unattractive, normally by giving the right to existing shareholders to buy shares at a very low price. This could be used by Mije Co, but the existing shareholders need to be willing to put additional funds into the business. The shareholders are unlikely to do this if the takeover is actually in their best interest.

A **golden parachute** involves offering large benefits to key management personnel who would lose their position in the event of a takeover. This would then make the takeover more expensive for Tianhe Co and acts as a deterrent. This could be a good option for Mije Co to take to defend against this takeover.

Mock exams

ACCA
Advanced Financial Management

Mock Examination 1
March/June 2017
Sample questions

Question Paper
Time allowed 3 hours and 15 minutes

Section A	THIS question is compulsory and MUST be attempted
Section B	BOTH questions to be attempted

DO NOT OPEN THIS PAPER UNTIL YOU ARE READY TO START UNDER EXAMINATION CONDITIONS

SECTION A: THIS QUESTION is compulsory and MUST be attempted

Question 1

The eight-member board of executive directors (BoD) of Chrysos Co, a large private, unlisted company, is considering the company's long-term business and financial future. The BoD is considering whether or not to undertake a restructuring programme. This will be followed a few years later by undertaking a reverse takeover to obtain a listing on the stock exchange in order to raise new finance. However, a few members of the BoD have raised doubts about the restructuring programme and the reverse takeover, not least the impact upon the company's stakeholders. Some directors are of the opinion that an initial public offering (IPO) would be a better option when obtaining a listing compared to a reverse takeover.

Chrysos Co was formed about 15 years ago by a team of five senior equity holders who are part of the BoD and own 40% of the equity share capital in total; 30 other equity holders own a further 40% of the equity share capital but are not part of the BoD; and a consortium of venture capital organisations (VCOs) own the remaining 20% of the equity share capital and have three representatives on the BoD. The VCOs have also lent Chrysos Co substantial debt finance in the form of unsecured bonds due to be redeemed in ten years' time. In addition to the BoD, Chrysos Co also has a non-executive supervisory board consisting of members of Chrysos Co's key stakeholder groups. Details of the supervisory board are given below.

Chrysos Co has two business units: a mining and shipping business unit, and a machinery parts manufacturing business unit. The mining and shipping business unit accounts for around 80% of Chrysos Co's business in terms of sales revenue, non-current and current assets, and payables. However, it is estimated that this business unit accounts for around 75% of the company's operating costs. The smaller machinery parts manufacturing business unit accounts for the remaining 20% of sales revenue, non-current and current assets, and payables; and around 25% of the company's operating costs.

The following figures have been extracted from Chrysos Co's most recent financial statements:

Profit before depreciation, interest and tax for the year to 28 February 20X7

	$m
Sales revenue	16,800
Operating costs	(10,080)
Profit before depreciation, interest and tax	6,720

Financial position as at 28 February 20X7

	$m
Non-current assets	
Land and buildings	7,500
Equipment	5,400
Current assets	
Inventory	1,800
Receivables	900
Total assets	15,600
Equity	
Share capital ($1 par value per share)	1,800
Reserves	5,400
Non-current liabilities	
4.50% unsecured bonds 20Y6 (from the VCOs)	4,800
Other debt	1,050
Current liabilities	
Payables	750
Bank overdraft	1,800
Total equity and liabilities	15,600

Corporate restructuring programme

The purpose of the restructuring programme is to simplify the company's gearing structure and to obtain extra funding to expand the mining and shipping business in the future. At present, Chrysos Co is having difficulty obtaining additional funding without having to pay high interest rates.

Machinery parts manufacturing business unit

The smaller machinery parts manufacturing business unit will be unbundled either by having its assets sold to a local supplier for $3,102 million after its share of payables have been paid; or

The smaller machinery parts manufacturing business unit will be unbundled through a management buy-out by four managers. In this case, it is estimated that its after-tax net cash flows will increase by 8% in the first year only and then stay fixed at this level for the foreseeable future. The cost of capital related to the smaller business unit is estimated to be 10%. The management buy-out team will pay Chrysos Co 70% of the estimated market value of the smaller machinery parts manufacturing business unit.

Mining and shipping business unit

Following the unbundling of the smaller machinery parts manufacturing business unit, Chrysos Co will focus solely on the mining and shipping business unit, prior to undertaking the reverse takeover some years into the future.

As part of the restructuring programme, the existing unsecured bonds lent by the VCOs will be cancelled and replaced by an additional 600 million $1 shares for the VCOs. The VCOs will pay $400 million for these shares. The bank overdraft will be converted into a 15-year loan on which Chrysos Co will pay a fixed annual interest of 4.50%. The other debt under non-current liabilities will be repaid. In addition to this, Chrysos Co will invest $1,200 million into equipment for its mining and shipping business unit and this will result in its profits and cash flows growing by 4% per year in perpetuity.

Additional financial information

Chrysos Co aims to maintain a long-term capital structure of 20% debt and 80% equity in market value terms. Chrysos Co's finance director has assessed that the 4.50% annual interest it will pay on its bank loan is a reasonable estimate of its long-term cost of debt, based on the long-term capital structure above.

Although Chrysos Co does not know what its cost of capital is for the mining and shipping business unit, its finance director has determined that the current ungeared cost of equity of Sidero Co, a large quoted mining and shipping company, is 12.46%. Chrysos Co's finance director wants touse Sidero Co's ungeared cost of equity to calculate itscost of capital for the mining and shipping business unit.

The annual corporation tax rate on profits applicable to all companies is 18% and it can be assumed that tax is payable in the year incurred. All the non-current assets are eligible for tax allowable depreciation of 12% annually on the book values. The annual reinvestment needed to keep operations at their current levels is equivalent to the tax allowable depreciation.

Details of the supervisory board

The non-executive supervisory board provides an extra layer of governance over the BoD. It consists of representatives from the company's internal stakeholder groups including the finance providers, employees and the company's management. It ensures that the actions taken by the BoD are for the benefit of all the stakeholder groups and to the company as a whole. Any issues raised in board meetings are resolved through negotiation until an agreed position is reached.

Required

(a) Explain what a reverse takeover involves and discuss the relative advantages and disadvantages to a company, such as Chrysos Co, of obtaining a listing through a reverse takeover as opposed to an initial public offering (IPO). **(9 marks)**

(b) Prepare a report for the board of directors of Chrysos Co which includes:

   (i) An extract of the financial position and an estimate of Chrysos Co's value to the equity holders, after undertaking the restructuring programme. **(18 marks)**

   (ii) An explanation of the approach taken and assumptions made in estimating Chrysos Co's value to the equity holders, after undertaking the restructuring programme. **(5 marks)**

BPP
LEARNING MEDIA

(iii)   A discussion of the impact of the restructuring programme on Chrysos Co and on the venture capital organisations.   **(10 marks)**

Professional marks will be awarded in part (b) for the format, structure and presentation of the report.

(4 marks)

(c)   Discuss why the attention Chrysos Co pays to its stakeholders represented on the supervisory board may change once it has obtained a listing.   **(4 marks)**

(Total = 50 marks)

SECTION B: BOTH QUESTIONS to be attempted
Question 2

Buryecs Co is an international transport operator based in the Eurozone which has been invited to take over a rail operating franchise in Wirtonia, where the local currency is the dollar ($). Previously this franchise was run by a local operator in Wirtonia but its performance was unsatisfactory and the government in Wirtonia withdrew the franchise.

Buryecs Co will pay $5,000 million for the rail franchise immediately. The government has stated that Buryecs Co should make an annual income from the franchise of $600 million in each of the next three years. At the end of the three years the government in Wirtonia has offered to buy the franchise back for $7,500 million if no other operator can be found to take over the franchise.

Today's spot exchange rate between the Euro and Wirtonia $ is €0.1430 = $1. The predicted inflation rates are as follows:

Year	1	2	3
Eurozone	6%	4%	3%
Wirtonia	3%	8%	11%

Buryecs Co's finance director (FD) has contacted its bankers with a view to arranging a currency swap, since he believes that this will be the best way to manage financial risks associated with the franchise. The swap would be for the initial fee paid for the franchise, with a swap of principal immediately and in three years' time, both these swaps being at today's spot rate. Buryecs Co's bank would charge an annual fee of 0·5% in € for arranging the swap. Buryecs Co would take 60% of any benefit of the swap before deducting bank fees, but would then have to pay 60% of the bank fees.

Relevant borrowing rates are:

	Buryecs Co	Counterparty
Eurozone	4.0%	5.8%
Wirtonia	Wirtonia bank rate + 0.6%	Wirtonia bank rate + 0.4%

In order to provide Buryecs Co's board with an alternative hedging method to consider, the FD has obtained the following information about over-the-counter options in Wirtonia $ from the company's bank.

The exercise price quotation is in Wirtonia $ per €1, premium is % of amount hedged, translated at today's spot rate.

Exercise price	Call options	Put options
7.75	2.8%	1.6%
7.25	1.8%	2.7%

Assume a discount rate of 14%.

Required

(a) Discuss the advantages and drawbacks of using the currency swap to manage financial risks associated with the franchise in Wirtonia. **(6 marks)**

(b) (i) Calculate the annual percentage interest saving which Buryecs Co could make from using a currency swap, compared with borrowing directly in Wirtonia, demonstrating how the currency swap will work. **(4 marks)**

(ii) Evaluate, using net present value, the financial acceptability of Buryecs Co operating the rail franchise under the terms suggested by the government of Wirtonia and calculate the gain or loss in € from using the swap arrangement. **(8 marks)**

(c) Calculate the results of hedging the receipt of $7,500 million using the currency options and discuss whether currency options would be a better method of hedging this receipt than a currency swap. **(7 marks)**

(Total = 25 marks)

Question 3

Toltuck Co is a listed company in the building industry which specialises in the construction of large commercial and residential developments. Toltuck Co had been profitable for many years, but has just incurred major losses on the last two developments which it has completed in its home country of Arumland. These developments were an out-of-town retail centre and a major residential development. Toltuck Co's directors have blamed the poor results primarily on the recent recession in Arumland, although demand for the residential development also appears to have been adversely affected by it being located in an area which has suffered serious flooding over the last two years.

As a result of returns from these two major developments being much lower than expected, Toltuck Co has had to finance current work-in-progress by a significantly greater amount of debt finance, giving it higher gearing than most other construction companies operating in Arumland. Toltuck Co's directors have recently been alarmed by a major credit agency's decision to downgrade Toltuck Co's credit rating from AA to BBB. The directors are very concerned about the impact this will have on the valuation of Toltuck Co's bonds and the future cost of debt.

The following information can be used to assess the consequences of the change in Toltuck Co's credit rating.

Toltuck Co has issued an 8% bond, which has a face or nominal value of $100 and a premium of 2% on redemption in three years' time. The coupon on the bond is payable on an annual basis.

The government of Arumland has three bonds in issue. They all have a face or nominal value of $100 and are all redeemable at par. Taxation can be ignored on government bonds. They are of the same risk class and the coupon on each is payable on an annual basis. Details of the bonds are as follows:

Bond	Redeemable	Coupon	Current market value
			$
1	1 year	9%	104
2	2 years	7%	102
3	3 years	6%	98

Credit spreads, published by the credit agency, are as follows (shown in basis points):

Rating	1 year	2 years	3 years
AA	18	31	45
BBB	54	69	86

Toltuck Co's shareholder base can be divided broadly into two groups. The majority of shareholders are comfortable with investing in a company where dividends in some years will be high, but there will be low or no dividends in other years because of the cash demands facing the business. However, a minority of shareholders would like Toltuck Co to achieve at least a minimum dividend each year and are concerned about the company undertaking investments which they regard as very speculative. Shareholders from both groups have expressed some concerns to the board about the impact of the fall in credit rating on their investment.

Required

(a)   Calculate the valuation and yield to maturity of Toltuck Co's $100 bond under its old and new credit ratings.
(10 marks)

(b)   Discuss the factors which may have affected the credit rating of Toltuck Co published by the credit agency.
(8 marks)

(c)   Discuss the impact of the fall in Toltuck Co's credit rating on its ability to raise financial capital and on its shareholders' return.
(7 marks)

(Total = 25 marks)

Answers

DO NOT TURN THIS PAGE UNTIL YOU HAVE
COMPLETED THE MOCK EXAM

BPP
LEARNING MEDIA

Plan of attack

Take a good look through the exam before diving in to answer questions.

Option 1

It is normally sensible to start with the compulsory Section A question on the basis that leaving it to later runs the risk of having to rush the 50 mark question, which is very difficult to do.

- **Question 1** focused on the valuations and restructuring sections of the syllabus. It was not unexpected to see a part of this question on reverse takeovers which was introduced to the syllabus in 2016 and featured in a recent article on the ACCA website.

    This question required careful reading because it was complicated to understand what was going on and, as you would expect, some of the numerical parts to the question in (b)(i) were challenging.

    It was important not to panic, and to try to adopt a logical approach, explaining your reasoning as you go.

- **Question 2** tests your understanding of currency swaps (again the subject of a recent article on the ACCA website) and overseas investment appraisal. A similar question was set in June 2011.

- **Question 3** tests your understanding of credit ratings and bond valuation. A similar question was set in December 2011.

Option 2

If you are a bit worried about question 1, as may be the case here, you could manage your exam nerves by doing a section B question first, selecting the one you are most comfortable with. However, make sure you don't spend too much time on this question, regardless of how much you think you can write. If you are comfortable with the question but cannot answer it in the time allowed then you are probably writing too much.

No matter how many times we remind you...

Always allocate your time according to the marks for the question in total and for the individual parts of each question. Also **always answer the question you were asked** rather than the question you wished you had been asked or the question you thought you had been asked.

You've got free time at the end of the exam...?

If you have allocated your time properly then you **shouldn't have time on your hands** at the end of the exam. If you find yourself with some time at the end, however, go back to **any parts of questions that you didn't finish** because you moved on to another question.

Forget about it!

Don't worry if you found the exam difficult – if you did, no doubt other students would too. If this was the real thing you would have to forget about it as soon as you leave the exam hall and **think about the next one**. If it was the last one, however – **celebrate!**

Question 1

Marking scheme

				Marks	
(a)		Explanation of what a reverse takeover involves	2		
		Advantages (up to 2 marks per well explained advantage)		Max	4
		Disadvantages (up to 2 marks per well explained disadvantage)		Max	4
				Max	9
(b)	(i)	Extract of financial position after restructuring programme			
		Appendix 1			
		Manufacturing business unit unbundled through an MBO			
		Estimate of cash flows	3		
		Estimate of amount payable to ChrysosCo	2		
		Selection of higher value unbundling option	1		
		Appendix 2			
		Chrysos Co, cost of equity	1		
		Chrysos Co, cost of capital	1		
		Appendix 3			
		Estimate of cash flows	3		
		Estimate of equity value	2		
				18	
	(ii)	Explanation of approach taken	1–2		
		Explanation of assumptions made (up to 2 marks per assumption)	3–4		
				Max	5
	(iii)	**Appendix 4**			
		Value from increased ownership	1		
		Additional value	1		
		Discussion of restructuring programme on the VCOs	3–4		
		Discussion of restructuring programme on Chrysos Co	4–5		
				Max	10

Professional marks for part (b)

Report format	1
Structure and presentation of the report	3
	4

(c) 1–2 marks per relevant point   Max   4
                                                                                        50

(a) A reverse takeover enables a private, unlisted company, like Chrysos Co, to gain a listing on the stock exchange without needing to go through the process of an initial public offering (IPO). The private company merges with a listed 'shell' company. The private company initially purchases equity shares in the listed company and takes control of its board of directors. The listed company then issues new equity shares and these are exchanged for equity shares in the unlisted company, thereby the original private company's equity shares gain a listing on the stock exchange. Often the name of the listed company is also changed to that of the original unlisted company.

Advantages relative to an IPO

(1) An IPO can take a long time, typically between one and two years, because it involves preparing a prospectus and creating an interest among potential investors. The equity shares need to be valued and the issue process needs to be administered. Since with the reverse takeover shares in the private company are exchanged for shares in the listed company and no new capital is being raised, the process can be completed much quicker.

(2) An IPO is an expensive process and can cost between 3% and 5% of the capital being raised due to involvement of various parties, such as investment banks, law firms, etc, and the need to make the IPO attractive through issuing a prospectus and marketing the issue. A reverse takeover does not require such costs to be incurred and therefore is considerably cheaper.

(3) In periods of economic downturn, recessions and periods of uncertainty, an IPO may not be successful. A lot of senior managerial time and effort will be spent, as well as expenditure, with nothing to show for it. On the other hand, a reverse takeover would not face this problem as it does not need external investors and it is not raising external finance, but is being used to gain from the potential benefits of going public by getting a listing.

Disadvantages relative to an IPO

(1) The 'shell' listed company being used in the reverse takeover may have hidden liabilities and may be facing potential litigation, which may not be obvious at the outset. Proper and full due diligence is necessary before the process is started. A company undertaking an IPO would not face such difficulties.

(2) The original shareholders of the listed company may want to sell their shares immediately after the reverse takeover process has taken place and this may affect the share price negatively. A lock-up period during which shares cannot be sold may be necessary to prevent this. [**Note.** An IPO may need a lock-up period as well, but this is not usually the case.]

(3) The senior management of an unlisted company may not have the expertise and/or understanding of the rules and regulations which a listed company needs to comply with. The IPO process normally takes longer and is more involved, when compared to a reverse takeover. It also involves a greater involvement from external experts. These factors will provide the senior management involved in an IPO, with opportunities to develop the necessary expertise and knowledge of listing rules and regulations, which the reverse takeover process may not provide.

(4) One of the main reasons for gaining a listing is to gain access to new investor capital. However, a smaller, private company which has become public through a reverse takeover may not obtain a sufficient analyst coverage and investor following, and it may have difficulty in raising new finance in future. A well-advertised IPO will probably not face these issues and find raising new funding to be easier.

(b)   **Report to the board of directors (BoD), Chrysos Co**

This report provides extracts from the financial position and an estimate of the value of Chrysos Co after it has undertaken a restructuring programme. It also contains an explanation of the process used in estimating the value and of the assumptions made. Finally, the report discusses the impact of the restructuring programme on the company and on venture capital organisations.

It is recommended that the manufacturing business unit is unbundled through a management buy-out, rather than the assets being sold separately, and it is estimated that Chrysos Co will receive $3,289 million from the unbundling of the manufacturing business unit (Appendix 1). This amount is recorded as a cash receipt in the extract of the financial position given below.

Extract of Chrysos Co's financial position following the restructuring programme

	$m
Non-current assets	
Land and buildings (80% × $7,500m)	6,000
Equipment ((80% × $5,400m) + $1,200m)	5,520
Current assets	
Inventory (80% × $1,800m)	1,440
Receivables (80% × $900m)	720
Cash ($3,289m + $400m – $1,200m – $1,050m)	1,439
Total assets	15,119
Equity	
Share capital ($1,800 + $600m)	2,400
Reserves **	10,319
Non-current liabilities	
Bank loan	1,800
Current liabilities	
Payables (80% × $750m)	600
Total equity and liabilities	15,119

** Balancing figure

Estimate of Chrysos Co's equity value following the restructuring programme

It is estimated that Chrysos Co's equity value after the restructuring programme has taken place will be just over $46 billion (Appendix 3).

Process undertaken in determining Chrysos Co's equity value

The corporate value is based on a growth rate of 4% on cash flows in perpetuity, which are discounted at Chrysos Co's cost of capital (Appendix 2). The cash flows are estimated by calculating the profit before depreciation and tax of the unbundled firm consisting of just the mining and shipping business unit and then deducting the depreciation and taxation amounts from this.

The bank loan debt is then deducted from the corporate value to estimate the value of the firm which is attributable to the equity holders (Appendix 3).

Assumptions made in determining Chrysos Co's equity value

It is assumed that Sidero Co's ungeared cost of equity is equivalent to Chrysos Co's ungeared cost of equity, given that they are both in the same industry and therefore face the same business risk. Modigliani and Miller's proposition 2 is used to estimate Chrysos Cos's restructured cost of equity and cost of capital.

It is assumed that deducting depreciation and tax from the profit before depreciation, interest and tax provides a reasonably accurate estimate of the free cash flows (Appendix 3). Other adjustments such as changes in working capital are reckoned to be immaterial and therefore not considered. Depreciation is not added back because it is assumed to be the same as the capital needed for reinvestment purposes.

It is assumed that the cash flows will grow in perpetuity. The assumption of growth in perpetuity may be over-optimistic and may give a higher than accurate estimate of Chrysos Co's equity value.

(**Note.** Credit will be given for alternative and relevant assumptions.)

Impact of the restructuring programme on Chrysos Co and on the venture capital organisations (VCOs)

By acquiring an extra 600 million equity shares, the proportion of the VCOs' equity share capital will increase to 40% ((600m + 20% × 1,800)/(1,800 + 600)) from 20%. Therefore, the share of the equity value the VCOs will hold in Chrysos Co will increase by $9,229m, which is 77·5% more than the total of the value of bonds cancelled and extra payment made (Appendix 4). As long as the VCOs are satisfied that the equity value of Chrysos Co after the restructuring programme has been undertaken is accurate, the value of their investment has increased substantially. The VCOs may want undertake a feasibility study on the annual growth rate in cash flows of 4% and the assumption of growth in perpetuity. However, the extent of additional value created seems to indicate that the impact for the VCOs is positive.

By cancelling the VCOs' unsecured bonds and repaying the other debt in non-current liabilities, an opportunity has been created for Chrysos Co to raise extra debt finance for future projects. Based on a long-term capital structure ratio of 80% equity and 20% debt, and a corporate value of $47,944 million (Appendix 3), this equates to just under $9,600 million of possible debt finance which could be accessed. Since the bank loan has a current value of $1,800 million, Chrysos Co could raise just under an extra $7,800 million debt funding and it would also have $1,439 million in net cash available from the sale of the machinery parts manufacturing business unit.

Chrysos Co's current value has not been given and therefore it is not possible to determine the financial impact of the equity value after the restructuring has taken place on the company as a whole. Nevertheless, given that the company has access to an extra $7,800 million debt funding to expand its investment into new value-creating projects, it is likely that the restructuring programme will be beneficial. However, it is recommended that the company tries to determine its current equity value and compares this with the proposed new value. A concern may be that both the 5 senior equity holders' group and the 30 other equity holders group's proportion of equity shares will reduce to 30% from 40% each, as a result of the VCOs acquiring an additional 600 million shares. Both these shareholder groups need to be satisfied about the potential negative impact of these situations against the potential additional benefits accruing from the restructuring programme, before the company proceeds with the programme.

Conclusion

The restructuring programme creates an opportunity for Chrysos Co to have access to extra funding and additional cash for investment in projects in the future. The VCOs are likely to benefit financially from the restructuring programme as long as they are satisfied about the assumptions made when assessing the value created. However, Chrysos Co will need to ensure that all equity holder groups are satisfied with the change in their respective equity holdings.

Report compiled by:

Date:

(Note. Credit will be given for alternative and relevant points)

Appendices

Appendix 1: Unbundling the manufacturing business unit

Option 1: Sale of assets

Net proceeds to Chrysos Co from net sale of assets of the manufacturing business unit are $3,102 million.

Option 2: Management buy-out

	$m
Sales revenue (20% × $16,800m)	3,360
Operating costs (25% × 10,080m)	(2,520)
Profit before depreciation, interest and tax	840
Depreciation (12% × 20% × ($7,500m + $5,400m))	(310)
	530
Tax (18% × $530m)	(95)
Cash flows	435

Estimated value = ($435m × 1·08)/0·10 = $4,698m

Amount payable to Chrysos Co = 70% × $4,698m = $3,289m

The option to unbundle through a management buy-out (option 2) is marginally better for Chrysos Co and it will opt for this.

Appendix 2: Calculation of cost of equity and cost of capital

Chrysos Co, estimate of cost of equity (Ke) and cost of capital (CoC)

Ke = 12.46% + [0.82 × (12.46% − 4.5%) × (0.2/0.8)]

Ke = 14.09%

CoC = 0.8 × 14.09% + 0.2 × 4.5% × 0.82 = 12.01, say 12%

Appendix 3: Estimate of value

	$m
Sales revenue (80% × $16,800m)	13,440
Costs prior to depreciation, interest and tax (75% × 10,080m)	(7,560)
Profit before depreciation and tax	5,880
Depreciation (12% × ($6,000m + $5,520m))	(1,382)
	4,498
Tax (18% × $4,498m)	(810)
Cash flows	3,688

Cost of capital to be used in estimating Chrysos Co's value is 12% (Appendix 2)
Estimated corporate value = ($3,688m × 1.04)/(0.12 − 0.04) = $47,944m
Estimated equity value = $47,944m − $1,800m = $46,144m

(**Note.** It is also acceptable to calculate cash flows after interest payment and use the cost of equity to estimate the equity value based on cash flows to equity instead of cash flows to firm.)

Appendix 4: Value created for VCOs

Value attributable to the VCOs = 40% × $46,144m = $18,458m
Value from increased equity ownership (this has doubled from 20% to 40%)
50% × $18,458m = $9,229m

Value of unsecured bonds foregone by the VCOs = $4,800m
Additional capital invested by the VCOs = $400m
Total of additional capital invested and value of bonds forgone = $5,200m

Additional value = ($9,229m − $5,200m)/$5,200m = 77.5% (or $4,029m)

(c) As a private company, Chrysos Co is able to ensure that the needs of its primary stakeholder groups – finance providers, managers and employees – are taken into account through the supervisory board. The supervisory board has representatives from each of these groups and each group member has a voice on the board. Each stakeholder group should be able to present its position to the board through its representatives, and decisions will be made after agreement from all group representatives. In this way, no single stakeholder group holds primacy over any other group.

Once Chrysos Co is listed and raises new capital, it is likely that it will have a large and diverse range of equity shareholders, who will likely be holding equity shares in many other companies. Therefore there is likely to be pressure on Chrysos Co to engage in value creating activity aimed at keeping its share price buoyant and thereby satisfying the equity shareholders. It is, therefore, likely that the equity shareholders' needs will hold primacy over the other stakeholder groups and quite possibly the power of the supervisory board will diminish as a result of this.

Question 2

Marking scheme

					Marks
(a)	Advantages		2–3		
	Disadvantages		3–4		
	Limit marks for (a) to 3 marks in total if answer does not mention Buryecs Co's situation			Max	6
(b)	(i)	Recognition that swap gives advantage	1		
		Swap mechanism	2		
		Net benefit after bank charges	1		
					4
	(ii)	Exchange rates	2		
		Correct translation of amounts swapped	1		
		Correct translation of other amounts	1		
		Net present value	1		
		Gain in € from the swap of the initial fee amount	1		
		Comments	2–3		
					8
(c)	Put option		1		
	$7.25 option calculations		2		
	$7.75 option calculations		2		
	Comments		2–3		
					7
					25

(a) The currency swap will involve Buryecs Co taking out a loan in €and making an arrangement with a counterparty in Wirtonia, which takes out a loan in $. Buryecs Co will pay the interest on the counterparty's loan and vice versa.

Advantages

Payment of interest in $ can be used to match the income Buryecs Co will receive from the rail franchise, reducing foreign exchange risk.

Buryecs Co will be able to obtain the swap for the amount it requires and may be able to reverse the swap by exchanging with the other counterparty. Other methods of hedging risk may be less certain. The cost of a swap may also be cheaper than other methods of hedging, such as options.

The swap can be used to change Buryecs Co's debt profile if it is weighted towards fixed-rate debt and its directors want a greater proportion of floating rate debt, to diversify risk and take advantage of probable lower future interest rates.

Drawbacks

The counterparty may default. This would leave Buryecs Co liable to pay interest on the loan in its currency. The risk of default can be reduced by obtaining a bank guarantee for the counterparty.

The swap may not be a worthwhile means of hedging currency risk if the exchange rate is unpredictable. If it is assumed that exchange rates are largely determined by inflation rates, the predicted inflation rate in Wirtonia is not stable, making it more difficult to predict future exchange rates confidently. If the movement in the exchange rate is not as expected, it may turn out to have been better for Buryecs Co not to have hedged.

Buryecs Co is swapping a fixed rate commitment in the Eurozone for a floating rate in Wirtonia. Inflation is increasing in Wirtonia and there is a risk that interest rates will increase as a result, increasing Buryecs Co's finance costs.

The swap does not hedge the whole amount of the receipt in Year 3. Another method will have to be used to hedge the additional receipt from the government in Year 3 and the receipts in the intervening years.

If the government decides to impose exchange controls in Wirtonia, Buryecs Co may not be able to realise the receipt at the end of Year 3, but will still have to fulfil the swap contract.

(b) (i)

	Buryecs Co	Counterparty	Interest rate benefit
Eurozone	4.0%	5.8%	1.8%
Wirtonia	Bank rate + 0.6%	Bank rate + 0.4%	0.2%
Gain on swap (60:40)	1.2%	0.8%	2.0%
Bank fee (60:40)	(0.3%)	(0.2%)	(0.5%)
Gain on swap after bank fee	0.9%	0.6%	1.5%

The swap arrangement will work as follows:

	Buryecs Co	Counterparty
Buryecs Co borrows at	4.0%	
Counterparty borrows at		Bank rate + 0.4%
Swap		
Counterparty receives		(Bank rate)
Buryecs Co pays	Bank rate	
Counterparty pays		4.6%
Buryecs Co receives	(4.6%)	
Advantage	120 basis points	80 basis points
Net result	Bank rate − 0.6%	5.0%

After paying the 30 point basis fee, Buryecs Co will effectively pay interest at the bank rate − 0.3% and benefit by 90 basis points or 0.9%. The counterparty will effectively pay interest at 5.2% and benefit by 60 basis points or 0.6%.

(ii) Using the purchasing power parity formula to calculate exchange rates:

$$S_1 = S_0 \times (1 + h_c)/(1 + h_b)$$

Year	1	2	3
	$0.1430 \times 1.06/1.03$	$0.1472 \times 1.04/1.08$	$0.1417 \times 1.03/1.11$
	$= 0.1472$	$= 0.1417$	$= 0.1315$

At Year 3, $5,000 million will be exchanged at the original spot rate as per the agreement and the remaining inflows will be exchanged at the Year 3 rate.

	0	1	2	3
	$m	$m	$m	$m
Initial fee	(5,000)			
Payment at end of franchise				7,500
Annual income		600	600	600
Year 0 Exchange rate	0.1430			
Years 1–3 Exchange rates		0.1472	0.1417	0.1315
	€m	€m	€m	€m
Swap translated at 0.1430	(715)			715
Amount not covered by swap				
(7,500 – 5,000) translated at 0.1315				329
Annual income		88	85	79
Cash flows in home country	(715)	88	85	1,123
Discount factor 14%	1.000	0.877	0.769	0.675
Present value	(715)	77	65	758

The net present value of the project is €185 million, indicating that it should go ahead. However, the value is dependent on the exchange rate, which is worsening for the foreign income. If there are also uncertainties about the variability of returns during the three years, the directors may consider the project to be in excess of their risk appetite and decline the opportunity.

As a result of the exchange rates on the initial fee being fixed at the year 0 spot rate, Buryecs Co has gained $5,000m \times (0.1430 - 0.1315) \times 0.675 = €39m$.

(c) Receipt using swap arrangement = €715m + €329m = €1,044m

Receipt if transaction unhedged = $7,500m × 0.1315 = €986m

Predicted exchange rate at year 3 is €0.1315 = $1 or $7.6046 = €1

Options

Buy $ put options as receiving $.

$7.75 exercise price

Do not exercise

Net receipt = €986m – (1.6% × $7,500m × 0.1430) = €969m

$7.25 exercise price

Exercise

Receipt from government = $7,500m/7.25 = €1,034m

Net receipt = €1,034m – (2.7% × $7,500m × 0.1430) = €1,005m

The $7.25 option gives a better result than not hedging, given the current expectations of the exchange rate. However, it gives a worse result than the swap even before the premium is deducted, because of the exchange rate being fixed on the swap back of the original amount paid. These calculations do not take into account possible variability of the finance costs associated with the swap, caused by swapping into floating rate borrowing.

Question 3

Marking scheme

		Marks	
(a)	Government yield curve	2	
	Toltuck Co spot-curve old and new	2	
	Bond valuation – old and new	3	
	Yield to maturity – old and new	3	
			10
(b)	Financial factors	4	
	Other factors	4	
	Limit marks for (b) to 3 marks in total if answer does not mention Toltuck Co's position and performance		8
(c)	1–2 marks per impact discussed		Max 7
			25

(a) The government yield curve can be estimated from the data available:

Bond 1: $\$104 = \$109/(1 + r_1)$
$r_1 = (\$109/\$104) - 1 = 4.81\%$

Bond 2: $\$102 = \$7/1.0481 + \$107/(1 + r_2)^2$
$r_2 = [107/(102 - 6.68)]^{1/2} - 1 = 5.95\%$

Bond 3: $\$98 = \$6/1.0481 + \$6/1.0595^2 + \$106/(1 + r_3)^3$
$r_3 = [106/(98 - 5.72 - 5.35)]^{1/3} - 1 = 6.83\%$

Year	Govt yield curve %	Spread old rating %	Toltuck Co spot old rating %	Spread new rating %	Toltuck Co spot new rating %
1	4.81	0.18	4.99	0.54	5.35
2	5.95	0.31	6.26	0.69	6.64
3	6.83	0.45	7.28	0.86	7.69

Valuation of bond under old credit rating

Year	Payment $	Discount factor	Discounted cash flow $
1	8	1/1.0499	7.62
2	8	1/1.0626²	7.09
3	110	1/1.0728³	89.09
Bond valuation			103.80

Valuation of bond under new credit rating

Year	Payment	Discount factor	Discounted cash flow
	$		$
1	8	$1/1.0535$	7.59
2	8	$1/1.0664^2$	7.03
3	110	$1/1.0769^3$	88.08
Bond valuation			102.70

Yield to maturity under old credit rating

Year	Payment	Discount factor	Discounted cash flow	Discount factor	Discounted cash flow
	$	8%	$	7%	$
0	(103.80)	1.000	(103.80)	1.000	(103.80)
1–3	8.00	2.577	20.62	2.624	20.99
3	102.00	0.794	80.99	0.816	83.23
			(2.19)		0.42

Using IRR approach, yield to maturity = 7 + ((0.42/(2.19 + 0.42)) × (8 − 7)) = 7.16%

Yield to maturity under new credit rating

Year	Payment	Discount factor	Discounted cash flow	Discount factor	Discounted cash flow
	$	8%	$	7%	$
0	(102.70)	1.000	(102.70)	1.000	(102.70)
1–3	8.00	2.577	20.62	2.624	20.99
3	102.00	0.794	80.99	0.816	83.23
			(1.09)		1.52

Using IRR approach, yield to maturity = 7 + ((1.52/(1.09 + 1.52)) × (8 − 7)) = 7.58%

Market value of $100 bond has fallen by $1.10 and the yield to maturity has risen by 0.42%.

(b)   The credit agency will have taken the following criteria into consideration when assessing Toltuck C's credit rating:

Country

Toltuck Co's debt would not normally be rated higher than the credit ratings of its country of origin, Arumland. Therefore the credit rating of Arumland should normally be at least AA. The rating will also have depended on Toltuck Co's standing relative to other companies in Arumland. The credit agency may have reckoned that Toltuck Co's recent poor results have weakened its position.

Industry

The credit agency will have taken account of the impact of the recession on property construction companies generally in Arumland. Toltuck Co's position within the industry compared with competitors will also have been assessed. If similar recent developments by competitors have been more successful, this is likely to have had an adverse impact on Toltuck Co's rating.

Management

The credit agency will have made an overall assessment of management and succession planning at Toltuck Co. It will have looked at business and financing strategies and planning and controls. It will also have assessed how successful the management has been in terms of delivering financial results. The credit agency may have believed the poor returns on recent developments show shortcomings in management decision-making processes and it may have rated the current management team poorly.

Financial

The credit agency will have analysed financial results, using measures such as return on capital employed. The agency will also have assessed possible sources of future earnings growth. It may have been sceptical about prospects, certainly for the short term, given Toltuck Co's recent problems.

The credit agency will also have assessed the financial position of Toltuck Co, looking at its gearing and working capital management, and considering whether Toltuck Co has enough cash to finance its needs. The agency will also have looked at Toltuck Co's relationship with its bankers and its debt covenants, to assess how flexible its sources of finances are if it comes under stress. It may well have been worried about Toltuck Co's gearing being higher than the industry average and concerned about the high levels of cash it needs to finance operations. It will also have assessed returns on developments-in-progress compared with commitments to repay loans. Greater doubt about Toltuck Co's ability to meet its commitments is likely to have been a significant factor in the fall in its rating.

The agency will also have needed reassurance about the quality of the financial information it was using, so it will have looked at the audit report and accounting policies.

(c)   Toltuck Co may not have increased problems raising debt finance if debtholders do not react in the same way as the credit rating agency. They may attach different weightings to the criteria which they use. They may also come to different judgements about the quality of management and financial stability. Debtholders may believe that the recent problems Toltuck Co has had generating returns may be due more to external factors which its management could not have controlled.

However, it is probable that the fall in Toltuck Co's credit rating will result in it having more difficulty raising debt finance. Banks may be less willing to provide loans and investors less willing to subscribe for bonds. Even if debt finance is available, it may come with covenants restricting further debt or gearing levels. This will mean that if Toltuck Co requires substantial additional finance, it is more likely to have to make a rights issue or issue new equity on the stock market. Shareholders may be faced with the choice of subscribing large amounts for new capital or having their influence diluted. This may particularly worry the more cautious shareholders.

Even if Toltuck Co can obtain the debt it needs, the predicted increase in yield to maturity may be matched by debtholders demanding a higher coupon rate on debt. This will increase finance costs, and decrease profits and earnings per share, with a possible impact on share price. It will also mean that fewer funds are available for paying dividends. Toltuck Co has been faced with difficult decisions on balancing investment expenditure versus paying dividends and these difficulties may well increase.

Additional debt may have other restrictive covenants. They may restrict Toltuck Co's buying and selling of assets, or it sinvestment strategy. Restrictions on Toltuck Co's decisions about the developments it undertakes may impact adversely on shareholder returns.

Loan finance or bonds will also come with repayment covenants. These may require Toltuck Co to build up a fund over time which will be enough to redeem the debt at the end of its life. Given uncertainties over cash flows, this commitment to retain cash may make it more difficult to undertake major developments or pay an acceptable level of dividend.

The fall in Toltuck Co's credit rating may result in its cost of equity rising as well as its cost of debt. In turn, Toltuck Co's weighted average cost of capital will rise. This will affect its investment choices and hence its ability to generate wealth for shareholders. It may result in Toltuck Co prioritising developments offering better short-term returns. This may suit the more cautious shareholders, but the current majority may worry that Toltuck Co will have to turn down opportunities which offer the possibility of high returns.

ACCA
Advanced Financial Management

Mock Examination 2
Specimen exam

Question Paper	
Time allowed 3 hours and 15 minutes	
Section A	THIS question is compulsory and MUST be attempted
Section B	BOTH questions to be attempted

DO NOT OPEN THIS PAPER UNTIL YOU ARE READY TO START UNDER EXAMINATION CONDITIONS

SECTION A: THIS QUESTION is compulsory and MUST be attempted

Question 1

Cocoa-Mocha-Chai (CMC) Co is a large listed company based in Switzerland and uses Swiss Francs as its currency. It imports tea, coffee and cocoa from countries around the world, and sells its blended products to supermarkets and large retailers worldwide. The company has production facilities located in two European ports where raw materials are brought for processing, and from where finished products are shipped out. All raw material purchases are paid for in US dollars (US$), while all sales are invoiced in Swiss francs (CHF).

Until recently CMC Co had no intention of hedging its foreign currency exposures, interest rate exposures or commodity price fluctuations, and stated this intent in its annual report. However, after consultations with senior and middle managers, the company's new board of directors (BoD) has been reviewing its risk management and operations strategies.

You are a financial consultant hired by CMC to work on the following two proposals which have been put forward by the BoD for further consideration:

Proposal one

Setting up a treasury function to manage the foreign currency and interest rate exposures (but not commodity price fluctuations) using derivative products. The treasury function would be headed by the Finance Director. The Purchasing Director, who initiated the idea of having a treasury function, was of the opinion that this would enable her management team to make better decisions. The Finance Director also supported the idea as he felt this would increase his influence on the BoD and strengthen his case for an increase in his remuneration.

In order to assist in the further consideration of this proposal, the BoD wants you to use the following upcoming foreign currency and interest rate exposures to demonstrate how they would be managed by the treasury function:

(i)   A payment of US$5,060,000 which is due in 4 months' time; and

(ii) A 4-year CHF60,000,000 loan taken out to part-fund the setting up of 4 branches (see proposal two below). Interest will be payable on the loan at a fixed annual rate of 2.2% or a floating annual rate based on the yield curve rate plus 0.40%. The loan's principal amount will be repayable in full at the end of the fourth year.

Additional information relating to proposal one

The current spot rate is US$1.0635 per CHF1. The current annual inflation rate in the US is three times higher than Switzerland.

The following derivative products are available to CMC Co to manage the exposures of the US$ payment and the interest on the loan:

Exchange-traded currency futures

Contract size CHF125,000 price quotation: US$ per CHF1

3-month expiry 1.0647
6-month expiry 1.0659

Exchange-traded currency options

Contract size CHF125,000, exercise price quotation: US$ per CHF1, premium: cents per CHF1

	Call options		Put options	
Exercise price	3-month expiry	6-month expiry	3-month expiry	6-month expiry
1.06	1.87	2.75	1.41	2.16
1.07	1.34	2.22	1.88	2.63

It can be assumed that futures and option contracts expire at the end of the month and transaction costs related to these can be ignored.

Over-the-counter products

In addition to the exchange-traded products, Pecunia Bank is willing to offer the following over-the-counter derivative products to CMC Co:

(i)   A forward rate between the US$ and the CHF of US$1.0677 per CHF1.

(ii)   An interest rate swap contract with a counterparty, where the counterparty can borrow at an annual floating rate based on the yield curve rate plus 0.8% or an annual fixed rate of 3.8%. Pecunia Bank would charge a fee of 20 basis points each to act as the intermediary of the swap. Both parties will benefit equally from the swap contract.

Alternative loan repayment proposal

As an alternative to paying the principal on the loan as one lump sum at the end of the fourth year, CMC Co could pay off the loan in equal annual amounts over the four years similar to an annuity. In this case, an annual interest rate of 2% would be payable, which is the same as the loan's gross redemption yield (yield to maturity).

Proposal two

This proposal suggested setting up four new branches in four different countries. Each branch would have its own production facilities and sales teams. As a consequence of this, one of the two European-based production facilities will be closed. Initial cost-benefit analysis indicated that this would reduce costs related to production, distribution and logistics, as these branches would be closer to the sources of raw materials and also to the customers. The operations and sales directors supported the proposal as, in addition to the above, this would enable sales and marketing teams in the branches to respond to any changes in nearby markets more quickly. The branches would be controlled and staffed by the local population in those countries. However, some members of the BoD expressed concern that such a move would create agency issues between CMC Co's central management and the management controlling the branches. They suggested mitigation strategies would need to be established to minimise these issues.

Response from the non-executive directors

When the proposals were put to the non-executive directors, they indicated that they were broadly supportive of the second proposal if the financial benefits outweigh the costs of setting up and running the four branches. However, they felt that they could not support the first proposal, as this would reduce shareholder value because the costs related to undertaking the proposal are likely to outweigh the benefits.

Required

(a)   Advise CMC Co on an appropriate hedging strategy to manage the foreign exchange exposure of the US$ payment in four months' time. Show all relevant calculations, including the number of contracts bought or sold in the exchange-traded derivative markets.   **(15 marks)**

(b)   Demonstrate how CMC Co could benefit from the swap offered by Pecunia Bank.   **(6 marks)**

(c)   Calculate the modified duration of the loan if it is repaid in equal amounts and explain how duration can be used to measure the sensitivity of the loan to changes in interest rates.   **(7 marks)**

(d)   Prepare a memorandum for the board of directors (BoD) of CMC Co which:

(i)   Discusses proposal one in light of the concerns raised by the non-executive directors; and

(9 marks)

(ii)   Discusses the agency issues related to proposal two and how these can be mitigated.   **(9 marks)**

Professional marks will be awarded in part (d) for the presentation, structure, logical flow and clarity of the memorandum.   **(4 marks)**

(Total = 50 marks)

SECTION B: BOTH QUESTIONS to be attempted
Question 2

You have recently commenced working for Burung Co and are reviewing a four-year project which the company is considering for investment. The project is in a business activity which is very different from Burung Co's current line of business.

The following net present value estimate has been made for the project:

All figures are in $ million

Year	0	1	2	3	4
Sales revenue		23.03	36.60	49.07	27.14
Direct project costs		(13.82)	(21.96)	(29.44)	(16.28)
Interest		(1.20)	(1.20)	(1.20)	(1.20)
Profit		8.01	13.44	18.43	9.66
Tax (20%)		(1.60)	(2.69)	(3.69)	(1.93)
Investment/sale	(38.00)				4.00
Cash flows	(38.00)	6.41	10.75	14.74	11.73
Discount factors (7%)	1	0.935	0.873	0.816	0.763
Present values	(38.00)	5.99	9.38	12.03	8.95

Net present value is negative $1.65 million, and therefore the recommendation is that the project should not be accepted.

Notes to NPV proposal

In calculating the net present value of the project, the following notes were made:

1   Since the real cost of capital is used to discount cash flows, neither the sales revenue nor the direct project costs have been inflated. It is estimated that the inflation rate applicable to sales revenue is 8% per year and to the direct project costs is 4% per year.

2   The project will require an initial investment of $38 million. Of this, $16 million relates to plant and machinery, which is expected to be sold for $4 million when the project ceases, after taking any taxation and inflation impact into account.

3   Tax-allowable depreciation is available on the plant and machinery at 50% in the first year, followed by 25% per year thereafter on a reducing balance basis. A balancing adjustment is available in the year the plant and machinery is sold. Burung Co pays 20% tax on its annual taxable profits. No tax-allowable depreciation is available on the remaining investment assets and they will have a nil value at the end of the project.

4   Burung Co uses either a nominal cost of capital of 11% or a real cost of capital of 7% to discount all projects, given that the rate of inflation has been stable at 4% for a number of years.

5   Interest is based on Burung Co's normal borrowing rate of 150 basis points over the 10-year government yield rate.

6   At the beginning of each year, Burung Co will need to provide working capital of 20% of the anticipated sales revenue for the year. Any remaining working capital will be released at the end of the project.

7   Working capital and depreciation have not been taken into account in the net present value calculation above, since depreciation is not a cash flow and all the working capital is returned at the end of the project.

Further financial information

It is anticipated that the project will be financed entirely by debt, 60% of which will be obtained from a subsidised loan scheme run by the Government, which lends money at a rate of 100 basis points below the 10-year government debt yield rate of 2.5%. Issue costs related to raising the finance are 2% of the gross finance required. The remaining 40% will be funded from Burung Co's normal borrowing sources. It can be assumed that the debt capacity available to Burung Co is equal to the actual amount of debt finance raised for the project.

Burung Co has identified a company, Lintu Co, which operates in the same line of business as that of the project it is considering. Lintu Co is financed by 40 million shares trading at $3.20 each and $34 million debt trading at $94 per $100. Lintu Co's equity beta is estimated at 1.5. The current yield on government treasury bills is 2% and it is estimated that the market risk premium is 8%. Lintu Co pays tax at an annual rate of 20%.

Both Burung Co and Lintu Co pay tax in the same year as when profits are earned.

Required

(a) Calculate the adjusted present value (APV) for the project, correcting any errors made in the net present value estimate above, and conclude whether the project should be accepted or not. Show all relevant calculations.   **(15 marks)**

(b) Comment on the corrections made to the original net present value estimate and explain the APV approach taken in part (a), including any assumptions made.   **(10 marks)**

(Total = 25 marks)

Question 3

Hav Co is a publicly listed company involved in the production of highly technical and sophisticated electronic components for complex machinery. It has a number of diverse and popular products, an active research and development department, significant cash reserves and a highly talented management who are very good in getting products to market quickly.

A new industry that Hav Co is looking to venture into is biotechnology, which has been expanding rapidly, and there are strong indications that this recent growth is set to continue. However, Hav Co has limited experience in this industry. Therefore it believes that the best and quickest way to expand would be through acquiring a company already operating in this industry sector.

Strand Co

Strand Co is a private company operating in the biotechnology industry and is owned by a consortium of business angels and company managers. The owner-managers are highly skilled scientists who have developed a number of technically complex products, but have found it difficult to commercialise them. They have also been increasingly constrained by the lack of funds to develop their innovative products further.

Discussions have taken place about the possibility of Strand Co being acquired by Hav Co. Strand Co's managers have indicated that the consortium of owners is happy for the negotiations to proceed. If Strand Co is acquired, it is expected that its managers would continue to run the Strand Co part of the larger combined company.

Strand Co is of the opinion that most of its value is in its intangible assets, comprising intellectual capital. Therefore, the premium payable on acquisition should be based on the present value to infinity of the after-tax excess earnings the company has generated in the past three years, over the average return on capital employed of the biotechnological industry. However, Hav Co is of the opinion that the premium should be assessed on synergy benefits created by the acquisition and the changes in value, due to the changes in the price/earnings (P/E) ratio before and after the acquisition.

Financial Information

Given below are extracts of financial information for Hav Co for 20X3 and Strand Co for 20X1, 20X2 and 20X3:

Year ended 30 April	Hav Co 20X3	Strand Co 20X3	20X2	20X1
	$m	$m	$m	$m
Earnings before tax	1,980	397	370	352
Non-current assets	3,965	882	838	801
Current assets	968	210	208	198
Share capital (25c/share)	600	300	300	300
Reserves	2,479	183	166	159
Non-current liabilities	1,500	400	400	400
Current liabilities	354	209	180	140

The current average P/E ratio of the biotechnology industry is 16.4 times and it has been estimated that Strand Co's P/E ratio is 10% higher than this. However, it is thought that the P/E ratio of the combined company would fall to 14.5 times after the acquisition. The annual after-tax earnings will increase by $140 million due to synergy benefits resulting from combining the two companies.

Both companies pay tax at 20% per annum and Strand Co's annual cost of capital is estimated at 7%. Hav Co's current share price is $9.24 per share. The biotechnology industry's pre-tax return on capital employed is currently estimated to be 20% per annum.

Acquisition proposals

Hav Co has proposed to pay for the acquisition using one of the following three methods:

1   A cash offer of $5.72 for each Strand Co share;

2   A cash offer of $1.33 for each Strand Co share plus 1 Hav Co share for every 2 Strand Co shares; or

3   A cash offer of $1.25 for each Strand Co share plus one $100 3% convertible bond for every $5 nominal value of Strand Co shares. In 6 years, the bond can be converted into 12 Hav Co shares or redeemed at par.

Required

(a)   Distinguish between the different types of synergy and discuss possible sources of synergy based on the above scenario.   **(9 marks)**

(b)   Based on the two different opinions expressed by Hav Co and Strand Co, calculate the maximum acquisition premium payable in each case.   **(6 marks)**

(c)   Calculate the percentage premium per share that Strand Co's shareholders will receive under each acquisition payment method and justify, with explanations, which payment method would be most acceptable to them.   **(10 marks)**

(Total = 25 marks)

Answers

DO NOT TURN THIS PAGE UNTIL YOU HAVE
COMPLETED THE MOCK EXAM

Plan of attack

Take a good look through the exam before diving in to answer questions.

Option 1

It is normally sensible to start with the compulsory Section A question on the basis that leaving it to later runs the risk of having to rush the 50 mark question, which is very difficult to do.

- **Question 1** was originally set as a real exam question in June 2014. Make sure you don't get too bogged down on individual figures. Ensure you leave enough time to answer the discursive parts, especially part (d) and take care to make your discussion points relevant to the company in question.

- **Question 2** was originally set as a real exam question in June 2014. Adjusted present value is a commonly tested technique for AFM.

- **Question 3** was originally set as a real exam question in June 2013. Business valuations are also a commonly examined area in AFM. In part (c) it is important to simplify the calculations as much as possible given the limited marks available for the numerical part of this question (estimating that about half of the ten marks are available for discussion areas).

Option 2

If you are a bit worried about question 1, as may be the case here, you could manage your exam nerves by doing a section B question first, selecting the one you are most comfortable with. However, make sure you don't spend too much time on this question, regardless of how much you think you can write. If you are comfortable with the question but cannot answer it in the time allowed then you are probably writing too much.

No matter how many times we remind you...

Always allocate your time according to the marks for the question in total and for the individual parts of each question. Also **always answer the question you were asked** rather than the question you wished you had been asked or the question you thought you had been asked.

You've got free time at the end of the exam...?

Looks like you've slipped up on the time allocation. However, if you have, don't waste the last few minutes; go back to **any parts of questions that you didn't finish** because you moved on to another task.

Forget about it!

Forget about what? Excellent – you already have!

Question 1

Marking scheme

		Marks
(a)	Calculation of payment using the forward rate	1
	Going short on futures and purchasing put options	2
	Predicted futures rate based on basis reduction	1
	Futures: Expected payment and number of contracts	2
	Options calculation using either 1.06 or 1.07 rate	3
	Options calculation using the second rate (or explanation)	2
	Advice (1 to 2 marks per point)	4–5
		Max 15
(b)	Comparative advantage and recognition of benefit as a result	2
	Initial decision to borrow fixed by CMC Co and floating by counterparty	1
	Swap impact	2
	Net benefit after bank charges	1
		6

				Marks
(c)		Calculation of annual annuity amount		1
		Calculation of Macaulay duration		2
		Calculation of modified duration		1
		Explanation		3
				7
(d)	(i)	2–3 marks per point	Max	9
	(ii)	Discussion of the agency issues		3–4
		Discussion of mitigation strategies and policies		4–6
			Max	9

Professional marks

Memorandum format		1
Structure and presentation of the memorandum		3
		4
		50

(a)   The US$ payment of 5.06 million due in 4 months' time exposes CMC to the risk of a devaluation in the CHF over this period.

This risk can be managed in a number of ways.

(i)   **Forward contracts**

The forward rate being offered of US$1.0677 per CHF would mean that the cost of this payment would be fixed at:

$5.06m/1.0677 = 4,739,159 CHF

This would completely remove the possibility of negative (or positive) exchange rate movements impacting on the cost of this payment in CHF.

Forward contracts are a simple way of starting to hedge risk and carry no transaction costs, although they do carry default risk.

(ii)   **Futures**

CMC would need to enter into contracts to sell CHF on the futures exchange. Six-month contracts would be needed.

The effective exchange rate on the futures market can be estimated as follows:

	Now	In 4 months
6-month future	1.0659	
Spot	1.0635	
Basis	0.0024	0.0008
	6 months remaining	2 months remaining
		(0.0024 × 2/6)

The closing future price is estimated at spot in 6 months (assume this is 1.0659) + 0.0008 = 1.0667.

The futures contracts would be set up as follows:

Number of contracts to sell ($5.06m/1.0659/125,000) = 38

In reality a margin payment would be needed to cover potential losses on these contracts.

Assuming that the closing spot = 1.0659 then the situation would be:

Actual transaction = a payment of $5.06m/1.0659 = 4,747,162 CHF

Contract to sell at opening future 1.0659
Contract to buy at closing future rate 1.0667
Loss on future = 0.0008

Total losses = 0.0008 × 38 contracts × 125,000 = $3,800 converted into CHF at closing spot = 3,800/1.0659 = 3,565 CHF

Final outcome = actual + future = 4,747,162 + 3,565 = 4,750,727 CHF

This is an effective rate of $5,060,000/4,750,727 = 1.0651

This can also be estimated as the opening futures price – closing basis = 1.0659 – 0.0008 = 1.0651

The treasury department would have to ensure that the future was closed out on the same date as the actual transaction.

There may be variation margin payments during the next four months if potential losses on these contracts exceed the initial margin.

This is less attractive than the forward contract.

(iii) **Currency options**

Because the contracts are in CHF, the contracts required will be to sell CHF ie put options. Six-month contracts will be needed.

As with futures, 38 contracts will be needed.

There is a choice of 2 options, 1.06 and 1.07 $ to the CHF. The 1.07 is the better rate and therefore is more expensive.

The potential outcome of using both is set out below.

	1.06	1.07
Cost of setting up 38 put options (in $)	102,600	124,925
	(2.16 premium)	(2.63 premium)
Cost in CHF at today's spot rate of 1.0635	96,474	117,466

Assuming that the option is exercised

	Use option			Use option	
	$5,035,000	$		$5,082,500	$
Cost in CHF	−4,750,000			−4,750,000	
		shortage in $			surplus in $
	−25,000	($5.06m − $5.035m) CHF at 1.0677		22,500	($5.06m − $5.0825m) in CHF at 1.0677
	−23,415	(fwd rate)		21,073	fwd rate
Premium in CHF	−96,474			−117,466	
Net in CHF	−4,869,889			−4,846,393	

This is an uncertain outcome, and may be better if the CHF gets stronger over the next four months (because then the option would not need to be exercised).

Summary

	CHF
Forward	4,739,159
Future	4,750,728
Option at 1.06	4,869,889
Option at 1.07	4,846,393

Based on this analysis I recommend using forwards which in any case are a simple and low cost way of beginning to hedge currency risk.

(b)

	CMC Co	Counterparty	Interest rate differential
Fixed rate	2.2%	3.8%	1.6%
Floating rate	Yield rate + 0.4%	Yield rate + 0.8%	0.4%

CMC Co has a comparative advantage in borrowing at the fixed rate and the counterparty has a comparative advantage in borrowing at the floating rate. Total possible benefit before Pecunia Bank's fee is 1.2% (1.6 – 0.4), which if shared equally results in a benefit of 0.6% each, for both CMC Co and the counterparty.

	CMC Co	Counterparty
CMC Co borrows at	2.2%	
Counterparty borrows at		Yield rate + 0.8%
Advantage	60 basis points	60 basis points
Net result	Yield rate – 0.2%	3.2%
SWAP		
Counterparty receives		Yield rate
CMC Co pays	Yield rate	
Counterparty pays		2.4%
CMC Co receives	2.4%	

After paying the 20 basis point fee, CMC Co will effectively pay interest at the yield curve rate and benefit by 40 basis points or 0.4%, and the counterparty will pay interest at 3.4% and benefit by 40 basis points or 0.4% as well.

(**Note.** Full marks will be given where the question is answered by estimating the arbitrage gain of 1.2% and deducting the fees of 0.4%, without constructing the above table.)

(c) Annuity factor, 4 years, 2% = 3.808
Equal annual amounts repayable per year = CHF60,000,000/3.808 = CHF15,756,303

Time	1	2	3	4	Total
Repayments (CHF'000)	15,756.3	15,756.3	15,756.3	15,756.3	
Df 2%	0.980	0.961	0.942	0.924	
PV ('000)	15,441.2	15,141.8	14,842.4	14,558.8	59,984.2
% of present value	15,441.2 ÷ 59,984.2 = 0.26	15,141.8 ÷ 59,984.2 = 0.25	14,842.4 ÷ 59,984.2 = 0.25	14,558.8 ÷ 59,984.2 = 0.24	

Macaulay duration
$(0.26 \times 1$ year +
0.25×2 years +
0.25×3 years +
0.24×4 years)
= 2.47 years

Modified duration = 2.47/1.02 = 2.42 years

The size of the modified duration will determine how much the value of a bond or loan will change when there is a change in interest rates. A higher modified duration means that the fluctuations in the value of a bond or loan will be greater, hence the value of 2.42 means that the value of the loan or bond will change by 2.42 times the change in interest rates multiplied by the original value of the bond or loan.

The relationship is only an approximation because duration assumes that the relationship between the change in interest rates and the corresponding change in the value of the bond or loan is linear. In fact, the relationship between interest rates and bond price is in the form of a curve which is convex to the origin (ie non-linear). Therefore duration can only provide a reasonable estimation of the change in the value of a bond or loan due to changes in interest rates, when those interest rate changes are small.

(d) **MEMORANDUM**

From:

To: The Board of Directors, CMC Co

Date: XX/XX/XXXX

Subject: Discussion of the proposal to manage foreign exchange and interest rate exposures, and the proposal to move operations to four branches and consequential agency issues

This memo discusses the proposal of whether or not CMC Co should undertake the management of foreign exchange and interest rate exposure, and the agency issues resulting from the proposal to locate branches internationally.

(i) **Proposal One: Management of foreign exchange and interest rate exposure**

The non-executive directors are correct if CMC Co is in a situation where markets are perfect and efficient, where information is freely available and where securities are priced correctly. In this circumstance, risk management or hedging would not add value and, if shareholders hold well-diversified portfolios, unsystematic risk will be largely eliminated.

The position against hedging states that in such cases companies would not increase shareholder value by hedging or eliminating risk because there will be no further reduction in unsystematic risk. Furthermore, the cost of reducing any systematic risk will equal or be greater than the benefit derived from such risk reduction. Shareholders would not gain from risk management or hedging; in fact, if the costs exceed the benefits, then hedging may result in a reduction in shareholder value.

There are two main situations where reduction in volatility or risk may increase cash flows – where a firm could face significant financial distress costs due to high volatility in earnings; and where stable earnings increase certainty and the ability to plan for the future, thus resulting in stable investment policies by the firm.

Active hedging may also reduce agency costs. For example, unlike shareholders, managers and employees of the company may not hold diversified portfolios. Hedging allows the risks faced by managers and employees to be reduced. Additionally, hedging may allow managers to be less concerned about market movements which are not within their control and instead allow them to focus on business issues over which they can exercise control. This seems to be what the Purchasing Director is contending. On the other hand, the Finance Director seems to be more interested in increasing his personal benefits and not necessarily in increasing the value of CMC Co.

A consistent hedging strategy or policy may be used as a signalling tool to reduce the conflict of interest between bond holders and shareholders, and thus reduce restrictive covenants.

It is also suggested that until recently CMC Co had no intention of hedging and communicated this in its annual report. It is likely that shareholders will therefore have created their own risk management policies. A strategic change in the policy may have a negative impact on the shareholders and the clientele impact of this will need to be taken into account.

The case of whether to hedge or not is not clear cut and CMC Co should consider all the above factors and be clear about why it is intending to change its strategy before coming to a conclusion. Any intended change in policy should be communicated to the shareholders. Shareholders can also benefit from risk management because the risk profile of the company may change, resulting in a reduced cost of capital.

(ii) **Proposal Two: International branches, agency issues and their mitigation**

Principal–agent relationships can be observed within an organisation between different stakeholder groups. With the proposed branches located in different countries, the principal–agent relationship will be between the directors and senior management at CMC Co in Switzerland, and the managers of the individual branches. Agency issues can arise where the motivations of the branch managers, who are interested in the performance of their individual branches, diverge from the management at CMC Co headquarters, who are interested in the performance of the whole organisation.

These issues may arise because branch managers are not aware of, or appreciate the importance of, the key factors at corporate level. They may also arise because of differences in cultures and divergent backgrounds.

Mitigation mechanisms could involve:

- Monitoring policies
- Compensation policies
- Communication policies

Monitoring policies: These would involve ensuring that key aims and strategies are agreed between all parties before implementation, and results monitored to ensure adherence with the original agreements. Where there are differences, for example due to external factors, new targets need to be agreed. Where deviations are noticed, these should be communicated quickly.

Compensation packages: These should ensure that reward is based on achievement of organisational value and therefore there is every incentive for the branch managers to act in the best interests of the corporation as a whole.

Communication: Branch managers should be made fully aware of the organisational objectives, and any changes to these, and how the branch contributes to these, in order to ensure their acceptance of the objectives. The management at CMC Co headquarters should be fully aware of cultural and educational differences in the countries where the branches are to be set up and fully plan for how organisational objectives may nevertheless be achieved within these differences.

(**Note.** Credit will be given for alternative, relevant approaches to the calculations, comments and suggestions/recommendations.)

Question 2

Marking scheme

		Marks
(a)	Inflated incremental profit	2
	Taxation	2
	Working capital	2
	Estimate of discount rate	2
	Net present value	1
	Issue costs	1
	Tax shield benefit	2
	Subsidy benefit	1
	Adjusted present value and conclusion	2
		15
(b)	Corrections made	4–5
	Approach taken	2–3
	Assumptions made	3–4
		Max 10
		25

(a) **All figures are in $ million – corrections are numbered**

Year	0	1	2	3	4
(error 1) Sales revenue (inflated, 8% p.a.)		24.87	42.69	61.81	36.92
(error 1) Costs (inflated, 4% p.a.)		(14.37)	(23.75)	(33.12)	(19.05)
Incremental profit		10.50	18.94	28.69	17.87
(error 2) Interest (not relevant)		n/a	n/a	n/a	n/a
(error 3) Tax (W1)		(0.50)	(3.39)	(5.44)	(3.47)
(error 4) Working capital (W2)	(4.97)	(3.57)	(3.82)	4.98	7.38
Investment/sale of machinery	(38.00)				4.00
Cash flows	(42.97)	6.43	11.73	28.23	25.78
(error 5) Discount factors (12%, W3)	1	0.893	0.797	0.712	0.636
Present values	(42.97)	5.74	9.35	20.10	16.40

Base case net present value is approximately $8.62 million.

Workings

1   *All figures are in $ million*

Year	0	1	2	3	4
Incremental profit		10.50	18.94	28.69	17.87
Capital allowances		8.00	2.00	1.50	0.50
Taxable profit		2.50	16.94	27.19	17.37
Tax (20%)		0.50	3.39	5.44	3.47

2   *All figures are in $ million*

Year	0	1	2	3	4
Working capital (20% of sales revenue)		4.97	8.54	12.36	7.38
Working capital required/(released)	4.97	3.57	3.82	(4.98)	(7.38)

3   $\beta a = \left(\dfrac{Ve}{(Ve + Vd(1-t))} \right) \beta e + \left(\dfrac{Vd(1-t)}{(Ve + Vd(1-t))} \right) \beta d$

Assuming the beta of debt = 0, Lintu Co's asset beta =

[$128m/($128m + $31.96m × 0.8] × 1.5 approx. = 1.25

Using the CAPM $E(ri) = R_f + \beta (E(R_m - R_f))$

So the all-equity financed discount rate = 2% + 1.25 × 8% = 12%

(error 6) Financing side effects

	$'000
Issue costs 2/98 × $42.97m	(876.94)

Tax shield
Annual tax relief =
On the subsidised loan = $42.97m × 60% × 0.015 × 20% = $77,346
On the rest of the loan = $42.97m × 40% × 0.04 × 20% = $137,504
Total = 77,346 + 137,504 = $214,850m p.a. for 4 years
This is discounted at the normal cost of debt which is 1.5% above the risk-free rate of 2.5% ie = 4%.

The present value of the tax relief annuity = 214.85 × 3.63	779.91

Annual subsidy benefit
$42.97m × 60% × 0.025 × 80% = 515.64 ('000)

The present value of the subsidy benefit annuity = 515.64 × 3.63	1,871.77
Total benefit of financing side effects	1,774.74

Financing the project entirely by debt would add just under $1.78 million to the value of the project, or approximately an additional 20% to the all-equity financed project.

The APV of the project is just under $10.4 million and therefore it should be accepted.

Note. In calculating the present values of the tax shield and subsidy benefits, instead of the discount factor being based on the normal borrowing/default risk of the company, alternatively, 2% or 2.5% could be used depending on the assumptions made. Credit will be given where these are used to estimate the annuity factor, where the assumption is explained.

(b)   **Corrections made to the original net present value (numbers are referenced in the above calculations)**

1   Cash flows are inflated and the nominal rate based on Lintu Co's all-equity financed rate is used (see below). Where different cash flows are subject to different rates of inflation, applying a real rate to non-inflated amounts would not give an accurate answer because the effect of inflation on profit margins is being ignored.

2   Interest is not normally included in the net present value calculations. Instead, it is normally imputed within the cost of capital or discount rate. In this case, it is included in the financing side effects.

3   The approach taken to exclude depreciation from the net present value computation is correct, but capital allowances need to be taken away from profit estimates before tax is calculated, reducing the profits on which tax is payable.

4   The impact of the working capital requirement is included in the estimate as, although all the working capital is recovered at the end of the project, the flows of working capital are subject to different discount rates when their present values are calculated.

Approach taken (relates to errors 5 and 6)

The value of the project is initially assessed considering only the business risk involved in undertaking the project. The discount rate used is based on Lintu Co's asset beta which measures only the business risk of that company. Since Lintu Co is in the same line of business as the project, it is deemed appropriate to use its discount rate, instead of 11% that Burung Co uses normally.

The impact of debt financing and the subsidy benefit are then considered. In this way, Burung Co can assess the value created from its investment activity and then the additional value created from the manner in which the project is financed.

Assumptions made

It is assumed that all figures used are accurate and any estimates made are reasonable. Burung Co may want to consider undertaking a sensitivity analysis to assess this.

It is assumed that the initial working capital required will form part of the funds borrowed but that the subsequent working capital requirements will be available from the funds generated by the project. The validity of this assumption needs to be assessed since the working capital requirements at the start of Years 2 and 3 are substantial.

It is assumed that Lintu Co's asset beta and all-equity financed discount rate represent the business risk of the project. The validity of this assumption also needs to be assessed. For example, Lintu Co's entire business may not be similar to the project, and it may undertake other lines of business. In this case, the asset beta would need to be adjusted so that just the project's business risk is considered.

It is also assumed that there are no adverse side effects of taking on the extra debt eg a worsening credit rating which could impact Burung's trading position.

(**Note.** Credit will be given for alternative, relevant explanations.)

Question 3

Marking scheme

		Marks	
(a)	Distinguish between different synergies	1–2	
	Evaluating possible financial synergies	2–3	
	Evaluating possible cost synergies	1–2	
	Evaluating possible revenue synergies	3–4	
	Concluding comments	1–2	
			Max 9
(b)	Average earnings and capital employed	1	
	After-tax premium	1	
	PV of premium (excess earnings)	1	
	Hav Co and Strand Co values	1	
	Combined company value	1	
	Value created/premium (P/E method)	1	
			6
(c)	Strand Co, value per share	1	
	Cash offer premium (%)	1	
	Cash and share offer premium (%)	2	
	Cash and bond offer premium (%)	2	
	Explanation and justification	4–5	
			Max 10
			25

(a) Synergies arise from an acquisition when the value of the new, combined entity is greater than the sum of the two individual values before the acquisition. There are three types of synergies: revenue, cost and financial.

Revenue synergies create higher revenues for the combined entity, also creating a higher return on equity and an extended period of competitive advantage.

Cost synergies arise from eliminating duplication of functions and also from economies of scale due to the size of the new entity.

Financial synergies may result from the ability to increase debt capacity or from transferring group funds to companies where they can be best utilised.

In this scenario, there may be financial synergies available as Hav Co has significant cash reserves, but Strand Co is constrained by a lack of funds. This means that the new entity may have the funds to **undertake projects** that would have been rejected by Strand Co due to a lack of funds. The larger company may also have an increased debt capacity and therefore additional access to finance. It is also possible that the new entity will have a lower cost of capital as a result of the acquisition.

Cost synergies may be available, through the removal of duplication in areas such as head office functions, but also in R&D. These synergies are likely to be more short term. Other cost synergies may arise from a **stronger negotiating position** with suppliers due to the size of the new entity, meaning better credit terms and also lower costs.

Revenue synergies have the potential to be the biggest synergies from this acquisition, although they are likely to be the hardest to achieve, and also to sustain. Hav Co can help Strand Co with the marketing of its products, which should result in **higher revenues** and a longer period of **competitive advantage**. Combining the R&D activity and the technologies of both companies may mean products can be brought to market faster too. To achieve these synergies it is important to retain the services of the scientist managers of Strand Co. They have been used to complete autonomy as the managers of Strand Co, so this relationship should be managed carefully.

A major challenge in an effective acquisition is to **integrate processes and systems** between the two companies efficiently and effectively in order to gain the full potential benefits. Often, this is done poorly and can mean that the acquisition is ultimately seen as a failure. Hav Co needs to plan for this before proceeding with the acquisition.

(b) **Maximum premium based on excess earnings**

Average pre-tax earnings of Strand Co = (397 + 370 + 352)/3 = $373m
Average capital employed = [(882 + 210 − 209) + (838 + 208 − 180) + (801 + 198 − 140)]/3 = $869.3m
Excess annual premium (pre-tax) = 373 − (869.3 × 0.2) = $199.1m
Post-tax annual premium = $199.1 × 0.8 = $159.3m
PV of annual premium in perpetuity = 159.3/0.07 = $2,275.7m

The maximum premium payable is $2,275.7m.

Maximum premium based on P/E ratio

Strand Co's estimated P/E ratio = 16.4 × 1.10 = 18.04
Strand Co's post-tax profit (most recent) = 397m × 0.8 = $317.6m
Hav Co's post-tax profit = 1,980 × 0.8 = $1,584m

Hav Co current value = $9.24 × 2,400m shares = $22,176m

Strand Co current value = 18.04 × $317.6 = $5,729.5m

Value of combined company = (1,584 + 317.6 + 140) × 14.5 = $29,603.2m

Maximum premium = 29,603.2 − (22,176 + 5,729.5) = $1,697.7m

(c) Current value of a Strand Co share = $5,729.5m/1,200m shares = $4.77 per share

Maximum premium % based on excess earnings = 2,275.7/5,729.5 × 100 = 39.7%
Maximum premium % based on P/E ratio = 1,697.7/5,729.5 × 100 = 29.6%

Cash offer: premium % to Strand Co shareholder

(5.72 − 4.77)/4.77 × 100 = 19.9%

Cash and share offer: premium % to Strand Co shareholder

1 Hav Co share for 2 Strand Co shares
Hav Co share price = $9.24
Price per Strand Co share = 9.24/2 = $4.62
Cash payment per Strand Co share = $1.33
Total return = 4.62 + 1.33 = $5.95
Premium = (5.95 − 4.77)/4.77 × 100 = 24.7%

Cash and bond offer: premium % to Strand Co shareholder

Each share has nominal value of $0.25 so $5 is 20 shares
Bond value $100/20 shares = $5 per share
Cash payment per Strand Co share = $1.25
Total return = 5 + 1.25 = $6.25
Premium = (6.25 − 4.77)/4.77 × 100 = 31.0%

Tutorial note. Although these evaluations have been carried out using the current share price given in the question, an equally valid approach would have been to have used a post-acquisition share price based on earlier calculations (although this would take longer and is less advisable given that it is likely that about half of the marks are available for the numerical element of this question).

Based on the calculations above, the cash plus bond offer will give the highest return to Strand Co shareholders. In addition, the **bond can be converted** to 12 Hav Co shares, giving a value per share of $8.33($100/12), which is below the current share price and so already **in-the-money**. If the share price increases over the 6-year period, then the value of the bond should also increase. The bond will also earn interest of 3% per year for the holder.

The 31% return is the closest to the maximum premium based on excess earnings and higher than the maximum premium based on P/E ratios. Thus this method appears to **transfer more of the value** to the owners of Strand Co.

However, this payment method gives the **lowest initial cash payment** of the three methods being considered. This may make it seem more attractive to the Hav Co shareholders as well, although they stand to have their shareholding diluted most by this method, but not until six years have passed.

The cash and share offer gives a return in between the other options. Although the return is lower than the cash and bond offer, Strand Co's shareholders could **sell the Hav Co shares immediately** if they wish to. However, if the share price of Hav Co falls between now and the acquisition, the return to Strand Co shareholders will be lower.

The cash only offer gives an immediate return to Strand Co shareholders, but it is the **lowest return** and may also place a **strain on the cash flow** of Hav Co, which may need to increase borrowings as a result.

It seems most likely that Strand Co's shareholder/managers, who will continue to work in the new entity, will accept the mixed cash and bond offer. This maximises their current return and also gives them the chance to gain in the future when converting the bond. The choice of payment method could be influenced by the impact on personal taxation situations, though.

ACCA
Advanced Financial Management

Mock Examination 3
September/December 2017
Sample questions

Question Paper	
Time allowed 3 hours and 15 minutes	
Section A	THIS question is compulsory and MUST be attempted
Section B	BOTH questions to be attempted

DO NOT OPEN THIS PAPER UNTIL YOU ARE READY TO START UNDER EXAMINATION CONDITIONS

SECTION A: THIS QUESTION is compulsory and MUST be attempted

Question 1

Conejo Co is a listed company based in Ardilla and uses the $ as its currency. The company was formed around 20 years ago and was initially involved in cybernetics, robotics and artificial intelligence within the information technology industry. At that time due to the risky ventures Conejo Co undertook, its cash flows and profits were very varied and unstable. Around ten years ago, it started an information systems consultancy business and a business developing cyber security systems. Both these businesses have been successful and have been growing consistently. This in turn has resulted in a stable growth in revenues, profits and cash flows. The company continues its research and product development in artificial intelligence and robotics, but this business unit has shrunk proportionally to the other two units.

Just under eight years ago, Conejo Co was successfully listed on Ardilla's national stock exchange, offering 60% of its share capital to external equity holders, whilst the original founding members retained the remaining 40% of the equity capital. The company remains financed largely by equity capital and reserves, with only a small amount of debt capital. Due to this, and its steadily growing sales revenue, profits and cash flows, it has attracted a credit rating of A from the credit rating agencies.

At a recent board of directors (BoD) meeting, the company's chief financial officer (CFO) argued that it was time for Conejo Co to change its capital structure by undertaking a financial reconstruction, and be financed by higher levels of debt. As part of her explanation, the CFO said that Conejo Co is now better able to bear the increased risk resulting from higher levels of debt finance; would be better protected from predatory acquisition bids if it was financed by higher levels of debt; and could take advantage of the tax benefits offered by increased debt finance. She also suggested that the expected credit migration from a credit rating of A to a credit rating of BBB, if the financial reconstruction detailed below took place, would not weaken Conejo Co financially.

Financial reconstruction

The BoD decided to consider the financial reconstruction plan further before making a final decision. The financial reconstruction plan would involve raising $1,320 million ($1.32 billion) new debt finance consisting of bonds issued at their face value of $100. The bonds would be redeemed in five years' time at their face value of $100 each. The funds raised from the issue of the new bonds would be used to implement one of the following two proposals:

(a) Proposal 1: Either buy back equity shares at their current share price, which would be cancelled after they have been repurchased; or

(b) Proposal 2: Invest in additional assets in new business ventures.

Conejo Co, Financial information

EXTRACT FROM THE FORECAST FINANCIAL POSITION FOR NEXT YEAR

	$m
Non-current assets	1,735
Current assets	530
Total assets	2,265
Equity and liabilities	
Share capital ($1 per share par value)	400
Reserves	1,700
Total equity	2,100
Non-current liabilities	120
Current liabilities	45
Total liabilities	165
Total liabilities and capital	2,265

Conejo Co's forecast after-tax profit for next year is $350 million and its current share price is $11 per share.

The non-current liabilities consist solely of 5.2% coupon bonds with a face value of $100 each, which are redeemable at their face value in three years' time. These bonds are currently trading at $107.80 per $100. The bond's covenant stipulates that should Conejo Co's borrowing increase, the coupon payable on these bonds will increase by 37 basis points.

Conejo Co pays tax at a rate of 15% per year and its after-tax return on the new investment is estimated at 12%.

Other financial information

Current government bond yield curve

Year	1	2	3	4	5
	1.5%	1.7%	1.9%	2.2%	2.5%

Yield spreads (in basis points)

	1 year	2 years	3 years	4 years	5 years
A	40	49	59	68	75
BBB	70	81	94	105	112
BB	148	167	185	202	218

The finance director wants to determine the percentage change in the value of Conejo Co's current bonds, if the credit rating changes from A to BBB. Furthermore, she wants to determine the coupon rate at which the new bonds would need to be issued, based on the current yield curve and appropriate yield spreads given above.

Conejo Co's chief executive officer (CEO) suggested that if Conejo Co paid back the capital and interest of the new bond in fixed annual repayments of capital and interest through the five-year life of the bond, then the risk associated with the extra debt finance would be largely mitigated. In this case, it was possible that credit migration, by credit rating companies, from A rating to BBB rating may not happen. He suggested that comparing the duration of the new bond based on the interest payable annually and the face value in five years' time with the duration of the new bond where the borrowing is paid in fixed annual repayments of interest and capital could be used to demonstrate this risk mitigation.

Required

(a) Discuss the possible reasons for the finance director's suggestions that Conejo Co could benefit from higher levels of debt with respect to risk, from protection against acquisition bids, and from tax benefits. **(7 marks)**

(b) Prepare a report for the board of directors of Conejo Co which:

(i) Estimates, and briefly comments on, the change in value of the current bond and the coupon rate required for the new bond, as requested by the CFO **(6 marks)**

(ii) Estimates the Macaulay duration of the new bond based on the interest payable annually and face value repayment, and the Macaulay duration based on the fixed annual repayment of the interest and capital, as suggested by the CEO **(6 marks)**

(iii) Estimates the impact of the two proposals on how the funds may be used on next year's forecast earnings, forecast financial position, forecast earnings per share and on forecast gearing

(11 marks)

(iv) Using the estimates from (b)(i), (b)(ii) and (b)(iii), discusses the impact of the proposed financial reconstruction and the proposals on the use of funds on:

- Conejo Co;

- Possible reaction(s) of credit rating companies and on the expected credit migration, including the suggestion made by the CEO;

- Conejo Co's equity holders; and

- Conejo Co's current and new debt holders. **(16 marks)**

Professional marks will be awarded in part (b) for the format, structure and presentation of the report.

(4 marks)

(Total = 50 marks)

SECTION B: BOTH QUESTIONS TO BE ATTEMPTED

Question 2

Eview Cinemas Co is a long-established chain of cinemas in the country of Taria. 20 years ago Eview Cinemas Co's board decided to convert some of its cinemas into sports gyms, known as the EV clubs. The number of EV clubs has expanded since then. Eview Cinemas Co's board brought in outside managers to run the EV clubs, but over the years there have been disagreements between the clubs' managers and the board. The managers have felt that the board has wrongly prioritised investment in, and refurbishment of, the cinemas at the expense of the EV clubs.

Five years ago, Eview Cinemas Co undertook a major refurbishment of its cinemas, financing this work with various types of debt, including loan notes at a high coupon rate of 10%. Shortly after the work was undertaken, Taria entered into a recession which adversely affected profitability. The finance cost burden was high and Eview Cinemas Co was not able to pay a dividend for two years.

The recession is now over and Eview Cinemas Co has emerged in a good financial position, as two of its competitors went into insolvency during the recession. Eview Cinemas Co's board wishes to expand its chain of cinemas and open new, multiscreen cinemas in locations which are available because businesses were closed down during the recession.

In two years' time Taria is due to host a major sports festival. This has encouraged interest in sport and exercise in the country. As a result, some gym chains are looking to expand and have contacted Eview Cinemas Co's board to ask if it would be interested in selling the EV clubs. Most of the directors regard the cinemas as the main business and so are receptive to selling the EV clubs.

The finance director has recommended that the sales price of the EV clubs be based on predicted free cash flows as follows:

1.   The predicted free cash flow figures in $millions for EV clubs are as follows:

Year	1	2	3	4
	390	419	455	490

2.   After Year 4, free cash flows should be assumed to increase at 5.2% per annum.

3.   The discount rate to be used should be the current weighted average cost of capital, which is 12%.

4.   The finance director believes that the result of the free cash flow valuation will represent a fair value of the EV clubs' business, but Eview Cinemas Co is looking to obtain a 25% premium on the fair value as the expected sales price.

Other information supplied by the finance director is as follows:

1.   The predicted after-tax profits of the EV clubs are $454 million in Year 1. This can be assumed to be 40% of total after-tax profits of EV Cinemas Co.

2.   The expected proceeds which Eview Cinemas Co receives from selling the EV clubs will be used firstly to pay off the 10% loan notes. Part of the remaining amount from the sales proceeds will then be used to enhance liquidity by being held as part of current assets, so that the current ratio increases to 1.5. The rest of the remaining amount will be invested in property, plant and equipment. The current net book value of the non-current assets of the EV clubs to be sold can be assumed to be $3,790 million. The profit on the sale of the EV clubs should be taken directly to reserves.

3.   Eview Cinemas Co's asset beta for the cinemas can be assumed to be 0.952.

4.   Eview Cinemas Co currently has 1,000 million $1 shares in issue. These are currently trading at $15.75 per share. The finance director expects the share price to rise by 10% once the sale has been completed, as he thinks that the stock market will perceive it to be a good deal.

5. Tradeable debt is currently quoted at $96 per $100 for the 10% loan notes and $93 per $100 for the other loan notes. The value of the other loan notes is not expected to change once the sale has been completed. The overall pre-tax cost of debt is currently 9% and can be assumed to fall to 8% when the 10% loan notes are redeemed.

6. The current tax rate on profits is 20%.

7. Additional investment in current assets is expected to earn a 7% pre-tax return and additional investment in property, plant and equipment is expected to earn a 12% pre-tax return.

8. The current risk-free rate is 4% and the return on the market portfolio is 10%.

Eview Cinemas Co's current summarised statement of financial position is shown below. The CEO wants to know the impact the sale of the EV clubs would have immediately on the statement of financial position, the impact on the Year 1 forecast earnings per share and on the weighted average cost of capital.

	$m
Assets	
Non-current assets	15,621
Current assets	2,347
Total assets	17,968
Equity and liabilities	
Called-up share capital	1,000
Retained earnings	7,917
Total equity	8,917
Non-current liabilities	
10% loan notes	3,200
Other loan notes	2,700
Bank loans	985
Total non-current liabilities	6,885
Current liabilities	2,166
Total equity and liabilities	17,968

Required

(a) Calculate the expected sales price of the EV clubs and demonstrate its impact on Eview Cinemas Co's statement of financial position, forecast earnings per share and weighted average cost of capital. **(17 marks)**

(b) Evaluate the decision to sell the EV clubs. **(8 marks)**

(Total = 25 marks)

Question 3

Wardegul Co, a company based in the Eurozone, has expanded very rapidly over recent years by a combination of acquiring subsidiaries in foreign countries and setting up its own operations abroad. Wardegul Co's board has found it increasingly difficult to monitor its activities and Wardegul Co's support functions, including its treasury function, have struggled to cope with a greatly increased workload. Wardegul Co's board has decided to restructure the company on a regional basis, with regional boards and appropriate support functions. Managers in some of the larger countries in which Wardegul Co operates are unhappy with reorganisation on a regional basis, and believe that operations in their countries should be given a large amount of autonomy and be supported by internal functions organised on a national basis.

Assume it is now 1 October 20W7. The central treasury function has just received information about a future transaction by a newly-acquired subsidiary in Euria, where the local currency is the dinar (D). The subsidiary expects to receive D27,000,000 on 31 January 20X8. It wants this money to be invested locally in Euria, most probably for five months until 30 June 20X8.

Wardegul Co's treasury team is aware that economic conditions in Euria are currently uncertain. The central bank base rate in Euria is currently 4.2% and the treasury team believes that it can invest funds in Euria at the central bank base rate less 30 basis points. However, treasury staff have seen predictions that the central bank base rate could increase by up to 1.1% or fall by up to 0.6% between now and 31 January 20X8.

Wardegul Co's treasury staff normally hedge interest rate exposure by using whichever of the following products is most appropriate:

- Forward rate agreements (FRAs)
- Interest rate futures
- Options on interest rate futures

Treasury function guidelines emphasise the importance of mitigating the impact of adverse movements in interest rates. However, they also allow staff to take into consideration upside risks associated with interest rate exposure when deciding which instrument to use.

A local bank in Euria, with which Wardegul Co has not dealt before, has offered the following FRA rates:

4–9: 5.02%
5–10: 5.10%

The treasury team has also obtained the following information about exchange traded Dinar futures and options:

Three-month D futures, D500,000 contract size

Prices are quoted in basis points at 100 – annual % yield:

December 20W7:   94.84
March 20X8:   94.78
June 20X8:   94.66

Options on three-month D futures, D500,000 contract size, option premiums are in annual %

	Calls		Strike price		Put	
December	March	June		December	March	June
0.417	0.545	0.678	94.25	0.071	0.094	0.155
0.078	0.098	0.160	95.25	0.393	0.529	0.664

It can be assumed that futures and options contracts are settled at the end of each month. Basis can be assumed to diminish to zero at contract maturity at a constant rate, based on monthly time intervals. It can also be assumed that there is no basis risk and there are no margin requirements.

Required

(a) Recommend a hedging strategy for the D27,000,000 investment, based on the hedging choices which treasury staff are considering, if interest rates increase by 1.1% or decrease by 0.6%. Support your answer with appropriate calculations and discussion.   **(18 marks)**

(b) Discuss the advantages of operating treasury activities through regional treasury functions compared with:

  • Each country having a separate treasury function.
  • Operating activities through a single global treasury function.   **(7 marks)**

(Total = 25 marks)

Answers

DO NOT TURN THIS PAGE UNTIL YOU HAVE
COMPLETED THE MOCK EXAM

Plan of attack

Question 1 mainly requires an analysis of the suggestions of three directors all in connection with risk management. Parts of this question are extremely challenging but part (a), part of (b)(ii) and parts (b)(iii) and (b)(iv) contain a number of areas where easier marks can be scored and it is essential that you allow sufficient time on these areas and do not get too distracted by the harder elements of (b)(i) and (b)(ii). Remember that you are not aiming for 100%!

You should target the easier areas and not worry about getting every aspect of the calculations correct (this is unlikely to be achievable under exam conditions).

- **Question 2** requires careful planning, do not rush into the numbers. Once you can see that the disposal value affects the assets and liabilities and therefore the earnings of the company then the question becomes much easier.

- **Question 3** looks at interest rate hedging, this looks like a very manageable question and tests a number of techniques in ways that you should be familiar with.

No matter how many times we remind you...

Always allocate your time according to the marks for the question in total and for the individual parts of each question. Also, **always answer the question you were asked** rather than the question you wished you had been asked or the question you thought you had been asked.

You've got free time at the end of the exam...?

Looks like you've slipped up on the time allocation. However, if you have, don't waste the last few minutes; go back to **any parts of questions that you didn't finish** because you moved on to another task.

Question 1

Marks

(a) Being able to bear higher levels of financial risk .... Up to 3
Better protection from predatory takeover bids .... Up to 3
Taxation benefit of higher levels of debt finance .... Up to 2
Max 7

(b) (i) Appendix 1
Conejo Co's yield curve based on BBB rating 1
Bond value based on BBB rating and spot yield rates 1
Comment on reason for virtually no change in value 1
Calculation of the coupon rate of the new bond 2
Comment on coupon rate 1
6

(ii) Appendix 2
Duration based on annual coupon and balloon payment of $100 in Year 5 ... 2
Amount of fixed annual repayments of capital and interest 2
Duration based on annual equivalent payments 2
6

(iii) Appendix 3
Financial position, Proposal 1 3
Financial position, Proposal 2 3
Interest payable on additional new debt finance 1
Interest payable on higher coupon for current debt finance 1
Return on additional investment 1
Gearing calculations 1
Earnings per share calculations 1
11

(iv) Discussion in report
Impact on Conejo Co .... Up to 6
Credit migration, credit rating agencies and CEO's opinion .... Up to 6
Impact on Conejo Co's equity holders .... Up to 4
Impact on Conejo Co's debt holders: current and new .... Up to 3
Max 16

Professional marks for part (b)
Report format 1
Structure and presentation of the report 3
4
50

(a) Increasing the debt finance of a company relative to equity finance increases its financial risk, and therefore the company will need to be able to bear the consequences of this increased risk. However, companies face both financial risk, which increases as the debt levels in the capital structure increase, and business risk, which is present in a company due to the nature of its business.

In the case of Conejo Co, it could be argued that as its profits and cash flows have stabilised, the company's business risk has reduced, in contrast to early in its life, when its business risk would have been much higher due to unstable profits and cash flows. Therefore, whereas previously Conejo Co was not able to bear high levels of financial risk, it is able to do so now without having a detrimental impact on the overall risk profile of the company. It could therefore change its capital structure and have higher levels of debt finance relative to equity finance.

The predatory acquisition of one company by another could be undertaken for a number of reasons. One possible reason may be to gain access to cash resources, where a company which needs cash resources may want to take over another company which has significant cash resources or cash generative capability. Another reason may be to increase the debt capacity of the acquirer by using the assets of the target company. Where the relative level of debt finance is increased in the capital structure of a company through a financial reconstruction, like in the case of Conejo Co, these reasons for acquiring a company may be diminished. This is because the increased levels of debt would probably be secured against the assets of the company and therefore the acquirer cannot use them to raise additional debt finance, and cash resources would be needed to fund the higher interest payments.

Many tax jurisdictions worldwide allow debt interest to be deducted from profits before the amount of tax payable is calculated on the profits. Increasing the amount of debt finance will increase the amount of interest paid, reducing the taxable profits and therefore the tax paid. Modigliani and Miller referred to this as the benefit of the tax shield in their research into capital structure, where their amended capital proposition demonstrated the reduction in the cost of capital and increase in the value of the firm, as the proportion of debt in the capital structure increases.

(b) **Report to the board of directors (BoD), Conejo Co**

Introduction

This report discusses whether the proposed financial reconstruction scheme which increases the amount of debt finance in Conejo Co would be beneficial or not to the company and the main parties affected by the change in the funding, namely the equity holders, the debt holders and the credit rating companies. Financial estimates provided in the appendices are used to support the discussion.

Impact on Conejo Co

Benefits to Conejo Co include the areas discussed in part (a) above and as suggested by the CFO. The estimate in Appendix 3 assumes that the interest payable on the new bonds and the extra interest payable on the existing bonds are net of the 15% tax. Therefore, the tax shield reduces the extra amount of interest paid. Further, it is likely that because of the large amount of debt finance which will be raised, the company's assets would have been used as collateral. This will help protect the company against hostile takeover bids. Additionally, proposal 2 (Appendix 3) appears to be better than proposal 1, with a lower gearing figure and a higher earnings per share figure. However, this is dependent on the extra investment being able to generate an after-tax return of 12% immediately. The feasibility of this should be assessed further.

Conejo Co may also feel that this is the right time to raise debt finance as interest rates are lower and therefore it does not have to offer large coupons, compared to previous years. Appendix 1 estimates that the new bond will need to offer a coupon of 3·57%, whereas the existing bond is paying a coupon of 5·57%.

The benefits above need to be compared with potential negative aspects of raising such a substantial amount of debt finance. Conejo Co needs to ensure that it will be able to finance the interest payable on the bonds and it should ensure it is able to repay the capital amount borrowed (or be able to re-finance the loan) in the future. The extra interest payable (Appendix 3) will probably not pose a significant issue given that the profit after tax is substantially more than the interest payment. However, the repayment of the capital amount will need careful thought because it is significant.

The substantial increase in gearing, especially with respect to proposal 1 (Appendix 3), may worry some stakeholders because of the extra financial risk. However, based on market values, the level of gearing may not appear so high. The expected credit migration from A to BBB seems to indicate some increase in risk, but it is probably not substantial.

The BoD should also be aware of, and take account of, the fact that going to the capital markets to raise finance will require Conejo Co to disclose information, which may be considered strategically important and could impact negatively on areas where Conejo Co has a competitive advantage.

Reaction of credit rating companies

Credit ratings assigned to companies and to borrowings made by companies by credit rating companies depend on the probability of default and recovery rate. A credit migration from A to BBB means that Conejo Co has become riskier in that it is more likely to default and bondholders will find it more difficult to recover their entire loan if default does happen. Nevertheless, the relatively lower increase in yield spreads from A to BBB, compared to BBB to BB, indicates that BBB can still be considered a relatively safe investment.

Duration indicates the time it takes to recover half the repayments of interest and capital of a bond, in present value terms. Duration measures the sensitivity of bond prices to changes in interest rates. A bond with a higher duration would see a greater fluctuation in its value when interest rates change, compared to a bond with a lower duration. Appendix 2 shows that a bond which pays interest (coupon) and capital in equal annual instalments will have a lower duration. This is because a greater proportion of income is received earlier and income due to be received earlier is less risky. Therefore, when interest rates change, this bond's value will change by less than the bond with the higher duration. The CEO is correct that the bond with equal annual payments of interest and capital is less sensitive to interest rate changes, but it is not likely that this will be a significant factor for a credit rating company when assigning a credit rating.

A credit rating company will consider a number of criteria when assigning a credit rating, as these would give a more appropriate assessment of the probability of default and the recovery rate. These criteria include, for example, the industry within which the company operates, the company's position within that industry, the company's ability to generate profits in proportion to the capital invested, the amount of gearing, the quality of management and the amount of financial flexibility the company possesses. A credit rating company will be much less concerned about the manner in which a bond's value fluctuates when interest rates change.

Impact on equity holders

The purpose of the financial reconstruction would be of interest to the equity holders. If, for example, Conejo Co selects proposal 1 (Appendix 3), it may give equity holders an opportunity to liquidate some of their invested capital. At present, the original members of the company hold 40% of the equity capital and proposal 1 provides them with the opportunity to realise a substantial capital without unnecessary fluctuations in the share price. Selling large quantities of equity shares in the stock exchange may move the price of the shares down and cause unnecessary fluctuations in the share price.

If, on the other hand, proposal 2 (Appendix 3) is selected, any additional profits after the payment of interest will benefit the equity holders directly. In effect, debt capital is being used for the benefit of the equity holders.

It may be true that equity holders may be concerned about the increased risk which higher gearing will bring, and because of this, they may need higher returns to compensate for the higher risk. However, in terms of market values, the increased gearing may be of less concern to equity holders. Conejo Co should consider the capital structure of its competitors to assess what should be an appropriate level of gearing.

Equity holders will probably be more concerned about the additional restrictive covenants which will result from the extra debt finance, and the extent to which these covenants will restrict the financial flexibility of Conejo Co when undertaking future business opportunities.

Equity holders may also be concerned that because Conejo Co has to pay extra interest to debt holders, its ability to pay increasing amounts of dividends in the future could be affected. However, Appendix 3 shows that the proportion of interest relative to after-tax profits is not too high and any concern from the equity holders is probably unfounded.

Impact on debt holders

Although the current debt holders may be concerned about the extra gearing which the new bonds would introduce to Conejo Co, Appendix 1 shows that the higher coupon payments which the current debt holders will receive would negate any fall in the value of their bonds due to the credit migration to BBB rating from an A rating. Given that currently Conejo Co is subject to low financial risk, and probably lower business risk, it is unlikely that the current and new debt holders would be overly concerned about the extra gearing. The earnings figures in Appendix 3 also show that the after-tax profit figures provide a substantial interest cover and therefore additional annual interest payment should not cause the debt holders undue concern either.

The current and new debt holders would be more concerned about Conejo Co's ability to pay back the large capital sum in five years' time. However, a convincing explanation of how this can be achieved or a plan to roll over the debt should allay these concerns.

The current and new debt holders may be concerned that Conejo Co is not tempted to take unnecessary risks with the additional investment finance, but sensible use of restrictive covenants and the requirement to make extra disclosures to the markets when raising the debt finance should help mitigate these concerns.

Conclusion

Overall, it seems that the proposed financial reconstruction will be beneficial, as it will provide opportunities for Conejo Co to make additional investments and/or an opportunity to reduce equity capital, and thereby increasing the earnings per share. The increased gearing may not look large when considered in terms of market values. It may also be advantageous to undertake the reconstruction scheme in a period when interest rates are low and the credit migration is not disadvantageous. However, Conejo Co needs to be mindful of how it intends to repay the capital amount in five years' time, the information it will disclose to the capital markets and the impact of any negative restrictive covenants.

Report compiled by:

Date

Appendices:

Appendix 1: Change in the value of the current bond from credit migration and coupon rate required from the new bond (Question (b) (i))

Spot yield rates (yield curve) based on BBB rating

1 year	2.20%
2 year	2.51%
3 year	2.84%
4 year	3.25%
5 year	3.62%

Bond value based on BBB rating

$\$5.57 \times 1.0220^{-1} + \$5.57 \times 1.0251^{-2} + \$105.57 \times 1.0284^{-3} = \$107.81$

Current bond value = $107.80

Although the credit rating of Conejo Co declines from A to BBB, resulting in higher spot yield rates, the value of the bond does not change very much at all. This is because the increase in the coupons and the resultant increase in value almost exactly matches the fall in value from the higher spot yield rates.

Coupon rate required from the new bond

Take R as the coupon rate, such that:
$(\$R \times 1.0220^{-1}) + (\$R \times 1.0251^{-2}) + (\$R \times 1.0284^{-3}) + (\$R \times 1.0325^{-4}) + (\$R \times 1.0362^{-5}) +$
$(\$100 \times 1.0362^{-5}) = \$100$
4.5665R + 83.71 = 100
R = $3.57
Coupon rate for the new bond is 3.57%.

If the coupon payments on the bond are at a rate of 3·57% on the face value, it ensures that the present values of the coupons and the redemption of the bond at face value exactly equals the bond's current face value, based on Conejo Co's yield curve.

Appendix 2: Macaulay durations (Question (b) (ii))

Macaulay duration based on annual coupon of $3.57 and redemption value of $100 in Year 5:

$[(\$3.57 \times 1.0220^{-1} \times 1 \text{ year}) + (\$3.57 \times 1.0251^{-2} \times 2 \text{ years}) + (\$3.57 \times 1.0284^{-3} \times 3 \text{ years}) + (\$3.57 \times 1.0325^{-4} \times 4 \text{ years}) + (\$103.57 \times 1.0362^{-5} \times 5 \text{ years})]/\$100$
= [3.49 + 6.79 + 9.85 + 12.57 + 433.50]/100 = 4.7 years

Macaulay duration based on fixed annual repayments of interest and capital:

Annuity factor: (3.57%, 5 years) = $(1 - 1.0357^{-5})/0.0357$ = 4.51 approximately
Annual payments of capital and interest required to pay back new bond issue = $100/4.51 = $22.17 per $100 bond approximately

$[(\$22.17 \times 1.0220^{-1} \times 1 \text{ year}) + (\$22.17 \times 1.0251^{-2} \times 2 \text{ years}) + (\$22.17 \times 1.0284^{-3} \times 3 \text{ years}) + (\$22.17 \times 1.0325 - 4 \times 4 \text{ years}) + (\$22.17 \times 1.0362^{-5} \times 5 \text{ years})]/\$100$

= [21.69 + 42.20 + 61.15 + 78.03 + 92.79]/100 = 3.0 years

Alternative presentation of duration calculations:

(Discount factors are based on the interest rates shown in previous presentation)

Based on annual rate of 3.57% and redemption in Year 5:

Time	1	2	3	4	5	Total
$	3.57	3.57	3.57	3.57	103.57	
df	0.978	0.952	0.919	0.880	0.837	
PV	3.5	3.4	3.3	3.1	86.7	100.0
% PV	0.04	0.03	0.03	0.03	0.87	1.0
% x year	0.04	0.06	0.09	0.12	4.35	**4.7**

Based on fixed annual repayments of interest and capital:

$	22.17	22.17	22.17	22.17	22.17	Total
df	0.978	0.952	0.919	0.880	0.837	
PV	21.7	21.1	20.4	19.5	18.6	101.3
% PV	0.22	0.21	0.20	0.20	0.19	1.0
% x year	0.22	0.42	0.60	0.80	0.95	**3.0**

Appendix 3: Forecast earnings, financial position, earnings per share and gearing (Question (b) (iii))
Adjustments to forecast earnings

Amounts in $ millions	Current	Proposal 1	Proposal 2
Forecast after-tax profit	350.00	350.00	350.00
Interest payable on additional borrowing (based on a coupon rate of 3.57%)			
3.57% × $1,320m × (1 − 0.15)		(40.06)	(40.06)
Additional interest payable due to higher coupon			
0.37% × $120m × (1 − 0.15)		(0.38)	(0.38)
Return on additional investment (after tax)			
12% × $1,320m			158.40
Adjusted profit after tax	350.00	309.56	467.96

Forecast financial position

Amounts in $ millions	Current	Proposal 1	Proposal 2
Non-current assets	1,735.00	1,735.00	3,055.00
Current assets	530.00	489.56	647.96
Total assets	2,265.00	2,224.56	3,702.96
Equity and liabilities			
Share capital ($1 per share par value)	400.00	280.00	400.00
Reserves	1,700.00	459.56	1,817.96
Total equity	2,100.00	739.56	2,217.96
Non-current liabilities	120.00	1,440.00	1,440.00
Current liabilities	45.00	45.00	45.00
Total liabilities	165.00	1,485.00	1,485.00
Total liabilities and capital	2,265.00	2,224.56	3,702.96

	Current	Proposal 1	Proposal 2
Gearing % (non-current liabilities/equity)	5.7%	194.7%	64.9%
Earnings per share (in cents)			
(Adjusted profit after tax/no. of shares)	87.5c	110.6c	117.0c

Notes

If gearing is calculated based on non-current liabilities/(non-current liabilities + equity) and/or using market value of equity, instead of as above, then this is acceptable as well.

Proposal 1

Additional interest payable is deducted from current assets, assuming it is paid in cash and this is part of current assets. Reserves are also reduced by this amount. (Other assumptions are possible)

Shares repurchased as follows: $1 × 120m shares deducted from share capital and $10 × 120m shares deducted from reserves. $1,320m, consisting of $11 × 120m shares, added to non-current liabilities.

Proposal 2

Treatment of additional interest payable is as per proposal 1.

Additional debt finance raised, $1,320 million, is added to non-current liabilities and to non-current assets, assuming that all this amount is invested in non-current assets to generate extra income.

It is assumed that this additional investment generates returns at 12%, which is added to current assets and to profits (and therefore to reserves).

(Explanations given in notes are not required for full marks, but are included to explain how the figures given in Appendix 3 are derived.)

(**Note.** Credit will be given for alternative relevant presentation of financial positions and discussion)

Question 2

		Marks
(a)	PV of free cash flows Years 1–4	1
	PV of free cash flows Years 5 onwards	2
	Desired sales proceeds	1
	Impact on statement of financial position	4
	Impact on eps	5
	Impact on WACC	
	Equity beta – cinemas	2
	Revised cost of equity – cinemas	1
	Revised WACC	1
		17
(b)	Arguments against sale	4–5
	Arguments for sale	4–5
		Max 8
		25

(a) **Proceeds from sales of EV clubs**

Year (all figures $m)	1	2	3	4
Free cash flows	390	419	455	490
Discount factor 12%	0.893	0.797	0.712	0.636
Present value	348	334	324	312
Present value	1,318			

Present value in Year 5 onwards = $490m × 1.052/(0.12 − 0.052) × 0.636 = $4,821m

Total present value = $1,318m + $4,821m = $6,139m

Desired sales proceeds (25% premium) = $6,139m × 1.25 = $7,674m

Impact on statement of financial position ($m)

Profit on sale = $7,674m − $3,790m = $3,884m

Current assets increase = current liabilities $2,166m × current ratio of 1.5 = $3,249m = increase of $902m compared to current level of $2,347m

Increase in non-current assets = increase in non-current assets = proceeds from sale of $7,674m less $902m increase in working capital, less $3,200m loan note repayment = $3,572m increase. This is then reduced by the sale of EV clubs with non-current asset value given as $3,790m. So the net change is a fall of $3,790m − $3,572m = $218m.

	Original $m	Adjustments $m	Final $m
Assets			
Non-current assets	15,621	(218)	15,403
Current assets	2,347	902	3,249
Total assets	17,968		18,652
Equity and liabilities			
Called-up share capital	1,000		1,000
Retained earnings	7,917	3,884	11,801
Total equity	8,917		12,801

	Original $m	Adjustments $m	Final $m
Assets			
Non-current liabilities			
10% loan notes	3,200	(3,200)	–
Other loan notes	2,700		2,700
Bank loans	985		985
Total non-current liabilities	6,885		3,685
Current liabilities	2,166		2,166
Total equity and liabilities	17,968		18,652

Impact on eps ($m)

	Current forecast	Revised forecast
Predicted post tax profits	1,135	1,135
($454m × 10/4)		
Less: profits from EV clubs		(454)
Add: interest saved, net of tax		256
($3,200m × 10% × (1 − 0.2))		
Add: return on additional non-current assets		343
($3,572m × 12% × (1 − 0.2))		
Add: return on additional current assets		51
($902m × 7% × (1 − 0.2))		
Adjusted profits	1,135	1,331
Number of shares	1,000m	1,000m
Adjusted eps	$1.135	$1.331

Impact on WACC

Equity beta

V_e = $15,750m × 1.1 = $17,325m

V_d = ($2,700 × 0.93) + $985m = $3,496m

βe = 0.952 ((17,325 + 3,496 (1 − 0.2))/17,325 = 1.106

Revised cost of equity

k_e = 4 + (10 − 4)1.106 = 10.64%

Revised WACC

WACC = 10.64 (17,325/(17,325 + 3,496)) + 8 (1 − 0.2) (3,496/(17,325 + 3,496)) = 9.93%

(b) Shareholders would appear to have grounds for questioning the sale of the EV clubs. It would mean that Eview Cinemas Co was no longer diversified into two sectors. Although shareholders can achieve diversification themselves in theory, in practice transaction costs and other issues may mean they do not want to adjust their portfolio.

The increase in gym membership brought about by the forthcoming sports festival could justify the predicted increases in free cash flows made in the forecasts. Although increased earnings per share are forecast once the EV clubs are sold, these are dependent on Eview Cinemas Co achieving the sales price which it desires for the EV clubs and the predicted returns being achieved on the remaining assets.

The proposed expansion of multiscreen cinemas may be a worthwhile opportunity, but the level of demand for big cinema complexes may be doubtful and there may also be practical problems like negotiating change of use. In Year 1 the EV clubs would be forecast to make a post-tax return on assets of (454/3,790) = 12.0% compared with 9.6% (12% × 0.8) on the additional investment in the cinemas.

Investors may also wonder about the motives of Eview Cinemas Co's board. Selling the EV clubs offers the board a convenient way of resolving the conflict with the management team of the EV clubs and investors may feel that the board is trying to take an easy path by focusing on what they are comfortable with managing.

There may be arguments in favour of the sale, however. The lower WACC will be brought about by a fall in the cost of equity as well as the fall in the cost of debt. A reduction in the complexity of the business may result in a reduction in central management costs.

Eview Cinemas Co may also be selling at a time when the EV clubs chain is at its most attractive as a business, in the period before the sports festival. The premium directors are hoping to obtain (on top of a valuation based on free cash flow figures which may be optimistic) suggest that they may be trying to realise maximum value while they can.

Question 3

		Marks
(a)	Impact of FRA for rate increase and decrease	2
	Go long on futures	1
	Selection of March futures and options	1
	Number of contracts	1
	Basis calculation	1
	Impact of interest rate increase/decrease with futures	3
	Buy call options	1
	Premium calculations	1
	Exercise options?	1
	Impact of interest rate increase/decrease with options	3
	Discussion	3–4
		Max 18
(b)	Regional functions compared with national functions	4–5
	Regional functions compared with global function	3–4
		Max 7
		25

(a) Forward rate agreement

FRA 5.02% (4–9) since the investment will take place in four months' time for a period of five months.

If interest rates increase by 1.1% to 5.3%

	D
Investment return 5.0% × 5/12 × D27,000,000	562,500
Payment to bank (5.3% – 5.02%) × 5/12 × D27,000,000	(31,500)
Net receipt	531,000
Effective annual interest rate 531,000/27,000,000 × 12/5	4.72%

If interest rates fall by 0.6% to 3.6%

	D
Investment return 3.3% × 5/12 × D27,000,000	371,250
Receipt from bank (5.02% – 3.6%) × 5/12 × D27,000,000	159,750
Net receipt	531,000
Effective annual interest rate as above	4.72%

Futures

Go long in the futures market, as the hedge is against a fall in interest rates. Use March contracts, as investment will be made on 31 January.

Number of contracts = D27,000,000/D500,000 × 5 months/3 months = 90 contracts

Basis

Current price (1 October) – futures price = basis

(100 – 4.20) – 94.78 = 1.02

Unexpired basis on 31 January = 2/6 × 1.02 = 0.34

If interest rates increase by 1.1% to 5.3%

	D
Investment return as above	562,500
Expected futures price: $100 - 5.3 - 0.34 = 94.36$	
Loss on the futures market: $(0.9436 - 0.9478) \times D500{,}000 \times 3/12 \times 90$	(47,250)
Net return	515,250
Effective annual interest rate $515{,}250/27{,}000{,}000 \times 12/5$	4.58%

If interest rates fall by 0.6% to 3.6%

	D
Investment return as above	371,250
Expected futures price: $100 - 3.6 - 0.34 = 96.06$	
Profit on the futures market: $(0.9606 - 0.9478) \times D500{,}000 \times 3/12 \times 90$	144,000
Net receipt	515,250
Effective annual interest rate as above	4.58%

Options on futures

Buy call options as need to hedge against a fall in interest rates. As above, 90 contracts required.

If interest rates increase by 1.1% to 5.3%

Exercise price	94.25	95.25
Futures price as above	94.36	94.36
Exercise?	Yes	No
Gain in basis points	11	0

	D	D
Investment return (as above)	562,500	562,500
Gain from options $(0.0011 \times 500{,}000 \times 3/12 \times 90)$	12,375	0
Premium		
$0.00545 \times D500{,}000 \times 3/12 \times 90$	(61,313)	
$0.00098 \times D500{,}000 \times 3/12 \times 90$		(11,025)
Net return	513,562	551,475
Effective interest rate		
$513{,}562/27{,}000{,}000 \times 12/5$	4.56%	
$551{,}475/27{,}000{,}000 \times 12/5$		4.90%

If interest rates fall by 0.6% to 3.6%

Exercise price	94.25	95.25
Futures price as above	96.06	96.06
Exercise?	Yes	Yes
Gain in basis points	181	81
Investment return (as above)	371,250	371,250
Gain from options		
Gain from options: $0{\cdot}0181 \times D500{,}000 \times 3/12 \times 90$	203,625	
Gain from options: $0{\cdot}0081 \times D500{,}000 \times 3/12 \times 90$		91,125
Premium as above	(61,313)	(11,025)
Net return	513,562	451,350

Effective interest rate		
$513{,}562/27{,}000{,}000 \times 12/5$	4.56%	
$451{,}350/27{,}000{,}000 \times 12/5$		4.01%

Alternative presentation of calculations:

Forward rate agreement:

FRA 5.02% (4–9) since the investment will take place in 4 months' time and last for 5 months.

Possible scenarios:	Rates rise by 1.1%	Rates fall by 0.6%
Base rate (now = 4.2%)	5.3%	3.6%
Return on investment (Base – 0.3%)	5.0%	3.3%
Impact of FRA (5.02% vs Base)	(0.28%)	1.42%
Net outcome as %	4.72%	4.72%
In Ds (% × D27,000,000 × 5/12)	531,000	531,000

Futures agreement:

March contracts to buy at 94.78 or 5.22% (100 – 94.78) are need to cover to the start of the investment (31 January). The number of contracts required will be D27m / D0.5m contract size × 5 months (investment term) divided by 3 months (contract term) = 90.

Opening basis on 1 Oct: future – base = 5.22% – 4.20% = 1.02% with 6 months to expiry of March future.

Estimated closing basis on 31 January = 1.02% × 2/6 = 0.34% with 2 months to expiry of March future.

So if rates rise to a base rate of 5.3% the estimated futures price is 5.3% + 0.34% = 5.64%.

If rates fall to a base rate of 3.6% the estimated futures price is 3.6% + 0.34% = 3.94%.

Possible scenarios:	Rates rise by 1.1%	Rates fall by 0.6%
Base rate (now = 4.2%)	5.3%	3.6%
Return on investment (Base – 0.3%)	5.0%	3.3%
Impact of Future:		
Opening rate 1 Oct (to receive)	5.22%	5.22%
Closing rate 31 January (to pay)	5.64%	3.94%
Net outcome on future	(0.42%)	1.28%
Overall net outcome (actual + future)	4.58%	4.58%
In Ds (% × D27,000,000 × 5/12)	515,250	515,250

Options agreement:

March call options at 5.75% (94.25) or 4.75% (95.25) can be chosen. There is an argument for either, this solution illustrates the outcome if 4.75% is chosen, which is the rate closest to the current base rate and provides compensation if interest rates fall at a lower premium compared to the 5.75% rate. Again 90 contracts will be needed, and contracts are closed out against the futures price on 31 January.

Possible scenarios:	Rates rise by 1.1%	Rates fall by 0.6%
Base rate (now = 4.2%)	5.3%	3.6%
Return on investment (Base – 0.3%)	5.0%	3.3%

Impact of Future:

	Rates rise by 1.1%	Rates fall by 0.6%
Call option rate 1 Oct	4.75%	4.75%
Closing rate 31 January (to pay)	5.64%	3.94%
Net outcome on future	Do not exercise	0.81%
Premium	(0.098)%	(0.098)%
Outcome (actual + option– premium)	4.902%	4.012%
In Ds (% × D27,000,000 × 5/12)	551,475	451,350

Discussion

The forward rate agreement gives the highest guaranteed return. If Wardegul Co wishes to have a certain cash flow and is primarily concerned with protecting itself against a fall in interest rates, it will most likely choose the forward rate agreement. The 95.25 option gives a better rate if interest rates rise, but a significantly lower rate if interest rates fall, so if Wardegul Co is at all risk averse, it will choose the forward rate agreement.

This assumes that the bank which Wardegul Co deals with is reliable and there is no risk of default. If Wardegul Co believes that the current economic uncertainty may result in a risk that the bank will default, the choice will be between the futures and the options, as these are guaranteed by the exchange. Again the 95.25 option may be ruled out because it gives a much worse result if interest rates fall to 3·6%. The futures give a marginally better result than the 94.25 option in both scenarios but the difference is small. If Wardegul Co feels there is a possibility that interest rates will be higher than 5·41%, the point at which the 94.25 option would not be exercised, it may choose this option rather than the future.

(b) **Regional functions compared with national functions**

Organising treasury activities on a regional basis would be consistent with what is happening in the group overall. Other functions will be organised regionally. A regional treasury function may be able to achieve synergies with them and also benefit from information flows being organised based on the regional structure.

If, as part of a reorganisation, some treasury activities were to be devolved outside to a bank or other third party, it would be simpler to arrange for a single provider on a regional basis than arrange for separate providers in each country.

A regional function will avoid duplication of responsibilities over all the countries within a region. A regional function will have more work to do, with maybe a greater range of activities, whereas staff based nationally may be more likely to be under-employed. There may be enough complex work on a regional basis to justify employing specialists in particular treasury areas which will enhance the performance of the function. It may be easier to recruit these specialists if recruitment is done regionally rather than in each country.

Regional centres can carry out some activities on a regional basis which will simplify how funds are managed and mean less cost than managing funds on a national basis. These include pooling cash, borrowing and investing in bulk, and netting of foreign currency income and expenditure.

Regional centres could in theory be located anywhere in the region, rather than having one treasury function based in each country. This means that they could be located in the most important financial centres in each region or in countries which offered significant tax advantages.

From the point of view of Wardegul Co's directors and senior managers, it will be easier to enforce common standards and risk management policies on a few regional functions than on many national functions with differing cultures in individual countries.

Regional functions compared with global function

Wardegul Co is being reorganised on a regional basis because of the demands of its global expansion. As discussed above, reorganising treasury functions regionally will be consistent with the way other functions are organised. Reorganising the treasury function regionally will be one way of dealing with the problem of having a single, overstretched, global function.

A regional function could employ experts with knowledge of the regulations, practices and culture of the major countries within the region. It may be more difficult for a global function to recruit staff with local expertise.

There may be practical issues why individual countries prefer to deal with regional functions rather than a global function, for example, a regional function will be based in the same, or similar, time zone as the countries in its region.

A regional function may have better ideas of local finance and investment opportunities. There may, for example, be better alternatives for investment of the surplus funds than the centralised function has been able to identify.

Mathematical tables and formulae

Formulae

Modigliani and Miller Proposition 2 (with tax)

$$k_e = k_e^i + (1-T)(k_e^i - k_d)\frac{V_d}{V_e}$$

The Capital Asset Pricing Model

$$E(r_i) = R_f + \beta_i\,(E(r_m) - R_f)$$

The asset beta formula

$$\beta_a = \left[\frac{V_e}{(V_e + V_d(1-T))}\beta_e\right] + \left[\frac{V_d(1-T)}{(V_e + V_d(1-T))}\beta_d\right]$$

The Growth Model

$$P_0 = \frac{D_0(1+g)}{(r_e - g)}$$

Gordon's growth approximation

$$g = br_e$$

The weighted average cost of capital

$$WACC = \left[\frac{V_e}{V_e + V_d}\right]k_e + \left[\frac{V_d}{V_e + V_d}\right]k_d(1-T)$$

The Fisher formula

$$(1+i) = (1+r)(1+h)$$

Purchasing power parity and interest rate parity

$$S_1 = S_0 \times \frac{(1+h_c)}{(1+h_b)} \qquad F_0 = S_0 \times \frac{(1+i_c)}{(1+i_b)}$$

Modified Internal Rate of Return

$$MIRR = \left[\frac{PV_R}{PV_I}\right]^{\frac{1}{n}}(1+r_e) - 1$$

The Black-Scholes option pricing model

$$c = P_a N(d_1) - P_e N(d_2) e^{-rt}$$

Where:

$$d_1 = \frac{\ln(P_a / P_e) + (r + 0.5s^2)t}{s\sqrt{t}}$$

$$d_2 = d_1 - s\sqrt{t}$$

The Put Call Parity relationship

$$p = c - P_a + P_e e^{-rt}$$

Present value table

Present value of 1 ie $(1 + r)^{-n}$

Where   r = discount rate
              n = number of periods until payment

Discount rate (r)

Periods (n)	1%	2%	3%	4%	5%	6%	7%	8%	9%	10%	
1	0.990	0.980	0.971	0.962	0.952	0.943	0.935	0.926	0.917	0.909	1
2	0.980	0.961	0.943	0.925	0.907	0.890	0.873	0.857	0.842	0.826	2
3	0.971	0.942	0.915	0.889	0.864	0.840	0.816	0.794	0.772	0.751	3
4	0.961	0.924	0.888	0.855	0.823	0.792	0.763	0.735	0.708	0.683	4
5	0.951	0.906	0.863	0.822	0.784	0.747	0.713	0.681	0.650	0.621	5
6	0.942	0.888	0.837	0.790	0.746	0.705	0.666	0.630	0.596	0.564	6
7	0.933	0.871	0.813	0.760	0.711	0.665	0.623	0.583	0.547	0.513	7
8	0.923	0.853	0.789	0.731	0.677	0.627	0.582	0.540	0.502	0.467	8
9	0.914	0.837	0.766	0.703	0.645	0.592	0.544	0.500	0.460	0.424	9
10	0.905	0.820	0.744	0.676	0.614	0.558	0.508	0.463	0.422	0.386	10
11	0.896	0.804	0.722	0.650	0.585	0.527	0.475	0.429	0.388	0.350	11
12	0.887	0.788	0.701	0.625	0.557	0.497	0.444	0.397	0.356	0.319	12
13	0.879	0.773	0.681	0.601	0.530	0.469	0.415	0.368	0.326	0.290	13
14	0.870	0.758	0.661	0.577	0.505	0.442	0.388	0.340	0.299	0.263	14
15	0.861	0.743	0.642	0.555	0.481	0.417	0.362	0.315	0.275	0.239	15

(n)	11%	12%	13%	14%	15%	16%	17%	18%	19%	20%	
1	0.901	0.893	0.885	0.877	0.870	0.862	0.855	0.847	0.840	0.833	1
2	0.812	0.797	0.783	0.769	0.756	0.743	0.731	0.718	0.706	0.694	2
3	0.731	0.712	0.693	0.675	0.658	0.641	0.624	0.609	0.593	0.579	3
4	0.659	0.636	0.613	0.592	0.572	0.552	0.534	0.516	0.499	0.482	4
5	0.593	0.567	0.543	0.519	0.497	0.476	0.456	0.437	0.419	0.402	5
6	0.535	0.507	0.480	0.456	0.432	0.410	0.390	0.370	0.352	0.335	6
7	0.482	0.452	0.425	0.400	0.376	0.354	0.333	0.314	0.296	0.279	7
8	0.434	0.404	0.376	0.351	0.327	0.305	0.285	0.266	0.249	0.233	8
9	0.391	0.361	0.333	0.308	0.284	0.263	0.243	0.225	0.209	0.194	9
10	0.352	0.322	0.295	0.270	0.247	0.227	0.208	0.191	0.176	0.162	10
11	0.317	0.287	0.261	0.237	0.215	0.195	0.178	0.162	0.148	0.135	11
12	0.286	0.257	0.231	0.208	0.187	0.168	0.152	0.137	0.124	0.112	12
13	0.258	0.229	0.204	0.182	0.163	0.145	0.130	0.116	0.104	0.093	13
14	0.232	0.205	0.181	0.160	0.141	0.125	0.111	0.099	0.088	0.078	14
15	0.209	0.183	0.160	0.140	0.123	0.108	0.095	0.084	0.074	0.065	15

Annuity table

Present value of an annuity of 1 ie $\dfrac{1-(1+r)^{-n}}{r}$

Where   r = discount rate
         n = number of periods

Discount rate (r)

Periods (n)	1%	2%	3%	4%	5%	6%	7%	8%	9%	10%	
1	0.990	0.980	0.971	0.962	0.952	0.943	0.935	0.926	0.917	0.909	1
2	1.970	1.942	1.913	1.886	1.859	1.833	1.808	1.783	1.759	1.736	2
3	2.941	2.884	2.829	2.775	2.723	2.673	2.624	2.577	2.531	2.487	3
4	3.902	3.808	3.717	3.630	3.546	3.465	3.387	3.312	3.240	3.170	4
5	4.853	4.713	4.580	4.452	4.329	4.212	4.100	3.993	3.890	3.791	5
6	5.795	5.601	5.417	5.242	5.076	4.917	4.767	4.623	4.486	4.355	6
7	6.728	6.472	6.230	6.002	5.786	5.582	5.389	5.206	5.033	4.868	7
8	7.652	7.325	7.020	6.733	6.463	6.210	5.971	5.747	5.535	5.335	8
9	8.566	8.162	7.786	7.435	7.108	6.802	6.515	6.247	5.995	5.759	9
10	9.471	8.983	8.530	8.111	7.722	7.360	7.024	6.710	6.418	6.145	10
11	10.368	9.787	9.253	8.760	8.306	7.887	7.499	7.139	6.805	6.495	11
12	11.255	10.575	9.954	9.385	8.863	8.384	7.943	7.536	7.161	6.814	12
13	12.134	11.348	10.635	9.986	9.394	8.853	8.358	7.904	7.487	7.103	13
14	13.004	12.106	11.296	10.563	9.899	9.295	8.745	8.244	7.786	7.367	14
15	13.865	12.849	11.938	11.118	10.380	9.712	9.108	8.559	8.061	7.606	15

(n)	11%	12%	13%	14%	15%	16%	17%	18%	19%	20%	
1	0.901	0.893	0.885	0.877	0.870	0.862	0.855	0.847	0.840	0.833	1
2	1.713	1.690	1.668	1.647	1.626	1.605	1.585	1.566	1.547	1.528	2
3	2.444	2.402	2.361	2.322	2.283	2.246	2.210	2.174	2.140	2.106	3
4	3.102	3.037	2.974	2.914	2.855	2.798	2.743	2.690	2.639	2.589	4
5	3.696	3.605	3.517	3.433	3.352	3.274	3.199	3.127	3.058	2.991	5
6	4.231	4.111	3.998	3.889	3.784	3.685	3.589	3.498	3.410	3.326	6
7	4.712	4.564	4.423	4.288	4.160	4.039	3.922	3.812	3.706	3.605	7
8	5.146	4.968	4.799	4.639	4.487	4.344	4.207	4.078	3.954	3.837	8
9	5.537	5.328	5.132	4.946	4.772	4.607	4.451	4.303	4.163	4.031	9
10	5.889	5.650	5.426	5.216	5.019	4.833	4.659	4.494	4.339	4.192	10
11	6.207	5.938	5.687	5.453	5.234	5.029	4.836	4.656	4.486	4.327	11
12	6.492	6.194	5.918	5.660	5.421	5.197	4.988	4.793	4.611	4.439	12
13	6.750	6.424	6.122	5.842	5.583	5.342	5.118	4.910	4.715	4.533	13
14	6.982	6.628	6.302	6.002	5.724	5.468	5.229	5.008	4.802	4.611	14
15	7.191	6.811	6.462	6.142	5.847	5.575	5.324	5.092	4.876	4.675	15

Standard normal distribution table

	0.00	0.01	0.02	0.03	0.04	0.05	0.06	0.07	0.08	0.09
0.0	0.0000	0.0040	0.0080	0.0120	0.0160	0.0199	0.0239	0.0279	0.0319	0.0359
0.1	0.0398	0.0438	0.0478	0.0517	0.0557	0.0596	0.0636	0.0675	0.0714	0.0753
0.2	0.0793	0.0832	0.0871	0.0910	0.0948	0.0987	0.1026	0.1064	0.1103	0.1141
0.3	0.1179	0.1217	0.1255	0.1293	0.1331	0.1368	0.1406	0.1443	0.1480	0.1517
0.4	0.1554	0.1591	0.1628	0.1664	0.1700	0.1736	0.1772	0.1808	0.1844	0.1879
0.5	0.1915	0.1950	0.1985	0.2019	0.2054	0.2088	0.2123	0.2157	0.2190	0.2224
0.6	0.2257	0.2291	0.2324	0.2357	0.2389	0.2422	0.2454	0.2486	0.2517	0.2549
0.7	0.2580	0.2611	0.2642	0.2673	0.2704	0.2734	0.2764	0.2794	0.2823	0.2852
0.8	0.2881	0.2910	0.2939	0.2967	0.2995	0.3023	0.3051	0.3078	0.3106	0.3133
0.9	0.3159	0.3186	0.3212	0.3238	0.3264	0.3289	0.3315	0.3340	0.3365	0.3389
1.0	0.3413	0.3438	0.3461	0.3485	0.3508	0.3531	0.3554	0.3577	0.3599	0.3621
1.1	0.3643	0.3665	0.3686	0.3708	0.3729	0.3749	0.3770	0.3790	0.3810	0.3830
1.2	0.3849	0.3869	0.3888	0.3907	0.3925	0.3944	0.3962	0.3980	0.3997	0.4015
1.3	0.4032	0.4049	0.4066	0.4082	0.4099	0.4115	0.4131	0.4147	0.4162	0.4177
1.4	0.4192	0.4207	0.4222	0.4236	0.4251	0.4265	0.4279	0.4292	0.4306	0.4319
1.5	0.4332	0.4345	0.4357	0.4370	0.4382	0.4394	0.4406	0.4418	0.4429	0.4441
1.6	0.4452	0.4463	0.4474	0.4484	0.4495	0.4505	0.4515	0.4525	0.4535	0.4545
1.7	0.4554	0.4564	0.4573	0.4582	0.4591	0.4599	0.4608	0.4616	0.4625	0.4633
1.8	0.4641	0.4649	0.4656	0.4664	0.4671	0.4678	0.4686	0.4693	0.4699	0.4706
1.9	0.4713	0.4719	0.4726	0.4732	0.4738	0.4744	0.4750	0.4756	0.4761	0.4767
2.0	0.4772	0.4778	0.4783	0.4788	0.4793	0.4798	0.4803	0.4808	0.4812	0.4817
2.1	0.4821	0.4826	0.4830	0.4834	0.4838	0.4842	0.4846	0.4850	0.4854	0.4857
2.2	0.4861	0.4864	0.4868	0.4871	0.4875	0.4878	0.4881	0.4884	0.4887	0.4890
2.3	0.4893	0.4896	0.4898	0.4901	0.4904	0.4906	0.4909	0.4911	0.4913	0.4916
2.4	0.4918	0.4920	0.4922	0.4925	0.4927	0.4929	0.4931	0.4932	0.4934	0.4936
2.5	0.4938	0.4940	0.4941	0.4943	0.4945	0.4946	0.4948	0.4949	0.4951	0.4952
2.6	0.4953	0.4955	0.4956	0.4957	0.4959	0.4960	0.4961	0.4962	0.4963	0.4964
2.7	0.4965	0.4966	0.4967	0.4968	0.4969	0.4970	0.4971	0.4972	0.4973	0.4974
2.8	0.4974	0.4975	0.4976	0.4977	0.4977	0.4978	0.4979	0.4979	0.4980	0.4981
2.9	0.4981	0.4982	0.4982	0.4983	0.4984	0.4984	0.4985	0.4985	0.4986	0.4986
3.0	0.4987	0.4987	0.4987	0.4988	0.4988	0.4989	0.4989	0.4989	0.4990	0.4990

This table can be used to calculate $N(d)$, the cumulative normal distribution functions needed for the Black-Scholes model of option pricing. If $d_i > 0$, add 0.5 to the relevant number above. If $d_i < 0$, subtract the relevant number above from 0.5.

Mathematical tables and formulae

Review Form – Advanced Financial Management (AFM) (02/18)

Name: _____   Address: _____

_____

_____

How have you used this Kit?
(Tick one box only)

☐ On its own (book only)

☐ On a BPP in-centre course_____

☐ On a BPP online course

☐ On a course with another college

☐ Other _____

Why did you decide to purchase this Kit?
(Tick one box only)

☐ Have used the complimentary Study Text

☐ Have used other BPP products in the past

☐ Recommendation by friend/colleague

☐ Recommendation by a lecturer at college

☐ Saw advertising

☐ Other _____

During the past six months do you recall seeing/receiving any of the following?
(Tick as many boxes as are relevant)

☐ Our advertisement in *Student Accountant*

☐ Our advertisement in *Pass*

☐ Our advertisement in *PQ*

☐ Our brochure with a letter through the post

☐ Our website www.bpp.com

Which (if any) aspects of our advertising do you find useful?
(Tick as many boxes as are relevant)

☐ Prices and publication dates of new editions

☐ Information on product content

☐ Facility to order books

☐ None of the above

Which BPP products have you used?

Study Text	☐	*Passcards*	☐	*Other*	☐
Practice & Revision Kit	☑	*i-Pass*	☐		

Your ratings, comments and suggestions would be appreciated on the following areas.

	Very useful	Useful	Not useful
Passing AFM			
Questions			
Top Tips etc in answers			
Content and structure of answers			
Mock exam answers			

Overall opinion of this Kit   *Excellent* ☐   *Good* ☐   *Adequate* ☐   *Poor* ☐

Do you intend to continue using BPP products?   *Yes* ☐   *No* ☐

The BPP author of this edition can be emailed at: accaqueries@bpp.com

Review Form (continued)

TELL US WHAT YOU THINK

Please note any further comments and suggestions/errors below.